Ecotourism and Sustainable Development

Who Owns Paradise?

Martha Honey

D1173649

ISLAND PRESS

Washington, D.C. • Covelo, CA

ISLAND PRESS is a trademark of The Center for Resource Economics.

Library of Congress Cataloging-in-Publication Data
Honey, Martha, 1945–
    Ecotourism and sustainable development : who owns paradise? /
Martha Honey.
        p.   cm.
    Includes bibliographical references and index.
    ISBN 1–55963–581–9 (cloth). — ISBN 1–55963–582–7 (pbk.)
    1. Ecotourism.   2. Ecotourism—Latin America.   3. Ecotourism—
Africa.   4. Sustainable development—Latin America   5. Sustainable
development—Africa   I. Title.
    G156.5.E26H66   1999   98–48342
    338.4'791—dc21   CIP

Printed on recycled, acid-free paper

Manufactured in the United States of America
10 9 8 7

Contents

Acknowledgments

This book grew out of my years living in East Africa and Central America, where my curiosity was peaked about whether nature tourism and later ecotourism could really contribute to sustainable economic development, particularly for rural communities. I was struck by the destructiveness of so many economic activities geared toward earning foreign exchange, from conventional mass tourism, to mining, logging, and bananas. And I was impressed by how the countries where I lived (Tanzania and Costa Rica) had, with foresight and sacrifice, established extensive systems of national parks and other protected areas, totaling, in each case, close to a quarter of their territory. One of my unfinished projects from these decades abroad was to look closely and systematically at ecotourism, to trace its origins, and to critically examine how it fit into the development strategies of a number of countries I know quite well. I arrived back in the United States in the early 1990s on the crest of the ecotourism wave, as environmental organizations, aid agencies, and the travel industry were all heralding ecotourism as a win-win proposition for Third World countries, conservation, and the traveling public.

What I initially conceived as being a quick and modest book turned into a lengthy and complex research and writing project. I am enormously grateful to the scores of people and institutions who provided assistance. Barbara Ras, former senior editor of Sierra Club Books, via my agent Gloria Loomis, first expressed interest and provided initial funding for this book. The bulk of the research and travel expenses were underwritten by grants from the Ford Foundation and Pew Charitable Trust, as well as several smaller foundations. I thank, in particular, Elaine Broadhead, Mike Conroy, Ole Gjerstad, Fran Korten, Josh Reichert, Stanley Selengut, and Genevieve Vaughan for providing support and encouragement. I am indebted to Chuck Savitt of Island Press for taking a keen interest in the project and to Todd Baldwin for patiently and thoughtfully guiding the rewrite of the manuscript.

My field work was facilitated and enriched by a number of experts, including Andy Drumm in Ecuador; Karen Wald in Cuba; Anne Becher in Costa Rica; Fatma Alloo, Abdul Sheriff, and Suhail Sheriff in East Africa; and David Fig, Eddie Koch, and Granville Shenker in South Africa. Others who helped in the field include Walter Bagoya, Amos Bien, Rodrigo Carazo, Marc Frank, Chris Gakahu, Harvey Haber, Michael Kaye, Steve Lawry, Pedro Leon, Jane

McManus, Ann Marie Saidy, Sue and John Trostle, Chris Wille, and Louis Wilson.

In the U.S., I received generous help from a number of ecotourism experts, including, most importantly, Costas Christ, who graciously gave me insights, analysis, and encouragement. Among the others who provided valuable assistance are Ray Ashton, Elizabeth Boo, Joe Franke, Bryan Higgins, Kurt Kutay, Deborah McLaren, and Megan Epler Wood. Others who helped collect information or share their research with me include Tony Avirgan, Katrina Brandon, Ronnie Casella, Tom Clements, Gillian Gunn Clissold, Molly Davis, Toby Ewing, Don Hawkins, Ellen Hoffman, Craig MacFarland, Sandy Munro, Meitamei Ole Depash, Miriam Pemberton, Susan Place, Anita Pleumaron, Ross Simmons, Stephanie Thullen, Marie Uehling, Scott Wayne, and Karen Ziffer.

The text was enhanced by the thoughtful and informed comments of a number of experts who took the time to read parts of the manuscript: Fatma Alloo, Johannah Barry, Anne Becher, Costas Christ, David Fig, Bob Hall, Diane Jukofsky, Bernie Kemp, Abdul Sheriff, Suhail Sheriff, Susana Struve, Karen Wald, and David Western.

Many assisted in the arduous tasks of editing, fact checking, and updating, including Marcus Lenzen, my marvelous German intern who tracked down many minute details. Joe Richey edited the initial chapters with great skill, while Maiah Jaskoski, Sandy Munro, Kimberly Pfeiffer, and Tommy Zarembka helped with editing during the final stages. I am enormously grateful for the meticulous skill and great care Pat Harris gave to copyediting the final manuscript.

Out of gratitude and for the sake of full disclosure, I want to thank the following companies that provided free or discounted "fam" trips, which made my research more affordable: Barker Campbell & Farley, The Boma, Conservation Corporation, Cubatur, Delamere Camp, Explora Lodge, Global Exchange, Horizontes Hotels (Cuba), Las Tortugas Lodge, Lasca Airlines, Lewa Downs, Lobo Lodge, Maho Bay, Marketing & Trade International, Mehenye, Oliver's Camp, Puesta del Sol, Sabi Sabi, Samoa Turismo (Ecuador), SATOUR, Spring O'Brien, Sun Game Lodges, Tamu Safaris, Tikal Tour Operators, Wilderness Safaris, and Wildersun Safaris.

I thank my colleagues at the Institute for Policy Studies and the Interhemispheric Resource Center, especially John Cavanagh, Meena Bhandari, Tom Barry, and Erik Leaver, for allowing me time to finish this book and picking up the slack on our other projects when I needed time off.

Finally I thank my family for once again putting up with all the weird hours and angst involved in writing a book. Our Tanzanian daughter, Deta Francis, provided logistical help in Tanzania and continual encouragement once she came to the U.S. So did my mother-in-law, Fran, who accompanied me to Monteverde. My husband Tony kept the household running for months on end and provided just enough pressure to keep me moving forward. My children, Shanti and Jody Avirgan, traveled with me in Africa, Cuba, and Costa Rica, taking pictures, offering support, and turning work into pleasure. I couldn't have done the book without them.

Part I

What Is Ecotourism?

Chapter 1

In Search of the Golden Toad

In 1987, Costa Rican Giovanni Bello and other investigators counted more than 1,500 adult golden toads in the Monteverde Cloud Forest Reserve. The next year, scientists and naturalist guides found just 10. In 1989, they found only one. Later that same year, there were two unconfirmed sightings of others. Since then, no golden toads have been found. Many scientists have by now concluded that the brilliant orange-colored toad, which was known to exist only in Costa Rica's Monteverde Reserve, is extinct. At the same time, scientists around the world began noticing a dramatic drop in numbers of other species of toads and frogs. There are many theories to explain why. Some speculate a connection with volcanic eruptions, the warming El Niño winds and currents, acid rain, depletion of the ozone layer, chemical pollution, habitat destruction, or disease caused by a lethal, single-celled protozoan.[1] Others warn that frogs, like canaries carried down a coal mine shaft, are giving a biological signal that conditions for survival are horribly out of balance, that catastrophe is close at hand.

Bello, for his part, continues to hope that the golden toads are simply in hiding, buried deep under the reserve's rich, moist biomass, and that one spring day they will again emerge, hopping from fern to vine to root. Nowadays, visitors to Monteverde see the golden toad only on postcards and on the entrance sign to one of the reserve's most popular tourist lodges, El Sapo Dorado.

In Monteverde, the disappearance of the golden toad has coincided with the phenomenal growth of tourism, in particular a relatively new "species" known as ecotourism. Although often equated with nature tourism, ecotourism, properly understood, goes further, striving to respect and benefit protected areas as well as the people living around or on these lands. The history of the golden toad and that of ecotourism are intertwined, and some speculate that an ecotourist (or perhaps a scientist) may have carried into Monteverde's rain forest an alien organism that caused a plague among the reserve's toad population.[2] If true, it is ironic, since Monteverde scientists and residents have consciously used conservation grants and ecotourism profits to protect the habitat of the golden toad and other exotic, endangered species, including the resplendent quetzal, one of the world's most majestic birds. Monteverde's farming community and conservation organizations began buying and incorporating surrounding land so that by the mid-1990s more than 10,000 hectares (some 26,000 acres) had been incorporated into this privately owned park, which is managed by a nonprofit scientific organization.[3] For several decades, the reserve attracted only scientists, some students, visiting friends and family (known in tourism lingo as VFFs), and a trickle of hardy travelers. But beginning in the mid-1980s—on the eve of the golden toad's disappearance—the worldwide growth of ecotourism brought a flood of visitors and a tidal wave of change to this small community. Tourist numbers grew from 450 in 1975 to 8,000 in 1985, to more than 50,000 in the late 1990s.[4] Eighty percent of Monteverde's hotels have been built since 1990. Ecotourism has now surpassed dairy farming as the community's main source of income. Bello himself now works as a naturalist guide, taking ecotourists through the rain forest.

Around the world, ecotourism has been hailed as a panacea: a way to fund conservation and scientific research, protect fragile and pristine ecosystems, benefit rural communities, promote development in poor countries, enhance ecological and cultural sensitivity, instill environmental awareness and a social conscience in the travel industry, satisfy and educate the discriminating tourist, and, some claim, build world peace.[5] Although "green" travel is being aggressively marketed as a "win-win" solution for the Third World, the environment, the tourist, and the travel industry, close examination shows a much more complex reality.

This book is about the search for ecotourism. Although nearly every country in the world, including the United States, Canada, Germany, Australia, and other developed countries, is now engaged in ecotourism, perhaps its most exciting potential is in its use as a tool for economic development and environmental protection in developing countries. I lived in East Africa and Central America for nearly twenty years, first as a graduate student and then as a journalist covering liberation struggles, civil and cold war–inspired conflicts, natural and humanmade disasters, popular protests, and a variety of economic development strategies spanning the political spectrum. Although tourism was only occasionally a central focus of my reporting, I was fascinated with its complexities and contradictions as they played out on the ground in East and southern Africa, Latin America, and the Caribbean.

For many of these economically poor countries with rich, unique, and largely unspoiled national parks and natural wonders, tourism offered a possible means for earning foreign exchange. But the infrastructure costs of conventional tourism are high, its adverse social effects are often great, and the economic benefits often meager, since most of the profits did not stay in the host countries. In the 1970s, I witnessed a lively and contentious political debate over tourism between socialist Tanzania and aggressively capitalist Kenya, which shared between them some of the world's finest game parks. By the early 1990s, these countries and the island of Zanzibar were all aggressively promoting nature tourism and ecotourism, with historically marginalized rural communities demanding a slice of the tourism pie. When I lived in Costa Rica during the 1980s, I saw the country transform itself from a low-key destination for nature lovers into the foremost ecotourism destination in the Americas. In the early 1990s, I was intrigued to see that both South Africa and Cuba, two countries that for very different political reasons had been considered international pariahs, were promoting tourism (and ecotourism) as the engine for economic growth and reintegration into the worldwide free-market system. And in the mid-1990s, I was alarmed by reports that the Galápagos Islands—a unique ecosystem and one of the world's most fragile, often cited as the place where ecotourism began—was being permanently altered by an uncontrolled influx of tourists, immigrants, and commercial fishermen.

In looking closely at Costa Rica, the Galápagos Islands, Cuba, Tanzania, Zanzibar, Kenya, and South Africa, I have assessed whether ecotourism is succeeding in its objectives of protecting the environment and benefiting local people and developing countries. I came to realize that to make such an assessment, it is necessary to examine the growth of ecotourism within each country's tourism strategy, its political system, and its changing economic policies. Just as scientists have come, over the past twenty years, to the realization that individual species cannot be studied in isolation but must be analyzed within their ecosystems, so, too, must tourism and ecotourism be placed within a country's overall development strategy, as well as within the context of a global economy that is systematically eliminating trade barriers and facilitating the penetration of foreign capital.

Research for this book involved journeys to all these countries as well as briefer forays to other destinations and international conferences. What I found was a mixture of hype and experimentation, superficiality and creativity, including industry promises before international forums and "green" imaging in slick brochures, juxtaposed, out in the field, with grassroots struggles around national parks and nature tourism by some of the world's poorest and most marginalized peoples. At its worst, when not practiced with the utmost care, ecotourism threatens the very ecosystems on which it depends. At its best, ecotourism offers a set of principles and practices that have the potential to fundamentally transform the way the tourism industry operates. As we reach the end of this millennium, the scorecard is very mixed: like the golden toad, genuine ecotourism is hard to find.

Defining and Measuring Ecotourism

In 1991, The Ecotourism Society coined what I have found to be the most
succinct yet encompassing definition of ecotourism: *"Responsible travel to
natural areas that conserves the environment and improves the well-being of
local people"* (italics added).[6] Ecotourism is often claimed to be the most
rapidly expanding sector of the tourism industry,[7] but when its growth is
measured, ecotourism is often lumped together with nature, wildlife, and
adventure tourism. In fact, ecotourism should be viewed as distinct from
these other categories. Nature tourism involves travel to unspoiled places to
experience and enjoy nature. It usually involves moderate and safe forms of
exercise such as hiking, biking, sailing, and camping. Wildlife tourism
involves travel to observe animals, birds, and fish in their native habitats.
Adventure tourism is nature tourism with a kick: it requires physical skill and
endurance (rope climbing, deep-sea diving, bicycling, or kayaking) and involves a degree of risk taking, often in little-charted terrain. Whereas nature,
wildlife, and adventure tourism are defined solely by the recreational activities of the tourist, ecotourism is defined as well by its *benefits* to both conservation and people in the host country.

"Real ecotourism," writes tour operator Kurt Kutay, "is more than travel
to enjoy or appreciate nature."[8] It also includes minimization of environmental and cultural consequences, contributions to conservation and community projects in developing countries, and environmental education and
political consciousness raising, such as the establishment of codes of conduct
for travelers as well as the various components of the travel industry.

There is at present no systematic effort to gather data worldwide on
ecotourism as a category distinct from nature, wildlife, and adventure
tourism. Therefore, estimates of ecotourism vary depending on the definition used. A 1992 survey conducted by the U.S. Travel Data Center estimated that 7 percent (8 million) of U.S. travelers had taken at least one ecotourism trip and noted that another 30 percent (35 million) said they
planned to take one during the next three years.[9] The survey described ecotourism as travel "during which travelers learn about and appreciate the
environment," a definition that encompasses nature and wildlife travel as
well. A 1994 study found that 77 percent of North American consumers had
already taken a vacation involving nature, outdoor adventure, or learning
about another culture. Estimates of ecotourism's annual growth in demand
range from 10 to 30 percent, and The Ecotourism Society projects that "no
drop off [is] foreseen as we head into the 21st century."[10] Ecotourism earnings soared as well, although estimates varied widely. A 1989 guesstimate
put the annual amount earned by developing countries at $2–$12 billion,[11]
and subsequent estimates have been as high as $30 billion per year.[12]

Ecotourism, or at least a revamped version of nature and wildlife tourism, is at the core of many Third World nations' economic development strategies and conservation efforts. Nearly every developing country is now promoting some brand of ecotourism. At international conferences and in the travel and environmental literature, the choice of countries seems endless: Dominica, Bolivia, Belize, Mongolia, Vietnam, Cambodia, Bhutan, Fiji, Indonesia, Senegal, Namibia, Madagascar, Uganda, and Zimbabwe are among the countries in the Americas, Asia, and Africa most actively marketing themselves as ecotourism destinations. Major international conservation organizations have initiated ecotourism-linked departments, programs, studies, and field projects, and many are conducting nature tours, adventure tours, or ecotours for their members. International lending and aid agencies, under the banner of sustainable rural development, local income generation, biodiversity, institutional capacity building, and infrastructure development, pump millions of dollars into projects with ecotourism components. The major travel industry organizations have set up programs, developed definitions and guidelines, and held dozens of conferences on ecotourism, and many of the leading corporate players have tried to "green" their operations. In the United States alone, there are scores of magazines, consultants, public relations firms, and university programs specializing in ecotourism. The Ecotourism Society (TES), a small, energetic, and influential nonprofit organization based in Vermont, includes among its 1,200 paid members travel industry representatives, government officials, academics, and consultants in more than seventy-five countries. There are, as well, a growing number of nationally based and regional ecotourism societies in countries and regions such as Kenya, Zanzibar, Australia, Ecuador, Indonesia, Belize, Brazil, and the Caribbean.[13]

And all this has happened in just two decades.

Origins of Ecotourism

The word *tourism*—describing travel as a leisure activity—first appeared in the *Oxford English Dictionary* in 1811, but the concept goes back as far as the ancient Greeks and Romans, whose wealthy citizens vacationed at thermal baths and explored exotic places around Europe and the Mediterranean region. A French monk, Aimeri de Picaud, is credited with writing the first tour guide. His book, published in 1130, was intended for pilgrims traveling to Spain. Early travel was often combined with religious pilgrimages, scientific investigation, geographic exploration, cultural and anthropological study, human and resource exploitation, or conquest, but from the beginning travelers have also sought out places of natural beauty for exploration and relaxation. Until the second half of the twentieth century, the number of travelers was small and their pace was slow. They traversed the globe by foot, sailing boat, horse, mule, and camel and, more recently, by ship, train, car, and plane.

In the eighteenth and nineteenth centuries, European aristocrats, British gentry, and, gradually, wealthy Americans took leisurely "grand tours" of the Continent's natural and cultural features, including the Swiss Alps.[14] With the industrial revolution, the first paid holidays and cheaper travel by railroad combined to create an annual mass exodus to seaside resorts in Europe. In 1841, Thomas Cook organized the first tourist excursion, a train ride through the English Midlands taking groups to temperance rallies, and by the mid-1850s, he was offering railway tours of the Continent. About the same time, in the United States, the American Express Company introduced traveler's checks and money orders.

Nothing, however, has altered tourism as profoundly as the airplane. Air travel for pleasure dates from 1948, when Pan American World Airways introduced tourist class. Mass international tourism really took off with the opening of commercial airplane routes between the United States and Europe, and in 1957, jet engines made air travel more accessible to the public. Not until the 1970s, with the advent of wide-bodied, high-speed airplanes, did Third World destinations come within reach of many people. In the mid-1970s, 8 percent of all tourists were from developed countries, traveling on holidays to developing countries. By the mid-1980s, the number had jumped to 17 percent, and by the mid-1990s it had climbed to 20 percent. International tourism to the Third World is increasing at 6 percent annually, compared with only 3.5 percent to developed countries. About 80 percent of these foreign travelers come from just twenty developed countries, with destinations in Asia, Africa, and the Americas growing at the expense of those in Europe. Between 1992 and 1997, the number of international tourists worldwide grew from 463 million to 594 million, a jump of 30 percent, and it will double between 1990 and 2010, according to the World Tourism Organization (WTO). Four to five times as many people travel inside their own countries.[15]

Changing work patterns, like improved modes of transportation, have also altered how and where people spend their leisure time. "In the past," Karen Ziffer, an ecotourism expert with Conservation International, points out, "people spent their limited free time relaxing from a grueling work week."[16] Leisure time and paid vacations have been increasingly recognized by the International Labor Organization (ILO) and other bodies as a fundamental human right. The ILO's first convention on holidays with pay, passed in 1936, provided for merely one week's leave per year; a 1970 convention expanded holidays to a minimum of three weeks with pay for all workers.[17] With paid vacation time, shorter hours of work, less physically taxing jobs, and better education, vacationers began to demand personal development as well as relaxation and entertainment. In the early 1990s, studies of U.S. consumers found, for instance, that 40 percent of U.S. travelers wanted "life-enhancing" travel, compared with 20 percent who were "seeking the sun."[18]

By the 1990s, tourism vied with oil as the world's largest legitimate business. In 1995, worldwide spending on travel totaled $3.4 trillion, and it was expected to reach $4.2 trillion by the year 2000. Tourism itself is the world's number one employer, accounting for 10 percent of jobs globally. If it were a country, it would have the second largest economy, surpassed only by that of the United States.[19] The United States is the world's biggest generator and beneficiary of tourism, accounting for about 15 percent of total spending, but tourism plays a major role in the economies of 125 of the world's 170 countries.[20]

For economy and convenience, most vacationers opt for prepaid packages on cruise ships and at beach resorts. Over the past four decades, mass tourism has become synonymous with the "four S's," sun, sea, sand, and sex, and has given rise to derogatory—and often accurate—stereotypes of the typical tourist.[21] Host countries, as well as tourists, began growing disappointed with this type of tourism. Although mass tourism was originally embraced by many countries as a "smokeless" (nonpolluting) industry that could increase employment and gross national product, evidence quickly grew that its economic benefits were marginal and its social and environmental costs high. Much of the money did not stay in the host country, and often the only benefit to the local community was found in low-paying service-level employment as maids, waiters, and drivers. Mass tourism often brought overdevelopment and uneven development, environmental pollution, and invasion by culturally insensitive and economically disruptive foreigners. In 1980, popular opposition within developing countries crystallized into a strongly worded statement drawn up at a conference in Manila convened by religious leaders. The Manila Declaration on World Tourism stated unequivocally that "tourism does more harm than good to people and to societies in the Third World." The Ecumenical Coalition on Third World Tourism, founded at this meeting,[22] has led the fight against sex tourism and other forms of exploitation.

In many cases, popular vacation spots are becoming degraded as a result of human activities linked to industrialization. In the Adriatic Sea, algae blooms have made the water unappealing to swimmers. Beaches have been closed in England because of radioactivity, in New Jersey because of hospital waste, and in Haiti because of sewage. In Canada, acid rain has depleted salmon stocks, threatening the closure of 600 fishing lodges. In some instances, such damage is caused by uncontrolled mass tourism; in others, by industrialization, overexploitation of natural resources, consumerism, and other forms of "unsustainable development that characterizes contemporary Western civilization," according to Héctor Ceballos-Lascuráin, an ecotourism expert with the International Union for the Conservation of Nature and Natural Resources (IUCN, now known as the World Conservation Union).[23]

From Nature Tourism to Ecotourism

In the United States, organized nature tourism—that is, travel to pristine places, usually involving physical activity—probably started with the Sierra Club Outing program. Begun in 1901, the first such expedition involved 100 hikers (plus Chinese chefs as well as pack mules and wagons) who trekked to the backcountry wilderness of the Sierra Nevada. The High Trip, as these large annual outings were known, continued until 1972. Although their purpose was "to take Club members into the Sierra to show them the natural wonders so that those persons could become active workers for 'the preservation of the forests and other natural features of the Sierra Nevada Mountains,'" these enormous caravans, which grew to an average of 115–125 people, were "anything but 'eco'" in terms of their effects on the environment, said Charles Hardy, director of Sierra Club Outings, in a 1996 interview.[24]

The rapid growth of nature tourism within the United States and overseas has been facilitated in recent years by the same ease and accessibility of modern transport that has fueled the rise in conventional tourism. The increasing number of people to whom these formerly remote natural areas are now available has resulted in serious damage to some of the most popular destinations. Visitors to the National Park System in the United States, one of the world's oldest, largest, and best-maintained park systems, rose by 20 percent in the decade 1980–1990, from about 190 million to more than 250 million. During the peak months of July and August, popular parks such as Yellowstone (the world's first national park, created in 1872) and Yosemite are anything but restful. Traffic jams resemble urban gridlock, exhaust fumes and loud music permeate the air, and the millions of visitors leave behind tons of garbage. The Grand Canyon, the second most visited U.S. national park, attracts nearly 3.8 million tourists per year,[25] and this is having a negative effect on the canyon's ecosystem. According to a January 6, 1995, press report, "Park rangers are killing off more than two dozen mule deer that have become hooked on . . . snack food and candy handed out at Phantom Ranch, losing their natural ability to digest vegetation." David Haskell, chief of resource management for Grand Canyon National Park, called junk food the "crack cocaine of the deer world."[26]

Turned off by overcrowded, unpleasant conditions and spurred by relatively affordable and plentiful airline routes, increasing numbers of nature lovers began seeking serenity and pristine beauty overseas. Between the late 1970s and mid-1980s, the new field known as ecotourism gradually took shape. The definition has often been vague: it is frequently referred to as "responsible," "sustainable," "conservation," or "low-impact" tourism[27] and is often listed by the travel industry in the category of nature or adventure tourism. The confusion over definition is partly due to its historical roots, which, broadly stated, can be traced to four sources: (1) scientific, conservation, and nongovernmental organization (NGO) circles; (2) multilateral aid institutions; (3) developing countries; and (4) the travel industry and traveling public. Almost simultaneously but for different reasons, the principles and practices of ecotourism began taking shape within these four areas, and by the early 1990s, the concept had coalesced into the hottest new genre of environmentally and socially responsible travel.

Conservation Organizations: Better Protection of Natural Areas

Most typically, ecotourism involves visits to areas that are under some form of environmental protection by governments, conservation or scientific organizations, or private owners or entrepreneurs. Around the world, many protected areas have been modeled after the U.S. National Parks System, which was created in the late nineteenth century by drawing boundaries around specific areas to preserve them in their natural state and free them of direct use. The United States Congress decreed that these national parks would serve as "pleasure grounds" for visitors, thus linking national parks to tourism from their inception. Other countries followed, setting aside land for national parks: Australia (1879), Mexico (1898), Argentina (1903), and Sweden (1909).[28] Since the 1970s, more protected areas have been established worldwide than during all preceding periods. By 1989, about 4,500 sites, totaling about 4.79 million square kilometers, or 1.85 million square miles—3.2 percent of the earth's surface—had been placed under some type of protection.[29]

But there is a downside to this impressive trend. By the late 1960s, the large international conservation organizations, together with environmentalists and scientists working in Latin America and Africa, began to reach two related conclusions. In Africa, they began to realize that "preservationist" conservation methods of separating (often forcibly) people and parks were not working. Most national parks and reserves in Africa were originally established for hunters, scientists, or tourists, with little or no regard for the local people. Park management emphasized policing—"fences and fines"—which forcibly evicted and kept out local community members, who were often politically and ethnically marginalized rural poor. These people, who received little or no benefit from either the parks or tourism, deeply resented being excluded from lands of religious and economic value and being restricted to increasingly unsustainable areas around the parks. Poaching, degradation of resources, and local hostility toward the parks and tourism were on the increase. The "preservationist approach," one study concluded, "requires an essentially militaristic defense strategy and will almost always heighten conflict."[30]

Some scientists, conservationists, park officials, and environmental organizations concerned about this clash between parks and people began to rethink the protectionist philosophy guiding park management. They began to argue that protected species, areas, and ecosystems would survive only if those people living nearest them benefited financially from both the parks and tourism. As David Western, director of the Kenya Wildlife Service (KWS) between 1994 and 1998 and first president of The Ecotourism Society, writes, these "conscientious concerns for nature were soon extended to local (usually indigenous) peoples. Implicit in the term is the assumption that local communities living with nature can and should benefit from tourism and will save nature in the process."[31] It was in Kenya that Africa's first official experiments with this new approach began. In the early 1970s, the government agreed to put several reserves, including Maasai Mara Game Reserve and Amboseli National Park, under the control of local county councils, which began receiving revenue from both park entrance fees and hotels and other tourism facilities. This "stakeholders" theory—that people will protect what they receive value from—has dovetailed with economic development theories holding that the road out of poverty must begin at, not simply trickle down to, the local community level. In the mid-1980s, as the concept of ecotourism began to take hold in East and southern Africa, the stakeholders theory was broadened to encompass environmentally sensitive, low-impact, culturally sensitive tourism that also helped educate visitors and local community members.

Parallel to this trend, scientists and environmental activists in South America were becoming increasingly alarmed that illegal logging, ranching, oil drilling, mining, and human settlement were destroying much of the world's remaining tropical forests. These rain forests are vital as both reservoirs of biological diversity and suppliers of oxygen necessary to maintain a balance in the earth's atmosphere. Initially, Latin Americans, from Mexico to Chile, tended to view ecotourism narrowly, as a conservation tool that could provide an economic alternative to these more invasive and extractive activities, promote public awareness of environmental issues, and increase funds for conservation. In a groundbreaking 1976 article, Gerardo Budowski, a Costa Rica–based conservationist, argued that the relationship between tourism and conservation can be variously one of conflict, coexistence, or symbiosis; he also outlined ways in which tourism can be used to support conservation.[32] Mexican architect and environmentalist Héctor Ceballos-Lascuráin defined ecotourism as travel "to relatively undisturbed or uncontaminated natural areas with the specific object of studying, admiring, and enjoying the scenery of its wild plants and animals, as well as any existing cultural aspects found in these areas." He argued that "the person who practices ecotourism will eventually acquire a consciousness that will convert him into somebody keenly interested in conservation issues." The emphasis is on building an activist constituency among the traveling public committed to environmental protection.[33]

In what may well be Costa Rica's earliest ecotourism-related news report, an October 1980 article in the weekly, English-language *Tico Times* hailed tour operator Michael Kaye's "new recipe" of "wilderness adventure" that was "being tossed into the traditional blend of museums, churches and 'pueblos tipicos.'" It described Kaye's recently formed company, Costa Rica Expeditions, which specialized in white-water rafting, as "the chief, if not only, alternative to traditional tourism" and quoted Kaye as saying, "Tourism should contribute to, rather than exploit (the land). . . . It should be active rather than passive, emphasizing cultural exchange rather than mere sightseeing."[34] These were pioneering words. Over the years, Kaye moved on to develop a fuller understanding of ecotourism, including a commitment to supporting Costa Rica's national park system, providing well-trained guides, and opposing megaresort developments.

Thus, the notion of ecotourism emerged almost simultaneously, although for somewhat different reasons, in Latin America and Africa. Quickly, however, there began to be a cross-fertilization of these concepts such that today ecotourism is usually seen as a tool for benefiting fragile ecosystems and local communities. While Ceballos-Lascuráin claims that he first coined the term *ecotourism* in 1983, other experts say it originated in Kenton Miller's pioneering 1978 work on national park planning in Latin America; there, it contains both dimensions of the definition. Miller argued that development must integrate biological considerations with economic, social, and political factors to meet both environmental and human needs. He contended that the potential for national parks to contribute to "ecodevelopment" had grown during the 1970s as greater numbers of well-trained personnel were able to work with larger budgets on more parklands. Kenton's concepts of ecodevelopment and ecotourism quickly entered the debate on sustainable development.[35] In 1980, the IUCN issued the *World Conservation Strategy,* which reflected the views of a growing number of organizations in stressing that protected area management must be linked with the economic activities of local communities. In 1982, conservationists at the IUCN's World Congress on National Parks in Bali endorsed this concept, arguing that conservation programs need to be community-friendly and promote economic development. The congress called for increased educational programs, along with revenue- and management-sharing schemes.[36] A decade later, at its IV World Congress on National Parks and Protected Areas in Caracas, Venezuela, the IUCN reaffirmed and expanded on these concepts, making a policy recommendation that "in developing greater cooperation between the tourism industry and protected areas the primary consideration must be the conservation of the natural environment and the quality of life of local communities."[37]

At this 1992 World Congress, the IUCN set up a small Ecotourism Consultancy Program, headed by Ceballos-Lascuráin, to offer IUCN members "technical consultation support service and a range of advice" for planning ecotourism developments.[38] (The IUCN brings together some 5,000 experts in governments, government agencies, and NGOs from more than 130 countries, with a central secretariat in Geneva.) In 1996, the Ecotourism Consultancy Program was expanded into the Task Force on Tourism and Protected Areas, with several dozen experts worldwide from park management agencies, academic institutions, tourism companies, and NGOs and a broader mandate to collect data on protected area tourism, develop case studies and tourism management guidelines for protected areas, and provide advice to the World Commission on Protected Areas (WCPA), a global network of more than 1,000 protected area managers and specialists that is supported by the IUCN. It does not, however, have the resources to serve other tourism-related institutions or to function as the tourism focus for the entire IUCN organization.[39]

Multilateral Aid Institutions: Responding to Environmentalism and the Debt Crisis

With the rise of both the environmental movement and Third World debt in the late 1970s, international aid and lending institutions also took a fresh look at tourism as a development tool and conservation strategy. By the mid-1990s, the United Nations Environment Programme (UNEP), the Inter-American Development Bank (IDB), the Organization of American States (OAS), the U.S. Agency for International Development (USAID), and other international assistance agencies were supporting a variety of ecotourism programs and projects. However, the trendsetter for the multilateral institutions has been the International Bank for Reconstruction and Development, or World Bank.

The World Bank, set up following World War II, has extended $300 billion in loans for some 6,000 economic and development projects in about 175 countries. Although tourism has represented a relatively minor part of its portfolio, during the 1970s the World Bank became the major source of finance for tourism-related projects. The bank's first tourism-related loan was made in 1967[40] by the International Finance Corporation (IFC), an arm of the institution that lends to private corporations rather than governments. It was for a hotel in Kenya that was partly owned by the Inter-Continental Hotel Corporation, which was then a subsidiary of Pan American Airways, signifying the interlinkage between large hotel chains and international airlines.

Between 1969 and 1979, the World Bank's Tourism Projects Department pushed developing countries to invest in conventional tourism as a strategy for encouraging foreign investment and earning foreign exchange, and in 1977, tourism was incorporated into the New International Economic Order doctrine as a means to redistribute wealth from rich nations to poor. During this period, the World Bank loaned about $450 million directly to governments for twenty-four tourism projects—referred to as "tourist plants"—in eighteen developing countries.[41] However, according to an official involved, as competition for bank funding grew, there was increasing criticism that the bank should be investing in low-cost housing and other poverty reduction programs, not in luxury hotels and large infrastructure projects to support international tourism and the private sector. This, coupled with a string of financially and environmentally disastrous projects in such countries as Egypt, South Korea, and Morocco, led the World Bank to close down its Tourism Projects Department in 1979.[42]

By the 1980s, failed tourism projects were not all that sullied the World Bank's reputation. The bank was under attack around the globe for its environmentally destructive big dams and other megaprojects that uprooted hundreds of thousands of people as well as for a pattern of lending that seemed to favor repressive regimes. Beginning in the 1980s, the bank linked its loans to crippling structural adjustment policies that forced poor countries to cut spending and social programs, privatize, and open their economies to foreign investment and trade. This also drew increasingly critical attention to bank practices. As Third World nations' foreign debt continued to climb, the bank looked for new directions. By the mid-1980s, the institution was once again contemplating tourism as part of its export promotion and debt repayment strategy. As Clark University professor Cynthia Enloe wrote in 1990, "The international politics of debt and the international pursuit of pleasure have become tightly knotted together."[43]

But the bank's rhetoric at least shifted to include sustainable development and environmental protection. In 1986, the bank issued its first official statement regarding protection of wildlands—defined as natural habitats relatively untouched by human activities—within development plans. Its guidelines, initiated more as an encouragement than as a "will-do" policy, state that the World Bank "promotes and supports" protection of wildlands and improved land use in its projects, which increasingly included tourism. They emphasize the need "to include local people in the planning and benefits" of wildland management projects and note that "rural development investments that provide farmers and villagers in the vicinity of [wildland management areas with] an alternative to further encroachment" can also help protect parks and reserves.[44]

In 1990, the World Bank, together with two United Nations agencies (UNEP and the United Nations Development Programme, or UNDP)[45] set up the Global Environment Facility (GEF), first as a pilot project and then, in 1994, as a permanent mechanism. The GEF's purpose is to facilitate and fund the integration of environmental concerns into development projects and to help implement the global environmental conventions agreed to at the 1992 United Nations Conference on Environment and Development (UNCED), known as the Earth Summit. One of the GEF's four focal areas is protecting biodiversity through, among other means, "development of environmentally sustainable nature-based tourism" and "participatory schemes for sustainable natural resource management, including . . . local communities, indigenous groups, and other sectors of society."[46]

Although the World Bank did not reconstitute a centralized, specialized unit for tourism, during the 1990s it undertook a large number of tourism studies and invested in a variety of multimillion-dollar tourism-linked loans under categories such as infrastructure, environment and biodiversity, rural development, and technical assistance.[47] These include a tourism infrastructure project involving Tanzania's national parks and tourism and recreational development within protected areas in Kenya and Mauritius. In addition, the portfolio of the IFC's Tourism Unit, which was never closed, has grown exponentially in recent years, although it has funded only a handful of ecotourism projects (see chapter 3).

No other international agency appears to be involved in more ecotourism projects than USAID. Ecotourism fits within two of the agency's four broad objectives—promoting national economic growth and conserving biodiversity—and this has facilitated the inclusion of ecotourism in many projects. Beginning in the 1980s, USAID, in tandem with the World Bank and other international funding agencies, saw a combination of the private sector, free trade, foreign investment, and expanded exports as the main engine for growth in poor countries. As a 1992 USAID study, carried out to establish a framework for the agency's programs, summarized, "AID's central environmental objective is to promote environmentally and socially sound, long-term economic growth. . . . At the same time, AID has placed high priority on stimulating private investment, free markets and free enterprise. Many officials within AID view nature-based tourism as well-suited for simultaneously meeting both objectives. As a result, there has been an increasing level of activity related to ecotourism within the agency."[48] In 1985, USAID began its support for ecotourism activities (loosely defined by the agency as nature-based tourism) by funding some twenty conservation and development projects in developing countries carried out by the World Wide Fund for Nature (WWF, known as the World Wildlife Fund in the United States and Canada);[49] in 1989, the agency initiated its Parks in Peril project to improve management as well as recreational and educational use of twenty parks in Latin America and the Caribbean;[50] and in 1992, it began funneling assistance for biodiversity projects in Asia and the Pacific region through a consortium of U.S. conservation NGOs. The agency also financed scores of major ecotourism studies focusing on a wide variety of issues and geographic areas.[51]

By the mid-1990s, USAID had 105 projects (totaling more than $2 billion in funding) with ecotourism components. They were in countries such as Belize, Costa Rica, Ecuador, Nepal, Kenya, Zaire, Madagascar, Jamaica, Sri Lanka, and Thailand. A number were transnational programs, such as one in southern Africa aimed at creating a cross-border megapark, including ecotourism and community development projects, within an ecosystem that encompasses South Africa, Swaziland, Mozambique, and Zimbabwe; another, Paseo Pantera (Panther Walk), aimed to establish national ecotourism councils in several Central American countries. These projects were all multidimensional but showed a strong emphasis on working with the private sector and channeling funds through U.S.-based NGOs, a shift from USAID's usual practice prior to the 1980s of primarily funding government programs in developing countries. Of these 105 projects, 52 involved the private sector, 37 involved community participation, 46 involved government capacity building, and 47 involved nongovernmental capacity building.[52]

Developing Countries: Seeking Foreign Exchange and Sustainable Development

During the mid- to late 1980s, many Third World countries turned to ecotourism as a foreign exchange earner that was potentially less destructive than alternatives such as logging, oil extraction, cattle, bananas, commercial fishing, or conventional mass tourism. They viewed ecotourism as minimizing negative effects through its emphasis on low-impact construction, controlled visitor numbers, and care in interacting with the local flora, fauna, and human population. Further, it could, in some instances, be more profitable. Studies in various countries have found that ecotourism and related economic activities may be a better form of land use than cattle ranching or agriculture, especially in arid and semiarid areas. On one ranch in Zimbabwe, for instance, a small wildlife operation incorporating tourism, hunting, and culling was estimated to generate three times more revenue per year than cattle ranching on the same amount of land; a similar study in South Africa found that net income from wildlife tourism was almost eleven times more than that from cattle ranching, and job generation was fifteen times greater.[53] In Kenya, it is estimated that one lion is worth $7,000 per year in income from tourism, and an elephant herd is valued at $610,000 annually.[54]

By the early 1990s, nearly every nonindustrialized country was promoting ecotourism as part of its development strategy. In several countries, nature-based tourism mushroomed into the largest foreign exchange earner, surpassing bananas in Costa Rica, coffee in Tanzania and Kenya, and textiles and jewelry in India. Namibia, which gained independence in 1990, purportedly became the first developing country to include what has been dubbed an "ecotourism plank" in its new constitution, pledging to protect "ecosystems, essential ecological processes and biological diversity . . . on a sustainable basis."[55] In 1994, Australia's government committed $10 million over a ten-year period to develop a national ecotourism strategy.[56] In 1997, Brazil announced it was launching a new $200 million program to develop ecotourism in its nine Amazonian states, and Latin American countries were reported to have invested $21 billion in ecotourism. Even places such as Zanzibar and Burma, which once were leery of tourism; the former Soviet Union, eastern Europe, China, and Vietnam, which once tightly controlled tourism; and onetime international outcasts such as South Africa and Cuba are now on the ecotourism bandwagon. Some entire countries, such as Costa Rica and Belize, are billed as ecotourism destinations. Elsewhere, pockets are promoted: Zanzibar, Mount Kilimanjaro, and the game parks in Tanzania; Amazonia, the highlands, and the Galápagos Islands in Ecuador; the habitat of the mountain gorillas in Uganda and, before its civil war, Rwanda. In 1998, the World Tourism Organization predicted that developing countries would continue to gain from the tourism boom and that international travelers would remain "interested in visiting and maintaining environmentally sound destinations."[57]

Throughout most of the world, the rise of ecotourism has coincided with the promotion of free markets and economic globalization, with the private sector hailed as the main engine for development. Nearly everywhere, state-run enterprises, including those in the tourism industry, are being sold off or shut down. The push toward privatization has been propelled by the international lending and aid agencies and major corporate players and is justified by the collapse of communism. These actors frequently promote "private–public partnerships," a term that often turns out to be a euphemism for state-provided subsidies and services for the private sector. State-run tourism operations (hotels, travel bureaus, and transportation services) have often—but not always—been overly bureaucratic and unresponsive to the standards of personal care that international tourists demand. But when unregulated and undertaxed, privatization means an influx of foreign companies, with most of the profits flowing away from those communities surrounding tourist attractions and often flowing out of the host country.

The Travel Industry: Tapping the Public's "Green" Sentiments

Although the travel industry did not originate the concept of ecotourism, it quickly adopted it, popularized it, mainstreamed it—and watered it down. The tourism industry, including the travel press, has come to view "green travel" as a marketing tool to attract the growing number of environmentally and socially conscious travelers and to open new, unexploited destinations. Ecotourism developed within the womb of the environmental movement, which took shape in the early 1970s and gained ascendancy in the 1980s. About 30 million Americans, for instance, belong to environmental organizations or profess an interest in environmental protection. The growing public concern with the environment and interest in outdoor-oriented travel, coupled with the growing dissatisfaction with conventional mass tourism, showed the tourism industry that there was a sizable market for ecotourism. As early as 1982, the WTO, together with the United Nations Environment Programme, declared: "The satisfaction of tourism requirements must not be prejudicial to the social and economic interests of the population in the tourist areas, to the environment, or above all to natural resources which are fundamental attractions of tourism."[58]

According to a 1995 survey by the Travel Industry Association of America (TIA), some 83 percent of travelers support "green" travel companies and are willing to spend more for travel services and products designed to conserve the environment. "The travel consumer's interest in environmentalism is not ending. More and more travelers are taking adventure and eco-vacations," said the TIA's president, William Norman, in 1995. "Consumers have made environmentalism part of their daily lives, and now they expect corporate America to be doing the same thing."[59]

Since the late 1980s, ecotourism has been endorsed, to various degrees, by the major tourism associations. These include, among others, the Madrid-based World Tourism Organization (WTO), created by the United Nations and made up of governments and private enterprises, which acts as a center to promote and monitor tourism development and compile industry statistics and market trends; the Travel Industry Association of America (TIA), based in Washington, D.C., and representing 2,300 travel-related businesses promoting travel to and within the United States; the American Society of Travel Agents (ASTA), the largest travel trade association in the world, with headquarters in Alexandria, Virginia, and representing 26,500 travel agents in 170 countries; and the World Travel and Tourism Council (WTTC), based in London and Brussels and made up of some seventy chief executive officers of major airlines, hotel chains, catering companies, and cruise lines.[60]

Because the tourism industry, more than any other, depends on a clean environment, it has embraced ecotourism as a means of survival. The 1992 Earth Summit, held in Rio de Janeiro, Brazil, resulted in the Rio Declaration on Environment and Development and Agenda 21, which together make up an environmental blueprint for the future that calls on industry, including the travel and tourism industry, to develop a strategy for sustainable development.[61] The tourism industry responded with *Agenda 21 for the Travel and Tourism Industry,* a lengthy document published in 1995 by the WTTC, the WTO, and the Costa Rica–based Earth Council, which is supposed to be overseeing implementation of Earth Summit directives. The report states, "The product that Travel & Tourism packages and sells ultimately relies on clean seas, pristine mountain slopes, unpolluted water, litter-free streets, well-preserved buildings and archaeological sites, and diverse cultural traditions." It contends that the industry has both a "vested interest" and a "moral responsibility to take the lead in making the transition to sustainable development"[62] and lists ten priority areas for action by travel companies, including energy efficiency, wastewater management, and sustainable design. It also lists nine broad priority areas for government agencies, national tourism administrations, and trade organizations, such as assessing carrying capacity, planning for sustainable tourism, and carrying out training, education, and public awareness efforts.[63]

ASTA, to which virtually every travel agent in the United States belongs, is potentially a strong mechanism for educating travel agents, developing ecotourism standards, and helping to monitor implementation. As one analyst puts it, travel agents need to "clearly assess and evaluate the environmental practices and responsibilities of the tourist suppliers they work with. Only then will they be able to satisfy environmental tourists by booking them with companies that are truly 'green.'"[64] In 1991, ASTA set up an Environmental Committee, which, committee member Marie Walters proclaims, shows that "the travel industry is really moving in a good direction to help preserve the environment." But in reality, its programs are inadequate. Although ASTA has taken a small but positive step in creating pilot training courses and a certification system for three specialty travel markets, including adventure tourism (which partially overlaps with ecotourism), the Environmental Committee's two main programs—the "Ten Commandments on Eco-Tourism" and its two annual environmental

(Washington, D.C.: Travel Industry Association of America, 1992), pp. 42–43.

10. World Travel and Tourism Council (WTTC), World Tourism Organization (WTO), and Earth Council, *Agenda 21 for the Travel and Tourism Industry: Towards Environmentally Sustainable Development* (London: WTTC, 1995), various pages; Héctor Ceballos-Lascuráin, "Tourism, Ecotourism, and Protected Areas," *Parks* 2, no. 3 (1991): 31; The Ecotourism Society, "TES Ecotourism Statistical Fact Sheet," on The Ecotourism Society's World Wide Web site (http://www.ecotourism.org/textfiles/stats.txt), February 1997; Brandon, *Ecotourism and Conservation*, p. 3; William Norman et al., *Green Evaluation Program and Compliance of Nature Tour Operators* (North Bennington, Vt.: The Ecotourism Society, February 1997), p. 4.

11. Karen Ziffer, *Ecotourism: The Uneasy Alliance* (Washington, D.C.: Conservation International and Ernst & Young, 1989), p. 9.

12. World Resources Institute, "Ecotourism: Rising Interest in Nature Vacations Has Mixed Results for Host Countries and the Resources They Promote," in *Environmental Almanac* (Boston: Houghton Mifflin, 1993), p. 149.

13. The Ecotourism Society's objectives include "finding the resources and building the expertise to make tourism a viable tool for conservation and sustainable development" and "documenting the best techniques for implementing ecotourism principles by collaborating with a growing global network of active professionals in the field." TES is a membership organization that publishes a newsletter and results of studies, conducts surveys, organizes education and training courses and seminars, and promotes media campaigns and lobbying regarding specific issues such as the raising of park entrance fees for foreigners in Costa Rica. Interviews with Megan Epler Wood, executive director of TES; literature from TES.

14. Héctor Ceballos-Lascuráin, *Tourism, Ecotourism, and Protected Areas* (Gland, Switzerland: IUCN, 1996), pp. 1–5; Nicholson-Lord, "Politics of Travel," pp. 11–18.

15. Anita Pleumarom, "The Political Economy of Tourism," *The Ecologist* 24, no. 4 (July–August 1994): 142; Anita Pleumarom, "Ecotourism: A New 'Green Revolution' in the Third World" (draft of article obtained from author, 1996), p. 2; Paula DiPerna, "Caution Must Be Exercised in Eco-tourism Growth," *Earth Times*, July 7, 1997; Ceballos-Lascuráin, *Tourism*, pp. 1–5; Nicholson-Lord, "Politics of Travel," pp. 11–18; World Tourism Organization statistics cited in "TES Statistical Fact Sheet," on The Ecotourism Society's World Wide Web site (Internet: http://www.ecotourism.org/textfiles/stats.txt), July 25, 1997; Brandon, *Ecotourism and Conservation*, p. 1.

16. Ziffer, *Uneasy Alliance*, p. 12.

17. International Labor Organization, *International Labor Standards: A Workers' Education Manual* (Geneva, Switzerland: International Labor Organization, 1990), pp. 52–54.

18. Brandon, *Ecotourism and Conservation*, p. 4.

19. "Exploring Tourism," *The Nation;* "TES Statistical Fact Sheet," July 25, 1997.

20. Nicholson-Lord, "Politics of Travel," p. 14; Ceballos-Lascuráin, *Tourism*, p. 9; Crossette, "Surprises," p. 5.

21. Ceballos-Lascuráin, *Tourism,* p. 23.

22. Nicholson-Lord, "Politics of Travel," p. 1⎺   subsequent conference in 1989 resulted in The Hague Declaration on T⎺   n, which reflects growing sensitivity to sustainable and community-b⎺   velopment. It calls on "states to strike a harmonious balance betwee⎺   iic and ecological consideration" and to give "priority attention to ⎺   and controlled development of tourist infrastructur⎺   d overall tourist capacity, in order to protect the envir⎺   lation." Although such agreements are nonbinding, ⎺   environmental considerations to the attention of ⎺   ourism industry. Ceballos-Lascuráin, *Tour⎺⎺

23.⎺   ⎺ism,* p. 19.

⎺oall, *History of the Sierra Club Outing Committee, 1901–1972* (San Francisco: Sierra Club, 1990), pp. 7–20; interview with Charles Hardy, director of the Sierra Club Outing program, 1996.

25. World Resources Institute, "Rising Interest in Nature Vacations," pp. 148, 156.

26. Associated Press, "Rangers Killing Deer Addicted to Snacks," *New York Times,* January 7, 1995. In the wake of this crisis, park officials began using "pretty blatant and graphic [educational] material" in order to "affect the visitors' behavior," explained Grand Canyon National Park biologist Elaine Lesley in a July 1997 telephone interview. She said they were seeing positive results: "The last deer was put down over a year ago, and the deer are in pretty good health now."

27. Malcolm Lillywhite claims to have coined the term low-impact tourism (LIT) in 1985. He defines LIT as establishing natural resource management through private investment in rural village–based tourism. In a study for USAID, he argues that LIT is distinct from ecotourism because it puts control and regulation of tourism development in the hands of the destination country and local communities, not in the hands of foreign travel agents and tour operators. However, Lillywhite's definition in fact fits within the definition of ecotourism used in this book. Malcolm Lillywhite, *Low Impact Tourism as a Strategy for Sustaining Natural and Cultural Resources in Sub Saharan Africa,* Mid Term Report (Washington, D.C.: U.S. Agency for International Development, Bureau of Africa, June 1990).

28. Ceballos-Lascuráin, *Tourism,* pp. 35–39.

29. Katrina Brandon and Michael Wells, "Planning for People and Parks: Design Dilemmas," *World Development* 20, no. 4 (1992): 558.

30. G. E. Machlis and D. L. Tichnell, *The State of the World's Parks: An International Assessment for Resources Management, Policy and Research* (Boulder, Colo.: Westview Press, 1985), p. 96, quoted in Michael Wells and Katrina Brandon, *People and Parks: Linking Protected Area Management with Local Communities* (Washington, D.C.: World Bank, World Wildlife Fund, and U.S. Agency for International Development, 1992), p. 1.

31. David Western, "Ecotourism: The Kenya Challenge," in C. G. Gakahu and B. E. Goode, *Ecotourism and Sustainable Development in Kenya* proceedings of the Kenya Ecotourism Workshop, Lake Nakuru National Park, Kenya, September 13–17, 1992 (Nairobi: Wildlife Conservation International, 1992), p. 15.

32. Gerardo Budowski, "Tourism and Environmental Conservation: Conflict, Coexistence, or Symbiosis?" *Environmental Conservation* 3, no. 1 (1976): 27–31.

33. Ceballos-Lascuráin, "The Future of Ecotourism," *Mexico Journal*, January 17, 1988, cited in International Resources Group, *Ecotourism: A Viable Alternative for Sustainable Management of Natural Resources in Africa* (Washington, D.C.: U.S. Agency for International Development, June 1992), p. 5.

34. Jean Hopfensperger, "Wilderness Adventures Spice Up Local Travel," *Tico Times*, October 10, 1980, p. 12.

35. Caballos-Lascuráin, *Tourism*, p. 21; Kenton Miller, *Planning National Parks for Ecodevelopment: Methods and Cases from Latin America* (Ann Arbor: University of Michigan, Center for Strategic Wildland Management Studies, 1978); Ray Ashton and Patricia Ashton, "An Introduction to Sustainable Tourism (Ecotourism) in Central America," unpublished paper prepared for Paseo Pantera: Regional Wetlands Management in Central America project (Gainesville, Fla.: Wildlife Conservation International, 1993), p. 18; Paul Eagles et al., eds., *Ecotourism: Annotated Bibliography for Planners and Managers*, 3rd ed. (North Bennington, Vt.: The Ecotourism Society, 1995), p. 41.

36. Wells and Brandon, *People and Parks*, p. 2.

37. Ceballos-Lascuráin, *Tourism*, p. 226.

38. Ibid., p. 213.

39. Correspondence with Paul Eagles, Department of Recreation and Leisure Studies, University of Waterloo, Waterloo, Ontario, Canada; IUCN, Commission on National Parks and Protected Areas, "Terms of Reference for the Tourism and Protected Areas Task Force" (Internet: http://www.ahs.uwaterloo.ca/rec/tmsofref.htm); information from World Commission on Protected Areas (Internet: http://www.iprolink.ch/iucnlib/themes/wcpa/wcpa.html)

40. The United Nations had declared 1967 the Year of the Tourist, an indication that tourism was increasingly viewed by multilateral institutions as an avenue for economic development in nonindustrialized countries.

41. This included huge resort complexes along the Black Sea and in Tunisia, Thailand, Mexico, and the Caribbean. Total investment in these projects was approximately $1.5 billion. In addition, the bank extended another $250 million in loans and credits for airport projects, for a total of about $1 billion.

42. Communications by Marcus Lenzen and author with various World Bank officials; Thanh-Dam Truong "The Political Economy of International Tourism," in *Sex, Money, and Morality: Prostitution and Tourism in Southeast Asia* (London: Zed Books, 1990), p. 122; Pleumarom, "Political Economy of Tourism," p. 143; International Resources Group, *Ecotourism*, p. 44.

43. Tourism is classified as an export industry because it earns foreign exchange. Cynthia Enloe, *Bananas, Beaches, and Bases: Making Feminist Sense of International Politics* (Berkeley: University of California Press, 1990), p. 32.

44. Telephone interview by Marcus Lenzen with Lou Scura, senior natural resource economist, Environment Department, World Bank, July 1997; World Bank, "Lending Policies: Sectoral, OP4.04," in *World Bank Operational Manual* (Washington, D.C.: World Bank, September 1995); Wells and Brandon, *People and Parks*, p. 3.

45. From the late 1960s onward, a variety of United Nations agencies, most importantly UNEP and the UNDP, financed and assisted international mass tourism through research, feasibility studies, master plans, education and training programs, and historic preservation projects.

46. Global Environment Facility, *Operational Strategy* (Washington, D.C.: Global Environment Facility, February 1996), pp. vii–viii, 18–19; International Resources Group, *Ecotourism,* p. 44.

47. International Finance Corporation, *IFC Tourism Sector Review* (Washington, D.C.: International Finance Corporation, Tourism Unit, February 1995), p. 12.

48. International Resources Group, *Ecotourism,* p. iii.

49. Wells and Brandon, *People and Parks,* p. 3.

50. U.S. Agency for International Development (USAID), *Parks in Peril,* Project Paper, Project No. 598-0782 (Washington, D.C.: USAID, 1990).

51. A list of USAID studies on ecotourism prepared for me in 1995 by the agency's Information Services Clearinghouse contained more than fifty reports.

52. "Table of USAID Environmental Projects with Ecotourism Components," mimeographed 7 page document compiled by Molly Davis, research associate, PPC/CDIE/DI Research and References Services Project, USAID, 1995.

53. David Grossman and Eddie Koch, *Ecotourism Report: Nature Tourism in South Africa: Links with the Reconstruction and Development Program* (Pretoria, South Africa: SATOUR, August 1995), p. 8; Price Waterhouse (1994) study discussed in Kreg Lindberg, "Economic Aspects of Ecotourism" (draft or article obtained from author, November 1997), p. 2.

54. Nicholson-Lord, "Politics of Travel," p. 16.

55. Republic of Namibia, *Constitution* (Windhoek: Rossing Uranium Ltd., 1990), p. 52.

56. Commonwealth Department of Tourism, Australia, *National Ecotourism Strategy* (Sydney: Australian Government Publishing Service, 1994), pp. iii, 1–6; Barbara Jones and Tanya Tear, "Australia's National Ecotourism Strategy," *Tourism Focus,* no. 1 (Paris, France: United National Environment Program, January–March 1995).

57. Ramesh Jaura, "Tourism: Developing Nations Expect Big Cut from Tourism Income," Inter-Press Service, March 11, 1998.

58. Quoted in U.S. Travel Data Center, *Discover America,* p. 15; Grossman and Koch, *Ecotourism Report,* p. 11.

59. Travel Industry Association of America, "Travelers Expect Environmental Responsibility," press release, March 17, 1995.

60. American Society of Travel Agents, "What Is ASTA?" (Internet: http://www.astanet.com/asta/pub/info/whatisasta.htmlx); World Travel and Tourism Council, "Media Information," Brussels, n.d.

61. United Nations, *Agenda 21: The United Nations Program of Action from Rio* (New York: United Nations, 1992). Even though travel and tourism may constitute the world's largest industry, the Earth Summit's Agenda 21 mentioned it in only a few sections. Chapter 11, for example, advocates that governments "promote and support the management of wildlife [and] . . . ecotourism," and chapter 36 calls for countries to "promote, as appropriate, environmentally sound leisure and tourism activities." Quoted in WTTC, WTO, and Earth Council, *Agenda 21 for the Travel and Tourism Industry,* p. 34.

62. WTTC, WTO, and Earth Council, *Agenda 21 for the Travel and Tourism Industry,* p. 34.

63. Ibid., p. 1.

64. Frederic Dimanche, "Greening Traditional Hotels," *Tour and Travel News,* August 29, 1994, p. G28.

65. Kutay, "Brave New Role," p. 40.

66. Western, "Ecotourism: The Kenya Challenge," pp. 15–16 (italics added).

67. Some other organizations posit similar definitions. The Canadian Environmental Advisory Council, for instance, states, "Ecotourism is an enlightening nature travel experience that contributes to conservation of the ecosystem, while respecting the integrity of host communities." However, although this definition speaks of respecting local communities, it does not state that the communities must benefit from ecotourism. Quoted in Pamela A. Wight, "North American Ecotourists: Market Profile and Trip Characteristics," spring 1996, on The Ecotourism Society's World Wide Web site (Internet: http://www.ecotourism.org/data.html).

68. The Ecotourism Society, *Ecotourism Guidelines for Nature Tour Operators* (North Bennington, Vt.: The Ecotourism Society, 1993), p. 3.

69. "The Tourist Trap: Who's Getting Caught?" *Cultural Survival Quarterly* 2, no. 3 (Summer 1982): 3.

70. William Schulz, "Conscientious Projectors: Tourists with an Eye on Human Rights Can Make a Difference," *The Nation,* October 6, 1997, p. 31.

Chapter 2

The World Travel Industry: Going "Green"?

As noted in the previous chapter, those in the tourism industry have recognized that the industry's very survival depends on a clean environment and pristine natural attractions. But *Agenda 21 for the Travel and Tourism Industry*, the travel industry's response to the Earth Summit's Rio Declaration on Environment and Development and Agenda 21, makes it clear that the industry couples sustainable development with free trade, privatization, and government deregulation. Two of the twelve "guiding principles" in the document state that "nations should cooperate to promote an open economic system in which international trade in Travel & Tourism services can take place" and "protectionism in trade in Travel & Tourism services should be halted or reversed."[1] Similarly, the Travel Industry Association of America (TIA), while applauding the growth of environmentalism, including ecotourism, opposes "governmental initiatives that would impede travel by discriminating against the traveler or the travel industry."[2] In developing countries, these prescriptions for open borders for trade and investment permit the penetration of multinational corporations, sometimes into previously closed markets, and are often directly at odds with local efforts to participate in and benefit from tourism. Economic globalization has been facilitated by international trade agreements, including the GATT (General Agreement on Tariffs and Trade), NAFTA (North American Free Trade Agreement), and the MAI (Multilateral Agreement on Investment), which have increased the power of foreign investors in developing countries, weakened fledgling domestic industries and businesses, and undermined efforts at environmental auditing and public scrutiny of these projects. Of particular import is the GATS (General Agreement on Trade in Services), which opens up signatory countries to 100 percent foreign investment in tourism services and disallows any protectionist measures. "This will edge out small, independent enterprises as TNCs [transnational corporations] and their affiliates, with the advantage of financial resources and technology, muscle their way in to control the tourist trade in countries in the South."[3]

These organizations also promote self-regulation rather than international or government directives. The WTTC's "Environmental Guidelines," for example, are a clear call for preemptive action to stave off outside regulation: "Travel and Tourism companies should seek to implement sound environmental principles through self-regulation, recognizing that national and international regulation may be inevitable and that preparation is vital."[4]

Despite its proenvironmental public stance, the WTTC vigorously opposes any tourism industry taxes, even those designed to promote environmental protection. At a forum preceding a Special Session of the United Nations General Assembly convened in June 1997 to review implementation of Agenda 21 over the five years since the Earth Summit the WTTC's president, Geoffrey Lipman, lobbied against and succeeded in killing a proposal for an international airline transportation tax to generate revenue to promote environmental protection. According to press accounts, Lipman argued that the tax would "simply create further bureaucracy that would stymie the innovations the travel and tourism industry were already making on their own." Since the tax was one of the "few viable new ideas for funding," as one observer noted in an *Earth Times* op-ed piece, "its demise is unfortunate. The WTTC should have been its ally, rather than opponent."[5] While talking the talk of environmental responsibility, the WTTC, which represents many of the world's largest tourism corporations, promotes only self-monitoring and "green" innovations that save money, while vigorously opposing any government or international taxes and regulations.

Structure of the Tourism Industry

The tourism industry that funnels American travelers to developing countries is a complex, multilayered maze. In the country of departure, it includes travel agencies (retailers), tour operators (wholesalers), airlines, cruise lines, car rental agencies, credit card companies, public relations firms, advertising companies, tourism bureaus, and the media. In the host country, it includes inbound tour operators, ground transporters, guides, accommodation facilities, national tourism bureaus, national and private parks and other recreational sites, cultural and craft centers, and special concessions such as providers of balloon, camel, and boat rides. The international travel industry is supported by government policies and regulations, infrastructure projects, and, frequently, direct subsidies, as well as by a wide array of commercial banks and international financial and aid institutions. Ecotourism receives support from conservation organizations and other NGOs, most of which are based in the United States and other developed countries but operate primarily in developing countries. Given the realities of overseas travel, "much of the trip cost, and thus the economic benefit," writes ecotourism expert Kreg Lindberg, "remains with outbound operators and source country airlines. To some extent this simply is due to the nature of the tourism industry; substantial funds are spent on marketing, commissions, and transport before tourists even reach the destination."[6]

The Big Players

The tourism industry is dominated by transnational corporations that are, on the one hand, becoming increasingly interlinked and consolidated and, on the other, spreading around the world and penetrating new markets. Since the 1960s, there has been a simultaneous and accelerating process of vertical and horizontal integration.

As Thanh-Dam Truong, a Vietnamese professor with the Institute of Social Studies at The Hague, explains, "When expanding into developing countries, the industry has required mass production and the standardization of services and quality. Given their late entry into the field, many developing countries have limited possibilities to develop their own stock of knowledge and control over the business. They have had to adopt the established standards and therefore must rely on foreign firms to run major sectors of the industry."[7]

Multinational institutions such as the World Bank, the International Monetary Fund (IMF), and the U.S. Agency for International Development (USAID), together with international trade agreements, have facilitated economic globalization and free trade and are forcing the removal of barriers, including investment regulations, labor standards, and environmental protection. Nevertheless, the American international travel industry, and especially the private airline companies, have always depended heavily on government subsidies and support. After World War II, the U.S. government unitized its surplus of military aircraft to subsidize the aerospace industry. It created financial institutions, such as the Export-Import Bank of the United States that gave low-interest loans to corporations for purchase of U.S.-made aircraft and equipment. U.S. assistance programs constructed and enlarged airports overseas, improved long-haul navigation, and financed development of long-range and wide-body aircraft. More recently, federal funds and powerful financial institutions also have underwritten research, development, and application of computer technology for the booking of airline reservations, hotel rooms, and car rentals. This, coupled with airline deregulation policies, has enabled the integration and consolidation of the travel industry. Pan American World Airways was among the first to develop an integrated global reservation system, with British Airways and Holiday Inn quickly following.

Nontourism companies in industrialized countries have also assumed a significant role in the industry as it has globalized. Major banks, along with firms specializing in brewing, food processing, gambling, media, tele-communications, shipping and real estate, have bought interests in airlines and hotel chains. ITT Corporation, for instance, bought 100 percent of the Sheraton hotel chain in 1968. Midland Bank bought 78 percent of the Thomas Cook Group's shareholdings, and the Rothschild Group pur-chased a sizable slice of Club Mediterranee (Club Med). As Thanh-Dam Truong writes,

> The general trend in integration in international tourism is that firms from industrialized countries tend to dominate the market through control of knowledge about the market, control of the means of distribution (travel agents, banks, department stores, business travel centers, etc.), and control over the advertising industry which, to a large extent, shapes and determines demand. This entails a division of labor according to which Third World countries, with few exceptions, merely provide the social infrastructure and facilities with little or no control over the process of production and distribution of the tourist-related services at an international level.[8]

What Truong calls "the four main economic agents in international tourism"—airlines, hotels, tour operators, and travel agents—have all become increasingly integrated in terms of their services, financing, man-agement, research, and development. Take, for instance, the American

fined to banking, that is, the sale of traveler's checks. In the 1960s, American Express moved beyond traveler's checks, buying shares in tour operations, tourism financing companies, and computerized reservation sys-tems. In 1971, it bought into CITEL, an electronic reservation system for hotel rooms, allowing it to provide reservation services for a half million rooms and some 5,000 car rental agencies in fifty countries. Today, American Express, with offices in every important city around the globe, is the largest travel agency in the United States, with gross sales of $8.7 billion in 1995.[9] It handles hotel reservations and airline, cruise, and ground travel and offers traveler's checks and credit cards, financial and small business advice, computer services, guidebooks, passport-processing assistance, and real estate services. Although American Express has been an industry trend-setter in modernizing, consolidating, and integrating various branches of the travel industry, it has not played a significant role in the development of eco-tourism. Since 1994, the American Express Foundation has offered "envi-ronmental grants" to conservation projects around the world. Its Environmental Protection Committee, however, after introducing some recycling and energy-saving procedures in the mid-1990s, has been largely inactive.[10]

Airlines

The biggest-ticket item in an overseas holiday goes to the airlines, that part of the industry (along with cruise ships and car rental companies) least infused with ecotourism principles or practices. Although the percentage varies with distance, size of group, carrier, and season, 61 percent of total U.S. travel agency sales went for airline tickets in 1995, with 14 percent going to cruise lines, 10 percent to hotels, 7 percent for car rentals, and 8 percent for other sales.[11]

For most developing countries and newly independent colonies, setting up a national airline that carried the country's flag and was fully or partially owned by the government was once an important symbol of sovereignty. Back in the 1950s, the founder of Hilton Hotels Corporation, which pioneered investments in developing countries, quipped, "No new nation has got it going until it has a seat in the United Nations, a national airline, and a Hilton Hotel."[12] Today, the United Nations membership remains, Hilton Hotels and other international hotel chains have probably multiplied, but the national airlines may well be gone.

Although they were symbolically important, these new national airlines—sometimes with a fleet of only two or three planes—were involved in a David and Goliath contest. Many bought jet aircraft, navigation equipment, and services from the Boeing Company and other U.S. corporations. These deals were frequently financed by the Export-Import Bank, which both made direct loans to foreign carriers and guaranteed loans made by commercial lenders. Other foreign airlines leased their planes and/or had management contracts with international commercial carriers such as Pan American, Compagnie Nationale Air France, and British Airways. As these nascent companies struggled to get a toehold in the international market, the big airlines from developed countries were acquiring wide-body aircraft with increased carrying capacity and decreased operating costs and were rapidly linking up with international hotel chains, travel agencies, tour operators, and car rental agencies for sales and promotional purposes and to offer discount tour packages. Inclusive tour packages offered by air charter companies also undercut the market for the new national airlines.[13] Whereas the national airlines offered travelers from overseas a bit of the flavor of the destination, thus becoming part of the holiday experience, today's big carriers provide increasingly homogenized and nondescript service.

During the 1990s, as economic liberalization and deregulation took hold, international carriers, with hefty marketing budgets, name recognition, and hookups with other sectors of the tourism industry, entered the most lucrative foreign markets in developing countries. In 1997, six of the top international carriers agreed to form Star Alliance, which they called "the first truly global airline network in the world." The carriers agreed to meld their frequent flyer mileage programs, ground services, and airport lounge services and to simplify ticketing and link schedules "to provide seamless service on every continent."[14] Without protective trade barriers to keep out competition and control fares, computer systems and other technological innovations, and integration with hotel chains, car rental agents, and tour operators, many small national airlines could not compete and were sold to foreign carriers. During the 1990s, Costa Rica's flagship airline, LASCA, a small but well-run operation, was gradually sold to foreign conglomerates. In the Caribbean, in 1995 alone, BWIA International Airways and Air Jamaica were privatized and Air Aruba, Bahamasair, and LIAT (based in Antigua) were discussing privatization. At the same time, American Airlines sold more than 65 percent of the tickets to the Caribbean.[15] So even if conscientious ecotravelers or tour operators try to patronize a host country's airline, they may find that though it still flies the national flag, the carrier is in reality owned by a foreign corporation.

With the rise of environmentalism and ecotourism, a number of the international carriers have given a nod to conservation by adopting some "green" practices. Cabin staff on U.S. Airways flights, for instance, separate used plastic for recycling if the airport where they are landing has a recycling program. Virgin Atlantic, which flies between Newark and Heathrow, has donated funds to help clean up New Jersey's beaches. More significantly,

A handful of airlines have promoted ecotourism in their in-flight magazines or movies (United Airlines), hooked up with national tourism boards to promote ecotourism (South African Airways), or sponsored ecotourism conferences and publications (USAfrica, before it collapsed). Most noted for its environmental programs is British Airways, which, along with the American Society of Travel Agents (ASTA) and travel associations in Great Britain and Asia, gives a series of well-publicized annual Tourism for Tomorrow Awards. British Airways also contributes to various environmental projects and has made efforts at improving fuel efficiency, ground energy consumption, and waste disposal, acquiring more environmentally friendly planes.[16]

Hotels, Resorts, and Cruise Ships

In the 1950s, Hilton, Inter-Continental, and Holiday Inn were among the first specialized hotel chains to invest abroad, before significant economic alliances were forged with air carriers and tour operators. Over the next four decades, more international chains expanded into developing countries, attracted by new investment opportunities for their excess capital, by low wages, and, increasingly, by the potential offered through integration with other sectors of the tourism industry. By 1980, 48 percent of all hotel rooms were located in ninety-three developing countries. By 1995, nineteen of the twenty largest hotel conglomerates were based in developed countries (the other was based in Hong Kong) and twelve of the top twenty operators were American multinational corporations. The leaders include U.S.-owned ITT Sheraton Corporation, Holiday Inn, Hyatt Hotels and Resorts, and Marriott International, as well as Inter-Continental Hotels and Hilton International (United Kingdom), Accor (France), and Grupo Sol Meliá (Spain).[17]

International hotel chains employ five different forms of investment in developing countries, most of which minimize their risks and maximize their ability to muscle aside small, locally owned hotels, lodges, and resorts. The types of investment used by multinationals are (1) ownership or equity investment; (2) management contracts; (3) hotel leasing agreements, whereby the multinational pays the hotel owner a percentage of the profits; (4) franchise agreements, whereby the owner uses the multinational's corporate name, services, and trademarks for a fee while maintaining certain operating standards; and (5) technical service agreements, whereby the multinational provides the local hotel with a consultant for management, marketing, and technology. Most common are the management contracts, which enable international corporations to parlay their expertise into often lucrative, long-term contracts that give them de facto control over the business without requiring them to put up any money. Developing countries have long paid a premium for such contracts. Whereas hotel management fees in industrialized countries range from 6 to 15 percent and average 12 percent, in developing countries they average 17 percent and can be as much as 23 percent. In addition, the international firm extracts additional fees for advertising and sales services, computerized reservation facilities, and routine inspections and consultations.

However, affiliation with international chains is frequently viewed as imperative in giving local investors a competitive edge over small, purely locally owned hotels in marketing, bookings, technology, training, and standardization of services, as well as access to goods at lower marginal costs. Therefore, whereas only about 2 percent of the hotels in western Europe are linked to multinational corporations through management contracts, in developing countries the proportion has approached or well exceeded 50 percent: 75 percent in the Middle East, 72 percent in Africa, 60 percent in Asia, and 47 percent in Latin America.[18]

Around the world, international conglomerates have, time and again, adopted the "eco" label for their mass tourism resort projects. Next to one of Belize's finest coral reefs, a $50 million venture billed as an "integrated and ecologically sound resort development" includes hotels, villas, golf courses, polo fields, and stables. Under the banner of sustainable tourism, the Tourism Authority of Thailand is promoting privatization of thirteen national parks; in one, Phu Kadueng National Park, Japanese investors are discussing construction of a cable car, hotels, and a golf course on a mountain summit. Today, mass tourism projects, marketed as "ecodevelopments," dot the Costa Rican landscape, and one nondescript downtown San José hotel markets itself as offering "Green Adventures." And then there's the advertisement for The Enchanted Garden in an ecotourism magazine that features a towel-draped female tourist lying on a massage table in the middle of a palm-shrouded garden. She's being rubbed down by a uniformed Jamaican woman, and the caption reads, "As Nature Intended . . ." But the Enchanted Garden is no ecoresort; it's a 112-room luxury spa complex managed by DHC Hotels & Resorts, a major international hotel chain. Typical of such places, most bookings are made in the United States, most profits flow back to the corporate headquarters, and Jamaicans receive scant benefits other than menial hotel jobs.[19]

Perhaps more than any other sector of the mass tourism industry, Caribbean cruise ships are anathema to the concepts and practices of ecotourism. These high-volume, prepaid, packaged holidays, with their celebration of sun-and-fun overconsumption and self-indulgence and their brief ports of call to allow tourists to buy souvenirs or duty-free First World luxuries, are the mirror opposite of the small-scale, locally owned, culturally sensitive, environmentally low-impact, and educational precepts of eco-

ciples. Even though tourism is the Caribbean's main industry and unemployment on many of the islands tops 20 percent, most of the 50,000 employees on cruise ships plying the waters between the United States and the Caribbean are neither West Indians nor Americans. Many of these low-wage workers are recruited by specialized labor contractors from depressed markets such as those in eastern Europe and Asia, and many work for only tips or commissions. Most of the ships are foreign owned and registered in tax havens such as Liberia and Panama.

The Caribbean cruise business is huge, bringing in $4–$6 billion annually and carrying more than 4.5 million Americans on some 130 ships each year. It is dominated by three companies—Carnival Corporation, Royal Caribbean Cruises Ltd., and Princess Cruises—which carry nearly half of all passengers worldwide.[20] But because it involves travel mainly in international waters by foreign-owned and foreign registered fleets, it is largely unregulated and untaxed. Under international maritime law, cruise lines are exempt from many national regulations other than those of their country of registry. Even though their ships carry U.S. passengers and are based or call at U.S. ports, these cruise companies are largely exempt from U.S. labor regulations, profit and income taxes, safety standards, sales tax, and environmental standards.[21] Similarly, they are exempt from most taxes and laws of the twenty-odd island countries, colonies, and dependencies in the Caribbean.

Not only does the cruise line business bring little income to the Caribbean, but over the past three decades, it has also used aggressive marketing and its exemptions from taxes and regulations to outcompete resort hotels in the islands. The Cruise Lines International Association, founded by the major lines in 1976, works closely with travel agents to promote cruises as less expensive and more glamorous alternatives to land-based Caribbean hotels. Cruise line sales have become a bread-and-butter business for U.S. travel agents, bringing in earnings of close to $600 million in commissions each year. Airlines also earn more than $650 million in ticket sales to cruise passengers flying to jumping-off points such as Miami. But almost all the money is spent either before the cruise begins or on board; cruise passengers buy relatively little onshore, and port taxes and other cruise line fees are low.

In recent years, however, the cruise industry has come under closer scrutiny by both the U.S. and Caribbean governments. Countries in the West Indies have begun to organize an effort to impose some taxes on cruise ships and set some standards for them. Proposed actions include increasing port taxes, insisting that cruise lines use land-based waste facilities rather than dumping at sea, prohibiting the dropping of anchor on coral reefs, limiting the number of cruise ships in port, and recruiting and training more islanders for shipboard work. The U.S. Congress and U.S. labor unions and trade associations have also begun looking into ways to force cruise lines that sail regularly to the United States to pay more in taxes, to pay at least federal minimum wage to crews, and to follow U.S. safety standards and environmental regulations.[22]

Cruise lines find these efforts at government regulation "a frightening prospect," according to Russell Nansen, who worked for Royal Caribbean for twenty-one years,[23] and they are striving to clean up and "green" their public image. Cruise ships dump some 20 million pounds of raw sewage and refuse into the world's oceans every day.[24] In the early 1990s, to the embarrassment of the cruise line's management, Greenpeace "ecowarriors" secretly trailed a cruise ship and videotaped some of these dumps. In 1993, when Princess Cruises was fined $500,000 for illegal dumping, it paid up and then went on the offensive to repair its reputation. Just a few years later, it succeeded in landing the annual ASTA/*Smithsonian Magazine* Environmental Award for its "strong corporate commitment towards protecting the environment to which they bring passengers and guests." ASTA's Environment Committee newsletter claimed that Princess Cruises "has chosen to make the incident a learning experience" through "a 'Save the Waves' feature in their brochures and cruise documents to educate their passengers about . . . their own environmental initiatives." The company launched, in effect, a public relations campaign targeting its customers. In announcing the award, ASTA stated that Princess Cruises' "environmental protection practices" include "model waste recycling programs," but the company has made no pledge that the line will completely stop dumping waste in the ocean.[25]

Other big industry players in mass tourism—for example, Inter-Continental Hotels and Resorts, Holiday Inn Worldwide, and Canadian Pacific Hotels & Resorts—have taken steps of some sort to "green" their operations. In the early 1990s, Hilton International and other hotel groups founded the International Hotels Environment Initiative (IHEI) "to increase general environmental awareness and to establish valid guidelines within the global hotel industry." In response to consumer demand for environmentally sensitive products and services, many conventional hotels, ranging from independent properties to major chains, had by the mid-1990s begun reuse and recycling programs, had installed energy-efficient lighting and water consumption control devices, and were using heat pumps. Many of these innovations are cost-saving strategies as well as environmental improvements. As Federic Dimanche wrote in a trade magazine, managers often view such "green" programs and practices as marketing strategies that "can improve sales and increase occupancy rates for hotels properly target-

travelers were more likely to chose a hotel if it had, for instance, recycling bins for guest use (67.5 percent of those surveyed said yes), has energy-efficient lighting (69.4 percent); turned off lights not being used in occupied guest rooms (65.6 percent); changed sheets only on request (58.9 percent); and used in-room displays printed on recycled paper (65.1 percent).[26] So far, these add up to useful, but largely token, measures that fall far short of the sound practices and principles of many of the ecolodges discussed in the following chapters. The hotel industry as a whole has not developed, as Dimanche puts it, a comprehensive and enforceable code of ethics and guidelines for interaction "with tourists, local communities and the environment."[27]

Outbound Travel Agents

Although the functions of tour operators and travel agents often blur and overlap, generally travel agents are retailers who sell airline tickets and off-the-shelf packages put together by overseas tour operators. These packages are featured in brochures and distributed through the national network of travel agencies.[28] The bulk of the retail trade consists of package tours. A package usually includes airfare, ground and internal air transportation, accommodations, some or all meals, transfers from airports to hotels, visa and other fees and taxes, often park entrance fees, and excursions such as white-water rafting, mountain climbing, and balloon rides—in short, all but incidentals, souvenirs, and tips. A package has a fixed departure date, length, itinerary, cost, and minimum (and often maximum) number of tourists.

Generally, the travel agent earns 10 percent of the cost of any package tour. Packages put together by overseas operators (in Costa Rica, for instance) normally include a 30 percent or more markup so that wholesalers, tour operators, and outfitters in the United States get 20 percent and the travel agent gets 10 to 15 percent. In addition, large travel agencies and tour operators can make significant commissions from airlines and hotels by selling large blocks of tickets.[29]

An estimated 75 to 80 percent of U.S. tourists book their air travel and 95 percent book their cruises through travel agents.[30] In response to travelers' demands for outdoor, nature-based holidays, some mass market travel agents have started to sell ecotours or conventional tours that include "eco-experiences"—say, a cruise that includes a day's hike in a rain forest and incorporates the lingo of "green" travel—and others are selling packages from a select few ecotourism wholesalers. According to ASTA, there are some 35,000 travel agencies in the United States. In 1991, the *New York Times* reported that there were nearly 500 U.S. "tour companies" (agents and operators) offering trips with environmental themes, mostly to developing countries.[31] Five years later, Marie Walters, a member of ASTA's Environmental Committee, stated that "all travel agents these days handle ecotourism," including prepackaged nature and adventure travel or "eco-" add-ons to conventional tours, although she conceded that "some are more professional than others." The Ecotourism Society (TES), in contrast, contends flatly that "travel agencies have not played a significant role in marketing or sales for the ecotourism industry." TES says that travel agencies lack the time to sell specialty products as well as lacking expertise, motivation, and training. Indeed, a 1997 *Washington Post* survey of area travel agents and their specialists found only one, Green Earth Travel, that stated it specialized in ecotourism.[32]

There is wide variance in quality of travel agents because the training and licensing procedures are very weak. The only regulatory bodies are the Airline Reporting Corporation (ARC) and the International Airlines Travel Agent Network (IATAN) through which travel agencies are licensed to write airline tickets. However, the industry has several professional organizations and associations. The Institute of Certified Travel Agents, for example, offers a two- to three-year professional travel counselor degree; however, only a small percentage of agents are so certified. ASTA, which lobbies on behalf of the industry, has 20,500 members in the United States and 26,500 worldwide.

Outbound and Inbound Tour Operators

U.S. tour operators are classified as wholesalers, although they sell both to travel agents and directly to the public. Those sending tourists abroad sell their own exclusive package tours and/or resell packages put together by tour operators in the host countries. Known as outbound tour operators or outfitters, they package the trips, oversee the creation of itineraries, select and contract with inbound tour operators in the host countries, arrange for airline tickets, and handle travel and liability insurance. They sell tour packages to the general public via either travel agents or special interest organizations such as environmental groups, alumni associations, and museums. Some market directly through magazine or newspaper advertisements or through catalogs, brochures, videotapes, CD-ROMs, and the Internet. Tour operators charge a markup of 15 to 40 percent, depending on how customized the tour is. Competition is very stiff, and tour operators try to entice travel agents to carry their packages by offering higher commissions, incentive programs, glossy advertising, news articles, contests, and free or reduced-rate trips.[33]

Standards, however, are lacking: there is no accrediting body or licensing procedure for tour operators, and because little capital is required to get started, virtually anyone can hang out a shingle. The United States Tour Operators Association (USTOA), with membership restricted to well-established operators, requires the posting of a $250,000 bond, which is applied to a consumer protection plan for tourists and travel agents using these companies. However, the USTOA evaluates tour operators only on the basis of their financial worthiness, not on whether they are promoting high-quality or socially and environmentally responsible travel.[34]

Outbound operators usually subcontract with inbound operators in host countries, who meet the travelers at the airport (or port or border); provide transportation throughout the trip; select local businesses to patronize; hire staff; and arrange accommodations (lodges, tented camps, inns, etc.), visits to parks, and specialty activities. As geography professor and ecotourism specialist Bryan Higgins put it, inbound operators are the essential link, making "upstream connections to industrialized countries" and "downstream economic ties to 'local' businesses within a particular country."[35] These firms are located in key urban centers, usually the capital city or the gateway town (Arusha, Tanzania, for example) to the main ecotourism attractions. With the exception of Cuba, where inbound tour companies are run by the government, in most countries nowadays they are all private or in the process of being privatized. They range from multinational companies, such as Abercrombie & Kent, that also own lodges and vehicles, to low-budget mom-and-pop shops with little more than a desk, a telephone, and a couple of employees.

The Travel Industry Press

When planning a vacation, many travelers rely on guidebooks, specialty travel magazines, travel supplements in newspapers, and television documentaries, nature programs, or travelogues. Members of the general public may look to the travel press for evenhanded and insightful assessments of prospective destinations. In contrast, the destinations, from specific hotels or restaurants to entire countries, view the travel press more as an in-house public relations arm of the industry that, properly cared for, can provide valuable, low-cost advertising. Several factors work to pull travel journalists into alliance with others in the industry.

The principal vehicle for wooing the writers, photographers, and television journalists who cover tourism and travel has been what are known as "fam" trips. *Fam* stands for *familiarization*; these are all-expenses-paid or highly subsidized trips to tourist destinations in the United States and overseas underwritten by national or local tourist boards, airlines, resorts, inns and lodges, hotel chains, restaurants, and overseas tour operators. Fam trips are usually organized by tourism offices or public relations firms in the United States hired by the destination. They are intended to garner good press in return for a good time.[36] An article in *Adventure Travel Business,* a monthly magazine that bills itself as "the voice of the adventure travel industry," is explicit about how to use the press: "Press trips are an important part of a public relations program as there is no substitute for the in-depth coverage that is generated by a media visit. It is the best 'advertisement' you can buy." The article goes on to give guidelines on how to "entice a journalist to cover your story" and "increase the chances that you'll get a return on the cost of hosting a journalist, in the form of a long, flattering article." It adds, "The most important part . . . is to have a good time."[37] For the travel press, especially its large stable of freelance writers and photographers, fam trips are standard operating procedure. "Unless you're writing for *National Geographic* [which pays well, besides covering expenses], you can't travel and survive without subsidized trips," says Diann Stutz, a public relations official who has been organizing fam trips since the late 1970s. Freelance writers are normally paid a pittance for travel articles and guidebooks: newspapers generally pay only a few hundred dollars for a supplement piece, and publishers typically pay a flat fee of $10,000–$15,000 for writing a guidebook from scratch, a project that could take a year or more.[38]

Given these realities, fam trips are imperative, but the obvious danger is of travel writers losing their independence. They may become—as is the intent of fam trips—a public relations arm for the travel industry rather than a watchdog for the public. As a *Washington Post* exposé on freebies given to guidebook writers put it, "Perhaps the biggest misconception about guidebooks is that they offer truly objective critiques of restaurants and hotels. . . . In reality, the objectivity of many guidebooks is undercut by 'comps'—free meals, lodging and entertainment accepted by the guidebook writer while on assignment." Edie Jarolim, who has written Fodor's and Frommer's guidebooks, calls fam trips and other comps "the dirty little secret of the industry."[39] Of the dozen-odd fam trip veterans I interviewed for this book, only one flatly denied that free trips influence what she writes. Others admitted that they find it awkward to write critically about a destination that has graciously hosted them. "It's difficult not to be influenced. I feel hesitant to lambaste [a place]," said one seasoned writer. Most said they simply opt not to write anything about a place that is bad.[40]

The issue of fam trips and comps has long been debated by travel writers and editors. Many of the largest-circulation newspapers have offi-cially stopped accepting articles by writers taking subsidized trips. These include the *New York Times,* the *Washington Post,* the *Los Angeles Times,* the *Philadelphia Inquirer,* the *Miami Herald,* and *Newsday.* In its exposé on comps given to guidebook writers, the *Washington Post* included the com-ment—twice—that it "does not permit contributors to accept any compli-mentary or discounted accommodations or meals, and our reporters usually travel incognito." The *Post* added, "We pay our writers' expenses or they pay their own."[41] *Newsday* goes as far as to require writers to turn in receipts showing that they have paid for the trip themselves. And some publications say they require their writers to travel incognito and show up unannounced to prevent their being given the red carpet treatment. But writers say that in practice, the policy is often "don't ask, don't tell": many editors and pub-lishers will turn a blind eye if they like the writer or the article. *Condé Nast Traveler,* started in 1987 by former journalists with the motto "Truth in travel," is one of the few travel magazines that does not accept articles writ-ten on the basis of subsidized trips. They contract with writers and photog-raphers to do particular stories, pay all expenses, and do not insist on only positive stories.[42] Much of the travel media would argue it cannot afford to underwrite all the travel expenses incurred by its journalists. However, one easy alternative would be to require travel articles, documentaries, radio reports, and books to state clearly all companies who provided free or discounted services. This "buyers beware" disclosure would at least let the public know what companies underwrote the information.

Travel writers say it is through advertising, as well as fam trips, that the travel industry works to keep the travel press tepid. Increasingly, travel advertisements are helping to underwrite entire publications. Some guidebooks go so far as to require destinations to pay a fee to be listed, sometimes letting the proprietor write the copy, and some magazines refuse to list establishments that don't advertise.[43] The travel press has therefore taken on a role as the "good news" branch of journalism, a genre that helps people escape from the cares and woes of the real world. As one writer put it, they are "more cheerleaders than critics."[44] Although travel sections in the *Washington Post,* the *New York Times,* and other major newspapers do carry travel advice, including articles warning, for instance, about airport luggage theft, the dangers of traveling to certain parts of the world, and even the effect of fam trips on the accuracy of guidebooks, they rarely pan specific companies, tourist attractions, restaurants, or lodgings. Writers say that some criticism is permitted if it is "balanced" with positive comments. "Horror stories do not fit the genre," explained one. He went on to say that he'd once received a stack of documents outlining severe health and sanitary violations on a number of cruise ships. He never pursued the story. "Who's going to run it? Certainly not a travel section." Why? "Because of the advertisers."[45]

Another travel industry institution—the professional associations—also helps keep travel writing light and in line. The most important of these is the Society of American Travel Writers (SATW), with 950 members, including 550 mostly freelance writers; the rest are public relations officials employed by resorts, tourism boards, airlines, and other parts of the tourism industry. Rather than promoting the independence of the press and its right and duty to critically examine the industry, the SATW helps create a cozy relationship between its travel press and industry public relations flacks. Admission requirements are rigorous, and membership is restricted and relatively expensive. Applicants must be nominated by two current members (who in turn are permitted to nominate only two members per year) and must either be a staff travel writer or have published at least twelve different major travel articles or one original travel book within the past year.[46] One writer described the SATW as "a closed shop"; another said, "It's designed to keep people out" because it is often through the SATW that journalists secure fam trips. For example, a public relations officer for a city in Virginia explained that before issuing invitations to a press event, she first checks to see whether particular writers are SATW members and then checks their reputation with her public relations colleagues. An official at the SATW said that despite the criticism of fam trips, she has "not noticed any decrease. They are still widely used."

Although the SATW's "Code of Ethics" states that "no member shall deliberately misrepresent his or her participation in a press trip in order to secure an editorial assignment" and "no member shall accept payment or courtesies in exchange for an agreement to produce favorable material about a travel destination," there is no enforcement.[47] These rules are routinely bent, travel writers say. But this coziness between the travel press and the industry does not serve the traveling public. Like the oil, nuclear, armaments, and automobile industries, the travel industry, including the branch known as ecotourism, needs to be scrutinized by a probing, investigative press.

Tourism Marketing

Although tourism executives recognize that the health, sustainability, and profitability of their industry depends in large part on protecting the environment, sophisticated marketing techniques often allow the travel industry to appear "green" without making fundamental or costly reforms. Marketing is one of the most important components of the travel industry, and promotional materials for nature tourism and ecotourism have developed a distinct style designed to sell "experiences," not products.[48] Through effective advertising, one tourism consultant writes, "a destination can literally be created in the traveler's mind."[49] Although travel brochures draw on imagery and language found in historical travel writing, they carefully weave adventure with safety, the unknown with the familiar, the primitive with the modern, ruggedness with comfort.

In his doctoral dissertation, which analyzed promotional brochures from fifteen educational tour companies conducting nature and cultural trips to Latin America, Ronnie Casella found tourists depicted as "time-travelers."[50] Voyagers International's brochure for the Galápagos Islands, for instance, promises, "Where we travel, it's a little piece of Eden—the world as it should be, at peace with itself and with you." The California Academy of Sciences' brochure for its trip to Panama includes a photograph of tourists landing on an isolated island beach with the caption, "Zodiacs give us the freedom to land virtually anywhere at will." The text explains, "The Kuna live in autonomous island communities, keeping their traditional lifestyle essentially intact. Adorned in their colorful embroidered fabrics, they invariably turn out to greet us when our Zodiacs arrive at one of their villages." This is well-managed time-travel, the "discovery" of a far-off culture aboard First World Zodiacs and the assurance of a warm welcome by Indians whose friendliness has been previously tested. The Cruise Company of Greenwich also offers a visit to unknown lands, in this case in one of Costa Rica's largest national parks: "The Corcovado area is so remote, inaccessible, and undisturbed that even most Costa Ricans have never visited." The notion that cruise ship passengers will machete their way through Corcovado's dense, steep, and rain-drenched tropical forest is ludicrous, but the image is appealing. Equally absurd is an Overseas Adventure Travel brochure's "special invitation to join us on [a seventeen-day safari to] Unexplored Serengeti" in Tanzania's most famous game park, which is visited by tens of thousands of tourists each year. These travel brochures promise, as well, a combination of both physical and intellectual rigor, often with tours led by a biologist guide, boats equipped with "onboard laboratories," and a clientele that includes environmental organizations, universities, and NGOs.[51]

Mainstream ecotourism, or "ecotourism lite," is often described with catchy phrases such as "treading lightly on the earth" and "taking only photos, leaving only footprints." The advertisements, brochures, and ecopublications contain buzzwords such as *quiet, rain forest, clean air, pure, lush, unspoiled, nature, breathtaking, bio-,* and, of course, *eco-* and *green.* In recent years, much of the mass tourism industry has adopted "green" language or even established environmental departments, but it has made only superficial changes in conventional tour packages, such as offering a brief walk in the rain forest or not changing guests' sheets and towels each day. In a press release headlined "Keep Your Towels—and Help Save the World!" British Airways' hotel division and International Hotels urged their hotels to "think green" by installing energy-saving showers and by laundering towels only when guests signal that they want them changed. These are sensible moves, but hardly ones that will change the world.[52]

The major U.S. nature tour and ecotourism operators rely heavily on glossy brochures with colorful photographs, advertisements in some of the estimated 250 tourism publications and travel supplements, and the *Specialty Travel Index* and other in-house trade publications. According to one survey, most nature tour operators that conduct tours to developing countries use magazines (94 percent) and brochures (91 percent) as their primary form of advertising in the United States. A large number also use direct mail to consumers (60 percent), appearances at tourism trade shows and travel markets (66 percent), and newspaper advertisements (56 percent).[53] Advertising and brochures are expensive. In just one year, the large California-based company Mountain Travel–Sobek spent $350,000 on its catalog; Overseas Adventure Travel in Massachusetts spent $150,000 on its catalog, and another $80,000 on media advertising.[54]

Given the cost of advertising and promotional material, tourism companies put a premium on getting free or inexpensive media coverage through fam trips, press releases, and public relations gimmicks. Classic Tours in Chicago uses press releases to hype specialty tours such as family safaris, grandparents' discounts, and "limited edition" departures led by experts in a given field.[55] Abercrombie & Kent (A&K) hosts an annual dinner to which members of the press are invited.

The Travel Industry's "Green" Tricks

Although travel writers have no union to represent their interests and fight on their behalf, the travel industry is protected and promoted by a variety of organizations, including ASTA, the World Tourism Organization (WTO), and the World Travel and Tourism Council (WTTC). Clearly, the travel industry has an interest in protecting the world's natural and cultural resources, which are at the core of its business activities. But it has other concerns as well, some of which run counter to the tenets of sound ecotourism. These travel associations advocate, for instance, self-regulation, expanded tourism markets, and a lowering of trade barriers. In the mid- to late 1990s, industry associations responded to the growth of environmental concerns and the rise of ecotourism by instituting certain changes that, when examined closely, often amount to promoting minor, cost-saving environmental reforms—ecotourism lite—rather than seriously grappling with the principles and practices of ecotourism.

In his column "Frommer's World" in February 1994, Arthur Frommer, a contributor to *Travel Holiday* magazine and certainly no ecotourism extremist, summed up the dichotomy between what many ecotravelers desire and what the industry is delivering.

> In a frantic rush to board the bandwagon, travel-related companies all over the world are proclaiming that they support—and practice—the principles of ecotourism. In many cases, they really don't. The evidence they cite includes such trivial steps as using recycled-paper menus and stationery or putting biodegradable soap in guest bedrooms. These sometimes exaggerated half-truths mislead an increasingly large number of travelers who are fervently determined to preserve the fragile and finite natural resources of the earth.[56]

ASTA's "Ten Commandments on Eco-Tourism" are among a growing number of voluntary codes of conduct written by various organizations. Widely distributed to travel agents and the traveling public, the "Commandments" are printed on green paper and designed to slip into an airline ticket folder. Directed at sensitizing travelers, not the travel agents who belong to ASTA, they include such platitudes as "Respect the frailty of the earth," "Always follow designated trails," and "Do not buy products made from endangered plants or animals." Although they urge travelers to "Patronize those . . . dedicated to strong principles of conservation," they do not specifically encourage travelers to patronize locally owned or community-based ecotourism ventures. Without further education of both travel agents and the public, ASTA's "Commandments" are not good ecotourism. An ASTA spokeswoman conceded that the organization has neither industry guidelines nor a monitoring system for travel agents involved in ecotourism.[57]

Codes such as this have no teeth but allow an organization to claim great sensitivity and responsibility. Few industry efforts demonstrate this more clearly than the WTTC's Green Globe logo program, endorsed by the Earth Council, which was set up to oversee implementation of the 1992 Earth Summit's Agenda 21. The WTTC's president, Geoffrey Lipman, unveiled the Green Globe program at a 1994 Montreal conference titled "Building a Sustainable World Through Tourism." Lipman told the delegates, "The Green Globe symbol means that a company is committed to environmental improvement. It does not mean that a company has achieved it. I describe this as a diagnostic and self-fitness program, not an accreditation program. It offers business benefits, it offers cost saving, and commercial positioning. I call this putting a Green Glove on Adam Smith's hidden hand of the marketplace." Under the scheme, for as little as $200, travel and tourism companies can purchase the right to use the Green Globe logo in all their publicity and thereby give the impression that they are "going green." In return, the company pledges to work toward more environmentally sound corporate practices as outlined in the United Nation's Agenda 21. To test Lipman's description, Worldwide Television News (WTN) in London set up a phony business called "Greenman Travel" and sent an application and $200 to Green Globe. In return, Greenman Travel received a certificate stating, "In recognition of commitment to environmental improvement." The WTTC did not verify Greenman Travel's authenticity or ask why it wanted to join Green Globe. Thus, Green Globe is, in essence, little more than a marketing ploy. As Lipman boasted to the conference participants, the WTTC had retained "a major public relations network around the world to help us promote this."[58]

Ecotourism Awards

There are, as well, a growing number of ecotourism awards that receive considerable press coverage and are used as marketing tools. At their best, these awards have helped give publicity and recognition to a number of less known but highly worthwhile projects.[59] For instance, in 1997, *Condé Nast*

Traveler's annual Ecotourism Award (cosponsored by a Russian vodka company) went to Clive Stockil, founder of an innovative CAMPFIRE program (Communal Area Management Programme for Indigenous Resources) in Gonarezhou National Park, in the southeastern corner of Zimbabwe. Stockil helped negotiate an agreement between the local Shangaan people and Zimbabwe Sun hoteliers to build a luxury ecotourism lodge, Mahenye. Through this project, which helped lay the foundation for other CAMPFIRE projects, the Shangaan village receives 10 percent of the profits from the ecolodge and helps to run photographic and hunting safaris. The Shangaan people, who have been transformed from poachers into protectors of the local wildlife, have used the proceeds for a variety of community projects, including building school classrooms, buying a grinding mill, and putting in electricity, telephones, and water pumps.[60]

However, these awards frequently do little to promote less known or locally owned projects that are struggling to break into the international market. Many recipients of the various ecotourism awards are either industry giants or already popular ecotourism projects. The same names keep popping up, and there is a revolving cycle of corporations giving awards to one another. Although the ASTA/*Smithsonian Magazine* Environmental Award, begun in 1991, has gone to the governments of Costa Rica (for rain forest protection) and Rwanda (for gorilla protection), between 1991 and 1996 those honored included seven airlines, two cruise lines, and two international hotel chains. Among these are British Airways, Inter-Continental Hotels and Resorts, Princess Cruises, American Airlines, and Canadian Pacific Hotels & Resorts. British Airways has also received awards for "environmental commitment" from the WTTC and the Pacific Asia Travel Association. British Airways' own Tourism for Tomorrow Awards (run in association with ASTA, the Pacific Asia Travel Association, and two British travel associations) have in turn gone to Inter-Continental Hotels, Carnival Cruises, Abercrombie & Kent's Friends of Conservation in Kenya and Tanzania, and the controversial Mnemba Club, on a small island off Zanzibar (see chapter 8). The Mnemba Club also won an award for ecotourism excellence from the WTTC's Green Globe program.

The Dangers of Ecotourism Lite

Much of what is marketed as ecotourism is simply conventional mass tourism wrapped in a thin veneer of green. Ecotourism lite is propelled by travel agents, tour operators, airlines and cruise lines, large hotel and resort chains, and international tourism organizations, which promote quick, superficially "green" visits within conventional packages. According to Diane Kelsay, a coordinator of the annual World Congress on Tourism for the Environment, "We've seen ecotourism used to mean all nature, adventure, and cultural travel. Someone even published a definition that includes Sunday afternoon drives. A lot of travel companies used it to call attention to anything they were selling."[61] Perhaps more than any other big player in the tourism industry, the Walt Disney Company has tried to cash in on the traveling public's desire to "go green" with an ecotourism lite theme park, Animal Kingdom. Disney spent $800 million to transform 500 acres of central Florida cow pasture into an African savanna, with fake wide-trunk baobab trees, a Zulu village, and some one thousand real imported animals. This largest of Disney's theme parks is designed to let the American public "go on safari" without leaving the shores of the United States. Although it has won praise from zoo-industry officials, Animal Kingdom opened in mid-1998 amidst protests from animal rights groups and an investigation by the U.S. Department of Agriculture into the deaths of some dozen animals, including representatives of endangered species. Two West African crowned cranes were run over by tour vehicles.[62]

A sizable segment of the traveling public wants this type of tourism. In recent years, there has been a gradual trend for many ecotourists to be less intellectually curious, socially responsible, environmentally concerned, and politically aware than in the past. Increasing numbers of older, wealthier, and "softer" travelers have begun opting for comfort over conservation. Ecotourism lite travelers are, as David Western puts it, "entertained by nature, but not unduly concerned with its preservation."[63] Biologist guides on the Galápagos Islands say that tourists these days, though far greater in number, are, overall, less interested in the details of the islands' unique ecosystem than they were in the past and want simply a quick historical and ecological overview of the islands. Several naturalist guides I interviewed said they were contemplating quitting because they were no longer getting much professional satisfaction. In a 1997 interview, Kurt Kutay of Wildland Adventures said he has also noticed that "the type of traveler is changing. Ecotourism is more mainstream. Today we sell environmental education in an indirect, informal, less obvious way."

Similarly, in Costa Rica, the women in charge of Horizontes Nature Tours, a highly respected tour company specializing in ecotourism, say that they have been forced to "soften" their brochures to emphasize beauty over adventure or environmental and cultural education. Both the owner, Tamara Budowski, and the company's Canadian consultant, Terry Pratt, said in interviews that since about 1993 they have noticed a shift toward more "mainstream" or "soft" ecotourists, and this has forced Horizontes to revise its itineraries and advertising. "They no longer seem to be the hard core nature-oriented traveler of the '80s," said Budowski, whose father, Gerardo, is a past president of The Ecotourism Society. Many tourists are coming now because Costa Rica is "in," not because they are interested in nature. Budowski says she has received complaints from clients that her guides talk too much. She quotes a trade adage: ten years ago, a naturalist guide was expected to talk on and on; five years ago, tourists expected at least half an hour; now, more than fifteen minutes is too much.

Horizontes' literature reflects this change. In 1991, the company's brochure emphasized physically challenging activities: "hiking up a dormant volcano . . . swimming under a jungle waterfall . . . rafting on a wild and pristine white water river." Horizontes' 1995 brochure is gentler, designed to appeal to the sensitive traveler seeking spiritual renewal rather than physical rigor. It urges the traveler to "open your eyes and heart to the power and beauty that surrounds you and rediscover your place in the natural world." Budowski says that "capitalizing on the peaceful energy of nature" is "very marketable" to today's overstressed workaholics. But she explains that even though these tourists don't think they want to be educated while on vacation, "in Costa Rica, you learn something almost anywhere you go. We realize that to be good teachers we have to adapt to different levels of interest. We've learned to show people nature from different perspectives."[64]

TAM, one of the oldest and most conventional Costa Rican–owned tour operators, is also shifting to meet the current market reality. Whereas Horizontes is becoming "softer" in its approach to nature, TAM has begun for the first time to sell new tours exclusively dedicated to nature tourism. In response to a market survey in the early 1990s, TAM created a new subsidiary, Adventure Tours, which it sells to foreigners during the dry season and to Costa Ricans during the rainy, or "green," season. Most of TAM's clients purchase packaged beach tours. Adventure Tours offers them light nature excursions such as a day of bird-watching or a visit to the rain forest's aerial tram, volcanoes, waterfalls, or coffee plantation.

These trends reflect the watering down of the true meaning of ecotourism—a movement from real ecotourism toward ecotourism lite. The ultimate goal of ecotourism should be to infuse the entire travel industry with the principles and practices of ecotourism and thereby transform tourism into an environmentally and culturally sensitive activity that contributes to sustainable growth in developing countries. Clearly, there is some movement in that direction on the part of many travelers and the mass market. According to a 1996 survey, "Overall, the characteristics of current and potential ecotourists suggest that interest in ecotourism is spreading to many population segments and that . . . some characteristics of the experienced ecotourist are being incorporated into mainstream markets."[65] But the movement toward ecotourism lite, toward industry "greenwashing" through advertising images and cosmetic changes, is stronger.

Once, some of the world's oldest and most prized nature destinations, including the Galápagos Islands, Nepal, and even Monteverde, were visited by only the most physically rugged and intellectually curious. Now, however, with improved air and ground transportation, better accommodations, and extensive publicity, these destinations are being marketed to a mass audience. When poorly planned, unregulated, and overhyped, ecotourism lite, like mass tourism or even traditional nature tourism, can bring only marginal financial benefits but serious environmental and social consequences. Nepal, for instance, was once visited by only a robust subset of adventure travelers, numbering fewer than 10,000 per year before 1965. By 1987, tourist numbers had skyrocketed to more than 240,000, and they continue to increase by about 17 percent per year. Between 1980 and 1991, the number of trekkers increased by 255 percent. The impact on this Himalayan kingdom's fragile environment has been tremendous. Careless trekkers wander off trails, destroy vegetation and leave behind tin cans, packaging, and other litter. According to the World Wide Fund for Nature, wood demanded by lodge operators for construction and by trekking groups for cooking, heating, and bathing has pushed back the timberline several hundred feet and forced local Nepalese to go long distances in search of firewood. Ridges once covered with rhododendrons are now barren, and deforestation is destroying the natural habitat of the rare snow leopard and red panda.[66] "Over the last two decades, the explosion of trekking tourism has upset the delicate ecological balance and contributed significantly to the loss of cultural integrity in the Annapurna region," commented Chandra Gurung of the Annapurna Conservation Area Project.[67] Nowadays, some visitors reach mountain summits via what is marketed as "ecotourism of the future"—and their only step upward is into a helicopter. "Helicopter treks" fly visitors to high mountain peaks, where they get out, stretch their legs, take photographs, and then fly back. Such tours clearly do little to educate the traveler and do nothing for conservation or local economic development.[68]

In Kenya's popular Amboseli National Park, Maasai Mara Game Reserve, and Nairobi National Park, hordes of camera-carrying tourists packed in minivans have endangered the cheetahs, which must hunt during the day to avoid having their kills snatched by lions and hyenas. The cheetah population in Amboseli has dropped to fewer than eight.[69] In Costa Rica, Manuel Antonio National Park, a tiny jewel of a park, is being trashed by overcrowding and unplanned overdevelopment of the adjacent community. On the Galápagos Islands, hordes of tourists and new immigrants have brought in new animal and insect species that are permanently altering and threatening to destroy the island's unique and delicate ecosystem.

The travel industry's efforts to water down ecotourism, to sell ecotourism lite in exchange for short-term profits, has led some travel experts to drop the word *ecotourism* and dismiss the concept as simply a fad. A columnist for *Travel World News,* for instance, wrote, "Is ecotourism dead? 'Not yet,' said the organizers of the 1994 World Congress on Tourism for the Environment. Then they added, 'but the word is on its way out!'" Adds Bob Harvey, one of the congress's organizers, "The word *ecotourism* became a buzz-word in the early 1990s, but so many people used it in so many different ways that it has become virtually meaningless."[70] This is, however, a classic case of throwing out the baby with the bathwater. As a concept, as a set of principles and practices, ecotourism is still in its infancy. "We've only just scratched the surface in realizing the potentials of ecotourism," says Daniel Jansen, a University of Pennsylvania biologist who has worked in Costa Rica for several decades. In identifying what is ecotourism lite and determining where genuine ecotourism is being practiced today, we need also to discover ways in which authentic ecotourism can move from being simply a niche market in the category of nature tourism to become a broad set of principles and practices that transform the way we travel and the way the tourism industry functions.

Notes

1. World Travel and Tourism Council (WTTC), World Tourism Organization (WTO) Earth Council, *Agenda 21 for the Travel and Tourism Industry: Towards Environmentally Sustainable Development* (London: WTTC, 1995), p. 34.
2. Travel Industry Association of America (TIA), *Travel Industry Association of America,* brochure (Washington, D.C.: TIA, n.d.); U.S. Travel Data Center, *Discover America: Tourism and the Environment: A Guide to Challenges and Opportunities for Travel Industry Businesses* (Washington, D.C.: Travel Industry Association of America, 1992).
3. Anita Pleumarom, "Ecotourism: A New 'Green Revolution' in the Third World" (draft of article obtained from author, 1996), p. 5.
4. Faxed copy of the World Travel and Tourism Council's "Environmental Guidelines," 1997.
5. In March 1997, various organizations and "stakeholders" (including Lipman) attended the Rio + 5 Forum in New York to draw up proposals to be presented to the special U.N. session known as Earth Summit + 5. Paula DiPerna, "Proliferation Ecotourism: Caution is Definitely Needed," August 1–15, 1997, p. 26.
6. Kreg Lindberg, "Economic Aspects of Ecotourism" (draft of article obtained from author, November 1997), p. 12.
7. Thanh-Dam Truong, *Sex, Money, and Morality: Prostitution and Tourism in Southeast Asia* (London: Zed Books, 1990), p. 116.
8. Ibid., pp. 110–111.
9. Ibid., pp. 108–111. American Express is almost twice as big as the second largest travel agency, Carlson Travel Network. Somerset R. Waters, *Travel*

Industry World Yearbook: The Big Picture—1996–97, vol. 40 (New York: Child & Waters, 1997), p. 150.

10. Interviews and correspondence by Marcus Lenzen with various American Express officials, August–October 1997.

11. Waters, *Travel Industry World Yearbook,* p. 150; International Resources Group, *Ecotourism: A Viable Alternative for Sustainable Management of Natural Resources in Africa* (Washington, D.C.: U.S. Agency for International Development, June 1992), p. 63; Lindberg, "Economic Aspects of Ecotourism," p. 12.

12. Truong, "Political Economy of International Tourism," p. 109.

13. Ibid., pp. 104–105.

14. Waters, *Travel Industry World Yearbook,* p. 6.

15. Ibid., p. 77.

16. Although British Airways did improve its emissions per available seat-mile, its emissions of total carbon dioxide and nitrogen oxides increased by 6 percent between 1991 and 1993 due to increased volume of business. B. Goodall, "Environmental Auditing: A Tool for Assessing the Environmental Performance of Tourism Firms," *Geographical Journal* 1, no. 161 (1995): 29–37, cited in Pleumarom, "Ecotourism: A New 'Green Revolution,'" p. 7.

17. Waters, *Travel Industry World Yearbook,* p. 153.

18. Stephanie Thullen, "Ecotourism and Sustainability: The Problematic Role of Transnational Corporations in Ecotourism" (Master's thesis, American University, 1997); Truong, "Political Economy of International Tourism," pp. 109–116.

19. Thullen, "Ecotourism and Sustainability," pp. 53–57; advertisements in various issues of the *Tico Times,* San Jose, Costa Rica; advertisement in *Going Green: The Ecotourism Resource for Travel Agents,* supplement to *Tour & Travel News,* October 25, 1993, p. 11; interviews with a representative of DHC Hotels; brochures from DHS Hotels.

20. Waters, *Travel Industry World Yearbook,* pp. 77, 165.

21. By 1997, cruise lines had to comply with new "safety of life at sea" regulations and were spending millions of dollars installing fire doors, sprinklers, and other safety devices. Ibid., pp. 77, 150, 164–165; Russell Nansen, "Hungry? Out of Work? Eat a Cruise Ship!" *Contours* 7, no. 10 (June 1997): 4–8.

22. Nansen, "Eat a Cruise Ship!" *Contours* 7, no. 10 (June 1997): 4–8.

23. Ibid., p. 4.

24. Global Education, *Tourism: Paradise in Peril* (Baltimore: Church World Service).

25. Nansen, "Eat a Cruise Ship!" pp. 4–8; American Society of Travel Agents (ASTA), Environment Committee, "Destination Earth—Save It, Share It," ASTA newsletter, September 1993; ASTA/*Smithsonian Magazine* Environmental Awards for 1991–1996.

26. Frederic Dimanche, "Greening Traditional Hotels," *Tour & Travel News,* August 29, 1994, p. G29; Kirk Iwanowski, *Taking the Black and Blue Out of Being Green: Developing Hotel Environmental Programs* (Mineola, N.Y.: HVS Eco Services, October 1994).

27. Dimanche, "Greening Traditional Hotels," G29; *London Hilton Hosts Environment Centre Film Launch and Executive Briefing* (London: The Earth Centre, November 5, 1993), cited in Anita Pleumarom, "The Political

Economy of Tourism," *The Ecologist* 24, no. 4 (July–August 1994): 147, n. 16.

28. Although travel agents are categorized as both corporate and leisure agencies, the focus here is on leisure. International Resources Group, *Ecotourism*, p. 23.

29. Interviews; Karen Ziffer, *Ecotourism: The Uneasy Alliance* (Washington, D.C.: Conservation International, 1989), p. 21.

30. Telephone interviews with ASTA officials in Alexandria, Virginia, in September 1998, and with Yvonne Rodgers, International Ecotourism Education Foundation, Falls Church, Virginia, in May 1996. In recent years, more travelers have been booking tickets via the Internet, and although this appears to be encouraging more travel, it also has cut into the business that typically goes to travel agents. Barbara Crossette, "Surprises in the Global Tourism Boom," *New York Times*, April 12, 1998, p. 5.

31. Another expert estimates "there are 50,000 travel agencies with over 300,000 travel agents selling travel in the U.S. alone." M.J. Kietzke, "The Role of Travel Agents in Ecotourism," *Earth Ways*, January 1996, p. EW4; Interviews with ASTA officials, September 1998; E. Weiner, "Ecotourism: Can it Protect the Planet?" New York Times, May 19, 1991, cited in Pleumarom, "Political Economy of Tourism," p. 144, n. 21.

32. Other travel agents listed adventure, bicycling, scuba diving, and various other sports as their area of specialization; nature tourism was not one of the categories included in the survey. The Ecotourism Society (TES) training course packet; interviews with Marie Walters and other ASTA officials; International Resources Group, *Ecotourism*, pp. 23–24; "Travel Agents and Their Specialties," *Washington Post*, September 28, 1997, p. E6.

33. International Resources Group, *Ecotourism*, pp. 23–25; TES training course packet.

34. International Resources Group, *Ecotourism*, pp. 27–28.

35. Bryan Higgins, "The Global Structure of the Nature Tourism Industry: Ecotourists, Tour Operators, and Local Business," *Journal of Travel Research* 35, no. 2 (fall 1996), p. 13.

36. I was very surprised when I first learned about fam trips. As a news reporter, I had always adhered to a creed of never taking favors from those I was covering. However, in the course of researching this book, I took three fam trips organized by public relations firms—one to Chile's Patagonia and two to the Virgin Islands of the United States. I also negotiated discounted or free hotel accommodations and airline tickets for some of my travels to Costa Rica, the Galápagos, Cuba, and Africa. My motivation was partly to learn how the travel press operates, but the reality is that I couldn't have covered the expenses involved in writing this book without fam trips (and several generous foundation grants).

37. Deborah Cooper, "Turning Press Trips into Client Trips," *Adventure Travel Business*, October 1997, p. 22.

38. Author's interviews; Tom McNicol, "Misguided," *Washington Post*, April 19, 1998, p. E6.

39. McNicol, "Misguided," pp. E6–E8.

40. I found myself torn emotionally and ethically by these fam trips. I went, with three other writers, on a fam trip to Chile's Patagonia that was billed by the public relations firm as ecotourism. We were fed the story with a silver spoon: everything was covered but tips; we were accompanied by guides, flown in

business class, and even had a day of sightseeing in Santiago en route to Patagonia. There, we were taken to an amazing new luxury hotel, Salto Chico, the only hotel in Torres del Paine National Park that is open year-around. The architect himself arrived to explain his marvelous creation. I was thrilled to hike through the windswept park, with its bonsai-like shrubs in tones of blue-green and burnt orange; jagged, snow-dusted Andean peaks; and dazzling blue-and-white icebergs floating across dark, choppy lakes. I never would have been able to visit this end of the earth otherwise. But in reality, we were experiencing luxury nature travel, not ecotourism. The hotel, owned by one of Chile's wealthiest families, which also owns the airline on which we flew, has no program for benefiting the park, scientific research, or the scattered homesteaders in the region. The guides working for the hotel are young, hip, bilingual college kids from Santiago without deep knowledge of Patagonia's unique ecosystem. The local park rangers I met on my own were far more informative. Salto Chico, though a beautiful, architecturally sensitive resort, does not qualify as an exemplary ecotourism project.

41. McNicol, "Misguided," pp. E6, E8.

42. Interviews with several *Condé Nast Traveler* editors and writers.

43. Interviews with travel writers and editors; McNicol, "Misguided," pp. E6–E8.

44. McNicol, "Misguided," p. E6.

45. Interviews by the author with some dozen travel writers between 1996 and 1998.

46. Society of American Travel Writers (SATW), "Membership Guidelines"; interviews with SATW officials and travel writers.

47. Faxed copy of the Society of American Travel Writers' "Code of Ethics."

48. Ziffer, *Uneasy Alliance*, p. 22.

49. International Resources Group, *Ecotourism*, p. 26.

50. Ronnie Casella, "Dinosaurs in Paradise: Off the Path with the Time-Traveling Tourist," in "The Educated Traveler" (Ph.D. diss., Syracuse University, 1996).

51. Brochures quoted are from Casella, "The Educated Traveler," or author's files.

52. British Airways, "Keep Your Towels—and Help Save the World!" press release, 96/MVLON/50, 1996.

53. Denise Ingram and Patrick Durst, "Nature-Oriented Travel to Developing Countries," FPEI Working Paper No. 28 (Research Triangle Park, N.C.: Southeastern Center for Forest Economics Research, October 1987), p. 6.

54. Ziffer, *Uneasy Alliance*, pp. 22–23; Ralph Sorenson, "Overseas Adventure Travel, Inc.," Case Study 9-391-068 (Boston: Harvard University, Harvard Business School, 1990); interviews; literature from agencies.

55. International Resources Group, *Ecotourism*, p. 27.

56. Arthur Frommer, "Frommer's World: Writing Reasonable Rules for Real Ecotourism," *Travel Holiday*, February 1994, p. 25.

57. ASTA literature; author's interviews with various ASTA officials.

58. "Ecotourism Investigation," *Agenda 21* series, Worldwide Television News, London, March 1995, produced by author; interview with Geoffrey Lipman, Montreal, September 1994.

59. ASTA and *Smithsonian Magazine*, "Environmental Award: Destination Earth—Save It, Share It," contains a complete listing of all recipients.

60. Author's visit to Mahenye and interviews with Clive Stockil and others; Marisa

Milanese, "Africa's Ghost in the Machine: Clive Stockil's CAMPFIRE Project Generates Tourism, Jobs—and Controversy," *Condé Nast Traveler*, June 1997, pp. 24–31.

61. "Ecotourism Case by Case: Conservation Travel," *Travel World News: The Monthly Review for Travel Agent* no. 72 (June 1994), p. 126.

62. Mireya Navarro, "New Disney Kingdom Comes with Real-Life Obstacles," *New York Times*, April 16, 1998; Jon Nordheimer, "Disney Goes Live with Its Newest Park," *New York Times*, April 26, 1998, pp. 8–9, 25.

63. David Western, "Ecotourism: The Kenya Challenge," in C. G. Gakahu and B. E. Goode, *Ecotourism and Sustainable Development in Kenya*, proceedings of the Kenya Ecotourism Workshop held at Nakuru National Park, Kenya, September 13–17, 1992 (Nairobi: Wildlife Conservation International, 1992), p. 16.

64. Interviews and correspondence with Terry Pratt and Tamara Budowski, 1995–1997; "Managing an Ecotourism Business," Section XIV, The Ecotourism Society training course packet.

65. Pamela Wight, "North American Ecotourists: Market Profile and Trip Characteristics," spring 1996, on The Ecotourism Society's World Wide Web site (Internet: http://www.ecotourism.org/data.html).

66. World Resources Institute, "Ecotourism: Rising Interest in Nature Vacations Has Mixed Results for Host Countries and the Resources They Promote," in *Environmental Almanac* (Boston: Houghton Mifflin, 1993), p. 150; Jim Motavalli, "Transforming Travel: Eco-tourism Is More Than a Buzzword; It's a Seismic Shift in a Trillion-Dollar Industry"; Motavalli, "Africa Wakes"; and John Ivanko, "Far-Flung Fantasies," *The Environmental Magazine*, April 1995, pp. 38–45; "TES Statistical Fact Sheet," on The Ecotourism Society's World Wide Web site (Internet: http://www.ecotourism.org/textfiles/stats.txt), July 25, 1997, p. 2.

67. "Nepal: How to Kill," InterPress Service, June 3, 1995.

68. Imtiaz Muqbil, "German Tourism Activist Sounds Warning on Bogus 'Ecotourism,'" *Bangkok Post*, tourism supplement, April 7, 1994, p. 3.

69. World Resources Institute, "Rising Interest in Nature Vacations," pp. 150–151.

70. "Ecotourism Case by Case," p. 126.

Chapter 3

Ecotourism Today

Throughout the international tourism chain are entrepreneurs marketing themselves as being involved in ecotourism. Strictly defined, everyone in ecotourism should practice the principles of low-impact, educational, and ecologically and culturally sensitive travel that benefits local communities and the host country. But the conscientious traveler can have a difficult time sifting tourism's wheat from the chaff to find genuine ecotourism projects. Guidebooks, brochures, press reports, and ecotourism awards are not always accurate. Frequently, it is only by going to a destination and spending vacation time and personal savings that the discerning traveler discovers that what is marketed as ecotourism is missing several key pillars of the definition.

Maho Bay: Some Missing Pillars

Maho Bay Camps, a tented camp facility, and Harmony Resort, an "off-the-grid" condominium complex, both located in a national park on St. John Island in the Virgin Islands of the United States, have succeeded in building reputations as two among a handful of the best-known ecotourism destinations. They have done so largely on the strength of international awards, press coverage, and the personal appeal of their owner and developer, Stanley Selengut. Selengut claims that his advertising budget is zero, yet Maho Bay and Harmony operate at nearly 90 percent occupancy. He has filled Maho Bay and Harmony (the two destinations are often referred to collectively as Maho Bay, after their location) through word-of-mouth referrals and repeat customers and by garnering more good media coverage and awards than any other ecotourism project. Maho Bay and/or Harmony have won the British Airways Tourism for Tomorrow Award, the first *Condé Nast Traveler* Ecotourism Award (1995),[1] and the ASTA/*Smithsonian Magazine* Environmental Award (1997). Maho Bay's promotional material includes a two-inch-thick packet of laudatory press coverage. The *New York Times* called Maho Bay "an ecological showplace," *Islands* magazine's first Ecotourism Award went to Maho Bay, and *Popular Science* gave it its 1995 grand award for environmental technology. The President's Council on Sustainable Development presented Selengut with a certificate of appreciation.

Maho Bay's appeal is enhanced by its setting. Unlike the heavily developed St. Thomas and St. Croix Island, two-thirds of the approximately fifteen-by-eight-kilometer (nine-by-five-mile) St. John is preserved in Virgin Islands National Park, thanks to philanthropist Laurance Rockefeller, who, in 1956, donated the land for conservation purposes. In 1976, Selengut leased a 5.7-hectare (14-acre) hillside on private land within the national park, just above secluded Little Maho Bay. He has since built four distinct resort complexes on St. John. The oldest is Maho Bay Camps, which consists of 114 platformed tent-cottages hidden in deep foliage overlooking the turquoise-blue bay. The wood-frame, canvas, and mosquito-net tents are set on posts, and nearly five kilometers (three miles) of elevated wooden walkways connect them to the beach, communal toilets, cold-water showers, and the large, gazebo-shaped dining-cum-meeting room. This construction protects foliage and minimizes soil erosion; during construction, no trees were cut down. Electrical cables and water lines, normally buried in the ground, were attached to the undersides of the ramps. Maho Bay does not, however, have solar energy, composting toilets, or other standard, environmentally sound innovations. Built in the 1970s, nearly two decades before ecotourism had gelled as a concept, this site-sensitive construction was both the cheapest and the least controversial technique, given the land's protected status. After *ecotourism* became the new marketing buzzword, Selengut began billing his tents as rustic ecotourism.

Above the tents, on about one hectare (two and a half acres) of land, stands Harmony Resort, consisting of a dozen upscale and innovative eco-condos. These luxury villas are built almost entirely of recycled materials (though not from St. John) and operate "off the grid," using solar and wind power and captured rainwater. The beams and girders are made from wood-scrap composites, the roof shingles from recycled cardboard and cement, the bathroom tiles from crushed lightbulbs, the doormats from old automobile tires, and the decks from recycled newspapers. Each villa has its own computer, which keeps track of how much electricity and water guests have used and when they might run out (as I did).

Selengut decided to build Harmony after the National Park Service and the Virgin Islands Energy Office in 1991 hosted a workshop on sustainable design at Maho Bay. The Park Service subsequently produced a how-to manual on sustainable design,[2] and Selengut put these principles into practice. He has received help from the Energy Office, which provided the computers, and the U.S. Department of Energy's Sandia National Laboratories, which supplied experimental products such as solar ovens, solar ice-making machines, and biodegradable detergents. "Harmony proves," says Selengut, "a delightful solution to comfortable living within a fragile environment."

Across the island on a dry, barren, and hot hillside, in sharp counterpoint to the lushness of Maho Bay Camps and Harmony Resort, are

Selengut's other two properties. The newest project is the Concordia Eco-
tents, perched on stilts overlooking Salt Pond Bay and a rough stretch of the
Caribbean sea. Each Eco-tent consists of a low-impact wooden structure
with mesh screens framing a full apartment that features solar- and wind-
generated electricity, energy-efficient kitchen appliances, composting toilets,
and space to sleep six. The Eco-tents, also made from recycled materials,
blend the best features of Maho Bay Camps' close encounter with nature
and Harmony Resort's environmentally sensitive construction and upscale
living. Next to the Eco-tents is Estate Concordia, which consists of nine luxury condominiums with passive solar design. Selengut has abandoned his
original scheme to build 120 such units, largely because, he says, they were
costly and because they are far less environmentally innovative than either
Harmony or the Eco-tents.

Selengut himself is the chief salesman for his ecoprojects; "the travel
industry's green guru"[3] is what United Airlines' in-flight magazine called
him. An engaging and affable New Yorker with a Bronx accent and signa-
ture white golf cap, white sport shirt, and white beard, Selengut has become
a popular speaker at ecotourism conferences and forums. "Ecotourism is a
kind of theater, and I'm doing the choreography," Selengut is fond of saying. Or, as he sometimes more bluntly puts it, "A lot of what we do [here] is
show business."[4] Selengut is also fond of saying that good ecotourism
is good business. His Maho Bay tents cost only about $7,500 each to put
up, and renting for between $60 and $105 double occupancy per night,
they earned back the investment in the first year. By 1993, Maho Bay was
taking in $3 million per year and its net income was close to $750,000. "It's
almost like stealing," Selengut told Forbes magazine.[5] Although the Maho
Bay tents are billed as appealing to "vacationers of a Sierra Club bent,"
Travel Weekly rates Harmony as the world's top "ecosensitive honeymoon
resort."[6] Harmony cost $70,000 per unit to build and rents for between
$95 and $195 double occupancy per night, making it impossible for Selengut to recoup the investment quickly. This is a main reason why, Selengut
says, he has moved to develop the far cheaper Concordia Eco-tents and is
negotiating to expand his ecoprojects to Puerto Rico, Bermuda, and
Hawaii.

When Selengut hosted The Ecotourism Society's International
Ecolodge Development Forum and Field Seminar in October 1994, Maho
Bay came under close scrutiny by ecotourism experts from around the
world. Virtually everyone in attendance praised Selengut for effectively and
creatively pushing the perimeters of ecolodge design in a blend of low-
impact construction, recycled materials, and renewable energy sources. But
a number of experts interviewed at the conference were deeply disturbed to
discover that Maho Bay and Selengut's other properties paid little heed to
other ecotourism principles involving the local community, conservation,

and tourist education. "I would give Maho Bay a mixed evaluation," said Ray Ashton, director of Water and Air Research, a Gainesville, Florida, consulting firm specializing in sustainable tourism program development for governments, private entrepreneurs, international agencies, and conservation organizations. In summing up his assessment, another expert concluded, "These are green lodges, not real eco-tourism." Joshua Reichert, who heads the Pew Charitable Trusts' environmental program, contends that sound ecotourism should meet four criteria: (1) it should be designed, built, and operated so that it leaves a "soft imprint"; (2) it should contribute money to the local economy and local community services; (3) it should contribute financially to environmental protection; and (4) it should educate visitors and members of the local community. Reichert concluded that under scrutiny, the Maho Bay properties, like much else that is advertised as ecotourism, falls short on a number of counts.

Maho Bay and Selengut's other properties, for instance, employ very few West Indians. Even though the Maho Bay tents have been around for two decades, the vast majority of Selengut's forty-five-odd staff members are young, single, white North Americans working for low wages in exchange for a stint in the Tropics. Selengut argues that he hires "off-island" because the Virgin Islands have no unemployment; according to the U.S. Virgin Islands Department of Labor, unemployment averaged between 3.5 and 5.9 percent between 1992 and 1997. Islanders I interviewed say that although unemployment is not high, there are people seeking work in tourism establishments. Employees, including senior staff members, at other resorts and tented camps on St. John are almost all West Indian. But, islanders say, Selengut does not attract West Indian workers because he pays less than other hotel owners, requires employees to live in tents on-site, and does not allow tipping.[7]

Those interviewed, including permanent residents and those with vacation homes on St. John, also complained that although Maho Bay is well-known internationally, it has done little for the island in terms of contributing to environmental or social welfare projects. Selengut says he has an informal fund from which he makes donations when he receives requests from employees or islanders to help with personal emergencies or special projects, but no percentage of profits is set aside for environmental initiatives or island development projects. Selengut himself lives in the United States and much of the staff works on short-term contracts, so few at Maho Bay have deep roots in the island or ties to the local community.

Although Selengut describes Harmony as balancing "both nature and culture," local crafts are not promoted, either in the condos' decor or in the gift shop. Good ecolodges should convey "a sense of place" and stimulate local artisanship. Harmony, however, is decorated with handicrafts from Bolivia and Brazil, all for sale and all from a previous Selengut venture,

Piñata Party, in which he imported South American handicrafts. He contends that St. John has few crafts and that those available are too expensive to display and sell. But the island's gift shops are full of locally produced baskets, pottery, and paintings, offered at a range of prices. American professor Bernard Kemp, who has studied the local arts and crafts, says that "Selengut has made no effort to utilize, display, or promote them to Maho Bay visitors."[8]

Selengut preaches that an ecoresort is far more profitable than a traditional resort. "What makes sense from an environmental and conservation point of view also saves money," he tells his audiences. Certainly, collecting rainwater and recycling wastewater at Harmony make environmental and financial sense, but as Ray Ashton warns, "There's a thin line between what's ecologically sound and what cuts overhead." He argues that although the Maho Bay tents "could use solar power to heat the showers and light the walkways," such upgrades may not be cost-effective because the property is leased. "If you're an ecologist you should go above and beyond and do more than just a cheap tented camp if you want to be touted as a model," says Ashton.[9]

Tracking True Ecotourism

As Maho Bay illustrates, the difference between good ecotourism and ecotourism lite or even "green" tourism projects may be difficult to discern. Throughout the entire ecotourism chain, in fact, there is frequently a blurring of the boundaries between nature tourism and the more multidimensional concept of ecotourism. This lack of precision makes it difficult, for instance, to quantify with scientific certainty the growth in the number of ecotourists. By the mid-1990s, estimates were that more than one-third of the U.S. traveling public (some 43 million people) had taken at least one ecotour, according to a U.S. Travel Data Center survey.[10] On the basis of these findings, ASTA's Environment Committee concluded, "The consumer preference for culturally and environmentally sound travel is well illustrated by a 30 percent annual increase in ecotourism, compared to a growth rate of 4 percent in the U.S. travel industry."[11] In 1996, the World Tourism Organization predicted that by the year 2000, most of the 86 percent increase in worldwide tourism receipts would come from active, adventurous, nature- and culture-related travel.[12] These statistics and projections are imprecise because they lump together nature travel, ecotourism lite, and real ecotourism, but they do demonstrate a growing public commitment to this type of travel.

Who are these ecotourists? Until recently, solid studies and statistics were few, and as discussed earlier, ecotourism was often lumped together with adventure or nature tourism.[13] In addition, tour operators and those who own and operate the accommodations, activities, and transportation all play a central role in whether the experience adheres to the principles and ethics of ecotourism. "No one can truly be called an ecotourist until they are 'on the ground' at the destination, behaving in accordance with the principles," says Canadian ecotourism researcher Pamela Wight.[14]

Nevertheless, experts say that ecotourists in the United States do fit a broad profile. Most are between thirty-one and fifty years of age, but there is also a considerable number of "mature" adults (older than fifty-five), equally divided by gender, and most are physically active. They tend to be better-educated professionals or businesspeople, often from dual-income families with a combined income of $50,000 or more who have a genuine interest in learning something about nature.[15] Tour operator Kurt Kutay says that ecotourists fall roughly into two main categories: "DINCs" (dual income, no children) and "empty nesters" (couples with grown children).[16] They are discriminating, and they recognize quality and are willing to pay for it. Many come from the some 30 million Americans who belong to environmental organizations or profess an interest in conservation.[17] Many are also socially minded and interested in the culture, history, and people in developing countries. Geographically, "the ecotourism market exists in virtually every major metropolitan area in North America," concludes Wight, from her survey in the United States and Canada of "experienced ecotourists"[18] and global companies offering nature, adventure, and cultural tours.

In recent years, as the number of ecotravelers has grown, the industry has attracted a less experienced clientele, which author Mary-Lou Weisman calls "neo-ecotourists." In "Confessions of a Reluctant Eco-Tourist," Weisman, a sixty-year-old American, recounts her ecovacation at Lapa Ríos, an ecotourism resort on a 1,000-acre private reserve in Costa Rica's Osa Peninsula. Described as "the most deluxe jungle and beach hide-away in Costa Rica," Lapa Ríos has won various international awards for its adherence to ecotourism principles of sustainable construction, educational hikes with naturalist guides, and contributions toward conserving the rain forest. Weisman writes that she and her husband "suffer from bipolar vacationing disorder": they seek physically strenuous daytime activities and comfort at night. "The oxymoronic pairing of the adjective 'luxury' with the noun 'jungle' appealed to our manic-depressive travel style. We booked three nights." However, after three hours of jungle hiking, Weisman determined that ecotourism wasn't really for her. "I opted out of the eco part of eco-tourism. Me no Jane. Instead, I headed for the pool, or the beach, where I spent one blissful afternoon kayaking and swimming with the other eco-flops."[19]

In general, Pamela Wight finds, ecotourists are better informed, more experienced, and more adventuresome travelers than the conventional tourist. They tend to seek wide-ranging activities and multidestination vacations and to prefer modest, intimate accommodations.[20] Many are former backpackers and are knowledgeable about the mechanics of travel, developing countries, and conservation. According to one survey of travelers, more than two-thirds had previous experience with overseas travel, and one-third were repeat customers.[21] Rather than consulting travel agents, ecotourists tend either to travel individually and independently ("foreign independent travelers," or FITs, in the industry jargon) or to use nature tour operators (known also as outfitters, wholesalers, or suppliers) to find an appropriate fixed-itinerary tour. By going directly to the tour operator, ecotourists may save some money, but their primary motive is to customize their tour or find a more ecologically sensitive package.

Ecotourism Structures in the United States: Outbound Ecotour Operators

Serious ecotourists, in contrast to conventional vacationers, often plan trips on their own or turn to specialist nature tour operators rather than generalist travel agents. These operators are usually located in the same country as the tourist, but they have an intimate, frequently firsthand, knowledge of the destination country, having lived there or traveled there frequently. They are, therefore, the ecotraveler's most important source of expertise and information; the choice of an outbound ecotour operator can make or break a vacation. As part of their oversight responsibility, outbound operators are supposed to ensure that ecotourism objectives and practices are followed. According to The Ecotourism Society (TES), "This may require extensive work with their in-bound operators to insure that guiding, business and conservation practices, as well as relations with local communities, are in line with ecotourism guidelines."[22] *Condé Nast Traveler* magazine outlines "seven golden rules" to guide travelers in choosing a tour operator and destination. Ideally, eco-operators should (1) link commercial tourism with local conservation programs; (2) provide money and other tangible support for development of parks and management of natural resources; (3) support indigenous businesses by buying local goods and services; (4) arrange and promote meaningful contact between travelers and local people; (5) promote ecological research programs; (6) develop sustainable tourist facilities that minimize environmental damage; and (7) help to repair the damage done by others (such as the Sierra Club's trail cleanup trips).[23]

An increasing number of specialized tour operators involved in ecotourism are acting as both travel agents, selling fixed-itinerary trips, and packagers, customizing trips to fit the interests, schedules, and budgets of particular groups or individual travelers. A number of outbound tour operators, such as Abercrombie & Kent (A&K), which has its own ground transport system and hotels at some destinations, are also inbound ground operators. Because of the time and added expense involved, the outbound tour operator charges 25 to 40 percent more for individually designed tours.

The number of nature and adventure tour operators in the United States has been growing by 10 to 20 percent per year, according to Canadian ecotourism consultant Carolyn Wild.[24] In 1901, there was just one, the Sierra Club, and in 1970, there were only nine.[25] By 1996, the number had jumped to 219 U.S. tour operators offering ecotours to developing countries.[26] Several studies have provided further breakdowns. An analysis of the 1987 edition of the *Specialty Travel Index* (*STI*) found that 78 U.S. firms were involved in nature tourism to developing countries. The number of clients handled by each ranged from 20 to 3,000 per year. The survey found that 81 percent of nature-oriented tours conducted in 1986 were to developing countries; the most popular destinations were Kenya, Tanzania, Nepal, Puerto Rico, Mexico, Costa Rica, and China. The most popular activities, in descending order, were trekking and hiking, bird-watching, nature photography, wildlife safaris, camping, mountain climbing, fishing, river rafting, canoeing, kayaking, and botanical study. A 1994 analysis of nature tour operators culled from a variety of sources, including the *STI*, identified 155 companies offering one or more nature tours to Latin America. The 82 firms (53 percent) successfully surveyed reported handling a total of 119,810 tourists during 1993–1994. Central America was the most popular region within Latin America, and Costa Rica was the most visited destination.[27]

In separate interviews during 1996, *STI* publisher Steen Hansen estimated there were about 40 U.S.-based tour operators marketing ecotourism, while Kurt Kutay stated there were only 25 to 30 U.S. tour operators marketing genuine ecotours. Some of the more successful operators have the commitment and capacity to make financial contributions to conservation efforts in the host country, whether from their own profits, from voluntary contributions solicited from the tourists, or from a combination of both. Their tours are small, usually including no more than eighteen persons, to minimize adverse impact on the resources and maximize the tourists' interaction with the natural environment, foreign culture, and tour leader, guide, and other experts. In an interview with ecotourism expert Carolyn Wild, she says that tour leaders are "very important in giving interpretation, making tracks come alive. Most are trained biologists, ecologists, or some other -ologists, and the tour companies are very proud of them and feature them in their literature. They are the ones who sell the next trip—

that make the ecotourist want to return next year and recommend the trip to a friend."

In her study for Conservation International, Karen Ziffer suggests that ecotour operators fall into one or more of four categories: (1) those "selling nature," who are trying to maximize profits from a lucrative market; (2) members of the "sensitive group," who try to design trips that are low impact and culturally respectful; (3) "donors," who give a portion of their revenues to local environmental or community projects; and (4) "doers," who take an active role in conserving or improving the areas they visit. Because travel is a highly competitive industry, most ecotour operators fall into the second and third categories rather than the fourth, which requires more time than most believe they have.[28]

Small Ecotour Operators

Most ecotour operators are small companies, often run by the founder. They range in size from tiny firms that specialize in a few countries and customize all their tours to ones that offer a mix of packaged and customized tours to those that sell only their own carefully compiled tours. They may specialize in particular activities, such as bird-watching, mountain climbing, hiking, or biking. What these companies broadly share is a social, environmental, and political sensitivity and a common operating ethic, hands-on involvement with their tourists and the destinations they are visiting, and carefully selected overseas operators, guides, accommodations, and destinations.

Take, for instance, tiny Tamu Safaris, based in the United States with an office in Nairobi and run largely via the internet. Founded in 1987 by Sally and Costas Christ, Tamu Safaris offers small (two- to fifteen-person), customized wildlife safaris of the highest quality. "Our philosophy has always been to stay small and effective, both in offering a personalized high-quality safari and in terms of making contributions to community development and keeping any negative environmental impacts to a minimum," Costas Christ explained. As part of its ecotourism ethic, Tamu Safaris supports small-scale community development projects such as the Lamu Town Conservation Society in Kenya. The company also actively participates in training workshops on ecotourism implementation and planning and has assisted government and nongovernmental organizations in developing national ecotourism strategies.

Sally and Costas Christ's commitment to responsible tourism grew out of years of living and working in East Africa, first as wildlife researchers and anthropologists, then as directors of college educational centers, and finally as private tour guides. Their goal is to hook up American travelers with the best local tour operators, guides, and ecotourism destinations in Kenya,

Tanzania, Seychelles, Madagascar, Namibia, Botswana, Zimbabwe, and South Africa. Everything they recommend they know firsthand and have assessed according to ecotourism principles. They conduct only about twenty tours per year, and their clients range from small groups of friends who like to travel together to families who want to blend learning and adventure, makers of documentary films casing locations, zoological groups seeking specialized natural history tours, and couples looking for a romantic adventure.

Tamu Safaris advertises very selectively, frequently through word of mouth, which is how I first learned of the company. At the October 1994 Ecolodge Forum at Maho Bay, I heard Costas give a thoughtful lecture about ecotourism developments in East Africa. When I first called Tamu, Sally began by listening—to my needs and desires, my time frame and budget. Mine was no easy trip to plan because it included my two teenagers, lots of interviews, many destinations, and a need to combine business and pleasure within a relatively modest budget. Over the course of two months, Sally helped me identify the most important ecotourism destinations and put together an increasingly refined and detailed itinerary. She prepared a packet of suggested reading and general travel tips and graciously and efficiently handled numerous last-minute changes. There were no glossy brochures, no off-the-rack packages; everything was personalized and tailored to our needs.[29]

Large Ecotour Operators

Overseas Adventure Travel (OAT), based in Cambridge, Massachusetts, and founded in 1979, is today one of the largest nature tourism outbound operators in the United States with a sophisticated marketing program for its exclusive, well-guided packaged tours. During its early years, it concentrated on camping safaris in East Africa using large, environmentally destructive Bedford trucks, but it gradually adopted a more sensitive and broad ecotourism mandate. Following a financial slump in the late 1980s,[30] OAT was acquired in 1993 by Grand Circle Corporation, which specializes in "senior" travel (for those older than sixty-five). The merger has proved financially successful. In 1994, OAT's sales jumped by 63 percent, and they rose by more than 100 percent over the following eighteen months.

In 1995, OAT asked Costas Christ to revamp its Africa division. He accepted the offer, welcoming the opportunity to find out whether the ecotourism principles that guide Tamu Safaris could be applied to a large outfitter. In evaluating the success of the effort, Costas said, "The final report card is still out on this. But one thing I learned is that large corporations like OAT do not always have the flexibility to make decisions based on what is best for the environment or for local people in their operations. There is a lot of emphasis on bottom-line financial returns." One year after Costas Christ redesigned all of OAT's Africa tours, the company reported that the trips he put together had achieved the highest quality rating of any tour packages in the company's fifteen-year history.

Although OAT specializes in East Africa and the Himalayas, it now offers trips to seven continents. Its choices include "Quick Escapes" for busy people, cost-saving "Affordable Adventures," "Family Adventures," and "Soft Adventures," offering inn and lodge accommodations rather than camping. OAT has set up a nonprofit foundation that provides material and financial assistance for a number of local projects, including the International University for Peace in Costa Rica, the Himalayan Trust in Nepal, and the Eastern Africa Environmental Network. It is also moving toward offering "home stays" with local families in order to increase the cross-cultural experience and bring more money into local communities. Although OAT has contributed tens of thousands of dollars to environmental and community projects, its size and volume preclude the flexibility of offering customized itineraries or working with many of the finer, wholly locally owned but invariably smaller, ground operators and ecotourism facilities in developing countries. The company is "like a big guy who is not very limber," says Costas Christ.

Midsize Ecotour Operators

Nestled between OAT and Tamu Safaris in size and approach is the Seattle-based Wildland Adventures. It has six employees, handles more than 1,000 tourists per year, and grosses about $2 million annually conducting tours to Central America, the Andes, East and southern Africa, Turkey, Egypt, Australia, New Zealand, and Alaska. The company's president, Kurt Kutay, says that Wildland Adventures offers three types of tours: private tours; tours with custom-made itineraries for couples, families, or small groups (40 percent of the company's business); exclusive tours put together by the company itself (30 percent); and fixed-itinerary tours that Wildland resells for reputable overseas ecotourism operators (30 percent).

Kutay, who once worked for Costa Rica's national park service and holds a master's degree in natural resource management, says he entered into ecotourism as a conservationist, not a businessman. In 1980, just as ecotourism was getting started, Kutay and a friend began informally putting together and leading tours to Central America and Nepal. "Our style was to take friends to countries we love," says Kutay. Gradually, through word of mouth and limited advertising, they put together a small company specializing in "culturally and environmentally responsible tourism."

In 1986, the young entrepreneurs created the Traveler's Conservation Trust, a nonprofit corporation affiliated with their for-profit business that contributes a portion of Wildland Adventure's earnings to community-level projects and conservation organizations in the developing countries they visit. Wildland Adventures routinely asks its clients to make voluntary contributions of $25 or more to the trust, and Kutay estimates that "95 percent contribute." Projects supported by the trust include scientific institutes in Costa Rica, monastery restoration projects in Tibet, the Charles Darwin Foundation on the Galápagos Islands, school wildlife clubs and a cheetah project in Africa, and fourteen projects in Nepal, including tree planting, solar water heating, environmental education, and medical programs. "The trick has been to identify organizations with English-language newsletters," Kutay explains. "We send the contributions and list of names to the local organizations and our clients automatically receive their newsletter for a year. Hopefully, they continue to make contributions." In 1994, *Condé Nast Traveler* cited Wildland Adventures and seventeen other outfitters worldwide as tour operators "that we believe are doing the right thing."[31]

Ecotours Sponsored by Nonprofit Organizations

A number of environmental, educational, and scientific organizations also offer nature, adventure, study, and service tours to their members. Usually, these travel programs contract with international or inbound tour operators in the host countries.[32] In the U.S., the best known of these organizations include the Smithsonian Institution, The Nature Conservancy, the Audubon Society, the World Wildlife Fund, the Earthwatch Institute, the Experiment in International Living, the Foundation for Field Research, and the Sierra Club. Increasingly, these travel programs are incorporating ecotourism principles, although they tend to use the larger, best-advertised U.S. nature tour operators and overseas ground operators, which are not always the most innovative and responsible ecotourism outfits. The main purposes of these trips are to promote the education and professional development of members, showcase the organization's projects in other countries, provide fun and relaxation for travelers, raise revenue for the organization, and give members a tax break.

Most of these organizations keep abreast of changes in the Internal Revenue Service's standards and regulations for tax exempt organizations by attending an annual "Non-profits in Travel" conference run by Travel Learning Conferences of Montana. Under the rules guiding nonprofit organizations, these trips cannot themselves be money-making or fund-raising activities. However, according to one study, such travel targets "the 'upscale market' [and] a key implicit objective is to win favor with present or potential donors and benefactors."[33] Ecotourism expert Ray Ashton, who used to run the natural history tours for the Massachusetts Audubon Society, says that some nonprofit organizations make a "ton of money" from the trips by tapping participants for contributions and gift giving.[34]

The Sierra Club's High Trip, a large annual camping and hiking expedition begun in 1901, was the first nature tourism expedition organized by an environmental group. However, in 1972, as environmental concern grew about the human "impact on the fragile High Sierra landscape,"[35] the Sierra Club's Outing Committee stopped conducting the High Trip and began organizing smaller trips (usually for twelve to fifteen people) featuring backpacking, biking, river rafting, and mountain climbing trips to a variety of U.S. locations and, beginning in 1964, overseas. Except for a small office staff, the Outings program is run entirely by authorized volunteers who scout destinations, organize itineraries, and lead the trips. The program currently offers about 340 trips per year, including some two dozen overseas, for about 4,000 members. In a 1996 interview, Sierra Club Outing director Charles Hardy argued that although "the spirit of adventure which grew out of the 1960s and 1970s has run its course" and people are now wanting "less strenuous trips," the service-oriented trips remain "very popular and healthy."

In 1993, the Sierra Club adopted a comprehensive ecotourism policy, which the Outings volunteers have augmented with "Emerald Guidelines" for "ecocultural tourism." These documents call for tourism that is low impact, respects "the carrying capacity and biodiversity of the environment," "encourage[s] and utilize[s] local enterprises," and is carried out in a "spirit of humility" and respect for "the privacy and dignity of local residents."[36]

Of the environmental organizations offering ecotours, The Nature Conservancy (TNC) has one of the best-known overseas tour programs, with about seventeen trips per year and twelve to fifteen destinations in Latin America and the Caribbean and, since 1997, Indonesia. Since 1988, the organization has been sponsoring trips for members only, "to show where we're working and meet with local conservation partners in these countries," as the travel program's director, Marie Uehling, explained in an interview. TNC, which handles 200 to 400 tourists per year, has also developed a set of ecotourism principles to guide its travel program. These include low-impact travel, respect for local cultures, provision of sustainable benefits to local communities, promotion of local conservation and educational efforts, and encouragement of government protection of parks. TNC, together with local conservation partners, operates thirty-nine projects with ecotourism components in Latin America and the Caribbean. Unlike those run by the Sierra Club, TNC's tours are organized through large U.S. nature tour operators, including International Expeditions, Victor Manuel Nature Tours, and Abercrombie & Kent, which "abide by ecotourism principles," Uehling explained. (In East Africa, Abercrombie & Kent's environmental track record is, in fact, somewhat tarnished; see chapter 7.) TNC's American staff members and experts serve as guides on the trips. Uehling added that TNC is continually evaluating the tour operators and destinations and has stopped offering tours to several sites because they are overused. "These trips have made us a little more wary of what ecotourism is and of the whole array of ecotourism wanna-bes,"[37] she stated. The cost of trips includes a $350 voluntary charitable contribution, which is used for TNC land acquisition and other projects in the countries visited. TNC raises about $100,000 per year from these contributions.

The World Wildlife Fund (WWF—known as the World Wide Fund for Nature outside the United States and Canada) also runs a travel program for its members, offering trips to twenty-seven destinations in Africa, Asia, North America, and Latin America. It has twelve to fourteen departures per year and handles approximately 700 travelers. The trips focus on wildlife observation but also include visits to WWF project sites and, occasionally, those of other organizations. Local guides are often, but not always, used. As does TNC, WWF uses major U.S. tour operators to run its program.[38]

Nature tours by nonprofit organizations constitute a "small but growing segment" of the ecotourism travel business, concludes Karen Ziffer of Conservation International. She adds that trips conducted by environmental organizations may offer "very effective models for how ecotourism should be developed in the future."[39]

Ecotourism Structures in Developing Countries: Inbound Ecotour Operators

Ecotourism, when viewed as a tool for sustainable development in poorer countries, means, in the main, the movement of travelers from the North to the South: from developed to developing countries. As Mexican ecotourism expert Héctor Ceballos-Lascuráin writes, "Tourist travel is still very much the privilege of people of the industrialized world. . . . Nevertheless, the shift in favored tourism destinations—from developed to developing countries—indicates that international tourism could become a means of redistributing wealth 'from north to south.'"[40] But this will happen only if host countries are able to retain the tourism dollars and stop the leakage of profits from the South to the North.

Tourists, travel agents, tour operators, and conservation organizations can help maximize the benefits to developing countries by utilizing, as much as possible, environmentally sensitive, socially responsible, and locally based companies and facilities in developing countries. Outbound tour operators and nonprofit organizations contract with inbound tour and ground operators in the host country, and it is these companies that are the most important component in ensuring high-quality ecotourism. Inbound operators are responsible for arranging all details of the trip, including assembling a network of lodges close to or within the nature viewing areas. The mid- to late 1990s have seen an upsurge in environmentally sensitive lodge construction, but there is still a shortage of good ecotourism facilities in some of the newer and fastest-growing destinations. Although ecotourism facilities run the spectrum from basic backpacker tents and cabins to small, exclusive, high-end luxury resorts, most ecolodges fall in the intermediate price range. Inbound ecotour operators also select locally owned restaurants featuring authentic cuisine and the best artisans and cooperatives selling local crafts or displaying local culture.[41]

The majority of the inbound operators involved in ecotourism are, like their counterparts in the United States, owned by their founders, who are either nationals or longtime foreign residents who keep most of the profits within the country. Costa Rica, more than most host countries, has a wide range of high-quality inbound operators; in 1996, the country had more than 200 registered tour operators. Virtually all of these companies now handle some nature tourism, but about a dozen are known for specializing almost exclusively in ecotourism.

In 1992, ecotourism researcher Ana Báez attempted to survey eighty-five tour companies in Costa Rica. She received responses from only eighteen, but her findings show that these companies, at least, have a high degree of environmental and social consciousness.[42] A majority, for instance, listed nature tourism as a priority and used the word *ecotourism* in their literature and with their clients, and all interpreted the word as signifying a "commitment" to conservation. Some said that ecotourism also encompasses cultural sensitivity, generation of economic benefits for local communities, and sound environmental practices by the company and staff. More than three-quarters of these companies reported that they had invested time and money in environmental training for their staff, and 86 percent listed well-trained naturalist guides as most important in providing information to tourists on nature tours. Two-thirds said that they make contributions, usually monetary, to the national parks service. Báez noted that this could be due to a "strong call" by the park service for help from tour operators. In 1992, for instance, Costa Rica's two leading ecotourism travel agencies, Costa Rica Expeditions and Horizontes Nature Tours, jointly contributed $25,000 to create a Park Guard Fund to buy uniforms and other equipment for park guards.

Michael Kaye, founder of Costa Rica Expeditions, rightly claims the mantle as Costa Rica's first nature and adventure tourism operator. Kaye, a New Yorker with a passion for outdoor adventure, came to Costa Rica in

1978 and opened Costa Rica Expeditions to promote white-water rafting and kayaking. In a 1996 interview, Kaye recalled, "There were six or seven commercially active tour companies in Costa Rica, but nobody was doing white-water or other nontraditional stuff."

Kaye's personal jump from adventure and nature tourism into eco-tourism is linked with his battle in the early 1990s to prevent the construction of Hotel Playa Tambor, Costa Rica's first real megaresort. Kaye lost the battle but gained national and international standing as a proponent of eco-tourism (see chapter 5). Costa Rica Expeditions has itself branched out into the accommodation business, with the construction of two lodges and a tent camp. Ironically, Kaye's lodge in Monteverde raised the ire of residents, who opposed an outside developer moving in and potentially draining business away from the locally owned pensions. Costa Rica Expeditions is today one of the country's largest inbound operators, handling some 20,000 clients per year and selling packaged tours to leading U.S. environmental organizations, zoos, and outbound ecotour operators.[43]

Although a number of companies have prospered with Costa Rica's eco-tourism boom, many smaller inbound operators in other countries have had difficulty breaking into the international market, even with tourism expanding. In Tanzania, for instance, Costas Christ wanted Overseas Adventure Travel to use Unique Safaris, an inbound tour operator owned by two long-time Tanzanian guides. "They are some of the best guides I know, and they are running the business very professionally," he says. However, Unique Safaris did not have enough vehicles and guides to secure subcontracts with OAT and other big U.S. outbound ecotourism operators or nonprofit organizations. Another small Tanzanian company, Black Mamba Travels, was created with the intention of using its profits to build schools and assist homeless children. Jointly owned by Joel Christenson, a young American schoolteacher who taught in Tanzania, and Leonard Lomayani, a Tanzanian Maasai and an experienced tour guide, the company had difficulty raising capital. As is the case in many developing countries, local banks in Tanzania charge 30 to 40 percent interest for loans; another major source of funding, the World Bank's International Finance Corporation (IFC), favors large, well-established, usually foreign-owned tourism projects. Black Mamba finally secured funding from private sources in the United States.[44]

Given the lack of ecotourism standards and regulation, outbound operators have difficulty assessing ground operators, especially if these firms are skillfully marketed. Although some of the best outbound and inbound operators consciously place long-term benefits ahead of short-term profits, many do not. There is a need for more regulation and independent evaluation of inbound tour operators as well as lodges and other facilities in developing countries to ensure adherence to the principles of ecotourism. In addition, the IFC and other multilateral funding agencies need to provide loans to well-run projects that are small in scale and locally owned.

The Conservation NGOs Alliance with USAID

Today, all of the major U.S.-based international conservation organizations are involved in ecotourism at some level, from issuing sets of principles and policy statements to establishing research departments, providing technical assistance and public education, operating projects in developing countries, and conducting travel programs. They have received millions of dollars in funding from the U.S. Agency for International Development (USAID) to implement scores of programs, projects, and studies in Africa, Latin America, the Caribbean, and Asia aimed at protecting threatened ecosystems and conserving biodiversity. Ecotourism is being hailed as a means of "giving nature value" and achieving sustainable development.[45] Many in these organizations view ecotourism as a way to promote small-scale private enterprise linked to free trade and economic liberalization. The World Wide Fund for Nature and the World Wildlife Fund (WWF), the World Conservation Union (IUCN), the World Resources Institute (WRI), The Nature Conservancy (TNC), Conservation International (CI), and other mainstream conservation organizations, as well as USAID and the World Bank, view ecotourism as one of a variety of "enterprise-based approaches to conservation"[46] that champion the marketplace and the private sector and diminish the role of government in economic growth. They often choose to enter into partnerships with private organizations, reserves, and parks rather than develop programs to strengthen and support financially strapped national park systems and government agencies in developing countries.

While recognizing the limits and contradictions of this ideological framework, it is possible to point to a number of ecotourism projects that are contributing to environmental protection *and* improving the lives of those living nearest to protected areas. In 1985, USAID began providing assistance to WWF's Wildlife and Human Needs Program, which included some twenty pilot projects in developing countries aimed at combining conservation and development.[47] One of the most successful was the Annapurna Conservation Area Project in Nepal, begun in 1985 to curb the adverse environmental effects of trekkers and to increase local income from ecotourism. Within its first decade, the Annapurna project trained 700 local people to work in lodges used by ecotourists, built a visitors' education center, and instituted a conservation fee of $12 per person, which generates more than half a million dollars annually for local conservation activities, including tree planting and trail maintenance.[48]

Although WWF does not have a separate ecotourism department, the organization undertook the first comprehensive analysis of ecotourism in a two-volume study of five Latin American and Caribbean countries,[49] and many WWF projects around the world include ecotourism components. WWF has, for instance, a variety of ecotourism-linked projects in the tiny Central American country of Belize (population 200,000), an important ecotourism destination that has 36 percent of its land under some form of protection and the second largest barrier reef in the world. WWF helped institute a $3.75 conservation fee, which is added to the airport departure tax charged to all foreign tourists and placed in a fund that can be used for activities related to biodiversity, cultural heritage preservation, and community-based ecotourism ventures. Viewed as a model for other developing countries, the fund is administered by the Protected Area Conservation Trust (PACT), made up of government officials and representatives from the tourism industry, village councils, and Belize NGOs. WWF has also extended technical and financial support to two Belize villages: the Maya Center, which runs a highly successful handicraft project near the Cockscomb Sanctuary, and Gales Point, which offers rustic home-stay accommodations near the Manatee Special Development Area. An important aspect of these activities is that although they have increased local incomes, they have not totally supplanted agricultural production. Should tourism decline, the villages will still have farms with which to earn a living.[50]

WWF is also involved, along with TNC and the WRI, in the Biodiversity Conservation Network (BCN), a $20 million USAID-financed program in Asia and the Pacific region. Begun in 1992, the BCN provides grants to community-based economic projects that depend directly on conservation. Of the twenty-projects under way in 1997, seven had ecotourism components, including ones in the mountain kingdom of Sikkim in northeastern India; Royal Chitwan National Park in Nepal; and Gunung Halimun National Park in West Java, Indonesia. Not all the local partners in these projects are community groups or conservation organizations: in Java, for example, McDonald's Corporation is involved, offering, the BCN's 1996 annual report states, "a unique opportunity to get private sector support and resources behind a conservation effort in Indonesia."[51] But given the restaurant chain's track record for aggressive expansion into developing countries, many suspect that these "resources" may include erecting golden arches in or near the national park.

The Nature Conservancy, together with local conservation organizations in each country, is also involved in a number of ecotourism projects in its main areas of operation, Latin America and the Caribbean. By 1997, thirty-nine of TNC's sixty-two sites in these regions included ecotourism projects.[52] In the Río Bravo Conservation and Management Area, a private reserve in the northwestern corner of Belize, for example, TNC and a Belizean NGO are working with local communities in a multiuse project aimed at making the area "a financially self-sufficient model" of long-term conservation. Taking advantage of the ecotourism boom, the project includes low-impact lodging and educational centers at several sites for both Belizean school groups and international tourists, students, and teachers. The project also involves sustainable harvesting of timber and other rain forest products.[53] Through TNC's International Trips Program, members can visit some of the organization's field projects.

In contrast with WWF and TNC, Conservation International (CI), the newest of the major U.S. organizations (founded in 1998), has a full-blown Ecotourism Program with a staff of six, operated from its headquarters in Washington, D.C. Although it receives USAID funding for a number of its projects, it is not part of the BCN consortium. By late 1997, CI had some thirty ecotourism projects in various stages of development in Latin America, Africa, and Asia. Its mandate is to "act as a liaison between local communities and the tourism industry in order to develop and support economically sustainable ecotourism enterprises . . . and . . . influence the broader tourism industry towards greater ecological sustainability." More systematically than the other organizations, CI is addressing the difficult challenge of effectively linking local ecotourism projects in developing countries with the international ecotourism market. Specifically, the program helps develop national and regional strategies for both governments and the private sector, helps teach skills to members of local communities so they can earn more from tourism, and develops and markets local ecotourism facilities—lodges, trail systems, concessions—as part of "a working ecotourism business network" connected to tour operators and ecotourists in the United States, Canada, and Europe.

CI's Chalalan Ecolodge project, for example, is in the 1.8-million-hectare (4.5-million-acre) Madidi National Park, Bolivia's premier Amazon reserve and a region of incredible biodiversity, containing more than 50 percent of the world's Neotropical bird species and 44 percent of the Neotropical mammals. In recent years, this ecosystem has been undergoing rapid destruction from logging and unrestricted hunting, particularly of a rare species of monkey. The ecolodge, which overlooks Lake Chalalan, is reached by a four- to six-hour boat trip down the Tuichi River. It accommodates twenty-four visitors in rustic, thatch-roof cabins built from local materials by traditional artisans. The Chalalan project works with a community inside the park's boundaries to integrate ecotourism with other economic projects in agroforestry, indigenous handicraft production, and non-timber forest product extraction. The Inter-American Development Bank has provided $1.4 million to finance the project.

As part of its marketing effort, CI has created a World Wide Web site, "The Ecotravel Center," which includes profiles of CI-affiliated destinations, tour operators, and lodges. Although CI does not officially "certify" any of the ecotourism facilities on its Web site, it does require that each company complete a "Responsibility Survey" to establish that it "truly benefits conservation and local people."[54] CI's ecotourism staff has been constantly exploring ways to involve local communities and move the ecotourism projects toward both sustainability and integration with other activities in the areas where they are located. CI, which maintains field offices in all countries where it works, has gradually "moved away from a concentration on product development such as specific ecotourism lodges and towards developing policy criteria" via a series of participatory workshops involving all stakeholders to discuss overall plans for development of its project areas, according to Donnell Ocker of CI's ecotourism department. In mid-1998, this process of developing mechanisms for local participation and empowerment was furthest advanced in Peru and Guatemala.

In recent years, many NGOs or some of their top officials have endorsed the free-trade, private sector, and structural adjustment agendas of the World Bank and USAID, even as local communities and NGOs with which they are in partnership have suffered under and, in some cases, organized in opposition to these policies. A USAID consultant contracted to evaluate the agency's ecotourism projects concluded that not infrequently its personnel failed to understand the full dimensions and complexities of implementing such projects. She found that despite its stated goal of fostering community-based development, in practice USAID showed a preference for working with the private sector and U.S. NGOs. In addition, she stated, "There's increasing pressure from Congress to get the money to come back to the U.S., not keep aid money in-country." The consultant concluded that many USAID functionaries are not "aware of all the complex web involved in ecotourism. AID is very linear in its thinking. There was a lot of enthusiasm at first, but now people are starting to see it's harder to implement on the ground than on paper. It's a great idea but hard to turn into a success."[55]

Multilateral Lending and Aid Institutions

Following the 1992 United Nations Conference on Environment and Development (UNCED), known as the Earth Summit, the World Bank heightened its emphasis on environmentally sustainable development. A 1995 press release titled "Greening of the World Bank" boasted that the bank had, since the Earth Summit, become "the world's leading financier of environmental projects in the developing world," including $10 billion in project loans in sixty-two countries and another $20 billion per year for "greening" its own operations.[56] For instance, the GEF (Global Environment Facility) and USAID committed $4 million to set up a trust fund for conservation of the recently established Bwindi Impenetrable Forest Gorilla Reserve, a biologically important tropical forest in Uganda, which contains about half (some 300) of the remaining population of mountain gorillas. The trust fund, jointly managed by representatives of Uganda's government, local and international NGOs, and the fifty local communities touching the reserve's boundaries, sets aside 60 percent of its net income for community development that is compatible with conservation. In addition, Uganda National Parks and a consortium made up of the African Wildlife Foundation (AWF), WWF, and other international NGOs have developed ecologically sound tourism, which, by the mid-1990s, was permitting twelve tourists at a time to visit the two groups of gorillas that have become habituated, that is accustomed, to the presence of people. Despite the steep cost—about $145 per person for a one-hour viewing— "gorilla tourism" runs at nearly 100 percent capacity. It earns about $400,000 annually, making Bwindi the highest revenue earner among Uganda's parks. Uganda National Parks also set aside revenues for community development, designating 10 to 20 percent of the combined earnings from gorilla viewing and accommodations for local community projects. Despite these benefits, the project has not been without problems. Tour operators are lobbying for more gorilla-viewing permits, most of the profits are not retained locally, and gorillas have been killed inside the park, although a World Bank study concluded that it is unclear how, if at all, these killings relate to gorilla tourism.[57]

While gorilla tourism in Bwindi is widely viewed as a successful tourism project, an independent evaluation of the GEF's pilot phase, which ran from 1990 to 1994, was critical of GEF-funded biodiversity projects, many of which included ecotourism components. "Most GEF work to date," the evaluation stated, "has been characterized by a top-down approach rather than responding to the needs of governments. It has not involved local communities in an effective way; it has sparked destructive competition among Implementing Agencies and other global organizations in the field of biodiversity; . . . and it has been overly dependent on international consulting firms."[58]

The World Bank's International Finance Corporation (IFC) was founded in 1956 to loan directly to the private sector, without government guarantees. It includes more than 170 member countries (125 of them considered developing countries) and, with annual investment approvals of nearly $3 billion, is the largest source of financing for private sector projects in developing countries. The IFC finances as much as 25 percent of project costs, may hold partial ownership in companies to which it extends loans, acts as a catalyst for private investors (both foreign and domestic), and works to develop capital markets in developing countries.

Like the World Bank, the IFC has had its share of environmentally and socially destructive megatourism ventures, in places such as Cancún, Mexico. Unlike the bank, however, the IFC has never stopped funding tourism projects, and it has a special Tourism Unit whose portfolio has been growing rapidly as worldwide demand for financial sources for hotel development has accelerated. Until 1987, the Tourism Unit was financing one to three new projects per year; between 1990 and 1994, it averaged thirteen to sixteen new tourism projects annually. The IFC works closely with the World Bank's Multilateral Investment Guarantee Agency (MIGA), established in 1988, which sells insurance against risks such as war or nationalization to tourism agencies and other companies operating in developing countries. In 1994, MIGA invested in its first ecotourism project, the Rain Forest Aerial Tram in Costa Rica, which it considers "quite a success"[59] (see chapter 5). By 1996, the IFC had invested in well over 100 tourism projects, totaling more than $600 million in loans and equity investments. This represented 5 percent of the IFC's dollar volume.[60]

Although the IFC has been striving to "green" its rhetoric and some of its procedures, its officials admit that ecotourism is not squarely on the agency's agenda.[61] Like the World Bank, the IFC conducts environmental impact studies for its projects in national parks and other fragile areas. It has also set up, together with the private sector, nongovernmental organizations, and other bilateral donors, a $25–$30 million fund to support biodiversity, conservation, and sustainable use "through a convergence of private profit and conservation objectives." A top World Bank official cited several IFC-financed projects (along Egypt's Red Sea and in Ghana, Costa Rica, and the Pacific island republic of Vanuatu) as illustrative of a "strong commitment to sustainable environmental development." IFC literature describes the agency's mission as "promot[ing] sustainable tourism development," and in 1995, the World Bank stated that the IFC had begun to develop "a pipeline of private sector activities compatible with GEF purposes." In 1996, the IFC and the GEF set up a very modest $4.3 million pilot project, the Small and Medium Scale Enterprise (SME) Program, to assist "enterprises in preserving biodiversity and reducing greenhouse gases." It listed ecolodges as one of its project areas and Costa Rica as one of the countries where projects would be based. However, in a 1996 list of the 113 IFC-funded tourism projects worldwide, Costa Rica projects include only the Hotel Camino Reál, a mass tourism complex owned by an international chain. The IFC had earlier turned down a request to fund Rara Avis, a pioneering ecotourism project in Costa Rica with strong community ties[62] (see chapter 5).

There are several reasons why this is the case. IFC officials complain that tourism projects are time-consuming to implement and coordinate, that finding suitable local investors with an established track record is difficult, and that most ecotourism projects are just too small to be given consideration. Typically, the IFC finances projects ranging from $5 million to $150 million, although some smaller projects have been supported via the African Enterprise Fund and the Pacific Islands Investment Fund.[63] The vast majority of loans continue to finance conventional mass tourism projects, or, in the case of nature-based tourism projects, the same well-heeled international companies, some with tarnished environmental track records, continue to receive IFC funding (see chapter 7). This is despite the fact that time and again, innovative and responsible locally owned ecotourism projects falter because they cannot get sufficient investment loans and, sometimes, because they are forced to compete with large foreign companies, some of which are financed by the IFC.

The United Nations Environment Programme (UNEP), based in Paris, has also set as a mandate working directly with the big players in the tourism industry as well as governments, with the aim, it says, of implementing voluntary "green" reforms.[64] In 1983, when the destructive effects of much conventional tourism had become apparent but before ecotourism had caught on, UNEP and the World Tourism Organization (WTO) signed a joint declaration on tourism and the environment. It stated, in part, "The protection, enhancement, and improvement of the various components of man's environment are among the fundamental conditions for the harmonious development of tourism. Similarly, rational management of tourism may contribute to a large extent to protecting and developing the physical environment and the cultural heritage, as well as to improving the quality of man's life." The 1992 Earth Summit's "action plan" for the environment, Agenda 21, further reinforced UNEP's mission of working with industry. "The tourism industry has a fundamental role to play," wrote UNEP official Jacqueline Aloisi de Larderel in a special tourism industry publication on ecotourism. She called on businesses to be proactive, through "self-regulation" and by adopting "codes of conduct and of good practice."[65] UNEP has assisted the tourism industry by conducting training sessions for hotel school directors and tourism experts in methods for reducing or avoiding the use of ozone-depleting products, developing environmental curricula for hotel schools, studying the use of low-impact technologies for tourism facilities, and investigating the use of "ecolabels" for tourism to certify companies following sound ecotourism principles and practices. Its publications include *Case Studies on Environmental Good Practices in Hotels*, published jointly with the International Hotels and Restaurants Association; *Awards for Improving the Coastal Environment*, produced with the World Tourism

Organization; numerous technical reports; and a quarterly magazine. UNEP officials work with the major tourism industry associations, regularly attend international ecotourism conferences, and sit on committees that give ecotourism awards to "green" projects and corporations.

The Marketing of Ecotourism

Ineffective or insufficient marketing is probably the primary reason why worthy ecotourism ventures in developing countries fail to attract visitors. Throughout Latin America, Cuba, and Africa, excellent locally run lodges, hotels, cultural centers, and ground operators founder for lack of know-how, financial resources, or government and industry assistance in carrying out proper marketing. In Costa Rica, for instance, the rustic, family-run Santa Clara Lodge nearly folded because the local telephone company suddenly changed the lodge's number just after it had taken out newspaper advertisements and distributed its promotional brochures. It had no money to redo its brochures and no political clout to regain its old telephone number. A key role of government tourism agencies should be to promote sound, locally owned ecotourism projects as well as national parks. But these agencies are often underfunded and under pressure to promote private resorts and reserves. South Africa's tourism board, SATOUR, and the Costa Rica Tourist Board (ICT), have, under the banner of ecotourism, put large amounts of time and money into promoting foreign-owned resorts, mass tourism developments, and private parks rather than concentrating on promoting abroad its national parks and the best locally owned ecotourism projects, including the smaller ones that cannot afford to do their own marketing.

Ecotourism's Promise—and Pitfalls

Tourism, including ecotourism, is at a crossroads. As David Nicholson-Lord, former environment editor of *The Independent* newspaper in London, puts it, "The world, clearly, is not going to stop taking holidays—but equally clearly we can no longer afford to ignore the consequences. And if one of the major culprits has been the industrialization of travel, a genuinely post-industrial tourism, with the emphasis on people and places rather than products and profits, could turn out to be significantly more planet-friendly."[66] But the path toward a more plane-friendly tourism, toward genuine ecotourism, is lined with pitfalls: ecotourism is not a panacea. At present, it is a set of interconnected principles whose full implementation presents multilayered problems and challenges. There are, in fact, pressing issues surrounding ecotourism that are crying out for deeper investigation, more rigorous analysis, more careful theoretical work. A discussion of the most important of these issues follows.

Local Communities, Sustainable Development, and Empowerment

Many of the most vibrant and militant rural social movements in developing countries center on national parks and tourism. These struggles have pitted local communities and NGOs not only against their own governments, the World Bank, and USAID but also, not infrequently, against the agendas of international conservation organizations. Fundamentally, these struggles are over who owns and controls the land's scarce and valuable resources. As Clark University professor Cynthia Enloe reminds us, "Tourism is not just about escaping work and drizzle; it is about power, increasingly internationalized power."[67] And as Anita Pleumarom, a Thai expert on tourism and development, elaborates, "For local people involved in immediate livelihood struggles in the Third World, such as protecting against illegally obtained title deeds to land and permits to start hotel construction or violation of environmental regulations, the issue of power is central, although this has been sidestepped by mainstream critics of tourism."[68]

In many places, these movements were for decades held in check by colonialism, military regimes, or one-party states that prohibited local organizing. Resistance took the form of individual or group acts of sabotage, poaching, fires, or cutting of trees or bush inside protected areas. However, since the mid-1980s, a number of factors have coalesced in Latin America and Africa to heighten the ability of rural people to organize. These factors include the economic and political liberalizations of the 1980s, the growth of local and international environmental organizations, the decline of military dictatorships in Latin America, an end to white rule in southern Africa and moves toward multiparty elections across the continent, and an increasing realization that sustainable development, even though supported by national and international programs and funds, must be carried out by empowering, educating, and providing tools and infrastructure to local communities.

In Tanzania, for instance, the Maasai living around Serengeti National Park and Ngorongoro Conservation Area have organized to demand a sizable slice of the tourism pie and the return of their rights to use land and water within the parks. In Zimbabwe and South Africa, rural people anticipated that with majority rule, national park lands would be returned to them. When this did not happen, they organized, often in alliance with local environmental and rural development groups, to win a stake in running the parks and tourism facilities. In Zimbabwe, CAMPFIRE (Communal Area

Management Programme for Indigenous Resources), a loosely organized nationwide network of communities that conducts hunting and camera safaris, is internationally acclaimed as a model of rural development through ecotourism. In Ecuador's Amazon basin, indigenous groups, occasionally with support from Quito-based or international environmental organizations, militantly resist oil-drilling operations and have set up alternative, environmentally respectful economic activities, including ecotourism camps, in the rain forest.

In these places as elsewhere, those living around or in parks, reserves, and other protected or fragile ecosystems have increasingly come to see ecotourism as an economic activity with the potential to provide both environmental protection and financial and material resources. In addition to securing employment as hotel workers, guides, drivers, and game scouts, people in many rural communities are negotiating or demanding the right to sustainable use of lands appropriated for national parks, rent or lease agreements with hotel and tour operators to use their traditional lands, and a percentage of park entrance fees or hotel profits. They are also demanding sole ownership of or joint partnership in campsites, cultural and handicraft centers, restaurants, lodges, and concessions such as those offering horseback riding, hiking, and fishing.

Despite the rhetoric of incorporating people and parks and the democratic developments in a number of countries, old ways and power relationships die hard. A 1992 study of various ecotourism projects concluded that "the results [of participation] thus far have been disappointing, to say the least,"[69] and although there are some wonderful and exciting exceptions, this still appears to be the norm. Even though Zimbabwe's innovative CAMPFIRE program has provided income and inputs for community development projects, the majority of rural Africans involved in CAMPFIRE are guides, porters, trackers, artisans, and waiters; rarely are they managers. Here and elsewhere, writes Anita Pleumarom, "Decision-making authority—including deciding whether a project should go ahead in the first place—has generally been denied."[70] During the 1990s, there were instances in Namibia, Botswana, South Africa, Rwanda, and Uganda of rural people being expelled from their land to create new parks and ecotourism projects. Many people resisted moving from their traditional lands, even when they were offered compensation. As one elderly South African in the Kosi Bay area put it, "Where do these people take the right to make money out of our land? We don't want compensation, we want our land. . . . They say they want to protect nature. But aren't people also part of God's nature?"[71] Although the ultimate outcome of many of these disputes remains unclear, the terms of discourse and forms of organizing have changed: environmental protection and the land and economic rights of rural people are now part of the debate. In these struggles, rural communities are building national and sometimes international alliances to demand an equitable slice of the economic pie, which now frequently includes ecotourism.

Free Trade versus Local Control

Ecotourism promotes locally owned enterprises, but with globalization and free trade, weak national capital often cannot compete with strong foreign companies. The lowering of trade barriers and opening up to unfettered foreign investment is again and again undermining the sustainability of smaller, locally owned ecotourism ventures in developing countries. Yet the World Travel and Tourism Council, the American Society of Travel Agents, and the major tourism industry organizations, together with the World Bank, USAID, and other international lending and development agencies, gloss over this central contradiction: they continue to advocate both community-based ecotourism *and* open trade and investment markets as if the two fit seamlessly together. As Anita Pleumarom writes,

> [M]ost of the profits are made by foreign airlines, tourist operators, and developers who repatriate them to their own economically more advanced countries. With increasing privatisation and deregulation of the global economy, there are now great and justifiable concerns that Southern countries will lose out even more. More liberalisation will lead to more foreign-owned tourist facilities and tour operations, and as a result, less income from tourism will remain in the local economy.[72]

Role of the State

Sound ecotourism, if it is to move beyond small individual projects and become a set of principles and practices on which tourism is based, will require careful planning and implementation. Within developing countries, for instance, ecotourism must become part of the country's overall development strategy. Although most countries have adopted national tourism plans, these often entail little more than sales promotion. In addition, planning is often carried out by a tourism department, without proper integration with agencies overseeing local development, conservation and the environment, and national planning. As ecotourism consultant and writer Katrina Brandon writes, "A strategy or overall plan for nature-based tourism, even in countries where the revenues from such tourism are high, is usually nonexistent."[73]

Whereas in the past, governments in socialist and communist countries such as the Soviet Union, eastern and central Europe, China, Vietnam, Tanzania, and Cuba owned, operated, and profited from their tourism industries, today the state is typically consigned to activities that do not generate income: setting broad tourism policies; carrying out overseas marketing and promotion; educating and training a workforce for the tourism sector (guides, interpreters, hotel staff and managers, drivers, etc.); establishing and maintaining the natural attractions (national parks and reserves, marine areas, waterfalls, mountaintops, forests, and other resources) on which tourism is based; putting in infrastructure such as airports, roads, electricity, ports, and waste and sewage treatment systems; and facilitating the entry of private, often foreign, capital, often by offering generous tax breaks and other enticements. In turn, the private sector in developing countries typically runs the travel and car rental agencies; the tour agencies and group operations; often the airlines, lodges, and hotels; the restaurants; and other specialized tourism facilities such as trekking, ballooning, and camel and horseback riding companies. Basically, the state provides the infrastructure, training, economic incentives, the national parks and reserves, and some promotional and other services, and private enterprise earns the bulk of the profits.

Although state-run tourism did not prove to be flexible and responsive to the demands of international tourism, wholesale privatization and reliance on market forces leads rapidly to overdevelopment, an outflow of profits, and myriad other problems. Within the field of ecotourism there is much facile talk about a "public–private partnership," but finding an equitable balance between the public and private sectors remains one of the unsolved challenges. At present—except in Cuba—the market, not the state, is the main vehicle for redistribution of tourism profits. Private enterprise, even many businesses involved in ecotourism, vigorously opposes new and higher taxes and seeks less regulation, yet it demands that the government provide well-trained workers, good infrastructure, and pristine, well-run national parks. In the centralized economies of the past, much of the profit was consumed by overblown government bureaucracies. Today, the bulk of the profit flows out of the host country—or never even enters it.

The growth of ecotourism should require *more*, not less from government, but these days, the state's role and income are being downsized. Even where tourism and ecotourism have grown enormously, the percentage of profits going into central government treasuries has frequently diminished as states have divested their ownership in tourism facilities. This has contributed to cutbacks in funding for national parks, public education and health care, and other environmentally and socially vital development programs. Parallel with this has been a push to keep more tourism dollars, particularly from park entrance fees, at the local level in order to better protect the most popular parks and channel a percentage of revenues to nearby communities. Although such policies are politically sound, they also have served to further reduce the national treasuries. In addition, many international organizations and aid agencies have shifted their funding toward the private sector. Taken together, these factors mean that national governments in developing countries typically have less authority and resources for careful planning of their economic activities and development strategies.

Leakage

A central issue facing developing countries that view ecotourism as a development tool is that of revenue capture—finding mechanisms to retain more of the profits within the country, not simply in the hands of the private sector but for use by local communities and the central government for conservation and economic development projects. In dividing up the profits from the mass tourism pie, the largest slice goes, predictably, to the tourism industry, especially for prepaid packaged tours. Major outflows of foreign exchange also come from payments for imported goods, management fees, expatriate salaries, tax breaks, and import content on local purchases. The local and national economies benefit through job creation; taxes on imported goods; park entrance fees; airport, hotel, and other user taxes; use of local hotels, transport companies, restaurants, tour operations, and concessions; and the domestic content on local purchases. The World Bank estimates that 55 percent of tourism dollars "leak out" of developing countries via foreign-owned tour operators, airlines, and hotels and by locally owned operators paying for imported food, drinks, and other supplies.[74] Some studies estimate this "leakage" to be 80 to 90 percent.[75] According to one study, less than 10 cents of every tourist dollar spent in Nepal's Annapurna region, long one of the world's leading nature and adventure tourism destinations, actually stays there.[76]

Mexican ecotourism expert Héctor Ceballos-Lascuráin notes that the size and style of tourism affects the amount of leakage. A study in the island of Antigua found that leakage was greater from large hotels than small ones, while another study in Bolivia found that the economic impact of unorganized "rucksack tourists" is "more than three times that of organized [or packaged group] tourists." While backpackers spend less per day, they stay longer and are more likely to patronage small, locally owned facilities. Ceballos-Lascuráin concludes that such comparative analysis "could be very useful in exploring whether the economic benefits of nature-based tourism, which typically involves small-scale facilities, are greater than those of resort-based tourism."[77] This has been one of the promises held out by ecotourism proponents: that the portion of the profits retained within the Third World

will be substantially greater, and the environmental and social consequences will be far less than with conventional tourism.

However, economic globalization, free trade, and privatization are
strong countervailing forces to the philosophy and promise of ecotourism.
In Costa Rica, which by the early 1990s was the number one overseas ecotourism destination for United States travelers, half of every tourist dollar
never left the United States, and only 20 cents actually went into the local
economy, according to a USAID study.[78] There is a need to work with local
communities and host governments to develop projects that capture more
of the ecotourism revenue.

Visitors: How Many and What Kind?

Ecotourism implies small-scale projects and small groups of tourists, yet
developing countries need to earn large amounts of foreign exchange.
In every developing country, there is a tendency for the government to
encourage the entry of more and more tourists, even when their numbers
exceed the capacity of certain parks, beaches, and reserves. Part of this
debate has revolved around the question of how to measure carrying
capacity, that is the number of visitors a protected area can sustainably
accommodate over the long haul. Although efforts have been made to
limit visitor numbers in many places, including the Galápagos Islands
and Costa Rica's Manuel Antonio National Park and Monteverde Cloud
Forest Reserve, in recent years many scientists have come to realize that
the very concept of setting fixed visitor numbers is flawed. As scientist
Craig MacFarland, former president of the Charles Darwin Foundation,
argues, "Pure numbers are not the answer." MacFarland says that park officials and scientists in the United States, Canada, Australia, and South Africa
"have all independently found the same thing: that about 90 percent of visitor management is not controlling numbers per se, it's controlling what
behaviors, activities, and equipment you allow and the time of day or time
of year you allow them in a particular place."[79] He and others note that a
handful of unruly tourists can do far more damage to a park than would
large numbers of environmentally sensitive and carefully managed ecotourists.

In addition to the scientific debate over carrying capacity, there is everywhere a tension between generating significant foreign exchange from ecotourism and dealing with the environmental and social costs. As Anita
Pleumarom observes, "To generate substantial revenue—whether for foreign exchange, tourism businesses, local communities or conservation—the
number of tourists has to be large, and that inevitably implies greater pressures on ecosystems."[80] In the drive to maximize profits, ecotourism has

become increasingly expensive and exclusive. Ecotourism promises a more ethical form of travel, but increasingly this means it is also exclusive, available only to the rich.

Coupled with this is the tension between international and domestic tourism. Developing countries put most of their tourism resources into attracting foreign visitors, but it is increasingly apparent that domestic tourism is important for numerous reasons, including the need to build a constituency that appreciates and wants to protect national parks, local culture, and fragile ecosystems. In 1992, just after peace accords ended the decades-long civil war in El Salvador, the Salvadoran Tourism Institute began a very popular government-subsidized program of "social tourism" to enable low-income Salvadorans to visit different tourist centers in national parks. "This may not have secured much income for the government, but doubtless considerable national interest in and support for protected areas were created," writes Héctor Ceballos-Lascuráin.[81] In other countries, such as South Africa, where most visitors to national parks have been nationals (though almost exclusively the white minority), domestic tourism can be an important source of income. In addition, domestic tourism provides a cushion when, for reasons beyond a country's control, international tourism suddenly drops off, as happened in East Africa during the 1990–1991 Persian Gulf War and following the August 1998 U.S. embassy bombings.

Effects on Local Cultures

By definition, ecotourism often involves seeking out the most pristine, uncharted, and unpenetrated areas on earth. Often, these are home to isolated and fragile civilizations. In some areas, ecotourism is the front line of foreign encroachment and can accelerate the pace of social and environmental degradation and lead to a new form of Western penetration and domination of the last remaining "untouched" parts of the world.[82] As Cynthia Enloe writes, "Tourism is as much ideology as physical movement. It is a package of ideas about industrial, bureaucratic life. It is a set of presumptions about manhood, education and pleasure. . . . A government which decides to rely on money from tourism for its development," she warns, "is a government which has decided to be internationally compliant."[83]

Ecotourism, as opposed to conventional tourism, holds out the twin promise of educating the visitor and respecting the local culture. Sometimes, however, these two goals conflict: people in Zanzibar, for instance, complain that backpackers who live in cheap guest houses or with families and try to learn from the locals are often the most intrusive of visitors. Ecotourism is still struggling to find models for authentic cultural exchange that respects the rights of the hosts and satisfies the curiosity of the visitors. But the road map is not clear, and there remains the danger that ecotourism may end up helping to destroy the culture and lifestyles it is seeking to protect.

Boom and Bust

Tourism is a skittish and fickle industry that tends to experience cycles: one place will be "in" for a number of years, and then another will rise to the top of the charts. Ecotourism, like tourism, frequently depends on extraneous factors beyond its control: natural disasters, AIDS and other diseases, civil wars, the stock market, hijackings, high levels of crime, and media coverage. Wildlife tourism in Kenya soared after Hollywood released *Out of Africa* in the late 1980s and then plummeted in the wake of the 1990–1991 Persian Gulf War. It sank again after the bombing of the U.S. embassies in Nairobi and Dar es Salaam in August 1998. Similarly, a murder on a golf course on St. Croix hurt tourism for a decade, and then, just as the numbers were starting to pick up, a hurricane devastated the island's port, preventing cruise ships from docking. Tourists can also become easy targets in broader political struggles, as illustrated by the killing of tourists in Egypt or their kidnapping in Costa Rica, Colombia, and Guatemala.

Locally based ecotourism can be less susceptible to the whims of the outside world if the communities maintain other forms of economic activity. Some of the most successful ecotourism projects are tied to scientific research stations, working farms, or fishing communities where there are several sources of income. Likewise, domestic tourism can cushion fall-offs in international visitor numbers. Moreover, some experts argue that, world-wide, tourism is more stable over the long term than are many other foreign exchange earners. Héctor Ceballos-Lascuráin contends, for instance, that "compared with other industries, which are prone to abrupt fluctuations and frequent sharp declines, tourism has seldom fallen into a serious long-term down-turn, making it seem a near recession-proof industry at the global level."[84] He finds further grounds for optimism in the fact that tourism to developing countries is growing. What this broad picture misses, however, are the sharp rises and falls that can occur among Third World countries, whose economies have little cushion to withstand the shortfalls.

Standards, Monitoring, and Evaluation: By Whom?

There is a dire need up and down the ecotourism chain to monitor, evaluate, and set standards. As the World Travel and Tourism Council's (WTTC's) Green Globe program and its *Agenda 21* illustrate, the industry would love to carry out its own oversight and regulation. This has proved unsatisfactory. However, determining who should do the monitoring and assessment and what criteria should be used is a complex matter. The Ecotourism Society (TES) and Clemson University, for instance, surveyed tourists in Ecuador to evaluate local tour operators and tourism facilities. The resulting six-part consumer survey was only quasi-independent, however, because it was administered by the tour operators themselves. Not surprisingly, the results, published in 1997, concluded that "nature tour operators appear to be practicing and generally following TES guidelines."[85] TES views this survey format as a model to be used around the world, but besides the fact that the survey was administered by tour operators, there are other drawbacks. Although tourists certainly need to be surveyed when ecotourism operations are evaluated, most tourists, realistically, cannot accurately assess important issues such as a company's relationship with the community or even with its own employees or its waste disposal and other environmental practices.

A much more thorough and objective model, carried out by two ecotourism researchers, Anne Becher and Jane Segleau, assesses every hotel, lodge, and resort that claims to be practicing ecotourism in Costa Rica, that is, those that have their own reserves and/or offer tours to nearby protected areas. This labor-intensive "sustainable tourism survey" (with sustainable tourism defined as "having a low impact on the environment, supporting the local economy, and promoting the best of local culture") involves an onsite visit and a detailed discussion with the managers and owners, staff, local community members, and tourists. Places that meet the standards of sound ecotourism are listed in each new edition of *The New Key to Costa Rica*, one of the oldest and best guidebooks. Written by Beatrice Blake and Anne Becher, two Americans who lived for many years in Costa Rica, *New Key* "aspire[s] to accommodate conscientious travelers."[86] The Sustainable Tourism survey covers or at least touches on all seven principles of real ecotourism (see chapter 1).

The *New Key* series has begun including "green rating" surveys of several other countries. Authors of the 1996 *New Key* edition on Ecuador, for example, surveyed tour operators and lodge owners and list twenty-four ecolodges that fit the green rating criteria; unfortunately, they did not survey the tour boats—the so-called floating hotels—operating around the Galápagos.[87] In Costa Rica, the *New Key* survey has also spurred the Costa Rica Tourist Board (ICT) to begin setting up its own classification system for hotels. Not only have the hotels been registered, for the first time, according to the internationally recognized five-star system, but the ICT also announced plans to categorize Costa Rican hotels by use of a series of green bands ranging from zero to five, to indicate how environmentally and socially responsible they are. Under this ambitious scheme, hotels in Costa

Rica and eventually, it is hoped, in all of Central America, will be evaluated in four areas related to sustainable development: (1) the hotels' effect on the surrounding physical environment; (2) their energy consumption, waste disposal, and use of biodegradable products; (3) their tourism education programs; and (4) their social integration with local communities, including benefits received by the communities, infrastructure development, and promotion of local culture.[88] However, in the late 1990s, large tourism interests opposed to the ICT's ecorating system forced the government to put its implementation on hold.

Ecotourism in Its National Context

As I investigated ecotourism and grappled with the foregoing issues and others, as well as the twin trajectories of real ecotourism and ecotourism lite, it became clear that these phenomena must be examined within their particular national settings and historical contexts. For this reason, I decided to study the growth of ecotourism on a country-by-country basis in order to fully understand the constraints on it and its possibilities of success. Just as conservationists and biologists have come to believe that individual species must be studied within their ecosystems, ecotourism must not be analyzed as an isolated phenomenon. Rather, it must be seen as part of the political economy and development strategy of each particular country. As Desmond de Sousa, former executive secretary of the Ecumenical Coalition on Third World Tourism, put it, "Tourism development is not isolated from, but rather an aspect of, the development process. So the tourism debate has to be situated within the development debate itself."[89]

My search for ecotourism entailed journeys through developing countries in the Americas and Africa as well as briefer forays to other countries and international conferences. The countries I visited—Costa Rica, Ecuador's Galápagos Islands, Cuba, Tanzania and the island of Zanzibar, Kenya, and South Africa—are all promoting ecotourism as a key component of their development strategies. Yet they have followed different routes toward ecotourism. Until the mid-1980s, the socialist governments in Cuba and in Tanzania and Zanzibar largely financed and conducted tourism with the aim of using the profits for social programs. At the other end of the political spectrum, the apartheid government in South Africa created parks and subsidized tourism for the benefit of its privileged white minority and a trickle of white foreigners. Postcolonial Kenya has had a roughshod brand of capitalism, laced with corruption and political patronage. Costa Rica and Ecuador have outstanding national park systems and mixed economies, with the governments playing an active but diminishing role in regulating their economies and social welfare programs. Costa Rica, the Galápagos Islands,

Tanzania, and Kenya are among the most popular ecotourism destinations in the world. Postapartheid South Africa and post-Soviet Cuba, respectively, have pushed international tourism as a main engine of growth and integration into the global economy. The chapters that follow examine how the principles underlying ecotourism are being played out in these seven locations and propose an "ecotourism scorecard" for each.

Notes

1. Peter Frank, "St. John: The Making of Harmony," *Condé Nast Traveler*, May 1995, pp. 24, 29.
2. U.S. Department of the Interior, National Park Service, *Guiding Principles of Sustainable Design* (Denver, Colo.: National Park Service, Denver Service Center, September 1993).
3. Ann Kalosh, "The Travel Industry's Green Guru: An Interview with Stanley Selengut," *Hemispheres*, United Airlines flight magazine, April 1994.
4. Interviews with Stanley Selengut, Maho Bay, St. John, December 1994 and January 1995; "Ecotourism Investigation," *Agenda 21* series, Worldwide Television News, London, March 1995, produced by author.
5. Suzanne Oliver, "Eco-profitable," *Forbes* 153, no. 13 (June 20, 1994).
6. "Clipboard," *Travel Weekly*, June 6, 1994.
7. Author's interviews on St. John, including with Ray Ashton, Joshua Reichert, and Stanley Selengut in 1994 and 1995, and telephone interview with Jossette Pacquin, Employment and Training Office, Department of Labor, St. Thomas Island, June 1998.
8. Interviews and correspondence with Bernard Kemp.
9. Interview with Ray Ashton, Maho Bay, St. John, October 1994.
10. Travel Industry Association of America, 1992, cited in "TES Statistical Fact Sheet," on The Ecotourism Society's World Wide Web site (Internet: http://www.ecotourism.org/textfiles/stats/txt), September 30, 1997.
11. American Society of Travel Agents (ASTA), Environment Committee, "Destination Earth: Save It—Share It," ASTA newsletter, September 1993.
12. Cited in Pamela A. Wight's two-part study "North American Ecotourists: Market Profile and Trip Characteristics" and "North American Ecotourism Markets: Motivations, Preferences, and Destinations," spring 1996 on The Ecotourism Society's World Wide Web site (Internet: http://www.eco-tourism.org/data.html).
13. Bryan Higgins, who has written a useful overview of the state of the literature on how the industry operates, concludes that "the global character, preferences, and significance of ecotourists remains a wide open topic for future research." Bryan R. Higgins, "The Global Structure of the Nature Tourism Industry: Ecotourists, Tour Operators, and Local Businesses," *Journal of Travel Research* 35, no. 2 (1996): 13. Available on The Ecotourism Society's World Wide Web site (Internet: http://www.ecotourism.org/retessel.html).
14. Wight, "North American Ecotourists" and "North American Ecotourism Markets."
15. Interview with Caroline Wild, Toronto-based ecotourism consultant, Montreal, September 1994.

16. Kurt Kutay, "Brave New Role: Ecotour Operators Take Center Stage in the Era of Green Travel," *Going Green: The Ecotourism Resource for Travel Agents*, supplement to *Tour & Travel News*, October 25, 1993, pp. 40–41, and author's interview with Kutay between 1995 and 1997.

17. David Grossman and Eddie Koch, *Ecotourism Report: Nature Tourism in South Africa: Links with the Reconstruction and Development Program* (Pretoria, South Africa: SATOUR, August 1995), p. 11.

18. Wight defined experienced ecotourists as those who had taken an out-of-state vacation in the past three years or planned to do so.

19. Mary-Lou Weisman, "Confessions of a Reluctant Eco-Tourist," *New York Times*, March 1, 1998, Section 5: *Travel*, p. 27.

20. Wight, "North American Ecotourism Markets."

21. Denise Ingram and Patrick Durst, "Nature-Oriented Travel to Developing Countries," FPEI Working Paper No. 28 (Research Triangle Park, N.C.: Southeastern Center for Forest Economics Research, October 1987), p. 8.

22. The Ecotourism Society (TES) training course packet.

23. Peter Frank and Jon Bowermaster, "Can Ecotourism Save the Planet?" and "Seven Golden Rules . . . and the People Who Stick to Them," *Condé Nast Traveler*, December 1994, pp. 138–139, 161–162.

24. Interviews with Marie Walters and Carolyn Wild, September 1994, Montreal.

25. Higgins, "Global Structure of the Nature Tourism Industry," p. 15.

26. *Specialty Travel Index (STI)* publication and interview. According to *STI* publisher Steen Hansen, some 550 tour operators, or about half the specialty companies in the United States, advertise in the *STI*, which is distributed to all travel agents. There are 11,000–12,000 tour operators in the United States.

27. Higgins, "Global Structure of the Nature Tourism Industry," pp. 13–16; Ingram and Durst, "Nature-Oriented Travel to Developing Countries."

28. Karen Ziffer, *Ecotourism: The Uneasy Alliance* (Washington, D.C.: Conservation International, 1989), pp. 19–20.

29. Numerous interviews with Sally and Costas Christ, plus Tamu Safari Tours' World Wide Web site (Internet: http://www.travelsource.com/safaris/tamusafaris.html).

30. Ralph Sorenson, "Overseas Adventure Travel, Inc.," Case Study 9-391-068 (Boston: Harvard University, Harvard Business School, 1990).

31. Author's interview with Kurt Kutay; Frank and Bowermaster, "Can Ecotourism Save the Planet?" pp. 138–139, 161–162.

32. International Resources Group, *Ecotourism: A Viable Alternative for Sustainable Management of Natural Resources in Africa* (Washington, D.C.: U.S. Agency for International Development, June 1992), pp. 34–40.

33. Jan Laarman, Timothy Stewart, and Jeffrey Prestermon, "International Travel by U.S. Conservation Groups and Professional Societies," *Journal of Travel Research*, summer 1989, pp. 12–17.

34. Quoted in Ziffer, *Uneasy Alliance*, p. 20.

35. H. Stewart Kimball, *History of the Sierra Club Outing Committee, 1901–1972* (San Francisco: Sierra Club, 1990), p. 20.

36. Sierra Club, "Guidelines for Ecocultural Tourism (Emerald Guidelines)," n.d.; "Sierra Club Policy: Ecotourism," Policy Code 13.1, adopted September 18–19, 1993.

37. Interviews with Marie Uehling, director, International Trips Program, The Nature Conservancy, between 1994 and 1997; program literature.

38. Marcus Lenzen's interview with WWF travel program office staff member, August 1997; travel program literature.

39. Ziffer, *Uneasy Alliance*, p. 20.

40. Héctor Ceballos-Lascuráin, *Tourism, Ecotourism, and Protected Areas* (Gland, Switzerland: IUCN, 1996), p. 6, 9.

41. TES training course packet.

42. Ana Báez, "Binomio turismo-conservación: Una alternativa de desarrollo," *Tecnitur: Costa Rica International Magazine* (published by the Professional Tourism Association of Costa Rica), no. 46 (June 1993): 48–53.

43. Other locally owned ecotourism operators in Costa Rica include Tikal, which pioneered ecotourism trips to Cuba as well; Sun Tours, which also owns lodges; and Horizontes, owned by two women, which in 1997 was one of nine runners-up for the *Condé Nast Traveler* ecotourism award.

44. Author's interview with Joel Christenson; Black Mamba's World Wide Web site (Internet: http://www.odsnet.com/blackmamba).

45. Anita Pleumarom, "The Political Economy of Tourism," *The Ecologist* 24, no. 4 (July–August 1994): 144.

46. World Wildlife Fund (WWF), The Nature Conservancy (TNC), and World Resources Institute (WRI), *Biodiversity Conservation Network: Getting Down to Business*, 1997 Annual Report (Washington, D.C.: WWF, 1997), p. iii.

47. Michael Wells and Katrina Brandon, *People and Parks: Linking Protected Area Management with Local Communities* (Washington, D.C.: World Bank, World Wildlife Fund, and U.S. Agency for International Development, 1992), p. 3.

48. Jonathan Adams, "Ecotourism: Conservation Tool or Threat?" *Conservation Issues* 2, no. 3 (June 1995).

49. Elizabeth Boo, *Ecotourism: The Potentials and Pitfalls*, vols. 1 and 2 (Washington, D.C.: World Wildlife Fund, 1990); author's interviews with Boo. This seminal study was financed by USAID.

50. Adams, "Ecotourism: Conservation Tool or Threat?"; Barry Spergel, *Belize's Protected Area Conservation Trust: A Case Study* (Washington, D.C.: World Wildlife Fund, June 3, 1996); Kreg Lindberg and Jeremy Enriquez, *An Analysis of Ecotourism's Economic Contribution to Conservation and Development in Belize*, vol. 1, *Summary Report* (Washington, D.C.: World Wildlife Fund, 1995).

51. WWF, TNC, and WRI. *Biodiversity Conservation Network: Stories from the Field and Lessons Learned*, 1996 Annual Report (Washington, D.C.: WWF, 1996), p. 18; interview with Connie Carroll, director, Biodiversity Conservation Network (BCN), September 1997; various BCN publications.

52. Information from Marie Uehling, director, International Trips Program, The Nature Conservancy, September 1997.

53. The Nature Conservancy, "Ecotourism," handout, n.d.

54. Conservation International, "CI Ecotourism Program Overview," and "The Ecotravel Center" World Wide Web site (Internet: http://www. ecotour.org/CIECO/overview.html); interview with Karen Ziffer and staff in Ecotourism Program; "Conservation International's Ecotourism Initiatives" and other CI documents collected by Marcus Lenzen.

55. Interviews with USAID contract official, who asked to remain anonymous, March–April 1996.

56. World Bank, "Greening of the World Bank: Notable Shift Since Rio Signals Billions for the Environment," press release no. 96/S/13, September 1995.

57. Katrina Brandon, *Ecotourism and Conservation: A Review of Key Issues,* Environment Department Papers, Biodiversity Series, No. 033 (Washington, D.C.: World Bank, April 1996), p. 56; Global Environment Facility, *Uganda: Bwindi Impenetrable National Park & Mgahinga Gorilla National Park Conservation,* project document (Washington, D.C.: The World Bank, January 1995).

58. United Nations Environment Programme (UNEP), United Nations Development Programme (UNDP), and World Bank, *Report of the Independent Evaluation of the Global Environment Facility Pilot Phases* (Washington, D.C.: UNEP, UNDP, and World Bank, 1993), p. 60, quoted in Anita Pleumarom, "Ecotourism: A New 'Green Revolution' in the Third World" (draft of article obtained from author, 1996), p. 9.

59. Various International Finance Corporation (IFC) documents and interviews with IFC Tourism Unit officials; Marcus Lenzen's telephone interview with Multilateral Investment Guarantee Agency (MIGA) official Roland Pladed, October 7, 1997; Ken Kwaku, global program manager, MIGA, "Challenges and Opportunities for Supporting Ecotourism Projects," speech delivered at International Ecolodge Development Forum and Field Seminar, Maho Bay, St. John Island, October 1994; documents from MIGA.

60. International Finance Corporation (IFC), Tourism Unit, *IFC Tourism Sector Review* (Washington, D.C.: IFC, Tourism Unit, February 1995), p. 12.

61. Interview with Maurice Desthuis-Francis, International Finance Corporation, Tourism Unit, IFC, Washington, D.C., April 1996.

62. International Finance Corporation, "Investing in Tourism" packet, 1996; International Finance Corporation, "IFC to Finance Small Environmental Enterprises," press release, September 12, 1996; interview with Amos Bien.

63. Kwaku, "Challenges and Opportunities"; literature from International Finance Corporation; interview with Maurice Desthuis-Francis, IFC, Tourism Unit, Washington, D.C., April 1996; Marcus Lenzen's interview with Carolyn Cain, tourism specialist, Technical and Environment Department, IFC, August 1997; various World Bank, IFC, and Global Environment Facility reports and tables.

64. Through its Industry and Environment Program, UNEP "works in cooperation with industry associations, international organizations and NGOs to provide decision-makers in government and industry with information and tools to achieve environmentally sound tourism development and management." United Nations Environment Programme, Tourism Section, "UNEP Industry and Environment: 1996 Achievements" (Internet: http://www.unep.org); various issues of UNEP brief papers, *Tourism Focus,* and other UNEP documents.

65. Jacqueline Aloisi de Larderel, "Building a Partnership for Sustainable Tourism," *Going Green: The Ecotourism Resource for Travel Agents,* supplement to *Tour & Travel News,* October 25, 1993, pp. 8–9.

66. David Nicholson-Lord, "The Politics of Travel: Is Tourism Just Colonialism in Another Guise?" *The Nation,* October 6, 1997, p. 18.

67. Cynthia Enloe, *Bananas, Beaches, and Bases: Making Feminist Sense of International Politics* (Berkeley: University of California Press, 1990), p. 40.

68. Pleumarom, "Political Economy of Tourism," p. 146.

69. Wells and Brandon, *People and Parks*, p. 34.

70. Pleumarom, "Political Economy of Tourism," pp. 145–146.

71. Medico International, "Project Dossier about Maputaland" (Obermainanlage 2, D-60314, Frankfurt am Main, Germany), quoted in Pleumarom, "Political Economy of Tourism," pp. 144–146.

72. Pleumarom, "Ecotourism: A New 'Green Revolution,'" p. 10.

73. Brandon, *Ecotourism and Conservation*, p. 32.

74. Cited in Boo, *Ecotourism: Potentials and Pitfalls*, vol. 1, p. 13.

75. Katrina Brandon, *Bellagio Conference on Ecotourism: Briefing Book* (New York: Rockefeller Foundation, 1993), p. 32.

76. World Resources Institute, "Ecotourism: Rising Interest in Nature Vacations Has Mixed Results for Host Countries and the Resources They Promote," in *Environmental Almanac* (Boston: Houghton Mifflin, 1993), p. 153.

77. Héctor Ceballos-Lascuráin, *Tourism, Ecotourism, and Protected Areas* (Gland, Switzerland: IUCN, 1996), pp. 10–11.

78. Interview with Phil Church, official with Center for Development Information and Evaluation, U.S. Agency for International Development, March 1995.

79. Interview with Craig MacFarland, October 1997. Ceballos-Lascuráin discusses several modifications of the traditional methods for measuring carrying capacity. One, the Limits of Acceptable Change (LAC) technique, focuses on identifying what management strategies are necessary to maintain or restore desired conditions. Another, Visitor Impact Management (VIM), seeks to measure the social impacts of increasing recreational use. Ceballos-Lascuráin, *Tourism*, pp. 133–146.

80. Pleumarom, "Ecotourism: A New 'Green Revolution,'" p. 7.

81. Ceballos-Lascuráin, *Tourism*, p. 9.

82. Pleumarom, "Political Economy of Tourism," p. 143. For an extensive and excellent discussion of these issues, see Deborah McLaren, *Rethinking Tourism and Ecotravel: The Paving of Paradise and What You Can Do to Stop It* (West Hartford, Conn.: Kumarian Press, 1997).

83. Enloe, *Bananas, Beaches, and Bases*, p. 31.

84. Ceballos-Lascuráin, *Tourism*, p. 9.

85. William Norman, "Green Evaluation Program and Compliance of Nature Tour Operators," on The Ecotourism Society's World Wide Web site (Internet: http://www.ecotourism.org/textfiles/sirak.txt), February 1997.

86. Beatrice Blake and Anne Becher, *The New Key to Costa Rica* (Berkeley, Calif.: Ulysses Press, 1997), pp. xvii–xxi.

87. David Pearson and David Middleton, *The New Key to Ecuador and the Galápagos* (Berkeley, Calif.: Ulysses Press, 1996), pp. xvii–xxi.

88. Jody Lekberg, "Hotels to Get Eco-Ratings," *Tico Times*, December 6, 1996; Jody Lekberg, "No Artificial Ingredients—A Study of Tourism in Costa Rica," *Mesoamérica* 16, no. 3 (March 1997).

89. Quoted in "Tourism, Environment, and Culture," *Wajibu* 10, no. 1 (1995): p. 7.

Part II
Nation
Studies

Chapter 4

The Galápagos Islands:
Test Site for Theories of
Evolution and Ecotourism

Standing on top of a sand dune, naturalist guide Jorge Marino gives his spiel to a small group of tourists. Sea lions lounge like huge gray rocks on the powder white beach. On a branch of a low flowering shrub, a yellow warbler sings; just three feet away, several people snap its photograph. Like all creatures on the Galápagos Islands, the warbler and the sea lions seem oblivious to the human spectators. Here, as nowhere else in the world, people can get within feet, sometimes inches, of sea lions, marine iguanas, giant tortoises, tropical penguins, songbirds, and rare birds such as the blue-footed booby, the flightless cormorant, the waved albatross, and thirteen kinds of Darwin's finches.

The Galápagos, originally known as the Enchanted Isles,[1] is often cited as the place where ecotourism originated. As one leading guidebook puts it, "Tourists from Europe started coming to [Ecuador's] Galápagos Islands more than 150 years ago. They may have called themselves sailors, scientists or adventurers, but in many ways they walked like, talked like, and looked like ecotourists."[2] This archipelago is universally viewed as one of the most unusual and precious ecosystems on earth:[3] 95 percent of the reptiles, 50 percent of the birds, 42 percent of the land plants, 70 to 80 percent of the insects, and 17 percent of the fish on the Galápagos live nowhere else in the world.

Since the 1960s, scientific research, sound park management, well-trained naturalist guides, and a fairly well regulated and responsible nature tourism industry have helped ensure that the wildlife of the Galápagos has been little disturbed by the steep rise in visitors. But since the late 1980s, the Galápagos Islands have had to cope with a variety of complex problems— new immigrants, introduced species, illegal fishing, and conflicts between towns people and park people—that have come in the wake of the ecotourism boom.

History

Located some six hundred miles off Ecuador's coast, the Galápagos Islands are a cluster of some 120 volcanic islands. Their significance was first recognized in 1835, when Charles Darwin, a young British aristocrat with a love of biology, stopped there while sailing around the world on the HMS *Beagle* as part of a five-year British expedition. Darwin spent just five weeks on the islands, but his observations there changed the course of Western scientific thought. Darwin noted two important phenomena: that the wildlife, with no natural predators, was unusually "tame" and that many of the islands had developed their own unique species of animals, birds, and plants. As Darwin recorded in his journal,

> [B]y far the most remarkable feature in the natural history of this archipelago . . . is that the different islands to a considerable extent are inhabited by a different set of beings. . . . I never dreamed that islands, about fifty or sixty miles apart, and most of them in sight of each other, formed of precisely the same rocks, placed under a quite similar climate, rising to a nearly equal height, would have been differently tenanted . . . [with] their own species of the tortoise, mocking-thrush, finches, and numerous plants.[4]

It is an irony of history that these idyllic islands, frequently described as a "Garden of Eden" or "peaceable kingdom," became the fountainhead for creationism's most serious challenge: the theory of evolution. In *On the Origin of Species by Means of Natural Selection,* published in 1859, Darwin outlined his theory of evolution by natural selection—that all living creatures adapt to and evolve in accordance with their environment—largely on the basis of observations made on the Galápagos.

Darwin's work put the Galápagos Islands on the map. As writer Kurt Vonnegut notes in his science fiction novel, *Galápagos,* "Darwin did not change the islands, only people's opinion of them."[5] For several centuries, a trickle of adventurers, naturalists, utopia seekers, aristocratic travelers, pirates, shipwrecked sailors, and ne'er-do-wells had sailed through and sometimes settled on the Islands. By the beginning of the nineteenth century, the archipelago, in particular Floreana Island (also known as Santa María Island or Charles Island) with its freshwater and its plentiful supply of tortoises, had become a favorite resting spot for passing whaling ships. Floreana also became the site of South America's first post office, a wooden barrel just off the beach (still functioning today). Crews on outbound whalers, whose voyages lasted as long as two years, would drop mail in the barrel; sailors on homebound ships would collect the letters and, eventually, deliver them.

By the time Darwin arrived the islands had in fact already begun experiencing the negative effects of human presence. Passing ships and the tiny permanent settlements on several islands had introduced into the archipelago rats, cats, pigs, goats, and other animals highly destructive to the local flora and fauna. Whaling vessels collected for fresh meat hundreds of thousands of Galápagos giant tortoises, which they piled upside down in the holds of their ships. The whalers had nearly decimated the tortoise population before the 1860s, when (fortuitously for both animals) the bottom fell out of the whaling industry.

Only gradually were steps taken toward conservation and rehabilitation, and the destructive trends were slowly reversed. In 1935, to mark the centennial of Darwin's visit, the Ecuadoran government passed legislation to protect the islands' wildlife. But the legislation was not enforced and serious conservation efforts did not begin until 1959. To commemorate the hundredth anniversary of Darwin's *Origins of Species,* Ecuador declared 97 percent of the islands a national park and restricted human habitation to the remaining 3 percent of the islands where settlements were already established. By then, scientists say, most of the twenty species and subspecies that have disappeared since people first arrived in the archipelago had already become extinct.[6] In the early 1960s, the Charles Darwin Foundation (headquartered in Quito, Ecuador, with an office in Virginia and a research station on the Galápagos) was set up under the auspices of UNESCO and the World Conservation Union (IUCN). In 1979, the islands were designated a UNESCO World Heritage Site, and in 1986, the Ecuadoran government declared approximately 50,000 square kilometers (19,300 square miles) of water a marine resources reserve intended to protect all internal waters within the archipelago and a zone of fifteen nautical miles around the islands. Over the decades, the government-run Galápagos National Park Service and internationally funded Charles Darwin Biological Research Station, located next to each other on Santa Cruz Island just outside the main town, Puerto Ayora, have maintained a symbiotic relationship in scientific research, protection, educational programs, and breeding of captive endangered tortoises and land iguanas (when the animals are sufficiently grown, they are repatriated to their original islands).

The Ecotourism Boom

Until recently, the islands' remoteness helped preserve the Galápagos as a unique living laboratory for observing evolution. Before the 1970s, the only "public" transportation to the islands was aboard infrequent and uncomfortable cargo ships from Ecuador's main port, Guayaquil. David Balfour, honorary British counsel and director of Metropolitan Touring's office on the Galápagos, recalls that when he first arrived, in 1969, "Tourism had not really started. Cargo ships were coming every three months or so, bringing groups of visitors." Numbers grew only after an old U.S. military base on the island of Baltra[7] was refurbished and regular commercial air links were established. Gradually, a tourism infrastructure within the islands began to be built.

Organized ecotourism began in the late 1960s, when two Ecuadoran companies headquartered in Quito, Metropolitan Touring and Turismundial, joined with a New York company, Lindblad Tours, and purchased two cruise boats, a twelve-passenger sailing vessel and a sixty-passenger luxury liner. Balfour says the Metropolitan began by doing "a feasibility study, especially from the point of view of conservation. Tourism was done in close conjunction with the Darwin Station and the new national park. It was pioneering work. The notes that we still publish and hand out to passengers about how they should conduct themselves were put out right at the start of our operations. So there was a close link between tour operations, scientists, and the national park."

During the early 1970s, tourism facilities grew slowly: about five small boats occasionally carried tourists on day trips, and Puerto Ayora had one "luxury" hotel with green, shaded lawns and individual bungalows, three small hotels, and a few restaurants. Then, between 1974 and 1980, tourism picked up (see table 4.1), and the number of vessels increased from thirteen to forty-two. As the industry expanded, ownership shifted: in the early and mid-1970s, with the exception of Metropolitan Touring's two boats, the "floating hotels" were owned by long-term island residents, most of whom lacked the capital and the foreign-language and marketing skills required to do business on an international scale. By 1982, about six tour agents from mainland Ecuador wholly or partially owned more than a dozen intermedi-

Table 4.1. The Galápagos Island's Tourism Growth: Visitors to Galápagos National Park

	Number of Visitors (in Thousands)								
	1972	1975	1979	1985	1989	1990	1993	1994	1996
Foreigners	6.7	7	10	12	27	26	37	41	46
Nationals	0.1	0	2	6	15	15	10	13	16
Total	6.8	7	12	18	42	41	47	54	62

Source: Bruce Epler, An Economic and Social Analysis of Tourism in the Galápagos Islands (Providence: University of Rhode Island, Coastal Resources Center, 1991), pp. 3, 15; "Tabla 1: Visitantes al Parque Nacional Galápagos entre 1979 y 1996," obtained from the Charles Darwin Foundation; José Rodriguez Rojas, Las islas Galápagos: Estructure geográfica y propuesta de gestión territorial (Cayambe, Ecuador: Talleres Abya-Yala, 1993), p. 107; George Wallace, "Visitor Management in Galápagos National Park," draft (Fort Collins, Colo.: College of Natural Resources, Colorado State University, January 1992), p. 1.

ate-size vessels catering to foreigners, but only Metropolitan maintained a full-time office on the Galápagos.

During the 1980s, as the ecotourism explosion brought world attention and new funds to the Galápagos, it also strained the islands' ecosystem and their resident human population. As one study put it, "Tourism . . . is the driving force which, directly and indirectly, dictates the pace and types of changes that are occurring in the islands."[8] Since 1979, the number of tourists has increased more than fivefold, facilitated by a second airport on San Cristóbal Island. Since the late 1980s, there have been tendencies toward both poorly done ecotourism and conventional tourism as well as uncontrolled immigration and commercial fishing. Yet here, more than almost anywhere else in the world, the *only* viable commercial activity is high-quality, limited, and carefully monitored ecotourism. This, combined with carefully regulated immigration and fishing, holds out a possibility of protecting the fragile environment and striking an equilibrium with the local population. If tourism and the problems it has spawned are not carefully managed, the ecosystem of the Galápagos will be pushed to the point of no return. "This is a critical time for the Galápagos," warns Smithsonian Institution biologist Tom Fritts. "We are constantly at threat of reaching that precipice of irretrievable damage to the islands' ecosystem."[9]

Current Tourism Trends in the Galápagos

Gradually, two competing tendencies developed in the Galápagos' nature-based tourism industry: toward low-budget, higher-volume, conventional sun-, beach-, and land-based tourism via on-land hotels and day boats and toward upscale, lower-density ecotourism aboard luxury tour boats or floating hotels, which have, at least in principle, less effect on the ecosystem. Whereas the first type of tourism is dominated by Galápagueños and Ecuadorans and serves primarily Ecuadorans, the second is controlled primarily by foreigners and wealthy Ecuadorans and caters mainly to foreigners. Each type produces, as Bruce Epler, a biologist with the University of Rhode Island's Coastal Resources Center, found in his 1991 tourism study, "a unique flow of economic, social, and environmental impacts."[10]

As Ecuador adopted free-market and structural adjustment polices in the mid-1980s and ecotourism became the latest buzzword within the travel industry, there was a flurry of tourism investment, producing new vessels, companies, and hotels, in the archipelago. There was talk, but fortunately no action, about building casinos and high-rise hotels. According to Epler, by the early 1990s, the islands' tourism industry was dominated by two main-land-based, vertically integrated inbound tour operators (Metropolitan

Touring and another company), both offering high-quality ecotourism. These companies owned several floating hotels and a part of the Ecuadoran airlines that fly to the islands, and they also conduct tours to other regions of Ecuador as well as to the Galápagos.[11] Since the late 1980s, their dominance has been challenged by the growth of other reputable ecotourism operators such as Quasar Nautica and Angermeyer's Enchanted Excursions. Tour companies and boat owners have responded to the growing international market by offering more comfort and safety, better sanitation, air-conditioning, higher-quality meals, and better-trained crews. Safety regulations were improved and annual inspections and rescue courses were instituted following the 1990 *Bartolomé* disaster. Faulty electrical wiring caused a fire and explosion aboard this tour boat, which sank, killing five passengers.[12]

By the late 1990s, the islands had eighty to ninety registered yachts, cabin cruisers, sailing vessels, and day boats. The floating hotels generally offer high-quality and well-managed nature tourism; what they do not offer is much direct benefit to the local community. Tourists sleep and eat on the boats and are usually discharged for only a few hours into Puerto Ayora where they visit the Darwin research station and national park headquarters and may buy T-shirts and other souvenirs, sometimes at the station's kiosk rather than in the town itself.

Local residents usually don't have the capital to buy or build luxury boats. "The operation now is run by companies in Guayaquil or Quito. Here, very little is in the hands of local people," says Georgina Martin de Cruz, a British woman who, with her Galápagueño husband, Agusto, runs the *Beagle III,* a small "standard tourist boat" with bunk beds, shared bath, and no air conditioning. These less luxurious, locally owned floating hotels are being increasingly marginalized by better-financed companies that are buying up operating permits and bringing in larger and more modern and luxurious vessels.

This high-end, foreign-dominated tourism has helped give rise to two other types of tourism on the islands: day cruises and on-land hotels, catering mainly to Ecuadoran and low-budget foreign tourists. Whereas elsewhere in the world, the percentage of domestic tourists has tended to decline in relation to international tourism, on the Galápagos the number of Ecuadoran visitors increased from less than 15 percent in the late 1970s to 40 percent by 1985 and has since dropped off to 25 to 30 percent. Local currency devaluations in the 1980s made the Galápagos affordable for many Ecuadorans, and, much earlier than in other countries, nationals began receiving deep discounts on airline flights, park entrance fees, and (space allowing) cruise boats. But most Ecuadoran visitors stay in land-based hotels in Puerto Ayora or Puerto Baquerizo Moreno (the archipelago's political capital, located on San Cristóbal), and use day boats to visit national park sites on other islands. Between 1981 and 1995, the number of on-land hotel rooms increased slightly faster (2.6-fold) than the number of berths in floating hotels.[13] Bruce Epler found that foreigners were spending on average 3.5 times more than Ecuadorans ($1085 and $300 per person, respectively) to tour the Galápagos, yet a much higher proportion of the money spent by Ecuadorans went into the local economy.

The day boats are locally constructed of wood and are locally owned and crewed by island residents. For example, Hugo Andrade, was born on the Galápagos and switched from fishing to tourism after the marine reserve was established. He describes making a living as "a constant struggle. It's easy to see among the tourist boats who are local Galápagueños and who are from the continent," as locals call mainland Ecuador.[14] Day boats are closely linked to the on-land hotels, which also are usually locally owned; it is common for a tour operator to own both a hotel and a day boat.[15] Epler concludes that "if the social well-being of the local population is a consideration, day boats and small hotels produce a wider stream of benefits to a poorer segment of society."[16]

Although domestic tourism to the Galápagos can be important in helping to build a national constituency committed to conservation and protection of the islands, it has a downside. Because domestic tourists as a class spend much less per day, greater numbers are needed to generate the same level of revenue gained from international tourism. Because Ecuadoran tourists can pay for airline tickets, hotels, and other services in local currency, they do not help the country to earn foreign exchange. In addition, naturalist guides and other scientists working on the islands note that Ecuadorans are often ill prepared by their travel agents: they may come expecting beach vacations and may learn little because they cannot afford top-quality naturalist guides and do not visit the most distant national park sites. Further, this sector of the industry has been poorly organized and regulated and has had a more negative effect on the islands' fragile ecosystem than have the floating hotels. The number of on-land hotels grew from only four in the 1970s to thirty-three in 1991; when I visited in 1994, tiny Puerto Ayora was filled with the sounds of construction of new hotels and wooden boats. Other land-based tourism businesses—restaurants, discotheques, museums, tour operators, and souvenir shops—have also expanded rapidly.

By 1997, tourism was providing an income for an estimated 80 percent of the people living on the Galápagos Islands and generating 60 percent of all tourism revenues earned by the Ecuadoran government.[17] The islands raise more money from tourism than does any other location in Ecuador—as much as $60 million annually in the mid-1990s—and in recent years there has been much debate over how to keep more of the profits on the islands for the benefit of both the park and the local community. In his 1991 study, Epler divides these tourism revenues into two components: (1) the total amount received by vessels, hotels, Galápagos National Park, and the airlines flying to the islands and (2) revenues attributable to Galápagos tourism but spent elsewhere in Ecuador. Visitors to the Galápagos must transit through Ecuador, and Epler found strong indications that foreigners spend as much for their vacations on the mainland as they do on the islands. He calculates that in 1995, for instance, the 55,782 tourists visiting the Galápagos spent $130 million, of which $69 million was spent on the islands.[18]

Regarding the total value of tourism on the islands, Epler found that in both 1990 and 1991 it equaled $32.6 million, of which roughly 85 percent ($27.5 million) was paid to vessels and airlines and a mere 3 percent each went for on-land hotels and park entrance fees. Airlines and vessels spend very little on the islands; most of the profits go off-island. The inequalities in distribution are also reflected in Epler's statistics showing that 92 percent of the tourist dollar was spent on floating hotels (most not owned by Galápagueños) and only 8 percent on day boats and land-based hotels (most locally owned). Epler calculates that less than $5 million, or 15 percent of the tourism income, directly enters the islands' economy and that the multiplier effect of this money is "exceptionally low" because "market linkages" between local farmers, cattle ranchers, fishermen, and the floating hotels is "virtually nonexistent": most food and other supplies are imported, and families of crew members live on the mainland. In contrast, day boats and hotels "significantly impact" the local economy because they are built by local craftsmen, their crews and employees are local residents, and they purchase food from local farmers and fishermen.[19]

The Ecotourism Industry's Role in Conservation Efforts

The ecotourism boom has brought expanded resources for Ecuador's national park service, INEFAN (Instituto Ecuatoriano Forestal y de Areas Naturales y Vida Silvestre). In the early 1990s, park entrance fee, paid at the airport and covering the entire stay, was low—$40 for foreigners and only $0.60 for Ecuadorans. This generated about $1 million in government revenues,[20] but only 10 to 20 percent went to support Galápagos National Park. In April 1993, park entrance fees were raised to $80 for foreign visitors, with the national park retaining a higher percentage of the intake. By the mid-1990s, tourism had become Ecuador's fourth largest foreign exchange earner, after petroleum, bananas, and shrimp, and was generally bringing in about $60 million annually to the Galápagos.[21] In 1994, however, the central government authorized the setting aside of 40 percent of the national park entrance fees to protect the islands, and this gave "a big boost" to Galápagos National Park, according to Arturo Izurieta, who was then the park's youthful superintendent. He said he was able to hire more staff, guards, and scientists and purchase more computers, fax machines, and radios and a patrol boat for rescue and inspection missions. In late 1997, entrance fees were again raised, to $100 for foreigners, which is projected to generate more than $5 million annually, or about $2 million for Galápagos National Park—than double the park's allotment from the central government.

The ecotourism sector, particularly the tour operators and floating hotels catering to foreigners, represents the island's largest legal commercial activity and a powerful economic and political force on the islands. Most of the profits from tourism, however, do not stay on the Galápagos, and direct taxation on hotels and boats has been very low. Tour boat owners are also moderately taxed per berth: in 1991, the government collected a mere $10,800 in vessel concession fees, and these fees were unfairly heavy for the lower-income day boat owners. Both the number of boats and the fees have increased considerably since then, but experts such as Craig MacFarland, who ran the Charles Darwin Biological Research Station in the 1970s and was president of the Charles Darwin Foundation from 1985 to 1996, argue that rather than "simply raising the park entrance fee over and over again," the government should levy a small "percent tax on the intake of the tourism industry, including hotels, restaurants, boats, and tour agencies." This, however, has been opposed by the tourism industry for what MacFarland labels "knee jerk, short-sighted reasons that it will hurt their numbers."[22]

Nevertheless, the ecotourism industry's contribution to conservation efforts on the Galápagos has, on the whole, been positive because the industry recognizes that its long-term success is based on a healthy and well-protected environment. A number of tour boat operators and guides work closely with the park service and research station to patrol for illegal fishing activities. Often, tour boat operators are the first to discover and photograph illegal encampments on the outer islands. For instance, Dolores de Diez of Quasar Nautica, one of the best-run and most responsible tour boat companies, works closely with Galápagos-based scientists to photograph and publicize destructive practices of shark and sea cucumber fishermen. "We are looking for a return on our investment in the long run. Our company is there to stay. We aren't out for fast money. So we want those islands to last," said Diez during an interview in Quito.

There have been several efforts to organize parts of the Ecuadoran tourism industry to more systematically support ecotourism principles and practices. The Ecuadoran Ecotourism Association (ASEC) started off with much promise as one of the first national ecotourism organizations in the world. Its president, Oswaldo Muñoz of Nuevo Mundo Tours, is also an official with The Ecotourism Society and a participant in many international forums. By the mid-1990s, ASEC had forty-two corporate members, mainly tour operators, divided into various committees, including one for the Galápagos headed by Dolores de Diez. Quasar Nautica, Metropolitan Touring, and a handful of other tour operators have been most active in pushing the government to control immigration and illegal fishing.

Unfortunately, some of these efforts have been undercut by ASEC's leadership (including president Muñoz) who, some members complain, favor the larger tour operators, refuse to run the organization democratically, and promote short-term interests over the broader principles of ecotourism. Muñoz, for instance, publicly opposed raising Galápagos National Park entrance fees from $40 to $80 fearing it would hurt tourism, despite the park service's urgent financial needs.[23] During militant actions by commercial fishermen and local residents in 1995 (described later in this chapter), Muñoz circulated a letter to the international press on behalf of ASEC saying that problems on the Galápagos were under control. Several association members who had not been consulted were angered by this move; as one put it, "I question the association's legitimacy as the defender of the marine and terrestrial ecology. They are more concerned with protecting tourism by hiding the problems."[24]

Disillusioned with Muñoz's unilateral actions and his failure to involve the wider membership, some tour operators refused to join and others dropped out of ASEC. For a time in the late 1990s, they participated in an informal working group, the Forum for Sustainable Tourism, with the aim of pushing both the government and the tourism industry to adhere to ecotourism principles and practices. In addition, the government-recognized Association of Galapagos Tour Operators (ASOGAS), includes the large, Quito-based companies, many of whom are Ecuadoran companies dedicated to raising the environmental, educational, and safety standards of tour boats and working for long-term environmental protection of the archipelago. In 1995, yet another group, the International Galápagos Tour Operators Association (IGTOA), headed by David Blanton of Voyagers International, based in Ithaca, New York, formed to lobby the Ecuadoran Congress for passage of the new comprehensive legislation on the Galápagos, to raise professional and safety standards of boat operators, and to raise funds for local conservation efforts. By late 1997, the IGTOA had twenty-three members who donated $5 per passenger to be used to support guide and crew training and programs of the park service and research station.[25]

Visitors' Effects on the National Park

Despite a more than tenfold increase in visitors since 1970, the National Park Service in the Galápagos has maintained extremely strict rules, and tourists *seem* to have had little effect on the animals. About one-third of the visitors are from the United States, and surveys invariably find that most tourists come away impressed. "I'm so astounded at what I've seen and the ambience of the islands. The whole environment, I would say, is as near as one could get to paradise on earth as is possible," mused Glenn Brisley of Norwich, England, as he boarded a plane to fly home. "It's absolutely fantastic; I'm very impressed by the national park system," commented Californian Meg Norton. "One thing that's been most striking to me is that for all the people who come here, there's very little mark left on the land. It's really nice to see what the earth looks like without man's imprint," commented Ben Mejia of Seattle, Washington.[26]

Keeping footprints off the Galápagos means carefully controlling all visitors. Tourists visiting any of the fifty-four designated land sites and sixty-two marine sites must be accompanied by naturalist guides; about a dozen sites are the most visited, and the vast majority of the islands are off limits to tourists. Although the guides work for the tour companies, they must attend special training courses given by the park service and Charles Darwin Biological Research Station. Most are not Galápagueños, and many hold degrees in biology or natural sciences and speak several languages. They function as both educators and guards. The guides make sure people stay on the narrow gravel paths, don't touch or take anything, don't take food onto the islands, don't litter, and don't disturb the animals. Before leaving an island, everyone carefully washes off so as not to transport anything, even grains of sand, from one island to another.

This hasn't always been the case. In the first years after the park was established, there were no rules for visitors. Scientists began noticing behavioral changes in the animals—such as iguanas waiting for tourists to give them bananas. But since the introduction of well-trained guides, marked trails, and strict rules, scientists say there has been little impact on animal behavior. However, some park officials, tour operators, and scientists say that since the tourism boom, they are beginning, once again, to detect adverse environmental effects on the most visited islands, including some trail erosion, loss of vegetation, and, perhaps, some change in behavior of certain animals. On a few beaches, male sea lions are reported to have become more aggressive in recent years, but it is not known whether this is caused by overpopulation of the animals themselves or by the presence of too many tourists. However, no behavioral change has been detected among other mammals or nesting birds, which live in high concentrations along the coast. "The system is getting a little weak here and there, but overall, it works. The changes in animal behavior are absolutely minimal," concludes Craig MacFarland.[27]

Some tourists, scientists, and boat owners complain that even though the Park Service must authorize schedules for all tour boats, some boats ignore the requirement or fail to file itineraries, so the most visited sites are becoming overcrowded. "You are having to wait behind perhaps ninety people, and that changes the whole flavor of your trip," complained one long time tour operator. The government is supposed to set limits on the number of tourists admitted each year, the number of passengers boats can carry, and the total number of boats. But these limits keep being raised. Although the government announced in 1992 that it was not issuing any new boat permits, enforcement was lax and some boat owners found ways to get around the restrictions, either by adding more berths to their boats or by buying permits from owners of smaller boat. "Definitely, more boats and larger boats are arriving," said David Balfour, who manages Metropolitan Touring. Chantal Blanton, director of the Charles Darwin Biological Research Station until 1996, said that at times "it's a bit like being in a theme park. To interact with nature, you just don't do that en masse."

Most controversial was the decision in early 1994 by Ecuador's national park service, INEFAN, to permit, for the first time, the entry of two cruise ships, with a combined total of more than 1,200 passengers, to visit Galápagos National Park. At $80 per head, that brought in considerable income, but many, including members the Permanent Galápagos Commission (appointed by Ecuador's president), local tour operators, and scientists, disapproved. Marta Lucia Burneo, an official with the commission, argued that the archipelago's tourism industry was moving in the wrong direction: "We should not have mass tourism, people who go traveling around the world in big comfortable ships with swimming pools and so on. We need to develop ecotourism." INEFAN subsequently announced a moratorium on visits by foreign cruise ship, admitting that the islands could not sustain such large numbers and that such visits would undercut local boat operators.

Decline in Quality of Ecotours

With the soaring tourist numbers on the Galápagos Islands, the guide "pool" has been forced to expand rapidly and to certify a new classification of "auxiliary" guides. These are most commonly native Galápagueños who know a great deal about the islands but often lack a depth of formal scientific training and knowledge and frequently speak only Spanish. Schisms have developed between the naturalist guides and the lower-paid and less trained auxiliary guides, leading to, as one naturalist guide put it, certification of some "substandard locals." "The level of interpretation has dropped," says biologist and former naturalist guide Andrew Drumm, who once ran Tropic, a small, Quito-based ecotourism company.[28] "Tourists before were getting a very clear education . . . in ecology, but also a lot [of them] were motivated to become conservationists by the guide. Now we're finding that there are a lot of guides who are not able to give that sort of experience to the tourists." Drumm notes that guides do not always exert adequate control over their groups, either because of a lack of conservation understanding or commitment or because they don't want to upset their passengers and jeopardize their end-of-cruise tip.[29]

In addition, as the number of ecotourists has expanded, it has also been diluted by less serious and less curious travelers. Tour boat operator Georgina Martin de Cruz describes many of the newer tourists as "softer," more concerned with comfort than conservation and with "ticking off a destination rather than having dreamt and saved up for it." In an informal survey of tourists I took during a sailing cruise, I found that none had read Darwin, few seemed aware of the scientific importance of the Galápagos Islands, and many were "savvy" travelers who had toured much of the rest of the world. Asked why she came, one Florida housewife said, "Well, we did Africa last year. We've done more luxurious cruising in the Mediterranean, to Greek Islands, around the world, so the Galápagos seemed like a good place to come." In 1993, Temptress Cruises, which was already well established in marketing ecotourism lite in Costa Rica, began operating around the Galápagos, offering passengers a choice between "a soft tour or hardcore natural history."[30] Some of the most qualified naturalist guides complain that many tourists today are not interested in detailed information about the islands and their habitat. This has led several of the most professional guides to quit.

As tourist numbers have grown and competition has increased, companies have taken cost-saving shortcuts that negatively affect the marine reserve. One of the most common practices is for boats to discharge their sewage and organic kitchen wastes into the ocean, which sometimes leads to unpleasant snorkeling experiences. Although there has been some improvement in this regard, some tour boats also dump inorganic trash and oil into the ocean when they think tourists are not looking rather than carry it back for disposal in port. "Naturalist guides are often in conflict with crews and owners on these issues," says former guide and tour company owner Andrew Drumm. "Crews can make life very miserable for a guide who tries to insist on responsible practices."[31]

By 1997, another threat loomed over the marine reserve. The government, under pressure from some dive boat operators and private Ecuadoran yacht owners, authorized "tag and release" sport fishing and, under restricted conditions, spearfishing. Supporters argue that these activities offer viable alternatives to commercial fishing within the marine reserve. Opponents, including a number of tour operators, tour boat owners, and scientists, contend that with overfishing already a pressing problem, sportfishing and spearfishing cannot be properly policed and will only lead to further exploitation. Jack Grove, head of Conservation Network International and author of the definitive book on the fish of the Galápagos,[32] calls this tag-and-release fishing "a facade" because "billfish such as marlin and sailfish are already showing up in the market in San Cristóbal. It's a sign of what is to come." He notes that the Galápagos Islands are "the only place in the world where divers can approach big fish. It's analogous to getting close to the "big five" game in the Serengeti, referring to the five African wildlife—lion, buffalo, rhino, leopard, and elephant—traditionally most prized by safari hunters. Grove says that sport fishing "is contradictory to selling ecotourism trips." It will attract a new type of clientele who want the best hotels and restaurants. They do not come to learn about the flora and fauna, but to capture it." The Charles Darwin Foundation's director, Johannah Barry, describes the introduction of sportfishing within the archipelago as "an attempt to put the camel's nose under the tent—to allow in fast fishing boats and then get tuna over into the packing plant in San Cristóbal."

Threats from Introduced Species

One of the most worrisome environmental threats to the Galápagos Islands has been the introduction of non-native species, whose numbers have accelerated in the wake of the ecotourism boom, endangering the survival of fragile and endemic species, that is, ones found only in one locale. At the top of the agenda of many scientists and park officials is tracking and eliminating introduced species—plants, animals, insects, fungi, bacteria—that are brought in by boat or plane by tourists, new immigrants, and illegal fishing operations. Scientists have estimated that by the mid-1990s, some 300 species of alien plants had been introduced—100 of them in the pervious decade.[33] Many of the exotic species are capable of outcompeting the unique native species of the Galápagos, which have evolved with few such threats.[34] "We are fighting very hard against introduced organisms which are arriving probably every day without us knowing it," explained Arturo Izurieta, then the national park superintendent, in a 1995 interview. "I think that the responsibility of preserving the ecosystems as they were formed millions of years ago is one of my greatest concerns. We have to fight against all introductions."

Although scientists working on the Galápagos had drawn up a comprehensive quarantine plan, including inspection and fumigation of cargo and people arriving by boat and plane, the Ecuadoran government had never approved the legislation or funds for it to be implemented. With no effective quarantine and control system to stop introductions, the park service and research station have concentrated on eradication. Much of the budgets of both institutions are spent trying to control alien species such as rats, goats, cats, and a wide variety of plants. On some islands, species of tortoise have become extinct because goats have eaten the vegetation they feed on and rats have eaten their eggs. On Isabela Island, home of more than one-third of the Galápagos giant tortoises, as many as 75,000 feral goats and burros, brought in by people living on the island's southern tip, have caused massive erosion, threatened the tortoises' habitat, and trampled their nests, forcing the park service to close Alcedo volcano as a visitor site. Together, the park and research station have adopted a multifaceted campaign to kill the goats and burros, relocate some of the endangered tortoises to a breeding center, and restore the island's ecosystem through fencing, seed banks, and reintroduction of native plants.[35]

Immigration & Colonization

Even more worrisome and, for political reasons, difficult to control has been the rapid acceleration in human arrivals, including colonists, fishermen, poachers, and job and fortune seekers. Historically, the tiny population of Galápagueños were subsistence farmers and fishermen; since the 1960s, some have worked for the Charles Darwin Biological Research Station or the park service. By the late 1980s, as word spread on the mainland that ecotourism was a *mina de oro* (gold mine) for the Galápagos, new arrivals began pouring in, lured by stories of plentiful jobs and high salaries.[36] Even though the cost of living on the islands was several times higher than on the mainland, salaries have been as much as seventy-five times higher.

The Galápagos Islands are now the fastest-growing area in Ecuador and one of the fastest-growing areas in the world, with a population that is increasing at a wholly unsustainable rate of 6 to 10 percent per year. The islands' permanent population leaped from a few hundred in the 1960s to 6,200 in 1982 to 15,000–20,000 by the late 1990s, all confined to the 3 percent of island territory not with the national park. Under Ecuadoran law, citizens have a right to move freely to the Galápagos because the islands constitute one of the country's twenty-one provinces. A constitutional amendment would be required to declare the entire archipelago a protected area, and this has proved impossible, given the powerful business and political interests supporting free access. Biologist Andrew Drumm says this immigration "is presenting the greatest threat the Galápagos have faced since perhaps the whaling industry in the nineteenth century."[37]

Whereas many national parks in developing countries are surrounded by culturally and ethnically stable rural peoples, new immigrants to the Galápagos are largely rootless and urban, coming from various parts of the mainland. Most of these immigrants end up in the main town, Puerto Ayora, on the island of Santa Cruz. Lyjia Ayove, for instance, is typical. She works in one of the town's small outdoor restaurants. Over the past decade, she and fourteen members of her family have moved to the Galápagos from their home in the crowded port city of Guayaquil. Ayove says, "It's easier to find work here than on the continent. Yes, it's certainly true that life is better here economically."

Geographically, the Galápagos are an anomaly: whereas elsewhere national parks are surrounded by human communities, here the tiny patches on four islands designated for human habitat are encircled by the national park and marine reserve. Government officials and island natives say the new arrivals are straining limited resources such as freshwater, electricity, telephone service, and schools; are increasing garbage and sewage disposal problems; and are demanding more fishing rights, timber, and parkland for houses and farms. The beaches on Santa Cruz are now devoid of sand, nearly all of which has been removed for construction. Equally worrisome, although Galápagueños have been taught from childhood to respect the animals and conserve supplies, many immigrants don't arrive with a similar respect for the islands' fragility. Tour boat owner and teacher Georgina Martin de Cruz says, "Obviously, the children, when they go to school, are taught about the Galápagos Islands and why we mustn't hit the iguanas over the head with rocks or let our dogs run loose. But the adult people who come here have no idea, and a lot of damage is being done that way."

Fishing and the Marine Reserve: Conflicts Between People and Parks

It is, however, around the issue of fishing within the marine reserve that the most serious conflicts have crystallized. Since the Galápagos Marine Resources Reserve (GMRR) was declared in 1986, it has been "run by everyone and no one," according to Andrew Drumm. The navy, the Ministry of Industry and Fisheries, and INEFAN (the national park service that falls under the Ministry of Agriculture and Livestock) have all held oversight responsibilities for this vast area, which is equal in size to Ireland.

There have been various ill-fated attempts to control fishing by limiting it to local fishermen using traditional methods, designating specific seasons, and issuing permits only for certain species. But again and again, the lack of clear management objectives and capacity to control has allowed the overexploitation of one resource after another. This has been exacerbated by the distance, weakness, and impoverishment of Ecuador's central government and by the exclusion of the Galápagos population from participation in real decision making about the use of the reserve. In October 1996, the government took a positive step by declaring the marine reserve a part of the Galápagos National Park system, moving it under the primary control of INEFAN, and appropriating more funds for its protection. But this followed years of serious exploitation by illegal commercial fishing interests.

Commercial fishing dates from the 1940s, when "whitefish" (grouper and sea bass) were first dried, salted, and exported to the mainland for the Lenten season. But by the late 1980s, the annual whitefish catch had dropped by 80 percent, suggesting that these species had been overfished. In recent years, far more serious problems have arisen as local fishermen (many of them new arrivals), commercial fishing operations, and trawlers (many foreign) have been engaged in illegal and highly destructive commercial fishing within the marine park for lobsters, tuna, sharks, grouper, and sea cucumbers. Japanese ships are frequently spotted just outside the reserve, where they rendezvous with local and mainland fishermen who sell them their illegal catches of shark fins and sea cucumbers. Dive guides report finding longlines and nets with dead sharks, sea lions, and turtles attached to them as well as finding live, but dying, sharks, including whale sharks, without their dorsal fins. British biologist David Day, who has worked on the Galápagos for more than two decades, says there's a multifaceted "battle going on about how the marine reserve should be used" between tour operators and fishermen; between the national park service and fishermen; and between permanent residents of the Galápagos and industrial fishing groups that are based on the mainland and tied to overseas commercial fishing interests.

In February 1994, Ecuadoran television showed shocking footage of large clandestine encampments of *pepineros* (sea cucumber fishermen) on Fernandina and Isabela Islands, two of the most pristine islands in the world. Scores of Ecuadoran fishermen were diving into the shallow waters and collecting an estimated 150,000 sea cucumbers per day. It was an industrial-style operation that involved cooking and drying the foot-long gray sea slugs. Garbage and empty cans littered the site, and the fishermen were shown bringing fresh food and other products onshore. They were also cutting for firewood the tall mangrove forests, which, according to a study by the Charles Darwin Foundation, provide "the only habitat for the rarest species of Darwin's finch, the tool-using Mangrove Finch. Cutting those heretofore undisturbed forests directly endangers that bird species."[38] Denouncing "these types of 'gold rush' fisheries," the foundation reported that by 1995, *every* suitable beach and cove—more than 500 separate localities—had been used by illegal fishermen.[39] From the Galápagos, the dried sea cucumbers and, recently, sea urchins, sea horses, and pipefish as well, are clandestinely exported to Japan, Taiwan, and Hong Kong (sometimes via the United States),[40] where they are eaten and used in medicines.

Most often, it is the naturalist guides, tour boat operators, scientists, and park officials, not Ecuador's tiny and ill-equipped navy, that discover such encampments, and this, in turn, has led fishing interests to launch verbal and physical attacks on the central government, park service, and research station. One of the original instigators of the illegal sea cucumber trade was Puerto Ayora businessman Luis Copiano, manager of the Coca-Cola distributorship on the Galápagos. Copiano admitted he had been involved in collecting and exporting sea cucumbers, and he blamed the antifishermen bias of the central government, park service, research station, and scientists for the closure of his fishing camps: "I don't know why they are against fishermen here in the Galápagos. They have no right to come here from nowhere, giving orders from a desk, from Quito, to the people living here, born here. I believe that's crazy." Copiano was, in fact, a recent arrival from the port city of Guayaquil, where he was linked to illegal commercial fishing operations tied to the Asian market.

Shortly after the illegal camps were exposed on television, park guards and tour guides discovered the carcasses of eighty-six butchered giant tortoises at five specific sites on Isabela Island—more than the total number killed by humans at these same locations between 1980 and 1992. Fishermen were widely suspected to have been behind the slaughter. Then, in April 1995, an enormous fire started on Isabela and burned for months, destroying more than 8,903 hectares (22,000 acres). Again, sabotage was suspected. Personnel at the research station and park officials mounted a rescue mission, airlifting fifty-six tortoises to a breeding center in Puerto Villamil, on Isabela Island.[41]

The Ecuadoran government was divided over how to handle the situation, with the Ministry of Industry and Fisheries and the Galápagos Islands member of Congress, Eduardo Véliz, favoring, and the national park service and Ministry of Agriculture (together with the tourism industry, scientists, and research station) opposing, collection of sea cucumbers inside the marine reserve. Finally, a compromise was struck: it was agreed that for a three-month period, beginning October 15, 1994, fishermen could harvest no more than 550,000 sea cucumbers. The experiment was disastrous. No effective controls or enforcement were put in place; even before the trial period had elapsed, the Charles Darwin Foundation estimated that 6 to 10 million sea cucumbers, along with a wide variety of other valuable species, including sea horses, oysters, and conchs, were "harvested." According to *Time* magazine, there were also reports "that boats coming to collect the sea cucumbers arrive with prostitutes and drugs from the mainland, and some prostitutes are said to be paid in bags of sea cucumbers, which they later trade for cash."[42]

When the government announced it was closing the fishing season in December 1994, a month early, the conflict quickly escalated. On the morning of January 3, 1995, a group of *pepineros,* some masked and wielding machetes and clubs, blockaded the road to the national park headquarters and research station outside Puerto Ayora. For four days, forty or more *pepineros* occupied the park and research station headquarters, harassing scientists, threatening to kill the tortoises, and forcing staff members to stay inside the buildings. "In effect," the Charles Darwin Foundation announced in an emergency bulletin, "the two institutions, their staffs, the facilities, and the breeding groups of tortoises and land iguanas are being held hostage." The siege ended after the government flew in military troops and representatives of the fisheries authority to negotiate.

Next, Congressman Véliz managed to push through the National Congress in Quito a law giving the islands near-autonomy in setting the rules for tourism and development. The populist bill had something for everyone, but nothing for conservation: the law doubled the salaries of public employees, required charter boat itineraries to include one night in a shore hotel, and put the national park under the control of a new bureaucracy, a provincial council. In September 1995, when Ecuador's president vetoed the legislation, Véliz led a three-week strike—the most militant action to date. Dozens of protestors blockaded and closed down the airport on San Cristóbal, blocked off the road from the main Baltra airport, and again occupied the park service buildings and Charles Darwin Biological Research Station. Station director Chantal Blanton hid out in the bush one night, and Congressman Véliz threatened "to kidnap tourists and if necessary burn any area of the national park."[43]

Needless to say, tourists on the Galápagos fled, and many others canceled their reservations. The Association of Galápagos Tour Operators estimated that reservations dropped by 15 percent, thus making, according to tour operator Drumm, "a bad year even worse."[44] The strikers were, in fact, an aggressive but small minority of the Galápagos population. In response, local people organized another group, the Committee for Peace and Wellbeing in the Galápagos, and the strike was finally called off in exchange for the president's pledge to set up a commission including Galápagueños to draft a new Special Law for the Conservation of the Galápagos. In March

1997, after sea cucumber fishermen who were illegally encamped on Isabela shot and severely wounded a park guard and masked men again attacked park headquarters and held officials hostage, more than three hundred people from the local fishing cooperatives, labor unions, municipality, civic organizations, tour boat companies, and research station marched through Puerto Ayora in a show of solidarity with the park service and a protest against violence and vandalism.[45]

The international community also weighed in with its concern over the political turmoil and deteriorating environmental conditions on the Galápagos. In December 1996, UNESCO's World Heritage Committee warned that the Galápagos would be designated a World Heritage Site in Danger if the Ecuadoran government did not adopt effective conservation measures. The government and the Galápagos Islands' tourism sector vigorously opposed this classification for fear it would hurt Ecuador's international image and tourism industry. As Jimena Flores, leader of a group of Galápagos women working in tourism put it, "Such a classification would have a direct repercussion on the economic prospects of our families, the islands, and the entire country."[46] At the same time, the government recognized that if it appeared recalcitrant, international organizations were likely to withhold funding for the Galápagos.

The Special Law for the Galápagos: A Victory for Conservation and the Community

"If there's one place in the world where we should draw a line in the sand, it's the Galápagos," a U.S. scientist told *Time* magazine in late 1995.[47] Over the next few years, this message was finally heard. Propelled by the mounting internal conflicts and strikes, the pro-peace citizens' coalition, and international pressure, Ecuador's government pledged to draw up and enact a comprehensive conservation law that would include a set of workable reforms for protecting the Galápagos. In April 1997, the president of Ecuador at last signed the Galápagos Decree, recognizing conservation of the archipelago as a national priority and listing a number of intended government reforms for controlling immigration, fishing, and introduced species.[48] In May, the government set up for the first time a process of consultation and negotiation led by the Permanent Galápagos Commission, which included representatives from conservation groups, the tourism industry, and various social sectors; industrialists; environmental authorities; and representatives from national and international organizations. The Charles Darwin Biological Research Station participated as an advisor. Both the process and the product—the Special Law for the Conservation of the Galápagos—were remarkable. Through a series of meetings, the islands' warring factions gradually began to reach agreement on how to ensure the long-term protection and profitability of the Galápagos. "Perhaps more than any other legislation, the document is the fruit of a true consensus reached among the various sectors involved with the Galápagos," said Jorge Anhalzer, president of the Charles Darwin Foundation.

But while what was dubbed the Galápagos Consensus was evolving on the islands, opponents of the law were busy lobbying the central government in Quito. In mid-November 1997, a vote was blocked by influential politicians, businessmen, and representatives of the fishing industry who wanted local control, open access to the marine reserve, and more liberal residence policies.[49] In January 1998, Ecuador's single-chamber Congress countered by passing the law, but in March, Ecuador's interim president issued a partial veto and proposed an alternative clause that would permit some industrial fishing within the marine reserve. The momentum, however, was shifting toward conservation. In early March 1998, while demonstrators dressed in black carried coffins through the streets on the Galápagos in a "march to mourn the archipelago," Congress again approved the law, thereby overturning the presidential veto.[50]

The Special Law, a complex set of some eighty articles, is a strong piece of environmental legislation that also provides support for residents of the Galápagos. It seeks to stabilize the islands' population by stipulating that only those who have lived on the Galápagos for more than five years will be eligible for legal residency; the rest could be deported. The Charles Darwin Foundation notes, however, one significant loophole: the law grants unlimited residence rights to all future descendants of Galápagos residents, whether or not they have ever lived in the archipelago, and this creates a sizable pool of potential immigrants. Giving in to pressures from the local community, the law also sets aside another 2 percent of the islands' territory for human settlement.

However, the law also sets aside more territory for conservation by extending the zone of protected waters surrounding the archipelago from fifteen to forty nautical miles, making it the world's second largest marine reserve. The law officially establishes the marine reserve as a protected area, to be managed by INEFAN, Ecuador's national park service, under the overall authority of an interinstitutional committee composed of four ministries and three stakeholder groups: tourism, fisheries, and a scientific and an educational group. The legislation divides the reserve into different use and protection zones. It also bans industrial fishing for sharks and sea cucumbers and permits local fishermen to fish seasonally for lobsters and specified types of fish. Although key issues remain to be negotiated—the precise definition of artisanal fishing and what measures should be taken to reduce overexploitation of the islands' resources—the Charles Darwin

Foundation concludes that in passing the law, the Ecuadoran Congress bucked the industrial fishing lobby and "took a bold decision to opt for something close to the Galápagos consensus. . . . [T]he law provides an excellent framework for conservation of the marine reserve."[51]

In terms of revenue, the law distributes park entrance fees by carefully balancing the need for conservation and the needs of the local community: 40 percent of the revenue is for Galápagos National Park; 40 percent is for town councils and other local authorities and must be used for the environment, tourism, and the Galápagos development agency that represents the communities; and 20 percent is to be divided among the quarantine program, the navy, the marine reserve, and Ecuador's other national parks.[52] The law also creates the National Institute for the Galápagos (INGALA), which is responsible for coordinating policies and planning throughout the Galápagos. However, since town councils enjoy autonomy under Ecuador's constitution, it is not clear how much authority this body will have. In an effort to control alien species, the legislation enacts and provides funding for the long-delayed quarantine inspection system, eradication programs, and environmental management plan. There are also requirements for environmental impact assessment and audits of the quarantine program.

The law says little about regulation of tourism, which, according to the Charles Darwin Foundation, "is both part of the introduced species problem and part of the solution."[53] There are some limits on expansion of tourism infrastructure, but no ceiling is set on the maximum number of tourists per year. In an effort to promote the local economy, permanent residents are given exclusive rights to future tourism opportunities and promotion of locally based tourism. Although this is a step in the right direction, assistance will need to be given to local entrepreneurs to ensure that land-based hotels are restricted and floating hotels meet standards for safety, high-quality ecotourism, and environmental protection. The law does promote improved environmental education in school curricula and for new immigrants as well as tax incentives for organizations that train and hire local residents.

Although much uncertainty remains, the momentum appears to have shifted toward conservation and sustainable development through well-regulated ecotourism, limited fishing by local residents, controlled immigration, and increased resources for both the resident community and conservation. In its analysis of the new law, the Charles Darwin Foundation concludes, "The law will do much to encourage all the Islands' residents to participate in, and take responsibility for, the conservation of Galápagos."[54] Craig MacFarland, who has some thirty years of experience with the Galápagos, concludes, "Things have turned around a lot. There's a groundswell in the islands, with lots of groups of people who are saying, 'Wait a minute, things aren't working right here.' People are starting to get fed up, and this is very positive."

The Galápagos Islands' Ecotourism Scorecard

The Galápagos Islands, with their geographic remoteness, well-run national park and biological research station, coterie of scientists and naturalist guides, and low-impact floating hotels and environmentally aware tourists, have been heralded as a model, a beacon light on the road to sustainable and sound ecotourism. However, in the latter half of the 1990s, headlines from the islands told of mysterious fires, slaughter of tortoises, illegal fishing camps, angry marchers with machetes, and other troubles in paradise. The Galápagos suddenly appeared to have become a warning light signaling the dangers of ecotourism that expands too rapidly without sufficient planning, government control, community benefits and involvement, tourism sector responsibility, and international concern. Then, just as the archipelago's fragile ecosystem seemed to have reached the point of no return, the Ecuadoran government did the right thing: it yielded to the Galápagos Consensus and passed the Special Law. The Galápagos Islands are now at a crossroads, an appropriate point to take stock of their ecotourism record and to evaluate how they stand up to the seven characteristics of real ecotourism.

- *Involves travel to natural destinations.* Nature *is* the allure of the Galápagos. This midocean moonscape of stark lava rock and scrub brush remains one of the world's most precious ecosystems. It offers ecotravelers both clues to understanding evolution and chances for close encounters with exotic as well as familiar creatures.
- *Minimizes impact.* Ecotourism's track record on the Galápagos has been remarkably good. Tour operators, naturalist guides, national park officials, and research station scientists have worked together for decades to create a model for low-impact, high-quality ecotourism. However, the steep rise in visitor numbers beginning in the late 1980s has caused some problems within the protected areas. There are signs of erosion at visitor sites, a slippage in the quality of guiding and enforcement of regulations, and too many incidents of tour boats dumping organic and inorganic waste within the marine reserve. "Tag-and-release" sportfishing and special types of spearfishing are inappropriately marketed as part of the ecotourism mix, whereas in practice they provide cover for commercial fishing activities. The most popular visitor sites are too often overcrowded; occasionally, cruise ships are permitted to discharge passengers on the islands; and too many substandard day boats and on-land hotels are marketing a more conventional type of "sun-and-sand" tourism.

The archipelago's land and sea parks are now divided into zones, but scientists such as George Wallace and Craig MacFarland argue that with more care and innovation, new types of recreational activities, such as hiking and horseback riding, can be introduced in certain areas of public and private land.[55] No effective system has ever been introduced to limit the number of either tour boats or tourists, and many scientists now believe it is sounder to analyze site impact. In summing up the effect of ecotourism on the parks, Tom Fritts, a wildlife biologist with the Smithsonian Institution's National Museum of Natural History, states, "The bottom line is that ... the Galápagos still have about 90 percent of their native [species of] flora and fauna. ... They're disturbed but not destroyed."[56]

Far more serious than this litany of minor problems are three other phenomena that have accelerated in the wake of the ecotourism boom: introduced species, immigration, and commercial fishing. This trio is threatening both the marine and land parks, as well as areas designated for human habitation and economic activity, and has led to repeated clashes between commercial fishing interests and those involved in environmental protection and ecotourism.

- *Builds environmental awareness.* Again, ecotourism has made a largely positive contribution to the broadening environmental awareness about the importance of these islands. Although Darwin's *Origin of the Species* put the Galápagos on the map as a laboratory for the study of evolution, the islands' significance was the concern of only a rather small and elite club of scientists. The growth of the environmental movement and of ecotourism has helped to expand the world's understanding of the islands' uniqueness and fragility. But as visitor numbers have grown, there has been a gradual watering down of environmental education. Naturalist guides, many of whom are scientists, have long provided high-quality educational tours to tourists traveling via the floating hotels. In recent years, this guide pool has been expanded to include auxiliary guides, who are less qualified and often speak only Spanish. Although this has provided an opportunity for a number of local people to move into guiding, it has meant that the most experienced guides command higher salaries and tend to work on the more luxurious and exclusive cruises. Simultaneously, many of today's international ecotourists are requesting less rigorous physical and intellectual experiences, and this, too, has served to water down the level of learning.

  The government and the travel industry have taken positive steps to promote domestic tourism by offering deep discounts to Ecuadorans. However, many nationals stay in less expensive land-based hotels and take day trips, which give them only a cursory view of the most popular islands. The upshot has been an overall decline in the vigor and quality of the educational experience, although those wanting and willing to pay for high-quality natural history can certainly find it.

The environmental understanding of the resident population has also been diluted by an influx of new immigrants who are seeking quick money and do not have a long-term commitment to the islands. The new law recognizes this latter problem and contains provisions for promoting environmental education in schools and for new immigrants.

- *Provides direct financial benefits for conservation.* The Galápagos Islands are Ecuador's biggest tourism destination, bringing in some 60 percent of the government's revenue from tourism.[57] The rise in visitor numbers, the steep hike in park entrance fees for foreigners, and the increase in the percentage of gate fees kept by the national parks service have greatly increased the amount of funds for environmental protection, allowing the park service to hire more staff and purchase badly needed equipment. This is a solid victory for conservation, but it comes at a time when the islands and marine reserve are facing greater environmental assaults than ever before, most linked directly or indirectly to the growth of ecotourism. In addition, the floating hotels, tour agencies, and other private businesses within the tourism sector continue to contribute only modestly to the national park system and conservation efforts.

- *Provides financial benefits and empowerment for local people.* Ecotourism has done both. Since the late 1980s, the standard of living and job opportunities on the islands have grown enormously, as have the political militance of the local population. The Special Law, the result of several years of legislative maneuvering, political conflict, sabotage, and violent protests, is a remarkable attempt to carefully balance the needs and demands of conservation with those of the local community. The law evenhandedly allots the same proportion of park entrance fees—40 percent each—to both Galápagos National Park and the local town councils. Moreover, it outlines measures to strengthen economic capacity and opportunities, educational level, technical skills, and social services of the resident community while attempting to curb its unsustainable level of growth. This is a clear victory for the islanders.

But the island community is a divided community. As Marc Miller, a law professor at Emory University, and Donald Kennedy, a professor of environmental science at Stanford University, caution, "This is not the familiar story of poor locals whose need for economic development is being fought by affluent outside conservationists." Rather, the struggle on the Galápagos has been largely between, on the one hand, newer immigrants who are aligned with international fishing interests and are pushing for political autonomy and, on the other hand, national park officials, research station and resident scientists, ecotourism operators, and many long-term Galápagueños who have traditionally relied on subsistence fishing and agriculture and, more recently, ecotourism. These long-term residents, Miller and Kennedy note, believe that "their economic

future will be improved more by preserving the ecosystem and promoting tourism than by exports of extracted natural resources."[58]
Undoubtedly, these two broad factions will continue to engage in political and economic wrestling matches, but the Special Law does offer the
best opportunity yet for building a stable and prosperous community
centered on ecotourism.

- *Respects local culture.* This is not a significant issue on the Galápagos,
  since much of the local community is imported. Planes arriving from the
  mainland often carry Otavalo market women bringing handwoven tapes-
  tries, thick sweaters, and woolen shawls from Ecuador's highland regions,
  but their culture is as alien as their woolen wares are inappropriate to life
  on the islands. The true Galápagueños who trace their roots to nineteenth-century sailors, prisoners, adventurers, and settlers do believe that
  they have a distinct culture, which includes both a spirit of independence
  and a deep understanding of and respect for the fragility of the islands as
  well as a code of conduct for protecting them. By aiming to strengthen
  the environmental education of schoolchildren and newcomers, the
  Special Law attempts to transfer some of these cultural and environmental norms to future generations.

- *Supports human rights and democratic movements.* For a long period,
  elected representatives from the Galápagos couched their populist campaigns in terms of local control and political autonomy. But they were primarily representing the interests of the fishing industry and newly arrived
  immigrants who worked, often illegally, for these international operations. Since 1997, a much broader and more representative movement
  has developed that has pushed for participatory democracy on the islands
  and passage of the Special Law by the national government in Quito. This
  highly significant development is in line with the principles and goals of
  ecotourism.

On the Galápagos, ecotourism operators can and must play a more
active role in promoting conservation and providing financial benefits for
the local population. But ultimately it is the Ecuadoran government and,
most important, the national park service, not enlightened ecotourism
operators or NGOs such as the Charles Darwin Biological Research
Station, that must be given the authority and resources to provide stew-
ardship for the islands. "Ecotourism concessions and NGOs obviously
provide an important complement to park management," writes George
Wallace, a specialist in ecotourism and environmental resources at
Colorado State University. "They should not, however, supersede or
replace park administrators, rangers, or interpreters as those primarily
responsible for the management of protected areas. There is no substitute
for the long term security, ecological and egalitarian management of pro-

tected areas that national and state systems—in this case the National Park Service in Galápagos—can provide," Wallace argues in a 1992 article. He concludes, "Protected areas like Galápagos are worth fighting for and protecting for all people, for their own sake, for all time. It is an achievable goal."[59] Wallace's sound but controversial thesis is that INEFAN, the national park service, should be viewed as primary among the various stakeholders in providing for the long-term health and protection of the archipelago. A recent but important caveat to this thesis is the need to strengthen the democratic participation of other local stakeholders who contributed to development of the Galápagos Consensus. Today, there is cautious optimism that with sound and careful implementation of the Special Law, the goal of finding an equilibrium between ecotourism, parks, and local people on the Galápagos Islands can be achieved.

Notes

1. In 1535, the archipelago's first recorded visitor, the bishop of Panama, Tomas de Berlanga, landed here and dubbed the hunks of lava rock the Enchanted Isles. The name stuck for nearly half a millennium before being replaced with Galápagos, Spanish for "giant tortoise."

2. David Pearson and David Middleton, *The New Key to Ecuador and the Galápagos* (Berkeley, Calif.: Ulysses Press, 1996), p. 9.

3. Bruce Epler, *An Economic and Social Analysis of Tourism in the Galápagos Islands* (Providence: University of Rhode Island, Coastal Resource Center, n.d.), preface.

4. Charles Darwin, *The Voyage of the Beagle* (New York: Penguin Books, 1988), pp. 340–343.

5. Kurt Vonnegut, *Galápagos* (New York: Delacorte Press, Seymour Lawrence, 1985), p. 16. This guidebook contains a useful "green rating" of tourist facilities on the mainland (but not the Galápagos) that advertise themselves as promoting ecotourism. Another important book details Ecuador's community-based ecotourism projects in the Amazon region: Rolf Wesche, *The Ecotourist's Guide to the Ecuadorian Amazon, Napo Province* (Quito: Panamerican Center for Geographical Studies and Research, 1995).

6. Consuelo Albornoz Tinajero, "Galápagos Threatened by Invasion," InterPress Service, June 13, 1995.

7. During World War II, the United States constructed a military base at Baltra and stationed several thousand people there. Godfrey Merlen, "Use and Misuse of the Seas around the Galápagos Archipelago" (unpublished paper obtained from author).

8. Epler, *Tourism in the Galápagos Islands,* p. 1.

9. Interview with Tom Fritts, Washington, D.C., 1996.

10. Epler, *Tourism in the Galápagos Islands,* p. 1.

11. Ibid., pp. 4–5.

12. Barry Boyce, *A Traveler's Guide to the Galápagos Islands,* 2nd ed. (San Juan Bautista, Calif.: Galápagos Travel, 1994), p. 78.

13. According to Epler, the number of hotel beds grew from 414 to 1,113 and the number of berths rose from 597 to 1,438 between 1981 and 1995. E-mail correspondence with Bruce Epler, December 1997.

14. Interview with Hugo Andrade, 1995.

15. Epler, *Tourism in the Galápagos Islands,* p. 8.

16. Ibid., p. 18.

17. Mario González, "Stoppage in Galápagos Urges Passage of Law," InterPress Service, November 20, 1997.

18. Epler, *Tourism in the Galápagos Islands,* p. 23; correspondence with Bruce Epler, December 1997.

19. Epler, *Tourism in the Galápagos Islands,* pp. 12–17.

20. Ibid., p. 29.

21. Economist Intelligence Unit (EIU), *EIU Country Profile 1995–96: Ecuador,* 1995, p. 27; Epler, *Tourism in the Galápagos Islands;* correspondence with Epler.

22. Epler, *Tourism in the Galápagos Islands,* p. 30; Telephone interview with Craig MacFarland, November 1997.

23. The increase in fees was vital to get more funds for managing and protecting the national park and it did not cause a drop in tourism. Rather, tourism dropped in the mid-1990s because of the conflicts between fishermen and the parks and because of the border dispute between Ecuador and Peru.

24. Interviews with association members, who asked to remain anonymous.

25. Telephone interview with David Blanton, November 1997.

26. Interviews in 1994; Bruce Epler found that 99 percent of tourists surveyed were "very satisfied or satisfied with the nature they observed in the islands." *Tourism in the Galápagos Islands,* p. 24.

27. Telephone interview with MacFarland.

28. Interview with biologist and tour operator Andrew Drumm. In mid-1998, Drumm joined the staff of The Nature Conservancy in Arlington, Virginia.

29. Research notes from Andrew Drumm.

30. Boyce, *Traveler's Guide,* p. 122.

31. Information from Andrew Drumm.

32. Telephone interview with Jack Grove, November 1997; Jack Grove, *Fishes of the Galápagos* (Stanford, Calif.: Stanford University Press, 1997).

33. Michael Lemonick, "Can the Galápagos Survive?" *Time,* October 30, 1995, p. 82.

34. George Wallace, "Visitor Management in Galápagos National Park," draft (Ft. Collins, Colo.: College of Natural Resources, Colorado State University, January 1992), p. 4.

35. Various Charles Darwin Foundation publications; Richard Harris, "Galápagos Islands at the Crossroads," *All Things Considered* (National Public Radio), December 18, 1995.

36. But as Craig MacFarland, a biologist who was president of the Charles Darwin Foundation for more than a decade, pointed out, the source of the trouble isn't tourism itself but the economic boom: "If the economic boom were goldmining or petroleum or fishing we might have had the same thing as tourism has brought. So it really isn't a function of tourism, *per se.* It's just

because tourism has become the boom [that] . . . really took off in the mid to late 1980s."

37. Interviews with Andrew Drumm and Craig MacFarland; González, "Stoppage in Galápagos."

38. Craig MacFarland, *Case Study: Biodiversity Conservation and Human Population Impacts in the Galápagos Islands, Ecuador* (Falls Church, Va.: Charles Darwin Foundation, 1995), p. 22.

39. *Galápagos Bulletin* (published by the Charles Darwin Foundation), special issue, fall 1995.

40. Interviews with scientists, including Grodfrey Merlen, Andrew Drumm, and David Day, as well as Luis Copiano and other businessmen in Quito, Guayaquil, and the Galápagos. In July 1997, the Clinton administration, at the request of the Ecuadoran government, announced it would prohibit the movement of illegally harvested Galápagos sea cucumbers and shark fins into or through the United States.

41. Interview and correspondence with Johannah Barry, executive director, Charles Darwin Foundation; Linda Cayot, *Recent Increase in Killings of Giant Tortoises on Isabela Island, Galapagos Archipelago* (Puerto Ayora, Santa Cruz Island: Charles Darwin Research Station, n.d.).

42. Lemonick, "Can the Galapagos Survive?"

43. Notes from Andrew Drumm; ibid.; Diana Jean Schemo, "*Homo Sapiens* at War on Darwin's Peaceful Isles," *New York Times,* November 28, 1995; *CNInews2 '97* (published by Conservation Network International), July 1997. In 1997, the Ecuadoran Congress charged Véliz and twelve other members of Congress with corruption and issued warrants for their arrest. Véliz's replacement, Fanny Uribe, was no better: she had been involved in trafficking of sea cucumbers.

44. Notes from Andrew Drumm; Schemo, "*Homo Sapiens.*" Official tourism statistics do not reflect this gloomy picture. Visits by foreigners dropped slightly between 1994 and 1995 but rose sharply in 1996, while the numbers of Ecuadoran visitors continued to climb. "Tabla 1: Visitantes al Parque Nacional Galápagos entre 1979 y 1996," obtained from the Charles Darwin Foundation.

45. *Noticias de Galápagos* (published by the Charles Darwin Foundation), no. 58 (May 1997): 2–3; *CNInews2 '97,* July 1997.

46. González, "Stoppage in Galápagos."

47. Lemonick, "Can the Galapagos Survive?"

48. *CNInews2 '97,* July 1997.

49. González, "Stoppage in Galápagos"; Galápagos National Park, "The Future of the Galápagos Marine Reserve," memo obtained from the Charles Darwin Foundation, November 7, 1997.

50. Mario González, "New Galápagos Protection Law in Force," InterPress Service, March 9, 1998.

51. Johannah Barry, "The Special Law for Galápagos: Comments by the Charles Darwin Foundation," document received via e-mail, March 24, 1998.

52. Telephone interview with Johannah Barry, executive director, Charles Darwin Foundation, December 1997.

53. Barry, "Special Law for Galápagos;" González, "New Galápagos Protection Law."

54. Barry, "Special Law for Galápagos."

55. Wallace, "Visitor Management"; interview with MacFarland.

56. Quoted in William Stolzenburg, "Collision at the Galápagos," *Nature Conservancy*, November/December 1996, p. 16.

57. González, "New Galápagos Protection Law."

58. Marc Miller and Donald Kennedy, "Saving the Galápagos," *New York Times*, op. ed., October 12, 1995, p. A23.

59. Wallace, "Visitor Management," pp. 16–17.

Chapter 5

Costa Rica: On the Beaten Path

Costa Rica is ecotourism's poster child. Since the mid-1980s, this tiny Central American country has been transformed from a staging ground for the covert U.S. war against Nicaragua and a testing ground for USAID's free-trade and privatization policies[1] into a laboratory for "green" tourism. More than any other event, President Oscar Arias Sanchez's 1987 receipt of the Nobel Peace Prize propelled Costa Rica onto the world stage, securing its image as a peaceful country and marking the start of the ecotourism boom. In the 1990s, Costa Rica jumped in popularity to the head of the ecotourism queue, ahead of older nature travel destinations such as the Galápagos Islands, Kenya, and Nepal. In 1992, the U.S. Adventure Travel Society dubbed Costa Rica the "number one ecotourism destination in the world," and a survey conducted by Costa Rica's government showed that most tourists were entering Costa Rica for ecotourism-related reasons.[2]

Ecotourism projects run a wide gamut in Costa Rica. Whereas many developing countries have only a handful of really fine ecotourism experiments, Costa Rica offers a cornucopia of choices, ranging from rustic to luxurious, from counterculture to indigenous culture, from spiritual to scientific, from purely Costa Rican to undeniably North American or European to eclectic, cross-cultural blends. The best of these ecolodges, totaling seventy-nine in 1997, are listed at the beginning of a tourism guidebook titled *The New Key to Costa Rica*.[3] This annual survey, begun as a pilot project in 1993[4] and perfected by researchers Anne Becher and Jane Segleau with the assistance of many of Costa Rica's leading ecotourism experts, was the world's first thorough, impartial assessment of nature tour destinations and ecolodges. It provides ecotourists with critical guidelines and gives the industry itself benchmarks for evaluating hotels and lodges.

It seems that every traveler from the United States who is interested in nature is heading for, or has already been to, Costa Rica. What they find is both a rich and a rough-hewn ecotourism tapestry, an industry full of creativity and experimentation as well as crass opportunism, marketing ploys, and downright scams. Costa Rica's ecotourism panorama is marked by both contradictions and potential. Although the country is marketed as an ecotourism haven, investment policies have favored large, foreign mass tourism developments. Despite Costa Rica's international reputation, ecotourism has so far only partially fulfilled its twin objectives of providing significant resources for national conservation efforts and benefiting local communities.

Costa Rica's natural wonders, encapsulated in the statistic that the country contains 5 percent of the world's biodiversity within just 0.035 percent of the earth's surface, were once a well-kept secret. When my family and I first moved to Costa Rica, in the early 1980s, the country was not yet on the radar screen of most U.S. travel agencies and tour operators. In Costa Rica itself, environmentalism was confined to a small cadre of scientists and national park offices. When we left, a decade later, ecotourism and environmental ethics had become part of Costa Rica's national consciousness. "Ecotourism has helped create the self-image of Costa Ricans. It's now their self-identity," says writer and activist Chris Wille, who together with Diane Jukofsky heads the Rainforest Alliance's office in San José. "That's tremendously important. There's a lexicon of environmentalism here, right up to the president."

Costa Rica has the right stuff, the proper building blocks, for ecotourism. As is the case in many developing countries, Costa Rica's ecotourism industry is built on its national park system. Here, however, it is complemented by other ingredients lacking in many developing countries: its well-functioning democracy, its political stability, the abolition of its army, its respect for human rights, and its (generally) welcoming attitude toward foreigners, particularly the *gringo* variety. Costa Rica has one of the highest standards of living, the largest middle class, the best public health care system, the best public education through the university level, and the highest literacy rate in Latin America. The country has produced an outstanding coterie of scientists and conservationists. More than a hundred local and international environmental NGOs have branches in the country. Costa Rica is physically compact and easy to get around in, with paved roads, telephones, electricity, and a pleasant climate, and it is just a few hours' flight from the United States.

Government Policy and the Private Sector

In the 1960s and 1970s, many tourist resorts, clubs, and parks were developed by Costa Rican entrepreneurs especially for the country's middle and upper classes. Domestic tourism (as in socialist Cuba) was substantial, and most foreign tourists were from other Central American countries. By 1980, tourism was the country's third largest foreign exchange earner (see table 5.1 for Costa Rica's overall growth in tourism since 1976). In the 1980s, the government began for the first time to invest seriously in tourism, reor-

Table 5.1. Costa Rica's Tourism Growth

	1976	1982	1984	1986	1989	1990	1992	1994	1995	1996
Arrivals (in thousands)	299	372	274	261	376	435	611	761	792	555
Gross receipts (in millions of U.S. dollars)	57	131	117	133	207	275	431	626	718	654

Source: Statistics are from the Costa Rican Tourist Board's Department of Statistics and Investigations, supplied by Anne Becher; Elizabeth Boo, *Ecotourism: Potentials and Pitfalls,* vol. 1 (Washington, D.C.: World Wildlife Fund, 1990), p. 26; the World Tourism Organization; the Economist Intelligence Unit; and various articles in the *Tico Times.*
Note: Figures include international tourist arrivals via land, sea, and air.

ganizing and beefing up funding (in part through hotel and airfare taxes) for the country's tourism board, the Costa Rican Tourist Board (ICT). The ICT's operating budget came from a 3 percent hotel room tax and an 8 percent airline ticket tax.[5]

Beginning in the mid-1980s, the visitor pattern began to shift: the number of tourists from North America and Europe grew while both the percentage of domestic tourism and the number of visitors from other Central American countries declined. Investment patterns also changed. In the 1980s, assistance from USAID, the World Bank, and the International Monetary Fund (IMF) mushroomed and helped engineer the shift toward overseas, particularly U.S., investment. This flow of dollars came with strings attached, including the requirement that Costa Rica quietly support the U.S. war against Nicaragua and adhere to wide-ranging structural adjustment policies such as privatization of government businesses and industries, promotion of exports and foreign investment, and cutting of funds for national parks, the ICT, and other public institutions.[6] Tourism was classified as an export industry because it earned foreign exchange.

In 1984, the government of Costa Rica passed legislation to provide investment incentives for hotels, air and sea transportation companies, car rental agencies, and travel agencies. Most of the shares of LACSA, Costa Rica's national airline since the mid-1940s, were gradually sold to Japanese and Salvadoran investors, and the government's share shrank to a mere 3 percent. With passage of the Tourism Development Incentives Law in 1985, tourism projects became eligible for ICT-administered incentives and tax breaks. These included exemptions from property taxes and from import duties for construction and remodeling materials and vehicles such as vans and cars, fishing and pleasure boats, jet skis, dune buggies, and golf carts.[7] To qualify, however, facilities needed to have more than twenty rooms and had to conform to strict standards on use of space and furnishings. "These restrictions often preclude local people from qualifying for incentives," wrote Carole Hill, a professor of anthropology and geography, in 1990.[8] In 1996, the government passed a new tourism incentive law providing hotel developers, car rental agencies, and tour operators with a twelve-year moratorium on taxes in return for investments in new tourism projects. Between 1985 and 1995, the number of hotel rooms nearly tripled, growing from 4,866 to some 12,000.[9] Although the ICT must approve all hotel construction, environmental impact studies were not required until 1995, when a new environmental law required such studies.

In 1987, the ICT kicked off a campaign to attract foreign investment in luxury tourism resorts, and ICT officials later signed a tourism incentives agreement with CINDE (Coalition for Development Initiatives, subsequently renamed Costa Rican Investment and Trade Development Board), an institute created and financed by USAID for the purpose of bringing in overseas investment. USAID's goal was to generate $1 billion in foreign exchange by 1995.[10] The agency began making tourism loans to the United States, as well as to some Costa Rican investors and developers via private Costa Rican banks that had earlier been created as part of USAID's structural adjustment program. USAID funded, for instance, Magil Forest Lodge, which is located on the slopes of a volcano in northern Costa Rica and owned by a former head of the ICT.

Tourism became Costa Rica's number one foreign exchange earner, surpassing coffee and bananas, in 1993, and between 1990 and 1994 thirteen new four- and five-star hotels were built, involving investments of nearly $1 billion.[11] As early as 1990, an ICT document warned that all along Costa Rica's coastlines, U.S., Canadian, Taiwanese, and Japanese investors were buying beachfront property for hotels, condominiums, and vacation homes at an astonishing pace, equal to the rate of all foreign property investment over the previous two to three decades. Experts estimated that by the early 1990s, 80 percent of the country's beachfront property had been purchased by foreigners. Alarmed by this trend, Congressman Gerardo Rudín asked the Tourism Ministry to investigate this "privatization of the coasts."[12] While Costa Rica's reputation as the leading ecotourism destination rose, in practice, under President José María Figueres (1994–1998) the government pursued a two-track policy supporting both ecotourism projects and conventional resorts, with the balance still tilted toward large, foreign-owned projects. "We believe that conservation and concern for the environment is the very centerpiece of creating good business opportunities," Figueres told members of the Botanical Research Institute in Texas in accepting the organization's 1996 International Award for Excellence.[13] Figueres touted ecotourism as one of the best business opportunities in Costa Rica, offered a variety of incentives to tourism investors, and launched a $15 million publicity campaign to attract U.S. and Canadian ecotravelers. Some tighter regulations were also instituted. A new Basic Environment Law, unanimously passed by the Legislative Assembly in September 1995, makes environmental impact studies mandatory for all tourism projects and other development projects. Figueres promoted legislation to give incentives to investors and to improve roads, ports, airports, and street signs, all of which primarily benefit large, foreign-owned tourism projects.

Papagayo

Despite his environmental agenda, Figueres decided in mid-1995 to give a green light to Papagayo, a $3 billion megaresort project—the largest in Central America. Papagayo is set to become Costa Rica's Cancún: a giant conventional resort complex on seventeen beaches strung around the Gulf of Papagayo. Its plans include vacation homes, condominiums, shopping centers, hotels, restaurants, two golf courses, a polo field, and marinas. When all three phases are complete, it will have 25,000–30,000 rooms— twice as many as the 13,000 hotel rooms in all of Costa Rica in 1994. The project's main developer was Grupo Situr, a huge Mexican resort development company that had been involved in the development of Cancún. A new, smooth, U.S.-style highway leads across miles of dry, overgrazed cattle pasture and barren brush country and then snakes down toward the sea, to Situr's first stucco hotel complex, named Caribbean Village even though it overlooks the Pacific Ocean. Equally incongruous is the large sign that reads Ecodesarrollo Papagayo (Ecodevelopment Papagayo), the name of Situr's Costa Rican company. Arnoldo Estaril, Situr's local infrastructure coordinator, conceded that Papagayo "is not an ecotourism project," but he insisted that the name *Ecodesarrollo* is appropriate because "we're trying to do sustainable development in tourism. We're going to plant trees and do an aviary for birds and a butterfly farm and things like that." Environmental activists were not impressed. "Everybody calls themselves 'eco developments,' but Papagayo is a city," reported environmental activist León González.[14]

Papagayo was, in fact, first proposed in the mid-1960s, when sun-and-sand megaresorts were still being pushed as an appropriate development strategy. It is unique because the Costa Rican government itself purchased the land, set it aside by law for tourism development, and then went looking for developers. The region's wars and economic woes kept developers at bay until the early 1990s, when Luis Manuel Chacón, tourism minister under Figueres's predecessor, Rafael Angel Calderón Fournier, and recipient of the "Green Devil" award from German environmentalists for his role in the development of Hotel Tambor, a large and environmentally destructive project on Costa Rica's Pacific coast, struck a deal with Situr. The developer received an uncustomarily long forty-nine-year lease (instead of the usual twenty years), generous tax exemptions, and unusually large plots of land, including islands normally protected from development. The ICT agreed to put in infrastructure (roads, electricity, water) and permitted construction to start before the government's master plan was prepared and approved.

Soon, the local municipality, university scientists, environmentalists, and the government's newly created ombudsman all launched complaints. Situr was charged with cutting down trees, dredging a mangrove swamp, building roads without proper permits, and building below the fifty-meter (approximately 164-foot) high-tide mark. Papagayo broke ground when such resort complexes were being repudiated worldwide and when Costa Rica was marketing itself as the world's premier ecotourism destination. Michael Kaye, owner of Costa Rica Expeditions, one of the leading ecotourism agencies, deemed Papagayo "yesterday's resort for tomorrow's market"[15] and predicted that it would become a white elephant. Even as a megaresort, Papagayo is problematic: offshore winds are strong, the beaches are narrow, and the ocean drops off sharply. Other opponents contended that Costa Rica's government does not have the capacity to control and police such a huge project. Over the first few years of construction, court actions repeatedly halted or slowed the Papagayo project.

Soon after the Figueres government took office, in May 1994, it ordered a thorough review of the project. In mid-1995, after conducting an environmental impact study, reviewing the legal issues, and preparing a legally binding master plan limiting building height to three stories and requiring green space, the government announced that the Papagayo project could proceed. Figueres's tourism minister, Carlos Roesch, explained that "it would be less damaging for the best interests of the nation to do whatever was necessary to salvage the Project instead of opting to cancel it" because cancellation would have "catastrophic effects."[16] In other words, Papagayo was too far along to stop.

Equally unstoppable is the pace of development up and down Costa Rica's coasts. "Until the early 1980s, the beaches were ours," bemoaned legislator and former planning minister Ottón Solís in a 1997 interview. "Now all the best ones are American and Canadian owned. Costa Rican families can't go anymore. It's too expensive, and it's an alien culture. The signs and talk are all in English." In a detailed 1996 survey of hotel ownership along most of Costa Rica's Pacific beaches, ecotourism analyst and writer Anne Becher found that the majority (57 percent) of hotels and resorts were foreign owned. Foreign investment is most dominant, Becher says, along "the most famous and ritzy" beaches, whereas Costa Rican–

owned hotels (and those most frequented by Costa Ricans) are along the least desirable beaches.[17]

With few exceptions, most beach resorts make no claim of being involved in ecotourism. Many, in fact, have been built in violation of the maritime zone, an imaginary 200-meter strip (approximately 656-foot) of land running along Costa Rica's coastline above the high-tide mark and intended to control beachfront construction. The zone is divided into a 50-meter (164-foot) strip closest to the shore, where no development is allowed, and the remaining 150 meters (492 feet), where land can be leased from local municipalities and construction is permitted so long as zoning, taxation, and ownership guidelines are followed. Most often, these guidelines are not followed. Foreigners, for instance, cannot obtain a concession for beachfront property unless they have resided in Costa Rica for at least five years, and foreign-based or foreign-owned companies do not qualify. Many foreigners get around this by applying for concessions in the names of Costa Rican partners.[18]

The struggles over Hotel Playa Tambor and Papagayo, though losses for the cause of ecotourism, helped build Costa Rica's environmental movement and stimulate public debate over mega- versus modest tourism projects. In the wake of these controversies, the ICT modified its regulations to permit *albergues* (lodges), *cabinas* (cabins), and *pensións* (pensions, or guest houses) with just ten (instead of twenty) rooms to qualify for incentives and tax breaks. But, as Ottón Solís pointed out in a 1997 interview, "To qualify you need a tourism contract, and to get a contract you have to have consultants and present feasibility studies, and all that is possible only for large companies. The big hotels get the tax exemptions, and the little things are left for locals."

Santa Clara Lodge

The Santa Clara Lodge, an economical six-room hostel on a Costa Rican-owned cattle ranch in Guanacaste that caters to Costa Ricans and foreign hikers and backpackers, has received a high rating in the *New Key to Costa Rica*'s survey of hotels practicing sustainable tourism. Its attractions include visits to three nearby national parks, horseback rides, and hikes in the surrounding countryside. In the early 1990s, when cattle prices were down, the ranch's owner, Marita Quesada, decided that tourism might offer a way for her to hold on to her 114-hectare (approximately 282-acre) family farm. The family took out a loan from a local bank, built two cabins and a small mineral-water swimming pool, put in a generator, printed brochures, invited the press and tour agencies to have a look, and began getting bookings. But

Ismael Mojica, Quesada's son-in-law, who has studied hotel management and runs the lodge, says that from the outset he has encountered only official obstacles: "Those in charge of the ICT classification system are very rigid. They do not support microbusinesses."

The Santa Clara Lodge was deemed too small to qualify for any ICT tax breaks, yet it has to pay 13 percent of its revenues in taxes to the government and the ICT. In addition, in just three years, the floating interest rate on its bank loan rose from 19 percent to an untenable 37.5 percent. San José and European travel agencies and tour operators take an additional 25 percent to 34 percent for bookings, raising the price to about $65 per night—too high, says Mojica, for the type of tourist Santa Clara targets. The lodge cannot afford the $500 fee to rent a booth at EXPOTUR's annual trade show, and, making matters even more difficult, soon after the lodge had distributed its brochures, listed itself with a number of travel agencies, and managed to get some press and guidebook coverage, the telephone company suddenly changed the guest house's number. The Santa Clara Lodge needs 60 percent occupancy to be profitable, but occupancy plummeted to approximately 5 percent, forcing Quesada and her family to consider selling the place. Congressman Ottón Solís argued that the ICT should be mandated to promote Costa Rican tourism projects, including awarding tax breaks and incentives to small local tourism projects, providing low-interest bank loans, and giving technical, quality control, and marketing assistance. Further, Solís argued, the ICT should negotiate with EXPOTUR to ensure that smaller establishments can exhibit at its trade shows and should negotiate with the telephone company and other government agencies to ensure that such places are properly supported.

Even medium-size ecotourism operators that could qualify for government incentives find ICT regulations weighted against them and toward the very largest projects. "Ecotourism operators find it very difficult to benefit from ICT's incentive program, where you need to bring in a container full of air conditioners or whatever to really get a tax break," Louis Wilson, owner of Las Tortugas Lodge, told me in an interview. While surveying for the *New Key to Costa Rica* the "sustainability" of hotels involved in nature tourism or ecotourism, researchers Anne Becher and Jane Segleau found that 60 percent of the operations they recognized for extraordinary efforts toward sustainable tourism were too small to receive ICT incentives. "The size barrier denies a majority of the ecolodgings we surveyed any government financial incentives," Becher explained in a 1997 interview. Like others, she concludes that "all the ICT breaks and concessions go to big projects. There is no government policy favoring small businesses." Yet often, these small- and medium-size ecotour operators conserve and protect the environment more vigilantly than do the large, mainstream tourism developments.

National Parks and Protected Areas

In 1502, when Christopher Columbus came ashore south of present-day Limón, he named the land Costa Rica (Rich Coast) under the mistaken belief that the country was full of precious minerals. Only in the past few decades has this misnomer seemed appropriate as scientists, conservationists, and tourists discovered Costa Rica's vast ecological richness. As part of the narrow isthmus joining North America and South America, Costa Rica has flora and fauna from both continents as well as its own endemic species. This country the size of West Virginia boasts more bird species (850) than are found in the United States and Canada combined and more varieties of butterflies than in all of Africa. It has more than 6,000 kinds of flowering plants (including 1,500 varieties of orchids), 208 species of mammals, 200 species of reptiles, and more than 35,000 species of insects. A long spine of volcanic mountains runs down the center of Costa Rica and the country contains twelve distinct ecosystems, ranging from mountain peaks some 3,840 meters (12,600 feet) high, cloud-covered peaks down to white- and black-sand beaches along the Pacific and Caribbean coasts. Costa Rica is, as former minister of natural resources Alvaro Umaña put it, a biological "superpower."[19]

Today, more than 25 percent of Costa Rica's territory, with an estimated land value of $2 billion, is under some form of protection. Worldwide, the average is just 3 percent. Costa Rica has a long tradition of environmental protection, dating from 1828, but it wasn't until 1969 that its first national park was officially created. By 1990, the country had 230 different protected areas, falling into eight categories, ranging from completely protected reserves to national parks where tourism, research, and infrastructure are allowed (but nothing can be extracted) to refuges where controlled development and extraction are permitted. Some 12 percent of Costa Rica falls under the rubric of national parks and other strictly protected areas. In recent years, the national parks and their surrounding buffer areas have been reorganized into nine regional conservation areas or megaparks, each financed autonomously and headed by a director who is responsible for both management and community outreach.

In creating parks and protected areas, Costa Rica's government pledged to buy out, rather than forcibly remove, those living within the park boundaries. Although this is a more humane approach, it has proved costly and time-consuming, with landowners often waiting years for payment and the park service legally unable to stop logging, farming, and grazing until land is completely acquired. By 1995, an estimated 12 percent of national park land still needed to be purchased.

Costa Rica's world-renowned system of national parks and protected areas has served as the springboard for ecotourism. Between 1984 and 1988, the number of foreigners visiting parks more than doubled, and the number doubled again between 1988 and 1992. By the early 1990s, 63 percent of foreign visitors to Costa Rica went to at least one park, according to Tourism Ministry statistics. Yet ironically, while tourism was becoming Costa Rica's largest foreign exchange earner and many private entrepreneurs were turning handsome profits from tourism in protected areas, the national park service itself was falling into crisis. The parks are plagued by insufficient funds, personnel, and infrastructure; incursions by loggers, gold miners, and homesteaders; and uneven usage, with some parks inaccessible to all but the hardiest backpackers and others overrun with visitors. With few exceptions—Poás Volcano, Irazú Volcano, and Santa Rosa National Parks—parks do not have visitor centers, roads, restaurants, or other facilities. There are campsites and hiking trails, but no hotels and often no trained naturalist guides. At the same time, the number of privately owned reserves has grown dramatically, and increasing numbers of tourists are spending their time and money in these reserves.

The founders of Costa Rica's park system[20] sought to preserve unique ecological areas for posterity, scientific investigation, and environmental education. They did not initially view national parks as areas for public recreation and did not seek to pay for them through tourism. During the 1970s, the Costa Rican government financed most of the parks' land acquisitions and operating budgets, and international conservation organizations provided scientists and technical advice. However, with the severe economic crisis of the early 1980s, the park system was forced to seek substantial external funding, mainly from U.S. environmental organizations and later from foreign governments. Between 1981 and 1995, Costa Rica's national park system received more than $50 million in foreign donations, equivalent to about half its total budget and covering 90 percent of all parkland purchases.[21] Although Costa Rica's economic crisis subsided by the mid-1980s, the park system continued to face financial problems, partly because new protected areas continued to be created and partly because the IMF, the World Bank, and USAID forced the government to cut park funding and staff. In the late 1980s, Alvaro Umaña, the Arias government's capable minister of natural resources, energy, and mines, succeeded in raising about $45 million in local currency for the park system through five debt-for-nature swaps, complex transactions involving international lending banks, Costa Rica's Central Bank, conservation organizations, and foreign governments. In these swaps, lending countries or institutions forgave part of Costa Rica's foreign debt in exchange for conservation projects including land purchases, reforestation projects, environmental education programs, and job creation for those living in buffer zone areas.[22]

By the mid-1990s, however, external grants had been sharply cut and the number of debt swaps had slowed.[23] Many international donors concluded that Costa Rica had conserved enough land and that funds should go to other countries.[24] Others began financing private reserves in Costa Rica. Faced with financial crisis, the government for the first time turned to tourism to provide substantial funding for the parks. In August 1994, Minister of Natural Resources, Energy, and Mines René Castro Salazar suddenly announced a steep rise in park entrance fees for foreigners: $15 at the gate, $10 for advance purchases, and about $5.25 for bulk purchases by travel agents. Until then, foreign and Costa Rican tourists had paid the same modest entrance fee (about $1), with an equally modest annual yield of $0.5-$1 million. The result of the fee hike was swift and dramatic. Despite a considerable drop in the number of foreigners visiting national parks, entrance fees netted $3.78 million during the first nine months of 1995, four times more than in all of 1994. Yet these additional funds did not expand the park service's overall budget: they were simply not enough to help offset the shortfall in government funds and external donations. In June 1995, National Parks administrator Fernando Bermúdez told Anne Becher that the park service's financial state was "very bad. We are operating below the minimum necessary for personnel, infrastructure, and land payments."

Although the concept of a two-tiered park entrance fee—a low rate for nationals and a higher one for foreign visitors—is widely accepted around the world, members of Costa Rica's tourism industry strongly criticized the fee formula as too high. Some tour operators stopped offering day tours to parks such as Poás Volcano and Irazú Volcano National Park, which tourists visited for only a few hours, or to parks without trail systems, guides, or other facilities offered in private reserves. In early 1996, after playing around with various other formulas, the government finally announced that entrance fees for foreigners would be lowered to just $6 at all parks. This compromise seemed to quell criticism while still guaranteeing increased income for the national park service.

Under the plan, 75 percent of park entrance fees go into the operating budget of the conservation area of origin and 25 percent supports conservation areas where tourism and income are still low. At the same time, foreign donors, including the Canadian, U.S., Dutch, and Swedish governments, have become *padrinos* (godfathers) of individual conservation areas and provide modest support. It is hoped that eventually each conservation area will create its own endowment and obtain its operating budget from interest earned. That, however, remains a dream even in the best-endowed conservation areas, and additional questions of how to adequately manage national conservation areas still loom.

Adverse Effects of Ecotourism

Costa Rica's national park system has received minimal benefit and many new problems from the ecotourism boom. Several small Pacific coast parks, such as Manuel Antonio National Park, Cabo Blanco Wildlife Reserve, and Carara Biological Reserve, have suffered environmental decay and loss of wildlife from far too many visitors. Tiny Manuel Antonio, whose curved, white-sand beaches and mountain backdrop have made it Costa Rica's most famous national park, received a staggering 250,000 visitors in 1994. The rapid, uncontrolled growth of more than a hundred mostly small hotels, as well as restaurants, bars, nightclubs, casinos, and other tourist concessions, along the road leading to Manuel Antonio is proof that small can also be ugly and destructive. The area around the park and the nearby town of Quepos both lack sewage systems, so refuse is dumped directly into the sea. Former park director Alvaro Ugalde calls Manuel Antonio "a red alert" signaling that government regulation, stricter zoning laws and enforcement, and environmental impact studies are needed for all tourism development, not just the large resorts. In the mid-1990s, the park service closed Manuel Antonio National Park and other parks on particular days and set limits on the number of visitors permitted to enter. Although these moves are welcomed by environmentalists, former park official José Courrau worries that the limits have simply been "pulled out of the air" and believes that much more scientifically based criteria for controlling numbers may be needed.[25] At the other end of the spectrum, a number of Costa Rica's largest parks, including Braulio Carrillo National Park, just fifteen minutes from San José, are rarely visited because they lack even basic infrastructure. Although they remain undamaged by visitors, they earn virtually nothing from tourism.

Parks and the Rural Poor

Parallel to these debates over how to finance and manage the parks in the wake of the ecotourism boom have been ongoing conflicts with rural poor people living around the parks. Costa Rican park officials and scientists did not initially view these protected areas as sources of income and employment for those living around their boundaries. Rather, as is the case in Africa, they adhered to a preservationist philosophy that sought to isolate the parks and prevent any outside encroachment. Costa Rican's conservationists had good reason for concern because outside the parks, environmental destruction has continued at an alarming pace. By the 1980s, Costa Rica had, outside its parks, the highest rate of deforestation in all of Latin America; in many areas, squatters and homesteaders have also felled forests and cleared land inside parks for grazing and agriculture.

Corcovado National Park

The most volatile, intractable, and long-running conflict between rural people and parks has centered on gold, not trees. Corcovado National Park, on the Osa Peninsula along the southern Pacific coast, is recognized by scientists as one of the richest tropical areas on earth and is widely considered "the jewel in the crown" of Costa Rica's park system.[26] In the early 1980s, large, well-financed mining companies consolidated control outside the park, driving hundreds of small gold miners (*oreros*) into the park, where they killed fish and wild animals for food and silted and poisoned the rivers with the mercury they used in panning. Over the years, the Rural Guard (rural police) and park authorities periodically rounded up and expelled the fortune seekers only to have them return on their release. On occasion, scientists were forced to abandon their research inside Corcovado and tourism camps were closed down. Even though tourism in Corcovado National Park was earning an estimated $1 million per year, twice as much as gold mining was netting, the *perception* was that mining was potentially more lucrative, especially for the region's poor.

In 1985, parks director Alvaro Ugalde asked University of Pennsylvania biologist Daniel Janzen, who had worked since 1972 in Santa Rosa National Park in Guanacaste province, to study the adverse environmental effects of the Corcovado gold miners and propose a way to get them out of the park. Janzen's findings were shocking—some 1,400 miners and hangers-on were living inside the park, game animals had been "practically eliminated," and most of the rivers had become "canals, sterile and full of sediment." The report predicted that the park's ecosystem would recover only after most of the miners were removed, but it said that police action was no long-term solution. Rather, Janzen proposed that to stop such invasions, "the [park service] should involve itself deeply with neighboring communities and other planning agencies to show the benefits of the park."[27] This early articulation of one of ecotourism's precepts proved, of course, much easier to propose than to implement. The miners showed little fear of arrest; the government itself was wary of confrontation because Costa Rica has traditionally tolerated peasant land invasions. Eventually, the park service decided to permit low-level incursions of as many as 200 *oreros* inside the park.

The *oreros* crisis did precipitate a rethinking of how ecotourism and other income-generating activities can become components in a new approach to community relations. By the mid-1990s, some former miners had found work in the dozen-odd ecotourism lodges, tent camps, and private reserves established in the buffer zone around the park.[28] In addition, *oreros* now own and run several income-generating projects. One multidimensional project, BOSCOSA, works with some of the estimated 5,000 families in Corcovado's buffer zone area in sustainable timber harvesting, improved agricultural methods, conservation education, and community development activities. One group, consisting of members of a once successful gold-mining cooperative, have formed a community association, Coope Unioro, to try living communally and self-sufficiently by growing vegetables, harvesting traditional jungle foods, experimenting with medicinal herbs, and hosting ecotourists. They have built a rustic lodge on fifty acres of land adjacent to the national park and offer hikes, horseback rides, and river excursions in the park and surrounding areas.

Guanacaste National Park

On a national level, the *oreros* crisis forced a number of Costa Rica's leading conservationists to rethink the way the national parks are run. "The concept of a national park," Janzen explained in an interview, "as a place that you set aside, administer with staff sent by the central office, and guard with a gun is dying here very, very rapidly, and we're trying to make it die as fast as possible." In 1987, Janzen adopted the new principles in expanding Santa Rosa from a small, unsustainable 10,000-hectare (24,710-acre) park into the 120,000-hectare (296,500-acre) Guanacaste National Park, making it the largest protected dry tropical forest in Central America or Mexico. The new park, financed through Costa Rica's first debt-for-nature swap, incorporates both biologically unique, unspoiled land and what Janzen describes as "trashed old pastures, land that had very little economic value and still had some people living on it here and there." The plan was twofold: restoration of pastureland to its original dry tropical condition and incorporation of the people. Janzen argued, "If you threw them out you had a social problem. We decided wherever there were people we were buying out who wanted employment in the conservation area, we'd employ them. This very quickly evolved into a new kind of administration." A number of farmers have been retrained to be caretakers, firefighters, research assistants, and guides, and their cattle help spread seeds to rejuvenate the original dry tropical forest. Although there was some resistance from middle-management park officials, the plan has worked: the land is recovering and there are, as Janzen puts it, "happy people" living around and the park working in it.

Villas del Caribe

On much of the Caribbean coast, such levels of community integration have not matched that of the Osa Peninsula or Guanacaste National Park on the Pacific coast. Costa Rica's Caribbean coast has its own distinct culture. A third of its people are Afro-Caribbean, and English dialects, Protestant denominations, and reggae music predominate over Spanish, Catholicism, and salsa. In recent years, Nicaraguan refugees, many of whom are Miskito-Afro-Caribbeans from Nicaragua's Caribbean coast, have settled here as well. Historically, most of the region's economic activities have involved exploitation of resources for sale to the international market. Yet until recently, this coastal region was an isolated and economically depressed backwater. Its population rose and fell with the boom and bust of exports: lumber, bananas, and turtle shells, meat, eggs, and *calipee,* a substance found under the lower shell and used to make soap.

From the main port of Limón southward to the Panama border are several protected areas and Caribbean towns, all scenes in recent years of conflicts between local people and outsiders for control of land, natural resources, and the tourism market. In the early 1990s, controversy flared around one of the area's foreign-owned beach resorts, which was built by Maurice Strong, arguably the most powerful man in international environmental circles. Strong, a Canadian multimillionaire, businessman, and diplomat, organized the 1992 Earth Summit (the United Nations Conference on Environment and Development, or UNCED) in Brazil, from which flowed the Costa Rica–based Earth Council and Agenda 21, an action plan intended to chart a path for corporate responsibility into the twenty-first century. In the spring of 1992, while Strong was gathering together world leaders, environmental activists, and indigenous groups for the Earth Summit, his company, Desarrollos Ecológicos (Ecological Development), was putting the finishing touches on his $35 million, twelve-suite luxury beach hotel south of the town of Puerto Viejo. Villas del Caribe uses recycling and composting containers and offers horseback rides and nature hikes, although, as one researcher stated, these add up to "very modest offerings of ecotourism" given Strong's position of leadership within the movement for sustainable development.[29] Even more troubling to area residents, Strong did not have clear title to the land: his 300-hectare (approximately 741-acre) property, including the hotel, falls inside both the Gandoca-Manzanillo Wildlife Refuge (where development is restricted) and the Kekoldi Indian Reserve (where only Indians or the government may buy property and any construction must be approved by the Indian association). Strong's Costa Rican partners included an architect and a lawyer who attempted, ultimately unsuccessfully, to use their influence with Costa Rican politicians to reduce the size of the reserve in order to exclude the hotel. In an interview prior to the Earth Summit, Strong denied he had built improperly within the Reserve and said he had met with Indian leaders, who did not object to his hotel.[30] The reserve's leaders, it turned out, had a different story. "He's supporting Indians and conservation around the world, that's what he's doing in Brazil, and here he's doing the complete opposite," declared Demetrio Mayorga, president of the Kekoldi Indian Association. Mayorga and other Indian leaders said they resented not being consulted about the project, and they expressed reservations about tourism development by outside entrepreneurs.[31] Costa Rican conservationists and government officials were equally annoyed. An advisor to the Ministry of Natural Resources, Energy, and Mines told the press that this was "not even tourism—just land speculation."[32]

The controversy, which was exposed by Greenpeace at the Earth Summit and published in the Costa Rican press and elsewhere, was clearly embarrassing to Strong, who abandoned plans to build a private home and other hotels in the area and quietly agreed to pay $5,000 to an organization representing the local Indians. He also pledged to "look for funds" to help the Indians buy out foreigners within the reserve. Strong did not, however, propose turning his hotel over to the reserve, paying rent for the land, or giving the Indians a share of his profits—options more commensurate with his international reputation. Over the next few years, Strong raised about $60,000 and transmitted it to The Nature Conservancy, earmarked for the Indian reserve. Strong, who never acknowledged his mistakes or apologized for them, continues to own the hotel. The public controversy has died down, but resentment remains among Indians living in the reserve. As one researcher who thoroughly investigated the controversy explained, "There's a huge gap between what could be done and what is being done. They [Strong's company] have the resources to have built a model eco-hotel, to have promoted ecotourism in the area, to have really developed and stimulated the economy. Instead they have a hotel built amidst controversy and with hostile attempts to change the status of the land it's on."[33] Villas del Caribe has never made it onto *The New Key to Costa Rica*'s list of true ecotourism hotels and lodges.

Tortuguero

Today, the turtle nesting hamlet of Tortuguero, along the canals running northward from Limón, is most frequently cited as the place where a national park and ecotourism have worked together to benefit both the cause of conservation and the economic well-being of the surrounding community. The only transportation is by boat—river taxis for tourists and wealthier Costa Ricans and dugout canoes, known as *cayucos,* for local residents. There's a small landing strip in Tortuguero but, so far, no roads, and this has helped stave off mass tourism. In recent years, however, the number of flights and the size of boat engines have increased substantially, and this has increased both noise pollution and tourism numbers.

As tour boat owner Modesto Watson maneuvers his awning-covered launch, *Riverboat Francesca* (named for his wife and partner, Fran, a former Peace Corps volunteer), up the 80.5-kilometer (50-mile) coastal canal linking Limón to Tortuguero, he points out sea turtles, crocodiles, sloths, monkeys, parrots, toucans, and iridescent blue morpho butterflies. Along the canals, ecotravelers pass homesteads and tiny hamlets where the wooden houses are built on stilts. "We're not just taking you from point A to point Z," Watson tells his mostly foreign clientele. "Traveling is like music: the pause between each musical note is what makes it beautiful. You should also enjoy the pause between where you're leaving from and where you're going to."

Watson, a Nicaraguan who opposed both the Sandinistas and U.S. interventionism in the 1980s, is part of the new breed of entrepreneurs riding Tortuguero's ecotourism wave. "Ecotourism has brought a 100 percent improvement to people in Tortuguero, and I've seen a change in mentality as well," he proclaims. "People now see that through conservation they realize more income." A closer examination shows, however, that although ecotourism has spawned both entrepreneurship and environmentalism, its effects on the local population are more mixed.

Tourists come to Tortuguero to visit the largest nesting beach in the Caribbean for green sea turtles and smaller numbers of leatherbacks, hawksbills, and loggerheads. Besides its remoteness, Tortuguero is protected by other conditions that make it unsuitable for resort tourism: the weather is almost always cloudy and rainy, the beach is composed of black, silty sand, the surf is rough, there are sharks, and the national park backs up to the beach, thereby reducing the land available for hotels. Although Puerto Viejo, Cahuita, Talamanca, and other spots along Costa Rica's Caribbean coast are promoted as ecotourism destinations, it is Tortuguero that has been most fully identified with sound conservation and small-scale ecotourism.

In the mid-1950s, American herpetologist Archie Carr founded the Caribbean Conservation Corporation's (CCC's) Green Turtle Research Station in Tortuguero, which has conducted widely acclaimed research, tagged and tracked some 26,000 green turtles, and played an active role in conservation efforts. By the 1970s, the turtle trade had declined, and in 1975, largely as a result of the CCC's work, Tortuguero National Park was established to protect most of the green turtles' nesting beach and nearly 20,000 hectares (49,420 acres) of lowland tropical forest and rivers.[34] In the late 1980s, the park was extended to create a corridor linking it with Barra de Colorado National Wildlife Reserve to the north. Creation of the park meant that turtling and forestry (at least until the late 1990s) were no longer allowed near Tortuguero, and some *campesinos* with farms within the park were bought out by the national park service. Prohibition of the use of natural resources profoundly changed the economic base of the village.[35] Tortuguero residents had little option but to turn to the new economic activity just getting started—tourism.

In 1988, there were just five tour boats carrying passengers from Limón and only two or three hotels. By 1995, there were forty-two boats and seventeen hotels and lodges in Tortuguero. In 1986, less than 20 percent of Tortuguero's tiny population made a living from tourism. By 1991, approximately 70 percent worked directly or indirectly in tourism, including work with the park and the CCC. During this same period, average income doubled, and new migrants brought the local population to some 500.[36] In addition, the number of tourists visiting Tortuguero National Park rose fifteen-fold, from 2,004 in 1986 (1,032 foreign visitors and 972 domestic) to about 30,000 in 1993.

However, surveys of ownership of Tortuguero's tourism infrastructure[37] reveal a more complicated and sobering reality: the rapid pace of tourism expansion has worked against local entrepreneurs, who need time to gather sufficient skills and capital; and there is a growing economic gap between those few local owners of tourism businesses and those who are either salaried employees or are totally outside the tourism sector.[38] This indicates that although the majority of tourism dollars at least stay within Costa Rica, most profits from the lucrative package tours do not stay in Tortuguero. Randy Leavitt, director of the CCC's research station, estimates that only 5 percent to 10 percent of the tourists who visit the area do so independently, using local hotels and restaurants and many of these purchase a tour package from their boatmen in Limón; they don't hire local guides or boats in Tortuguero.

The ability of Tortuguero residents to control and benefit from ecotourism has been hindered by a lack of organization and by weak kinship, community, and institutional ties. Community cohesiveness and participation have been impeded by "powerful internal and external obstacles . . . from factionalism within the village to state policies that promote centralized planning and the accumulation of capital among large . . . tourist facilities," writes geographer Susan Place.[39] Place argues that promotion of domestic tourism could strengthen Tortuguero's local entrepreneurs and counterbalance foreign-oriented tourism.

Although its effects on the local community have been mixed, ecotourism has been largely good for conservation. "Because Tortuguero is really a little enclave and all around it is a national park, I can see the turtles surviving and Tortuguero being a good example of how ecotourism can be successful forever," says former CCC ecologist Bob Carlson. Most local people now *do* see economic value in protecting the turtles and their eggs as well as other threatened species, such as the West Indian manatee and the macaw.

The CCC, the park service, and the Canadian-financed Cabo Palma Biological Station have played a positive role both in training local turtle guides and in organizing a guides' cooperative, which has become a model for good turtle protection and viewing. Tourists must visit the nesting sites in groups of ten or fewer led by a trained guide, and only one group at a time is permitted near a nesting female. The CCC has also designed, and the town has adopted, a zoning plan—purportedly the first such plan in Central America—based on the needs of the turtles. There are, however, some worrisome trends. Lodge owners, whose tourism profits depend completely on the national park, offer night tours, which are harmful to the wildlife. Waterfowl, kingfishers, and herons, for example, safely perch near the banks during twilight, when they can still see. Night tours on the canals disturb the birds, forcing them to relocate after dark, when they are more likely to be eaten by caimans.

The biggest threat to conservation, however, will come from a road currently under construction that is certain to bring a sharp increase in tourism. There has been suspicion that lumber interests are behind this project, which in 1995 opened a wide swath through several miles of the park's rain forest. The Tortuguero community was divided, with those involved in tourism and conservation adamantly opposing the road and farmers and owners of small businesses supporting it. If completed, this road could ruin the balance between conservation and tourism.

In 1998, loggers began felling trees along the canal's banks, beside the illegal dirt road, and on properties within the corridor where owners had refused to sell. Investigations revealed that the 5,500 hectares (13,590 acres) of forest along the canals had been inexplicably left out of the national park expansion when the corridor was created in the late 1980s and, further, that the Forestry Law of 1996 permitted persons without property title to obtain logging permits. Many feared, as the *Tico Times* put it, that the "bad old days" of profiting from environmental destruction rather than conservation were returning to Tortuguero.[40]

Private Reserves

Costa Rica's history of private reserves and refuges is even older than its national park system. By the mid-1950s, the country was already home to a number of foreign conservationists and scientists, including ornithologist Alexander Skutch, botanist Leslie Holdridge, and herpetologist Archie Carr, who were interested in preserving particular types of land, flora, or fauna.

From the 1960s until the late 1980s, the number of private reserves grew modestly. Most were intimately connected to scientific research and had a close relationship with the national parks. Since the 1980s, the number of private reserves and refuges has grown rapidly, totaling several hundred by 1996 and equal to an estimated 2 percent to 5 percent of Costa Rica's territory. About 50 of these belong to an association of private reserve owners. Most are forest reserves; many have been bought by foreigners or international conservation organizations such as the World Wildlife Fund, Conservation International, and the Rainforest Alliance; and an estimated 50 to 150, ranging in size from 10 to 5,000 hectares (approximately 25 to 12,355 acres), are involved in ecotourism. Private reserves do not need to register with the government, but if they do, they receive a package of benefits including tax exemption on fixed assets, exemption from real estate tax, technical assistance with projects, and guaranteed expulsion of squatters within three days.[41]

Although most ecotourists are drawn to Costa Rica by the international reputation of its large, well-protected national park system, increasingly these visitors spend their time and money in private reserves, which offer accommodations, more infrastructure, and higher-quality interpretation. In one survey, Canadian ecotourists ranked four private reserves—Monteverde, La Selva, Rara Avis, and Marenco—as "the most impressive natural areas visited."[42] Three of these are discussed in detail in the sections that follow: Monteverde Cloud Forest Reserve and La Selva Biological Station[43] are two of Costa Rica's oldest private reserves that have expanded from scientific research into ecotourism, and the third, Rara Avis, can be considered Costa Rica's first "intentional" ecotourism project. All have grown with the ecotourism wave sweeping Costa Rica.

Monteverde Cloud Forest Reserve

Monteverde Cloud Forest Reserve is located in the Tilarán Mountains, several hours' drive up a bone-jarring, muffler-mashing, switchback dirt road off the Pan-American Highway. It is the most famous of Costa Rica's private reserves and the country's leading ecotourism destination. Internationally acclaimed for its sound conservation and tourism strategies, Monteverde is blessed by its relative inaccessibility, careful monitoring by scientists, well-trained guides, and cohesive, socially responsible local community. Today, ecotourism earnings are helping to finance the purchase and protection of the 50,180 hectares (124,000 acres) in the Monteverde area that have been set aside in both private reserves and public parks. Since the late 1980s, however, as the tourism explosion has brought world attention and new funds to Monteverde, it has also put strains on its ecosystem and nearby population.

Monteverde, a bucolic, misty mountaintop on Costa Rica's continental divide, was "discovered" in 1951 by twelve North American Quaker farming families who moved to Costa Rica to protest the peacetime military draft in the United States. (Costa Rica had abolished its army in 1948.) The new immigrants found that environmental destruction was already moving up the slopes toward Monteverde: Costa Rican loggers, agriculturalists, and cattle ranchers were rapidly clear-cutting the dense cloud and mountain forest in an agrarian settlement program supported by the government.

In the 1950s, the Quaker immigrants bought 1,200 hectares (2,965 acres) at the top of the mountain from a local land company, began dairy farming and set up a milk and cheese factory, which was run as a profit-sharing cooperative and quickly became the economic hub of the area. The factory is run democratically by its 500 shareholders (who must be area residents, and none can own more than 5 percent of the capital) and has from the outset been actively involved in community affairs. "In one way or another, we always participated in the community, with education, health, roads, and general services," explains José Luis Vargas, the cheese factory's general manager.

Although the Quakers were a minority, until recently most newcomers shared their values, and thus their original ideals were preserved. Monteverde, as well as the two neighboring, largely Costa Rican communities of Santa Elena and Cerro Plano, developed strong, self-reliant local systems of governance that blended Quaker values of simplicity, democracy, nonviolence, and personal and community responsibility with Costa Rica's strong traditions of participatory democracy, nonmilitarism, and cooperative societies. At the outset, the Monteverde settlers set up a town meeting, and this is still the basic governing body, wherein everyone has a voice and decisions are made by consensus rather than majority vote.

The Monteverde Cloud Forest Reserve, on which Monteverde's ecotourism industry is based, began when the original Quakers set aside 554 hectares (1,370 acres) of virgin tropical forest, known as the *bosque eterno* (eternal forest), to protect their watershed and buffer the force of wind on their pastures. In the early 1970s, George Powell, a biologist working in Monteverde, proposed that the *bosque eterno* and another 328 hectares, or 810 acres (for which he raised funds to purchase), be joined to create the Monteverde Cloud Forest Reserve in order to protect the primary breeding area of Monteverde's rare endemic golden toad. The Monteverde community granted a ninety-nine-year lease and management of the reserve to the San José–based Tropical Science Center (TSC), a nonprofit scientific research and educational organization. The TSC built a field station at the entrance to the reserve, and increasing numbers of biologists, students, and bird-watchers came to study the cloud forest's flora and fauna. Through land purchases financed by U.S. conservation organizations and private individuals, the reserve has grown to 10,522 hectares (26,000 acres), encompassing eight ecological zones and linked physically to purchases of Monteverde Conservation League (a local nonprofit organization) and to Costa Rica's national park system.

According to longtime Monteverde residents John Trostle and Wilford "Wolf" Guindon, the Quakers who settled here did not initially have a strong environmental ethic. Guindon told me he arrived as a "chain saw expert," and his "vision of development was clearing pastures and building roads and schools" until he began working with George Powell and got "converted to a philosophy of protection." Today, Guindon is the most respected forest guard in the reserve. Sadly, however, the Quakers' conservation efforts did not save the golden toad, which now appears to be extinct. One of the lessons learned, Guindon says, is that "protection of forests and primary habitat doesn't guarantee survival of all species. It's all linked together to a much larger area and much bigger problems than we'd attempted to solve here."

Originally, the Monteverde Cloud Forest Reserve was intended for research and protection, not tourism. The twenty-five-mile trek from the Pan-American Highway up a steep, frequently impassable dirt road meant that only the most hardy travelers made the journey during the early decades. The first pension, Irma's, opened in 1952, and additional dormitory space in the reserve's field station adequately accommodated visiting friends, students, and scientists until the mid-1970s. In 1974, when the reserve first opened, Monteverde had a mere 471 visitors. In 1980, there were 3,257 visitors; in 1983, there were 6,786; and in 1985, there were 11,762.[44]

During the last half of the 1980s, tourism in Monteverde increased by 36 percent per year, and in the early 1990s, it grew at a rate of 50 percent per year. In 1992, the number of visitors reached 49,580, an incredible hundred-fold increase in the eighteen years since the reserve opened; it has since averaged about 50,000 per year. By 1996, twenty-six places offered lodging, most of them along the road from Santa Elena to the reserve. Tourism-linked employment steadily increased as well. By 1992, there were some seventy services related to ecotourism in the Monteverde area, including a souvenir and crafts store, a horse rental facility, art galleries, restaurants, transportation services, and a discotheque-bar, employing a total of 231 people.[45]

One of the clearest beneficiaries of the ecotourism wave has been CASEM (Comité de Artesanías Santa Elena–Monteverde), a women's handicraft cooperative. Since its founding in 1982, it has grown from 8 to some 150 members (including 4 men)[46] and has greatly improved the quality, variety, and marketing of its embroidery, hand-painted stationery and clothing, T-shirts, jewelry, wooden crafts, and other products. Sales doubled between 1987 and 1988[47] but had slowed by the mid-1990s as tourism leveled off. With the help of a few outside experts, the members of the cooperative, most of whom had never before earned an income, "created a handicraft environment that didn't exist before," explains Monteverde resident Sue Trostle, who worked with CASEM in the beginning. "CASEM has been a wonderful way for women to feel empowered, to gain self-esteem, and to build a sense of sisterhood to address family problems such as alcoholism and domestic violence." The ecotourism boom has brought expanded resources for conservation as well as for the community. Entrance fees to the private reserve have always been higher than to the national parks—roughly $2.75 versus $0.65 during the 1980s. The reserve's income grew from $10,000 in 1983 to $33,750 in 1987, adequately covering maintenance costs.[48]

However, as tourist numbers climbed, reserve officials began to foresee huge problems. In response, the Tropical Science Center limited visitors in 1991 to 100 at a time (later raised to 120), restricted most tourists to well-marked trails through only about 2 percent of the reserve, hired and trained more naturalist guides, and sharply increased entrance fees for foreigners to $23, including a guided tour and a slide show, in hope of curbing the number of visitors, particularly those on package tours. Fees for Costa Ricans are $2 ($1 for students). By 1994, the Monteverde Cloud Forest Reserve was bringing in $850,000 per year—more income than from all of Costa Rica's national parks combined. Ninety percent of this was going into the reserve's operating expenses, an endowment fund, and a fund for scientific research; the rest was sent to the TSC's head office.[49] The number of staff members expanded from two or three in the mid-1980s to forty-five in the mid-1990s. Tourist facilities improved, and new equipment was purchased. Some Monteverde leaders, however, complain that the reserve has not contributed its share to support community services, which have had to expand as a result of the tourism boom.

Several smaller private reserves have been opened adjacent to the Monteverde Cloud Forest Reserve. The most innovative is the 314-hectare (775-acre) Santa Elena Cloud Forest Reserve, opened in 1992, that is owned and run by the local high school and assisted by the Monteverde Cloud Forest Reserve. The tourism boom has also helped spawn new scientific and educational projects. The Monteverde Institute hosts U.S. college students, who live with local families and study both rain forest conservation in the reserve and agricultural ecology in the surrounding areas. The

Monteverde Conservation League purchases primary forest and teaches environmental education and reforestation techniques in the surrounding communities. It began in 1986 as an all-volunteer organization, but by mid-1995 it had forty-three paid staff members, 70 percent of whom were Costa Ricans from the Monteverde area. Through land purchases, including the purchase of pastureland to allow it to regenerate, the league has succeeded in more than doubling the size of the protected area in the region. Most purchases were made possible by individual contributions, some from international conservation organizations, and by three debt-for-nature swaps. The league's most successful international campaign has been the Children's Rain Forest, through which schoolchildren in forty-four countries have raised more than $2 million to buy and protect 17,199 hectares (42,500 acres) that share common boundaries with the Monteverde Cloud Forest Reserve. Part of the purchases were financed, as well, through a $540,000 debt-for-nature swap involving the Rainforest Alliance and several other conservation organizations.[50] A small section of the Children's Rain Forest known as the Bajo del Tigre Trail, which was donated by a U.S. family, is open to the public. Eventually, the league plans to open much more of the Children's Rain Forest to visitors, but only after carefully devising plans for the local communities to participate in and benefit from ecotourism.

But along with ecotourism's accomplishments and aspirations have come some new problems. "The main problem we have now is the impact of tourists on tourists," said reserve director Francisco Chamberlain in 1995 as he looked at the crowds gathered at the entrance to the Monteverde Cloud Forest Reserve. "Everyone shows up here at 8 A.M. So, if you come here you'd say, there's so many cars, so many people." In response, the reserve has begun promoting early morning, afternoon, and night tours, limiting density to twenty-five persons over a one-and-a-quarter-mile trail, and has opened two new trails and may open a second entrance at a different location. Although the resplendent quetzal, the reserve's the main tourist attraction, does not seem to be affected by the increased tourism, scientists are convinced that other animals and birds have moved away from the main trails.

Some in Monteverde worry that the area has become too dependent on its ecotourism "monocrop." It is estimated that 65 percent to 70 percent of the area's income now comes from tourism—up from just 10 percent in the late 1980s. Some local residents have successfully entered into ecotourism. Near Monteverde's hotels, for instance, Jorge Rodríguez manages a farm with abundant wildlife but terrain so steep that his cattle kept falling into ravines and breaking their necks. With the absentee owner's permission, Rodríguez put in trails and a parking lot and changed the property's name to Ecological Farm. "For the first time," says Rodríguez, "the farm is mak-

ing a little profit, just enough to maintain the paths and sustain my family."
Four miles down the road, fifteen farmers in the hamlet of Los Olivos have
not been so fortunate. They borrowed $50,000, built a rustic lodge and
cabins overlooking a pond, and put in nature trails. But their Eco Verde
Lodge suffers from poor marketing, a hard-to-find location, and stiff competition from dozens of ecohotels in Monteverde. By 1997, occupancy was
less than 4 percent. "It's easy to talk about ecotourism and sustainable development, but the reality is very difficult," says Huber Barquero, a farmer and
Eco Verde's main investor.[51] Although most hotels and restaurants around
Monteverde are small and owned by local families, several of the biggest are
owned by outsiders, and, as in Tortuguero, increasing numbers of visitors
arrive on prepaid package tours.

Monteverde's ecotourism boom has also brought an influx of immigrants seeking jobs. According to a 1992 survey, the population of the three
communities, Monteverde, Santa Elena, and Cerro Plano, grew by more
than 130 percent between 1984 and 1992, and 600 of the area's 3,500
residents had moved in over the previous five years.[52] This has forced up
the cost of living, led to housing shortages, and put pressure on schools, the
health clinic, and electrical, water, and other services. Land value has also
been driven up by purchases for tourism and conservation purposes. As is
the case elsewhere in Costa Rica, land use planning and zoning laws are not
enforced to control construction of hotels, restaurants, and other tourist
facilities. Until 1993, there was also no community garbage collection or
recycling. Individual families disposed of their own waste, usually by burying it or throwing it over hillsides or into rivers.

Social inequality has increased as well. "You have people with capital
who can afford to build the hotels and people who come in and work as
chambermaids and cooks," says Nathaniel Scrimshaw, former codirector of
the Monteverde Institute. "Yes, it benefits the whole community, but it's
creating increasing differences in wealth as well." The price of land has shot
up, and Carlos Vargas, a Costa Rican Quaker and manager of the Santa
Elena banking cooperative, worries that too many people have abandoned
dairy farming, either selling their land to outsiders or converting their farms
into pensions, hostels, and restaurants. "Now we say we can sell what we
have, but we cannot afford to buy. We are losing the properties that we
have," says Vargas. And many fear that the tourism boom will not last. In
1996, the number of hotel rooms exceeded the number of visitors and some
Monteverde hotels were defaulting on their loans. For this reason, the cooperative's board of directors decided not to give loans for tourism projects;
instead, its loans are for what it views as more stable and long-term, if not
always so environmentally benign, economic options: dairy farming, coffee
growing, and handicrafts.

The survival of local community values and institutions may be most threatened by the ecotourism boom. The Monteverde way of doing things is symbolized by the community's decision—which took twelve years of discussion to reach—to grade but not pave the road. (A paved road would bring even more tourists; the dirt-and-stone road keeps down the number of visitors and ensures that they must spend at least one night in Monteverde, and this is good for the local economy.) Growth has taken a toll on the community's social fabric, as Scrimshaw describes: "In the past, there was a lot of moral force that acted to shape whether something happened or somebody did something. And that is simply no longer true. Now there's no time, and it's too diverse. And that has been pulling at the texture of the traditional town meeting that used to run everything." Many of the new economic immigrants don't understand or appreciate Monteverde's community activism and participatory style of governance. Carlos Vargas and others are concerned about the fact that tourism is not a cooperative activity, as is dairy farming. He says dairy farmers have to work together, but hotels, restaurants, and tour companies compete with one another. It's been very difficult to get those involved in the local tourism industry together to exert control over their activities. For example, in the mid-1990s, Monteverde had three different tourism associations, each claiming to represent the industry.

Ecotourism has changed Monteverde forever. The community is no longer a tiny and remote utopian experiment. Monteverde is sharing its wealth with the world, not only through ecotourism but also through scientific and educational programs and through deep interaction with the surrounding Costa Rican communities. The results have been both positive and negative. As Nathaniel Scrimshaw reflects, "Monteverde is doing all the right things, and making all the mistakes. It is dealing with the ecotourism boom as best as any community can, and it's also having all the disappointments of overdevelopment."

Private Reserves of the Organization of Tropical Studies

More modest and controlled ecotourism flourishes at three private reserves run by the Organization for Tropical Studies (OTS). The OTS is a consortium of fifty-six research institutions and universities in the United States, Puerto Rico, Costa Rica, and Honduras that offers scientific courses at its Costa Rican field stations in areas such as tropical biology, ecology, plant systems, agriculture, and tropical forestry. With its headquarters at Duke University and an office in San José, Costa Rica, the OTS was founded in 1963 by the National Science Foundation (NSF) in Washington, D.C., and U.S. biologists who wanted to learn more about the Tropics. "In terms of science, the Tropics were as unknown as the far side of the moon," says

Chuck Schnell, a lanky biologist with an M.B.A. degree who became OTS's associate director in the mid-1990s. The OTS is partially financed by annual dues from member institutions and grants from the NSF and private foundations, and, as Schnell explains, about half of its income comes from "the business side of running field stations, tuition for courses, and so on." Each year, some 6,000 people, including scientists, university students and professors, government and national park officials, ecologists, and environmental journalists, attend OTS courses, which are taught in both English and Spanish. Schnell explained that the OTS's three ecologically distinct field stations are closely linked to Costa Rican national parks, are used to support the courses, and are now involved in ecotourism.

The oldest and best known of OTS's reserves is La Selva Biological Station, a 1,538-hectare (3,800-acre) tract of humid lowland rain forest along the Sarapiquí River's watershed in northern Costa Rica. In 1968, when the OTS acquired the core of the reserve, a 619-hectare (1,530-acre) cacao farm, from American forester Leslie Holdridge, the area was extraordinarily rich in wildlife and was part of a much larger unbroken forest. The OTS registered La Selva as a natural forest reserve in order to protect it from cutting and to avoid problems with squatters who might claim it as unused land. However, the OTS soon found that registration was not enough to ensure the survival of a piece of pristine land. Over the next fifteen years, roads, settlers, farmers, and loggers cut into the region. By the early 1980s, only a two-mile-wide, nine-mile-long neck connected La Selva to the 31,768-hectare (78,500-acre) Braulio Carrillo National Park, which had been created in 1978.

The alarming rate of deforestation forced the OTS to rethink its preservationist conservation philosophy and strategy. Since small islands of habitat tend to lose much of their biodiversity, expanding the size of La Selva and linking it to the enormous Braulio Carrillo National Park became vital to its survival. The government did not have the $2.2 million necessary to buy the corridor, so the OTS helped raise the money from private U.S. foundations and conservation organizations and bought up enough land to double the reserve's original size. A 1986 presidential decree officially added this corridor to Braulio Carrillo and, in the process, saved La Selva.

OTS staff members also came to realize that since successful conservation means contented neighbors, La Selva must provide benefits to its surrounding community. As Gary Hartshorn, a former OTS student who went on to become a vice president of the World Wildlife Fund and then director of the OTS, puts it, "There are some 10,000 families of colonists in an area going two-thirds the way around La Selva and on 50,000 hectares of land. If La Selva doesn't deliver useful outreach [to them]—whether tree seedlings, environmental education, or community services—the reserve won't survive into the next century."[53] La Selva employs more than 100 local people and runs a variety of programs, including training naturalist tour guides, technicians, and research assistants; offering environmental education programs such as tours, seminars, and classes for schoolchildren, teachers, and parents; and helping local farmers start small-scale tree plantations with native species.

Down near the Panama border, with a pleasant mountain climate, is the OTS's Las Cruces Biological Station, 146 hectares (360 acres) of tropical rain forest and cultivated plantings that includes the 8.1-hectare (20-acre) Wilson Botanical Garden, a diverse and beautifully landscaped nursery of tropical and subtropical plants. The botanical garden, established in 1960 by Florida horticulturalists Robert and Catherine Wilson, contains ferns, bromeliads, gingers, and 680 species of palms—the world's second largest collection. In 1964, the Wilsons invited the OTS to use the property for graduate training programs, and in the early 1970s, they transferred ownership of Las Cruces to the OTS for use as a center for research, scientific training, and public education. It is being developed as a model site for sustainable land use and conservation in the Tropics. Like La Selva, Las Cruces and the botanical garden have many outreach and educational programs with the surrounding communities. In 1994, a devastating fire of unknown origin burned to the ground the botanical garden's laboratory, library, lodging rooms, and other facilities. Although the buildings have since been replaced with others of more modern and functional design, lost were irreplaceable collections of data, photographs, files, artwork, and many books and documents spanning the previous forty years.

The OTS's third field station, Palo Verde Biological Station, is located in a dry forest area in Guanacaste Province that encompasses mountains, wildlands, and wetlands that are noted for their numerous bird species. Rather than being adjacent to a national park, Palo Verde sits in the middle of a national park of the same name. "Dan Janzen originally picked it out for us in the late 1960s as the best place to do a comparative ecosystems study with the wet forest at La Selva," Chuck Schnell explains. The OTS leased the land from its Costa Rican owners for a token $1 per year. In 1990, the government declared the area a national park and expropriated a number of farms, including the one being used by the OTS. The OTS offered to turn over its field station to the national park, but instead the government asked the OTS to remain and to orient the field station toward practical research and management.

In recent years, these three field stations have branched out into ecotourism, and the OTS as a whole supports ecotourism in a variety of ways. "In some sense, we're a scientific travel agency, and I would say that OTS is one of the reasons that Costa Rica has the privileged position in the ecotourism market," Schnell contends. Only about 6 percent to 8 percent of the 6,000 annual visitors to these three field stations are ecotourists. They are accommodated only when space is available, so as not to interfere with the OTS's research and teaching functions, and this serves to keep the numbers low. Schnell conceded that the OTS could cater better to its ecotourists, especially since they are charged "a pretty penny," in part to offset the OTS's free programs for the local community.

The OTS's role in promoting ecotourism is broader than simply hosting tourists at its research stations. "Many of the interesting little stories about organisms and natural history have grown out of OTS [work]," Schnell says, "and former OTS people are now working all over the country." He lists, for instance, Daniel Janzen, who first came to Costa Rica with the OTS in the 1960s; Larry Gilbert, from the University of Texas, who for twenty years has run a butterfly and forest ecology field station on the Osa Peninsula; Amos Bien, at Rara Avis; many of the biologists now at Monteverde; and a number of Costa Rican scientists, professors, resource management experts, and national park officials.

Rara Avis

Amos Bien wears a beard, tall rubber boots, a brimmed canvas hat, and a machete strapped to his waist as he briskly strides into the rain forest. He's followed by a small band of hikers. Bien knows how to read the rain forest, and he's also a good storyteller. He weaves together what we're seeing in one small patch of forest: a black-and-white butterfly, a passion flower, white dots on the leaves, a caterpillar, and a fruit called a *granadea*. "A good guide," Bien contends, "without using a single scientific name or technical word, will explain how the forest works, will build up whole concepts based on interesting natural history stories."

Amos Bien's name and attire conjure up the image of a Pennsylvania Dutch farmer, but he is a transplanted New Yorker who has lost most of his city accent and become *puro Tico* (pure Costa Rican), with deep roots, including a wife and children, in his adopted country. In many ways, Bien is the pioneer of ecotourism in Costa Rica. Whereas Monteverde and the OTS backed into ecotourism, Bien set out to build his lodge and private reserve, Rara Avis (Latin for *rare bird*), in accordance with what are now viewed as sound ecotourism principles. Bien first came to Costa Rica in 1977 to take an OTS biology course at La Selva. There he spent a lot of time talking with farmers who had cut out small homesteads on the reserve's periphery. "When I sat down and did the math with them about how much money they hoped to make and how much they really could make from cattle," Bien says, "the two things were widely different." He was convinced he could demonstrate that rain forest left intact could be more profitable than clear-cut land. "The rain forest is becoming scarce, and because of that scarcity, people are going to want to come as tourists and see it," Bien contends.

In 1983, Bien spent six months backpacking around Costa Rica and finally found 607 hectares (1,500 acres) of virgin rain forest on the Caribbean side of the country. It is adjacent to Braulio Carrillo National Park and has a good climate, four spectacular waterfalls, and an old jungle prison colony, which became Rara Avis's first lodge. Bien recounts that he initially approached the World Bank's private sector branch, the International Finance Corporation (IFC), for funding, "and they said if I could find a way of doing it for $4 or $5 million they would finance it, but if it was less, they weren't interested." Bien instead talked some friends and relatives into becoming stockholders and took out a modest loan from a Costa Rican bank. "We were the very first project to get bank financing for ecotourism. It was considered totally radical, and the banks thought they were taking a substantial risk. But in the end, they were happy because we paid back all our loans, and they have gone on to finance other ecotourism projects."

The townspeople of Las Horquetas helped Bien find the land, build the dirt road (really consisting of deep mud and slippery clay), construct small bridges, repair the prison camp, and rescue stranded vehicles and people. "I felt that if the surrounding community of Las Horquetas—the potential chain saw wielders—were not part of the project, then it would never work," Bien explains.

Initially, Rara Avis was based at the very rudimentary El Plastico prison colony's dormitory; today, this is used by visiting scientists and students. Tourists stay in either the eight-room Waterfall Lodge; Las Cabinas, designed especially for bird-watchers; or a treetop cabin that is reached by climbing a rope (accompanied by a guide). Accommodations are fairly basic: there's no electricity, but there are excellent communal meals and hot showers. The main activity is the guided hikes along narrow forest trails, where three types of monkeys, anteaters, and deer are common and tapirs, jaguars, and three-toed sloths are occasionally seen. As the name of the reserve implies, the bird-watching is unparalleled. More than 300 species have been identified, including the great green macaw, the salty-tailed trogon, the keel-billed toucan, and other unusual species.

One of Bien's first two managers was from Las Horquetas; nearly all his employees, including guides, are from the town; and he buys most of his goods and services locally. Employees have received English-language instruction and training in cooking, guiding, and other skills. Those who have been with the company for two years become stockholders, and there is also a profit-sharing scheme for lower-level employees. The community is involved in other ways as well. Rara Avis gives free tours to elementary and secondary school groups and has made in-kind donations to the local clinic and schools. Each year, Bien provides two scholarships to outstanding students from poor families to continue their education through secondary school. "With the director of the school and sixth-grade teacher, we pick two students who are at risk of dropping out. We provide, for the rest of their academic career, 50 percent of their school fees, including books, uniforms, bus transport, and school lunches. The other half is paid by the family, so they feel an equal responsibility," Bien explains. "This has worked very well. And we have the students up here once or twice a year to learn about the rain forest. Our door is open for them." Bien calculates that Rara Avis generates about $80,000 annually for the local community, making it one of the most important sources of income and employment.[54]

Bien says that Rara Avis has successfully demonstrated to people in the area that "the rain forest offers a higher income-producing potential for ecotourism than for any other use." Rara Avis's World Wide Web site describes it as "a fascinating project in commercial rainforest conservation—using ecotourism to make the rainforest profitable without destroying it, and using publicity to teach others to do the same." However, like Daniel Janzen, Bien sees ecotourism as just one of the "products" that can be harvested from protected lands. Rara Avis grows tree seedlings for reforestation programs in Costa Rica and raises and exports butterfly chrysalises and the endemic "stained glass window" palm, which makes a lovely ornamental plant. Bien also plans to collect seeds from dozens of species of orchids and package them in test tubes for the overseas market.

Until a few years ago, Rara Avis's most famous "product" was the "mechanical web," a mobile perch that permits scientists to move horizontally and vertically through the forest canopy. Fellow OTS biologist Don Perry first built this engine-powered cable car over Rara Avis's main waterfall and some twenty acres of forest. However, Rara Avis lost the mechanical web, which Perry moved to another, more accessible rain forest twenty miles away. This, combined with a fierce increase in competition among ecotourism facilities and a shift toward "softer" ecotourists, who don't want to spend hours on Rara Avis's awful "road" before reaching the lodge, have all hurt business. Rara Avis is not, Bien readily admits, for everyone. "After we tell people they have to wear boots, take a difficult tractor ride, [and] slough around in the mud, the people who come here are the right sort." Over the years, more than 5,000 of the "right sort" have made the journey to Rara Avis, which remains Costa Rica's most authentic ecotourism experiment.

Newer Private Reserves

Since the late 1980s, increasing numbers of both foreigners and Costa Ricans have been actively buying up rain forest and other pristine patches of

Costa Rica and turning them into private reserves and ecotourism resorts. There are today probably hundreds of ecolodges and private reserves, mostly nestled in the mountains, often next to a national park.

One of the newest is the Rain Forest Aerial Tram, a state-of-the-art "soft" ecotourism project designed by biologist Don Perry as an upscale version of his Rara Avis mechanical web. Opened in 1994 and just a fifty-minute drive from San José, the tram quickly became one of the country's most popular ecotourism attractions. The $2 million project is financed by sixty U.S. and Costa Rican investors and MIGA, the World Bank's risk insurance fund. The tram's lift, 30.5 meters (100 feet) high and 1.3 kilometers (0.81 mile) long, carries visitors and their naturalist guides in green cable cars through the treetop canopy, giving them a spectacular bird's-eye view of where two-thirds of all rain forest species live. The 450-hectare (1,000-acre) private reserve is adjacent to the magnificent Braulio Carrillo National Park, which is 100 times bigger but largely inaccessible. Perry wanted none of the canopy cut during construction of the tram, so he hired sixty-five local laborers and a Russian-built helicopter from the Nicaraguan air force to lower the twelve 100-foot-high towers into holes carefully dug among the trees. (Trees were cut, however, for an entrance road, a parking lot, and a restaurant and other buildings.) Many of these workers, cattle ranch hands from around the hamlet of La Unión, have continued to work for the Rain Forest Aerial Tram, now the area's largest employer. Perry calls his project "the school of the treetops," and each year the tram offers free trips for several thousand Costa Rican schoolchildren. Tourists pay a hefty $47.50, plus transportation and food, but numbers are kept to a maximum of 250 per day and the guides are excellent. The Rain Forest Aerial Tram meets important ecotourism criteria: it's educational, accessible to elderly and handicapped tourists, ecologically quite sensitive, and, apparently, beneficial to the surrounding community. One major drawback is that although the tram's rich canopy comes from its proximity to a vast national park, the park itself receives no direct benefit from this ecotourism project.

Another "soft" ecotourism project, Villablanca Hotel and the Los Angeles Cloud Forest, just a two-hour drive north of San José, near San Ramón, is *puro Tico*. Its owner is former Costa Rican president Rodrigo Carazo, who also founded the Costa Rica–based United Nations University for Peace and is an avid proponent of ecotourism. "There's no other way for Costa Rica to earn the foreign exchange and protect its national parks and protected areas," Carazo explained as he showed me around his beautiful mountaintop ecolodge, whose food, furnishings, and whitewashed adobe cottages with red tile roofs and cement fireplaces are authentically Costa Rican. Carazo frequently lectures his mostly elderly American guests, interweaving Costa Rican history, politics, and folklore with environmental matters. His 804-hectare (2,000-acre) private reserve has well-maintained trails, biologist guides, quetzals and other fauna and flora, spectacular vistas, rain and fog, and an entrance fee on par with Monteverde's.

On the Caribbean coast just adjacent to Panama, another ecotourism project caters to a very different clientele. Hardy ecotourist backpackers can hike eight hours through the Gandoca-Manzanillo Wildlife Refuge, near the border with Panama, to another private reserve and simple, inexpensive lodge owned cooperatively by ASACODE, a small farmers' association. ASACODE is dedicated to reforestation with native trees and selective harvesting and processing of hardwoods. Its thirteen *campesino* families receive technical support from ANAI, a U.S.-based organization that, since the 1970s, has been involved in organic farming in the Cordillera de Talamanca, a mountain range in southern Costa Rica. Guests, who are mainly biologists, Costa Ricans, and agro-tourists, can view the association's experimental plots, canopy exploration areas, water buffalo pastures, and sawmill.[55] The 1997 edition of *The New Key to Costa Rica* gives ASACODE its highest, three-sun "sustainable tourism" rating.

The proliferation of private reserves[56] that protect unspoiled land and promote ecotourism is widely endorsed by Costa Rican government and national park officials; members of the tourism industry; officials of conservation organizations, the World Bank, and other lending agencies; academics; and scientists. They argue that private reserves protect land that the government cannot afford to buy and therefore are the most expedient way to expand Costa Rica's protected areas. Private reserves provide facilities for ecotourism that the national parks cannot afford or do not want to provide. Private reserves bypass government bureaucracy and red tape, are often more efficiently run than national parks, can respond quickly to conservation and ecotourism needs, offer an opportunity for community-run conservation and ecotourism, and provide resources to support other activities such as scientific research, organic farming, and sustainable harvesting from the forest.

Drawbacks of Private Reserves

Several studies have concluded that private reserves are, overall, enormously beneficial.[57] However, in studying private reserves in Costa Rica (and then in Africa), I became convinced of a number of pitfalls and problems that need to be addressed. What happens, for instance, to the rural poor who are displaced when private reserves are created by foreigners or wealthy Costa Ricans? Whereas Costa Rica's national parks are, at least in principle and on paper, committed to paying a fair price for land that is incorporated into parks, there is no such requirement for private reserve owners. The backbone of Costa Rica's economic and social stability has been the yeoman farmer, but in recent years increasing numbers of small landowners have sold out, often too cheaply, and joined the ranks of rural or urban laborers. Environmentalist and former legislator Guillermo Barquero says, "In the name of ecotourism, our poor peasants are giving away their land for pennies." Not only are there no restrictions on foreigners owning land, but also, in a break with its historic support for squatters (*precaristas*[58]), the Costa Rican government now pledges to quickly remove squatters from private reserves.

Although private reserves are often praised as a low-cost means to help governments establish protected areas, they may not include the most ecologically important land. In Costa Rica, many are too small or too remote to fit into the country's system of megaparks. Further, Costa Rica's main problem is financing and preserving the existing park system. Private reserves are siphoning off NGO funds, scientists, and tourists from the national parks. International conservation organizations that in the past would have donated funds and experts to the national parks are today investing in private reserves, where they find more flexibility and fewer bureaucratic hassles. Increasing numbers of ecotourists are visiting private reserves, which, though much more expensive than the national parks, offer more amenities.

Justifiably, Costa Rican park officials are wary of their parks becoming full-service parks like those in North America and South Africa. Nevertheless, the country's national parks must develop better guides and trails and provide basic visitor services either within or just on the perimeter of protected areas. The raising of entrance fees for foreigners was a positive step toward tapping ecotourism dollars, but the national parks need to develop more sophisticated types of ecotourism and explore other income-generating fields, such as bioprospecting for medical plants, sustainable forestry, and harvesting of rain forest products.

A number of private reserves do voluntarily work closely with neighboring publicly protected areas by training guards and guides or lending buildings for park meetings. Private reserve owners should, however, be compelled to contribute more systematically to national conservation efforts through, for instance, a visitors' tax, educational programs, lower entrance fees for Costa Ricans, hiring and training of employees from the surrounding area, and cooperation in scientific research with Costa Rica's universities and national parks. If the popularity and profitability gap between private reserves and public parks continues to widen, pressure will surely mount, as it is in the United States, to privatize national parks. This would be a tragic mistake: Costa Rica's megaparks are an important part of the national patrimony, and their long-term protection is best ensured by the government, not private owners, who increasingly are not Costa Ricans.

Leatherbacks, Yellow Lights, and "Green Luxury" at Playa Grande

In February 1995, an article titled "Green Luxury in Costa Rica" appeared in the American Institute of Architect's (AIA) magazine *AIArchitect*. "Ecotourism will meet the high life in a luxury beach resort planned for Costa Rica," the article began, and it went on to describe plans for a $50 million "village for 5,000 vacationers and full-time residents," including shops, restaurants, a hotel, condominiums, a casino and nightclub, a health spa, a swimming pool, an auditorium, orchards and gardens, and a marina and yacht club with space for 150 sailboats. The article claimed that "environmental considerations are an integral part of the design," including electric golf carts, solar panels, and structures no more than three stories high. The resort's "most interesting" environmental feature: "the special yellow lighting that will be installed outdoors in deference to the giant turtles that come on land at night to lay eggs. The turtles are averse to regular lighting systems, but testing found the yellow lights to meet reptilian and human needs alike."

The project's main developer, financier, and architect was AIA member Heydar Ghiai & Sons, an Iranian father-and-son firm that had been architects for the shah, with offices in France, Costa Rica, and San Francisco. In a telephone interview, Yves Ghiai described his project as "the most luxurious resort in all of Central America. Rooms will rent for $350 a night, no discounts. We want a luxury clientele." He added reassuringly that the project "is totally geared and fitted for ecotourism. We're the only group of developers really caring about the environment in Costa Rica. No one else gives a damn." Stylistically, Ghiai explained, the hotel will "meld Modernist concepts with a strong Middle Eastern influence," which does not fit with ecotourism's precept that architecture should be culturally sensitive and reflect its locale. The beach, Ghiai revealed, is Playa Grande, on the Nicoya Peninsula, and the turtles are leatherbacks, the world's largest reptiles.

Miguel Rodríguez, the Costa Rican administrator of the Ghiai's Playa Grande project, has produced a glossy brochure for the project showing a large swath of land along the beach and the interior subdivided into more than 300 lots for vacation homes and a hotel. About half the lots had already been sold to foreigners, a handful of the houses had been built, and construction of the hotel was about to begin, Rodríguez said. The brochure promised investors "public water systems, street lighting, fire hydrants, electricity, and sewage systems, as well as a 24-hour security service." Rodríguez said he knew nothing about plans for solar power or any other ecologically sensitive features listed in the *AIArchitect* article.

Fortunately, this article provoked responses from several socially responsible architects. The Andersen Group, the Minneapolis-based architectural firm that built the environmentally acclaimed Lapa Ríos Lodge and private reserve on Costa Rica's Osa Peninsula, wrote, "We are appalled to see a project of this nature described as somehow 'green.'" Costa Rica's Chamber of Consultants in Architecture and Engineering wrote, "We were horrified at the implications" of this project for the leatherbacks and "the arrogant approach held by Architect Yves Ghiai concerning development in Costa Rica."

As to the yellow-lights experiment, Ghiai recalled in an interview that "the tests" had been performed at neighboring Playa Flamingo, a glitzy beach resort where his company had built condominiums. Project manager Rodríguez confirmed that he had overseen the yellow-lights experiment. But, he said, it had been designed to keep away mosquitoes, not to protect the nesting habits of turtles. And a half dozen scientists dismissed Ghiai's claims that the yellow lights do not disturb nesting turtles. Claudette Moe, director of wildlife management at Costa Rica's National University, explained, "It's just not true that yellow lights don't affect turtles. They are less susceptible to certain colors. Red light is one of the least noticeable, but they will eventually have some perception of any type of artificial light." She and others said that the only solution was to keep all lights, no matter what color, facing away from the beach.[59]

The "green luxury" project has for several years been at the eye of a storm of controversy over how to protect Playa Grande and the leatherbacks, promote sound conservation and ecotourism, and stop megaresorts. The issues are broader than the leatherbacks: they involve competition with the local community for freshwater, the question of how to properly protect the mangrove swamp, the influx of non–Costa Rican developers and speculators, and corruption, bribes, and payoffs to government officials.

Playa Grande is now recognized as the most important leatherback nesting beach in the entire Pacific Ocean. Every year between October and March, as many as 2,500 females,[60] each about five feet long and some weighing more than a ton, lumber out of the sea to lay their eggs on the broad, smooth bank of this white-sand beach. Guided by little-understood primordial instincts, leatherbacks travel thousands of miles under the sea, returning year after year to the same nesting areas—as long as these areas remain largely undisturbed. Unfortunately, their nesting season coincides with the peak tourist season, and their preferred nesting beaches are also prime tourist spots.

Among the leatherbacks' protectors is Louis Wilson, a North American who has lived in Costa Rica since 1973. Back then, he ran guided excursions and deep-sea fishing expeditions with his brother out of the oldest luxury hotel at Tamarindo, the beach next to Playa Grande. In recent years, Wilson has become increasingly involved in environmental issues, advocating the release of all billfish (an issue still under debate by the Costa Rican government but now practiced by most sportfishing operators), preservation of the mangrove estuary, a host of measures to protect the nesting turtles, and carefully managed tourism development. Part of what spurred him to action was rapid and uncontrolled development of Tamarindo in the late 1980s that turned the tranquil, low-key fishing village–cum–vacation spot into a honky-tonk strip of signboards, fast-food restaurants, cement hotels, and, during peak season, bumper-to-bumper cars and blaring music. As the sunbathers and surfers poured into the brightly lit hotels, the leatherbacks, which had once nested along Tamarindo's wide, soft-sand beach, stopped coming.

As tourist numbers rose, turtle viewing at neighboring Playa Grande and illegal collection of eggs grew out of control. Wilson recounts how, over the Christmas holiday in the mid-1980s, tourists arrived by the boatload and busload, roaming Playa Grande with flashlights and flash cameras and handling the eggs and baby turtles. On occasion, 150 tourists would be gathered around a single nesting mother. Costa Ricans made a sport of riding on the leatherbacks and a business of collecting the eggs. "There was a *huevero* [a turtle-egg poacher] every fifty meters with a bag under the turtle catching all the eggs," Wilson relates. "We would arrive with our group of tourists and literally buy the turtle. We would explain to the *huevero* in Spanish that we wanted him to leave, and then we'd have to lie to the tourists and tell them that the eggs would be untouched. Oftentimes, the *huevero* would come back later and dig them up."

An increasingly frustrated and vocal Wilson, along with his partner, Costa Rican Marianela Pastor, moved from Tamarindo across the estuary to Playa Grande, built a small hotel and a turtle station, and become guardians of the leatherbacks. Through CINDE, an institute created by USAID to promote foreign investment, Wilson found several other investors willing to put up capital for the project. Wilson and Pastor also solicited help from members of the Rural Guard and Boy Scouts in patrolling the beach and spoke on local radio about the need to protect the turtles.

In early 1990, the efforts of Wilson, Pastor, and others bore fruit: Costa Rica's Legislative Assembly approved the Tamarindo Wildlife Refuge, protecting the estuary, its unique saltwater mangrove forest, and, along Playa Grande, the first 50 meters (164 feet) above the highwater mark. This wildlife refuge became part of Costa Rica's national park system, with its own budget and rangers. That same year, Wilson opened Hotel Las Tortugas, a lovely stucco-and-tile hotel built with the leatherbacks in mind: no lights shine on the beach; no rooms face south, where the nesting beach is located; and the entire hotel has low lighting. For Wilson's conservation efforts and the hotel's design, *The New Key to Costa Rica* listed Las Tortugas as one of the few beach lodges practicing sustainable tourism.

When the Calderón administration took office in May 1990, several key government officials, including Maria Teresa Koberg, director of the Sea Turtle Conservation Program, and Mario Boza, vice minister of the Ministry of Natural Resources, Energy, and Mines took an active interest in Playa Grande and began urging that it be more rigorously protected as a national park rather than simply a wildlife reserve. In 1991, President Calderón, at the urging of Boza and Koberg, issued an executive decree creating Las Baulas (*baulas* means *leatherbacks* in Spanish) National Park to include an additional 50 meters (164 feet) of beachfront above the public zone. A number of investors in the Playa Grande area, led by a German-owned hotel development, agreed voluntarily to set back their buildings the additional 50 meters, reduce the size of their buildings, and keep lights off the beach. Ironically, Wilson's Las Tortugas, the only completed hotel along Playa Grande, fell within the park's boundaries and, in theory, the government could have expropriated the lodge and compensated Wilson. But the park existed only on paper: the government decree committed no money to buy out Wilson, control new construction, or protect the park; even the land donated by other developers was never legally incorporated into the park.

Immediately, as well, the Ghiai and other investors in the "green luxury" project began using their influence with certain top government officials to get the park decree nullified. In early 1993, the Minister of Natural Resources, Energy, and Mines suddenly issued new instructions that the area should be managed only as a national wildlife refuge, not a park, thereby allowing urbanization and construction to proceed with almost no restrictions.[61] Maria Teresa Koberg and Mario Boza both resigned from their government positions in protest.

For the next several years, Playa Grande's legal status was disputed, but the national park service, together with the local municipality, some scientists, and Wilson and Pastor, continued efforts to professionalize the turtle tours and stop the poaching. Scientists have, however, detected signs that nesting patterns are being affected by the scattered development that has already taken place along the beach. In 1996, only 450 turtles came to Playa Grande, down from about 700 over the prior five years. Leatherbacks are being drowned in tuna nets and decimated by poachers worldwide, but the bright lights from Tamarindo and newer hotels near Playa Grande may be affecting nesting habits as well.[62] Although longer-term studies are needed,

those done so far indicate less nesting along stretches of the beach where
there is construction and where vegetation near the dunes has been
removed. Wildlife refuge administrator Sergio Obando de Torres, deeply
worried that the "green luxury" resort and other development schemes
threaten the leatherbacks' nesting, argued in a 1995 interview that Playa
Grande can be properly protected only if it is a national park. In mid-
1995, the Legislative Assembly and Costa Rica's president, José
María Figueres, finally approved a bill officially creating Las Baulas National
Marine Park, a much stronger action than the earlier government decree.
"Formation of Las Baulas is the most important step taken to preserve
the leatherback in the last 30 years," said Indiana University biology professor Frank Paladino. "Now the park needs to be consolidated so that it can
complete its job."[63] However, according to Wilson, the exact boundaries of
the 400-hectare (988-acre) park remain unclear. The law creates a buffer
zone between the beach and any development, but a hill on the Ghiai's
property that was to be included in the park was, in the end, mysteriously
exempted. Environmentalists warn that lights on the hill will shine on the
beach and disturb the turtles.

The "green luxury" scheme is proceeding slowly, but the developers
have not started construction of the hotel and will probably be barred from
ever building the marina and yacht club. Their development has, it appears,
been slowed and constricted but not completely revamped—or stopped.
Meanwhile, Rancho Las Colinas Golf and Country Club, another megaresort with 220 lots and condominium sites, a golf course, shopping and dining facilities, tennis courts, a marina, artificial lakes, and equestrian facilities,
is going up on another good-sized hill overlooking Playa Grande. In a script
that could have been written by Yves Ghiai, Jack Osborne, one of the
resort's American owners, claims, "We are pioneering an eco-sensitive development, saving trees and working to save nature in our area. Our lakes on
the golf course have already become sanctuaries for birds."[64] Although the
long-term protection of leatherback nesting is not guaranteed, Playa Grande
and Las Baulas National Marine Park represent a victory of sorts, especially
compared with the high-profile but unsuccessful battles fought against the
Hotel Playa Tambor and Papagayo megaresorts.

Ironically, one upshot of this struggle may be that Wilson's Hotel Las
Tortugas Lodge is expropriated because it is too close to the beach. Wilson
is philosophical, saying he wouldn't mind stepping back and letting the government and others continue the fight. "We've come so far," he concludes.
"You're looking right now at a place that is a model for sustainable development in Costa Rica. What happens here is going to be a testing ground.
Win, lose, or draw, this is going to be an important educational tool for what
happens in other areas."

Costa Rica's Ecotourism Scorecard

During the first half of the 1990s, the number of tourist arrivals to Costa Rica grew by a vigorous 17 percent per year, tourism became the country's top dollar earner, and Costa Rica's international image was transformed from that of a Central American banana republic to an ecotourism mecca. This tiny country has become the second most frequented tourist destination in Latin America, following Mexico. Although this transformation has not been without problems and drawbacks, Costa Rica has the right conditions for high-quality nature tourism and, on a number of fronts, the country has fulfilled the seven main criteria for sound ecotourism.

1. *Involves travel to natural destinations.* It is Costa Rica's fine national park system and its growing number of outstanding private parks and reserves that draw most visitors.

2. *Minimizes impact.* The majority of Costa Rica's hotels and lodges are small: by 1997, some 73 percent of the 360 registered hotels had sixteen or fewer rooms.[65] However, in recent years, the fastest-growing tourism sector has been megaresorts by big international hotel chains, according to the Costa Rican Chamber of Hotels.[66] Even though this development has been around, rather than in the national parks and much of the development within the private reserves is environmentally sensitive, the steep rise in numbers of tourists has caused environmental decay in some of the most popular parks. It is, however, along Costa Rica's coasts that the negative effects of tourism are most apparent. With a few exceptions, such as Hotel Las Tortugas at Playa Grande and a few lodges in Tortuguero, ecotourism has bypassed Costa Rica's beach developments. There has been serious overdevelopment of lodges and hotels in areas such as Manuel Antonio National Park, Montezuma, Tamarindo, and Jaco. In several controversial projects, Papagayo and Hotel Playa Tambor, for instance, government officials, from ministers to municipal functionaries, were accused of taking bribes in return for granting licenses for environmentally inappropriate construction. In other areas, most notably Manuel Antonio, lack of enforceable zoning has led to uncontrolled growth of small tourism establishments.

   Scant official attention is paid to the need for low-impact construction. Without enforceable zoning regulations and environmentally strict construction standards, few of Costa Rica's hotels have been built with an overall rigor intended to limit impact. A number of ecolodges, however, have some ecological features, such as solar-heated water, natural ventilation or ceiling fans instead of air conditioning, and use of thatch and other local construction materials.

   Environmental impact can be minimized through good government planning, enforceable regulations, coordination among various ministries, and an overall development plan. In her seminal 1990 ecotourism study, Elizabeth Boo wrote that "concrete governmental actions . . . and coordinating efforts of the National Park Service and the Costa Rican Tourism Institute, still must be taken"[67] if ecotourism in Costa Rica is to improve. As the decade neared an end, little had changed. In 1997, Costa Rica's tourism minister, Carlos Roesch, declared, "Costa Rican tourism is a baby who cannot stand by himself, but his parents think he is already in college."[68] Costa Rica's tourism planning has been fragmented, characterized by a lack of coordination and overlapping responsibilities among the different government agencies and ministries and an absence of (or at least an absence of enforcement of) regulations, including laws, mandatory environmental impact studies, and controls on foreign ownership. The lack of a master plan for ecotourism development at the national level has meant that local communities such as Monteverde have been forced to cope with the tourism explosion on their own, without guidelines or technical expertise from the central government.

3. *Builds environmental awareness.* Ecotourism has clearly helped to build environmental awareness among both visitors and Costa Ricans. The twin concepts of environmental protection and sustainable development are now nationally endorsed, although they are haphazardly and often superficially defined and implemented. There are scores of Costa Rican and international environmental organizations, environmental classes are now taught in many schools, and at least one university offers a degree in ecotourism. And the "sustainable tourism rating" carried in *The New Key to Costa Rica* guidebook has pioneered techniques and criteria for independent and in-depth surveying of ecotourism lodges and has spurred the government to design its own rating system. Such surveys not only are extremely useful to tourists but also help set national standards and definitions of what constitutes high-quality ecotourism. They are therefore important educational tools for the traveling public, government officials, NGOs and community organizations, and the tourism industry.

Traditionally, Costa Ricans have vacationed along their beaches, but with the rise of ecotourism, increasing numbers are visiting parks and reserves. Local visitors can enter the national parks for a very modest fee, and some private reserves also have reduced entrance fees for local visitors. Guanacaste National Park, in particular, has developed nature programs for schoolchildren, and the privately owned Rain Forest Aerial Tram admits free of charge a limited number of local school groups. In 1996, the government took a positive step by instituting a new program offering vacation loans and deep (40 to 60 percent) hotel and other travel-related discounts to *Tico* (Costa Rican) tourists, particularly during the rainy, or "green," season. All of this is helping to build a solid national base of support for both conservation and ecotourism.

In terms of tourist education, most tour companies and private parks have well-qualified, bilingual naturalist guides who are also knowledgeable about the country's history and culture. The national parks, however, frequently are understaffed and their best guides are often drawn away to better-paying jobs in the private sector. In addition, many tourists themselves are demanding vacations that are less rigorous both physically and intellectually. Thus, some of the best ecotourism companies have been forced to water down their programs, and conventional tour operators have moved in to offer ecotourism lite experiences that include only quick overviews of both nature and the country, such as a visit to a volcano or a botanical garden.[69]

4. *Provides direct financial benefits for conservation.* The growth of ecotourism in Costa Rica has helped support conservation efforts and scientific research, particularly in the older private reserves, such as Monteverde and La Selva, and has undoubtedly slowed the rate of deforestation within protected areas. But although Costa Rica's national parks remain among the world's finest and, with the hike in entrance fees for foreigners, are earning more from ecotourism, they are far from self-supporting. Greater effort should be made to open parts of the larger national parks to visitors as well as to better limit tourist numbers in the smaller, most popular parks. Because most national parks offer little in terms of naturalist guides, trails, lodging, and restaurants, they are being aggressively challenged by private reserves, which typically provide better services and attract more foreign visitors. The government needs to ensure that the private parks, which benefit from the international reputation and often the boundaries of the national parks, make appropriate economic and educational contributions to conservation and community development efforts.

5. *Provides financial benefits and empowerment for local people.* More than in many other developing countries, a sizable number of local people have managed to benefit from Costa Rica's ecotourism boom. Even Costa Ricans of modest means have moved into the ecotourism market by operating concessions (handicrafts, horseback riding, tour boats, white-water rafting, butterfly farms, trout fishing, bird-watching, orchid and organic farms, etc.); building a few tourist *cabinas* and hiking trails on their *fincas* (farms); and opening small restaurants serving *comida típica* (local food). Costa Rica's countryside is now dotted with locally owned tourism enterprises, many of them wisely combined with other economic activities, such as farming. Increasing numbers of Costa Ricans have also been trained as naturalist guides, park rangers, hotel managers, tour drivers, or multilingual tour operators. Parallel with the growth of locally owned or managed ecolodges, small hotels,

and bed-and-breakfasts has been a proliferation of Costa Rica–based travel agencies and tour operators, which totaled 265 in 1996. Almost all of them handle nature tourism, and about a dozen specialize in high-quality ecotourism.[70] A majority of Costa Rica–based tour companies and about half of the seventy-nine ecolodges receiving *The New Key to Costa Rica*'s sustainable tourism rating in 1997 are locally owned,[71] either by Costa Ricans or by long-term foreign residents.

But there is a downside as well. The demands of Costa Rica's rural poor for land and for access to gold, timber, and resources within the parks have been only partially and often temporarily addressed. Under pressure from foreign investors, the government has become less tolerant of squatters who move onto private lands set aside for tourism or other economic activities. In addition, the cost of land and the cost of living have skyrocketed in ecotourism havens such as Monteverde and along the beaches, making it impossible for Costa Ricans with modest resources to cash in on the ecotourism boom without borrowing heavily and at high interest rates. Hotel construction continues to outpace demand, and most hotel owners say that they need 70 percent occupancy to recover from the mid-1990s downturn. A number of hotels declared bankruptcy during that time, and by mid-1996, 47 percent of tourism businesses had fallen behind in repaying their bank loans to the Central Bank.[72] Unlike the situation in many other developing countries where there is captial flight, in Costa Rica, overall political stability has meant that most of the profits from locally owned tourism projects are kept in the country. There has been, however, a sharp rise in the number of tourists who arrive on prepaid packages, charter flights, and cruises, from which Costa Ricans receive only minimal benefit.

6. *Respects local culture.* This is somewhat more difficult to measure, in part because on the surface the country appears to lack a strong national character and culture. Costa Ricans often refer to themselves as more pro–United States than any other Latin Americans, and middle- and upper-class Costa Rican values are linked to those of the United States via music and movies, vacations at Disney World, and shopping in Miami. The ecotourism boom has brought in its wake U.S.-style fast-food chains and shopping malls, transactions in dollars, and signs in English, all of which have further diluted Costa Rica's culture. On the other hand, ecotourism has helped stimulate and improve local crafts, increased interest in folkloric dancing, the national theater, and museums, and stimulated pride in and protection of regional cultures such as those of the Afro-Caribbeans along the Caribbean coast, the pockets of indigenous Indians, and the Guanacaste cattle ranchers and cowboys. The number of guidebooks and historical and cultural books about Costa Rica has grown enormously since the 1980s. One

tiny gem, *Costa Rica: A Traveler's Literary Companion,* compiles English translations of some of Costa Rica's finest literature, arranged geographically to give visitors a flavor of regional distinctions.[73] And despite the tourism onslaught, Costa Ricans continue in various ways to hold on to strong cultural traditions such as a commitment to the extended family, a respect for the elderly and a loving indulgence of children, a pride in Costa Rica's pacific and democratic traditions, and an adherence to religious holidays. At both Easter and Christmas, for instance, the country literally shuts down and goes on holiday, despite pressure from the tourism industry to keep open stores and banks.

7. *Supports human rights and democratic movements.* Costa Rica has the oldest democracy in Latin America, a strong tradition of respect for human rights, and an absence of both a military force and armed guerrilla groups. These favorable social and political conditions, together with the country's parks and reserves, have provided a solid foundation for the growth of ecotourism. Many people attribute the start of the ecotourism boom to President Oscar Arias Sánchez's receipt of the 1987 Nobel Peace Prize, which helped the world to distinguish Costa Rica from its war-torn and largely undemocratic neighbors. Ecotourism has helped expand international awareness of Costa Rica's pacific and democratic traditions and has probably increased Costa Ricans' pride in their fine national heritage, although this is hard to gauge. The principles of ecotourism have helped stimulate government actions to expand and better protect the national parks and to promote other environmental programs, to strengthen NGOs, and to create some concrete projects to improve the political rights and economic conditions of the rural poor, Afro-Caribbeans, and indigenous Indians living around the parks and reserves and along the beaches. On the other hand, the simultaneous growth of conventional tourism has worked to undermine the rights of local people to ownership of land, particularly beach front property and has increased government removal of squatters.

Future Prospects

When stacked against other land-based, foreign exchange–generating activities such as cattle ranching, banana growing, and logging, Costa Rica's ecotourism industry has appeared economically and environmentally viable and its future has looked bright. However, there have been warning signs that these trends may not continue. In 1996, a chill swept through Costa Rica with the announcement that for the first time in a decade, the tourism industry had slumped. Tourism revenues dropped by 2.8 percent during the first five months of 1996; airport arrivals were down by 2.2 percent, with numbers of European visitors falling by 30 percent and those of Canadians by nearly 23 percent; and hotel room occupancy plummeted to an unsustainable 25.7 percent.

Analysts pointed to some obvious causes for the downturn.[74] Bad publicity from urban street crime and several high-profile attacks on tourists, including two kidnappings for ransom, damaged Costa Rica's reputation for peace and tranquility. Costa Rica's "green" image became tarnished as visitors encountered dirty rivers and beaches,[75] widespread deforestation outside the national parks, and heavy vehicular pollution in San José. In addition, Costa Rica had become relatively expensive compared with Cancún, the Dominican Republic, or Cuba, and a campaign in Canada encouraged tourists to vacation in Cuba to protest the U.S. government's draconian Helms-Burton law, which seeks to punish Canadian and other foreign companies doing business in Cuba.

Some of these factors were beyond Costa Rica's control, but others stem from poor government planning and lack of a clear strategy. In response, the government sought to stop the slide by launching a $3 million advertising campaign targeting the United States and Canada, inviting members of the press on "fam" trips (see chapter 2) to Costa Rica, and promoting domestic tourism. In addition, under heavy pressure from the tourism industry, the government lowered park entrance fees from $15 to $6, eliminated the 3 percent hotel tax, and shelved plans to increase airline tickets while hotel owners and tour boat operators cut prices for their advertised packages by 10 to 15 percent.[76] Within the first five months of 1997, tourism increased by a modest 3 percent over the previous year, and by the end of the year, it appeared to have rebounded.

However, Costa Rica's government continues to pursue a risky, two-track policy of heavily marketing its parks and ecotourism while trying to increase visitor numbers by means of hugh beach resorts and urban hotels owned by international chains, cruise ships, and prepaid air charter tours.[77] This strategy is flawed. In the international market, all of tiny Costa Rica is being promoted as an ecotourism destination, unlike the situation in Tanzania and South Africa, where ecotourism is promoted only in certain areas. Since image is so important, it seems unlikely that Costa Rica will, over the long haul, be able to get away with selling this dual identity.

Notes

I am extremely grateful to ecotourism expert and writer Anne Becher for all her assistance in gathering materials and doing follow-up interviews in Costa Rica.

1. Martha Honey, *Hostile Acts: U.S. Policy in Costa Rica in the 1980s* (Gainesville: University Press of Florida, 1994).
2. "What's Wrong with Mass Ecotourism?" *Contours* (Bangkok) 6, nos. 3–4 (November 1993): 16; Costa Rica Tourist Board (ICT) statistics cited in Polly

Jo Morrison, "The Monteverde Area of Costa Rica: A Case Study of Ecotourism Development" (master's thesis, University of Texas, Austin, 1994), p. 31.

3. Beatrice Blake and Anne Becher, *The New Key to Costa Rica* (Berkeley, Calif.: Ulysses Press, 1997), pp. xvii–xxi. The Sustainable Tourism Rating survey was conducted by Anne Becher and Jean Segleau, but Segleau is not one of the authors of the book.

4. The first survey was done by Richard Holland, who directed the Costa Rica-based Department for Responsible Tourism and promoted a code of ethics for the industry. Interviews with Richard Holland; "Paradigm Shift from Reinventing the Wheel to Improving the Wheel?" *Mesoamérica,* September 1996.

5. Costa Rica set up its first tourism board in 1931, and in 1955 it became the Costa Rican Tourist Board (ICT), which continues to the present. Somerset R. Waters, *Travel Industry World Yearbook: The Big Picture—1996–97,* vol. 40 (New York: Child & Waters, 1997), p. 89.

6. Honey, *Hostile Acts,* pp. 51–196.

7. Ibid., p. 179.

8. Carole Hill, "The Paradox of Tourism in Costa Rica," *Cultural Survival Quarterly* 14, no. 1 (1990): 17.

9. Somerset R. Waters, *Travel Industry World Yearbook,* p. 89.

10. Honey, *Hostile Acts,* pp. 65–66, 114–123.

11. Economist Intelligence Unit (EIU), *EIU Country Profile, 1994–95: Costa Rica* (London: EIU, 1994), p. 22.

12. Honey, *Hostile Acts,* pp. 179–180; Hill, "Paradox of Tourism in Costa Rica," p. 17.

13. Randy Lee Loftis, "Costa Rica: A Model of Ecotourism," *Santa Barbara News Press,* April 28, 1996.

14. John Brown, "Officials, Tourism Leaders Dispute Papagayo Project," *Tico Times,* January 21, 1994, p. 13.

15. Ibid.

16. Carlos Roesch, "ICT Straightens Out the Situation of the Tourist Development Project on the Papagayo Gulf," advertisement, *Tico Times,* March 24, 1995, p. 17.

17. **Hotel Ownership on Selected Pacific Coast Costa Rica Beaches, 1995–1996**

Beach	Costa Rican	Foreign	Costa Rica/Foreign[a]
Brasilito	2	3	0
Carrillo	3	2	0
Conchal	0	1[b] (in process)	0
Dominical-Ballena	8	9	1
Dominical (town)	5	4	0
Esterillos Oeste	0	0	0
Esterillos Este	0	2	0
Flamingo	1	2	0
Garza	0	2	0

Grande	1	1	0
Hermosa	1	2	0
Jacó	22	21	1
Junquillal	0	6	1
Manuel Antonio	12	23	1
Matapalo	3	1	0
Negra y Avellanas	3	4	1
Nosara	2	10	0
Pan de Azúcar	0	1	0
Penca	2	1	0
Playa Tortuga	0	7	0
Potrero	2	4	0
Quepos	16	3	0
Sámara	7	13	0
Tamarindo	4	16	0
Zancudo	4	5	1
Total	98	143	6
% of total	40%	58%	2%

[a] Costa Rican/Foreign couple, partners, or foreigner who is a naturalized Costa Rican.
[b] In process.
Source: Anne Becher's notes, which she used in compiling the Sustainable Tourism Rating Survey for *The New Key to Costa Rica*.

18. Under the farsighted but complex law, passed in 1977, no building can legally take place on maritime zone land within parks, reserves, and other protected areas (about two-thirds of the total land area), and municipalities must regulate construction on the rest. Corruption and violations have become the norm: by 1997, some 15,000 "concessions," including most hotels and tourist facilities, had been built within the maritime zone, of which only about 200 were properly registered. The Figueres government proposed a controversial plan to sell off the remaining maritime zone land to private developers in order to raise money to pay the country's debt. Guillermo Escofet, "Beach Zone 'Chaos,'" *Tico Times*, Real Estate and Construction supplement, February 28, 1997; Christine Pratt, "Debt Plan Hailed, Assailed," *Tico Times*, December 20, 1996; Guillermo Escofet, "Interested in Beach Land? Know the Rules," *Tico Times*, March 6, 1998.

19. Katrina Brandon and Alvaro Umaña, "Rooting for Costa Rica's Megaparks," *Américas*, August 1991.

20. For an excellent history of Costa Rica's national park system, see David Rains Wallace, *The Quetzal and the Macaw: The Story of Costa Rica's National Parks* (San Francisco: Sierra Club Books, 1992).

21. Wallace, *The Quetzal and the Macaw*, pp. 100–106.

22. "Costa Rica's Megaparks," p. 29; "Unique Debt Swap to Protect Forest," *The Canopy*, published by The Rainforest Alliance, Spring 1991, pp. 1–2.

23. In 1998, INBio, a Costa Rican scientific research center that catalogs the

country's biological resources, arranged an $11 million (in Canadian dollars) debt-for-nature swap with the Canadian government. The innovative project involves the construction of a "bioprospecting" laboratory and biodiversity garden as well as several projects in protected areas. Carol Weir, "New Lab, Garden for INBio," *Tico Times,* April 24, 1998.

24. The annual operating budget for the national park service runs between $7 million and $12 million. In 1995, only $2.28 million came from international NGOs and $1.68 million came from the Costa Rican government. The park service was able to budget a mere $347,000 of the estimated $10–$36 million needed to buy the remaining inholdings.

25. Park officials decided to allow only 600 visitors per day into Manuel Antonio National Park and to close the park on Mondays. These moves cut visitor numbers almost in half, giving some relief to the park but incensing hotel owners and other local businesspeople, some of whom are being forced to sell or close. Larry Rohter, "Quepos Journal: Today's Garden of Eden, Fouled by Adam and Eve," *New York Times,* December 19, 1996, p. A4; Anne Becher's interview with Jose Courrau in 1996.

26. Wallace, *The Quetzal and the Macaw,* p. 128.

27. Ibid., pp. 134–136.

28. Brandon and Umaña, "Costa Rica's Megaparks,"p. 28; Blake and Becher, *The New Key to Costa Rica,* pp. 338–342.

29. Correspondence with a North American writer and researcher who has studied Costa Rica's Caribbean coast, but who asked, given Maurice Strong's prominence, to remain anonymous.

30. This videotaped interview was done for Greenpeace USA, where I was working as director of media.

31. Author's interviews with Maurice Strong and several researchers and journalists who investigated the controversy and requested that their names not be used; Michele Sheaff, "Summit Organizer Charged with Violating Nature Laws," *Tico Times,* June 5, 1992.

32. "UN 'Earth Summit' Organizer Involved in Conflict as Costa Rica Struggles with the Meaning of Ecotourism," Tropical Conservation News Bureau, Costa Rica, 1992, quoted in Anita Pleumarom, "The Political Economy of Tourism," *The Ecologist* 24, no. 4 (July–August 1994): 144.

33. Author's correspondence with an anonymous North American writer and researcher.

34. Blake and Becher, *New Key to Costa Rica,* pp. 202–203; Susan Place "Nature Tourism and Rural Development in Tortuguero," *Annals of Tourism Research* 18, no. 2 (1991): 186–201.

35. Place, "Nature Tourism," pp. 186–201; Guillermo Escofet, "Loggers Menace Park," *Tico Times,* February 27, 1998.

36. Eliot Wajskol, "Abstract: Ecotourism-Based Entrepreneurship and Wealth in Tortuguero, Costa Rica: Patterns in a Noncohesive Community with Ill-Defined Land Rights" (proposal for master's thesis, Duke University, 1994).

37. In the mid- to late 1990s, Anne Becher, Susan Place, and Beatrice Blake all conducted ownership surveys. As of 1995, of Tortuguero's seventeen hotels and lodges, six of the eight very modest ones in town were mostly locally owned; the two less expensive package-tour lodges were owned by nonresident Costa Ricans from the Central Valley; and seven higher-priced package tour lodges were owned by either nonlocal Costa Ricans or foreigners. Two of

the three foreign owners, including Michael Kaye, live permanently in Costa Rica. Most of these bigger lodges bring in managers, leaving only the menial jobs for local people. Five simple restaurants, two souvenir shops, and two small grocery stores are owned by Tortuguero residents. Most of the canal boat owners are from Limón; some live in San José.

38. Place, "Nature Tourism," pp. 186–201.

39. Susan Place, "Ecotourism for Sustainable Development: Oxymoron or Plausible Strategy?" *GeoJournal* 35, no. 2 (1995): 170, 171.

40. Anne Becher's interviews; Brian Harris, "Furor over Road Link to Tortuguero" and "Biological Corridor Plagued by Problems," *Tico Times,* January 26, 1996; Escofet, "Loggers Menace Park"; Guillermo Escofet, "Debate Rages over Road through Park," *Tico Times,* March 6, 1998.

41. Statistics from Amos Bien, president of the Association of Private Reserve Owners.

42. Paul Eagles, Jennifer Ballantine, and David Fennell, *Marketing to the Ecotourist: Case Studies from Kenya and Costa Rica* (Waterloo, Ontario: University of Waterloo, Department of Recreation and Leisure Studies, n.d.), p. 5.

43. Wallace, *The Quetzal and the Macaw,* pp. 12–13.

44. Elizabeth Boo, *Ecotourism: The Potentials and Pitfalls,* vol. 2 (Washington, D.C.: World Wildlife Fund), p. 44.

45. Morrison, "Monteverde Area of Costa Rica," p. 42; author's interviews and correspondence.

46. Interview with Sue Trostle; Ilse Abshagen Leitinger, "Survival of a Women's Organization over the Long Term: Growing Sophistication of Institutional Strategies and Responses at CASEM, the Artisans' Cooperative in the Santa Elena–Monteverde Region of Costa Rica, and New Challenges" (paper presented at the Nineteenth International Congress of the Latin American Studies Association, Washington, D.C., September 1995).

47. Boo, *Ecotourism: Potentials and Pitfalls,* vol. 2, p. 39.

48. Ibid., p. 38.

49. Interview with Francisco Chamberlain, director, Monteverde Cloud Forest Reserve.

50. "Unique Debt Swap," *The Canopy.*

51. John Burnett, "Ecotourism in Costa Rica," *All Things Considered* (National Public Radio), September 3, 1997.

52. Morrison, "Monteverde Area of Costa Rica," p. 47.

53. Jon Kohl, "No Reserve Is an Island," *Education* (September–October 1993): 77.

54. Interview with Amos Bien; Rara Avis' World Wide Web site (http://www. interlog.com/~rainfrst/; Yanina Rovinski, "Private Reserves, Parks, and Ecotourism in Costa Rica," in Tensie Whelan, ed., *Nature Tourism: Managing for the Environment* (Washington, D.C.: Island Press, 1991), p. 49.

55. Blake and Becher, *New Key to Costa Rica,* pp. 227–228.

56. Other fine examples of ecotourism on private reserves include the 486-hectare (1,200-acre) Marenco Biological Station, which is dedicated to "conservation, education, tourism, and adventure" and located on a hilltop overlooking the Pacific Ocean and adjacent to Corcovado; El Mirador de San Gerardo, a 300-hectare (741-acre) primary forest located on a working Costa Rican–owned

dairy farm with a simple lodge overlooking Arenal Volcano; the Chacón family's Albergue de Montaña Río Savegre, a 300-hectare forest and *finca* with cabins, quetzals, trout fishing, home cooking, and mountain walks; the Dúrika Biological Reserve combines primary and secondary growth and is owned by a community aspiring to self-sufficiency, has impressive terraced gardens with sixty-six crops, and is using its ecotourism profits for purchase of a corridor to La Amistad International Park; and Costa Rican agronomist Peter Aspinall's idyllic Tiskita Lodge, featuring fruit trees, hiking trails, a twenty-meter (sixty-five-foot) waterfall, and a view of the Pacific. Blake and Becher, *New Key to Costa Rica*, pp. 354, 392–393, 423, 439, 446–447. Notes from Anne Becher; Nicki Solloway, "Back to Nature: Costa Rican Commune Opens Its Doors to Ecotourism," *Costa Rica Today*, March 2, 1995.

57. Claudia Alderman, Environment Division, Latin America and the Caribbean, World Bank, "The Economics and the Role of Privately Owned Lands Used for Nature Tourism, Education, and Conservation" (paper presented at the Fourth World Parks Congress of National Parks and Protected Areas, Caracas, Venezuela, February 1992); Jeff Langholz, "Economics, Objectives, and Success of Private Nature Reserves in Sub-Saharan Africa and Latin America," *Conservation Biology* 10, no. 1 (February 1996).

58. Costa Ricans benignly refer to squatters as *precaristas*, a reference to their precarious existence, rather than the common Spanish term, *paracaidistas*, meaning "parachutists."

59. Michael Jack, "Green Luxury in Costa Rica," *AIArchitect*, February 1995, p. 19; letters objecting to scheme sent to Stephanie Stubbs, *AIArchitect* and copies obtained by author; author's interviews in U.S. and Costa Rica.

60. It is estimated that only 34,500 female leatherbacks remain in the world, of which approximately 6,000 live in the Pacific Ocean. Mexico, where 50,000 leatherbacks once nested, now has fewer than 1,000 per year. Stefano Ambrogi, "Efforts to Save Leatherback Get a Boost," *Tico Times*, October 4, 1996.

61. Letter from architect Julia Van Wilpe, Chamber of Consultants in Architecture and Engineering of Costa Rica, to Stephanie Stubbs, *AIArchitect*, September 18, 1995.

62. Xenia Guido, "Is Tourism Hurting Turtles?" *Tico Times*, February 28, 1997.

63. Ambrogi, "Efforts to Save Leatherback."

64. Catalina Calderón, "Luxury, Golf Offered in 'Eco-Sensitive' Project," *Tico Times*, special expotur supplement, May 23, 1997.

65. Jody Lekberg, "No Artificial Ingredients—A Study of Tourism in Costa Rica," *Mesoamérica* 16, no. 3 (March 1997): 13.

66. Guillermo Escofet, "Mega-Resorts the Trend in C.R.," *Tico Times*, special expotur supplement, May 23, 1997.

67. Boo, *Ecotourism: Potentials and Pitfalls*, vol. 1, pp. 27–28.

68. Allen Clinton, "Costa Rica," *Mesoamérica* 16, no. 8 (August 1997): 12.

69. David Petritz, "Cruise Covers Caribbean," *Tico Times*, Weekend section, January 3, 1997.

70. Information supplied by Anne Becher; Ana Báez, "Binomio turismo-conservación: Una alternativa desarrollo," *Technitur: Costa Rica International Magazine* (published by the Professional Tourism Association of Costa Rica), no. 46 (June 1993): 48–53.

71. Blake and Becher, *New Key to Costa Rica,* pp. xvii–xxi; information from Anne Becher.

72. Stefano Ambrogi, "Hoteliers Cheer End of Room Tax," *Tico Times,* November 8, 1996; Ambrogi, "Hotel Files for Intervention," *Tico Times,* October 11, 1996.

73. Barbara Ras, ed., *Costa Rica: A Traveler's Literary Companion* (San Francisco: Whereabout Press, 1994).

74. Peter Brennan, "Drop in Tourism Sparks Alarm," *Tico Times,* July 26, 1996; Stefano Ambrogi, "Tourism Has Other Worries," *Tico Times,* August 30, 1996; Stefano Ambrogi, "Tourism Plans Push," *Tico Times,* September 6, 1996; Clinton, "Costa Rica," p. 12; Lekberg, "No Artificial Ingredients," p. 11–13; "A Warning to Visitors of Street Crime," *New York Times,* Travel section, February 16, 1997, p. 12.

75. A 1996 survey by the National Water Service's Ecological Blue Flag Program found that forty-three beaches did not meet sanitary and safety standards, five were considered unsuitable for bathing, and only ten achieved the program's highest rating. Those beaches surveyed constitute about 80 percent of Costa Rica's main tourist beaches. "Forty-Three Beaches Flunk Test," *Tico Times,* December 6, 1996.

76. A tour package to any of these three countries—Cuba, the Domican Republic, or Mexico—may cost as much as $600 less. Lekberg, "No Artificial Ingredients," p. 12; David Todd, "Why Tourism Is Suffering," letter to the editor, *Tico Times,* August 2, 1996; Guillermo Escofet, "Tourism Off to a Slow Start," *Tico Times,* March 7, 1997; Catalina Calderón, "It Was a Terrible Year for Tourism," *Tico Times,* December 27, 1996; Ambrogi, "Hoteliers Cheer End of Room Tax."

77. By 1996, there were seven international hotel chains operating in Costa Rica. They had either built new hotels or acquired Costa Rican–owned hotels. "Radisson to Administer Hotel Europa Zurquí," *Tico Times,* September 13, 1996.

Chapter 6

Cuba: Growth of Tourism and Ecotourism During the "Special Period"

In October 1994, Moka Ecolodge, a twenty-six-room white stucco, wood, and glass ecotourism lodge nestled into a hillside above the community of Las Terrazas in Cuba's Pinar del Río Province, was officially opened to foreign tourists. I was among the first guests at the lodge, part of a group of fifty Americans who had come to Cuba despite the U.S. travel ban.[1] Moka is the pride of Cuba's ecotourism aficionados, and the symbolism of opening its doors first to U.S. citizens was fitting, since Cuban tourism officials are convinced that ecotourism will succeed on their island only if the U.S. government ends its travel and trade embargoes.

Just an hour outside Havana, Moka is a world apart from the capital's vibrant culture and steamy urban decay. Here, the air is sweet and gentle, the rolling hills are a kaleidoscope of variegated greens, and the tempo of daily life is harmonized to nature's timetable. The four-star Moka Ecolodge is surrounded by ferns and flowers, a tiny stream runs through its lobby, and large trees shoot through the roof. No forest was cut down or hillside razed to build the hotel. Part of its electricity comes from solar panels, and some of the food served at the lodge is grown in hydroponic and organic gardens. The resort complex includes a swimming pool, a tennis court, sulfur springs, and hiking and horseback riding trails; a health spa and a campsite are being added. This is upscale (about $82 for a double room), low-density, environmentally and culturally sensitive tourism—a sharp departure from Cuba's typical low-budget, high-volume package tourism.

Moka was built between the community of Las Terrazas and the Sierra del Rosario, a tropical mountain forest (declared a biosphere reserve by UNESCO in 1985 in recognition of its unique ecosystem), so that tourists could spend time and money at both locations. "What we've tried [to do] is to incorporate the natural environment and the local community. The idea is that the tourists and the community together participate in all this," explained Tourism Minister Osmany Cienfuegos in an interview in the lounge at Moka.

Our group went on guided hikes through the biosphere, had lunch at a restored nineteenth-century coffee plantation, met with scientists at the biosphere reserve's research station, and visited Las Terrazas' health clinic and herbal medicine garden, day-care center, schools, various craft workshops, and small museum displaying the history of the community. We chatted with young people at the communal game area and joined community members crowded into an open-air boathouse for an evening of singing.

Las Terrazas, whose red-tile-roof apartments are built on terraces around an artificial lake, is one of Cuba's oldest and best-functioning postrevolutionary rural communities. It was formed in 1968 when some seventy scattered farm families, charcoal makers, and construction workers elected to move together to gain access to schools, health care, and other amenities. From the outset, Las Terrazas was an experiment in sound environmental and human management, and its progress has been carefully nurtured and monitored by government officials, scientists, environmentalists, sociologists, and other Havana intellectuals, a handful of whom have moved there. Most of the adults in this 850-member village are involved in reforestation work in and around the biosphere reserve.[2] Some 150 work at Moka, either as guides in the reserve or in community tourism projects, including a bakery, craft workshops, a coffee shop, and a small restaurant.

Moka Ecolodge was the brainchild of Cuba's tourism minister Cienfuegos, an architect, and close confidant of Fidel Castro who, from the beginning, played a central role in Las Terrazas.[3] In 1990, as Cuba rapidly slid into economic crisis, Cienfuegos proposed building a small ecotourism lodge to help provide a steady income for Las Terrazas in keeping with the community's ecological and social goals. After a series of community meetings, a team of psychologists and sociologists carried out a detailed house-to-house survey, soliciting opinions on all aspects of tourism. The community gave the green light and chose a special neighborhood council to handle all issues relating to the hotel and tourism. "It's a community hotel, developed and managed by the community," says Jorge Ramón Cuevas, president of ProNaturaleza, a nongovernmental environmental organization that works with Las Terrazas.

Cuba's Ministry of Tourism financed and built the hotel complex at a cost of about $6 million; the community is scheduled to repay the investment over a period of fifteen to twenty years. Forty percent of the profits from the hotel go into a community development fund overseen by the neighborhood committee, and another 10 percent go directly to the community's health clinic, which has begun promoting herbal medicines. In addition, 60 percent of profits from tourism-related businesses (the bakery, coffee shops, craft workshops, etc.) go into the community development fund. At a meeting with community members and scientists who work in the biosphere, one woman explained that the ecotourism hotel is not intended to replace their normal activities: "Tourism is not essential. It's complementary to our other work within the bioreserve. And the profits will support the community's schools and day-care center." Tourism earnings have been used, for instance, to finance the production of a small newsletter; buy shoes, school uniforms, and books for the children; and purchase radios so that people can hear Las Terrazas' community-run station.

Cuevas explains that in addition to providing employment and funding for Las Terrazas, Moka has also helped "increase [community] awareness about the environment and natural resources," including spurring the creation of a children's branch of his organization. Cuevas says, "We've found we can introduce, through the kids, elements of environmental education, and get into the family this way." He says, for instance, that the sixty-nine-member children's committee learned recycling techniques from the hotel and from ProNaturaleza experts and then set about putting recycling boxes in each home and teaching families the proper techniques.

Moka encapsulates the best of Cuba's efforts in ecotourism. This lodge and the concept of ecotourism have captured the imagination and harnessed the talents of many Cuban environmentalists, scientists and social scientists, activists, and community leaders. Although Moka is unique, elsewhere on the island there are scores of other ecotourism projects in various stages of development. Indeed, ecotourism is an outgrowth of Cuba's broader movement toward more environmentally sensitive, locally based technologies and of earlier types of domestic and "solidarity" tourism; it is also a reaction to Cuba's notoriously exploitative and ecologically destructive, prerevolutionary style of tourism.

But the reality is that in Cuba today, large-scale beach and urban tourism is capturing the international contracts and bringing in the bulk of the hard currency. Through environmental impact studies and other forms of monitoring and planning, Cuba is trying to make mass tourism more environmentally responsible. Many Cubans openly worry, however, that their society might be sliding back toward typical conventional foreign-owned mass tourism. There is debate over whether ecotourism is a catalyst for creating a new, "greener" tourism industry or whether it is, as one Cuban intellectual put it, simply "window dressing" for the island's mushrooming conventional tourism. Cienfuegos admits that ecotourism accounts for "very little" of Cuba's overall tourism market. Although as minister of tourism he is the country's highest-ranking ecotourism promoter, he is only cautiously optimistic about its potential: "Ecotourism is something we've just begun to imagine, and we have to modify it. All we've been selling so far is sun and beaches. And so, naturally, if we want this dream to be successful, we have to work at it."

The Metamorphoses of Tourism in Cuba

Sun and beaches have always sold the Caribbean region, and Cuba, the largest Caribbean island and the United States' nearest overseas neighbor, has plenty of both: some 5,794 kilometers (3,600 miles) of coastline, 289 beaches, more than 1,600 small islands and cays *(cayos),* coupled with nearly year-round good weather. In the 1920s, prohibition in the United States helped turn Cuba into an American Riviera for wealthy, famous, and thirsty pleasure seekers. Cuba legalized gambling, and American developers built villas, luxury resorts, casinos, race tracks, country clubs, golf courses, polo and tennis grounds, and marinas on the island. On New Year's Eve 1919–1920, New York hoteliers opened Havana's grandest hotel, the Sevilla-Biltmore, and along Varadero Beach's fine white sands, E.I. du Pont began building mansions for American business executives. In October 1927, Pan American Airways inaugurated passenger service between Key West, Florida, and Havana, and the winter of 1927–1928 broke all previous visitor records. But Cuba's first tourism boom lasted less than a decade: it was brought to an abrupt close by the Great Depression, the end of prohibition in the United States, and Cuba's 1933 revolution.[4]

Cuba's second tourism boom came in the 1950s, spurred by falling sugar prices, the Fulgencio Batista dictatorship's promotion of foreign investment, and the introduction of jet service and package tours. The elite tourism of the 1920s was greatly expanded to include middle- and working-class American vacationers. Pan Am began operating sixty to eighty flights per week from Miami, and steamers and car ferries shuttled between Key West and the island. Cuba's overwhelmingly American clientele, some 350,000 per year by the late 1950s, made it the regional powerhouse, with 20 to 30 percent of the Caribbean's tourism traffic.[5] But Batista's ruthless rule and close personal and business ties to organized crime, prostitution, illegal drug dealing, and gambling cast a dark shadow over the good times. Cuban American Enrique Fernandez graphically writes, "Even in the heyday of Cuba's appeal—in fifties Havana, with its gambling casinos, frozen daiquiris, nightclub extravaganzas, live sex acts, girls and boys for hire, controlled substances out of control, and, a couple of hours away, a beach with sand so fine you could snort it. Even then," the author recalls, Cuba's violent underbelly—"bodies bloodied with bullets and young faces ripped apart by torturers"—got "in the way of paradise."[6] Under Batista, the island's U.S.-dominated tourism became a symbol of the decadence and corruption that paved the way for revolution.

After Castro's forces seized power in January 1959, the American travel industry and the new revolutionary government briefly tried to carry on business as usual. The Castro government, determined to make tourism Cuba's number one foreign exchange earner, quickly committed millions of dollars to expand and modernize hotels, highways, and airports. In October, some 2,500 delegates from the American Society of Travel Agents (ASTA), the largest U.S. travel organization, held their weeklong annual convention in Havana. It was a red-carpet affair, underwritten with $1 million raised from Cuba's travel industry. Castro attended, glad-handing the travel agents and assuring them that his government wanted to expand tourism. Cuba's new tourism commission published a thick, glossy promotional magazine incongruously proclaiming 1959 the "Year of Liberation" and Cuba the "Playground of the Americas" and promising investors "virtually unlimited possibilities for profit-making ventures."[7]

But halfway through the conference, the atmosphere of goodwill suddenly changed. On October 18, an old World War II B-26 bomber, piloted by Cuba's former air force chief, who had defected to Miami, dropped anti-Castro leaflets over Havana. "At first, I thought it was just some tour operator dropping advertisements," recalled Eric Friedheim, executive editor of *Travel Agent Magazine,* who attended the ASTA conference, "but then Cuban antiaircraft gunners opened fire." The next day, a passenger train was machine-gunned by another aircraft.

Although the cold war had not yet reached its peak, Cuba already aligning itself politically with the Soviet Union, and tenuous relations between the United States and Cuba were easily snapped. The U.S. government moved to seal off the island to tourism and most other forms of contact, with U.S. Department of State advisories warning citizens not to travel there. In January 1961, the U.S. government broke off diplomatic relations with Cuba and imposed an economic blockade, and beginning in 1962 it barred U.S. citizens from visiting the island. This, along with the 1961 Bay of Pigs invasion, the 1962 Cuban missile crisis, and general press hysteria, effectively killed U.S. tourism by the early 1960s.

Cuba's radical new government, in turn, expropriated U.S.-owned land, factories, and businesses, including some hotels and other tourist facilities, and moved to wipe out the more repugnant aspects of Cuba's prerevolutionary style of tourism. "Fidel Castro padlocked Cuba's fabulous gambling casinos and taught Havana's prostitutes new trades," writes historian Rosalie Schwartz. "Revolutionary Cuba effectively ended a financially profitable, but morally bankrupt, tourist industry."[8]

Beginning in the late 1960s, the Cuban government developed vacation facilities designed for its own people, much of which was nature oriented: smaller beach resorts, health spas, mountain lodges, fishing clubs, campgrounds, hiking and bicycle trails, and other recreational facilities, all made available to Cubans as part of their employment benefit packages. For

decades workers and their families enjoyed government-subsidized vacations, while Cuba's bureaucratic and military elite relaxed at a network of exclusive retreats.

But international tourism to Cuba took decades to recover. Covertly,
right-wing Cuban exiles and other anti-Castro militants, together with the
Central Intelligence Agency (CIA), worked to terrorize tourists and the
travel industry. Acts of political sabotage included the 1976 bombing of a
Cuban flight out of Barbados, which killed all 73 passengers on board; the
bombing in the late 1970s of the JFK Airport offices of Caribbean Holidays,
which was conducting charter tours to Cuba; and, in the late 1980s, the
bombing of the office of Marazul Tours, the killing of its president, and the
blowing up of several of its planes in Miami.[9] In 1997, anti-Castro militants
again targeted tourism. Within a five-month period, some dozen small
bombs exploded in luxury tourist hotels and restaurants in Havana and elsewhere, injuring several people and killing an Italian Canadian businessman.
Cuban authorities arrested fifteen people who they said were part of a terrorist "network" financed by a Miami-exile organization. One, a former
U.S.-trained Salvadoran soldier who admitted to planting at least six of the
bombs, said in a televised confession that the purpose was "to create panic
among tourists." These widely reported incidents marred Cuba's reputation
as a safe holiday destination and, although Cuban officials deny any such
effect, they may have contributed to the slight slowdown during 1997 in the
rapid growth of tourist numbers.[10]

In 1976, Cuba created a single government agency, the National
Institute of Tourism (INTUR), to conduct international tourism, collect
data, and develop policy; a subsidiary, Cubatur, was created as the country's
only travel agency. Then Cuba started moving very cautiously into state-run
package tourism to beach resorts and Havana nightclubs. At first, most foreign tourists were Canadians; gradually, small numbers came from Germany,
France, Spain, Italy, Argentina, and Mexico. Russians and eastern Europeans
vacationed in the same hotels, but on a barter system that reimbursed Cuba
in kind with vacations in Soviet bloc countries. No money changed hands.
In 1977, tourist arrivals totaled 66,600 (including some 17,000 from the
Soviet bloc), a 700 percent increase over 1974 but less than 20 percent of
the prerevolution levels.

Nearly all of these tourists went only to Varadero and Guardalavaca
beaches and to Havana. Varadero was the first area refurbished and expanded during the 1970s to handle foreign tourists, who were isolated
in the deluxe International Hotel and other large resort hotels.[11] "These
were 'Club Med' tours," says Bob Guild, program director for the New
York–based Marazul Tours, which has conducted educational tours to Cuba
since the 1970s. "There was a desire to put a wall around the people going

down and isolate them from the Cuban people." In the late 1970s, the International and several other Varadero hotels began accepting only dollars, a practice later extended to Havana's larger hotels. Cubans could not legally possess dollars (until 1993), so they were barred from these hotels and restaurants; virtually the only Cubans whom tourists met were hotel employees and tour drivers. This state-run enclave tourism was limited in numbers, but the bulk of its profits went to the government. Except for overseas travel agencies and, on occasion, foreign airlines, the government owned all the links in the tour package. Bob Guild estimates that 80 percent or more of the tourism dollars stayed *in* Cuba—a sharp contrast from package tourism elsewhere, where often 80 percent of tourism dollars either never enters the developing country or "leaks out."

Cuba's enclave tourism did have problems. The new hotels were architecturally uninsipiring and often environmentally insensitive, the service lackluster, the food notoriously poor. "People came for other reasons, because the beaches were empty, the weather predictably good, or the price a bargain," Guild noted in a telephone interview. Jane McManus, who has lived in Cuba since the mid-1960s and has written an English language travel guide for the island, says that the government bureaucracy was the main obstacle to well-run tourism. "It's very inefficient, and it's not agile enough," she contends. "Tourism is a sensitive market, and the people who are running it have to be aware of what the client wants. Unfortunately, the government always managed everything and it just doesn't work in tourism," McManus said in an interview in her Havana apartment.

When sugar prices fell in the early 1980s, the Central Community of Cuba's Communist Party embarked on a protracted debate over how to expand and modernize tourism and whether to permit gambling by foreigners on some of Cuba's beautiful offshore cays. The party finally said yes to tourism expansion, including the docking of cruise ships, but no to gambling on the island or in its territorial waters. In 1982, Decree No. 50 on Economic Association Between Cuban and Foreign Entities authorized, for the first time, foreign investment in tourism through joint ventures in which the government "aspires to" majority control. By 1984, international tourism was growing but still modest: earnings totaled $80 million per year[12] from fewer than 200,000 tourists.

Tourism was being revamped in other ways as well. In 1987, Cuba's government broke the INTUR-Cubatur monopoly by creating the first "autonomous"—that is, semigovernmental—development corporation, Cubanacán, to seek foreign capital on a fifty-fifty basis in hotels and tourism infrastructure projects. Most of the early deals were with Spanish hotel chains, including several new luxury hotels in Varadero. By the late 1980s, a major hotel construction program was under way and joint tourism ventures had been signed with Mexican, German, Italian, Argentine, Jamaican, and Canadian companies. By 1991, tourism was earning $400 million per year and had become the country's third highest foreign exchange earner.[13]

The U.S. Travel and Trade Embargo Against Cuba

Never had the United States tried so long and hard to isolate internationally and economically, as well as politically destabilize another country. From 1962 onward, with a brief hiatus during the Jimmy Carter administration in the late 1970s, the United States imposed various trade and travel bans against Cuba. The impact on tourism was enormous: in the 1950s, more than 90 percent of tourists were from the United States; in 1987 Cuba reported only 8,727 Americans, less than 5 percent of the total 208,241 visitors.[14] According to a May 1992 study, Cuba's tourism sector was losing $3.5 billion each year as a result of the embargo.[15] (Total losses were estimated at $29 billion, plus another $9 billion in indirect costs.)

In an effort to isolate Cuba, the United States tried to strong-arm its allies into breaking off diplomatic relations with the island. By 1965, only Mexico and Canada in the Western Hemisphere recognized the Castro government. After the 1989 collapse of the Soviet Union and "fall" of communism, most countries normalized their relations with Cuba; the U.S. government, however, tightened its unilateral trade embargo and travel ban and imposed new sanctions. In April 1992, President George Bush closed U.S. ports to any ships that had stopped in Cuba during a previous six-month period. In October 1992, the United States Congress passed the draconian Cuban Democracy Act, popularly known as the Torricelli bill, which prohibits subsidiaries of U.S. companies based in "third" or other foreign countries from trading with Cuba and put in effect Track II, an effort to undermine Castro by funding dissidents on the island.

Relations soured even further when, in February 1996, Cuban MiG jets shot down two small airplanes belonging to a Miami-based exile group, killing their crews. For months, planes flown by Brothers to the Rescue had defied Cuban government warnings by repeatedly overflying the island's airspace and, on several occasions, dropping anti-Castro leaflets. President Bill Clinton denounced the shoot-down and reacted by stopping humanitarian aid, family visits, and financial remittances from Cuban Americans in the United States. But his strongest retaliation was signing the Helms-Burton bill, which gave U.S. nationals the right to sue in U.S. courts foreign companies investing in expropriated Cuban property. The law expands the definition of U.S. nationals to include those who became American citizens after their properties were expropriated, opening the way for nearly 6,000 claims. In signing the bill, Clinton relinquished the presidential right to end the

Cuban embargo, which can now only be lifted by Congress, thus compli-
cating any efforts to normalize relations. The Helms-Burton law provoked
widespread international anger. The Economist Intelligence Unit wrote that
"most democratic governments saw [Clinton's] crack down on third-coun-
try investment in Cuba as an extreme reaction and as an unwarranted inter-
ference in free markets."[16] Although Cuban officials have maintained that
the Helms-Burton law has not caused any established investors to withdraw
from Cuba, outside observers say the threat of legal action has made new
foreign investors more carefully weigh the pros and cons of doing business
in Cuba. In 1997, the oldest and largest of Cuba's foreign investors, the
Spanish hotel group Grupo Sol Meliá, received U.S. assurances that it would
not suffer retaliation under Helms-Burton.[17] In 1998, following Pope John
Paul II's historic visit to Cuba, Clinton rolled back some of the restrictions
he had imposed, but the Helms-Burton law remained on the books.

Since the 1960s, most Americans who have traveled to Cuba have done
so illegally. The U.S. travel ban—actually a series of rulings by the Department of Treasury that prohibit Americans from spending money in Cuba—
exempts only a few approved categories of visitors, including academics,
charity workers, and journalists. In an effort to circumvent the ban,
the Cuban government began financing "solidarity" visits for Americans
wanting to see the social and political changes under way in Cuba, show support for the Cuban people, and contribute materials (medicine, books, bicycles, etc.) or labor (such as help in harvesting sugarcane). Technically,
these were legal visits because Cuba picked up the tab and the Americans, at
least in theory, spent no money on the island. Cuba lost financially but
gained some political support in the United States.

The U.S. government's criminal penalties for unauthorized travel to
Cuba are up to ten years' imprisonment and $250,000 in individual and
$1 million in corporate fines, but it has never been fully enforced. Over the
years, some of those challenging the travel and trade bans have been
harassed and questioned, been detained by immigration officials, had their
passports seized, been fined, or been taken to court. Treasury Department
officials say that between September 1993 and September 1996, they initiated 159 civil cases alleging forbidden trade with Cuba and collected
$192,198 in fines.[18] Only one American, Dan Snow, has actually spent time
in jail. During the Carter administration, when travel was legal, Snow, a fish-
erman from Kingwood, Texas, began taking groups of bass enthusiasts to
Cuba. "There are ten great bass lakes in the world, and they are all in Cuba,"
says Snow. Although he doesn't use the term, Snow's Bass Tours have from
the outset incorporated many of the principles of ecotourism: "We tag the
bass, keep records, and don't eat, mount, or keep any catch. We work with
Cuban scientists and the local communities living near the lakes." When

President Ronald Reagan reimposed the travel ban in 1982, Snow ignored warnings and continued taking more than 1,000 fishermen per year to Cuba. He was eventually arrested and, after a lengthy court battle, sentenced to forty-five weekends in jail, a $5,300 fine, and 1,000 hours of community service. In June 1995, he finally completed this "sentence," and, Snow says, "quick as I could, I began going again. Maybe I'll also become the second person to go to jail." But by 1995, tourism to Cuba was in high gear and increasing numbers of Americans—estimates ranged from 15,000 to as many as 60,000[19]—were defying the travel ban.

The "Special Period"

The engine driving both Moka's and Cuba's current fast-paced tourism expansion was the "Special Period," as Cubans dubbed the catastrophic economic crisis brought on by the 1989 collapse of the Soviet Union. Before the collapse, 85 percent of Cuba's foreign trade had been with the Soviet bloc: the Soviets had supplied nearly all of Cuba's oil, raw materials, equipment, spare parts, and imported food, and Cuba had exported 75 percent of its sugar and nickel to Russia and eastern Europe. The abrupt end of Soviet aid and trade, coupled with the U.S. trade embargo and travel ban, plunged Cuba into its worst economic crisis and threatened to undo the national health care system, free schooling through the university level, and other social programs that many Cubans viewed as the major gains of the Cuban Revolution. To protect such programs as well as its political control, the Cuban government embarked on wide-ranging economic reforms, including opening up to foreign investment, a "dollarization" of the economy, and small-scale Cuban private enterprise. Although most Cubans welcomed the economic (and the more tentative and limited political) liberalizations begun during the Special Period, they continued to favor some more flexible and benign form of socialism over raw capitalism. As one high-level official explained, the Cuban people "think they want more free enterprise, but they are too accustomed to free education and health care to ever give that up. . . . Things here are difficult now, but there is absolutely no question that life under Batista was far worse for most Cubans."[20]

By early 1995, however, the island appeared to have turned the corner from the black days of severe food and fuel shortages, electricity cuts, factory closures, the plummeting peso, and the exodus by sea of an estimated 33,000 Cubans aboard makeshift boats and rafts. In February 1995, Castro proudly, and accurately, told *Time* magazine, "No other country has been able to endure the collapse of the socialist camp and the loss of its imports in the midst of a blockade."[21] Despite predictions that Cuba would remain locked in a Stalinist model incapable of adapting to either the end of the cold war or the economic crisis, Castro's government proved considerably flexible and innovative. During 1995, the economy grew for the first time in a decade, by a modest 2.5 percent, about the same rate as the U.S. economy. Then, in 1996, GDP jumped an impressive 7.8 percent. However, Cuba's foreign debt, much of it in the form of extremely costly short-term loans, rose from 2.8 billion in 1983 to $9 billion in 1995. [22]

Tourism Growth in the 1990s

In facing down economic collapse and political unrest, Cuba undertook the twin challenges of reinserting itself into the global free-market economy and transforming its domestic economy along more decentralized, more market-oriented, and often more sustainable, less import-dependent lines. Central to the first challenge of moving into the global economy via export promotion and foreign investment has been the revving up of international tourism. Central to the second challenge of building a more self-sufficient economy has been a "greening" of Cuba's agriculture, medicine, energy, transportation, and, more modestly, its tourism. These twin challenges are not always in harmony. For instance, although Cuba pursues ecotourism with a thoughtful, carefully planned, interagency government strategy, the pace is slow and environmental regulation is at times compromised by the need for quick hard currency from foreign investors and package tours.

Tourism is being looked to as the country's new "engine of growth" to replace the Soviet bloc's aid and market.[23] Cuba's strategy parallels that of other socialist countries, from Tanzania, Zimbabwe, and Mozambique in Africa to eastern Europe and the former Soviet Republics, all of which began, in the 1990s, concentrating on tourism as they moved from centralized planning toward various degrees of market economics. However, Cuba

Table 6.1. Cuba's Tourism Growth

	1958	1977	1984	1988	1989	1991	1993	1995	1996
Arrivals (in thousands)	350	67	207	298	315	418	544	738	995
Gross receipts (in millions of U.S. dollars)	—	—	76	—	204	387	720	1,100	1,300

Source: Economist Intelligence Unit (EIU), *EIU Country Profile, 1994–95: Cuba* (London: EIU, 1994); *Cuba: EIU Country Report,* 3rd quarter 1997, p. 23; Somerset Waters, *Travel Industry World Yearbook: The Big Picture—1996–1997* (New York: Child & Waters, 1997); World Tourism Organization (WTO), *Yearbook of Tourism Statistics,* 47th ed. (Madrid: WTO, 1995); other publications.
Note: Figures are unavailable where there are blanks.

is unique in that its economic liberalizations have not been directed by a structural adjustment program imposed by the World Bank, the International Monetary Fund (IMF), and the U.S. Agency for International Development (USAID). As a result, the Cuban government has arguably retained more control in deciding on the pace and specific components of its economic transformation.

After 1990, both investors and tourists began flocking to Cuba (see table 6.1). Between 1990 and 1994, Cuba's tourism industry grew by more than 16 percent annually, compared with 4.7 percent for the Caribbean region as a whole. By 1995, tourism ranked as Cuba's second highest gross foreign exchange earner ($1.1 billion for 1995) after sugar ($1.2 billion), and within a year it had become number one.

Cuba's tourism expansion is financed through both state and foreign investment, and a key tool has been joint ventures between domestic government-controlled enterprises and foreign companies. In 1994, the government established a Foreign Investment Ministry, which is seeking overseas capital for all sectors of the economy except defense, national security, public health, and education. One hundred forty-four of the estimated 220 such joint investment projects established by the end of September 1995 were in the field of tourism.[24] By December 1995, the Ministry of Tourism was negotiating 200 possible joint venture projects with companies from twenty-eight countries, mainly Italy, Spain, Canada, and France. And by 1997, even China was negotiating a joint venture, for a motel and restaurant in Varadero.[25] Much of this involved expansion of facilities at Varadero but also projects in other regions and the offshore cays. Spanish capital is driving development on the island of Cayo Coco, and an Austrian company plans to spend $100 million on a tourist village on Cayo Sabinal. The deals have increasingly diverged from straight investment as investors, including a German investment and management company, LTI International Hotels, signed less risky management agreements.[26]

New Cuban legislation granted enormous tax breaks and other incentives to investors. In 1992, Decree 50 of 1982 was substantially broadened to allow transfer of state property to joint ventures with foreign capital, unrestricted repatriation of profits and dividends, freedom to hire foreign managers, and government insurance covering losses from accidents, nondelivery of goods, and other problems.[27] In September 1995, the government announced further liberalizations permitting 100 percent foreign ownership and foreign capital in partnerships with private Cuban investors.

Investors and economic analysts were clearly pleased. "The market opportunities for Cuba are overwhelming," concluded a 1994 report by the Canadian accounting firm Price Waterhouse.[28] In another study, luxury hotels "all reported profitability and occupancy rates well above levels in their

other Caribbean properties. . . . Occupancy rates were also excellent," ranging from 77 to 88 percent year-round.[29] Carlos Pereda, a representative of
Spain's Sol Meliá hotel chain, which has six investment and management
contracts as well as cruise tourism in Cuba, ticked off the benefits: "We have
had every tariff facility, no taxes, no extortion from a single official, we export our profits and have absolute liberty to acquire on the international
market all of the products and articles to offer quality service at the four- and
five-star hotels of Sol Meliá."[30]

All this has left the U.S. travel industry chomping at the bit to get back
into this tourism "paradise," where it once was dominant. Executives from
companies such as Marriott International, Hyatt Hotels and Resorts, and
Radisson Hotels International have quietly gone to Havana, and according
to John Kavulich, president of the New York–based U.S.–Cuban Trade and
Economic Council, by early 1995 "damn near everybody" else involved in
tourism had called his office expressing an interest in investing in Cuba.
Dozens of American firms have signed nonbinding letters of intent to invest
in tourism, medicine, and biotechnology[31] once the embargo is lifted, and
other U.S. entrepreneurs have become silent partners in tourism projects
with companies from Canada, Mexico, Jamaica, and other countries. One
hotel investor from Rochester, New York, who entered into a covert partnership with a Canadian hotel management company, angrily told a journalist in Havana, "It's absurd why we can't officially do business here. The
Cold War is over. The Russians have left. What are we waiting for?"[32] An increasingly powerful business bloc, including the U.S. Chamber of
Commerce and the American Society of Travel Agents, has called for an end
to the U.S. trade embargo and travel ban.

Despite the joint ventures and management agreements, four of every
five dollars fueling the country's tourism expansion have been Cuban, according to the Ministry of Tourism's vice minister, Eduardo Rodríguez de
la Vega. By the year 2000, the Cuban government will have spend 2.4 billion pesos on infrastructure (roads, sewage systems, communications, etc.),
transportation, and other tourism-related projects.[33] This amounts to a
tremendous economic and considerable political and social cost. While the
economic crisis forced Cubans to eat less, ride bicycles or walk, and queue
for nearly everything, La Sevilla (the old Sevilla-Biltmore) and several other
stately Havana hotels were being extensively remodeled—murals repainted,
marble repaired, brass polished. In the early and mid-1990s, electricity cuts
routinely plunged much of Havana into nightly darkness, but tourist hotels
always have electricity, air-conditioning, cable television, and plenty of food.
Time magazine described this as the "stark contrast between the fantasy
playground being built for foreigners and the gritty reality that ordinary

Cubans must contend with."[34] Such discrepancies have led to a lot of grumbling and, on occasion, unrest. In street riots on August 5, 1994, which helped unleash the rafters' exodus, hundreds of protesters hurled rocks at Havana's foreigners-only Hotel Deauville and nearby "dollar" stores that sell hard currency imported or hard to acquire Cuban goods. "You work, and you earn 100 pesos a month, and you can't afford to live in this country," one protester told the *New York Times*. "It is we Cubans who have become tourists here."[35]

In August 1993, the government announced that for the first time in several decades, Cubans could legally possess dollars. Cuban society was instantly divided between those with and those without access to dollars. Tourist hotels quickly became magnets for Cubans desperate to earn hard currency. The 54,000 people the tourism finance division, FINATUR, calculated in 1995 as directly employed in tourism included among their ranks highly trained professionals who could no longer live on their peso salaries. Tour guides and waiters can often earn more from a day or two's worth of dollar tips than they were receiving in a month as a scientist, physician, or teacher. Cubans not connected to the tourism industry are still barred from patronizing many luxury hotels and restaurants (apparently at the discretion of the manager), a much-resented policy that *Condé Nast Traveler* labeled "tourist apartheid."[36] In scenes reminiscent of pre-Castro Cuba, there has appeared outside Havana's grandest hotels tourism's informal sector of prostitutes, black marketers, hawkers, artists and artisans, beggars, free lance guides and interpreters, and unlicensed taxi drivers.

Gradually, the Cuban government has come to permit or at least tolerate more dollar-based private enterprises linked to tourism, including the renting of rooms and operation of small restaurants in private homes. By 1997, more than one-fifth of all tourists (67,900) were reported to be staying in private homes, at a revenue loss to the state of an estimated $20 million per year. This was relatively little—less than 2 percent of gross tourism revenue—but it affected particularly the smaller, Cuban-managed, three-star hotels.[37] Even more popular, given the mediocre fare and service in most government-run restaurants, are the *paladares* (named after a restaurant in a popular Brazilian soap opera), small family-run restaurants in private apartments and houses. They are allowed to seat only twelve persons, must be run only by family members, and must pay taxes to the government. But the boundaries are often pushed: for example, one excellent, reasonably priced *paladar* I visited had several additional dining rooms behind closed doors and a bank of young male waiters who showed no family resemblance. Individual Cubans continue, however, to be barred from entering into joint ventures with foreign partners, in part because under socialism no Cuban would legally have been able to accumulate enough capital to invest in a major tourism project, or any other kind of project, for that matter.

Between 1991 and 1995, the number of tourists grew by nearly 80 percent, most of them from Canada, Germany, Italy, Latin America, and Spain. The majority continue, as in the past, to arrive by way of inexpensive beach resort package tours.[38] Optimistically, the government has announced that it expects to have 50,000 hotel rooms (up from 23,255 in 1995), 2 million visitors, and a gross revenue of more than $3 billion by the year 2000. According to the Center for Studies on the Cuban Economy in Havana, the long-term goal is to develop sixty-seven tourist areas, concentrated in eight regions and with some 200,000 rooms capable of housing 10 million tourists, who will bring in $10–$15 billion dollars per year.[39] If this goal is met, it would clearly equal mass tourism par excellence.

Despite Cuba's impressive growth, by the end of 1995 it was still a small player in the region: it ranked fourteenth among twenty Latin American destinations and had captured only 4.2 percent of Caribbean visitors—compared with 20 to 30 percent in the 1950s. But its rapid expansion, heavy infrastructure investment, and potential capacity (estimated at almost 4 million visitors if it regains its pre-1959 share of the regional traffic[40]) is making other tourism-dependent Caribbean and Central American countries very nervous. Puerto Rico's executive director of tourism, Luis Fortuno, warned that the resurgence of the Cuban tourism industry is creating "the possibility of a disastrous impact here as well as in the rest of the Caribbean." The situation will only worsen when the U.S. blockade is lifted, since more than half of the 13 million tourists to the Caribbean each year are Americans.[41] Cuba, for its part, is concerned that tourism competition might jeopardize newly established diplomatic and trade ties within the region. By the mid-1990s, nearly the entire Caribbean had defied the United States and normalized relations with Castro. Cuba has joined the thirty-two-nation Caribbean Tourism Organization (CTO), and in 1994 the CTO met in Cuba for the first time in more than thirty years. Cuban officials stress regional cooperation rather than competition and are working with Jamaica and Costa Rica to promote multiple destination tour packages. "We want the Caribbean to become a giant tourism area and not for any particular island to be the champion," declared Cuba's minister of foreign relations, Roberto Robaina González.[42]

By the mid-1990s, Cubans were generally convinced that tourism, despite its downside, had proved vital in countering the country's economic crisis. Tourism dollars were being used to purchase fuel, medicines, and other urgently needed imports; reduce the national debt; and prevent the collapse of the country's day-care centers, clinics, schools, and other social programs. According to 1995 Ministry of Tourism statistics, the government was using about 30 percent of tourism's net profits for health care, education, and other government programs; the rest was being reinvested in the tourism industry.[43]

However, the tourism sector's heavy dependence on imports, together with the economic concessions given to foreign investors, means that a sizable portion of net and gross profits now either never reach Cuba or "leak" out of the island. For instance, between 1992 and the end of September 1995, FINATUR, the government's tourism finance arm, spent more than $193 million on tourism sector imports. An estimated 70 percent of the foreign exchange earnings from tourism go to purchase tourism-related imports,[44] higher than the Caribbean average. In addition, because the embargo precludes Cuba from purchasing imports from the United States, transport costs are also high. "This is probably the most fundamental problem faced today by Cuban tourism, since its import component radically limits any major increase in profitability," concludes one study.[45]

Although this situation will improve as Cuban factories reopen and agricultural production picks up, a more fundamental issue is the fact that Cuba owns and controls a decreasing share of its tourism sector. Not only has the state given up its monopoly over the tourism infrastructure on the island, but also the number of foreign airlines and cruise ships bringing package tours to Cuba has increased greatly. Most tourists arrive on prepaid, low-budget package tours and charter flights, marketed by some 150 private travel agencies in thirty countries.[46] Evidence indicates that although the overall revenue from tourism is growing, Cuba's tourism today is less profitable per tourist than in the 1970s and 1980s because imports are high and the government now has less ownership and control of segments in the tourism chain.

Clearly, the rapid growth of mass tourism has provided Cuba with a critical short-term, hard-currency fix for getting out of the Special Period. But many Cubans see the long-term implications of this type of mass tourism as worrisome. The government argues that it is implementing regulations and oversight to ensure that Cuba does not return to the pre-1959 era of uncontrolled, unregulated, foreign-owned mass tourism. There have been crackdowns on "sex tourism" involving both prostitutes and minors, and harsh penalties have been imposed on foreigners involved in organizing the trade. In addition, the Tourism Ministry is trying to move from low-cost packages for mass tourism toward higher value-added tourism involving the development of new, smaller resorts.[47] The government is continuing to play a central role both in running and monitoring tourism, and in this process the philosophy and principles of ecotourism are crucial, both in "greening" conventional tourism, and in developing new types of locally based, educational, and environmentally sensitive tourism.

The Emergence of Ecotourism in Cuba

By the late 1980s, ecotourism had become the hottest new market niche in the Central American and Caribbean travel industry, and Cuba, desperate for hard currency, began efforts to cash in on the concept. In addition to the financial motivation, there were, as well, several antecedents that helped propel Cuba's ecotourism development. More than any other country in the region, Cuba knows firsthand the social and environmental pitfalls of conventional tourism, and Cuban environmentalists had observed with dismay the unchecked tourism development in Mexico and Spain. Gisela Alonso, who in 1996 headed the Cuban Academy of Sciences' Department of Natural Resources and Tourism, explains "Several years ago we started to see some dangers within our traditional tourism. We don't want to have the problems of Cancún and the Mediterranean. We want to make sure that ecotourism is well handled." The roots of Cuba's ecotourism are found both in Cuba's people-to-people "solidarity" tourism, through which visitors learned about the country and interacted with its people, and in its extensive network of small, nature-based lodges, spas, and parks built for domestic tourism.

The origins of Cuba's ecotourism are also found in the island's broader environmental movement, which was greatly strengthened during the Special Period in the 1990s. Like the Chinese character for the word crisis, Cuba's Special Period contained within it elements of both danger and opportunity. In the face of enormous hardships, Cubans demonstrated a strong resilience and determination, and on some fronts daily life has become more healthy and environmentally friendly. People ride bicycles or walk, recycle nearly everything, and throughout the island plant small garden plots. Farmers plow fields with oxen instead of tractors and use organic instead of chemical fertilizers and pesticides. Acupuncture and hypnosis have replaced anesthesia for some dental and medical procedures, and sutures are being made from locally grown hemp. The country has also embarked on an impressive program to grow, manufacture, and promote herbal medicines based on Cuba's traditional home remedies.[48]

Ecotourism has gained popularity as part of this wider effort to construct a new sustainable, less externally dependent economic model. Although these measures were initially spurred by the economic crisis, many Cubans have come to see organic fertilizers and pesticides, herbal medicine, bicycles, and ecotourism as superior alternatives. As one Cuban tourism official put it, "From the point of view of beaches, we don't have a big advantage [over others in the region]. But from the point of view of nature, we do. The country is very well preserved, with extraordinary scenic beauty. Tourists traveling the world are searching for places that are tranquil. And

that is what we should be offering: a sane tourism, a well-conceived ecotourism."

Cuba's ecotourism potential is clearly enormous. The island is the
largest in the Caribbean and has the greatest biodiversity, with seventy-three
wildlife sanctuaries, biosphere reserves, and national parks covering more
than 12 percent of the national territory. Indeed, as *Condé Nast Traveler*
notes, "Once out of Havana, one is silenced by the majesty of this country
and finally understands what everyone has been fighting about. With its limitless expanses of rolling hills, rivers, and ocean, Cuba is truly God's country."[49] Among the island's natural attractions are some 8,000 species of
trees, flowers, and plants and 350 species of birds, including the red, white,
and blue–feathered Cuban trogon, which is the national bird, and the
Zunzunzito, the world's smallest hummingbird, which is indigenous to
Cuba. The island's scenic beauty and variety, coupled with "the wonderful
warmth of the people, good climate, [and] tremendous infrastructure in
areas of ecological interest," including small lodges, restaurants, health spas,
campgrounds and hiking trails, surpass even the attractions of Costa Rica,
says Bary Roberts, owner of the San José–based Tikal Tours and the first foreign tour operator to market ecotours to Cuba.

Ecotourism is not only part of Cuba's "green revolution," but also part
of its effort to build and strengthen civil society at the community level.
While the Central Committee had, in the early 1980s, debated the efficacy
of moving more aggressively into mass tourism, Roberts says that, in the
early 1990s, the committee debated long and thoroughly about moving into
ecotourism, in part because this "greener" form of tourism had political implications. With ecotourism, tourists are no longer confined to beach enclaves or the hotel district in Old Havana; rather, they travel throughout the
country and have close contact with rural communities. From the outset,
however, ecotourism had an important ally: Osmany Cienfuegos (brother of
Camilo Cienfuegos, who, after Che Guevara, is Cuba's most respected
revolutionary martyr), who in 1994 was named Cuba's first minister of
tourism.[50] Roberts, who has worked closely with Cienfuegos, says his support has been crucial: "The person who finally really caught on to what ecotourism is all about is Osmany Cienfuegos, and it's because of the vertical
power structure [and] totalitarian government that Cuba can establish very
clearly what are the proper parameters for ecotourism."

Once the government agreed to move forward, ecotourism proponents
began studying Cuba's competitors (particularly Costa Rica, Belize, and
Ecuador), holding symposiums, developing guidelines, choosing sites, creating ecotourism facilities, putting together ecotour packages, training
guides, and so forth, as well as striving, through new legislation and government institutions, to make conventional tourism projects more environ-

mentally sound. The Cuban government began formulating a carefully planned, interdisciplinary national ecotourism strategy under a broad banner incorporating culture, history, architecture, agriculture, health care, and rural community life, along with nature exploration and education. As Roberto Perez Lazar, tourism director for Pinar del Río Province, told me in an interview, "We consider ecotourism to be tourism which integrates, in addition to nature, the history and culture of the location. Nature is the basis, but we see the local population, with its culture, its history, its traditions as an integral part." Of the countries profiled in this book, only South Africa comes close to having such a comprehensive definition and such a multidimensional government strategy. But whereas in South Africa the impetus for ecotourism has come from rural shantytowns, community activists, NGOs, environmental consultants, and the private sector, Cuba's large, well-educated pool of government scientists, its academics and environmentalists, and Minister Cienfuegos and some other tourism officials have been the chief catalysts.

Government Support for Ecotourism

Since the early 1990s, a variety of government agencies, at both the national and provincial levels, have been preparing the ground for the move into ecotourism as well as working to make conventional tourism more environmentally sensitive. Following the 1992 Earth Summit—where Cuba was one of only two countries in the world to be given an A+ rating for implementation of sustainable development practices—Cuba pledged to implement the summit's environmental program, Agenda 21, and adopted a constitutional amendment to protect its environment. In 1993, the government set up a National Program for Environment and Development and created a series of new institutions, as a government document states, as "a concrete and clear expression of the political will to continue along a [course of] sustainable development." The new institutions include a National Commission on Ecotourism, made up of tourism officials, scientists, and environmentalists. According to commission member Gisela Alonso, "This Commission approves any marketing which will be done of particular areas, not only from the point of view of selecting the areas of biodiversity, but also from the point of view of managing these areas in an ecologically integrated way." The commission is helping to train multilingual naturalist guides, developing visitor conduct manuals, and establishing criteria for determining carrying capacity for ecotourism sites. In keeping with the principles of ecotourism, the authorities have decided that a percentage of profits should be used for park maintenance and improvement.[51] The government has also created several legal bodies to reinforce environmental protection, including ones on environmental impact assessment and environmental inspection with authority to analyze the environmental effects of any new tourism and other construction projects.

In 1994, the government set up a new Ministry of Science, Technology, and Environment, superseding the National Commission for Protection of the Environment and the Rational Use of Natural Resources (COMARNA), roughly equivalent to the Environmental Protection Agency (EPA) in the United States. This ministry overlaps with the Ministries of Tourism, Culture, and Agriculture in handling ecotourism, and there continues to be tension and conflict over the best way to balance environmental protection and economic development. The ministry's researchers complain that the tourism officials commission them to carry out studies and then do not always abide by the results. For instance, there is an ongoing controversy over construction of causeways to Cayo Coco and other cays where tourism is being developed. The government rejected scientific recommendations for a series of bridges to permit water circulation, opting instead for less effective, less expensive underwater tunnels in the causeways.[52] In Varadero as well, overdevelopment has continued virtually unabated despite recommendations for preventing erosion and protecting the dunes.[53] Many hotels in this prime tourism location are badly constructed, built too close together and too near the ocean, and have introduced non-native plants and trees, according to the Cuban Institute of Physical Planning. A 1995 *Condé Nast Traveler* cover story on tourism in Cuba found the expansion excessive. "Although the Cubans have repeatedly vowed that they will never overdevelop, Varadero is already showing the early symptoms of 'Cancúnization,' since Spanish, Canadian, and Mexican investors have put up nearly a dozen hotels in the last ten years, [and] with more on the drawing board Varadero is now barely recognizable from what it was only a decade ago."[54]

In 1997, at the United Nations' Rio + 5 Forum, called to assess national implementation of Agenda 21, Cuba's report hinted at some of these problems. It stated that although the Ministry of Tourism and the Ministry of Science, Technology, and Environment were "working together" in a "Tourism Development" program, "there is a need to consider even more the different environment variables in the planning and execution of the tourist centers." It added that the national program of coastal management had been hurt by a lack of financial and material resources and a legal framework for integrated coastal zone management. In order to rectify some of these shortcomings, tourism enterprises were, beginning in 1997, supposed "to define their specific environmental policies, based on the guidelines established by the Ministry of Tourism," including "use of environmentally safe technologies and low water consumption sanitation facilities, systems for the use of alternative energy sources, the use of indigenous plant species in gardening," and "training programs for executives and workers in the tourism sphere."[55] All of this shows an impressive degree of national and regional planning and use of scientific expertise in environmental protection and tourism development, which have not been found in the other countries surveyed.

Cuba still remains exempt from the scale of overdevelopment and environmentally destructive construction that is widespread on many Caribbean islands. Jorge Mario García, who is with the Ministry of Science, Technology, and Environment's Center for Environmental Education and Information, argues that "there is a clear consciousness and will at the top levels to protect the environment, to manage development of tourism in a rational and sustainable way. Cuba has suffered very few major environmental effects from the rapid development of tourism because we did exhaustive environmental studies prior to development, and while some concessions had to be made from time to time, on the whole they normally opted in favor of the environment."[56]

In addition to major reshuffling at the top, ecotourism policy has also been partially decentralized to the fourteen provinces and myriad government-owned hotel and tour agency chains. Until the early 1990s, INTUR and its tourism agency subsidiary, Cubatur, operated 95 percent of all tourism in Cuba. In 1994, the tourism industry was restructured: INTUR was abolished, its functions dispersed among a number of new specialized agencies, and a Ministry of Tourism was created to handle planning, policy, and coordination.

Today, an alphabet soup of new semiautonomous government companies have fingers in the tourism pot and are signing joint ventures with foreign investors. All have their own ecotourism divisions, and many have their own tour operators, marketing departments, vehicles, hotels, guides, and sometimes planes and boats, as well as ecotourism divisions. These include Grupo Cubanacán, which in the late 1980s started developing hotels and took about 20 percent of the tourism market; Fantastico, which belongs to Cubanacán and handles specialty tourism such as ecotourism; Gaviota (Seagull), the armed forces' international tourism wing, which offers health, hunting and fishing, and other specialized holidays and has some of the most luxurious ecotourism resorts; Cubamar, the national camping organization, which in 1994 began focusing on international ecotourism excursions including camping, youth hostels, and bike tours; Gran Caribe, which operates four- and five-star hotels and by 1997 had approximately 40 percent of the tourism market;[57] and many more. Most joint ventures have been with either Cubanacán or Gaviota. In addition, there are other specialized agencies, such as Puerto Sol (marinas and other nautical services), Transtur (transport), Abatur (supplies), Publicitur (publicity), Caracol (hotel shops), and UNECA, a government-owned construction company, which built Moka Ecolodge and many other new hotels.[58]

Despite the government's reorganization, political commitment, and professional competence, finding funds for ecotourism has been a problem; there has been no foreign investment in any ecotourism projects. "Until now we have talked but there have been no deals," said Tourism Minister Cienfuegos in 1994, and this situation has persisted. (Cuba has, however, received some modest international assistance for its national parks and biosphere reserves.) It may be that the government wants to keep control of its more politically sensitive, community-linked ecotourism projects. The government has, for instance, reportedly rejected several offers from foreign investors wanting to buy into Moka, and there are stories of other potential ecotourism investors running into insurmountable bureaucratic difficulties.[59] Officials from the Ministry of Tourism and the Chamber of Commerce, among others, say that the main reason is that foreign investors are currently making quick profits in conventional tourism and view the ecotourism market in Cuba as too uncertain, undeveloped, and long term. "We meet with potential investors, but only a minority is interested in ecotourism," says government ecologist Julio Pérez García. "We ourselves are unfamiliar with the market, and we can't do what we don't know about."

Ecotourism Attractions: Cuba's Greener, Cleaner Alternatives

Cuba's international ecotourism industry is being built, in part, on the foundation of its collapsing domestic tourism infrastructure. With the economic crisis, including the grave shortages of gasoline and transportation, the government was forced to cut back on vacation packages for workers. (Still intact are the three-day, state-paid honeymoon packages to certain hotels, which account, Cubans quip, for the country's high rate of divorce and remarriage.) As a result, some of Cuba's favorite domestic tourist spots were closed and rapidly fell into disrepair. The National Commission on Ecotourism has identified some half dozen of the country's best-equipped areas for immediate ecotourism development. These include Pinar del Río Province, Ciénaga de Zapata, the Escambray Mountains, Holguín Province, Sierra Maestra National Park, and Pinares de Mayarí.[60] All these areas have domestic tourism infrastructure that is being prepared for ecotourism, and new hotels, restaurants, health spas, hiking trails, and other facilities are being added.

The agriculturally rich and breathtakingly beautiful Pinar del Río Province, to the west of Havana, has long been a favorite vacation region for

Cubans and is now the heartland of Cuba's international ecotourism expansion. On a drive through the Sierra de los Órganos shortly after the Cuban Revolution, Castro envisioned developing Pinar del Río for what he called "agrotourism," which would "locate here a new wave of national and international tourists, precisely in those places that offer such beauty and natural attractions."[61]

The province includes several distinct zones, ranging from the island's oldest mountain ranges to beaches and cays; vast fields of tobacco and sugarcane, quaint rural towns with cobble-stone streets and adobe houses; and the Viñales valley, whose spectacular vistas include ecologically unique rock formations called *mogotes,* which rise like huge, green-robed pincushions[62] from a floor of intensely cultivated farmland. The ecotourism possibilities seem limitless: the *mogotes* and mountains are laced with hiking trails, thousands of species of plants and trees (including a small, rare endemic pine), subterranean rivers, waterfalls, and some 5,000 caves.

Several of Pinar del Río's lovely smaller hotels that were used before the 1990s for domestic tourism have now been renovated for foreigners. Villa Soroa, for instance, includes forty-nine mountainside cabins and an enormous swimming pool; several restaurants; hiking, bicycle, and horseback riding trails, and exquisite gardens with some 700 varieties of orchids. Two other lovely older hotels formerly catering to Cuban tourists, La Ermita and Los Jazmines, have spectacular views overlooking the Viñales valley and have been thoroughly upgraded for ecotourism. In addition to Moka Ecolodge, Pinar del Río's new ecotourism offerings include twenty A-frame cottages built with raised walkways and local mangrove poles on Cayo Levisa, a short boat ride from the fishing village of La Esperanza. At the western tip of the island is Guanahacabibes Peninsula National Park, a vast, remote flatland of forest and wildlife reserve that the government plans to further develop for ecotourism.

In sharp geographic contrast to Pinar del Río is the hot, humid Ciénaga de Zapata, a big, boot-shaped lowland peninsula of saw grass swamp and thick woods southeast of Havana. At the time of Castro's victory, the Zapata Peninsula was the island's most backward region, sparsely inhabited by charcoal makers, fishermen, and crocodiles. The new government put in roads, schools, health clinics, and tourist facilities,[63] including three hotels: Villa Guamá on Treasure Lake and two large, mediocre resorts along beautiful stretches of Playa Larga and Playa Girón (on the Bay of Pigs), catering to package tours from Canada, Germany, and France.

The Castro government's first resort, Guamá, was an idyllic black bass fishing and honeymoon resort catering to foreign, but attracting mainly domestic, tourists. Constructed on thirteen tiny islands in Treasure Lake to resemble a pre-Columbian Indian village, it has fifty-nine thatch-roof bungalows raised on stilts and connected with arched wooden bridges. (Castro used to stay in bungalow #33.) Despite the fragility of the Guamá area, writes Smithsonian Institution scientist Ross in a 1995 paper, "proper sewage disposal, environmental education, and integration into a sound environmental management scheme for the Zapata Swamp [were] completely absent."[64] By 1994, the resort was virtually empty, although the staff remained employed. The bridges were collapsing, the roofs were full of holes, the swimming pool was crisscrossed with deep cracks, and, tourism officials said, they were seeking a joint venture with foreign capital to do the repairs. This did not happen; instead, Horizontes, which operates two- and three-star hotels, financed the refurbishing, and Guamá is now open for foreign tourists and a small number of Cuban honeymooners and outstanding workers.

Provincial tourism director Mario Díaz says the peninsula has about fifty other tourist attractions, mostly restaurants and multiple-use recreation areas. "We believe that our region is one of the ones which today offers the best potential for the development of ecotourism," Díaz explained in a 1995 interview. Described as the biological mirror of the Florida Everglades,[65] the Zapata Peninsula is Cuba's major tropical wildlife reserve, with reptiles, mammals, 160 species of birds, and a wide range of wild orchids and other unusual flora and fauna. The Caleta Buena restaurant is among its newest ecotourism facilities. It sits on a bluff overlooking the sea, surrounded by a series of natural, well-protected pools where visitors can swim safely among tropical fish. Just off the main highway is El Cenote, a limestone sinkhole, and nearby, Cueva de los Pescos, Cuba's deepest lagoon, which connects to a series of underwater caves and caverns ideal for scuba diving. Nestled among the trees and overlooking El Cenote is another attractive, ranch-style restaurant, with a red tile roof and wooden tables.

Karen Wald, an American journalist who has lived in Cuba for some three decades, is the foremost foreign expert on Cuba's ecotourism. She has interviewed many of Cuba's main ecotourism promoters; analyzed the legislation, institutions, and companies handling ecotourism, and visited a number of existing and proposed sites. She concludes that despite the hardships posed by the Special Period, Cuba is solidly committed both to ecotourism and to a "greener" type of conventional tourism. But Wald has also found although there is a strong cadre of Cubans involved in ecotourism, they face a number of problems: insufficient funds, marketing difficulties, and ecological degradation of some sites.

Wald is especially enthusiastic about developments under way in the mountains and along the coasts of eastern Cuba, particularly in Cienfuegos, Holguín, and Santiago de Cuba Provinces. For instance, Gran Piedra National Park, located near Santiago de Cuba, takes its name from a huge rock balanced on a peak more than half a mile above sea level from which, on clear days, Jamaica and Haiti are visible. The park's varied topography includes giant ferns, giant pine woods, and wild orchids. There are trails for hiking and horseback riding, and camping expeditions are conducted by specially trained guides. These specialists told Wald that swaths of land have been denuded by agriculture and logging; that the park was, for decades, overused for national tourism; and that its rustic cabin hotels need to be modernized and made more environmentally sensitive. However, ecotourism is providing impetus and some resources for reforestation, new trails, and scientific investigations.

On the island's eastern tip, the slow-paced Baracoa, the site of Christopher Columbus's 1492 landing and Cuba's first capital (1512–1515), is just getting into ecotourism. Until after the revolution, no road ran to this remote outpost, located in Guantánamo Province, which also uncomfortably houses the U.S. naval base. Baracoa is fronted with miles of unspoiled beaches behind which El Yunque (The Anvil), a flat, square mountain, rises some 610 meters (2,000 feet) above the sea, long serving as a point of reference for sailors. Hikers can climb to the top of this peak, which was declared a national monument because for centuries Indians, runaway slaves, and rebel fighters sought shelter here. Cubanacán, Horizontes, and other tour companies are offering ecotourism packages to Guantánamo and neighboring Granma Province, and more small hotels, hiking trails, and other ecotourism attractions are being built. The high Sierra Maestra range is crisscrossed with winding trails and rivers, including the Toa, the island's widest river, and filled with caves, beautiful waterfalls, Taíno Indian artifacts, and tropical birds, royal palms, and other fauna and flora. At Casa Campesina, a rural house surrounded by flowering and fruit-bearing trees, visitors see how local farmers live, make chocolate and cocoa, and grow *achote,* star fruit, *guayaba, guayacoqui,* and other local fruits and vegetables. The region includes Cuchillas de Toa, a tropical rain forest that is one of Cuba's four biosphere reserves; Bahia de Mata, a black-sand beach described in Columbus's diary; and beautiful Playa Duaba, where a river flows into the sea from the mountain backdrop and important Taíno archaeological remains have been found.

Cubamar, a reincarnation of the old national chain that provided camping, hosteling, hiking, bicycling, and boat trips to Cuban youth, was formed in 1994 to revamp these facilities for international ecotourism. Cubamar's director, Oscar Rodríguez, says that the company, run mostly by young people, has hired an ecotourism specialist and is training guides, labeling plants and trees, and upgrading its infrastructure. In Pinar del Río, Cubamar offers Sendero Maravilla, a guided walking tour through the rich Viñales valley, and a stay at Aguas Claras, a small hotel and campsite with a typical creole restaurant. At Varadero, Cubamar also offers sunbathers day excursions of ecotourism lite: bird-watching, caves, fresh water springs, an archaeological site, horseback riding, and swimming in a river. Although some camping is still offered to Cuban nationals, Rodríguez says Cubamar is focusing on international tourism in order to gain resources so that it can eventually provide camping for everyone.

Cuba's broadly defined ecotourism industry also includes health and stress reduction spas, an offshoot of the country's excellent public health and medical services. (In fact, nature tourism and health tourism have long been linked, as illustrated by the European "Grand Tours" of the eighteenth and nineteenth centuries, which included visits to supposedly curative hot springs. In Cuba, health tourism was also practiced on an organized basis in the nineteenth century, when wealthy Cubans sought curative waters at Santa María del Rosario, outside Havana.) The Castro government has long offered its citizens and a limited number of foreigners three types of health tourism: inpatient and outpatient hospital care in Havana, sanatoriums, and health spas. The spas use, as one tourism brochure puts it, "the healing effects of lovely landscapes, fresh air, splashes in the sea and sunbathing." Although the curative power of sunbathing is debatable, in the mid- to late 1990s several mountain spas have been integrated into ecotourism programs. Run by medical specialists, the spas handle a wide range of physical and psychological ailments, offering weight and stress reduction programs and treatments focused on sleep disorders, alcoholism, drug addiction, and asthma. Treatment combines traditional Western medicines and high-tech equipment with herbal medicines, mud baths, medicinal and hot springs, acupuncture, massage, relaxation techniques, hypnosis, exercise, and, increasingly, low-fat and vegetarian diets. A growing number of international tourists are coming to Cuba's high-quality, relatively inexpensive, and beautifully situated spas such as Topes de Collantes and El Saltón,[66] making this one of the fastest-growing types of tourism. Like cultural tourism, this type of health tourism is frequently linked by the tourism industry and travelers themselves to ecotourism. At its best, health tourism does fit at least some of the criteria of sound ecotourism, involving travel to natural destinations, being low impact and educational, and involving and benefiting the local communities.

Within Cuba there is, in fact, an ongoing debate over how ecotourism interfaces with and benefits local communities. In Pinar del Rio, the provincial tourism director Roberto Perez has a clear vision: "Part of the benefits have to go to the preservation of what we have here. In addition, part should contribute to improving the living standard of these people. That's how we see ecotourism," Perez says in a 1995 interview. Cubanacán, Horizontes, and other newer tourism companies are mandated to ensure that local communities are involved in and benefiting from their projects. The country's proudest example—Moka Ecolodge—is clearly benefiting the Las

Terrazas community financially, and according to experts at the Man and Nature Foundation, several other communities, including the fishing village of Las Morlas on the Varadero Peninsula, are working on similar profit-sharing arrangements with ecotourism projects. At an ecotourism conference in Santiago de Cuba Province in late 1994, however, several speakers questioned the extent to which local communities are actually involved in and benefiting from ecotourism. Although the Cuban government has been actively signing agreements with foreign investors, apparently as yet there is no move to systematically work out written contractual arrangements with local communities.[67]

All of Cuba's tourism companies have developed ecotourism sites and packages, but three—Cubanacán, Horizontes, and Gaviota—have the best-developed programs and are most aggressively promoting ecotourism excursions internationally, particularly in Canada and Spain. Costa Rican tour operator Barry Roberts, who runs ecotourism tours in Cuba, says that the Cuban government has been able to maintain control over these new semi-autonomous companies "so you don't have a bunch of people abusing ecotourism when they're doing eco-commercialism instead of being responsible." However, some of what these companies market as ecotourism is dubious. Horizontes, for instance, lists in its ecotourism brochure the hotels at Playa Girón and Playa Larga, which were built and designed for large, conventional package tours. In Pinar del Río, Horizontes is taking ecotourists to the Indian Cave, where they travel by motorboat down an underground river that winds through a series of sculptured chambers lit by artificial colored lights. Indian Cave was originally opened as a domestic tourism attraction in the 1970s, and environmentalists now recognize that gasoline from the motorboats is polluting the river and the fumes are damaging the cave's rock formations. Motorboats are not used in other caves in, for instance, Cienfuegos Province. In addition, the tour agency Rumbos, which operates restaurants and kiosks, often lacks environmental sensitivity: Cuban environmentalists quip that this agency's idea of a nature trail is a cement path with metal handrails, and Karen Wald has found cheaply built Rumbos kiosks selling beer, soda, and snacks in otherwise beautiful parks and scenic monument sites. In 1996, however, Rumbos hired an ecotourism specialist and a new president and began making improvements.

One of the most bizarre and inappropriate ecotourism destinations is Cayo Saetía, an islet off Cuba's northeastern coast containing thousands of Indian and African animals, including zebra, ostrich, gazelle, antelopes, and even white rhinos, where Gaviota has been conducting camera and hunting safaris. The animals were imported for zoos or given as gifts to Cuba over the past thirty years. In Cuba's mild climate and with no natural predators, they have bred rapidly, so the Ministry of Agriculture has permitted controlled hunting. A Gaviota brochure reads, "At Cayo Saetía you feel attracted by the enchantments of an African jungle combined with the pleasures of an excellent beach in the Caribbean." Another brochure, prepared for Canadians, shows several camouflage-suited hunters and states, "Big game hunting? YES! These one-week trips offer the challenge and excitement of hunting in the rolling red grasslands and hardwood forests of a 42 sq. km. island." By the mid-1990s, however, Gaviota had discontinued the hunting safaris.

Cuba's move into ecotourism brings other challenges and obstacles. Marketing has been slow and cautious, and at least in Europe and Canada, Cuba is saddled with the image of offering cheap, often fairly mediocre, package beach tours. According to one study, Cuba's "two main appeals at the present time remain 'sun and sand' and 'value for money.' . . . It is clear that a generic 'sun and sand' positioning makes the Cuba destination vulnerable to shifts to other locations, due to price or novelty."[68] Over the long run, ecotourism, which often involves less costly and more environmentally sensitive infrastructure and retains more of its profits, will prove more lasting than mass tourism. But, says tour operator Barry Roberts, to market ecotourism successfully, "You have to change the image first. The purchasing power of the ecotourist is generally higher than [that of] the mass tourists. This requires developing new marketing, better infrastructure, and better services."

For Cuba's minister of tourism, Osmany Cienfuegos, ecotourism's most serious obstacle to growth is, in a sense, beyond the industry's control: the U.S. travel and trade blockade. "If the blockade were lifted," states Cienfuegos, "ecotourism would jump dramatically with the influx of North American tourists. Lifting the blockade is a major factor in our success with ecotourism." Although this undoubtedly is true, ending the blockade will also cause a dramatic increase in mass tourism and could conceivably overwhelm Cuba's ecotourism efforts.

Cuba's Ecotourism Scorecard

Where is it all leading? This is the question that Cubans and close observers are pondering. The *it* may refer to ecotourism, to Cuba's overall tourism development strategy, or to the even broader question of market reforms. Cuba is at a crossroads, a country in transition from state ownership and centralized planning to more decentralized decision-making and a mixed economy of state ownership, communal ownership, foreign private ownership, and, in certain areas, private local ownership. The old model is dead, but the process toward and final shape of the new model emerging from the Special Period are not yet clear. In assessing how well Cuba is meeting the criteria of genuine ecotourism, it is necessary to assess both the development of ecotourism as a niche market and efforts to "green" its much more powerful cousin, conventional nature tourism.

So far Cuba gets mixed reviews when its ecotourism efforts are compared to the following seven criteria that are necessary for real ecotourism.

1. *Involves travel to natural destinations.* In terms of its natural attractions, Cuba has a fine network of unique, diverse, and largely unspoiled beaches and offshore islands, and a wide variety of underexploited natural wonders rivaling those of Costa Rica and surpassing those in the rest of the Caribbean. These attractions, however, are largely a well-kept secret, with most visitors continuing to be drawn to Cuba by its reputation for inexpensive sun-and-surf tourism and Havana nightlife.

2. *Minimizes impact.* A tourism analysis in the mid-1990s by the Canadian investment firm Price Waterhouse argued optimistically that Cuba is uniquely capable of making a complete transformation to a cleaner, healthier form of tourism. The study, commissioned by the Cuban government, concludes that this island, unlike others in the Caribbean, is in an enviable position of having "a tourism industry that can be fashioned and expanded to meet current and future demands, rather than those of 20 years ago. We believe there to be no [other Caribbean nation with] the same ability to re-engineer their tourism industry from the ground up, or to benefit and learn from the experiences and mistakes of other destinations."[69]

   In reality, however, Cuba is not a tourism tabula rasa. The government must adapt its old enclave tourism infrastructure, much of which is environmentally insensitive and architecturally unattractive, to current needs and the modern market. Many of the large foreign firms involved in joint ventures have little interest or know-how in environmental protection or community involvement. In the rush to expand tourism, sound environmental practices have, on a number of occasions, been sacrificed. Cuba is also saddled with an international reputation as a bargain destination for mass tourism, and the government has not had sufficient time, money, or market know-how to revamp this image.

   On the other hand, Cuba's impressive ecotourism infrastructure has been built on the back of its crumbling domestic tourism infrastructure. Ecotourism has inherited a wealth of small hotels, spas, cabins, chalets, and campgrounds, which are being refurbished and upgraded for international visitors. Many were constructed with little attention to their physical effect on the environment, but there are now standards and systems in place to ensure, funds and time permitting, that they are rebuilt with greater environmental sensitivity. New ecotourism facilities are being held to much higher standards to ensure that they are small, are low impact, and blend into their surroundings.

In assessing the environmental effects of both tourism and ecotourism, David Collis, former Deputy Director of Georgetown University's Cuba Project, concludes, "Cuba has neither the financing nor the construction capability to turn itself into an environmental disaster overnight. The number of proposed ecotourism sites remains small and tourist visits are limited. The current prospects for severe environmental degradation appear low. However, this could change if development plans are redesigned to maximize hard currency earnings."[70]

Out of economic necessity, Cuba has experimented with low-cost, environmentally responsible, locally available, and renewable alternatives. Collis is guardedly optimistic: "Growing environmental awareness at the grass roots, the population's relatively high level of scientific education, the lower cost of some environmentally sound methods, and the acknowledged importance of environmental protection to long-term tourism revenues all provide limited grounds for hope. However," he cautions, "the economic and political forces militating against environmental protection remain formidable and should not be underestimated."[71]

3. *Builds environmental awareness.* Through legislation, new ministries and institutes, and participation in national and international conferences, Cuba has laid an impressive theoretical foundation for ecotourism, carefully mapped out areas targeted for ecotourism development, and set standards for "greening" conventional tourism. Cuba probably surpasses even Costa Rica in its well-trained experts (scientists, engineers, architects, etc.) and well-educated workforce. Those involved in ecotourism, as drivers, guides, tour company officials, park rangers, and hotel employees, frequently have a deep and multifaceted conception of ecotourism that encompasses environmental protection, community development and empowerment, careful planning, and protection of social services. Much ecotourism planning, however, continues to be from the top down, a result of enlightened national and provincial policies and an outgrowth of struggles among government agencies rather than a result of popular grassroots campaigns. Even Moka Ecolodge, Cuba's most comprehensive ecotourism project, is popularly referred to as "Osmany's hotel," a recognition that it is a creation of the minister of tourism, not the Las Terrazas community. Yet Moka does have close ties to the Las Terrazas community and has helped to spur environmental awareness and stimulate cultural activities and local crafts. By the late 1990s, no other ecotourism ventures had so successfully enhanced environmental education and cultural activities at the community level.

4. *Provides direct financial benefits for conservation.* Unlike in Cost Rica, the Galápagos Islands, and other places where a percentage of park entrance fees are designated for both the particular park and the overall park system, in Cuba there are no separate entrance fees to national parks and biosphere reserves. (Entrance to certain parks, such as the very fragile Ciénaga de Zapata National Park, is restricted and visitors can only enter by hiring a guide.) Foreign visitors usually go through one of the government's tour agencies and pay for the entire package. Tourism-related profits go into the government's coffer and are used to finance the tourism section, imports, social welfare programs, the government bureaucracy, and other state expenses. In the early 1990s, the government designated that a portion of tourism profits should be used to upgrade national parks and other protected areas. Rehabilitation has been concentrated in those parks, reserves, beaches, and other conservation areas earmarked for international tourism.

5. *Provides financial benefits and empowerment for local people.* During the 1990s, tourism became Cuba's main engine of growth. In the wake of the collapse of the Soviet Union, tourism was widely credited with pulling the island back from the brink of economic disaster during the difficult era known as the Special Period. The government has invested hundreds of millions of dollars in tourism, and although a majority of the profits have either gone to foreign investors or been reinvested in refurbishing, expanding, and supporting the tourism industry itself, tourism dollars have also provided funds for vital imports and propped up public health, education, and other social programs. For instance, Cuban government statistics for 1995 indicate that the country's gross hard currency receipts from tourism were $1.1 billion, whereas net earnings were only about $340 million.[72]

Tourism has been a controversial development strategy. Cubans openly grumbled about the large slice of public funds poured into luxury tourism projects while islanders queue for basic necessities; about the "apartheid" system that excludes Cubans from certain hotels and restaurants; and about the growth of prostitution, gambling, the black market, and other social ills. Many Cubans, however, particularly in Havana, are personally benefiting from international tourism. Some have found work in the tourism industry; others have turned their homes into guest houses or small restaurants and their cars into taxis. By 1997, for instance, slightly more than one-fifth of all tourists were staying in private homes.[73] In the countryside, a few whole communities, most notably Las Terrazas, are benefiting financially from ecotourism.

But despite its investment in infrastructure, the Cuban government has not effectively marketed ecotourism via, for instance, reputable and experienced ecotourism operators in Canada and Europe. As a result, many of the fine ecotourism facilities are underutilized and not profitable.

6. *Respects local culture.* There is widespread concern in Cuba that the rapid growth of conventional tourism is leading to a return to the prerevolutionary days of prostitution, gambling, black-marketing, and other vices. The government has sought to control prostitution and limit casinos, but these ills are evident to all visitors. In Italy, Mexico, and elsewhere, Cuba is being marketed as a place for cheap, easy, and safe sex (since its rate of AIDS has been low and well controlled). The number of Italian tourists, many of them pursuing "sexual tourism," jumped almost eightfold between 1991 and 1996, from some 24,000 to more than 192,000, according to the Ministry of Tourism. Two Cuban authors sought to counter the trend by publishing, in Italian, *Travel to the Identity of an Island,* which concentrates on Cuba's cultural offerings, including art, festivals, and music.[74]

7. *Supports human rights and democratic movements.* Ironically, the collapse of the Soviet Union, not the U.S. embargo, has been the proximate cause of Cuba's economic and political reforms. In this process, ecotourism is contributing to ongoing discussions about how to strengthen local communities and civil society and how to evolve a new, "greener," model of development. Most Cubans supporting these liberalizations argue that more, not fewer, ties and contacts with foreigners, including Americans, will help strengthen the democratic forces within the island.

Future Prospects

Some of those trying to predict the future worry that ecotourism and the "greening" of conventional tourism may prove a mere passing fancy as Cuba plunges headlong into mass tourism, a development model that is doomed to failure. At a February 1995 meeting in Havana, Cuban economists concluded that it would be unwise for the country to become overly dependent on tourism, given the volatility of both investors and tourists.[75] Historian Rosalie Schwartz concurs that the current "cycle of investment, promotion, and construction intended to salvage the Cuban economy" could fail. She warns rather ominously, "Two previous waves of tourism [in the 1920s and 1950s] ended in financial loss and revolution. History never repeats exactly, but it sometimes comes close."[76]

For the near future, barring a major catastrophe, both tourism and ecotourism will continue to coexist. Cuba's minister of tourism, Osmany Cienfuegos, the man with his finger most closely on the pulse of what's possible, is very clear: "We need to make ecotourism more important," but "we're continuing to market the beaches as well." Havana-based journalist and economist Marc Frank, who has lived in Cuba for a decade, agrees that it's not "an either/or question. I think that Cuba is very serious about protecting the natural environment. That's not in any way a hoax. At the same time, Cuba does need to develop mass tourism, with all its negative impacts. And the best they can do is try to make it as healthy as possible. But they can't stop its development because they need it in order to survive. And they are trying to find a balance." But the reality is that major change—whether through Castro's eventual death, political upheaval, or normalization of relations with the United States—is just off center stage. One way or another, Cuba will almost certainly be reconnected with the U.S. market. How this happens will affect the future of ecotourism and, undoubtedly, everything else in Cuba.

Notes

I am especially grateful to Karen Wald for her enormous assistance in collecting and analyzing information for this chapter.

1. In recent years, increasing numbers of Americans have visited Cuba to challenge the U.S. travel ban. The most organized challenge has been mounted by Global Exchange, a San Francisco–based human rights organization supporting economic, political, and social justice movements around the world.

2. Through reforestation programs, the government has increased the island's forest area from 14 percent at the time of the revolution to almost 20 percent by the mid-1990s.

3. Interview with Jorge Ramón Cuevas during "The Caribbean Environment: Issues of Mutual Concern" conference sponsored by Cuba Project, Georgetown University, Washington, D.C., December 5–6, 1995.

4. Rosalie Schwartz, "Cuban Tourism: A History Lesson," *Cuba Update*, winter–spring 1991.

5. Francoise Simon, "Tourism Development in Transition Economies: The Cuba Case," *Columbia Journal of World Business*, spring 1995, p. 27.

6. Enrique Fernández, "Fidel's Limbo," *Condé Nast Traveler*, July 1991, p. 72.

7. Harry Tomlinson, ed., "Cuba . . . 1959: Land of Opportunity, Playland of the Americas," *CUBA Magazine* (Havana: Cuban Tourist Commission, 1959), p. 50.

8. Schwartz, "Cuban Tourism," p. 24. Anticolonialists and Third World activists hailed Cuba's bold stand against both U.S. domination and the decadent tourism industry. In the early 1970s, for instance, Tanzanian Marxist Issa Shivji, wrote that "the 'Hiltons' were put to proper use—accommodating students and workers on their way to participate in literacy campaigns and weekend sugar-cane cutting. The property had reverted to its rightful owners." I.G. Shivji, ed., *Tourism and Socialist Development* (Dar es Salaam: Tanzania Publishing House, 1975), p. x.

9. There are numerous books detailing the litany of sabotage and terrorist actions by Cuban exiles and the CIA aimed at killing Castro and toppling his government. Among the most thorough is Warren Hinckle and William Turner, *Deadly Secrets: The CIA-Mafia War against Castro and the Assassination of*

JFK (New York: Thunder's Mouth Press, 1992). Originally published as *The Fish Is Red* (New York: Harper & Row, 1981), this new edition describes various attacks on tourism facilities. "Inside a six-week span [in 1976] the Cuban United Nations Mission in New York was bombed; a bomb exploded in a van carrying luggage to a Cubana airliner in Kingston, Jamaica; the office of British West Indies Airlines in Barbados was bombed; the Air Panama office and Cuban Embassy in Bogotá, Colombia, were attacked [and] the Cubana office in Panama was bombed" (p. 382).

10. Latin American Data Base, University of New Mexico; "Salvadoran Is Bomb Suspect," *Tico Times*, October 10, 1997; Economist Intelligence Unit, *Cuba: EIU Country Report*, 3rd quarter 1997, pp. 25–26; Larry Rohter, "Wave of Bombings Stops in Cuba but Tensions Persist," *New York Times*, October 13, 1997.

11. Jane McManus, *Getting to Know Cuba: A Travel Guide* (New York: St Martin's Press, 1989), p. 99. Even though the Cuban government also built several dozen simple cottages and put in lockers so that some Cuban workers could use this sparkling white-sand beach, Varadero remained, according to travel writer Jane McManus, "a little tourist ghetto." Interview with Jane McManus in Havana, December 1996.

12. Marc Frank, *CUBA Looks to the Year 2000* (New York: International Publisher, 1993), p. 156.

13. Ibid.; McManus, *Getting to Know Cuba*, p. 39.

14. Gareth Jenkins and Xavier González-Paz, eds., *Cuba Business*, vol. 3, no. 3, June 1989 and *Cuba Business: Report '89 Preview*, n.d., London.

15. Simon, "Tourism Development," p. 38.

16. Economist Intelligence Unit, *Cuba: EIU Country Report*, 2nd quarter 1996, p. 7; Christopher P. Baker, *Cuba Handbook* (Chico, Calif.: Moon Travel Handbooks, 1997), pp. 44–45, 57–59.

17. Economist Intelligence Unit, *Cuba: EIU Country Report*, 1st quarter 1997, p. 24.

18. "Warning Letter," Department of the U.S. Treasury, in possession of author; Christopher Reynolds, "The Secret Vacation Americans Don't Talk About," *Los Angeles Times*, April 20, 1997; Peter Greenberg, "The Forbidden Business Trip," *Frequent Flyer*, February 1994, p. 30.

19. Ibid.; Baker, *Cuba Handbook*, p. 87.

20. Elinor Lander Horwitz, "Return to a Forbidden Island," *Washington Post*, May 18, 1997, p. E10.

21. Cathy Booth, "Castro's Compromise," *Time*, February 20, 1995, p. 58.

22. Baker, *Cuba Handbook*, p. 78.

23. Iraida Calzadilla Rodríguez, "Turismo, hoy algo mas que una perspectiva," *Granma*, November 28, 1995.

24. Baker, *Cuba Handbook*, p. 76; Interview with Cuba–based economic journalist Marc Frank; Economist Intelligence Unit, *Cuba: EIU Country Report*, 2nd quarter 1996, p. 13; Interview with John Kavulich, president of the New York–based U.S.–Cuba Trade and Economic Council, which provides information to U.S. businesses exploring investment possibilities on the island.

25. Dalia Acosta, "Cuba-Economy: Tourism Sweeter Than Sugar," InterPress Service, December 20, 1995; Christopher Baker, "Fifteenth Cuba Tourism Convention Augurs a Healthy Future," *Cuba Update*, October 1995, p. 13;

Economist Intelligence Unit, *Cuba: EIU Country Report,* 3rd quarter 1997, p. 26.

26. Economist Intelligence Unit (EIU), *EIU Country Profile 1994–95: Cuba* (London: EIU, 1994), pp. 27–28.

27. Simon, "Tourism Development," p. 33.

28. Quoted in Baker, "Fifteenth Cuba Tourism Convention," p. 14.

29. Simon, "Tourism Development," p. 33.

30. Gareth Jenkins and Lila Haines, *Cuba: Prospects for Reform, Trade, and Investment* (London: Economist Intelligence Unit, 1994), p. 88.

31. Booth, "Lion in Winter."

32. Greenberg, "Forbidden Business Trip," p. 33.

33. Interview with economist Eduardo de Llano, Havana, December 1996; Economist Intelligence Unit, *Cuba: EIU Country Report,* 1st quarter 1997, p. 24, and 2nd quarter 1996, p. 13.

34. Cathy Booth, "Open for Business," *Time,* February 20, 1995, p. 54.

35. Maria Newman, "Collars Define Cuba's Haves and Have-Nots," *New York Times,* August 28, 1994, p. 1.

36. Ann Louise Bardach, "Cuba Fever," *Condé Nast Traveler,* November 1995, p. 312.

37. Economist Intelligence Unit, *Cuba: EIU Country Report,* 3rd quarter 1997, p. 26.

38. Tourists flock to Cuba in part because its package tours continue to be a bargain. For instance, a one-week package tour from Toronto to a Varadero Beach resort might cost just $650, with airfare, lodging, meals, sports activities, and unlimited drinks included. As Shawn Rank, a Canadian from Ottawa on a two-week vacation in cinder block bungalows at the Bay of Pigs, explained, "It's 25 percent less than other islands for Canadians. I've been to most islands in the immediate area. Cuba isn't on the top of the list, but with the price factor, you overlook that." By 1997, the *Tico Times* was reporting that Canadian snowbirds "had abandoned Costa Rica and picked Cuba as their winter retreat," making the island "the top winter hot spot for Canadians." Author's interviews with tourists in Cuba; Michael Puchnaty, "Canada Snowbirds Fly Away," *Tico Times,* March 7, 1997, pp. 1,14.

39. Rodríguez, "Turismo"; Acosta, "Cuba-Economy."

40. Simon, "Tourism Development," pp. 30–31.

41. Larry Rohter, "Cuba's Drive for Tourists Stirs Neighbors to Action," *New York Times,* September 17, 1995, p. 3.

42. Bert Wilkinson, "Caribbean Tourism: No Need to Worry, Cuba Reassures Neighbors," InterPress Service, August 4, 1995.

43. Economist Intelligence Unit, *Cuba: EIU Country Report,* 2nd quarter 1996, p. 13; Simon, "Tourism Development," p. 30.

44. Economist Intelligence Unit, *Cuba: EIU Country Report,* 2nd quarter 1996, p. 13.

45. Simon, "Tourism Development," p. 34.

46. Ibid., p. 32.

47. Economist Intelligence Unit, *Cuba: EIU Country Report,* 1st quarter 1997, p. 25, and 3rd quarter 1997, p. 25.

48. Based on author's interviews and on radio documentaries for the BBC's *Women's Hour* and National Public Radio's *Marketplace* and *Living on Earth*. Among the numerous articles and books about Cuba's "green revolution" are Joel Simon, "An Organic Coup in Cuba?" *Amicus Journal,* winter 1997; Peter Rosset and Media Benjamin, *Two Steps Backward, One Step Forward: Cuba's Nationwide Experiment with Organic Agriculture* (San Francisco: Global Exchange, n.d.); Peter Rosset and Shea Cunningham, "The Greening of Cuba: Organic Farming Offers Hope in the Midst of Crisis," *Food First Action Alert* (published by the Institute for Food and Development Policy, San Francisco), Spring 1994.

49. Bardach, "Cuba Fever," p. 311.

50. Cienfuegos lost some of his political power when in October 1997 he and seven others were dropped from the Political Bureau, the party's most powerful deliberative body, apparently to make way for some younger members. Larry Rohter, "Cuba's Party Peers Ahead and Then Votes to March in Place," *New York Times,* October 12, 1997.

51. Interview with Gisela Alonso; Alina Cepero, "Ecotourism: New Option for Cuba," *Cuba Update,* September 1992, p. 43; David Collis, "Environmental Implications of Cuba's Economic Crisis," *Cuba Briefing Paper Series,* No. 8 (Washington, D.C: Georgetown University, July 1995), p. 7; Baker, *Cuba Handbook,* p. 22.

52. Collis, "Environmental Implications," p. 2; Notes from Karen Wald. Oceanographer Pedro Acolado told Wald that subsequent modifications have improved circulation, decreased salinity, and increased the fish population.

53. Cepero, "Ecotourism."

54. Bardach, "Cuba Fever," p. 312.

55. Summary of workshop, "Environment and Development—National Consultation Rio + 5," Havana, January 1997, posted on-line by the Earth Council. (Internet: http://www.ecouncil.ac.cr/rio/national/reports/america/cuba/cub2.htm).

56. García cited, for instance, the government's decision to restrict oil exploration at Varadero and Cardenas despite the country's tremendous need for fuel. Undoubtedly, the government recognized as well that a major oil spill along these beaches could ruin tourism. Interview conducted by Karen Wald.

57. Other important agencies with ecotourism divisions include Havanatur, a tour agency with offices in Panama and other countries; Mercadu, the University of Havana's travel agency, which conducts study tours; Rumbos, which runs tourist restaurants and kiosks, not hotels; Horizontes, which operates two- and three-star hotels; Isla Azul, which has facilities at the lower end of the international tourism market; and ServiMed, which runs spas and health tourism facilities. Author's interviews; Notes from Karen Wald; Economist Intelligence Unit, *Cuba: EIU Country Report,* 2nd quarter 1997, p. 23.

58. UNECA has also carried out dozens of projects overseas, in Nicaragua, Angola, Ethiopia, and other countries allied with Cuba. A number of UNECA construction workers building Grenada's new international airport were killed during the U.S. invasion in 1983. Interviews; Simon, "Tourism Development," p. 28; Jenkins and Haines, *Cuba: Prospects for Reform,* p. 86; "UNECA: Construction Multinational," *Cuba Business,* August 1989, p. 12.

59. Interviews by author and Karen Wald.

60. Data from Karen Wald; Collis, "Environmental Implications," p. 7.

61. Antonio Nuñez Jimenez, *En marcha con Fidel 1959* (Havana: Editorial Letras Cubanas), 1982, p. 249.

62. McManus, *Getting to Know Cuba,* p. 90.

63. Ibid., pp. 107–109.

64. Ross Simmons, assistant provost for science, Smithsonian Institution (written comments presented at The Caribbean Environment Conference, Georgetown University, Washington, D.C., December 1995). In addition, Guama's "tranquility is destroyed by excessively loud piped music by day and the disco by night," Baker, *Cuba Handbook,* p. 464.

65. Randy Wayne White, "Havana in the Rearview Mirror," *Outside,* July 1994.

66. Topes de Collantes, one of Cuba's oldest spas, is located 20 kilometers (about 12 miles) outside the historic city of Trinidad in the Escambray Mountains where sea breezes mingle with the scents of a conifer, fruit tree, and fern forest. Built in the 1950s as a tuberculosis sanatorium, it was converted into a teacher training school after tuberculosis was eradicated in the 1960s. Currently owned by the military's tourism wing, Gaviota, the Topes health resort has a full medical staff, modern diagnostic and therapeutic equipment, pools, gyms, and other recreational facilities. According to a Gaviota official, the people living in the area "are totally involved," working on staff in the resort, baking bread for the restaurant, and growing herbs used by the spa.

   One of the newest health spas is El Saltón, located in the Sierra Maestra, two hours outside Santiago de Cuba. Built beside a natural pool at the base of one of the area's many waterfalls, the lodge has a panoramic view of the valley, which is dotted with citrus orchards, coffee plantations, and cattle farms. Karen Wald wrote in her notes prepared for this chapter, "The hotel was first inaugurated in 1991 primarily as an antistress center, complete with doctors, nurses, psychologists, a physical therapist, sauna, jacuzzi, gym, etc. But really all you need to relieve stress is a swim in the natural pool, looking up at the streams of water sparkling in the sun as they pour over the moss- and fern-covered cliff." Wald says that El Saltón has been incorporated into Cubanacán's ecotours to La Gran Piedra, Pinares de Mayarí, and Guardalavaca Beach.

   Although Wald found the staff and guides extremely professional, the facilities and programs impressive, and the surroundings beautiful and tranquil, some problems have not been fully resolved. There is, for instance, a certain tension over the preferences of different types of tourists: those who come solely for medical treatment tend to want urban amenities such as satellite dishes, video games, and telephones, whereas the ecotourists want simplicity, quiet, and time to interact with nature and the people of the area. Most important, the spa has not worked out ways to maximize the benefits to farmers living in the immediate vicinity. Wald found that although all staff members are from the general region, only one nearby campesino family is directly benefiting from the health spa. This family has worked out a contractual arrangement with El Saltón to receive tourists in their home, serve them refreshments, and share their knowledge of the area. The hotel guide brings the tourists on a set schedule; in exchange, the family gets 70 percent and the hotel 30 percent of what the tourists pay.

67. Interviews by author and Karen Wald.

68. Simon, "Tourism Development," p. 37.

69. Price Waterhouse, *An Assessment of Tourism Developments and Investment Opportunities in Cuba* (report prepared for Cubalink Canada, Ltd., Toronto), quoted in Baker, "Fifteenth Cuba Tourism Convention," p. 13.

70. Collis, "Environmental Implications," pp. 7–8.

71. Ibid., p. 8.

72. Somerset R. Waters, *Travel Industry World Yearbook: The Big Picture—1996–97*, vol. 40 (New York: Child & Waters, 1997), p. 83.

73. While this meant a loss of $20 million to the state sector, on the positive side, home-stay tourism was putting dollars directly into the hands of individual Cubans, allowing them to purchase scarce goods in the dollar stores. Economist Intelligence Unit, *EIU Country Report: Cuba,* 3rd quarter 1997.

74. Dalia Costa, "Cuba Brushes Up Its Tourist Image," InterPress Service, September 19, 1997.

75. Acosta, "Cuba-Economy."

76. Schwartz, "Cuban Tourism," p. 27.

Chapter 7

Tanzania: Whose Eden Is It?

As our safari van followed a dirt track across the Serengeti grassland dotted with canopied, thorn-covered acacia and yellow fever trees, we spotted in the distance a tall, thin, slightly stooped figure wrapped in a red-checkered toga and leaning on a walking stick. Apparently oblivious to our arrival, he slowly walked away toward a *manyatta,* or circle of cone-roofed rondavels (cylindrical one-room houses). It was a classic East African scene: a Maasai[1] elder, caught in a time warp, entering his *kraal,* as his ancestors had done for hundreds of years. But there was a twist to this photo-perfect panorama. The Maasai was Moringe Parkipuny, former member of Parliament, former college professor, and social activist, and his compound was a newly built Maasai secondary boarding school. The school is in Loliondo District, just outside Serengeti National Park, where the only visible boundary on the seamless savanna is the swinging pole at a recently built checkpoint, where a handful of Tanzanian park guards and police officers live with their families. Seamless as well is the boundary that separates the park from Maasai Mara Game Reserve, its extension in Kenya. Political animosities and economic competition between the two countries dating from the 1970s have officially closed this border. But it is a boundary ignored by some 2 million wildebeest, gazelles, and zebras, which migrate twice each year between the Serengeti and Maasai Mara. The 250,000 Maasai in Tanzania and the 150,000 in Kenya also scoff at this "boundary decided in Berlin" (with the signing of the 1886 and 1890 Anglo-German agreements) and, despite their different nationalities, consider themselves one people.

Serengeti National Park, a 14,763-square-kilometer (5,700-square-mile) swath of the African continent, contains some 4 million animals and birds, giving it the greatest concentration of wildlife in the world. Just outside the entrance to Serengeti is the famous archaeological site known as Olduvai Gorge. The Serengeti is one of Tanzania's twelve national parks. Other world-famous parks include Kilimanjaro National Park, containing the snow-capped, 5,895-meter (19,341-foot) Mount Kilimanjaro, Africa's highest peak, which is located just south of the equator, and Lake Manyara National Park, a compact lakeside park renowned for its flamingos and its lions, which lounge in the trees. There are also fourteen game reserves where licensed hunting is permitted. Among these is Selous Game Reserve, the biggest wildlife area in Africa and home to some of the continent's largest herds of elephants. There are, as well, fifty-six "controlled areas" where humans and wildlife both live. Finally, there is the Ngorongoro Conservation Area, housing Ngorongoro Crater, a wildlife-filled extinct volcano crater 259 square kilometers (100 square miles) wide and 610 meters (2,000 feet) deep that is often called one of the natural wonders of the world. All together, the government estimates, 25 percent of Tanzania is under some form of protected area status.[2] Four conservation areas—Serengeti, Ngorongoro Crater, Mount Kilimanjaro, and Selous—have been designated World Heritage Sites by the United Nations because of their "outstanding universal value," a remarkably high number given that there are only seventy-seven such sites in the world.

Tanzania is one of the poorest countries in the world. But it is arguably the richest in wildlife, and today many predict that wildlife tourism will pull Tanzania out of poverty. Since the late 1980s, Serengeti and the other parks that make up the tourism belt known as the Northern Safari Circuit have been undergoing an enormous boom, with new hotels and tented camps, dozens of new tour companies, and an exponential rise in numbers of tourists. Tanzania's national parks are marketed under the umbrella of nature and adventure tourism, both of which are frequently described as ecotourism. As Tanzania's director of tourism, Hassan Kibelloh, put it in a 1995 interview, "What we have now is basically ecotourism, and we think this is the line we're going to take. We're revising our policy whereby ecotourism will feature very high, including community development and involvement."

A British travel brochure promises that visitors to Tanzania will discover "a vast Garden of Eden." It continues, "Tanzania provides travelers with a profoundly rewarding glimpse of a land unspoiled by the ravages of modern civilization. Its game viewing experiences are widely regarded as the best in Africa." Cambridge-based Overseas Adventure Travel (OAT) describes its seventeen-day Serengeti safari as follows: "If you've ever yearned to see the wilds of Africa—lions, zebras, antelope, elephants—roaming freely. Or experience the sublime beauty of the Serengeti plain with its violent sunsets and golden dawns. Then please accept this special invitation to join us on Unexplored Serengeti." Except for the preposterous claim that the Serengeti Plain is unexplored, these advertisements don't exaggerate: after decades of travel, I still find the Serengeti, in fact all of the Northern Safari Circuit, to be among the most awe-inspiring and thrilling game parks I know.

Parkipuny and the young men gathered at the secondary school deeply revere the Serengeti. But they describe a reality far from the community-

sensitive ecotourism discussed by government officials or the Garden of
Eden most tourists seek in East Africa. "We don't get any benefits from
the tourists, from the national parks, from the wild animals. It all goes to the
government," one of the teachers says in an interview. "We don't understand why the Maasai don't get benefits from the wild animals that we have
always been keeping." By "keeping," the Serengeti's wild animals, the
Maasai explain, they don't mean corralling or domesticating them but rather
living side by side and in harmony with them. Except for young Maasai warriors, or *morans,* who must kill a lion with a spear as a rite of passage into
manhood, the Maasai do not normally hunt wildlife or eat game meat. "We
have been keeping animals from the beginning and naturally know how to
[do so] better than those who go to college," the Maasai teacher explains,
referring to the park rangers, scientists, and tour guides charged with protecting, studying, and interpreting the wildlife. Since the colonial period, the
Maasai have been barred from using prime grazing lands and water sources
within the Serengeti, and in recent years they have witnessed the growth of
tourism bypassing their impoverished communities. They see the tourist
dollars flowing in and out of what they contend is their land, and yet they
receive almost no benefit.

Today in Tanzania, the national parks and protected areas not only are
at the heart of the tourism boom but also are center stage for rural social
movements, experiments, and struggles. Moringe Parkipuny has been one of
the key players. He is the founder of Korongoro Integrated Peoples
Oriented to Conservation (KIPOC), an NGO concerned with the rights of
the Maasai and other pastoralists. They deal with legal and political issues,
economic empowerment, social justice, educational advancement, and cultural preservation. Land is a key issue: *kipoc* is a Maasai word meaning "we
shall recover." Once, the Maasai and their cattle roamed freely across the
Serengeti Plain, following the seasonal rains. The Sukuma and Dorobo peoples, as well as several other groups of hunters and cultivators, also claim
smaller sections of the Serengeti. Today, the Maasai and other ethnic groups
are excluded from the Serengeti, the result, their oral history and the written record both document, of a long trail of broken promises.

"Conservation without Representation" in Colonial Tanganyika

Serengeti National Park—like many of Africa's most famous national
parks—dates from colonial times. The first international conservation treaty,
the Convention for the Preservation of Animals, Birds and Fish in Africa,
which was signed in London in 1900 by all the continent's colonial pow-
ers—Britain, Germany, France, Italy, Portugal, Spain, and Belgium—laid the

foundation for the top-down, preservationist style of management[3] that came to characterize African conservation policies. Under the treaty, only a few animals, including the giraffe, the gorilla, and the chimpanzee, were accorded complete protection.[4] Big game hunting, a favorite sport of the European aristocracy, was permitted for all other species and was even encouraged for lions, leopards, wild dogs, and other animals considered threats to settler farming. Hunting required a license, something Africans could not obtain or afford; further, the colonial governments did not permit Africans to own rifles. Historically, Africans had killed wild animals only for food, ritual use, or self-protection, never for sport or pleasure. But now, these traditional practices were banned, and, writes Ray Bonner in *At the Hand of Man*, "Africans who shot wild animals for meat . . . or to protect their livestock became, *ipso facto*, poachers."[5] The 1900 treaty became the basis for most subsequent legislation that demarcated game reserves and subsequently national parks without consideration of traditional land-use systems or the consent of those living in or around the protected areas.[6]

The colonialists' premise was that Africans, left to their own devices, were wiping out the continent's wildlife. But, by 1900, the record had already proved it was the white interlopers, not the indigenous peoples, who were most swiftly and systematically killing off Africa's wildlife. Not covered by the treaty, for instance, was the Cape Colony in South Africa because the European settlers had already slaughtered all the big game there. This mistaken belief—that parks and the surrounding people must be separated—guided nearly a century of colonial and postcolonial conservationist policy in Africa.

By 1912, the German colonial rulers had declared thirteen game reserves, covering 30,000 square kilometers (11,583 square miles), and mapped Ngorongoro Crater in German East Africa (later known as Tanganyika and then Tanzania).[7] Following Germany's defeat in World War I, the League of Nations gave Tanganyika to Great Britain Tanganyika to rule as a "mandated territory" or protectorate. Tanganyika was a political and economic stepchild to Kenya, Britain's most important East Africa colony. But from the outset of British rule, Tanganyika was viewed as a prime piece of real estate by international conservationists, big game hunters, and wildlife adventurers. In ordinances passed between 1940 and 1951, the Serengeti was upgraded to a national park, the first in East Africa. All hunting was banned. No other national parks were declared in Tanganyika until 1960, when the Ngorongoro Conservation Area and Arusha and Lake Manyara National Parks were gazetted. Another nine parks have been declared since independence, the most recent in 1992.

The law declaring Serengeti a national park contained an unusual promise: that the Maasai could continue to live there. But it was a promise that didn't hold for a decade. From the outset, conservation organizations in Europe and the United States and scientists and technocrats in Tanganyika weighed in to build an increasingly powerful lobby to expel the Maasai, arguing that the Serengeti's soil was too fragile and its water too scarce to support both humans and wildlife. Among the most influential was British paleontologist Louis Leakey, who, with his wife, Mary, excavated in the Serengeti's Olduvai Gorge, a sand-swept canyon that turned out to be a gold mine for the origins of humankind. While his wife dug, Leakey lectured, arguing that the Maasai should have no legal right to remain in the Serengeti.[8] Equally influential was Bernhard Grzimek, director of the prestigious Frankfurt Zoo, who, together with his son, studied the park's wildlife migration patterns. His 1959 book *The Serengeti Shall Not Die* made an impassioned plea for expelling the Maasai and maintaining Ngorongoro Crater and the Serengeti as a single national park.[9] The Maasai, marginalized politically, resorted to "everyday" forms of confrontation born of necessity, including illegal hunting, fires, grazing, and collection of fuelwood.[10]

Then, on the eve of independence, a compromise was struck. Under the amended National Park Ordinance, passed in 1959, the Maasai and other Africans were excluded from the western Serengeti, and the Ngorongoro Crater sector was removed from the park and reconstituted as a separate conservation unit known as the Ngorongoro Conservation Area (NCA), where Maasai pastoralists were permitted.[11]

In concluding this agreement, British colonial officials convinced a group of twelve Maasai elders to sign off on these new boundaries, putting their marks on a document that stated, "We understand that as a result of this renunciation we shall not be entitled henceforth in the years to come to cross this line which will become the boundary of the new Serengeti National Park. We agree to move ourselves, our possessions, our cattle and all our other animals out of this land by the end of the next short rains."[12] National park officials breathed a sigh of relief: with the removal of the Maasai from most of the Serengeti, they were successfully "eliminating the biggest problem" they faced.[13]

The Maasai, however, continued to be haunted by this agreement. More than thirty years later, Ray Bonner tracked down one of the dozen elders, Tendemo Ole Kisaka, who revealed, "We were told to sign. It was not explained to us." None of the signers, he said, knew how to read or write. The elderly Maasai recalled how, shortly after they had put their marks on the paper, six large trucks arrived and moved the Maasai and their few possessions outside the park. "You white people are very tough," Ole Kisaka told Bonner.[14]

Tanzanian Socialism and State-Run Tourism

Just as Serengeti National Park blends seamlessly with Maasai Mara Game Reserve, Tanganyika's colonial conservation policy made a transition virtually unaltered in ideology and, frequently, in personnel into postcolonial Tanzania. It was a transition carefully scripted and controlled by the major international conservation organizations, which, in the early 1960s, feared that the end of colonialism would mean the end of Africa's wildlife. "We felt that under the new African governments, all prospects for conservation of nature would be ended," related E. M. Nicholson, the first head of the World Wide Fund for Nature–International.[15] In September 1961, WWF and the International Union for the Conservation of Nature and Natural Resources (IUCN, now the World Conservation Union) summoned the newly independent African leaders to a meeting in Arusha to discuss what they described as a state of emergency facing Africa's wildlife. Julius Nyerere, as the titular host of the meeting and the first prime minister of Tanganyika, delivered the brief opening address. These three paragraphs, known as the Arusha Manifesto, have often been quoted over the years by Western environmental organizations:

> The survival of our wildlife is a matter of grave concern to all of us in Africa. These wild creatures amid the wild places they inhabit are not only important as a source of wonder and inspiration but are an integral part of our natural resources and our future livelihood and well being.
>
> In accepting the trusteeship of our wildlife we solemnly declare that we will do everything in our power to make sure that our children's grand-children will be able to enjoy this rich and precious inheritance.
>
> The conservation of wildlife and wild places calls for specialist knowledge, trained manpower, and money, and we look to other nations to co-operate with us in this important task—the success or failure of which not only affects the continent of Africa but the rest of the world as well.[16]

Nyerere, though a gifted writer and orator, did not draft this proclamation. Nicholson and several others from WWF wrote it in order to commit Africa's new rulers to both wildlife protection and a continued reliance on European and American expertise. With its expansive and rich natural reserves, Tanzania (as the new country became after its 1964 union with Zanzibar) quickly became a central focus for international conservation organizations. The IUCN-WWF gathering in Arusha kicked off an intense effort by the major international environmental NGOs to funnel money, technical support, and management training into Tanzania's park system. Under British colonialism, African participation in wildlife conservation had been limited to jobs as trackers, gun bearers, cooks, game scouts, and reserve guards rather than positions of management or authority. Tanzania's tiny white population, made up of retired soldiers, civil servants, farmers, big game hunters, and adventurers with little formal wildlife training, played a disproportionately powerful role in managing the country's colonial and postindependence wildlife services.

Just after independence, concern over carefully managing the inevitable process of "Africanization of the game service" led the African Wildlife Leadership Foundation (now known as the African Wildlife Foundation, or AWF) to found the College of African Wildlife Management in Mweka, Tanzania, at the base of Mount Kilimanjaro. This was the first such training school in black Africa, and it remains one of only two on the continent today.[17] "As a result," writes Roderick Neumann, a professor of international relations who specializes in Tanzania, "they helped to create in Tanzania an elite class of conservation bureaucrats, trained in western ideologies and practices of natural resource conservation which essentially replicated the top-down, repressive practices of colonial rule."[18] As Tanzania gazetted dozens of new protected areas over the next three decades, much of the colonial legislation and land tenure system giving ownership to the central government was maintained, despite the negative effects on surrounding communities. The postindependence policies continued to include mass relocations from new parks, increasingly militarized patrolling and antipoaching techniques, and a bureaucratic structure that concentrated authority and revenue at the top. Conservation practices were generally unsympathetic to the needs of the local communities, whose members were deprived access to ancestral homelands, grazing land, water, and wildlife and saw few tangible benefits from either the parks or tourism.[19]

Tourism Policy

The history of Serengeti National Park, Ngorongoro Conservation Area, and Tanzania's other parks and reserves has always been interwoven with tourism. Initially, tourism meant hunting. The gathering spot for hunters was the New Safari, a rambling hotel surrounded by English flower gardens in the center of Arusha. In the 1970s, its wood-paneled bar featured signed photographs of Ernest Hemingway and various members of British royalty surrounded by safari gear and African porters. In 1934, the first game park hotel, Ngorongoro Crater Lodge, was built on the oft misty rim of the escarpment. Gradually, hunting was restricted to certain blocks of land, and tourists with cameras began to arrive at the crater and then continue on camping safaris into the Serengeti. By the time of independence, the

Serengeti had won a place in the hearts of the conservation elite in the United States and Europe. The first director of Tanzania National Parks (TANAPA), J. S. Owen, urged that his agency "encourage by every means the growth of a tourist industry."[20] Likewise, Julius Nyerere—the platitudes of the Arusha Manifesto aside—clearly saw the monetary value in this international interest in wildlife. "I do not want," Nyerere said shortly after independence, "to spend my holidays watching crocodiles. Nevertheless, I am entirely in favor of their survival. I believe that after diamonds and sisal, wild animals will provide Tanganyika with its greatest source of income."[21]

However, in reality, Tanzania's tourism policies over the next fifteen years were ambivalent, constrained financially by the country's extreme poverty and lack of infrastructure and politically by the new government's unique brand of socialism. When Tanganyika gained independence in 1961, its annual per capita income was about $15 and its population of some 20 million included fewer than 100 university graduates. As did most other newly independent African countries, Tanzania declared itself a one-party state. Nyerere argued forcefully that a single political party, together with a common language—Swahili—and a carefully balanced tribal and religious composition within the government, the military, and parastatal bodies (semiautonomous government-owned companies), was essential to weld the new country's 120 tribes into a unified nation. Tanzania thus avoided the tribal and ethnic conflicts that have wracked its neighbors (Kenya, Uganda, Rwanda, and Burundi), though its single-party socialism meant that internally, ethnic rights and struggles were suppressed for the sake of nation building and the common good. Maasai leader Moringe Parkipuny complains bitterly that under socialism, the profits from tourism and the national parks first went to the centralized bureaucracy in Dar es Salaam, and then a mere trickle came back to the Maasai. "This is our land, from which we were illegally evicted to create these parks. The profits should have gone first to us for development projects and then we would funnel them upwards, not the other way around," Parkipuny explains. It wasn't until the political liberalizations begun in the late 1980s, when Tanzania agreed to hold multiparty elections, that the Maasai and other pastoralists could legally organize to express their views through a nongovernmental organization such as KIPOC.

Although international conservationists were fond of quoting the Arusha Manifesto, it was Julius Nyerere's 1967 Arusha Declaration, delivered in the same city, that set Tanzania apart from other newly independent African states. In this speech, Nyerere laid out the road map for his country's policy of "socialism and self-reliance," declaring that the country should not rely on foreign aid or investment; that political leaders and top civil servants should not be involved in capitalist activities (the so-called

Leadership Code), and that the foundation of the country's socialist development should be *ujamaa* (familyhood) villages, where agricultural work and social services were communally shared.

As did Cuba, Tanzania pumped a large proportion of its limited resources into primary education, health care, and provision of potable water. The results were impressive. During the 1970s, 92 percent of Tanzanian children attended primary school, and the country developed one of the best primary health care systems in Africa, with "barefoot doctors" providing basic medical care free of charge to rural communities. Despite Nyerere's warnings about reliance on foreign capital, Tanzania's emphasis on basic human services, its Leadership Code, and its nonaligned foreign policy made the country the darling of foreign aid donors. Tanzania forged politically eclectic trade and aid alliances with China, the Soviet Union, Cuba, Scandinavian countries, and Canada as well as with Britain and the United States.

But while foreign aid flowed in, foreign investment shied away from socialist Tanzania. Following the Arusha Declaration, the government nationalized large sectors of the economy—banks, insurance companies, large trading companies, industries, plantations—that had been owned mainly by British and local Asian (as East Africa's Indian and Pakistani immigrants are collectively known) firms, creating instead a number of new parastatal bodies. Many of these nationalizations were done hastily, without proper planning or trained personnel, and the companies quickly began to operate in the red.[22]

Following the Arusha Declaration, the government created the Tanzania Tourist Corporation (TTC) which owned and operated fifteen luxury hotels and lodges along the Northern Safari Circuit; in Tanzania's capital, Dar es Salaam; in Arusha; and along the Indian Ocean. Like that of Cuba in the 1970s, Tanzania's national tourism industry was intended to help support health care, education, and other social programs. Tanzania similarly sought to confine tourism to specific enclaves, but given the country's distance from Europe and the United States, it targeted the luxury safari market, not the overseas mass market, as Cuba had. These government-owned hotels showed architectural sensitivity, incorporating local materials and designs. Interestingly, in this era before ecotourism, "all the hotels and lodges were designed to conform with the environment and culture of this country," according to the TTC's development officer, Phillip Bukuku.[23] I was particularly impressed by Tanzania's game lodges, which were beautiful, innovative, first-class structures positioned to capture spectacular views and to blend into their surroundings. My favorite has always been Lobo Wildlife Lodge, built in the northern Serengeti, just south of Kenya's Maasai Mara Game Reserve. Completed in 1970, Lobo is a multitiered, 150-bed hotel built of East African woods, local stone, and glass and nestled among a group of ancient granite boulders known as *kopjes*. It is virtually invisible to tourists approaching on the dirt road from the south, but once inside, guests have a magnificent view of the vast Serengeti Plain.

Unlike Cuba, Tanzania did not nationalize any already existing privately owned hotels or tour operations. However, following the Arusha Declaration, the country really didn't want and certainly didn't attract much foreign investment. "At that time, no foreign investment was coming in, so it was necessary that government take the lead," recalled Costa Mlay, director of the Serengeti Research Institute, in a 1995 interview. During the 1970s, Mlay had been part of Julius Nyerere's government, which included many of the country's best and brightest young bureaucrats. There was very little domestic capital as well. Government and party officials were barred by the Leadership Code from engaging in private enterprise. Local capitalists, most of whom were Arab and Asian immigrants, feared that if they invested, the government might nationalize or simply seize their businesses, as was happening in Kenya and in Uganda under dictator Idi Amin. Except for the privately owned Ngorongoro Crater Lodge and a handful of other settler-, Asian-, or foreign-owned hotels in the Northern Safari Circuit, the TTC held a monopoly over accommodations in and near the game parks. During the 1970s, some private local capital did quietly move into smaller tourism enterprises, including taxi services, tour companies, and more modest hotels.

Tanzania's state-run tourism was, however, heavily dependent on foreign expertise, capital, and imports. Initial tourism studies were carried out by the World Bank and the Boston-based consulting firm Arthur D. Little.[24] The TTC's hotels were developed jointly with the British company Hallmark Hotels, and they were designed and built by foreign architectural and construction companies. Because Tanzania's industrial base was very small, an estimated 40 percent of the government's tourism budget went toward importation of construction materials, furniture, cutlery, petroleum, motor vehicles, foodstuffs, liquor, and the whole range of consumer goods.[25] In addition, there were not enough qualified Tanzanians to run these hotels, so the TTC hired Hallmark and an Israeli company to manage its facilities. The Hallmark arrangement, however, ended in 1974, by which time Tanzania had developed a solid cadre of middle- and upper-level tourism professionals.

The TTC's broad functions included promoting all aspects of tourism, including "engaging in the business of tour operators, travel agents, hotel developers and managers, publicity and advertising agents, publishers, [and] film exhibitors" and any other activities related to the industry. The TTC opened five overseas offices, including one in New York. It set up several

other parastatal bodies, including the Tanzania Film Company, Tanzania
Duty Free Shops, Tanzania Wildlife Safaris, Ltd., which conducted hunting
safaris, and, most important, Tanzania Tourism Ltd. (TTL), later renamed
the State Travel Service, to run ground handling facilities with more than
200 vehicles as well as driver-guides.[26]

Building and operating the tourism sector represented an enormous financial investment for the government. Between 1969 and 1974, the TTC
budgeted TSh 194 million (roughly U.S.$40 million) for tourism projects
including hotels, tour operations, roads, airports, water supplies, and upgrading of existing national parks and creation of new ones.[27] By 1979, the
TTC's investment in its hotels and lodges totaled about TSh 250 million
(which, due to currency devaluation, equaled about U.S.$27 million).[28]
Although tourist numbers did rise sharply from 51,000 in 1969 to 63,000
in 1972 to a peak of 167,000 in 1976 (see table 7.1),[29] the investment was
so high that Tanzania's government coffers gained little. Reliable statistics
are hard to find, but according to Frank Mitchell, a Kenya–based researcher,
in the early 1970s Tanzania was earning only $1–$2.5 million per year from
tourism, which ranked a lowly eighth among the country's foreign exchange
earners.[30]

While some Tanzanian intellectuals and student leaders argued that
state-owned tourism was not a sound development strategy for socialist
Tanzania, others worried it would bring negative social practices, such as
prostitution and corruption. Despite the fears of critics, Tanzania's tourism
industry was too tiny and too concentrated in the remote Northern Safari

Table 7.1. Tanzania's Tourism Growth

	1969	1972	1976	1979	1985	1989	1992	1993	1994	1996
Arrivals (in thousands)	51	63	167	78	59	138	202	230	262	326
Gross receipts (in millions of U.S. dollars)	—	20	95	—	14	60	120	147	192	322

Source: Economist Intelligence Unit (EIU), EIU Country Profile, 1994–95: Tanzania
(London: EIU, 1994), p. 11; various editions of the EIU Country Report for Tanzania,
including 3rd quarter 1997 and 1st quarter 1998; Somerset R. Waters, Travel Industry
World Yearbook: The Big Picture—1996–1997, 40 (New York: Child & Waters, 1997), p.
142; World Tourism Organization (WTO), Yearbook of Tourism Statistics, 47th ed., vol.
1 (Madrid: WTO, 1995); I. G. Shivji, ed., Tourism and Socialist Development (Dar es
Salaam: Tanzania Publishing House, 1975), p. 95; Estrom Maryogo, "Tourism in
National Development," in Karibu Tanzania: A Decade of TTC's Service to Tourists
(Dar es Salaam: Tanzania Tourist Corporation, 1983), p. 107.
Note: Figures are unavailable where there are blanks.

Circuit to do much cultural or social damage. Even though Tanzanians were never barred from visiting the game parks or tourist hotels, the vast majority could not afford to do so. Unlike the situation in Cuba, the Tanzanian government did not have the resources to develop a domestic tourism infrastructure for peasants and workers to enjoy. So, as Tanzania's ministry of information argued in an article published in 1970, tourism, like diamonds, became an industry designed only for foreign consumption: "We need a socialist discipline to reject the product—tourism—for our own consumption, as much as we do not encourage our women to dangle diamonds."[31]

Conflict with Kenya

In reality, Tanzania's tourism industry during the decade 1967–1977 did not fit neatly into either a socialist or a capitalist mold. Whether it ultimately could have become profitable without compromising the country's cultural norms or socialist values was never fully tested. Just after the costly capital investments had been made and tourism numbers had begun to rapidly rise, the industry crashed. It fell apart because it carried within it, Tanzanian socialists contended, a fatal flaw: dependence on Kenya. The nub of the problem was that Kenya had the tourists and Tanzania had the best tourist attractions. The vast majority of visitors flew into Nairobi, Kenya, located just a few hours' drive from Tanzania, where they hired a tour van and a guide to take them to the Serengeti and other Tanzanian parks. (Some Nairobi tour agencies went so far as to claim that Mount Kilimanjaro was in Kenya.) The tourists crossed the border, but the tourism dollars did not. Tanzanian Mervin Nunes, who ran the TTC office in Nairobi, said in an interview that although "statistics at that time were not really kept, it would be safe to say 90 percent of the tourism benefits stayed in Kenya."

Efforts to negotiate a more equitable arrangement proved impossible because of the deep animosity between the two countries, stemming from Kenya's most-favored-colony treatment by the British. The friction accelerated after independence as the two countries followed radically different economic and political strategies. Whereas Tanzania under Julius Nyerere was pursuing its brand of African socialism, Kenya under Jomo Kenyatta opened its doors wide to international investment in tourism and other fields. Tanzanians accused Kenya of being a "man-eat-man" society; Kenyans countered that Tanzania was a "man-eat-nothing" society. The conflict came to a head in February 1977, when the East African Community—the economic alliance between Kenya, Tanzania, and Uganda—collapsed. Just hours after Kenya announced it was seizing East African Airways planes and other community assets in Nairobi, Nyerere announced he was sealing off all road and air links between Tanzania and Kenya.

The border closure caught virtually everyone by surprise. It appeared at the time to be an impulsive retaliatory action, but it took many years to undo, and in the process, it brought down Tanzania's state-run tourism industry.

Right after the border closure, the Tanzanian government launched an ambitious overseas marketing campaign to sell the country as a "self-contained tourist destination." Using such slogans as "Tanzania welcomes the world" and "Tanzania, the land of Kilimanjaro," the TTC "really went on a shopping spree," providing tours to foreign travel agents, tour operators, and filmmakers.[32] It didn't work. By the early 1980s, visits by nonresidents to Tanzania's national parks fell to fewer than 50,000 per year[33] and tourism ranked just seventh among Tanzania's foreign exchange earners. Most of it was business and conference tourism; holiday tourism had come to almost a complete stop.[34] During this same period, more than 360,000 tourists per year were visiting Kenya, and tourism was that country's second highest foreign exchange earner.

The situation was further exacerbated by a recession in Europe and the United States and, most important, by Tanzania's war against Idi Amin, the ruthless and erratic dictator of Uganda. In October 1978, Amin's troops invaded and attempted to annex a section of western Tanzania. The Tanzanian army retaliated by invading Uganda and pursuing Amin and his troops across the country, forcing Amin out of office.[35] The toppling of Amin, though hailed by many Africans as a great moral victory, further hurt tourism and cost Tanzania dearly—including some $608 million in direct costs and a staggering $5.12 *billion* in forgone production as resources were diverted from economic production and toward military activities.[36] "Before, this was a profitable hotel. But with the border closure and war with Uganda, tourism stopped completely. We were losing money," recalled Damien Qamara, resident manager of the Ngorongoro Crater Lodge, in a 1995 interview. Tanzania's economic situation was further compromised by a fall in the world price of its principal agricultural exports, a steep rise in the cost of imported oil, and a severe drought at the end of the 1970s.

The state was left holding the bag on an extremely expensive tourism infrastructure, but without foreign exchange for imports, upkeep, and marketing, this infrastructure rapidly fell into disrepair. For years after the border was closed, only a handful of guests were to be found in the government's lovely Ngorongoro and Serengeti hotels. With road and air traffic cut from Kenya and conflict in Uganda, only the most adventuresome and determined overseas tourists could fly into Tanzania, usually via Ethiopia, Mauritius, or the Seychelles Islands. "Lobo would be empty for a week and the government was subsidizing it," Telesphor Mukandara, the lodge's manager, told me in an interview. The TTC needed at least 45 percent occupancy just to break even in the Northern Safari Circuit.[37] "It was disastrous for us," recalls Margaret Gibb, whose hotel, Gibb's Farm, survived by attracting foreign residents living in Tanzania. Besides guests, these hotels lacked virtually all imported commodities, which had in the past come mainly from Kenya. To this day, one American visitor tells the story of how, during a 1978 visit, he became afflicted with the usual traveler's scourge and, finding no toilet paper in his room, rushed to the front desk. The clerk, noting his desperation, told him reassuringly not to worry—toilet paper from China was expected to arrive within the next two weeks.

Economic and Political Liberalizations

When I returned to Tanzania in the summer of 1995, I found a tourism boom. Everyone seemed to be in on the action—major hotel chains, the World Bank, international conservation organizations, TANAPA, South Africans, Arab hunters, the Aga Khan, a Congolese importer-exporter, and a burgeoning class of Tanzanian entrepreneurs, including the president of the country, Ali Hassan Mwinyi. This "mixed grill of investors," as described by Hassan Kibelloh, then director of tourism, was involved in projects running the gamut from conventional five-star city hotels to the refurbishing and upgrading of existing government and private game lodges, construction of new luxury lodges and tented camps inside the parks, creation of the country's first marine park, and a handful of more modest, innovative, ecologically and community sensitive projects. The tourism director said that Tanzania is seeking "quality" tourism, not "mass tourism," yet its push to improve roads, airports, and other infrastructure appears geared to increasing tourist numbers. "Tanzania's Tourism Department has a strong bias for large-scale hotels," one World Bank official told me. Tanzania wants "exclusive, upscale tourism, and lots and lots of it," another bank official wryly quipped.

Those in the tourism industry I met displayed the energy and confidence of pioneers on a new frontier. According to one press report, "National and foreign investment are in the race to capture the free market atmosphere created by the government's liberalization policies, and invest in tourism."[38] In this race, Tanzania's main competitor is, as always, Kenya. "With the restructuring of our tourism sector, Kenya's tourism has to watch it. The new drive is going to turn the pathetic state of tourism in Tanzania into a tourism mecca," proclaimed Paul Lyimo, chairman of Tanzania Hotels Investment (TAHI), a parastatal body charged with attracting private investment.[39] From a low of about 50,000 tourists in the early 1980s, tourist numbers grew to 153,000, with gross receipts of $63 million, in 1990. Tanzania projected, overoptimistically, that it would be attracting

500,000 tourists per year by 1995. But by 1992, tourism was Tanzania's leading foreign exchange earner,[40] and by 1993, Tanzania's tourism sector was the second most rapidly growing in Africa, with numbers of tourists rising by an astonishing 28 percent each year since 1985. However, tourism in Tanzania, despite the country's nationalist bravado, broader mix of investors, and modern Kilimanjaro International Airport, just outside Arusha, which has attracted some direct flights from Europe, remained heavily linked to Kenya. By 1993, for instance, 70 percent of all tourists visiting Tanzania still came through Kenya.[41]

Although the border closure accomplished little at the time and cost state-run tourism (and ultimately the Tanzanian people) dearly, nearly everyone I interviewed (except for hotel owners and managers) looked back on it as a good decision because, ironically, it forced Tanzania to allow the growth of local capitalists. This was a sign of how thoroughly free-market liberalism has supplanted Tanzanian socialism. Former TTC official Mervin Nunes, for instance, explained in an interview that he "wholeheartedly" backed the decision to close the border. "Tanzania's tourism didn't die at that point; it was born. The closure of the border gave rise to local entrepreneurs to start off businesses within Tanzania," said Nunes, who in 1980 started a highly successful tour agency, Wildersun Safaris, based in Arusha. Danford Mpamibea, a former journalist who is now an official with the Association of Tanzanian Travel Operators (ATTO), concurred, saying that "the closure of the border was a blessing to Tanzanians" involved in private enterprise. He recalled that afterward, "all these [Kenyan] companies left. There was a vacuum, and this is where indigenous Tanzanians began establishing tour operations." Mpamibea explained that Tanzanians invested first in tour companies because they required less capital and offered faster returns than hotels.

Although clearly not foreseen by Julius Nyerere, the border closure set in motion a process that gradually led to the privatization of Tanzania's state-run tourism industry. This privatization proceeded in two stages. The first, beginning in 1977, involved mainly new investments with local capital. State-run tourism ended up doing little more than laying the foundation—in roads, hotels, transportation, national parks, trained personnel, and overseas marketing—for the local private sector. By 1983, for instance, there were at least sixty private tour companies, in addition to the TTC's two subsidiaries.

The second stage, involving substantial investment by foreign capital, began in the mid-1980s, after Nyerere stepped down. Under Nyerere's hand-picked successor, Ali Hassan Mwinyi, a Zanzibari Muslim without Nyerere's political vision or commitment to Tanzanian socialism, the border reopened, and Tanzania embraced the economic liberalizations and structural adjustment policies dictated by the World Bank and the IMF. Under the terms of the 1984 agreement that reopened road and air links between Tanzania and Kenya, tour operators from each country are barred from "plying their trade within the national parks of the other country," as Nunes explained. In practice, most tourists change tour companies at the border town of Namanga. No comparable agreement was ever reached for the border dividing Serengeti National Park and Maasai Mara Game Reserve, which remains closed today. Although statistics are lacking, this system undoubtedly means that more hard currency actually enters Tanzania. However, large portions still leak out and are banked overseas.[42] In addition, the largest foreign ground operators, such as the Kenya-based Abercrombie & Kent (A&K) and the British company United Touring Company (UTC, a Kenya-based company), have opened local offices and put fleets of minibuses and other vehicles in Arusha, but they still make most of their bookings and receive payments outside Tanzania.

In compliance with the terms of World Bank and IMF loans, Tanzania enacted a new investment code that offered foreign capital broad incentives and declared tourism a "high priority" area for foreign investors.[43] In 1993, Mwinyi dissolved the already weakened TTC and set up the Tanzania Tourist Board (TTB), whose task is narrowly defined as promoting tourism. These steps have accelerated the influx of foreign capital from private companies in Europe, South Africa, Kenya, and the United States. In the late 1980s, the Mwinyi government hired the French firm Accor/Novotel to refurbish and market seven government-owned hotels and game lodges, financed with a $16.5 million loan from the German Investment Bank, Swiss International Finance for Development in Africa, and the East African Development Bank.[44] By mid-1994, more than sixty foreign investors had applied for tourism projects and forty-three applications had been approved.[45] Sheraton and Hilton built large hotels in Dar es Salaam.

And, for the first time, the investors included South Africans. In 1991, following a decision by the Commonwealth countries to partially lift sanctions against South Africa, Tanzania "announced the scrapping of tourism sanctions against the country, thus opening the Tanzanian industry to the South African market." In 1994, South Africa's huge Protea Hotels chain took over management and acquired 40 percent of the shares of four government hotels.[46] That same year, Conservation Corporation, South Africa's leading company marketing upscale ecotourism, acquired the Ngorongoro Crater Lodge from Kenya-based A&K as part of a complex merger scheme.

In 1994, as well, the World Bank and fifteen other donors approved a $900 million transportation and infrastructure project for upgrading and expanding a number of tourism-related roads, bridges, and airports (including Kilimanjaro International Airport). At the same time, the bank began a tourism project also designed to upgrade some infrastructure, including the road from Arusha to Ngorongoro Crater and on across the Serengeti. This tourism project, estimated at $50 million, also included upgrading personnel, improving government efficiency, and undertaking tourism master plans for both the mainland and Zanzibar with the main purpose of helping to increase numbers of tourists and private investment. Although the World Bank's plans do not include ecotourism, they do require the Tanzanian government to unify its two environmental departments and carry out a national environmental assessment and impact study. When, by 1996, the Tanzanian government had failed to do the impact study for the Ngorongoro-Serengeti road or to adopt the stipulated bureaucratic reforms, the World Bank suspended the project. Privately, bank officials argued that a paved road through the Serengeti would be an "eco-disaster," while Tanzanians widely asserted that a good road was necessary both for tourism and development of the areas surrounding the national parks. As former Tanzanian president Julius Nyerere retorted, "I don't like the case of preserving the environment being used against development in the South. The Serengeti road is a case in point."[47]

Large-Scale Tourism Projects in Tanzanian Parks

The World Bank's private sector arm, the International Finance Corporation (IFC), has financed a number of projects in national parks and other fragile areas. But it is not actively supporting either ecotourism or locally owned projects in Tanzania.[48] The projects in Tanzania receiving IFC financing include foreign-owned hotels and tour companies, which contribute little more than jobs to the local economy. Among these projects is a $9 million loan and equity package for four luxury game park hotels built by the Aga Khan, one of the world's richest men and leader of the most powerful Indian religious community in East Africa; a small luxury lodge owned by a Kenyan-British company, Nomad Safaris, for photographic (not hunting) safaris in Selous Game Reserve; and a $450,000 loan to Abercrombie & Kent (Tanzania) to purchase thirty diesel-powered minivans.

Although the A&K proposal passed the IFC's environmental impact review, longtime Tanzanian tour operator Mervin Nunes says he is concerned that A&K and other companies are switching to less expensive but more polluting diesel engines. "If fifty companies decide to go to diesel vehicles, there will be a lot of smoke in the parks," he contends. A&K, whose nonprofit arm, Friends of Conservation, finances environmental education projects, has a poor track record in other ways. In 1992, the Tanzanian government closed down A&K's luxury camp site inside Ngorongoro Crater because its diesel engines, lights, latrines, garbage pit, and other infrastructure were causing environmental damage and disturbing the wildlife.[49]

By the early 1990s, new lodges were being built in the Northern Safari

Circuit, despite recommendations by conservation organizations and park officials that only temporary camps, not new hotels, be permitted inside these national parks. For more than two decades, Tanzania had successfully barred construction of private resorts inside its national parks. Now this taboo, like so many others, has been broken, and the new projects are pitting tourism more directly against both conservationists and the Maasai. The largest of these investors is the Aga Khan Fund for Economic Development (AKFED), headquartered in France, which owns Serena Lodges and Hotels. AKFED, together with the World Bank's IFC and Great Britain's Commonwealth Development Corporation (CDC), are collectively investing $33 million in three luxury lodges and a tented camp in Ngorongoro Conservation Area and Serengeti and Lake Manyara National Parks.[50]

The other major investment group, Sopa Lodges, owned by the Kenya-based Consolidated Tourist and Hotels Investment Ltd., has put up new luxury lodges in Tarangire National Park, Ngorongoro Conservation Area, and Serengeti National Park and has permits to build lodges and permanent tented camps in other parks. The corporation is owned by S. Murjik, a Congolese Asian who made his fortune in the import–export business and had close ties to former Zairean dictator Mobutu Sese Seko. The Sopa and Serena lodges almost double the tourist bed occupancy in the Serengeti and Ngorongoro. However, they have raised an array of questions and concerns about the way the contracts were awarded and the environmental impact of the hotels on wildlife, the environment, and the Maasai.

"They were forced down our throats by the president's office—by the president [Mwinyi] himself," a Tanzanian government official told Ray Bonner,[51] a view corroborated by a well-placed World Bank official. In an attempt to block construction, the Ngorongoro Conservation Area (NCA) board unanimously voted to oppose the new hotels and appealed to the minister of natural resources and tourism and directly to the president, finally recommending that a tourism master plan be done first—all to no avail. The five-star hotels went up. Among the various ecological concerns, water draw-off was the most acute. In 1990, before the new hotels were approved, a government report had warned, "The current water supply system [in the NCA] is inadequate to meet the demands of over a quarter of a million head of livestock, and some 25,000 resident pastoralists."[52] Both new hotels are built next to water sources used by the Maasai. The Ngorongoro Sopa Lodge is beside the Munge River, which runs into the Ngorongoro Crater. With the hotel promising $200-per-night "safari comfort," including "luxuriously appointed bedrooms, a swimming pool, conference facilities, shopping boutiques, nightly wildlife films and CNN programs, opulent bar . . . and close and personal attention," it is likely that the Ngorongoro Crater's wildlife, livestock, and local residents will do without water long before the tourists do.[53]

Although Sopa's lodges are pure glitz, the Serena Lodge in the Ngorongoro Conservation Area (NCA) is billed as embodying the principles and sensitivities of ecotourism. Architecturally, this is true. The Ngorongoro Serena Lodge is built into the side of the crater's rim and constructed of local stone, which will eventually become covered with plants and blend into the landscape. The original site was moved six feet to accommodate a fig tree; plans to install bathtubs, a swimming pool, and a water slide were scrapped and a rooftop rainwater collection system was installed after the Maasai objected to pumping from a nearby spring; solar panels produce hot water; and the diesel generator for electricity is housed in a double-skinned shed to reduce noise and fumes.[54] According to *African Business* magazine, "The Aga Khan, who appears to have taken on environmental protection as a personal crusade, was insistent that the development should merge into the habitat and cause the minimum of disruption to human, animal and environmental needs."[55] A press release from the World Bank's IFC claims the project will provide money for conservation, reduce poaching, and "promote the welfare of the local communities"[56] and an IFC official contended that the agency was "entirely satisfied" by the results of three environmental impact assessments done for the lodge project.

Ngorongoro Conservation Authority officials were not. They were angered that the Serena Lodge had proceeded to build its staff housing in the overcrowded crater village despite the NCA's plans to move all hotel employees and park staff to a new location just outside the conservation area's boundary. An IFC official dismissed this relocation plan as "a nonstarter," but it has been endorsed by conservationists, TANAPA, and even some World Bank officials as an ecological and human imperative. There are presently some 3,000–4,000 such employees living in near slum conditions on the crater's rim, without adequate water, sanitation, farmland, schools, and so forth. TANAPA, in fact, plans eventually to move hotel and park staff out of the Serengeti and all its other parks.

Moreover, KIPOC contends that the lodge is built on land belonging to the Maasai village of Oloirobi, that the villagers were never consulted, and that "the site was given in person to Serena by [Mwinyi,] the President of the United Republic of Tanzania." The hotel is next to the Maasai's main route for taking cattle in and out of Ngorongoro Crater. An official involved in the hotel project complained that this cattle path is "incredibly disruptive" and a "tremendous erosion problem." The Maasai counter that certainly more damage is done by the movement of 150,000 tourists and some 20,000 vehicles per year in and out of the crater along two steep, narrow dirt roads. They fear that under the press of tourism, they will be expelled from the vicinity of the lodge and, ultimately, from the entire conservation area.[57]

Their fears are grounded in reality. Ever since the government's 1959 agreement to permit the Maasai and wildlife to share the crater, the Maasai have found themselves confined to an increasingly smaller space and circumscribed by ever stricter regulations. Since 1974, they have been precluded from living on the crater's floor, and now they need a special permit to take their cattle into the crater by day for water and salt. In 1975, the government banned cultivation inside the Ngorongoro Conservation Area, and police continued to arrest farmers and destroy crops into the late 1980s. In recent decades, the Maasai have turned more to agriculture, growing grains to supplement their diet. One reason is that their cattle herds have decreased sharply—from an average of ten per person in the mid-1960s to just three in 1993—due mainly to several diseases. As pastoralists, the Maasai traditionally move to avoid disease, but this is increasingly difficult because they are surrounded by parks and agricultural farms.

Since the early 1990s, the Maasai have felt under assault as never before by tourism developers, agriculturalists, private big game hunters, and corrupt officials, all wheeling and dealing, bribing and strong-arming their way onto the lands where the Maasai now live. Although the luxury safari lodges in the Northern Safari Circuit market themselves as "green" and caring, in practice they continue to ignore the rights and needs of the Maasai and carelessly exploit limited resources such as water. Further, even though the World Bank and its IFC division claim to have adopted rigorous environmental standards, to be sensitive to local communities, and to be contributing to national development, they continue to support huge infrastructure projects that promote mass tourism and foreign-owned companies that provide scant benefits to Tanzania. As Ray Bonner writes, "The Maasai had been evicted from the Serengeti and Ngorongoro Crater in the name of protecting the environment. Now everything that conservationists had fought for was being sacrificed on the altar of tourist profits."[58]

Community Involvement and Ecotourism

In contrast with these multimillion-dollar, multiinstitutional projects, there are in Tanzania some modest efforts at ecotourism and community involvement by the park service (TANAPA), the Wildlife Division, which regulates hunting, NGOs, and the private sector. These projects began in the late 1980s, when several factors coalesced to give them impetus. First, the top-down, centralized, police-like approach to national parks had led to poaching and other forms of encroachment and a deep hostility toward the parks. Second, ecotourism had emerged as both a sound development tool and a category of tourism distinct from simple nature travel. Third, political liberalizations, particularly the multiparty elections that followed on the heels of the country's economic liberalizations, provided a new opening for popular dissent and legal recognition of nongovernmental and grassroots organiza-

tions. And fourth, the central government, plagued by severe cutbacks in social programs and bureaucratic weakness, ineptness, and corruption, turned
to both the national parks and the tourism industry to provide basic services
in rural areas.

The most ambitious of Tanzania's projects that fit broadly into the category of ecotourism is the Community Conservation Service (CCS), started
by TANAPA in 1989. The director of the Serengeti Research Institute,
Costa Mlay, outlined in an interview the philosophy behind the CCS: "The
world now knows that protected areas will continue to survive only if they
bear a relationship to the surrounding community. If not, then it's a sure
loss. Protected areas are now important only to the extent that they relate
to and contribute to the health of the community living around them.
TANAPA [is] spearheading a program of activities that make communities
benefit from what [parks] earn in tourism." Under the slogan "*Ujirani
mwema*" ("Good neighbors"), TANAPA is providing both social services—
primary schools, dispensaries, safe water systems, cattle dips—and environmental education to the villages nearest the parks. As TANAPA's director,
Lota Melamari, explained in 1995, "Basically these [development projects]
should have been done by the District Development Authorities, which normally get their funding through the central government. But the economic
situation of this country is so low that with its little resources, the government is not able to reach all the needy areas."[59]

Given the enormity of the task, TANAPA's commitment to the CCS is
modest. In 1992, its contribution equaled 2.5 percent of the park's budget,
and in 1994, it rose to 5 percent. In 1995–1996, TANAPA was providing
7.5 percent of the CCS's budget and projects had been established in all
twelve parks. The goal is to provide 10 percent of the park's income, including contributions from the private sector and NGOs. Melamari describes the CCS not as a donor but as a "partner [with the community] in
social-economic development." TANAPA supplies the expertise and some
funds, and the villagers choose the project and supply the labor.

Although TANAPA appears wealthy compared with other parts of the
government, its earnings, about $5 million per year, are a mere fraction of
the $24–$48 million that international experts calculate Tanzania really
needs to adequately protect its parks and wildlife.[60] One ecotourism operator who works closely with the CCS program praises its "cadre of young,
bright, and dedicated staff who, where they have been active, have been in-
strumental in turning people's perceptions of parks and conservation toward
[a] most positive" direction. Others, however, complain that TANAPA, like
other government agencies, has been plagued by corruption and mismanagement.[61]

The relationship between the CCS and local communities is not always
harmonious, as illustrated by the CCS's first pilot project in the conflictive

Loliondo District, where KIPOC is based. Martin Tobias Loibooki, CCS's officer for Serengeti National Park, is himself a Maasai, a fact that, as noted in a study by the African Wildlife Foundation (AWF) and the World Bank, "has been a key factor in maintaining an open dialogue between TANAPA and the local community."[62] A soft-spoken, thoughtful young officer, Loibooki talked freely about his work in his barracks-like office at the park headquarters in Seronara. He said the initial project, which received financial support from the AWF, grew out of public meetings in each of three villages to identify major problems and needs. Loibooki listed security from cattle rustling as the major need. In contrast, KIPOC officials, interviewed at their secondary school, said the villages had listed water, followed by health and education, as the most pressing needs.

The first concrete project—the new ranger post I had crossed through in my visit to see Moringe Parkipuny—was supposed to address several of these concerns. Financed by the AWF, this post was also to become the new zonal headquarters for TANAPA officials and Lobo Wildlife Lodge staff—part of an environmentally sound plan to get all park and hotel employees to live outside the national parks. It was also to house a clinic for the three area villages. When finished, however, the ranger post contained no clinic because, Loibooki said, it is located too far from the villages. "But we've done a lot instead," the CCS officer insisted. "Two classrooms, a teacher's house, a dispensary, and a medical assistant's house. We're also helping them make eighty desks and start campsite and walking safari projects run by local communities." KIPOC officials say that nevertheless, they feel short-changed: they had wanted a clinic at the ranger post, as well as five teachers' houses and three classrooms.

Asked to describe his dealings with KIPOC, CCS officer Loibooki appeared a bit perplexed and hesitant. "I don't know how to put it. Everyone has their own complaints. So CCS is trying to be fair, to go to every village adjacent to the park and give them what they want. And Loliondo has more projects proportionally than other places." He is struggling as well to meet the needs of four other villages outside Loliondo. This is undoubtedly a common picture: even the best-qualified CCS officers feel frustrated; even the best-organized villages feel shortchanged. While TANAPA and NGO officials often talk of CCS as a brave new "partnership," it's more like a tug of war taking place on a field littered with decades of mistrust and broken promises.

In the late 1980s, the IUCN undertook a detailed evaluation of how well the Ngorongoro Conservation Area (NCA) was carrying out its triple mandate of protecting the interests of the Maasai, conservation, and tourism. An NCA official familiar with the report said its findings were highly critical of how the NCA had treated the Maasai. In an interview at the crater, the official argued that "the Maasai should have rights, should be

assisted, given grain, health clinics, schools. Their livestock should get vet-
erinary care. The Maasai should have members on the [NCA] board and be
involved in development issues. Most of this," he contended, "has now been
implemented." The NCA created the Community Development Department, or CDD (equivalent to TANAPA's CCS), through which "about
half" of Ngorongoro's budget "goes to the Maasai." The funds have been
used to build grain storage facilities, a maize mill, and grinding machines. In
addition, he said, the Maasai are now allowed to grow grain in certain areas,
and the authorities distribute grain to them in times of need. Certain areas
have been designated for the Maasai to sell beads and perform traditional
dances for tourists, and two of the nine NCA board members are Maasai.

Although all this sounds impressive, many Maasai complain that they
were not properly consulted as the report was being prepared. Among those
to bitterly attack the IUCN study was Tipilit Ole Saitoti, a Maasai elder,
writer, and activist who holds a Ph.D. degree from an American university.
He said the Maasai have suffered "repression" and have "virtually been reduced to museum pieces whose sole function is to show-case their art and
culture for the benefit of the tourism and conservation industry." A local
Maasai organization, the Ngorongoro Pastoralist Survival Trust, recorded
twenty hours of videotape in five villages in which people voiced "the depth
of [their] mistrust, disappointment and anger."[63]

This reveals that despite some shifts by government and conservation
officials in philosophy and practice, a wide gulf still exists between what the
government is willing to do and what the Maasai are, with increasing mili-
tancy, demanding. Conditions are still far from perfect, funds are insufficient, and tensions remain. Employment, for instance, continues to be a
major issue. Although in the late 1990s about 20 percent of the NCA's staff
were Maasai—up from just 1 to 2 percent a few years earlier—incredibly, by
the mid-1990s, none of the hotels at the Ngorongoro Conservation Area or
in Serengeti National Park had any Maasai employees. The glib assertions of
hotel managers—"The Maasai are just interested in grazing," one told me—
ring hollow when one looks at Kenya's Maasai Mara Game Reserve where a
sizable percentage of hotel and park staff are Maasai.

Community Hunting: Ecotourism's
Ultimate Paradox

Parallel to TANAPA's CCS projects in national parks, the Wildlife Division
has been developing a community wildlife management program aimed at
helping rural villages derive benefits by conducting hunting safaris and hunting for their own consumption. The Wildlife Division is working with communities located in buffer zones near national reserves and controlled areas

where there is commercial hunting. "We want to create good working relationships between hunters and villagers," explains a Wildlife Division official, Hashim Sariko. Tanzania, as do Zimbabwe and South Africa, permits trophy hunting in designated "blocks" in game-controlled areas and reserves. Historically, sport hunting was conducted by private companies owned by foreigners and white Tanzanian settlers, and colonial Tanganyika developed the first block and quota (designating how many animals can be shot) system in Africa. Just after independence, in the 1960s, the government began giving 25 percent of hunting profits to district councils around game reserves. The scheme was intended to promote rural development and enlist local support for trophy hunting and conservation, but as in Kenya, most of these funds just didn't trickle down to the grass roots. In the early 1970s, Julius Nyerere's government began granting hunting operators longer-term concessions to encourage them to invest in their particular blocks.

In 1973, Tanzania banned all commercial hunting in an unsuccessful effort to curb poaching. Hunting was reopened in 1978 as a state monopoly run by the Tanzania Wildlife Corporation (TAWICO). (Kenya prohibited hunting in 1977, and it remains banned.) No private companies were permitted to participate, although TAWICO subcontracted a few blocks to private professional hunters. TAWICO's monopoly ended in 1988 "with the liberalization of business under pressure from the IMF and World Bank and also from private hunters. This change affected our income very much," TAWICO's senior professional hunter, Eliab Orio, told me in a 1995 interview at his office in Arusha. The number of hunting safaris run by TAWICO dropped from more than 200 to a mere 25 per year. There are currently some three dozen private hunting companies, none of which is 100 percent locally owned.

That same year, the government, with German aid and technical advice, undertook an experimental pilot project, the Selous Conservation Project, the country's first community wildlife management program aimed at working with and providing direct benefits to villages near hunting areas. Selous Game Reserve, an enormous, rugged game reserve in southern Tanzania that is famed for its large elephant herds, had suffered from two decades of unprecedented levels of poaching carried out by highly organized gangs of as many as fifty men, backed by a network of corrupt government officials. A 1986 aerial count showed that elephants had been reduced from more than 100,000 to less than half of that number and only a few of the 3,000 black rhinos remained.[64] The park is too remote and undeveloped to be adequately supported through photographic tourism alone. The Selous Conservation Project therefore started with an understanding that half of all hunting revenues would be retained by the reserve itself. With these funds, the project has initiated programs with villages in the buffer zone. "Poachers come from the villages surrounding the reserve. To root this out one has to go into the villages and involve the population," writes German scientist Rolf Baldus, who has been involved in the project. Each village has elected a Wildlife Management Committee and appointed young game scouts to patrol for poachers and keep wild animals out of villages and cultivated areas. Like the CCS, the Selous Conservation Project has provided assistance and technical advice for various small-scale development schemes, including wells, fish ponds, and classrooms. Communities are expected to contribute half of the cost plus labor.

The project has also helped establish clear boundaries and legal title for farms, villages, and new wildlife management areas, where villagers now can hunt legally specified quotas of wild game for their own consumption. Although the government has been very slow in getting promised resources and revenues to the local communities and in setting up the legal framework to enable villagers to hunt, by 1993 thirty-one villages in three districts were involved in the project. Eventually, these villages will be licensed for both subsistence hunting and commercial hunting, along the lines of the hunting safaris run by the CAMPFIRE project in Zimbabwe.[65] According to Costa Mlay, "We hope in the future the total revenue earned by the Selous will be applied for water supply projects, schools, dispensaries. In this way, the Selous will be seen to be contributing meaningfully to the welfare of the people. It will be a catalyst for their rural development efforts."

Selous's elephant population is increasing, and poaching has decreased significantly. "Now we have a model. We know we need to give guardianship of the resource to those who are closest to it, to the local community," says Hashim Sariko, a Wildlife Division official who has been involved in drafting a bill to expand the Selous model of village-owned wildlife management areas for both trophy hunting and subsistence hunting to all game reserves. "The concept is now accepted. But how to do it still needs to be decided," he explains.[66]

Sport hunting is, as one official put it, the ultimate paradox for ecotourism. Although most of those involved in conservation and nature tourism find hunting distasteful, cruel, and ethically reprehensible, many admit that if properly managed, trophy hunting helps curb poaching and does less environmental damage and brings in much more foreign exchange than do photographic safaris. "The 500 tourist hunters coming to Tanzania each year cause a lot less damage than the 300,000-odd camera tourists," argues Sariko. He ticks off the evidence: less garbage; less pollution; less damage to—or even need for—roads; mobile camp sites instead of game lodges or permanent tented camps, and, ironically, harassment of fewer wild animals. Trophy hunters need to find their target only once; often, photographic safari tourists crave quantity, wanting to "bag" on film as many elephants, lions, cheetahs, or leopards as possible. Too many camera tourists, hungry for close-ups and action shots, drive off the roads, following very closely as lions and cheetahs stalk their prey. Further, the presence of big game hunters in remote, often poorly patrolled reserves and controlled areas helps deter poaching.

Costa Mlay, who was head of the Wildlife Division in the early 1990s, calculates that a hunter brings in 100 times more revenue than a nonhunting tourist; the Wildlife Conservation Society of Tanzania estimates it is 55 times more.[67] Either way, the difference is enormous. A typical twenty-one-day hunting safari costs $25,000 to $50,000, excluding airfare to Tanzania. The price for shooting an elephant, for instance, is $4,000; a leopard or lion, $2,000; a zebra, $590. (Rhinos, cheetahs, and wild dogs cannot be hunted.) Between 1988 and 1993, the number of hunting safaris in Tanzania rose from some 200 to around 500 and the gross income increased from $4.6 million to $13.9 million.[68]

Although the arguments for commercial hunting are impressive, they presume that the system functions well, and in Tanzania this has, sadly, not been the case. For decades, commercial hunting has been infected with corruption and mismanagement, and the government, the parastatal body TAWICO, and private hunting companies have all been responsible. According to Tanzania's Wildlife Conservation Society, hunting blocks continue to be given out in secret and quotas raised "with no scientific justification," the Ministry of Tourism, Natural Resources, and Environment has overridden earlier allocations and offered blocks to new bidders with political or financial clout, and there are repeated charges of "financial irregularities."[69]

The 1994 case of the Amboseli bulls exposed some of these problems. In Kenya's Amboseli National Park, located in the shadow of Mount Kilimanjaro and along the border with Tanzania, elephants have become unafraid of vehicles and people. The elephants also regularly cross the unfenced border into Tanzania in search of food, water, and shade. For years, Tanzania had not assigned hunting blocks along this border, but in late 1994, a German Tanzanian hunter—a descendant of the von Trapp family of *The Sound of Music* fame—obtained a hunting block right on the border and brought in a German hunter. They shot at least three, possibly five, of the Amboseli bull elephants that had wandered across the border. "It's about as sporting as shooting your neighbor's poodle," said Cynthia Moss, an American scientific researcher in the park. The shootings were not illegal, but as Moss put it, they were clearly "immoral."[70]

And they were very bad press. *National Geographic* reported, for instance, that the Amboseli bulls "were a major tourist attraction. Three eco-

tourism companies pay a group of Kenya's Maasai about $60,000 per
year to let them bring visitors to Maasai lands to view wildlife, especially
elephants. Moss has been working to persuade the Tanzanian government
to encourage such community-based ecotourism on its side of the border."[71] The Tanzanian government needed little encouragement to quickly
announce that it would no longer issue hunting concessions along the
border.

Abuses remain. The most famous is the tale of the Arab hunters, known
as "Loliondogate," that rocked the local press and hit the *New York Times*
in 1993. Under highly unusual and still-shrouded circumstances, the minister of natural resources and tourism, Abubaker Mgumia—on orders, it's
widely said, from President Ali Hassan Mwinyi and over the written objec-
tions of the Wildlife Division—gave exclusive ten-year hunting rights to
Brigadier Mohammed Abdulrahim al-Ali, deputy defense minister of the
United Arab Emirates (UAE). The brigadier was granted a monopoly to
hunt in TAWICO's two prize hunting blocks in the Loliondo game-controlled area. These blocks were so rich in game that they brought in 70 percent of TAWICO's total revenue.[72]

Beginning about 1991, the brigadier, accompanied by a sixty-member
entourage, plus food, drinking water, falcons, and an arsenal of weapons, periodically arrived aboard a military cargo plane and camped for a month or
two in Loliondo. His luxury safari camp was set up and run by Abercrombie
& Kent. What ensued, according to accounts by safari operators, other
hunters, local Maasai, government officials, and the press, was indiscriminate
wildlife slaughter and no community projects. There were reports of Arab
hunters machine-gunning large herds of animals, sometimes leaving the carcasses behind and at other times loading the meat (and sometimes live animals) into their plane to take back to the UAE. In 1991, for instance, the
hunters in Loliondo were reported to have shot cheetahs and wild dogs,
both of which are endangered species and off limits to hunters; in 1992,
they illegally shot seven lions and two leopards; and in 1993, they are said
to have shot a sizable number of gerenuks, an unusual antelope with a long,
giraffe-like neck. A safari operator came across three giraffes that had been
machine-gunned and abandoned. A Tanzanian scientist came across a pride
of thirty lions that had been machine-gunned. A hunter who stumbled upon
a small corral containing a dozen live gerenuks warned their captors that if
left in the sun like that, the delicate animals would die.[73] The scandal eventually cost Mgumia his job, but the Arabs kept operating in Loliondo.

Although the Arab hunters and the Amboseli bulls incident brought
Tanzania negative publicity, there are, fortunately, at least a handful of qui-
eter and happier stories of hunters, safari operators, and international organizations working to support both conservation and local communities.

Robin Hurt, for instance, is a widely respected professional hunter and safari operator from Kenya who, in the early 1970s, took clients hunting in the Maswa Game Reserve, on the southern edge of the Serengeti. Elephants, rhinos, leopards, elands, roan antelopes, and other highly prized game animals were bountiful. When Hurt returned to the area in 1985, after the hunting ban and the government monopoly on hunting had been lifted, he was shocked to find the reserve's animals decimated by poachers. Hurt says he realized that this could be reversed only if the local Makao villagers were turned from poachers into conservationists. He conceived of a three-pronged antipoaching and community assistance program. It involved setting up a salaried, uniformed village antipoaching team; paying individual villagers $2.50 for each poacher's snare they collected, $75 for each poacher's rifle, and $100 for information leading to the arrest and prosecution of an elephant or rhino poacher; and providing social services through contributions from his clients equal to 20 percent of the cost of a license fee.

Hurt enlisted the cooperation of American Friends of the Game Conservancy, a small Louisiana-based NGO that advocates hunting, and then he turned to selling the project to the villagers. Nearly the entire village, led by the elders, the only schoolteacher, and the one health worker, showed up. "Robin explained to us the value of the game and what benefits we could get by protecting the game instead of poaching, and he offered to help us," one of the villagers later told Ray Bonner. After hours of discussion, the villagers agreed to cooperate. They selected a team of rangers—most of them former poachers—who were given uniforms, rations, bicycles, and a salary of TSh 500 per day, which equals less than $1 but is considerably more than government rangers earn. Within six months, sixty-eight poachers had been captured and convicted, seven poachers' camps had been destroyed, and 2,000 snares had been turned in. With donations from Hurt's clients, the village bought an automatic grinding mill the first year and a tractor the second.[74] Hurt's scheme, known as Cullman Wildlife Project Benefits, has since expanded to fund antipoaching teams and community projects including wells, classroom buildings and teachers' housing, desks, and pit latrines, in a half dozen villages scattered around Tanzania.[75] Even those most critical of sport hunting, including Maasai activist Meitamei Ole Dapash, concede that Robin Hurt is an unusual hunter. "In the eyes of many Maasai, all hunters are the same. But Hurt *has* done some good work," says Ole Dapash.

Despite the government- and privately sponsored antipoaching patrols and community development projects, as well as several major antipoaching operations, poaching has continued to deplete Tanzania's elephant population. The numbers declined from 600,000 in the 1960s to only about 100,000 in the late 1990s. Unlike Kenya, Tanzania has not banned hunting.

However, following the 1989 CITES (Convention on International Trade in Endangered Species of Wild Fauna and Flora) ban on the international sale of ivory, the Tanzanian government, like others, was forced to stockpile ivory it seized from poachers or obtained from elephants that had been culled or had died.

In 1997, the CITES Secretariat, under pressure from Botswana, Zimbabwe, and Namibia, all countries with unsustainable, growing elephant populations, partially lifted the ban to permit a onetime sale of stocks. In early 1998, Tanzania's Ministry of Tourism, Natural Resources, and Environment prepared to sell the government's ivory stocks, estimated to be worth $20 million. Although hunters welcomed the move, conservationists feared it would encourage more poaching and hurt game-viewing tourism.[76]

Private Ecotourism Projects

Parallel with the efforts of Robin Hurt and several other socially responsible professional hunters have been a variety of ecotourism projects started by private tour and safari camp operators and several conservation organizations. As with hunting, the government has offered no guidance or real support for private ecotourism investors. An example is Oliver's Camp, a beautiful, privately owned tented camp located on the edge of Tarangire National Park that has successfully negotiated written agreements with the Maasai communities that own the land.

Oliver's Camp is reached by driving through Tarangire, Tanzania's fourth largest park, which is noted for its baobab forests and the country's second highest concentration of wildlife (after the Ngorongoro Conservation Area) during the dry season. Just a two-hour drive from Arusha on an atypically good paved road, it is a gem of a park. Oliver's Camp is located just outside the far gate, down a dirt road and under a spread of acacia trees. It's an inconspicuous collection of long green canvas tents designed to accommodate eighteen guests by treading as lightly on the earth as possible, with solar electricity and hurricane lamps, pit latrines, and gravity showers. The camp is simple and comfortable and has a well-deserved reputation for serving the finest food in East Africa. What Oliver's Camp promises—and delivers—is an "intimacy and closeness to nature" with "no crowds, no long drives, just wilderness Africa." It specializes in walking safaris and nighttime drives, which, though common in South Africa and Zimbabwe, are just beginning to gain popularity in East Africa. It also promises personalized service, with tours tailored to the desires and stamina of guests and led by one of the two owners.

The owners, Paul Oliver and Jim Howitt, are two British adventurers who have spent years running safaris and now call Tanzania home. When I interviewed Howitt at Oliver's Camp in 1995, he explained that beginning in the late 1970s, the area around Tarangire was hard hit by poaching. "The rhino were gone and elephants were suffering. We often came across carcasses," recalled Howitt as he perched on a huge *kopje* at sunset. Through his binoculars he spotted a familiar herd of young elephants beside the Tarangire River. "All the old bulls were killed by poachers. With them died the knowledge of how to survive, which they teach to the youngsters. Now, for instance, these young ones don't know how to find water or food in times of drought."

Howitt continued, "In 1990, Paul and I decided to join forces to set up a permanent camp. We wanted the experience of being in one place, of seeing the seasons change, and of promoting community conservation. And we wanted to have a business with morals so we could be happy as we worked with it." They decided to try to negotiate a contractual agreement with the Maasai villages in the area. This is a game-controlled area, or open area, with a patchwork of conflicting interests: established communities, new immigrants, farming, hunting concessions, Maasai pastoralists, wildlife, and important migration routes to and from the national park.

The two British owners worked closely with Dorobo Tours and Safaris, a mobile tented safari company that was also hoping to negotiate a lease agreement for land to the south of Oliver's Camp. The two sets of entrepreneurs embarked on a yearlong series of meetings with the local village councils and the Wildlife Division. "The Maasai enjoy debating," said Howitt, "so these were always five- or six-hour sessions. We were keen to convince them that it was in their interest to preserve the land as it is. We wanted to work out some financial arrangement—fees for using the area and also an employment agreement. They suspected we were working for TANAPA and would grab the land for the national park." Ownership boundaries also were not clear, so the negotiators had to help the Maasai villages demarcate correct boundaries. Then there were disagreements over the best way to use the land. The younger Maasai wanted to sell or farm the land, but the village elders and women's section opted for conservation and ecotourism, and their views prevailed.

Howitt says they eventually signed agreements with two Maasai villages to pay $12 per night for each overseas tourist and $6 for tourists from Tanzania. These funds go into a Wilderness Conservation Fund, which is split evenly between the two villages. Oliver's Camp also has four Maasai on its sixteen-member staff. In return, the Maasai gave the camp a thirty-three-year lease for a 2,023-hectare (5,000-acre) "core area" and a 32,375-hectare (80,000-acre) "activity area." In the core area, used for the base camp and the one-day walking safaris, the villagers have agreed not to graze cattle, farm, or cut trees except in times of real need. Oliver's Camp is using the activity area for longer walking safaris and remote wilderness camping, but the villagers retain grazing and water rights.

Howitt explained that although he and Oliver have not specified how the villages are to use the funds, they have tried to set up a corruption-proof method of disbursement. "We were concerned that these payments might become an internal village problem," he explained. By agreement, every two months Oliver's Camp deposits the funds into a bank account in Arusha. Each village has selected four people to handle the accounts, all projects are approved by the whole village, and periodically Oliver's Camp posts in the villages a notice showing exactly how much money it has deposited, what it was used for, and who withdrew it. Between October 1992 and early 1997, the camp paid the villages approximately $40,000, and these funds have gone for a variety of communal projects that Tanzania's central government was unable to finance. One village used the funds to construct a borehole, build a cattle dip, and repair classrooms. They plan next to build teachers' housing and get desks for the classrooms. During a drought, both villages used some funds to buy corn for resale to families at a guaranteed price in order to prevent starvation. In addition to these direct benefits to nearby villages, Oliver's Camp helps support national park conservation by paying $20 per person per day to TANAPA for rights to pass through and use Tarangire National Park.

Although Oliver's Camp's negotiations with the local villages were tacitly supported by the Wildlife Division and TANAPA, there is no government requirement that other tour operators do the same. There are currently a number of camps, lodges, photographic safari operators, and hunting companies operating in this game-controlled area. An Oliver's Camp pamphlet states, "We strongly feel that these operators should get involved with Village Councils and pay directly to these councils a fee." Few have done so, but Oliver's Camp has been approached by village councils, conservation organizations, and TANAPA officials to share their expertise on executing community contracts and carrying out ecotourism.

Already in and around the Serengeti are several other ecotourism projects. An American couple who are longtime Tanzanian residents, Jeanette Hanby and David Bygott, live on a small farm off the beaten track between Ngorongoro Conservation Area and Serengeti National Park, where they write books and work with the local Mbulu people in a variety of farming and livestock projects. To help generate income for these projects and provide employment, Hanby and Bygott have built a small hotel and campsite.

Dorobo Tours and Safaris is considered by many to be the best ecotourism outfit in the Northern Safari Circuit. Dorobo is owned by three brothers, David, Thad, and Mike Peterson, who, as sons of American Lutheran missionaries, grew up among the Maasai. Concerned by rapid and unplanned agricultural expansion, increased cutting of trees and bushes for charcoal production, and the fall in value of cattle (by 1994, it cost about 200 cattle to buy the same tractor it had cost 30 cattle to buy in 1986), the Peterson brothers came to see nonconsumptive ecotourism as one of the few viable alternatives for the Maasai adjacent to the Serengeti. They worked with the residents of three villages in Ngorongoro District, who first had to secure legal title deeds to their land and then convince the Wildlife Division to stop giving away land for hunting concessions. "For the projects to succeed it would be necessary for the Wildlife Division to excise these areas from the hunting concessions as the non-consumptive type of tourism we were proposing directly conflicted with hunting," states a Dorobo background paper. The Wildlife Division agreed, and the Petersons then negotiated five-year lease agreements with the three villages. In the legally binding contracts signed by Dorobo and the village governments, the brothers agree to pay annual lease payments and visitor night fees "in return for exclusive control of tourist activities in the areas." Dorobo argues that exclusivity, "while controversial, is a critical project component from a marketing perspective," since prospective tourists are seeking "an exclusive wilderness experience with an option of walking." In making payments to the villages, Dorobo says it has "attempted to walk the fine line between ensuring suitable use of funds [and] dictating use." The funds have gone for village priorities, including acquisition of a truck, rehabilitation of borehole, and construction of an office building. David Peterson writes that although their projects outside the Serengeti as well as the one on land outside Tarangire are "community conservation successes, the time required to work more closely on the community side [e.g., rather than just paying the fees per agreement] is hardly justifiable in a business sense for such small operations as ours and Oliver's." He argues that although the Wildlife Division gave tacit approval for these projects, it has not "recognized or supported" them, "which means that our position is tenuous." He warns that powerful hunting interests could intervene and reclaim these lands as hunting blocks.[77]

In addition to Dorobo and Oliver's, Gibb's Farm Safaris (connected with the excellently run Gibb's Farm and its sister hotel, Ndutu Sarai Lodge, near Olduvai Gorge) is operating environmentally responsible camping safaris in and near Serengeti National Park. "The famous word called *ecotourism,* we're all striving for it," says Nigel Perks, the company's young British owner, who first came to Tanzania in 1987. Perks's company uses special low-impact tents, brings in all its own food and water, takes out all its garbage, uses biodegradable chemical toilets, and cooks with coffee wood, pruned from Gibb's Farm trees, instead of charcoal. There are some fifteen big companies doing mobile tented safaris, and, Perks says, "rubbish is now a big problem. The laws are not enforced, so many are burying or dumping the garbage inside the park." At one point, Perks found out, to his dismay, that "our guys were burying tin cans. So we began counting the cans and fining workers if not all are carried out. Now our guys are fanatics." Perks works on teaching his guests as well, giving them leaflets explaining how they should behave. "What we try to portray is educative and supportive of Tanzania. We're getting people into the conservation mode," Perks explains. Describing himself as a "converted hunter who used to shoot elephants," Perks now shuns even cameras, advocating that visitors use binoculars instead: "The whole world has been photographed. Using binoculars gets you close up so you don't have to drive off the roads."

In terms of community empowerment through ecotourism, a project in Loliondo District, initiated by Maasai youth and women and financed in part by a Dutch NGO, Retour Foundation, is the most advanced. On the premise that "sustainable development and empowerment are very much interrelated," the project aims to involve Loliondo-area Maasai "in decision making, planning, development and evolution of tourism" on an equal footing "with other tourism interests." The project, which is still in the pilot stage, includes two campsites with a capacity for fifteen tents each; two other, more basic, campsites; cooperatives selling and exhibiting beadwork; and a range of walking safaris. In launching such a project, a competent and sensitive NGO is usually vital to help maneuver through the government bureaucracy and assist with financing and marketing. Retour, for instance, has supplied the necessary training, advised about the development of tourism infrastructure, lobbied various levels of the government, and organized pilot tours from Holland. After just three months, the project was employing, at least part-time, 200 people and had realized $3,000 in profits, which was put in a communal bank. In addition, the project is helping to improve the participant's capacity to challenge the power structure and, through its income-generating activities, has improved the economic position of women, involved them in decision making, and helped build a women's organization.[78]

There are, in addition, several other types of tourism projects in Tanzania that can be broadly classified as ecotourism. Zoe and Roland Purcell (Roland is former director of the Mountain Gorilla Project in Rwanda) operate two tented camps in small, remote national parks south of Kigoma, on the eastern edge of Tanzania. One, Mahale Mountain Tented Camp, on the sandy shore of Lake Tanganyika, offers "Great Ape Escape" and "The Beast Retreat" tours, specializing in walking safaris and chimpanzee viewing as well as snorkeling, fishing, bird-watching, and sunset cruises on one of the world's deepest lakes. Mahale is a tropical rain forest where since 1965 Japanese researchers have been studying chimpanzee. It became a national park in 1985, and although it is less well known than nearby Gombe National Park, the site of Jane Goodall's research on chimpanzees, it is, according to a Fodor's travel guide, "much more exciting terrain, and ecologically stunning." And unlike Gombe, Mahale Mountain Tented Camp is accessible to ecotourists. Mahale's guides are scientifically trained, "with emphasis on chimps," says Zoe. "They can identify most chimps by name, and they enforce strict rules for viewing to ensure no stress for chimpanzees."

The Purcells also run a traditional bush camp in Katavi National Park, one of Tanzania's last genuine wildernesses, which is noted for its concentrations of waterbirds. It offers tours by vehicle, on foot, and by plane. Both camps are ecologically sensitive, using solar power and biodegradable soaps, and are completely dismantled at the end of each season. Most visitors fly in aboard charter planes, but it is possible, although difficult, to get to Mahale by chartered fishing boat from Kigoma, the principal Tanzanian town on Lake Tanganyika.[79]

On the other side of Tanzania is a new, innovative conservation and ecotourism project headed by the World Wide Fund for Nature (WWF) through both its U.S. and international divisions. Based on Mafia Island, which in past centuries was in turn a Persian, Arab, Portuguese, and German trading outpost along Tanzania's southern coast (and which bears no relation, Tanzanian tourism brochures are quick to point out, to organized crime), the project, begun in 1991, is creating the country's first marine park and linking it to sustainable fishing, handicrafts, small-scale industries, and ecotourism. The marine park, covering 400 square kilometers (155 square miles) and including a massive coral reef, four islands, and an extremely rich fishing area, was declared in 1995. Set up as a parastatal body under the department of fisheries rather than national parks, since TANAPA has no experience with ocean protection, it is managed by a board of trustees composed of local government officials, businessmen, and scientists.

Mafia Island Marine Park suffers from some of the same problems as do the Galápagos Islands. In recent years, outside fishermen have camped on the islands, mined large quantities of live coral for construction, and engaged in illegal fishing with dynamite and longlines. According to Lucy Kashaija, a Tanzanian WWF officer, "Local fishermen have been calling for a park. They, together with the Mafia community [of some 35,000], are very keen, and a very big priority [for WWF] is to see that the community is involved in the project." Mafia residents are allowed to fish inside the marine park using traditional hand lines, and the park is being patrolled by both park rangers and local fishermen, Kashaija explained in an interview.

The project involves controlling tourism development as well as fishing practices. All new hotel projects were stopped while WWF developed guidelines for ecotourism. These require hotels to undergo environmental impact

studies, educate guests about how to behave in the marine parks, and contribute a percentage of their profits to the park. There are already two functioning fishing lodges—one government run and one private—and a luxury
hotel is being built by Zanzibar-based hotelier Emerson Skeen on tiny Chole
Island, in the middle of the marine reserve. Just before the moratorium went
into effect, Emerson (as he is known) obtained permission to build an
architecturally unique "exclusive hotel" in the midst of eighteenth-century
stone ruins on Chole. "It will be like living in tree houses among ruins
in the middle of a jungle," explained Emerson. The hotel, he says, will be
environmentally sensitive, using all local materials (except cement), solar
and wind energy, composting toilets, saltwater showers, and biodegradable
soap. Emerson contended that whereas the two other hotels provide "no
social benefits," he has formed an "NGO partnership" with the Chole villagers and is financing a primary school and a clinic on the island. He has established two community-based funds, the Chole Development Society and
the Chole Community Support Society, which will administer donations
made by his hotel and its guests for microenterprises and social welfare
projects.

In a series of bound reports aimed at attracting other investors, Emerson writes, "The primary goal of the project is to develop a profitable hotel,"
but adds that it is also "designed to bring maximal socio-economic benefits
to the local community, to support the objectives of the marine park and to
integrate the hotel into the community and the marine park." However,
those familiar with the Chole project say Emerson's scheme is more a marketing ploy—ecotourism lite—than solid ecotourism. One marine park official who visited Chole says, "I doubt the reality. The teacher had left, and all
I found were people wearing T-shirts Emerson had given them."

Tanzania's Ecotourism Scorecard

Tanzania's conservation and tourism strategies have undergone significant
changes since the mid-1980s. During the 1990s, tourism has become the
country's most important foreign exchange earner, and there are real efforts
by some government departments and private entrepreneurs to give a portion of the profits to local communities and conservation.

Tourism dollars are, for the first time, providing funds to run Tanzania's
national parks and support local community projects. There is optimism and
conviction among TANAPA officials that if local people are involved in conservation and benefit from tourism, Tanzania's wildlife will survive.
Scattered around the country are some fine examples of private entrepreneurs running tourism projects with sensitivity for the environment and the
community. But genuine ecotourism projects are few, small in scale, and

often underfunded. And despite the rhetoric, the government has developed no overall tourism strategy. "Tanzania is going to kill its goose," contends Kenya ecotour operator Steve Turner. "There's no effort to control tourism. It's the biggest make-for-all I've ever seen."

Tanzania's president, Benjamin Mkapa, who took office in 1996, also believes that the government, not the marketplace, must implement economic policies and provide social services. Mkapa, who was a foreign minister and ambassador to the United States under Julius Nyerere, quickly staked out a position supporting sustainable tourism development. "We will not let our short-term needs for money obscure our long-term commitment to conservation and preservation," Mkapa said. With a none-too-veiled reference to Kenya, Mkapa contended that "while others have overexploited and over-commercialized their natural resources . . . we have the advantage of being able to learn from the experience of others and, therefore, avoid costly mistakes."[80]

The Mkapa government's minister of natural resources and tourism, Zaneb Mejia, is a competent and principled former university professor who has taken several wise measures to improve conservation, tourism, and tourism revenues. One of her first moves was to halt construction of new hotels in Serengeti National Park and Ngorongoro Conservation Area, while actively courting investors for the southern parks and those along the coast. In early 1998, Mejia made the controversial decision that Tanzania should sell its ivory stockpiles as part of an effort to raise funds for improving tourism facilities.[81] Parallel with these moves, however, corruption remains widespread and Mkapa's government failed to carry out many of its pledges, including a long-scheduled nationwide environmental impact study and master plan. In August 1998, terrorist bombs exploded at the U.S. embassies in Dar es Salaam and Nairobi, Kenya, killing 258 and wounding some 4,000. The blasts shattered Tanzania's international image as a safe and stable country. When the U.S. State Department responded by warning Americans against travel to East Africa, Tanzania feared tourism would be hard hit.

Tourism is now viewed as Tanzania's best hope for development, and ecotourism, loosely defined to include nature tourism, ecotourism lite, and genuine ecotourism, is widely hailed by government and tourism officials as the model Tanzania is pursuing. In terms of the definition of real ecotourism, Tanzania stacks up as follows.

1. *Involves travel to natural destinations.* Tanzania rates high on this criterion. Its Northern Safari Circuit includes some of the finest and least spoiled wildlife and game parks in the world, and the government is making a concerted effort to open up to both wildlife viewing and sport hunting the largely vast and little-explored southern game parks.

Along the coastline and on islands such as Mafia and, most important, Zanzibar, Tanzania is viewed as a pristine alternative to Kenya's over-developed coastline. Tanzania's tourism sector remains largely "enclave" tourism, with the game parks and islands, rather than the entire country, being marketed for ecotourism.

2. *Minimizes impact.* To date, damage has been done mainly in the heavily visited destinations, Kilimanjaro National Park and Ngorongoro Conservation Area. Although poaching has taken a serious toll, the negative environmental effects of nature tourism have been relatively limited. After independence, the Tanzanian government built game parks that were architecturally respectful though not very environmentally sensitive in terms of conservation of freshwater, waste disposal, or staff housing. There is a recognition that no new hotels should be built inside the parks of the Northern Safari Circuit, that hotel staff and park guards must be moved outside the park boundaries, and that only tented camps should be permitted. But these principles continue to be bent and broken. And with a few exceptions, most notably WWF's Mafia island project, Tanzania is pushing conventional beach tourism, based on overseas package tours, and supports no real community involvement. The fact that Tanzania's extraordinary natural resources are largely unspoiled reflects the reality that tourist numbers are still relatively low, the number of game lodges is still small, and the parks themselves are difficult to reach. New roads, particularly a paved road from Arusha into the Northern Safari Circuit, could rapidly change this, and the government, now locked into tourism as its principal source of foreign exchange, has failed to make an overall environmental strategy.

3. *Builds environmental awareness.* In this category, Tanzania receives high marks for education of foreign visitors but not for that of Tanzanians. Since independence, Tanzania has worked to build up a coterie of local, high-quality naturalist guides, park rangers and guards, scientists, and, on Mount Kilimanjaro, mountain guides and porters. In addition, there are now a number of private camps, lodges, and tour companies practicing solid ecotourism and giving their guests highly informative tours. Some tour companies prepare visitors beforehand with articles and lists of books. Environmental education is, however, far less widespread among Tanzanians themselves, for whom even a basic primary education is not always available, particularly in rural areas. Visiting Tanzania's parks is expensive (even with cut-rate prices for those living in the country), so domestic tourism remains low. Although the number of local and international environmental organizations in Tanzania has grown in recent years and there is more popular awareness of environmental issues, for most Tanzanians the na-

tional parks are simply a source of foreign exchange and, for the Maasai, a source of their own exploitation.

4. *Provides direct financial benefits for conservation.* Conservation is being benefited, but much more needs to be done. Unlike the situation in Kenya, Costa Rica, and South Africa, there are virtually no private parks or reserves, so all foreigners who go on safari do so in the national parks. In the late 1990s, the government made an appropriate decision to raise park entrance fees in the Northern Safari Circuit from $20 to $25 per day, while lowering them from $20 to $15 in the less visited parks in the Southern Safari Circuit in an effort to better disperse visitors. It addition, it raised to $100 the entry fees to special chimpanzee and other primate research stations, such as Mahale Mountain Tented Camp in western Tanzania, which can accommodate only very limited numbers of visitors. With the increase in tourism numbers and the hike in entry fees, more money is coming into the national parks' coffers. But TANAPA also faces many more demands, including several new parks to manage, the need for new or upgraded facilities and infrastructure, and the necessity of training more guards and park officials. At the same time, a rising percentage of its profits are going to CCS projects in local communities. Therefore, both TANAPA and the Wildlife Division, remain severely underfunded.

5. *Provides financial benefits and empowerment for local people.* There is some small, but largely positive, progress in this area. Although benefits have greatly increased, local development and ecotourism projects rarely lead to real empowerment of local people. Many of the communities around Tanzania's parks are now getting tangible benefits from gate fees, tourism projects, and hunting concessions. Although all these projects speak of a "partnership" with the local communities, it is an uneven and often paternalistic partnership in which rent is paid for land use but local people have no say in the way the tourist project or park is run. Financial and material benefits are, therefore, sometimes little more than bribes or buyouts. But there are some exceptions, including the Retour project in Loliondo, the interactive negotiations between the Maasai and Dorobo and Oliver's Camp, and some of TANAPA's CCS projects. The CCS projects represent an important movement from individual ecotourism projects to a national program, a step toward moving ecotourism from a niche market to a set of principles and practices to reshape the country's tourism and conservation policies as a whole. But as Tanzania's failure to develop an environmental impact assessment and strategy illustrate, the government remains weak and lacks consistent national planning, a clear sense of direction, and strong leadership.

258   Part II. Nation Studies

6. *Respects local culture.* Tanzania scores poorly in this regard. Despite some efforts, much prejudice remains toward the Maasai and other pastoralists. They continue to be viewed by government officials, tour operators, and visitors as tourist attractions and sources of souvenirs. Most tourists continue to come to Tanzania to see the wildlife, not to learn about local culture or history. Little seems to have changed: dollars are exchanged for photographs or beads, but there is little real interchange or understanding on either side. Although Tanzania's tourism has not resulted in serious problems with prostitution or other social ills—largely because the game parks are fairly isolated from population centers—there is a need to develop more culturally sensitive and educational forms of interaction.

7. *Supports human rights and democratic movements.* Indirectly, ecotourism has done so. Tanzania, though not fully democratic, is not a dictatorship, and in recent years there has been an increase in the number of NGOs and independent community and rural organizations and in political activism. The rise of ecotourism is one of the forces giving impetus to these struggles. Some Maasai leaders, TANAPA officials, private tour operators, and local and international NGOs are trying to use ecotourism to provide both financial support and political empowerment to local people.

   The Mkapa government has done disappointingly little to curb corruption, revamp basic social services such as public health and education, or build a national development strategy that incorporates the principles and practices of ecotourism. The democratic "flowering" seen around the 1996 elections remains very fragile. It is uncertain how much political leeway will be given in the future to grassroots democratic organizations and how much the Maasai and others living around the parks will really be included in decision making and profit sharing. Mainland activists are worried by the government's continuing support of Zanzibar's unpopular and undemocratic leader, Salmin Amour, whose 1995 reelection has been widely disputed[82] (see chapter 8). Regrettably, tourists traveling to Tanzania remain largely ignorant of the demands, desires, and aspirations of those living around the parks. Because Tanzania's political struggles have been largely peaceful and low-key, many tourists are not aware of them, and tour operators and naturalist guides rarely discuss politics unless urged to do so.

Notes

1. Although colonial officials generally used the spelling Masai, those who belong to this ethnic group prefer *Maasai.*
2. Ministry of Tourism, Natural Resources, and Environment, *National Policy on*

Tourism (Dar es Salaam: Ministry of Tourism, Natural Resources, and Environment, 1991) p. 3; Raymond Bonner, *At the Hand of Man: Peril and Hope for Africa's Wildlife* (New York: Vintage Books, 1994), p. 195. The IUCN calculates that a more modest 12 percent of Tanzania's territory is in either parks or reserves.

3. I am grateful to Roderick Neumann for the phrase *conservation without representation* to describe this style of management, as well as many of the other insights and analysis I have found in his writing. Roderick Neumann, "Local Challenges to Global Agendas: Conservation, Economic Liberalization, and the Pastoralists' Rights Movement in Tanzania" *Antipode* 27, no. 4 (October 1995): 364.

4. Bonner, *At the Hand of Man,* pp. 39–41.

5. Ibid., pp. 42–43.

6. International Institute for Environment and Development (IIED), *Whose Eden? An Overview of Community Approaches to Wildlife Management* (London: Overseas Development Administration, July 1994), pp. 11–12.

7. From the 1880s through World War I, the colonial name for Tanzania was German East Africa. Then it became Tanganyika until 1964, when the postcolonial government merged with Zanzibar to form Tanzania.

8. Bonner, *At the Hand of Man,* p. 174.

9. Ibid., pp. 174–175.

10. Neumann, "Local Challenges," p. 365.

11. This is frequently cited as an example of enlightened conservation policy, although until very recently the cash-strapped and top-down management of the NCA did virtually nothing to assist the Maasai.

12. Quoted in Bonner, *At the Hand of Man,* p. 178.

13. Roderick Neumann, "Ways of Seeing Africa: Colonial Recasting of African Society and Landscape in Serengeti National Park," *Ecumene* 2, no. 2 (1995), p. 163.

14. Bonner, *At the Hand of Man,* p. 178.

15. Neumann, "Local Challenges," p. 366; Bonner, *At the Hand of Man,* p. 65.

16. Bonner, *At the Hand of Man,* p. 64.

17. Ibid., p. 58.

18. Neumann, "Local Challenges," p. 366.

19. IIED, *Whose Eden?*, pp. 11–12.

20. Neumann, "Local Challenges," p. 367.

21. Ibid., p. 361.

22. For instance, a 1962 study found that Tanganyika had proportionately "amongst the lowest figures of high-level manpower encountered in any country, even the least industrially developed." Cranford Pratt, *The Critical Phase in Tanzania, 1945–1968: Nyerere and the Emergence of a Socialist Strategy* (Cambridge: Cambridge University Press, 1976), p. 21.

23. Phillip Bukuku, "Tanzania Tourist Corporation Development Decade," in *Karibu Tanzania: A Decade of TTC's Service to Tourists* (Dar es Salaam: Tanzania Tourist Corporation, 1983), p. 139.

24. I.G. Shivji, ed., *Tourism and Socialist Development* (Dar es Salaam: Tanzania Publishing House, 1975), pp. 36, 90–94.

25. Ibid., p. 37.

26. Bukuku, "Tanzania Tourist Corporation," p. 138.

27. United Republic of Tanzania, *Second Five Year Plan for Economic and Social Development* vol. 1 (Dar es Salaam: Government Printer, 1969), cited in Mohan Ranjit Wikramanayake, "The Development of Tourism in Tanzania" (master's thesis, George Washington University, 1970), pp. 63–64.

28. Bukuku, "Tanzania Tourist Corporation," p. 139.

29. Shivji, *Tourism and Socialist Development,* p. 95; Estrom Maryogo, "Tourism in National Development," in *Karibu Tanzania,* p. 107.

30. Shivji, *Tourism and Socialist Development,* pp. 50, 32, 45.

31. Ibid., p. 87.

32. Interviews; Esrom Maryogo, "The Tanzania Tourist Corporation Reintroduced," in *Karibu Tanzania,* p. 4.

33. United Republic of Tanzania, *The Changing Face of Tanzania: Business Prospects: Tourism Potential and Investment Opportunities in Tanzania* (Dar es Salaam: Investment Promotion Center, May 1992), paper presented at Investment Promotion Seminar, London, May 21–22, 1992, p. 4.

34. Esrom Maryogo, "Tanzania Tourist Corporation," pp. 4–5.

35. Tony Avirgan and Martha Honey, *War in Uganda: The Legacy of Idi Amin* (Westport, Conn.: Lawrence Hill Books, 1982).

36. Joyce Francis, "War as a Social Trap: The Case of Tanzania" (Ph.D. diss., American University, Washington, D.C., 1994), pp. 128, 146–155, 222.

37. Maryogo, "Tourism in National Development," p. 109.

38. Lugano Mbwina, "Tanzania Tourism Begins to Attract Foreign Investment," InterPress Service, April 28, 1993.

39. Ibid.

40. Economist Intelligence Unit (EIU), Tanzania/Comoros (London, EIU, 1994), p. 23.

41. Mbwina, "Tanzania Tourism."

42. One early estimate, made in 1980, was that local tour operators were illegally banking 20 percent to 40 percent of their hard currency earnings overseas. Maryogo, "Tourism in National Development," p. 111.

43. Ibid.; Interviews with World Bank officials who asked not to be named.

44. United Republic of Tanzania. "Tanzania: Opportunities for Investors in the 1990s and Beyond," n.d. Obtained from Tanzanian Embassy in Washington, D.C.; Mbwina, "Tanzania Tourism"; EIU, *Country Profile,* pp. 22–23; Neumann, "Local Challenges," pp. 368–369.

45. Paul Chintowa, "You Are Safe, Visitors Assured," InterPress Service, June 10, 1994.

46. United Republic of Tanzania. *Changing Face of Tanzania,* p. 5; Alpha Nuhu, "South African Firm to Run Hotels," InterPress Service, December 30, 1994.

47. Interviews by author and Marcus Lenzen with various World Bank officials. Author's correspondence with Dr. Julius Nyerere, November 1998.

48. Interview with Maurice Desthuis-Francis, International Finance Corporation Tourism Unit, Washington, D.C., April 1996. This IFC official explained, "I don't know of one [IFC project] in Tanzania that would fit into a real definition of ecotourism."

49. Interviews with tour operators and hotel officials in Tanzania; Bonner, *At the Hand of Man,* p. 183.

50. Neumann, "Local Challenges," p. 369; Anver Versi, "Dawn of a New Age?" *African Business,* November 1994, p. 40.

51. Bonner, *At the Hand of Man,* p. 196.

52. Ibid., p. 197.

53. Sopa's lodge in Tarangire National Park also became involved in controversy. Sopa was originally granted a site next to the park's main river, where wildlife drink, and the hotel planned to dump its waste into the river. Tour operators and conservationists raised a storm of protest, and a TANAPA management plan drawn up by the IUCN recommended that no more hotels be built in the park. In 1992, when Lota Melamari became TANAPA's director, he "went to war" with Sopa and extracted a compromise that the hotel be built on a ridge, away from the river. The hotel, with seventy $240-per-night suites, opened in January 1995 and caters to Americans. Sopa's brochure states that the hotel's "concept is . . . one of environmental care and conservation." Its Kenyan manager, Susan Wachira, explained in an interview, "We are trying to adhere to the principles of ecotourism. We use as much local materials as we can." But the hotel's marble interior and its staff, clad in garish Punjabi-style batik clothing, hardly appear either local or culturally appropriate.

54. Hrvoje Hraniski, "Tanzania Is Developing 'Environmentally Sound' Tourism Policies," *Environmental Times,* September 1996.

55. Versi, "Dawn of a New Age?" pp. 40–41.

56. IFC documents; Interviews with IFC officials in Washington, D.C., 1996–1997; Neumann, "Local Challenges," pp. 374–375.

57. Neumann, "Local Challenges," pp. 374–375.

58. Bonner, *At the Hand of Man,* p. 193.

59. These areas—education, health, and water—had been priorities of Tanzania's post-independence socialist government, but they have been hard hit by structural adjustment policies that demanded sharp reductions in public spending. Between 1984 and 1994, government spending on education dropped from 35 percent of the budget to just 4.8 percent and health care from 35 percent to less than 5 percent. Paul Chintowa, "SAPs Blamed for Declining Standard," InterPress Service, March 16, 1995; Tafadzwa Mumba, "Unbridled Structural Adjustment a Sure Recipe for Ill Health and Female Illiteracy, Warns Nyerere," InterPress Service, September 12, 1995.

60. Bonner, *At the Hand of Man,* p. 195.

61. Interviews with David Peterson and Costas Christ.

62. Deborah Snelson and Peter Lembuya, "Kenya and Tanzania: Pilot Projects: Protected Areas: Neighbors as Partners Program," in Agnes Kiss, ed., *Living with Wildlife: Wildlife Resource Management with Local Participation in Africa,* World Bank Technical Paper No. 130 (Washington, D.C.: World Bank, 1993), p. 110.

63. "Tanzanian Wildlife Conservation Project Threatens Local Community," *EcoNews Africa* 5, no. 1 (January 12, 1996).

64. Rolf Baldus, "The Selous Project: Saving Many By Killing a Few," *Miombo* (newsletter of the Wildlife Conservation Society of Tanzania), no. 12 (January 1995): 8.

65. Interviews; Baldus, "Selous Project," p. 8; IIED, *Whose Eden?* p. 41; Werner Rohs, *The Environmental Impact of Tourism in the Northern Selous Game Reserve*, SCP Discussion Paper No. 9 (Dar es Salaam: Selous Conservation Programme, 1991).

66. Interviews; Baldus, "Selous Project," pp. 8–9; IIED, *Whose Eden?* p. 41.

67. Bonner, *At the Hand of Man*, p. 244; "The Hunting Industry in Tanzania: From World Leadership to National Concern," *Miombo*, no. 12 (January 1995): 2.

68. Interviews; "Hunting Industry in Tanzania," pp. 1–2.

69. "Hunting Industry in Tanzania," pp. 1–3.

70. "They're Her Elephants," *60 Minutes* (CBS) June 11, 1995, transcript, vol. 27, no. 40, pp. 8-14.

71. "Earth Almanac: Famed Bulls Dead or Missing," *National Geographic*, July 1995, p. 142.

72. "Loliondogate," editorial, *Miombo*, no. 10 (July 1993): 2, 17–18.

73. Interviews; "Loliondogate," pp. 2, 17–18; Caroline Alexander, "The Brigadier's Shooting Party," *New York Times*, November 13, 1993.

74. Bonner, *At the Hand of Man,* pp. 235–250.

75. Interviews; literature from American Friends of the Game Conservancy.

76. Paul Chintowa, "Tanzania Secures Ivory Markets in China and Japan," InterPress Service, February 10, 1998.

77. Correspondence with David Peterson; Directors, Dorobo Tours and Safaris, "Community Centered Conservation"(paper presented to Tanzania Community Conservation Workshop, Arusha, Tanzania, February 1994).

78. Marcus Lenzen's correspondence with Theo Noten, Retour Foundation, Nijmegen, The Netherlands, September 1997; Frans de Man, managing consultant, Retour Foundation, "Contributions of Tourism to Empowerment of Local People: The Case of Maasai in the Loliondo District," unpublished excerpt from manuscript, n.d.

79. *Fodor's Kenya and Tanzania* (New York: Fodor's Travel Publications, 1992), p. 126; correspondence with Zoe Purcell.

80. Hraniski, "Tanzania Is Developing 'Environmentally Sound' Tourism"; Interview with Benjamin Kapa, November 1996 in Washington, D.C.

81. George Owuor, "How Tourism Can Play a Major Role in Development," *Earth Times,* July 8, 1997; Chintowa, "Tanzania Secures Ivory Markets."

82. L. Muthoni Wanyeki, "Mkapa Losing Marks over Zanzibar," InterPress Service, May 3, 1996.

Chapter 8

Zanzibar: Ecotourism on a Muslim Island

At the Ecotourism Society's International Ecolodge Developers Forum and Field Seminar held at Maho Bay, St. John island, in October 1994, I was surprised to find a Zanzibari government official listed among the participants. Dr. Ahmada Hamadi Khatib, then head of marketing and promotion for Zanzibar's Commission for Tourism, explained that his Indian Ocean island had turned to ecotourism after "the mishaps of conventional tourism had worried everyone." Asked what were Zanzibar's main ecotourism attractions, Khatib replied that the island was promoting "four main product lines": (1) the culture and history of the old Stone Town (also known as Zanzibar Town, once a major financial center); (2) spice tours; (3) the sea, including coral reefs and deep-sea fishing; and (4) white-sand beaches. And, Khatib added, Zanzibar (like Kenya) was forming an independent ecotourism society "to see that we get the type of tourism appropriate for the environment and culture of the country." (The Zanzibar and Kenya ecotourism societies were both officially registered in 1996.)

I was skeptical. I had done research for my doctoral dissertation in Zanzibar during the 1970s and early 1980s, and at that time tourism was viewed with suspicion and not actively promoted. It seemed unlikely that over the subsequent dozen years ecotourism had really reached this distant, culturally conservative, and fairly insular island. I was sure that Zanzibar (which is made up of two main islands, Unguja, where the famed Stone Town is located, and Pemba, where most of the cloves are grown) had never *really* experienced conventional, or mass, tourism. And the four "product lines" listed by Khatib were identical to ones that had always been hawked by a handful of elderly *kanzu*-clad (white-robed) tour guides who hung about outside Old Stone Town's hotels. What, I wondered, was really new? What was "eco" about Zanzibar's present-day tourism? Wasn't this simply another example of repackaging, or "greenwashing"?

Eight months later, I boarded a hydrofoil in Dar es Salaam's harbor for a high-speed passage from the Tanzanian mainland to Zanzibar. For centuries, Zanzibar was a cosmopolitan crossroads for ivory, slave, and other traders from the East and West and the center of Swahili culture, with an influence penetrating into the heart of the African continent. Although separated by twenty-five miles of emerald blue Indian Ocean, Zanzibar and the Tanzanian mainland, known as Tanganyika, had (along with Kenya and Uganda) been part of Great Britain's East African colonial empire. During the nineteenth century, Zanzibar emerged as the clove-growing capital of the world. Beginning in 1880, Britain ruled Zanzibar nominally through the islands' Arab sultanate. In 1963, Britain granted independence to a country that was politically divided and had a shaky coalition. Just five weeks later, in January 1964, a brief but bloody populist revolution toppled the government, killed thousands of Arabs and Indians, and sent Sultan Seyyid Jamshid ibn Abdullah and remnants of the British colonial service fleeing by boat.[1]

Zanzibar's new "revolutionary" government quickly established diplomatic relations with the communist world, including the Soviet Union and eastern Europe, China, and North Vietnam. Horrified, the U.S. government denounced Zanzibar as "the Cuba of Africa" and then, just a few months later in early 1964, breathed a sigh of relief when newly independent Tanganyika and Zanzibar announced they were uniting to form a new country, Tanzania. Dar es Salaam was the capital, and Julius Nyerere, a nonaligned socialist and one of Africa's great statesmen, was the president. Nyerere viewed the union with Zanzibar as a step toward the cause of African unity, a dream that has remained illusory. Under the union's quasi-federal structure, Zanzibar retained authority for most of its internal affairs. But it was always an uneasy alliance, with each side suspecting that the other was gaining more.

The First Tourism Debate: From State-Run to Free-Market Tourism

In a small book titled *Tourism and Socialist Development,* published in 1975, Issa G. Shivji, a Marxist law professor at the University of Dar es Salaam, laid out a major critique of tourism, reprinting articles and letters from Tanzania's English-language newspaper. This "tourism debate" represented, Shivji wrote, the first "serious political debate in print in Tanzania."[2] Shivji argued that Tanzania needed to evaluate tourism from three angles: (1) by analyzing the nature of underdevelopment; (2) by studying the experiences of other developing countries; and (3) by assessing tourism's contribution to Tanzania's socialist goals (known as *ujamaa,* or familyhood). Relecting the views of many socialists, the youth wing of Tanzania's ruling TANU party argued "[T]ourism reinforced the existing colonial and neo-colonial social, cultural and economic relationships."[3] The value of this critique was in its suggestion that Tanzania, including Zanzibar, should concentrate on more socially beneficial and stable activities such as food production, manufacturing of textiles and other basic goods for the domestic and regional markets, and processing of agricultural exports.

In the 1970s, the bulk of tourism on Zanzibar was carried out, in a lackluster manner, by the government's Zanzibar Friendship Tourist Bureau (ZFTB) and confined almost exclusively to the main island, Unguja (popularly referred to as Zanzibar). During the decade when I visited Zanzibar, from 1973 to 1983, I never saw more than a handful of other foreigners. Most of the tourists were youthful backpackers, aid workers, or diplomats from the mainland. The trickle of tourism was confined to a few badly run government-owned hotels in converted Arab houses or former British colonial hotels in the Stone Town and the overpriced "modern" Bwawani Hotel, a 114-room, eastern European–style cinder block monstrosity built next to the sewage outlet on the edge of town. The original architectural plans for the hotel, which was designed by Zanzibar's dictator, Abeid Amani Karume, shortly before his assassination in 1972, reportedly included no hallways, the world's largest outdoor swimming pool, and an artificial beach. During construction, someone remembered to add hallways, but the swimming pool, built according to Karume's plan, never functioned and slowly degenerated into a gigantic garbage-filled and mosquito-infested swamp. By the time I left Tanzania and Zanzibar in 1983, tourism, like Karume's pool, had dried up almost completely.

Two decades after this first "tourism debate," Zanzibar is experiencing both a tourism boom and a lively debate over tourism and ecotourism. In the mid-1980s, after Nyerere stepped down, Tanzania and Zanzibar shifted gears and gradually began to promote both tourism and manufacturing export zones. The impetus on Zanzibar was twofold: plummeting clove prices (down from $9,000 per ton in the early 1980s to a mere $600 in the mid-1990s)[4] and pressure from the World Bank, the International Monetary Fund (IMF), and USAID for more liberal trade and investment policies. In 1986, the terms of an IMF structural adjustment loan dictated profound economic "liberalizations" in Zanzibar and on the mainland, including a denationalization of the banks and many other government-owned enterprises; opening of the country to private, including foreign, investment; promotion of new exports; an easing of regulations on repatriation of profits; and abolition of duties and taxes on the import of raw materials for industry.[5]

To facilitate this shift from a state-run to a free-market economy, the Zanzibari government enacted a series of new laws and created new institutions. The 1985 Trade Liberalization Policy advocated diversification of the economy and a greater role for the private sector. That same year, the Stone Town Conservation and Development Authority was established to promote restoration and rehabilitation. In 1987, Zanzibar's Economic

Recovery Program stressed, for the first time, that tourism was an important component in Zanzibar's economic development, and in 1989, the Investment Protection Act, designed to attract foreign capital, was amended to include tourism as an export, thereby qualifying it for an array of investment incentives. In 1992, the Zanzibar Investment Promotion Agency (ZIPA) was established to facilitate "one-stop shopping" for both local and foreign investors, and the Commission for Tourism was created to promote Zanzibar as a tourism destination and to regulate and monitor the tourism industry.[6] As the World Bank's private investment arm, the International Finance Corporation (IFC), summed up, between 1985 and 1995 Zanzibar moved to facilitate investment "through a generous system of incentives."[7] In 1994, the World Bank itself began a multimillion dollar Tourism Infrastructure Project in Tanzania and Zanzibar whose objective was, according to Barbara Koth, the bank's first tourism advisor in Zanzibar, "to 'unstick' private investment through infrastructure improvements,"[8] including roads, electricity and water facilities, and Zanzibar's main airport. The World Bank project also included assistance to upgrade Zanzibar's statistical and data collection capabilities and training of local personnel.[9]

Taken together, these reforms moved Zanzibar from the socialist camp to the neoliberal USAID–World Bank–IMF camp. Between 1982 and 1992, tourism grew quickly, averaging an 18.5 percent increase per year (see table 8.1).[10] (Tanzania as a whole is the second fastest growing country in tourism receipts in Africa, with a 28 percent average increase since 1985.)[11] A study by the IFC, however, warns that official statistics on Zanzibar's tourism arrivals and earnings are notoriously unreliable, both because of "deficient data collection methods" and because they are based solely on occupancy in hotels whose owners underestimate visitor numbers in order to avoid taxes. The IFC estimates that "the figures probably underestimate Zanzibar's visitation by 25% to 30%."[12] In the 1990s, international visitors have become

Table 8.1. Zanzibar's Tourism Growth

	Number of Visitors (in Thousands)						
	1985	*1987*	*1990*	*1992*	*1993*	*1995*	*1997*
Foreigners	16	29	39	55	43	56	86
Nationals	35	—	20	40	33	—	—
Total	51	—	59	95	75	—	—

Source: International Finance Corporation (IFC), *Zanzibar: Tourism Investment Study: International Finance Corporation Annexes* (Washington, D.C.: IFC, March 1995), p. 14; Statistics obtained for 1994 to 1997 by Fatma Alloo from the Commission on Tourism, Zanzibar, June 1998; Economist Intelligence Unit (EIU), *EIU Country Profile, 1994–95: Zanzibar* (London: EIU, 1994), p. 42.

more important than Tanzanian visitors from the mainland. Tourists from Europe consistently account for about two-thirds of Zanzibar's international visitors; Americans typically visit the island as an "add-on" to visits to game parks in Tanzania or Kenya. The average stay is short, lasting only two nights.

Most of Zanzibar's tourism growth, in both visitor arrivals and numbers of hotels, has taken place since 1990. Between 1991 and 1993, for instance, the number of hotel rooms increased by 42 percent. By mid-1993, ZIPA had approved 204 projects totaling a proposed investment of some U.S.$265 million. Of these projects, 53.4 percent were for foreign-owned "hotels and tourism," a mere 1.1 percent were "joint ventures" involving foreign and local capital, and 6.3 percent were for tour operators, a category restricted to Tanzanian nationals.[13] A *Condé Nast Traveler* poll published in July 1994 included Zanzibar on a list of the fifty-five "most desirable islands," even though almost all the other islands had more and better tourism facilities.[14] By mid-1995, tourism had dislodged cloves (for which the world price had plummeted) as Zanzibar's number one foreign exchange earner.[15]

The Second Tourism Debate: Ecotourism Workshops

Despite its rapid growth, Zanzibar's tourism was, according to a government report, "completely unplanned." A 1983 tourism development plan prepared by the World Tourism Organization (WTO) and the United Nations Development Programme (UNDP) had never been followed.[16] So in the early 1990s, in an effort to establish guidelines, the Zanzibari government held three conferences. The most significant of these was the March 1994 International Workshop on Ecotourism and Environmental Conservation, sponsored by the Department of Environment in collaboration with the Commission for Tourism.

Some one hundred people attended the four-day workshop, including twenty-two from overseas, sixty-four from Zanzibari government institutions, and sixteen from the private sector. The aim of the conference was to review ecotourism experiences in other countries, give government officials and tour operators a practical introduction to ecotourism, discuss plans to establish the island's first national parks (referred to as nature conservation areas), and examine the benefits of local community involvement in tourism. However, no representatives of local communities were invited to the conference, an unfortunate decision necessitated, organizers said, by the fact that proceedings were in English. Instead, one day was spent on field trips to several communities interested in tourism.

The delegates made ultimately sixteen recommendations that collectively set forth a dynamic and thorough blueprint for implementing sound ecotourism as a strategy for community development and environmental protection.[17] The most innovative of these recommendations was a set of resolutions to involve local communities in tourism development that would benefit the communities and protect the environment.

At the time, tourism was just picking up in Zanzibar, with construction on most proposed projects not yet under way. In theory, the island had the opportunity to choose the path of sustainable tourism development. But in reality, many contradictions already existed within Zanzibar's tourism sector, and the island's government lacked the sound, publicly accountable leadership necessary to implement a strategy to protect the environment and benefit local communities, entrepreneurs, and workers. Zanzibar had never known popular democracy, had no tradition of independent organizations or of community-based involvement in development schemes, was politically and economically subservient to the mainland government, and was locked, together with the mainland, into a development strategy based on foreign investment, privatization, and a diminished economic and political role for government. The tourism and environment departments lacked bureaucratic power and effective coordination with other parts of the government. And the political trajectory was, in fact, moving toward greater instability, with rising tensions both within Zanzibar and between the island and the mainland. The Zanzibari government has therefore never systematically implemented these recommendations, although debate over tourism and ecotourism has continued through the 1990s.

Part of this ongoing debate has been over the type of tourism projects Zanzibar should seek to attract: whether it is preferable to concentrate on luxury-oriented conventional tourism in order to earn more foreign exchange or whether construction of more moderate but environmentally sound bungalows, guest houses, and small hotels should be encouraged. There was unanimous agreement that Zanzibar no longer wanted low-budget "backpackers" and "low-grade hotels," which had dominated its tourism in the past. A 1993 Tourism Consultancy Mission carried out by the International Labor Organization found that 80 percent of the island's rooms were "below a level" likely to attract tourists other than backpackers,[18] despite, the island's 1989 Investment Protection Act, which sought to encourage "high-class tourism" by requiring that all new hotel projects involve an investment of more than $4 million[19] or $35,000 per bed.[20] However, the final resolutions of the workshop warned that the government "should recognize that 'high class tourism' which follows the principles of ecotourism, and which may bring many economic benefits to Zanzibar, is frequently not produced by conventional resorts with concrete structures, television, air-conditioning etc. The 'primitive luxury' market, with simple *makuti* (palm frond) and wood structures, can command very high prices, and is often favourable to the principles of ecotourism."[21]

At the same time, supply of hotel rooms has been outstripping demand. Zanzibar's overall occupancy rate dropped from 38 percent in 1983 to an "unacceptable" 30 percent in the mid-1990s, leading the Commission for Tourism's marketing director, Ahmada Khatib, to pledge that the government would "focus on the improvement and upgrading of hotels rather than increasing their number."[22] But with sixty hotels (excluding guest houses) and 1,500 beds already available in 1995, and plans for Zanzibar to have 6,000 beds by the year 2000 and a total of 15,000 beds by 2015, many of these hotels faced a crisis unless visitor numbers increased. By the late 1990s, prospects looked better as Kenya's political violence sent more charter flights of Germans and Italians directly to Zanzibar and tourism from South Africa grew as well. But Zanzibar's own political turmoil following its 1995 elections was also threatened to undermine tourism.

Zanzibar's Unusual Offerings: Promoting Responsible Urban and Oceanside Tourism

Unlike virtually every other destination seriously involved in ecotourism, Zanzibar has no national parks (other than the ill-kept Masingini Forest Reserve which was established in the 1950s to conserve the town's groundwater). The 1994 ecotourism workshop passed several resolutions urging the creation of nature conservation areas (NCAs), to be administered by a newly formed Zanzibar Nature Conservation Trust, a nongovernmental organization with some government representation on its board. By 1996, three NCAs had been declared: Jozani Forest Reserve, home of the endemic red colobus monkey; beautiful Misali Island, off Pemba Island's western coast, one of East Africa's richest marine areas, with great potential for sport diving; and a marine park off Chumbe Island, just outside the Stone Town. A resolution adopted at the workshop recommended that guidelines for tourism investment in or adjacent to these parks include the involvement of local communities and "high standards of ecotourism guiding and environmental protection in NCAs."[23] Misali Island, for instance, is being damaged by destructive fishing practices, illegal anchoring by Kenyan cruise boats, mining of coral rocks (it takes as long as 300 years to restore destroyed coral reefs), dumping of sewage and chemical pollutants, and cutting of trees. Although some foreign investors and their Zanzibari collaborators argued against the reserve and pushed to be allowed to develop a luxury hotel and other economic activities on this island, the scales tilted toward conservation. The U.S.-based African Wildlife Foundation (AWF) has been the main

promoter and financier of the Misali Island Trust, which the AWF's East
African director, Mark Stanley Price, called a "test case" for future preserves.
However, following the October 1995 elections, the AWF's involvement in
the project was put on hold indefinitely because of escalating political
unrest.[24]

The Stone Town

Without national parks, Zanzibar's tourism development has been concentrated in the Stone Town and the island's coastal beaches and offshore
islands. The World Bank's tourism advisor, Barbara Koth, has argued that
the Stone Town distinguishes Zanzibar from its Indian Ocean island rivals,
the Seychelles, Mauritius, and Réunion, and is "the centerpiece of
Zanzibar's tourism image—with its architecture, the art, dance, ceremony
and way of life [and] its history. [It] would seem an authentic form of
tourism."[25] The narrow, winding streets and tall stone buildings of the
Stone Town, the heart of the old Arab and Asian financial monopoly, still
appear much as they did more than 100 years ago. Zanzibar, together with
Lamu (on Lamu Island, off Kenya) and, to a lesser degree, Mombasa, are
the only functioning historic stone towns along the East African coast.[26] The
United Nations Environment Programme (UNEP) and the German government have been helping with conservation efforts, and Zanzibar has
applied to have the Stone Town recognized by UNESCO as a World
Heritage site.[27] In the mid- to late 1990s, some of the elegant stone homes
with ornate wooden balconies and carved wooden doors, as well as several
of the main cobblestone streets, were restored. Curator Abdul Sheriff[28] put
together an impressive three-story museum in the sultan's former oceanfront palace, which contains many of the island's finest antiques. Until international funding ceased because of political violence after the 1995 elections, he was also restoring the Sultan's House of Wonders, built originally
as a ceremonial palace and converted by the British into government offices.
After the revolution, it was turned into a museum displaying toys and gad-
gets that Zanzibar's rulers had collected from around the world.

These days, the Stone Town's bustle is its most striking feature. After
years of austerity and shortages of basic consumer goods, the town is undergoing an economic revival brought on by economic liberalizations and
increased trade. The port where hydrofoils from Dar es Salaam dock is now
lined sky-high with rows of empty containers, brought in mainly from
Dubai. A dozen years ago most stores either were boarded up or sold meager piles of dates, spices, and cornmeal. Now—for a price—there are plenty
of imported rubber sandals, cloth and clothing, umbrellas, suitcases, spices,
fruits, and tinned foods.

Between 1989 and early 1994, about half of the hotel projects approved by the government involved the conversion of the Stone Town homes into guest houses. A 1993 survey reflects the phenomenal growth of the private sector over the previous few years, listing fourteen existing hotels and thirteen guest houses in the Stone Town and another seven guest houses near the town. Of the Stone Town hotels, only four were state owned,[29] the same ones that had been in government hands since the 1970s. Private accommodations range from low-budget guest rooms in traditional houses to lavishly restored suites in some of the town's finest structures. Among the most luxurious is the fifty-two-room Zanzibar Serena Inn, which comprises two blocks of beautifully restored buildings near the ocean. The Serena Group received a generous ninety-nine-year lease for this multimillion-dollar hotel, one of ten East African hotels and lodges owned by the Switzerland-based Aga Khan Fund for Economic Development (AKFED). It has also been given land for a beach hotel at Mangapwani, eight miles north of town. The fund was set up by Karim al-Hussain Shah, the Aga Khan IV, leader of the Ismailis, one of several Muslim sects with followers in Zanzibar and elsewhere in East Africa. The Ismailis had been the most economically powerful of the Asian (as the traders from the Indian subcontinent were collectively known) communities in East Africa. Many left East Africa during political troubles in the 1970s, but in the 1990s, some Asian capital began returning. Although AKFED represents foreign investment, it does have deep ties to Zanzibar and has set up a social welfare arm that funds some community-based projects.[30] In return for being granted permission to turn prime Stone Town property into a luxury hotel, the Aga Khan Trust for Culture funded and supervised restoration of the town's historic dispensary and plans to do other restoration work in the Stone Town. The Zanzibar Serena Inn received financial assistance from Tanzanian and Commonwealth development corporations as well as the World Bank's International Finance Corporation (IFC). By the late 1990s, this represented the only loan the IFC had given for tourism projects in Zanzibar.[31] The IFC certified that the refurbishment and construction plans met World Bank environmental, health, and safety guidelines.[32] However, according to ecotourism expert and tour operator Costas Christ, Serena's Stone Town hotel is "following some noteworthy environmental guidelines, including better efforts at waste management, in seeking to be ecotourist friendly. If measured by the yardstick of corporate hotels, it's more than just window dressing. But it still lacks the detailed principles of sustainable design found among some smaller ecotourism properties."[33]

Another is Emerson House, two restored homes decorated with fine Zanzibari antiques. One has a small rooftop restaurant lined with cushions, long low dining tables, billowing scarfs, spicy curries, and a panoramic view of the town. The owner of Emerson House is a transplanted New Yorker, Emerson Skeen—known simply as Emerson—who projects himself as the unofficial spokesman for the Stone Town. Emerson is one of the "oldest" (having arrived in 1989) and most successful of the foreign hoteliers, and is aggressively buying up other properties. Like Stanley Selengut at Maho Bay, Emerson is a superb host and master at marketing through the media, and his clientele includes a steady stream of travel writers.

Emerson admits his community and ecotourism endeavors are minimal. He supports the Zanzibar Ecotourism Society, is highly critical of what the big Italian beach hoteliers are *not* doing, and has developed a culturally sensitive dress code that he distributes to his guests. He says he hires too many employees and pays them too much, yet he's building houses for his staff. But, he adds, "I still get four times my annual investment in gross profits per year." And he is blunt about his limitations in the Stone Town: "I can't deal with the community. It's too complex. Village law is the only way and there's no village government in Zanzibar Town."

Indeed, Emerson is right in that for Zanzibar and much of the rest of world ecotourism strategizing has concentrated on how to involve and benefit rural and indigenous communities, not urban folks. The tourism boom, while helping to promote urban renewal and local employment, is undermining both the historical authenticity and the cultural life of the Stone Town. According to the proceedings of the 1994 workshop on ecotourism, "This [construction] is endangering the life of the town, and if it continues unabated it is likely that the Town's aesthetic value will rapidly decrease."[34] Likewise, Zanzibari tourism expert Fadhil Ubwa warns that tourism "is growing very fast and may soon grow out of control. We want to ensure the culture of the Stone Town is not lost."[35]

White Sand and the Sea

There has been a parallel concern that development along Zanzibar's beaches and on its small islands is also getting out of hand. Most of the new beachfront construction is on the island's eastern coast, where in 1994 facilities for more than 1,000 hotel beds were under construction and the lack of planning and control were most apparent. Many of these are local guest houses built by Zanzibaris who, the authorities found, often lacked sufficient capital "either to meet desired standards of service or to incorporate measures for environmental protection into their design and operation." Some of these guest houses have been built "irrespective of wider social impacts, the wishes of the community in general or tourism policy considerations."[36] Resolutions established during the ecotourism workshop warned that this eastern coast development "was a matter of great concern and national importance" because "guest houses have developed very close to the beach front and within villages, causing environmental and social problems."[37]

Land speculation is also rampant, with would-be developers and middlemen buying up tracts, often for almost nothing. Since all land is state owned, potential developers must obtain a lease from the government and pay the local farmers or villages for their assets, which are usually coconut trees or small garden plots. Ecotourism advocates say the government has unfortunately granted a number of exorbitantly long (ninety-nine-year) leases, without having in place proper guidelines or monitoring procedures and without requiring projects to be completed within a specified time frame. World Bank representative Barbara Koth proposed that the government cancel leases if nothing is built within a prescribed period. Further, despite calls for contracts between investors and villages and for equity share agreements for the land, the government has not yet required them.

Conflicts between tourism and local communities have arisen over a variety of issues, including access routes, use of freshwater, boat moorings, cemeteries, seaweed farming in intertidal areas, and standards of dress. It is at two of the beach resorts along the northeastern coast that the most vocal conflicts, as well as the best experiments between villagers and tourist hotels, are taking place.

Mnemba Club

Guidebooks and travel articles give the Mnemba Club, located on its own small island, rave reviews. "One of the world's classiest small tropical resorts sits on its own sandy coral cay in dazzling seas just off the northeast coast of Zanzibar," reads an article in *Condé Nast Traveler*.[38] It has, the article continues, "the kind of stylishly simple accommodations that only serious money can buy. [Doubles start at $500 per night.] The clientele is appropriately wealthy—Bill Gates once rented the entire thing to entertain close friends. As [writer] William Dalrymple said, 'If you have been somewhere nicer than this, you are probably dead and in heaven.'"[39] The resort has been given both British Airways and Green Globe's ecotourism awards.

Mnemba has received good marks on environmental design. Its fourteen bungalows are, according to another hotel owner, "very expensive but locally made" with palm fronds, and they were constructed without disturbing the area. The Mnemba Club specializes in diving and deep-sea fishing and has a well-protected reef that runs halfway around the island where fishing is prohibited. The government has been monitoring the reef and says it has improved since fishing was banned at the insistence of the hotel owners. In many respects, the Mnemba Club appears to be the type of "primitive luxury" resort many ecotourism specialists say is appropriate for Zanzibar.

But just below the surface there has been a great deal of tension. The original owner was Bruno Brighetti, an Italian entrepreneur whose resorts along the Kenyan coast are associated with rumors of prostitution, money laundering, and even drug trafficking, and these stories have followed Brighetti to Zanzibar. Opened in 1988 as one of the first foreign-owned hotels in Zanzibar, the Mnemba Club was given a ninety-nine-year lease for exclusive use of the island, a decision many government officials now regret. "After having been closed for twenty-five years, we had no experience, no standards, and no international references," says former director of the Department of Environment Abdulrahman Issa. Many suspect that Brighetti obtained this sweetheart deal by sweetening the pot of key government functionaries. What is clear is that Zanzibar itself is gaining very little from the hotel. Guests take charter flights directly from Italy to Zanzibar, and the hotel transports them to the island. Most of the tourism dollars are paid abroad and never even enter Zanzibar.

Perhaps most contentious is the issue of exclusivity: the Mnemba Club has made it impossible for Zanzibaris from this part of the island to land on the island or fish on the reef. Traditionally, fishermen from the nearby coastal villages fished in the waters around the island and dried their fish and nets on the island. "Brighetti swindled the locals out of their island," says one ecotourism operator. Former environment director Issa says that the "missing link" in the deal involved failure to consult the fishermen beforehand. "Fishermen *were* destroying the reef. We [the government] supported stopping fishermen, but they needed to benefit from what was done on the island and also work out where they would fish instead," he says. Brighetti paid no compensation to the local fishermen or villagers, and the club wouldn't even permit fishermen to make emergency landings on the island during storms. Zanzibaris hired to work in the hotel did not come from the village. As tempers boiled in mid-1995, one angry villager charged that he and other local people knew who was responsible for four different thefts of outboard motors, gasoline, and boats from the hotel. But because of the conflict, they had not given the information to the club's management or the hotel. Instead, he claimed, the fishermen were plotting to mount an "armada" of fifty small boats to provoke "an armed confrontation with Mnemba. We want to be able to use the island as in the past."

When the Conservation Corporation, South Africa's premier ecotourism company (see chapter 10), bought the Mnemba Club in July 1996, many anticipated swift improvements in management and community relations. This has only partially been true. Costas Christ was among those whom the Conservation Corporation approached for advice on improving relations with the local villagers. Christ, who speaks Swahili and knows Zanzibar well, had spent time with the village before Brighetti took over control of the island. He advised a senior Conservation Corporation official to quickly sack the old Mnemba Club management team as a sign to the local villagers that better relations were a priority. The company balked, apprehensive of taking such drastic action so quickly. Six months later, however, when the Zanzibari government threatened to close Mnemba if the Italian manager was not removed immediately, the Conservation Corporation took the desperately needed action. Since then, the corporation has sought to provide some benefits locally by buying produce and fish directly from the villagers and hiring only villagers for work projects. Unfortunately, however, it has continued to deny local fishermen access to the island.[40] Ecotourism experts contend that the South African company could be doing a lot more for the local community but has been reluctant to go beyond the easy and obvious steps for fear it will end up having to allow villagers access to the island, thereby destroying its image for luxurious exclusiveness.

Matemwe Bungalows

The counterpoint to the Mnemba Club is Matemwe Bungalows, located along an enormous stretch of dazzling white-sand beach on the edge of the village and within eyeshot of the island housing the Mnemba Club. It is owned by two young Swedish sisters, Len and Katharina Horlin,[41] who grew up in a national park on a small island in the Baltic Sea where their father worked. In 1989, the Horlin sisters set off on a round-the-world trip, first stop Zanzibar. They were enchanted by the island's beauty and intrigued by all the talk of tourism and foreign investment. "We decided to make a company here," says Katharina. "We didn't yet know the term *ecotourism,* but the concept was an old habit because we came from a national park. We wanted to build the hotel in the local style, to help the people of the area, and to try not to disturb their way of life." Along with two other European partners, they decided on location and obtained a lease from the government. "The land was uninhabited," Katharina explains. "The village people were afraid of it because there's a burial ground here. We paid for two coconut trees and some *shambas* [gardens]that were on the land."

Their entrée to the 5,000–6,000 villagers living nearby was assisted by a government bureaucrat whose relatives live in the village. "From the beginning, we've had good communication with the villagers," says Katharina. "We talked with the villagers beforehand, and there was some opposition. We agreed to sign a special agreement not to disturb the graveyard. It's always been a friendly relationship. If there's a problem, for example, kids begging on the beach or tourists sunbathing topless, we have a meeting. We try to be sensitive to the culture. We provide guests with a dress code of what to wear in the village, and several times we've stopped women from bathing topless on the beach."

The hotel's brochure, which is placed in each room, sets the tone for proper behavior: "The local population of this area is predominantly Muslim. Their hospitality and friendliness should be reciprocated through the utmost consideration from our side. Tourism is a completely new and unknown phenomenon in the lives of these people. Please be aware of this when you venture into villages in the neighborhood, and respect their culture. The dress code in the area is one of extreme modesty—please respect this." The brochure concludes, "Through the years the hotel has established a good and fruitful relationship with the local population. Our biggest challenge will be to preserve this unique atmosphere while different cultures meet in mutual respect."

Five of Matemwe's employees come from the Stone Town; the remaining thirty-three are from the village. "We had to train fishermen to be waiters," explains Katharina. "And we employed a local teacher to teach them English. We've been amazed at how quickly and well they have learned their jobs." Matemwe salaries are well above minimum wage, but Katharina estimates that employees make about as much as they do by fishing. Despite this, she says, "We have more people who want to work here than we have positions, and [there are] always a lot in training." She says she has many small problems, such as Muslim employees who refuse to serve liquor, and food "walking away" from the kitchen—a problem she's tackled by training a kitchen manager. A more serious problem and a great expense is freshwater. A hotel's brochure warns guests, "Insufficient fresh water is one of the major problems for the inhabitants and also for the hotel. Please use it carefully." There are no wells and little rainwater, since Matemwe is on the driest side of the island. Therefore, the hotel has water brought thirty miles by truck from the Stone Town and supplements this by buying buckets of water from two dozen village women, who haul it from communal village taps.

The hotel interacts with the villages in other ways as well. It buys its fish, fruit, and vegetables from the surrounding area and has helped village women set up a restaurant and a small shop. Through a partner in the hotel, Matemwe Bungalows obtained Dutch aid for the shop, several new fishing boats, and a poultry project. The hotel's brochure tells visitors, "During the last part of your trip to Matemwe you might have noticed small shops along the road selling sea shells and corals. We do not encourage such enterprises and kindly request you to leave the treasures of the sea where they belong: the ocean in front of you. However, shop owners are encouraged to sell locally made handicrafts. May we draw your special attention to the

[women's] shop . . . close to the bungalow. . . . [They] have started a cooperative and now try to run their own business."

However, Katharina admits that it isn't easy to organize the village
women. "The women need an alternative to collecting shells. We would like
them to make mats or baskets to sell to the tourists. They already know how,
but it's hard to get them to do it for sale. And there are fights among the
women, so it's hard to get them to work together." Katharina explains that
"eventually we want to have the hotel co-owned with the [nearest] village,
but they don't have their association officially declared. When they do, we
will give them shares."

As she speaks, three women with very erect bearing and clad in brightly
colored *khangas* (traditional cotton cloth) walk into the hotel compound,
balancing buckets of water on their heads. Several young boys pass by on
their way to the beach, carrying small balsam wood boats that they hope to
hawk to tourists. "The beach belongs to the village," Katharina says. "They
pass freely through our property. We don't want big fences. We have problems with cows, not with the people."

Later, a local villager, who has just rattled off a litany of complaints
against the Mnemba Club, agrees. "Relations with Matemwe have been very
positive. We've had no problems, no complaints. They help the local people.
If a boat breaks down, they sail out to rescue it. They use their vehicles to
take sick villagers to the hospital. And the employment gives us a way to
diversify because we can't all make a living from fishing. In turn, we help
protect the hotel. Several times, we've helped arrest thieves. So the relationship is mutually beneficial."

Katharina says that in constructing the hotel, "We tried to build in the
local style. We used limestone and coral from inside the island, not from the
reef, and mangrove pools and *makuti* [palm fronds] for the roof. One of our
owners had architectural training, and he designed it with the local people."
Two solar panels provide electricity for the dining room and kitchen. A generator runs the refrigerators, and the bungalows are lit with kerosene lamps.
The structures are intended to capture the sea breezes; there are no fans or
air conditioners. The result is a beautifully relaxing and refreshing oblong-
shaped dining room and veranda with coconut wood furniture, huge pil-
lows, and a spectacular view of the beach and ocean. In contrast, the twelve
bungalows, built by local *fundi* (artisans), are "primitive," without much
luxury. The doors are too low and the windows too small, and it's easy to
imagine the rooms getting oppressively hot in summer. But each has its own
porch, privacy, and a beautiful oceanfront view.

Besides sunbathing and relaxation—the trees and flowers planted
around the hotel are lovely—the hotel offers diving, fishing, and snorkeling,
either in its own boats or in boats hired from the villages. The guests are

mostly Europeans, with a smattering of Americans and Australians, and at $80 per night for full board (less with a shared bath), they are a cut above the ordinary backpackers. The owners do very little promotion, relying instead on word of mouth and the press. Since opening in 1990, the hotel has operated at 60 percent occupancy. Katharina says, "The hotel may be a bit too small to make a profit. We reinvest all our money into new construction and new rooms."

A detailed tourism study carried out in 1995 by the International Finance Corporation (IFC) praises Matemwe Bungalows and concludes that "Matemwe is well viewed by the Government as the sort of development it would like to encourage."[42] But in practice, the IFC, the Zanzibari government, and international promoters of ecotourism have done little to help Matemwe. Despite its excellent community involvement programs and architectural and environmental sensitivity, Matemwe Bungalows has received no international ecotourism awards (which would have boosted occupancy) and has less favored status with the government than the Mnemba Club. It was given only a thirty-three-year lease for the land and a two-year rather than a three-year reprieve on paying taxes. The Commission for Tourism's visitors' guide urges tourists traveling to Matemwe to "take a boat and visit Mnemba Island. It is a real Paradise: very clear waters, coral reefs, white sand beaches." It makes no pitch for Matemwe Bungalows.[43]

Chumbe Island

On a half-mile long island just a short boat ride from the Stone Town is another foreign-owned project that, like the Matemwe Bungalows, is marketed as ecotourism but, like Mnemba Club, has suffered from poor community relations. On the million-year-old coral-rag island, Sibylle Riedmiller, a German woman and former consultant with the Department of Lands and Environment, negotiated a lease and set up the Chumbe Island Coral Park Company, with the intent, she said, of using the island for ecotourism and environmental education for the benefit of both tourists and Zanzibaris. Riedmiller, with German aid funds and the help of several other foreign residents, built simple but well-marked nature trails through the forest. The fine coral reefs off the island's western coast, home of 367 species of fish (including some extremely rare ones), was gazetted as a marine park in 1995 and the European Union has provided funds for the marine park and rehabilitating the existing buildings for visitors. By 1995, construction was under way on both a nature educational center and fourteen high-vaulted, environmentally low-impact, guest cabins built on stilts using a combination of cement, coral, and mangrove poles.

But, sadly, even those supportive of the ecotourism endeavor on

Chumbe say that Riedmiller has alienated fishermen, other hoteliers and tour operators, government officials, and local environmentalists alike by her often brusk personal manner and her unwillingness to work out arrangements so that Zanzibaris can have some access to the island. Riedmiller initially worked closely with local youth groups and schools, as well as the nature tours, but by 1997, she was no longer giving discounts to Zanzibaris and only occasionally permitted school groups to visit the island. "She was previously a development worker and, unlike the Mnemba people, she knows what to say," says one environmentalist. "But her claims to be working with us are just not true." Moreover, continuous battles between Riedmiller and government officials have slowed progress. The government granted only a ten-year lease, which at the present pace will mean the hotel will only just be completed when the lease runs out.[44]

Ecotourism Rhetoric versus Reality

Time is running out for Zanzibar to commit to a steady ecotourism course. Participants at the March 1994 ecotourism workshop attempted to lay out a set of guidelines and principles that, if followed, would put Zanzibar in the forefront of ecotourism development. (See resolutions listed in footnote 17.) It called for a review of every hotel project approved so far and recommended that all future projects undergo environmental, social, and cultural impact assessments and that the government give economic incentives to those who follow ecotourism principles and punish violators.

By and large, Zanzibar's government officials and private sector talk the right talk about ecotourism. As Zanzibar's former chief minister, Dr. Omar Juma, stated, "If local residents benefit from tourism, they will take an interest in the resource base of tourism. It is by this way our people will take the meaningful responsibility to safeguard both [environmentally and ecologically] friendly tourism. It is imperative for the local community to be creative enough to think through the multitude of local business opportunities."[45] But government support for local communities has been largely absent. It is essential, for instance, that the government lay down criteria for collaboration between villages and the private sector, but as yet, no comprehensive policy has been enacted. Instead, private sector involvement with the community remains ad hoc, voluntary, and, with a very few exceptions, minimal.

On the surface, the statistics look good in terms of local ownership: 50.5 percent of tourism projects are owned by Tanzanians; 30.5 percent by Europeans; 8.3 percent by other Africans; 4 percent by Asians and Australians; 3.5 percent by North Americans; and 3.2 percent by investors from the Persian Gulf states.[46] But most of the Tanzanian- and Zanzibari-owned facilities are either older hotels built and owned by the government or newer, low-investment guest houses catering to the domestic market. Zanzibar's bloody revolution and socialist policies either eliminated or nationalized most economic activities of the island's capitalist class. According to tourism director Ramadhan Mwinyi, during the island's "long period of suppression the private sector was inept," with the result that today the private sector is crippled by "immaturity as well as low financial capabilities [and] shortfalls. [in] technological, managerial, marketing, and organizational skills."[47] Virtually all the hotel contracts approved by the government went to foreign investors.[48]

A similar ownership pattern exists with the tour operators. In 1991, the government adopted a sensible policy of restricting ownership of tour operation businesses to Tanzanian citizens or joint local and foreign ventures. However, according to a knowledgeable foreign expert, of the 54 tour agencies existing in 1995, three were Kenyan owned and all of the largest were either foreign-owned or joint ventures. Further, little new investment has gone into tour companies: of the 109 tourism projects initiated between 1988 and November 1993, only 12 were tour operators.[49]

Although many Zanzibaris express an interest in starting up auxiliary tourism enterprises,[50] so far this has been largely confined to guiding, providing taxi service, and establishing restaurants and curio shops in the Stone Town. One innovative, educational project in the countryside is Zala Park, a snake and reptile zoo started by a retired schoolteacher. Another ecotourism attraction is a natural aquarium featuring sea turtles, run by members of the Nungwi fishing village. At the island's extreme northern tip, some dozen hotels specializing in scuba diving and surfing are either open for business or under construction. At another fishing village where tourists come to see local boat building, two groups of villagers have opened restaurants. After visiting rural areas, ecotourism workshop participants "could see opportunities for small-scale, village-based tourism activities in all areas visited [but] most were deemed unsuitable for large-scale tourism."[51]

In its study of tourism in Zanzibar, the IFC, the World Bank's private sector arm, recognized the difficulties local entrepreneurs and rural communities face in obtaining investment funds either from their government or from international agencies. "The differences between developing foreign-financed tourism investments and providing capital for tourism enterprises reserved for Tanzanian ownership are enormous," the IFC study states. "Institutional arrangements have been disadvantageous to Tanzanian nationals and resident foreign investors seeking to use local capital."[52] By mid-1998, neither the IFC, which extends loans to big tourism projects, nor the IFC's Africa Enterprise Fund, which can make loans for smaller projects, had provided assistance for any locally owned or ecotourism projects on Zanzibar or Pemba.

Likewise, the World Bank itself, with its tourism and infrastructure project, was long on proper rhetoric but short on innovative programs to involve local communities. At the World Bank–sponsored 1995 Tourism Infrastructure Workshop, Barbara Koth, the person in change of the bank's Zanzibar program, bluntly challenged government officials by stating that it was "imperative for Zanzibar to set tourism policy *now*, at the beginning of the growth period, in order to control its tourism future three, five, or fifteen years from now. I suggest that it is very late for Zanzibar to be talking in generalities about wanting 'high-spending, upscale tourists and not budget backpackers.' This statement is not a comprehensive tourism policy."[53] In early 1996, the bank withdrew Koth, who had ruffled local sensibilities. The bank's tourism infrastructure project was itself a fairly routine, though necessary, plan to upgrade airports and roads, professionalize government departments, and pave the way for foreign investment. As one bank official candidly admitted, the project "was focused on hard-core infrastructure. It was missing how to involve and integrate local communities." It had no component for working with the government to forge a new path toward culturally sensitive tourism that would respect the island's Muslim prac-tices, benefit local communities, and facilitate local ownership. Significantly, the World Bank did require, as a precondition of implementation, that the Tanzanian government adopt a national environmental strategy and single environmental department (see chapter 7). When the government dragged its feet, the bank put the tourism project indefinitely on ice[54]

As is typical of tourism elsewhere, the majority of the estimated 2,600 jobs directly flowing from Zanzibar's tourism industry are low-paid service positions in hotels. The March 1994 ecotourism workshop resulted in the proposal that locals be given preference in all tourism jobs and that the government provide economic incentives to encourage tourism projects that employ Zanzibaris. (Workshop participants did recognize, however, that in the short run, foreigners are required for certain positions, such as dive instructors and hotel managers.) But once again, contrary to its rhetoric, the government appeared to be bungling even its most minimal commitment to job training. In 1992, the International Labor Organization (ILO) and the United Nations Development Programme (UNDP) established the Hotel and Tourism Training School at Maruhubi to teach basic skills in hotel management, tour guiding, housekeeping, and food management. The school is financed by the ILO and the UNDP, which require only that the Zanzibari government contribute 1 percent of its 15 percent hotel levy as a sign of its commitment to the project. But by mid-1995, the government had failed to contribute anything and the UNDP was threatening to close down the school.

The Zanzibari government has continued to be weak in its tourism planning and regulation and in the implementation of even its most straight-forward ecotourism projects and goals. The IFC study of Zanzibar noted that "tourism development within the Tanzanian Government has usually taken a back seat to other uses of funds" and that the Tourism Ministry has a "relative lack of bureaucratic power within the Government." Participants at the ecotourism workshop found that government agencies failed to coordinate with one another and the special committee for approval of construction that was to monitor projects did not meet regularly or visit projects. Because of the government's reluctance to cancel permits, most infractions go unpunished.[55]

As has long been typical of the Zanzibari bureaucracy, even minor decisions, such as whether to register the Zanzibar Ecotourism Association, can take years to make. The association, whose steering committee includes conservationists, hotel and tour company owners, and a few government officials, is modeled after The Ecotourism Society in the United States and similarly named organizations in Kenya and Ecuador. Its fourteen page constitution outlines a broad array of functions, including assisting local communities to participate more fully in tourism; setting guidelines for tourists, hotels, and tour operators; acting as an advisor to potential investors and tour operators; initiating demonstration projects; and serving as a bridge between its members and the government. Clearly, such a body is needed. But although the 1994 ecotourism workshop endorsed the association and its first meeting was held at the end of that conference, the government did not approve its registration as an NGO until 1996. Under the leadership of Matemwe Bungalows' co-owner, Len Horlin, the association is striving to help set standards and raise public awareness.

Instead of Zanzibar's leaders grappling with pressing issues, there has frequently been a reductionist tendency to narrow the debate over the cultural and social effects of tourism to one issue: a dress code for female tourists. Whereas elsewhere, increased tourism has frequently led to liberalization of social mores and strengthening of movements by women, gays and lesbians, and other oppressed groups, Zanzibar's tourism boom coincides with a rise in conservative Muslim practices. This marks a shift from the island's tradition of religious moderation and tolerance stemming from its location as a cultural, commercial, and intellectual crossroads. For example, during my visit to the island in the 1970s, I usually wore long skirts, but this time I was cautioned (although not compelled) to wear clothing that covered my elbows as well as my knees. Whereas in the past, many Zanzibari women wore their *buibuis* (black nylon robes) rather casually, this time I saw more women fully veiled, with only narrow eye slits in their face covers. In 1993, there were a number of minor acts of violence against places serving liquor and other tourist facilities deemed offensive to Islamic law. There have also been several incidents of Islamic extremists threatening to obstruct the passage of visitors to the island.[56] This is a potentially volatile situation, especially since the government is run largely by conservative Muslim men.

The situation worsened and Islamic populist zeal rose in the aftermath of Tanzania's October 1995 parliamentary and presidential elections, which were marred by poor organization and charges of massive fraud and corruption. In Zanzibar, President Salmin Amour of the ruling CCM party was declared the winner by a mere 0.4 percent of the vote over the opposition CUF (Civic United Front) party, whose charismatic leader, Seif Shariff Hamad, claimed that the victory was rigged—a view accepted by much of the international press.[57] The CUF's campaign called for "equal rights for all," a "more just" government in Zanzibar, and a renegotiation of the terms of alliance with the mainland—something the Tanzanian political leadership feared meant ending the union. No one, not even the international observers, believed the official election results.

In the subsequent months, tensions escalated between Zanzibar's two islands, Unguja, controlled by the CCM, and Pemba, where the CUF is dominant. Government officials from Pemba and those suspected of having any sympathy for the CUF were fired, including the competent and principled director of the department of environment, Abdulrahman Issa. The CUF responded by keeping its twenty-four members of Parliament away from Zanzibar's fifty-member Parliament, refusing to recognize President Amour, and staging demonstrations and acts of civil disobedience. The government arrested and charged with treason some forty people accused of trying to blow up a power station. In a shocking move, the army was brought out to bulldoze homes of suspected opposition supporters. As fear spread that the political turmoil might deteriorate into chaos and killings, as in the populist revolution of 1964, young men reportedly fled to Great Britain and the Persian Gulf states, and British government announced it was considering deporting 900 asylum seekers believed to be from Pemba. As more arrests, including those of some opposition members of Parliament, continued into 1998, Tanzania's president, Benjamin Mkapa, stood by Amour and refused to take action to quell the unrest that was threatening the union between the island and the mainland.[58] In the wake of the crisis, foreign investment slowed and U.S. and European aid, along with economic support from several international conservation organizations, was suspended. Parallel with but not directly linked to the political chaos, the World Bank put on hold its tourism infrastructure project. In 1996, tourism was estimated to have earned Zanzibar a meager $1.6 million.[59]

One of the few major developers apparently not turned off by the political turmoil was Thomas Wells, a British entrepreneur whose $4 billion investment scheme on the Nungwi Peninsula included eleven hotels, a resort village, time-share village, eighteen-hole golf course, racecourse, airports, trade and conference center, and offshore banking facilities. Wells, who cultivated highly placed government officials, also promised to build schools, a university, and a mosque. In October 1997, the Zanzibar investment agency ZIPA announced Wells' Nungwi Peninsula project, the "largest leisure resort development in East Africa," was "ready to start." Less than a month later, Wells was briefly detained in Tanzania based on an Interpol alert that he was wanted on fraud charges in the sultanate of Oman. Investigators tracked Wells' "corporate headquarters" in Britain to a walk-up mail drop above a Chinese take-out restaurant. Wells claimed to have raised only $300 million for the project, the IFC had turned down his request for financing, and no construction had begun. Undeterred, ZIPA announced in May 1998 that Wells' Nungwi Peninsula project was moving ahead, with the government holding 26 percent of the shares.[60]

As Zanzibar tries to find both political stability and a niche in the international tourism market, it is being pulled by conflicting forces of which ecotourism is a vocal, but not powerful, element. Ecotourism experts say that Zanzibar's government may be too far along the path of conventional tourism development to seriously implement ecotourism. On Zanzibar's main island, Unguja, much of the land has already been leased and not many options are left open to potential investors. But, fortunately perhaps, construction has yet to begin on more than half of the hotels.[61] The government can still review and revoke these permits if construction does not get under way quickly or does not comply with sound ecotourism standards. In addition, Unguja's remoter and much less developed sister island, Pemba, is still largely a blank slate in regard to tourism and ecotourism. It has only three low-grade government guest houses (eight rooms each, with no running water or electricity) and two new foreign-owned hotels catering to divers. The 1995 IFC study described proposals for two innovative ecotourism projects. One, the Wete Dhow House Club, consists of twenty-four locally constructed *dhow* houseboats designed to minimize "social, cultural and environmental intrusion, while maximizing employment and benefits to the local population." The second, Wambaa Village Guest Houses, proposes building small, three-star village guest houses that take advantage of Pemba's numerous small beaches. These "ecologically friendly accommodations" would be staffed by local people and would help bring improved infrastructure—roads, electricity, water, sewage disposal, and the like—to the village operating the guest houses. This was envisioned, the IFC report states, as part of "a network of improved, village based, ecological guest houses throughout Zanzibar, constituting an alternative form of visitation for tourists and a highly efficient village owned and managed accommodation facility that would allow villagers to take part directly in Zanzibar's tourism development."[62] However, by the late 1990s, the political turmoil in Zanzibar had halted virtually all foreign aid and private development projects and neither these schemes nor plans to make Misali Island a national park had been implemented. The silver lining to this dismal cloud is that no construction has been permitted on Misali except for a simple open-air palm leaf shelter, and no visitors were being allowed except for research or ecological education trips.

Zanzibar's Ecotourism Scorecard

I was wrong: ecotourism *has* reached Zanzibar, a sign of how this concept has literally taken hold around the world as poor countries seek new, sustainable forms of economic development. In the quest for ecotourism, Zanzibar has, in theory at least, an advantage over two other island destinations, Cuba and the Galápagos. Unlike Cuba, Zanzibar was not saddled with a great deal of conventional tourism infrastructure, and unlike the Galápagos, Zanzibar is not a highly fragile ecosystem that allows little room for error. It has been, in essence, a sort of tabula rasa on which some tinkering could be tolerated.

1. *Involves travel to natural destinations.* Although ecotourism in Zanzibar is not built on the foundation of a strong national park system, as it is in most countries, the island has its own alluring attractions—the Stone Town and Arab ruins, pristine beaches, tiny offshore islands, and coral reefs—that can be marketed as complements to ecosafaris in Tanzania and Kenya.

2. *Minimizes impact.* The record is mixed on this point. Several of the beach hotels, such as Matemwe Bungalows, Chumbe Island, and the Mnemba Club, used local building materials and architectural styles and have made attempts to adopt other environmentally sensitive practices. Despite efforts to set environmental building standards and require environmental impact studies, the government has permitted construction of far too many typical cement block hotels that are heavy on imports and use of energy and water. Because of the failure of both the mainland and Zanzibari governments to implement an overall environmental strategy, the World Bank in mid-1996 suspended its tourism infrastructure project. According to a World Bank official,

both the island and mainland governments "downgraded environment protection because land leases are so profitable. They did not want anything to interfere" in what he described as "corruption [bribes] in the Tanzanian way."[63] The government's 1998 decision to approve Thomas Wells' mega project on the Nungwi Peninsula signals an even higher level of disregard for environmental preservation.

In the Stone Town, however, the effects of tourism appear, at least on the surface, to be far more positive. Most construction involves the repair of existing historic buildings, and again, though environmental impact has not been rigorously assessed or monitored, these urban hotels are clearly an improvement over the unsanitary conditions that were the norm for many decades. The rise of tourism and increased environmental awareness have stimulated other basic rehabilitations in the Stone Town, including repair and paving of the streets, an overhaul and modernization of the sewage system, and remodeling and preservation of historically important sites such as the Sultan's House of Wonders and the sea-front dispensary, which was restored by the Aga Khan Trust for Culture.

3. *Builds environmental awareness.* Environmentalism is today an issue of public concern and popular organizing in Zanzibar; before the 1990s, this was not the case. Some of the first and most active of the new NGOs are involved in environmental issues, many linked to eco-tourism and promotion of protected areas and endangered species such as sea turtles. There has been more education by NGOs and the government via the schools, radio programs, and publications. The Stone Town has undergone a remarkable cleanup and rehabilitation, making it more environmentally sound and attractive and preserving its unique culture and history. Ecotourism has given impetus to and been reinforced by this heightened environmental awareness. Together with Kenya, Zanzibar has the first ecotourism society in Africa. However, those spearheading it have been primarily foreigners, a fact that has prevented it from having much political muscle. Few of the ecotourism projects are actively involved in providing environmental programs for Zanzibaris at affordable prices. Regrettably, Chumbe Island, with its marine reserve and nature walks, has canceled its low entrance fees for islanders, and government-run environmental education trips to Misali Island, off Pemba, are also very expensive.

4. *Provides direct financial benefits for conservation.* The growth of both environmentalism and ecotourism has given impetus to the designation, for the first time, of national parks and marine reserves in Zanzibar. International conservation organizations pledged funds to help in these efforts, but these donations, along with bilateral and multilateral aid, were suspended when political tensions and repression escalated following the 1995 elections. Although there has been some

discussion about what type of tourism would be appropriate in and around these areas, there has been no effort to specifically tap tourism dollars to support conservation efforts.

5. *Provides financial benefits and empowerment for local people.* Here, the record is poor. So far, the tourism boom's social and economic effects on local communities in Zanzibar have been "very dismal," according to two environmental experts.[64] Despite the laudable recommendations resulting from the 1994 ecotourism workshop, villagers and townspeople have continued to be enticed into selling their property[65] to tourism investors who do not guarantee any profit sharing, joint ownership, or other form of sustained benefit. Land speculation has forced up prices and competition for government-issued leases along the coast and on the tiny islands around Unguja and Pemba.

   The tourism boom has caused competition for services, especially water. Fatma Alloo, an official with a local development agency, says that in Nungwi, villagers were promised that tourism development would bring them "abundance"; instead, "with the coming of rich tourist hotels," they have "ended up buying buckets of water."[66] The 1995 IFC study concluded, "There has been little involvement of local communities in most tourism developments, although Matemwe Bungalows is a notable exception."[67] The government had provided no protective policies until 1997, when it created a special committee of the House of Representatives to investigate complaints. However, its 1998 decision to approve the development project on Nungwi Peninsula could mean the removal of hundreds of people, against their will, from this area.

   Although some Zanzibaris have moved into tourism as guides, taxi drivers, tour operators, and owners of lower-end hotels and guest houses as well as auxiliary services such as restaurants, taxis, and various concessions, the main benefit has been employment in foreign-owned hotels. However, even this has been limited because the government has not required that workers be given any social benefits.[68]

6. *Respects local culture.* This is a subject of major concern to the Zanzibaris, particularly religious and government leaders. There has been much public discussion about the effects of tourism on the island's predominantly Muslim culture. Often, this has centered on a dress code for women. The debate has, however, led several leading hoteliers to distribute rules of acceptable behavior to their guests and to negotiate specifically designated beaches where tourists can sunbathe. In the Stone Town, historic cultural attractions are being preserved, and most tourists come to Zanzibar seeking a combination of nature tourism (whether ecotourism or more traditional sun-and-surf tourism) and cultural tourism.

7. *Supports human rights and democratic movements.* At present, the

unpopular, unstable, and undemocratic Zanzibari government is largely adrift. Within this milieu, there is strong undercurrent pulling against ecotourism and toward foreign-owned sun-and-surf package tourism that offers little, not even skilled and well-paying jobs, to the people of Zanzibar.

Despite its poverty, Zanzibar has, in addition, a reasonably good physical infrastructure, especially on the main island Unjuga; improved transportation to the outside world; a relatively experienced civil service; and a fairly literate urban work force, many of whom speak English and other languages. Counted among its blessings, as well, are a healthy suspicion of unbridled capitalism as the path to development, a concern about the cultural impact of western-dominated tourism, and a weariness with years of highly centralized state-run economic austerity. What it lacks, most centrally, is a compass for guidance toward a new development strategy that combines a popular and democratic government, strong independent NGOs, and activist local communities. So far, Zanzibar has failed to formulate and then stay the course on a new model that encompasses ecotourism instead of merely small-scale, upscale, foreign-owned conventional tourism.

Notes

1. The precise death count remains uncertain, since there were no independent observers on the island at the time. The *New York Times* reported that an estimated 10,000 had died. John Okello, the revolution's messianic leader, wrote that 13,656 had been killed, whereas A. M. Babu, leader of the revolution's left-wing party, claimed that "the real casualty figure was minimal." Cranford Pratt, *The Critical Phase in Tanzania, 1945–1968: Nyerere and the Emergence of a Socialist Strategy* (Cambridge: Cambridge University Press, 1976), pp. 138, 279, n. 21; A. M. Babu, "The 1964 Revolution: Lumpen or Vanguard?" in Abdul Sheriff and Ed Ferguson, eds., *Zanzibar under Colonial Rule* (London: James Currey, 1991), pp. 240–241.

2. I. G. Shivji, ed., *Tourism and Socialist Development* (Dar es Salaam: Tanzania Publishing House, 1975), p. vii.

3. Ibid., p. x.

4. Moyiga Nduru, "Turning to Services as Clove Prices Fall," InterPress Service, April 19, 1996.

5. Office of East African Affairs, U.S. Department of State, *Investment Climate Report: Tanzania* (Washington, D.C.: U.S. Department of State, Office of East African Affairs, February 1995).

6. *Proceedings of the International Workshop on Ecotourism and Environmental Conservation in Zanzibar*, held at Inn By The Sea, March 21–24, 1994 (Zanzibar: Commission for Lands and Environment of the Department of Environment, 1994), p. 14.

7. International Finance Corporation (IFC), *Zanzibar Tourism Investment Study* (Washington, D.C.: IFC, March 1995), p. 9.

8. Barbara Koth, "Zanzibar Tourism Policy," in *Proceedings of speech to Tourism Infrastructure Workshop,* Bwawani Hotel, Zanzibar (Zanzibar: Commission for Tourism, January 18, 1995), n.p.; Interviews with Koth in Zanzibar and World Bank officials in Washington, D.C., 1995–1998.

9. Ahmada Khatib, Commission for Tourism, Zanzibar, "The Present State of Tourism Development in Zanzibar," in *Proceedings of Workshop on Ecotourism,* March 1994, annex 3, p. 5; Nduru, "Turning to Services."

10. Ramadhan Mwinyi, director of tourism, speech in *Proceedings of Tourism Infrastructure Workshop;* Khatib, "Present State of Tourism Development," p. 4.

11. IFC, *Zanzibar,* p. 11.

12. Ibid., pp. 9, 13. Sometimes the inaccuracies go the other way. At the 1994 ecotourism workshop, Dr. Khatib announced that between 1983 and 1993, tourists visiting Zanzibar had spent $31,913 million, a figure that is clearly a gross overstatement. Khatib, "Present State of Tourism Development," p. 5.

13. IFC, *Zanzibar,* p. 15, and annex 6; Mwinyi, *Proceedings of Tourism Infrastructure Workshop.*

14. Ibid.

15. Features Africa/InterPress Service, "Tourism Dislodges Cloves in Zanzibar," *East African Chronicle,* May 19–26, 1995. The article does not, however, quote figures for earnings, and five months earlier, director of tourism Mwinyi had stated, "No effort has been done to rank tourism among other sectors of the economy and therefore it becomes difficult to quantify its contribution to the national economy." Mwinyi, *Proceedings of Tourism Infrastructure Workshop.*

16. Robert Bensted-Smith, Zanzibar Integrated Lands and Environmental Management Project. *An Environmental Policy and Programme for Zanzibar* (Zanzibar: Commission for Lands and Environment, Department of Environment, 1991), p. 29.

17. Executive Summary with Key Resolutions, *Proceedings of Workshop on Ecotourism,* pp. 5–8. The most important points in these sixteen resolutions are as follows:

    (1) "The system of approval and monitoring of tourism projects should be strengthened" and should include "an assessment of their environmental, social and cultural effects."

    (2) The government's Technical Committee should "urgently review the 111 approved hotel projects."

    (3) "To enhance local community benefits from tourism, villagers' opinions should be taken into consideration before any project is approved," and the government should lay out "the legal framework with clear rules as to the rights of villagers" and ensure "that benefits from tourism go to all villagers."

    (4) The government "should educate villagers about tourism, especially about what tourists like, how to run a tourism business, potential negative effects of tourism, government plans for tourism development, and their legal rights."

    (5) "Hotel projects should be required to have a written agreement with local villagers" and "such an agreement could be made a condition of either the interim certificate or the land lease."

(6) "Intermediaries will be needed to assist in negotiations between investors and local communities, and then to monitor compliance."

(7) "[V]illage funds [should] be set up to channel benefits from tourism development to local communities."

(8) "The people concerned with establishing Nature Conservation Areas (NCAs) and the Zanzibar Nature Conservation Trust should have further consultation with the tourism sector to agree on [a] specific mechanism of cooperation," including ways in which the tourism industry can help conservation efforts.

(9) The Zanzibar Nature Conservation Trust and the NCA should be created immediately and then legally reinforced, defined, and expanded. "Clear guidelines should be written concerning procedures and rules for investment in or adjacent to NCAs."

(10) "The Trust, once formed, should ensure high standards of ecotourism guiding and environmental protection in NCAs."

(11) "Zanzibar should not be marketed as an ecotourism destination," as this could raise tourists' expectations regarding the environmental standards of Zanzibar's tourism industry, resulting in disappointment during their visits. This would lead to criticism and negative publicity. This is especially true given the high-tech nature of much ecotourism, with completely recycled water, composting of sewage, and other measures that Zanzibar is a long way from achieving. However, the government of Zanzibar should make its commitment to the principles of ecotourism known.

(12) "The Government should take action to decrease the growing trade in marine curios (e.g. shells, coral and sea turtle products)."

(13) "To maximize benefits to Zanzibaris from tourism, there should be a system where preference is given to locals for all jobs. However it should be recognized that in the short run foreigners are required for some jobs and that for the long run training is needed."

(14) "The Government of Zanzibar should stop policies such as setting high investment thresholds which encourage large conventional cement structures."

(15) "The Government should actively support the creation and implementation of a National Conservation Policy" and "support efforts to create an Ecotourism Association in Zanzibar."

(16) "Tourism businesses should take responsibility for the behaviour of their clients (such as how they dress, what they buy and how they treat the coral) and educate them, through 'do's and don'ts' notices, environmental literature, talks and the example of the behaviour of their own staff. 'Village tours' should be discouraged, as experience from other countries shows that this has negative influences with lack of privacy and loss of respect and dignity especially of children."

18. IFC, *Zanzibar,* p. 18.

19. *Proceedings of Workshop on Ecotourism,* p. 22.

20. "Running an Ecotourism Enterprise," *Proceedings of the Workshop on Ecotourism,* p. 28.

21. Ibid., pp. 8, 28.

22. Khatib, "Present State of Tourism Development," *Proceedings of Ecotourism*

Workshop, annex 3, p. 5. The IFC study said that government statistics put occupancy at "a worrying 23% in 1993." IFC, *Zanzibar,* p. 19.

23. *Proceedings of Workshop on Ecotourism,* Resolution 10.

24. Interviews with Africa Director Mark Stanley Price and other AWF officials between 1996 and 1998.

25. Koth, "Zanzibar Tourism Policy," *Proceedings of Tourism Workshop.*

26. Ulrich Malisius, *The Stone Town of Zanzibar* (Zanzibar: Ministry of Water, Construction, and Energy, 1985). Lamu is classified as the only "living preindustrial" stone town (i.e., no cars), in sub-Saharan Africa.

27. A 1983 study by the United Nations Center for Human Settlements (HABITAT) found that of the Stone Town's 2,497 buildings (including 48 mosques), almost 40 percent were dilapidated. Malisius, *Stone Town,* foreword.

28. Dr. Abdul Sheriff, who was my dissertation advisor at the University of Dar es Salaam, remains a reserved skeptic of tourism, including its ecotourism permutation. He is a product of both a conservative Muslim family and the milieu surrounding the heated intellectual debate over tourism that engulfed the University of Dar es Salaam and the Tanzanian press in the mid-1970s. His son, Suhail, is a founder of the youth environmental group Roots and Shoots, one of the island's new NGOs that has been involved with several ecotourism projects.

29. IFC, *Zanzibar,* p. 19.

30. Martha Honey, "An Economic History of Asians in Tanzania and Zanzibar" (Ph.D. diss., University of Dar es Salaam, Tanzania, 1983); Interview with Fatma Alloo, an employee of the Aga Khan's social welfare NGO in Zanzibar, April 1998.

31. A loan for a beach resort in Pemba was approved but not disbursed; the project was put on hold because of the political unrest. Interview with Carolyn Cain, International Finance Corporation, Tourism Unit, May 1998.

32. James Mwakisalya, "Serena Inn Gives Zanzibar Tourism Shot in the Arm," n.s., n.d.; IFC, "Tanzania: Tourism Promotion Services (Zanzibar) Ltd. (TPS): Environmental Review Summary," *Zanzibar,* annex 6 (November 30, 1994); other IFC reports and interviews with Tourism Unit officials.

33. Interview with Costas Christ, May 1996.

34. *Proceedings of Workshop on Ecotourism,* p. 15.

35. Paul Chintowa, "Zanzibar-Economy: Cloves Take a Back Seat to Tourism," InterPress Service, May 10, 1995.

36. Abdulrahman Issa and Colin Poulton, Commission for Lands and Environment, Zanzibar, "Environmental Impacts of Tourism" *Proceedings of Tourism Infrastructure Workshop,* p. 3.

37. *Proceedings of Workshop on Ecotourism,* p. 15.

38. Ron Hall, "New Dawn in the Indian Ocean," *Condé Nast Traveler,* April 1995, p. 128.

39. Ibid.

40. Interview with Costas Christ, October 1997.

41. Interviews with Katharina Horlin and visit to Matemwe Bungalows, June 1995.

42. IFC, *Zanzibar,* p. 51.

43. Commission for Tourism, *A Tale of Two Islands . . .* (Zanzibar: Commission for Tourism, n.d.), E28.

44. Author's visit to Chumbe Island, August 1995 and interviews; Salim Salim, "Tanzania's Marine Park on Chumbe Island Set to Open Next Year," *The East African*, April 24–30, 1995.

45. Omar A. Juma, chief minister of the Revolutionary Government of Zanzibar, inaugural speech, *Proceedings of Tourism Infrastructure Workshop*.

46. Khatib, "Present State of Tourism Development," *Proceedings of Ecotourism Workshop*, annex 3, p. 4.

47. Mwinyi, *Proceedings of Tourism Infrastructure Workshop*.

48. IFC, "ZIPA," *Zanzibar*, annex 3, p. 4

49. Interviews; *Proceedings of Workshop on Ecotourism*, pp. 14–15.

50. In their field trips to villages, ecotourism workshop participants found villagers very interested in getting involved in tourism projects. *Proceedings of Workshop on Ecotourism*, pp. 33–36.

51. Ibid., p. 35.

52. IFC, *Zanzibar*, p. 53.

53. Koth, "Zanzibar Tourism Policy," *Proceedings of Tourism Infrastructure Workshop*.

54. Various interviews with World Bank officials, Washington, D.C., 1996–1998.

55. IFC, *Zanzibar*, p. 53; *Proceedings of Workshop on Ecotourism*, March 1994, p. 22; Interviews.

56. Economist Intelligence Unit (EIU), *EIU Country Profile, 1994–95: Zanzibar*, p. 41; James Mwakisalya, "Serena Inn Gives Zanzibar Tourism Shot in the Arm," n.d.

57. The Economist Intelligence Unit subsequently referred to them as "the rigged Zanzibari presidential elections." *Tanzania: EIU Country Report*, 1st quarter 1998, p. 6.

58. Ibid.

59. Interviews; Nduru, "Turning to Services"; Moyiga Nduru, "Commonwealth Steps In to Resolve Conflict," InterPress Service, January 13, 1998; Anaclet Rwegayura, "Political Storm Brewing," InterPress Service, February 8, 1996; Penny Dale, "Opposition Groups Protest in London," InterPress Service, January 13, 1998.

60. "A Joint Report: The East African," *The East African*, November 13, 1997; Joseph Mwamunyange, "Zanzibar's Controversial $4 Billion Tourism Project Gets Go-Ahead," *The East African*, May 20–26, 1998, and other articles.

61. Mwinyi, *Proceedings of Tourism Infrastructure Workshop*, January 1995.

62. IFC, *Zanzibar*, pp. 46–49.

63. Off-the-record interview, December 1997.

64. E-mail communication with Fatma Alloo, who gathered information from local environmentalists, September 1997.

65. Since all property is owned by the government, which grants leases to users, Zanzibaris sell the assets on their leased land—often only coconut or clove trees—to investors, who then negotiate new leases with the government.

66. E-mail communication with Fatma Alloo, September 1997.

67. IFC, *Zanzibar*, p. 38.

68. Ibid., p. 23.

Chapter 9

Kenya, The *Mzee* of Ecotourism in Africa: Early Experiments, Foreign Aid, and Private Reserves

The horrible state of the road into the reserve was the first tip-off that all was not as positive as I had heard and read. In Tanzania's Serengeti National Park, Maasai leaders had pointed north to Kenya, to Maasai Mara Game Reserve, and said, "We should get schools, dispensaries, and other benefits like our brothers in Kenya. They get money and jobs from the game reserves, campsites, and lodges, from tourism and from wildlife." Most fundamentally, these leaders said, Kenya had recognized, as Tanzania had not, that the Maasai own the land and therefore should control it. Moreover, a World Bank study of ecotourism in Africa concludes that Maasai Mara "is arguably Africa's most sustained success in incorporating local communities in conservation."[1] I had expected to find the area around Maasai Mara dotted with small development projects—primary schools, clinics, water pumps, cattle dips—and, I naively thought, good roads.

This was July, and some 2 million wildebeest, gazelles, and zebras were pouring into the 1,700-square-kilometer (656-square-mile) Maasai Mara from the Serengeti to the south. Together these areas form a natural ecosystem containing the largest concentration of wildlife anywhere in Africa and accommodating the greatest land migration of animals anywhere in the world. No tourist vehicles, however, could cross between the Serengeti and Maasai Mara, a lingering remnant of Tanzania's 1977 border closure spat with Kenya (see chapter 7). Tourists traveling by road are therefore forced to make an 805-kilometer (500-mile) detour, driving back across the Serengeti to Arusha, across the border at Namanga, to Nairobi, and then west to Maasai Mara. Although Maasai Mara Game Reserve is Kenya's most popular park and my party was traveling at the height of the tourist season, our van, it seemed, was the only one plying the dust-swept and deep-rutted tracks across the largely empty savanna. There was no evidence of either development projects or other tourists. When we finally reached the hotel, I quickly learned that most tourists fly into Maasai Mara and then rent vehicles for game viewing. When I left, I flew out.

The Growth of Nature Tourism

Kenya is the *mzee,* or elder statesman, of nature tourism and ecotourism in Africa. From the end of British colonialism (in 1960) onward, Kenya's vibrant, wide-open capitalism helped turn the country into Africa's most popular wildlife tourism destination. By 1987, tourism had become Kenya's number one foreign exchange earner, surpassing both tea and coffee. By the early 1990s, no other African country was earning as much as Kenya from wildlife tourism,[2] and Kenya was being hailed as "the world's foremost ecotourist attraction."[3] In 1990, Kenya hosted a regional workshop on ecotourism; in 1993, Kenyan conservationists, tour operators, and lodge owners formed the continent's first ecotourism society; and in 1997, Kenya hosted an international ecotourism conference. In 1994, David Western, a wildlife scientist and first president of The Ecotourism Society (based in the United States), became the director of the Kenya Wildlife Service (KWS), the semiautonomous institution that runs the country's national park system. Western, who views ecotourism as "a set of evolving principles and practices for improving nature tourism as a whole," vowed to remold systemically Kenya's national park service to involve and benefit local communities and sustainably protect the environment and wildlife.[4]

As in Tanzania, nature tourism and ecotourism in Kenya have been built on a foundation of national parks and big game hunting. "The era of big game hunting in East Africa coincided with the establishment of colonial rule," and hunting safaris became "a symbol of western dominance over nature" and European racial and class domination over black Africans, writes John Akama, a Kenyan lecturer in tourism.[5] The slaughter by some of these Western travelers, military officers, politicians, and aristocrats was astounding. Theodore Roosevelt, for instance, who, together with 200 trackers, porters, skinners, and gun bearers, went on a yearlong hunting safari through East Africa, shipped back to Washington, D.C., 3000 specimens of African game.[6]

The earliest wildlife legislation dates from 1898, when Kenya enacted regulations to control indiscriminate hunting. In 1907, the colonial government created a game department to oversee hunting. The National Parks Ordinance of 1945 marked "a shift in conservation policy from protection through hunting legislation to preservation through land protection"[7] and eviction of local people. Gradually, about 12 percent of Kenya's territory was set aside for protection in twenty-six parks, twenty-eight reserves, and one sanctuary.[8] With the exception of Tsavo East and Tsavo West National Parks, most are small, incomplete ecosystems whose wildlife migrates into surrounding areas, where the animals must compete with both people and cattle.

Following independence, nature tourism in Kenya took off, increasing at the extraordinary rate of more than 300 percent between 1960 and 1972.[9] By the early 1970s, writes Western, wildlife was viewed as "a golden egg, a gift needing little promotion or management," and tourists seemed to arrive spontaneously,[10] drawn by wildlife films, good airline connections, and package tours. However, by the mid-1970s, this laissez-faire attitude was shattered: poaching was on the rise, and the quality of wildlife viewing was declining sharply.[11] In 1977, in an effort to stop this deterioration, Kenya banned sport hunting.

Between 1978 and 1983, tourism stagnated due to these internal problems and international factors including the 1979 oil crisis and resulting recession in Kenya, the border closure with Tanzania, and the regional consequences of Tanzania's war against Ugandan dictator Idi Amin. Then, in 1984, tourism began once again to pick up sharply, both because the international climate improved and because Kenya's economic liberalizations, promoted by the World Bank and USAID, provided new incentives and tax breaks for private investment. The Foreign Investments Act, for instance, guarantees repatriation of capital and profits. International airlines were offered tax exemptions on capital investments and property to encourage them to invest in game lodge and hotel development. As a result, a number of airlines promoted package tours combining airfare with stays in particular hotels.[12] Kenya also received technical assistance and funds for tourism projects from British, German, Swiss, and Italian development agencies, as well as USAID. And in 1987, boosted by the Hollywood film *Out of Africa*, tourism became Kenya's number one foreign exchange earner, bringing in some $350 million annually. By 1990, wildlife-based tourism was earning $480 million per year, or 43 percent of Kenya's total foreign exchange.

Parallel with this, increasing numbers of Kenyan entrepreneurs and politicians moved into tourism. According to Perez Olindo, former director of Kenya's Wildlife Conservation and Management Department (WCMD), Kenya's 1977 ban on commercial hunting inadvertently provided an impetus for a number of former hunters, guides, and trackers to move into nature tourism under the slogan "Come shooting in Kenya with your camera." Sport hunting had been dominated by whites, who were the tour operators and guides while Africans served as porters, gun bearers, and skinners. Various colonial regulations had made it virtually impossible for Africans to cross this color line. Olindo says this shift from hunting to camera safaris helped to break the white monopoly, allowing "the more enterprising" (or politically influential) black Kenyans to start their own companies or move into management positions in hotel, ground transportation, and tour companies.[13]

The Kenya Tourist Development Corporation (KTDC), established by the Jomo Kenyatta government in 1966, became primarily a vehicle for using public funds to help handpicked private capitalists get pieces of the tourism pie. In addition, a Kenyan law requires that all businesses be at least partly owned by Kenyans. The KTDC's mission of buying shares in foreign-owned tour companies, travel agencies, hotels, and lodges and then selling these shares "to promising Kenyan entrepreneurs on special terms,"[14] served to subsidize the business activities of the rich, powerful, and politically well connected. Foreign investors, in turn, found it advantageous to form partnerships with powerful politicians and businessmen who could help them cut through red tape and provide a shield against expropriation or expulsion.

Kenya's tourism grew rapidly in the early 1980s, helping to finance, together with foreign aid receipts, Kenya's growing trade imbalance (see table 9.1).[15] However, despite the growing importance of tourism, conditions in its national parks and reserves continued to decline: poaching of elephants and rhinos remained high; and, in 1989, several times armed bandits attacked tourists while they were on game drives.[16]

In addition to world-famous game parks, Kenya has an extensive ecosystems that include several marine parks and reserves. Since the late 1970s, beach resort tourism, based north and south of the main coastal city of Mombasa, has grown enormously. At present, the majority (more than 60

Table 9.1. Kenya's Tourism Growth

	1955	1980	1985	1988	1990	1993	1995	1996	1997
Arrivals (in thousands)	36	362	541	695	814	826	690	728	750
Gross receipts (in millions of shillings or U.S. dollars)	KSh 80	KSh 183	$249	$394	$466	$413	$486	$465	$502

Source: Correspondent, "Tourist Arrivals Worse in Kenya," Nairobi Daily Nation, August 5, 1998 (Internet: http://www.nationaudio.com/news/dailynation/050898/business/business3.html); Steve Shelley, "Marketing Strategies for Ecotourism in Africa," in C. G. Gakahu and B. E. Goode, eds., Ecotourism and Sustainable Development in Kenya, proceedings of the Kenya Ecotourism Workshop, held at Lake Nakuru National Park, September 13–17, 1992 (Nairobi: Wildlife Conservation International, 1992), pp. 133–137; David Western, "Handling the Wildlife Time-Bomb That Is KWS," The Eastern African, November 17–23, 1997; Economist Intelligence Unit, Kenya: EIU Country Report, 3rd quarter 1997, p. 23; Economist Intelligence Unit, Kenya: EIU Country Report, 1st quarter 1998, p. 6; World Tourism Organization (WTO), Africa: Trends of Tourism Receipts by Country, 1989–1993 (Madrid: WTO, 1994), p. 32; World Tourism Organization (WTO), Yearbook of Tourism Statistics, vols. 1 and 2 (Madrid: WTO, 1995).

percent) of holiday visitors spend time at Kenya's coast. The bulk of the beach tourism consists of relatively cheap conventional package tours for Europeans, particularly Italians and Germans. But despite the growth of sun-and-sand tourism, wildlife remains at the heart of Kenya's tourism industry. More than 90 percent of tourists visit a game park, and 79 percent cite "nature and wildlife" as their major reason for visiting Kenya, according to the Kenya Wildlife Service.[17] Further, Kenya earns more from wildlife tourism than from beach tourism. According to the World Bank, "[T]he value added [profit] to the Kenyan economy from wildlife-based tourism was about 60 percent, in comparison to a value added of only 20 percent by coastal tourism."[18]

Overall, however, the 1990s have not been a good decade for tourism in Kenya. Tourism to all of East Africa slumped during the Persian Gulf War in 1990–1991, and then Kenya began to face stiff competition from South Africa, Tanzania, Uganda, and Zimbabwe. Kenya's share of the African market shrank from 9.3 percent in 1989 to 7.1 in 1993, and its receipts dropped from $420 million to $413 million during the same period.[19] In 1995, there was a 20 percent drop in tourism, blamed in part on press reports of muggings and harassment of tourists.[20] In 1996, the government finally created the Kenya Tourism Board but was heavily criticized for failing to give it an adequate budget, especially for overseas promotional work. As the country's second multiparty elections neared, internal political turmoil began to take its toll. The December 1997 elections, which international as well as Kenyan observers charged were riddled with fraud, gave President Daniel arap Moi his fifth consecutive term.

Between 1997 and mid-1998, election unrest, politically instigated ethnic clashes and killings along the coast, a crime wave, a deteriorating infrastructure, and unusually heavy rains combined to cause coastal tourism to plummet by some two-thirds. By mid-1998, about 50 percent of Kenya's tourist hotels—most along the coast—had closed down or reduced their staffs, and about 50,000 workers, or 30 percent of the tourism sector workforce, had been laid off.[21]

But an even bigger blow hit in August 1998, when a terrorist bomb ripped apart the U.S. Embassy and neighboring buildings in downtown Nairobi, killing and wounding thousands, mainly Kenyans. The State Department immediately issued a travel warning, advising Americans against traveling to both Kenya and Tanzania, where another bomb had exploded almost simultaneously. The Kenyan government, business leaders, and even the Council of [Muslim] Imams called on the United States to rescind the advisory, arguing that, as Mike Kirkland of the Kenya Association of Tour Operators, Coast branch, put it, there was "absolutely no danger or anti-U.S. feelings in Kenya and no reason for any tourist to cancel their

holiday." Several weeks later, the State Department did withdraw the warning, but many Kenyans feared, as the *Daily Nation* predicted, that these
events would plunge their "country's tourism industry into greater problems." [22]

Innovations in National Park Management and Nature Tourism: Good Theory, Poor Performance

By the mid-1970s, it was clear to many wildlife experts in Kenya that uncontrolled tourism could be harmful to wildlife conservation and that communities around parks could not continue to be excluded from tourism's benefits. In an effort to better address tourism and conservation issues, the
Kenyan government amalgamated several agencies and established the
Wildlife Conservation and Management Department (WCMD). In 1975,
the government approved a broad, bold national strategy that encompassed
many of the principles of ecotourism and attempted to expand the concept
beyond the Maasai Mara and Amboseli National Park experiments (discussed in the following sections). This wildlife management policy for
national parks as well as game reserves was "based on local participation in
all forms of wildlife utilization . . . including tourism, hunting, cropping for
meat and trophies, game ranching, live animal captures for restocking or
export, and the associated value-added processing of animal products." The
policy stated that wildlife must "pay its way"; that the vigor of wildlife
depended on access to larger ecosystems, which included private and communal lands around protected areas; and that wildlife officials should be
"facilitators, advisors and assessors working with landowners rather than
'policemen' working against them." [23]

The following year, Kenya secured a $37.5 million loan package from
the World Bank to help implement this policy, including strengthening
antipoaching activities, preparing the country's first tourism development
plans, and devising programs to involve local communities around the parks.
In 1977, as a condition for continued World Bank funding,[24] Kenya banned
hunting and outlawed commercial trade in wildlife trophies and products.
From this date forward, all forms of consumptive utilization of wildlife
ceased, except for limited game cropping in national parks and reserves and,
under a quota, on some private ranches. But the wave of poaching continued, fueled by the WCMD's incompetence, by corruption among top government officials and their family members, and by the high world price of
ivory and rhino horns. Even after President Daniel arap Moi succeeded
President Jomo Kenyatta, who died in 1978, cronyism and corruption continued to hold sway over economic and political life. Between 1975 and
1990, Kenya's elephant population dropped by 85 percent, to approxi-

mately 20,000, and its rhino population fell by 97 percent, down to fewer than 500.[25]

In addition, the broader objectives of the government's policy and the World Bank project were never implemented, and according to one critique, the WCMD continued to deal with conflicts between people and parks "through its role as a 'policeman.'"[26] Even the World Bank's own 1990 evaluation report was devastatingly critical. Despite the massive influx of aid, the bank's evaluation found that "park and reserve infrastructure [had] deteriorated badly and maintenance of roads, vehicles, plant, and equipment virtually ceased. The WCMD was unable to guarantee the safety of tourists and unable to address their growing dissatisfaction with poor facilities. . . . Unregulated tourism was seriously damaging numerous wildlife habitats." Further, the bank's evaluation found, the project failed to deal with the growing conflict between wildlife and increasing agricultural activities around parks and reserves. "The conversion of range to agricultural lands has not only permanently destroyed certain wildlife habitat zones, but has also changed the symbiotic relationship between nomadic pastoralists and wildlife to one of continual conflict between the sedentary farmer/herder and wildlife, as wildlife has become a major pest," the report stated.[27]

Under pressure from international conservation organizations and the U.S. Embassy, the Moi government, which had permitted the slaughter of wildlife, finally took action. In April 1989, it scrapped the inept WCMD and replaced it with a new parastatal body, the Kenya Wildlife Service (KWS), headed by Richard Leakey, a museum director and son of the world-renowned paleontologists Louis and Mary Leakey. As a semiautonomous institution, the KWS had its own board of trustees, managed its affairs internally, and was financially independent from the government. Income from user fees and donations was retained for park management. The KWS was given, at least in theory, presidential backing and wide authority to clean up corruption, remove officials involved in poaching and skimming of gate fees, implement the integrated tourist and wildlife management plans, initiate new programs involving local participation, and "tackle the thorny issues of improved distribution of benefits derived from tourism."[28] The national parks and two reserves are directly under KWS management; the other reserves, including Maasai Mara and Samburu Game Reserves, continue to be owned and managed by the county councils.

In late 1989, Leakey won international acclaim when he endorsed the campaign to have elephants listed as an endangered (or Appendix I) species under CITES (the Convention on International Trade in Endangered Species of Wild Fauna and Flora), thereby imposing a worldwide trade ban on ivory and other elephant parts. As Ray Bonner details,[29] the lobby that led to a total ban on sale of ivory and other elephant products was orchestrated by a handful of Western environmentalist and animal rights groups, which portrayed elephants as near extinction throughout Africa when in reality poaching was rampant only in East Africa, not southern Africa. They succeeded in convincing the United States, Great Britain, Canada, and other Western governments to endorse the ivory ban, and at the October 1989 CITES meeting they had African elephants declared an endangered species.

Earlier that year, Leakey had proposed selling Kenya's ivory to raise money for the KWS's antipoaching operations. However, when the CITES Ivory Trade Review Group reached the conclusion that although "sustainable utilization" (controlled hunting) was an ideal goal, poaching had so decimated the elephant and rhino populations in East Africa that nothing but a complete ban would prevent the slaughter, Leakey revised his views. Leakey says that he came to realize "we were never going to stop the ivory trade in time if we didn't do something very dramatic, and I was heavily influenced by the mortal blow Bridget Bardot's burning of fur coats in Paris and London had dealt to the spotted cat trade."[30] Just a few months before the CITES meeting, Leakey staged his own dramatic demonstration to prove Kenya's commitment to elephant and rhino protection. Although Kenya had banned hunting since 1977, the park service had ivory stocks from culling operations, confiscations from poachers, and animals that had died of natural causes. With the eye of a theater director, Leakey orchestrated a public burning of the country's entire ivory stock. In Nairobi National Park, twelve tons of ivory were piled into a gigantic twenty-foot-high tepee, and as the cameras rolled, President Moi lit the pyre. To the dismay of many Africans and the cheers of Western animal rights activists, $3 million worth of ivory went up in smoke. Leakey's calculation was shrewd: this stunt improved Kenya's conservation and wildlife tourism image, served to legitimize Moi as an "environmental leader," and contributed to Leakey's success in landing foreign aid.

Further, the ban and the ivory burning did work. The international price of ivory plummeted, and so, too, did poaching in both Kenya and Tanzania. As Leakey put it in a 1996 interview, "The ivory burning had an enormous impact on people's attitudes and permanently affected the use of ivory in the west. Before the ban we were losing 4000 to 5000 elephants a year, and afterwards, up to this moment, we are losing less than 100 a year."[31] Parallel with the ban, Leakey treated his mandate to protect wildlife in the parks as sacrosanct, arming rangers with automatic rifles and orders to shoot to kill poachers.[32]

Following the 1989 ivory debate, Leakey quickly set about reorganizing the wildlife service, retiring a lot of the dead wood, weeding out corrupt elements, and implementing sounder revenue collection methods. Within the first year, the KWS doubled its income from gate fees simply by use of stricter collection practices. Leakey and his staff also drew up a new policy framework and development program known as the Zebra Book. This document outlined the KWS's wide-ranging goals for developing a sound and integrated national conservation and ecotourism strategy. The Zebra Book pledged, for instance, that the KWS would minimize the environmental impacts of tourism, contribute to the national economy, train and license guides and drivers, monitor visitor impact, require environmental assessment studies of lodging units, and provide better visitor information. The Zebra Book also stressed that the KWS must "forge an effective partnership with communities living adjacent to parks and reserves,"[33] including protecting people and their property from wildlife damage. To this end, Leakey announced in 1992 the formation of the Community Wildlife Service (CWS) to assist communities outside the parks and reserves with funds and development projects. Its mission was to fund both microenterprise, income-generating activities and community development projects such as construction of schools and water systems. And Leakey made an ambitious pledge: that the KWS would give 25 percent of gate revenues from all parks to the surrounding communities. It was a promise he quickly discovered he could not fully deliver.

At the time, however, international lending and conservation organizations enthusiastically welcomed these pronouncements and reforms. USAID proclaimed that the KWS "marks a radical departure from the previous conservation approach under the WCMD."[34] Donors lined up with checkbooks and in-kind contributions, including eighty vehicles and seven airplanes. By 1992, Leakey had landed a hefty $153 million, five-year World Bank loan package and a pledge for a second loan package if the first program were successfully carried out.[35] With the World Bank as the umbrella organization, the U.S., Dutch, and Japanese governments, as well as the European Economic Community (EEC) and Britain's Overseas Development Administration (now called the Department for International Development), all signed up to handle specific parts of the PAWS (Protected Area and Wildlife Service) project, including an elephant conservation program, wetlands and coastal conservation, antipoaching training and equipping, infrastructure, and institution building. The goal, Leakey explained, was to rehabilitate the national parks and reserves, increase their revenue-generating capacity, and make the KWS self-supporting within five years, by the end of 1996. This was a second promise that Leakey soon discovered he could not fulfill.

The rather modest piece of the pie taken by USAID was known as COBRA (Conservation of Biodiverse Resource Areas) and was aimed, according to official documents, at assisting the KWS's Community Wildlife Service "to implement its new community conservation approach in order to demonstrate that it is in people's financial and social interest to promote and protect wildlife."[36] While other components of the World Bank's project concentrate inside parks and reserves, COBRA works in the surrounding areas to "decrease competition between people/livestock and wildlife." COBRA's "core objective" is the "development of income-generating activities for local landholders and communities," and its mandate includes helping the Community Wildlife Service to develop a system for "sharing revenue from gate receipts directly with communities."[37] However, a COBRA evaluation was sobering regarding the possibilities that enterprises open to rural communities. It found that "the most lucrative opportunities have already been seized by the private sector" and "the management requirements are usually considerable, generally beyond the means of communities." The study concluded that "considerable assistance (extension, training, and technical) will be needed to ensure the successful operation of enterprises promoted or developed" by COBRA.[38]

COBRA's community projects were to be financed partly by a long-term loan of U.S.$7 million long-term loan from USAID's Development Fund for Africa[39] and partly from the 25 percent Leakey pledged from the KWS's gate receipts. USAID projected that over the course of five years, the KWS would distribute $8.3 million in revenue sharing to communities in selected areas, including $4.7 million for the COBRA projects. This didn't happen. A special government inquiry concluded that between 1991 and 1994, the KWS spent only 2 percent of gate fees on communities surrounding the park.[40] Gate fees were only about $5 per person in local currency until the end of 1993, when they were raised to the more realistic $20 for foreigners; thus, the KWS's earned income was simply too meager to turn over one-quarter to local communities. Since the service lacked clear revenue-sharing guidelines, its disbursements were delayed, and communities themselves often had limited involvement in deciding how the funds should be used. Leakey's pledge therefore raised expectations among communities that the KWS simply could not meet.

Despite these early shortcomings, there were some promising projects. The KWS supported, for instance, creation of the Mwaluganje-Golini Community Wildlife Reserve on Kenya's southern coast. A coalition of local subsistence farmers, NGOs, tour operators, and government agencies worked to protect and use for tourism a vital corridor for elephants and other wildlife, with its income going to the local community. But, as often happens with small projects, its marketing was extremely poor and it failed to make a profit. According to the head of one international NGO, beach resorts only twenty miles away were unaware of the reserve and so were not sending guests there.[41]

Leakey's failure to fulfill his pledge to contribute the 25 percent of gate revenue to local communities became one of the issues raised by President Moi that led to Leakey's resignation under pressure in Januray 1994. By then, Leakey himself had doubts about the program. "By the time I left," Leakey said in an interview, "it was very clear that the 25 percent made no sense. The ability for many of the communities to absorb some of that money simply wasn't there. We were beginning to see problems of accountability, all sorts of political shenanigans as to who should receive and control the money."[42] Two years later, Leakey voiced even blunter and broader doubts: "I don't believe community-based conservation has a hope in hell," he told the press.[43]

Despite Leakey's international support and successes in reorganizing and strengthening Kenya's wildlife department, he made other strategic errors and some powerful enemies. There was strong pressure, for instance, for the KWS to share its international funding with other government agencies, something Leakey steadfastly refused to do. As a condition for the World Bank loan, Leakey had promised that he would make the KWS self-supporting within five years by setting up a trust fund. However, he quickly found he could not deliver because the KWS had too many programs that did not generate revenue, including research, antipoaching work, and infrastructure maintenance. A further drain were the fifty-five expatriate and Kenyan experts the KWS employed at international-scale salaries as part of the PAWS project. This inflated the institution's salaries at the top end and created resentment among the majority of the personnel, whose salaries were on the local pay scale. In addition, tourism slumped during the Persian Gulf War, so by 1993, the KWS had an operating deficit of more than $6 million.[44]

In late 1993, Leakey's light plane mysteriously crashed: the KWS's director lost both of his legs and nearly lost his life. Although Leakey, fitted with artificial limbs, continued to work, by January 1994 he had had enough. Telling the press that "the stress and pain of being vilified by senior politicians and others is more than I think is good for my health," he resigned. Once out of office, he also hinted that his plane had been sabotaged.[45]

Leakey was a hard act to follow. The World Bank and other foreign donors were not pleased to see him driven from office. President Moi's choice of another white, David "Jonah" Western, for the top conservationist slot helped ease their fears. Although Western lacked Leakey's international reputation, charisma, and management experience, he was a highly respected wildlife scientist who had directed the Nairobi-based Wildlife Conservation International and had accrued decades of hands-on field experience. Western had grown up in Tanzania, where his father was a part-time hunter and honorary game warden, and in the late 1960s he had begun research in Amboseli National Park, where he pioneered conservation projects with the Maasai. He spent much of the next two decades in Amboseli, developed a deep respect for the Maasai, and became a naturalized Kenyan citizen.

Although Leakey and Western appeared to be "two boys from the same neighborhood," there was, as one associate put it, "no love lost between them." Western did, however, seem to be the right person to carry on Leakey's Community Wildlife Service, which was subsequently officially renamed the Wildlife for Development and Benefits Sharing Program. He was deeply committed to the concept that sound conservation and eco-tourism depended on involving and benefiting the local people. He argued that this was especially necessary in Kenya, where 70 percent of the wildlife migrated or lived outside the national parks and reserves, on land occupied by farmers and herders. He was also convinced that ecotourism could not remain as "a small and very exclusive upper-end market," à la Kenya's string of white-owned private ranches. "To be a positive force for conservation," he argued, "ecotourism had to pump billions of dollars into the economies of cash-strapped developing countries to compete against loggers, farmers, and herders."[46]

Recognizing that Leakey's pledge to turn over one-quarter of park revenue to local communities was too ambitious, Western quickly announced that the KWS would strive to reach 10 percent. This remains—as it has with TANAPA's Community Conservation Service in Tanzania—the target, but one that has not been fulfilled for most parks. Western argues, however, that he has broadened and deepened the mandate of the KWS's ecotourism initiatives and restructured the organization to reflect three principal goals: (1) conserving biodiversity; (2) linking conservation and tourism; and (3) creating partners among local, national, and international interests. The KWS began decentralizing its administration away from Nairobi to ecologically determined regional units and, via the COBRA project, accelerated its funding of income-generating activities for local landholders and communities in the dispersal areas.

By the end of 1995, KSh 80 million (some U.S.$1.6 million) had been disbursed to communities, local associations, and local governments, and almost 300 projects had been approved and financed. About one-third of these projects involved either school construction or bursaries (school scholarships); however, in recent years more emphasis has been placed on productive community investments, capacity building, and the development of income-generating activities linked to wildlife and conservation. These included provisions of funds and training to start locally owned and managed tourist enterprises and encouragement of lodge designs that incorporate local materials and culture. A 1996 evaluation of the COBRA project perceptively notes, "While social investments such as schools, bursaries, clinics, and social infrastructure represent genuine community priorities, they are not overtly tied to conservation practices. Furthermore, in some cases they appear to be creating a sense of entitlement based simply on living in proximity to protected areas rather than being tied to positive measures taken by the community to improve wildlife conservation and management."[47] Overall, however, the evaluation's conclusions were positive. It stated, "Significant progress has been made toward attaining the stated purpose of the COBRA project" and "Benefits have been generated for communities, primarily through revenue sharing and to a more limited extent from enterprise development. Perhaps more important," the report concluded, "community attitudes toward KWS and toward the possibility of deriving meaningful economic and other benefits from community-based conservation have changed radically, especially in the focal areas of the COBRA project."[48] In 1997, Kenya's national parks celebrated their fiftieth anniversary with the theme "Parks Beyond Parks" to signify the aim of conserving wildlife and creating diversified tourist destinations in dispersal areas for the benefit of local communities.

However, all was not well: tourism was in a three-year slump, and with 95 percent of the KWS's revenue coming from tourism, the agency's deficit was mounting. Western toyed with another hot-button income-generating idea: reopening limited commercial hunting for certain species, but not elephants and rhinos. Western envisioned permitting not only certain private ranches but also communities in the dispersal areas to offer hunting safaris on an experimental basis, similar to the CAMPFIRE program in Zimbabwe, to see whether this could generate significant income. A joint study by the KWS and the African Wildlife Foundation in 1995 and the draft Wildlife Policy of 1996 both recommended lifting the hunting ban and permitting "wildlife utilization" in dispersal areas and on private ranches, including hunting of certain animals (other than elephants) as well as bird shooting, game farming, and live animal trade.[49] Some private, largely white, ranchers and some local communities weighed in to endorse the resumption of "sustainable utilization" of wildlife, that is, controlled hunting. This was strongly opposed by Maasai organizations, which traditionally opposed hunting, and by much of Kenya's powerful wildlife tourism industry, which feared that lifting the ban would hurt Kenya's international image for camera safaris and conservation.

On the world stage, Western played a more nuanced role than had Leakey in the ivory debate, an issue that was frequently intertwined with debates over hunting. As the 1997 CITES meeting neared, the ivory-ban consensus was weakening, with both international organizations and African countries divided, and pressure was mounting to lift the ban in southern Africa. Powerful hunting advocacy groups joined with financially strapped southern African countries to argue for ending the ban. At the Zimbabwe meeting, Kenya (led by Western) and South Africa ended up playing a key role in brokering the unusual compromise that partially altered the 1989 ban. CITES voted to downgrade the large elephant populations in Namibia,

Botswana, and Zimbabwe to Appendix II (designating "protected" but not "endangered" species), allowing these countries to sell their stockpiled ivory to one country, Japan, in 1999, subject to certain conditions. The small elephant populations in Kenya, Tanzania, and elsewhere remain classified as Appendix I (endangered). Animal rights groups, as well as the Maasai Environmental Resource Coalition (MERC), contend that poaching has increased, even in East Africa, because trophy hunters now anticipate a worldwide ivory market. "The date CITES voted, we lost rhino and elephant in Kenya and we hold Western responsible for it," said MERC's leader Meitamei Ole Dapash. Western, however, disputes this, saying that by the end of 1997, the KWS had determined that "there had been no increase in poaching over the long term background level."[50]

But by late 1997, both Western's personal reputation and the promising picture of the community conservation projects were becoming tarnished as the KWS was buffeted by both internal weaknesses and external troubles. While Western tirelessly promoted the KWS and ecotourism across the United States and in Europe and the KWS hosted an international ecotourism conference in Nairobi, the local press began lobbing criticisms. Soon, the chorus of critics widened to include some overseas journalists, officials of aid agencies and conservation organizations, and finally President Moi himself. Beginning in late 1997, the three-year slump in tourism deepened in the wake of political violence surrounding Kenya's elections and torrential rains brought by El Niño. This caused a 50 percent drop in the KWS's revenue, forcing Western to cut the agency's payroll by 30 percent, lay off hundreds of staff members, and close more than thirty field stations. Institutional morale plummeted and notices were posted ordering employees not to talk with the press.[51] Citing a host of statistics, a Kenyan newspaper, The People, charged that KWS was continuing to pay "inflated salaries to a well-connected circle of cronies," including a hefty $148,000 annual salary for the director himself.[52] There were, as well, accusations that Western was a poor administrator, that the organization was adrift, and that the institutional decentralization was likely to weaken the KWS's financial position and ability to carry out its core mandate. One local paper claimed the KWS was verging on "operational and financial breakdown," another called it "a facade held together by a demoralized field staff," and a third contended that foreign donors had "given up on KWS."[53] Western countered that he had eliminated all expatriate positions at KWS, was implementing other cost-saving and income-generating measures, and had convinced USAID to extend the COBRA project into 1998.[54]

More fundamentally, some donors and conservationists voiced concern that Western was concentrating too heavily on community projects in the buffer zones and neglecting conservation, protection, infrastructure improvement, and income generation priorities within the KWS's parks and reserves. The World Bank accused Western of not properly implementing the PAWS program and clung to its unrealistic demand that the KWS become financially independent by rehabilitating its few most commercially viable parks. Agi Kiss, principal ecologist for the bank's African Environmental Group, told *Science* magazine, "We've been increasingly concerned and dissatisfied about how KWS manages its resources and sets priorities," and World Bank officials said privately that they did not intend to renew the PAWS project when its funding runs out, in 1999.[55] Consultant Robert Hall, who assessed the COBRA project, had somewhat different concerns. He worried that Western's very active role in community conservation would "pull KWS further into land management conflicts in areas outside the Parks—both with residents and with sectoral agencies that were already a bit miffed with KWS for interfering in agriculture and livestock activities. As KWS tries to solve problems in its external environment, it is likely to be seen as an interloper and the source of problems."[56]

Then, in May 1998, President Moi weighed in, announcing that he was removing Western, just months after extending his contract as KWS director for another two years. Moi gave no reason for the decision, but Western quickly contended that it had nothing to do with the KWS's financial or other problems. Rather, Western asserted, he was fired because he had rebuffed efforts by cabinet ministers to open new gemstone mines in Tsavo West National Park and grab other land owned by the KWS.[57]

Through it all, Western held his ground, arguing that although there were inevitably problems in implementing community-based conservation projects, it was the only viable course for Kenya. "Protecting parks alone, as the World Bank would have KWS do, carries a high cost," Western wrote in answer to one critical article. "Although still KWS's top priority, protected areas cover less than 8% of the land surface and simply don't give adequate biodiversity coverage. Furthermore," he contended, "few if any are ecologically viable. Difficult or not, the human-wildlife conflict must be tackled if Kenya's wealth of species and migratory herds is to be preserved." Quickly, other advocates of community-based conservation rallied to support Western. A letter signed by nine American and British scientists stated in part, "The real issue in Kenyan wildlife conservation is not management style, but science. [I]t is that conserving nature in small, isolated reserves will not work. Western's pivotal biological contribution here was to reverse the insularization of Kenya's parks."[58] In Nairobi, a group of international conservationists and donors (minus the World Bank) met privately with Moi and threatened to withhold millions of dollars if Western were not reinstated. Within ten days, Moi reversed his decision, and Western returned to the helm of the beleaguered KWS.[59]

But the battle was not over. In September 1998, following the U.S. Embassy bombings and fears of further drops in tourism numbers, Moi again forced Western to resign. The underlying reason, Western made clear, was the same: "that pressure to allow mining on conservation land [was] at the heart of the issue." And, to the surprise of many, Moi replaced Western with his old rival, Richard Leakey—despite Leakey's own acrimonious exit as KWS chief in 1994. While Leakey brings enormous talent, energy, and connections to the job, many Kenyans and international observers see the political instabilities within the once-promising KWS as a sign that Kenya's national experiment with sound ecotourism was ending.[60]

Community Conservation and Early Ecotourism: Experiments in Amboseli and Maasai Mara

Even before the WCMD in the 1970s and the KWS in the 1990s began testing the principles of community-based ecotourism, Kenya had begun experiments with revenue sharing of park fees and tourism in several of its most famous protected areas.

People living on the parks' boundaries have always borne the brunt of wildlife protection in terms of deaths and injuries, crop and livestock losses, and restricted access to resources.[61] Kenya, in contrast with Tanzania, has an estimated 60 to 75 percent of its wildlife living *outside* the national parks. This has caused conflict over land use, particularly as pastoralists have diversified into agriculture, new farmers have moved into these areas, and Kenya's population has tripled in size since independence. Throughout the colonial period and much of the postcolonial period, most national preserves were administered with a centralized, top-down philosophy requiring that all park entrance fees be sent to the central park authority.

However, three decades ago, long before ecotourism had entered the popular lexicon, two areas—the Maasai Mara Game Reserve and Amboseli Game Reserve (now Amboseli National Park)—began programs that embodied the principles of local community participation in wildlife conservation, mixed land use in the buffer zones, and tourism. These are often considered the earliest ecotourism programs in Africa. Maasai Mara and Amboseli are both located on land historically used by Maasai pastoralists for grazing and watering their herds of cattle, goats, and sheep. Historically, the Maasai have not hunted; their domestic herds have shared land with wildlife, but the Maasai have derived no financial benefit from it. Under the treaties of 1904 and 1911 between the British colonial administrators and the Maasai's spiritual leader, pastoralists in the Southern Reserve encompassing these two areas were to be left unmolested "for as long as the Maasai shall exist as a race."[62]

This, of course, was not to be. It was challenged by the 1945 National

Parks Ordinance, which marked the start of efforts to curb Maasai access to both Amboseli and Maasai Mara.[63] In the late 1940s, both areas were declared national reserves within the Royal National Parks of Kenya, and the Maasai pastoralists were allowed only limited entry and use of the reserves. The Maasai rightly saw this as yet another step toward taking away their remaining grazing, water, and spiritual sites. They began to call the reserves *shamba la bibi*, literally "the old lady's garden," a reference to the British queen.[64]

Then, in the late 1950s, as independence neared, a new plan was proposed. The Maasai, along with the Game Department and the wildlife advisor to the Kenyan government, opposed efforts to turn these reserves into full-blown national parks. "Their rationale, very innovative for the time," write Lee Talbot and Perez Olindo, "was that if the areas were to be conserved for the benefit of the country and posterity, they would have to be supported by the people who lived near them. To accomplish this, those people would have to receive a share of the tangible benefits of the areas and, ideally, they should participate fully in their creation and management."[65] The reality was that as much as 70 percent of the wildlife either migrated or lived permanently in so-called dispersal areas, which were inhabited by pastoralists and their livestock. It was imperative that these people come to see wildlife as a positive economic benefit, worth protecting. Under the agreement reached in 1961, Amboseli, Maasai Mara, and a few other Kenyan reserves were to be managed by the local district or county councils rather than the central government.

Maasai Mara Game Reserve

Today, Maasai Mara receives more visitors than any other wildlife area in East Africa, and about 30 percent of tourists visiting Kenya go to this reserve. Even though it is twelve times smaller than Serengeti National Park, each year Maasai Mara Game Reserve receives more than twelve times as many tourists as its Tanzanian counterpart: 250,000, compared with 20,000.[66] More than any other place in Africa, Maasai Mara, as the continent's longest-running experiment in government-sanctioned ecotourism, reveals how difficult it is to create and maintain democratically run local institutions and how struggles over control of land, wildlife, other resources, and tourism revenues can undermine both the tourism experience and the wildlife reserve.

Back in 1961, under a plan proposed by Maasai Mara's longtime colonial game warden, Major Lynn Temple-Boreham, management of the reserve was granted to the Narok County Council (NCC),[67] with the central portion of the game reserve set aside solely for wildlife-viewing tourism. The NCC was responsible for developing tourism facilities, establishing and maintaining roads, appointing the warden, rangers, and other staff, and collecting entrance and other fees. The Game Department provided training for the staff. In 1962, the NCC built the first permanent tourist facility, which included a number of self-catering bandas (thatched-roof bungalows) at a lovely location near fresh water. Three years later, these were replaced with a private hotel, Keekorok Lodge. All subsequent lodges and tented camps in and around the reserve have been built by private developers, who lease the land from the NCC. In addition, the dispersal area surrounding the reserve, which is twice the reserve's size, was divided into hunting and photographic blocks. The NCC set and collected the fees for visitor entry, camping, trophy collection, and vehicle use in these blocks. It was supposed to use the funds derived from these various tourism sources within and on the periphery of Maasai Mara to do upkeep of the reserve and to benefit the group ranches in the surrounding area. Most of the Maasai in the reserve are part of group ranches that organize their economic and social activities and hold their land communally but often have no legal documentation or title to the land.

By the end of the first decade, the reserve was being hailed as "a complete success" in terms of both conservation and community involvement.[68] Neither poaching nor livestock grazing was a serious problem within the reserve and tourist numbers increased steadily, making the Maasai Mara a mainstay of Kenya's nature tourism industry. The NCC used its revenue for a variety of community projects, including mobile and fixed dispensaries and schools, water pumps, cattle dips, and road maintenance. In terms of equitable distribution of the Narok County Council's revenue, these early years were by far the most successful.

With the 1977 border closure between Tanzania and Kenya, Maasai Mara suddenly became the terminus of what had been a popular circuit through the Serengeti to Ngorongoro Crater. This caused a sharp rise in visitor numbers in Maasai Mara, "triggering inadequately planned development of ecotourism infrastructures," according to biologist and founder of the Ecotourism Society of Kenya (ESOK) Chris Gakahu, who worked in the reserve.[69] That same year, Kenya imposed its hunting ban, eliminating the income the Maasai group ranches had been receiving from the leasing of hunting blocks. Some of this loss was offset by an increase in entrance fees to the reserve and construction of new lodges and tented camps on communal lands as many hunters shifted over to wildlife tourism. By 1987, about half of the tourism development was in the dispersal area and Maasai landowners were found to "have a positive attitude toward tourism."[70] With tourism proving so lucrative, both poaching and the cost of antipoaching efforts had dropped to almost nothing. Contrary to the situation in most of the rest of Kenya, numbers of elephants and rhinos were increasing. In

1990, Maasai Mara recorded only five elephant deaths (three from natural causes) and the killing of only one rhino—the first in six years.[71] But despite its high income and low incidence of poaching, Maasai Mara was in trouble. "The problems have always centered around money, and how the money is being spent," says one dissident Maasai leader. There are three intertwined issues regarding allocation of funds. One is that the Narok County Council began using its tourism revenues to support projects throughout the entire district, not just for upkeep within the reserve and development programs in the dispersal area surrounding it. As elsewhere in East and southern Africa, deciding what constitutes the community living around a protected area is a delicate political issue. The Maasai in the dispersal areas nearest the reserve compellingly argue that they are the ones barred from grazing and watering their livestock in the reserve and on whose lands wildlife live or migrate. Historically, these Maasai have borne the costs of wildlife that kill their cattle, compete for grazing land, transmit diseases, and destroy property.[72] They want fair compensation, but for many years the NCC's disbursements have been minimal and spread thinly among all NCC's constituents, not just those living nearest the park. One of NCC's few projects has been bursaries to students, but even these are given out by ward chairmen, usually to politically powerful rather than the most needy families.

The second issue is corruption, with powerful politicians on the NCC or within the central government simply pocketing large sums of the tourism money or using their power to get both permits for hotels and other concessions and land for farming. Tourism experts report that ripoffs are routine with gate fees, hotel levies, and various other concessions. Game-viewing balloon rides, for instance, cost around $300 per hour. Of this, the company retains only a small fraction; the rest is paid to local officials as "administrative fees." William Ole Ntimama, Kenya's longtime minister of local government and former chair of the Narok County Council, is widely reputed to be one of Kenya's most corrupt politicians. Ntimama owns two luxury lodges in Maasai Mara. One of his classmates referred to him as "half Maasai," noting that he dons the traditional dress and behavior "only when he comes to see us, and quickly forgets who we are once his car is turned toward Nairobi."[73] Those I interviewed said that Ntimama and several other Maasai officials had also been behind many of the illegal transactions to get tracts of land for tourism projects or wheat farms in Maasai Mara. Increasing numbers of non-Maasai have moved in and managed to get land title, some changing their names so they can claim to be Maasai. "People who want land go through these big bosses," said Maasai group ranch leader and game driver James Morinte. "They then go to the Lands Office in Nairobi, take out a map and say they want such and such a piece and they are given the title."

The third issue is lack of transparency in terms of where the funds go and lack of democratic selection of Narok County Council members. The NCC and group ranches are supposed to hold regular annual meetings to distribute tourism revenues, but those interviewed said that even when these meetings occur, there is no way to tell how much money has actually been collected. Council members and group ranch officials are supposed to be elected, but for years, no membership lists have been kept or public meetings held, so no elections could take place. A World Bank official estimated that by the mid-1990s, the Narok County Council was collecting $1.5–$2 million per year. "No one knows for sure how much because the Council doesn't say," the official said. "But what is clear is that the Council puts absolutely nothing or very little into the local community." This lack of public accountability led some group ranches to break away and form the Transmara County Council.

By the early 1990s, the evidence was in that the game reserve, local people, and tourism were all suffering from the corruption, land grabbing, and lack of investment. A 1991 survey of Maasai Mara Game Reserve by Wildlife Conservation International (WCI) found a deterioration of the tourism experience, infrastructure, and visitor facilities as well as wildlife protection. The two dozen lodges and permanent tented camps were clustered into two main areas in the northwestern and southeastern parts of the reserve, causing problems with waste disposal and shortages of firewood for cooking and heating water. With the poor distribution and condition of the roads, this has meant overuse of the parts of the reserve nearest the lodges. Drivers prefer to stay in these areas because they know where the game animals are likely to be found and they want to reduce gasoline costs and wear and tear on the vehicles. Off-track driving is illegal but very common, and this causes deep ruts and destroys grasses and shrubs eaten by the animals. Vehicles often crowd and harass the animals, especially the cheetahs and lions.[74]

The WCI study found further that although the quality of the tourism experience is declining, visitors themselves are more environmentally aware, more discriminating in choosing destinations, and willing to pay more to support conservation and community projects. Tourists surveyed complained that they received insufficient information before beginning their safaris, and only 15 percent were given copies of the reserve's list of "Dos and Don'ts" for visitors and drivers. Drivers-cum-guides are the tourists' main source of information, but the visitors surveyed rated the drivers' knowledge of ecology, animal behavior, conservation problems, and other areas as low.[75]

Over the years, there have been several attempts to bring Maasai Mara Game Reserve under the control of the national park system. In the early 1990s, for instance, Richard Leakey, as the first director of the Kenya

Wildlife Service, devised a plan to make Maasai Mara a game park managed by the KWS. But even though Leakey had World Bank and other external backing for his plan, he was bitterly opposed by the Narok County Council and Minister Ntimama, and this was a factor in Leakey's replacement in 1994 by Western, who is viewed as pro-Maasai. Western says he subsequently "drew up a Memorandum of Understanding with both the [breakaway] Transmara and Narok County Councils saying that it was not KWS's intention to take over Maasai Mara." However, President Moi, in an effort to exert some limited national control over the reserve, announced that the armed Maasai Mara rangers should be under the jurisdiction of the KWS.[76]

By the mid-1990s, the NCC was being challenged by a rival county council, seven group ranches, and one association, all officially registered and all trying to collect fees. The mood just below the surface was ugly as these mini-fiefdoms vied for control of the tourism dollars. There were stories of tourist vans in Maasai Mara being stopped and charged entrance fees multiple times as they crossed the invisible dividing lines between group ranches. At the upscale tented camp Kichwa Tembo, for instance, guests witnessed a nasty scene between the desk clerk and a British couple who were arguing that they had already paid the 10 percent nightly hotel tax to a travel agency in Nairobi. This levy is supposed to be collected at the hotels and turned over to the nearest group ranch, but the NCC uses the Kenya Association of Tour Operators (KATO) to collect the fees via travel agencies selling prepaid safari packages to Maasai Mara. Interviews with the hotel staff revealed that two rival group ranches were claiming to own the land on which Kichwa Tembo is located. Under a lease agreement, the hotel had since 1977 been paying the 10 percent levy to a group ranch connected to the Transmara County Council, which seemed to have the support of most of the local people. The group ranch had used the profits to build a primary school, three nursery schools, and a dispensary. In 1993, another group had suddenly appeared, claiming title to the land and backing from the NCC.

In the mid-1990s, ownership of the hotel itself was transferred from Abercrombie & Kent (A&K) to Conservation Corporation (ConsCorp), a South African ecotourism company that was expanding aggressively into East Africa. When Conservation Corporation bought Kichwa Tembo, 50 percent of the staff were Maasai, already more than the Maasai Mara's average. Although Maasai Mara's antipoaching and other reserve staff have long been largely Maasai, by 1987 only 39 percent of the tourism workforce (hotel and campsite operators, drivers) were Maasai, and most upper-level managers were non-Maasai.[77] A much larger percentage of Maasai Mara residents, however, were involved in tourism-related activities. A 1992 survey found that more than half of the respondents had two or more family members working in tourism, and nearly half indicated that their family received income from tourism through jewelry sales, camping concessions, or fees paid to visit cultural centers.[78]

For Maasai women, cultural centers and handicrafts have long been the most important legitimate sources of income. Maasai dancers perform at many of the hotels, although they are often hotel employees who are asked by management to dance for the guests for a very minimal fee. There are numerous cultural villages, known as *bomas*, scattered around both Maasai Mara and Amboseli, where Maasai dance, sing, and sell their famous beaded jewelry. Visitors pay an admission fee in return for being allowed to see and photograph "traditional" activities. However, most *bomas* are not professionally run, and many concentrate on hustling sales rather than educating tourists about Maasai traditions and culture. One Maasai leader called these cultural centers "black holes of exploitation," since a lion's share of the entrance fees goes to a few big businessmen and to the safari drivers, who get commissions for bringing in tourists. [79]

Some *bomas* have become fronts for prostitution, pornography, or drugs. Not infrequently tourists and their agents offer small fees to get women to pose bare breasted and men to expose their buttocks. These photos are used in postcards, brochures, and books. "In return," writes John Ole Kisimir in the *Nairobi Daily Nation*, "the Maasai have earned a reputation as a symbol of backwardness and savagery."

Such crude cultural exploitation reached new heights when *Sports Illustrated* used the Iltilal Maasai village in Kajiado District as a setting for its winter 1998 swimsuit edition. The magazine paid "the chief" one thousand dollars, and he delivered the village's young men. "The idea was to capture the raw, unspoiled beauty of this place and people," writes Walter Chin. "We [arrived] with models. A camera crew. T.V. people. A whole international, multimedia traveling circus. 'Oh,' we said, 'we won't bother anyone, and besides it'll be fun!'" When the first model dropped her sarong, leaving her only in a bikini and high heels, the "warriors pressed forward to touch her."[80]

The Kenyan press related a different story—that "the Massai women screamed" and hid in their houses, "elders herded their children away," while "the young warriors stayed put as the cameramen went wild with their flashes." MERC leader Meitamei Ole Dapash, among others, protested. He charged this incident shows the lengths that Kenya's tourism industry "is willing to go to capture the tourist dollar at the expense of the rights and values of the Maasai people" and he urged the Kenya Association of Tour Operators (KATO) to draw up a code of conduct to govern operators and tourists. KATO's executive committee replied that it could not possibly "police" the activities of all tour operators in the country. [81]

A handful of cultural centers are, however, trying to avoid such exploitation. One is the Olonana Maasai Cultural Center opened near Kichwa Tembo, which began offering tourists an authentic and informative ninety-minute tour to view traditional Maasai cattle keeping, cooking, crafts, construction, and ceremonies. Olonana was started with professional advice and financial backing from a group of South African whites (not connected to Conservation Corporation) who have been involved in setting up high-quality Zulu and other cultural villages. The village employs seventy Maasai and uses a portion of its income to support community projects, including five schools. According to Jackson Ole Looseyia, Olonana's cultural advisor in 1995, "Our aim is to educate without harassing the tourists, as well as to help to keep alive our traditions and culture, which our young people are forgetting."

One of the most clearly successful multidimensional, locally run eco-tourism projects was developed by the Olchoro O'rowu Association and is made up of eight local landowning families.[82] Unlike most of the group ranches in Maasai Mara Game Reserve, the association families all have legal title to their land, which collectively totals 8,903 hectares (22,000 acres) and, including extended families, supports some 500 people. The association was formed in 1992 in opposition to the Narok County Council and through the impetus of Willie Roberts, a white Kenyan who had leased land in the area for wheat farming. The farming did not work out, so Roberts conceived of forming the association and became its executive director. The association went to court to get permission to collect revenue from tourism on its land. Not only was it given permission, but the court also ruled that the Narok County Council had to pay the association KSh 14 million (U.S.$467,000) in back revenue. The association began collecting entrance fees—$20 from foreigners and KSh 100 (U.S.$3.30) from Kenyans—plus land rent from the Paradise Lodge and three other luxury tourism lodges located on association land, all of which was averaging a handsome KSh 10 million (U.S.$333,333) per month in the mid-1990s. Every six months, the association held a meeting to announce how much had been collected. Thirty percent of the proceeds were divided evenly among the eight families, another 30 percent went for management, and 4 percent went for development projects. Association members as a whole selected the development projects, which included a primary school, school fees and uniforms, teachers' salaries, a dispensary, and wells.

With the support of several NGOs and using 6 percent of its profits from tourism, the Olchoro O'rowu Association has also begun a rhino protection and wildlife education project aimed primarily at the local Maasai rather than tourists. The Natal Parks Board in South Africa donated ten white rhinos to Kenya and two of these were given to the association. (Others went to Lewa Downs, a private reserve discussed later in this chapter.) The association has fenced off a large tract of land for the rhinos and had plans to build an environmental center at this site to teach wildlife conservation. Steven Kuluo, the association's warden in 1995, said that since the association was formed, he had "seen a change in just a few years. People see wildlife as an economic benefit and young people are learning to appreciate and understand them." Chris Gakahu, founder of the Ecotourism Society of Kenya, said that although the association is unique because it involves a small group of individual landowners, "it has done something very good which should happen elsewhere, on the group ranches."[83]

But sadly, all did not proceed smoothly for the association. Two neighboring group ranches aligned with the Narok County Council began demanding a large cut of the association's profits to compensate for tourists' viewing of game on these ranches while staying at lodges on association land. Kuluo said that frustrated members of his association were threatening to kill off the wildlife and turn from tourism to wheat farming. "It's not what we want, but we're pushed into a corner and we don't have a choice. Given options, I think wildlife and tourism are better for this land than agriculture. But the future is not good." The association finally agreed to start a revenue-sharing program with the neighboring group ranches, but what they offered was not enough, and tensions persisted. Then, in 1997, Kuluo died suddenly from a rare genetic disease. The association has continued, but it is weaker without Kuluo's energetic presence.

Whereas some talented, young Maasai leaders such as Kuluo chose to stay and challenge the Narok County Council's authority, other organizers have been forced to flee, some into exile. One is Meitamei Ole Dapash, who in 1993 fled to the United States after he was repeatedly arrested and, he says, tortured because he and others protested environmental destruction and overdevelopment in the reserve. In the 1980s, Dapash, who grew up in Maasai Mara and attended college in Nairobi, joined the East African Wildlife Society, a conservation organization led and staffed largely by Kenyans. Dapash's duties included work with the Green Tourism Program in which he talked with tourists about ecotourism, conservation, and wildlife protection. Dapash now heads the U.S.-based Maasai Environmental Resource Coalition (MERC), which, like KIPOC in Tanzania, works for the rights of pastoralists and environmental protection of the land.

Over the years, a series of studies, ecotourism conferences, and press exposés have enumerated the litany of problems in Maasai Mara and suggested solutions, including proposals that no more lodges be built inside the reserve and that new ones built outside be better dispersed; that new viewing circuits be established in remote areas within and outside the reserve; and that tourists receive better presafari educational materials and guides receive professional training backed up by a code of conduct. More fundamental, Chris Gakahu writes, is the need for a closer working "relationship between policy makers, planners, tour operators and the local community" as well as "coordinated and integrated national planning."[84] But improvements have not come, and the quality of ecotourism has continued to decline. As a 1995 article in the Kenyan magazine *Wajibu* concluded, "Measures to preserve the unique environment in the Mara are long overdue if we wish to continue to attract visitors to this area. As things stand now, the visitors' perception of 'wild Africa' as viewed through the eyes of discerning tourists has gone; instead they see hordes of vehicles surrounding animals, and their anticipated experience of enjoyment in the wild is replaced with something more akin to a mobile visit to a zoo."[85] By the late 1990s, Maasai Mara Game Reserve remained, according to NGOs leaders and local activists, "a mess" and a "political hot potato," and its once-promising and pioneering ecotourism experiment lay largely in shambles.

Amboseli National Park

In the 1930s, Ernest Hemingway and, before him, Teddy Roosevelt trekked to Amboseli Game Reserve (later to become Amboseli National Park) on big game safaris, hunting lions and elephants against the backdrop of snow-capped Mount Kilimanjaro. Amboseli, Kenya's other early ecotourism experiment, has moved in a different trajectory, toward gradually curbing the authority of the county council by giving more authority to the national park system and more revenue to the local group ranches. Although it is more successful than Maasai Mara, Amboseli has also suffered from decades of conflict and corruption that have stunted the growth of both local development projects and community-run tourism.

In 1961, the colonial government handed control of the Amboseli reserve to the Kajiado County Council, the local authority for a 20,000-square-kilometer (7,722-square-mile) district that included the 600-square-kilometer Amboseli basin. The council secured agreement from the local Maasai group ranches to set aside a 78-square-kilometer area within the basin solely for wildlife. Tourism in Amboseli, which is located just a few hours' drive south of Nairobi, grew quickly, and by 1968 the council was getting 75 percent of its annual income from the reserve.

From the outset, however, there were serious conflicts between the council and the local Maasai and their traditional leaders over how the

reserve and the revenue were being used. Out of necessity, the Maasai continued to move their cattle into the basin for water and grazing, leading to
complaints that they were interfering with tourism. As in Maasai Mara,
development projects, built with tourism profits, were widely scattered, and
those in the settlements closest to the reserve complained that they were not
receiving sufficient benefits. In addition, the council had little expertise or
training in finances, and there was a series of incidents involving mismanagement.[86]

By the late 1960s, the conflict had intensified, with the local Maasai
demanding that they be given title to the entire region and conservationists
urging that Amboseli be declared a national park from which the Maasai
would be totally excluded. In 1971, Kenya's president, Jomo Kenyatta, pre-
cipitously decreed that the government was taking over a large area within
the basin and that the Maasai would be compensated with alternative water
sources. The Maasai retaliated by spearing rhinos, lions, leopards, and elephants. Their message was clear: take the land and the Maasai would take
the animals.

At this point, David Western, who was working as a biologist in
Amboseli, together with several New York Zoological Society and World
Bank experts and local Maasai leaders, became deeply involved in negotiating a settlement that would protect much of the original Maasai-based ecotourism experiment, integrate the livestock and wildlife economies, and
focus primarily on providing the Maasai nearest the reserve with benefits
from tourism and wildlife utilization.[87] For the first time, there were public
meetings between local leaders and Ministry of Tourism and Wildlife officials, a development Western calls the "most enduring impact" of this crisis.
They sought to create, Western says, a "Maasai park rather than a national
park, and that was accepted—begrudgingly—by the government, but was
overturned in the late 1960s during the general elections. It was only later,
when the government unilaterally took over Amboseli, that we tried to
negotiate some compromise between the state and local participation."[88]
Finally, in 1974, a compromise was struck by which Amboseli became a
national park under central government control and administered by the
newly created Wildlife Conservation and Management Department
(WCMD). The agreement contained, however, a number of innovative pro-
visos to encourage local support: (1) the government would construct boreholes and a pipeline to pump water from the swamp to surrounding communal lands; (2) the Kajiado County Council would be guaranteed income
from land surrounding tourist lodges located inside the park as well as a portion of the gate entrance fees; (3) the government would use its share of the
entrance fees for park maintenance and development; (4) the government
would retain all local staff members as rangers, scouts, and lodge employees;

and (5) the Maasai group ranches would receive title to the remainder of the land. In addition, nearly $6 million of a $37.5 million World Bank Tourism and Wildlife Project was allocated for Amboseli.[89]

Problems, however, continued, and so did power- and revenue-sharing negotiations between the central government, the county council, group ranches, and park authorities. Eventually, another parcel of land, containing proposed sites for tourist lodges, was annexed from the park and given to local Maasai. The plan was that the four group ranches outside the park would get increasing revenues from tourist lodges and campsites, game cropping, and safari hunting as well as a "wildlife utilization fee" or rent to compensate for the loss of grazing lands to wildlife. In addition, a school, dispensary, and community center were built on the edge of the park, and roads inside the park were improved. Western recounts that at a *baraza* (meeting) held to distribute to the group ranches the first payments from hunting concessions—KSh 1.9 million (U.S.$271,000)—the Maasai responded, once again, that they considered wildlife to be valuable. As the elders told the government officials, "The national park has gained two thousand extra pairs of eyes to help watch out for poachers."[90] Feeling confident that this deal would hold, the Maasai agreed to vacate the park completely by 1977.

But despite some early successes, after several years conflicts again arose, in part because there was no written agreement and the terms of the oral understanding were never fully implemented. The WCMD was severely underfunded and plagued with ineptitude, corruption, and nepotism. The agency proved to be, Western wrote, "disastrous not just for Amboseli, but for the locally based approach and Kenya's wildlife generally."[91]

However, by the mid-1980s, the situation began to improve slightly as tourist numbers increased and Amboseli's group ranches began, for the first time, to take the initiative in implementing wildlife and tourism projects. By this time, the Amboseli Maasai were in the process of making a rapid transition from subsistence pastoralism to a mixed economy of farming, salaried employment, and—as beef prices rose—commercial livestock ranching. A new generation of Maasai leaders emerged and began to devise new ways of relating to wildlife and tourism.

In one highly successful project, each of 200 families on one group ranch contributed KSh 300 to build a 9.7-kilometer (6-mile) solar-powered electric fence to keep out wildlife.[92] Another group of Maasai opened a campsite, which by 1987 was earning more than KSh 300,000 (U.S.$18,000) per year. The four group ranches all contracted with safari operators to bring in tourists. For instance, in 1991, the Olalarashi Group Ranch negotiated a $20,000-per-year deal with two big tour operators, Abercrombie & Kent (A&K) and Ker and Downey, for eight campsites.[93]

These self-initiated and profitable ecotourism schemes once again led to an overall decline in poaching, which was on the rise elsewhere in Kenya, except in Maasai Mara. As Western wrote, "Despite the failure of the government program, WCMD's contribution to the collapse of park infrastructure, and a much-publicized poaching scandal . . . the Maasai's own wildlife programs sustained and improved their development activities as well as wildlife numbers."[94]

By 1989, Amboseli National Park ranked, with Maasai Mara Game Reserve and Nairobi Park, among Kenya's top tourist attractions. It was receiving some 100,000 visitors and earning an average of KSh 9 million (more than U.S.$200,000) per year, giving it an enviable revenue base to share with the local communities, county council, and central government.[95] But those living closest to the park, and suffering the most from wildlife eating crops and killing livestock and sometimes people, continued to benefit little. In early 1990, after the Kenya Wildlife Service (KWS) replaced the WCMD, government officials and the Amboseli group ranches reached several broad agreements, including one to resume revenue disbursements and another to create a team of local Maasai scouts to protect wildlife. As part of KWS director Richard Leakey's pledge to distribute 25 percent of gate revenues to local communities, the Amboseli group ranches became, in 1991, the first to receive payment. The ranches used part of this KSh 4 million (more than U.S.$100,000) to build four schools and several cattle dips and to hire twenty Maasai game scouts to protect wildlife.

But when the KWS failed to follow through and systematically implement the 25 percent revenue-sharing scheme, several Amboseli group ranches set up their own wildlife association to undertake conservation programs and tourist concessions.[96] In 1996, for instance, the Kimana Group Ranch opened its own 40-square-kilometer (15.4-square-mile) wildlife sanctuary in a stretch of swampy land east of Amboseli,[97] financed by USAID as part of the COBRA program and supported by the Kilimanjaro Safari Club and the KWS. The ranch's chairman, Paul Ole Nangoro, admitted that the sanctuary is a gamble because many Maasai fear it is simply a device to turn more of their land over to wildlife protection. Nangoro estimated that for the sanctuary to win solid support from the ranch's 840 families, it must take in about $130,000 per year. "We want every family to get a share at the end of the year, knowing it was from the sanctuary and from wildlife," he said. In its first week of operation, however, only seventeen tourists, each paying just $10, visited the sanctuary. "The whole idea can still be killed," Nangoro told the *New York Times*. "Kimana is like a calf. It has just been born and it is still trying to walk."[98]

Despite continuing disputes, David Western remains cautiously optimistic. He concludes the evidence shows that "the original aim of maintaining the integrity of the Amboseli ecosystem and improving the welfare of the Maasai landowners is being achieved. Poaching levels remain low, attitudes toward wildlife are fairly positive, and wildlife income is steadily becoming a more significant component of Maasai income."[99] Biologist Chris Gakahu said in an interview that by the mid-1990s, "Amboseli had become much better than Maasai Mara. People know their rights, they run the show, and they are managing to keep the politicians out." He adds, "It's taken time to evolve, through small, successful activities where everyone saw success."

Kenya's Private Ranches and Reserves: Two-Tiered "Ecotourism"

Today, with the overcrowding and the deteriorating conditions within the national parks and council-run reserves, many visitors with sufficient funds are seeking "wild Africa" elsewhere, in Kenya's growing number of privately owned parks. These private ranches and reserves offer both illusion and luxury. In part because of the crowds, crime, and poaching in the national parks, a growing number of private estates have been converted to exclusive conservation and wildlife-viewing areas. Most are owned by white Kenyans from settler families who stayed on after independence and, in many cases, obtained citizenship. Some are using their large tracts of land as conservation sanctuaries, protecting and raising endangered species such as black rhinos, Rothchild's giraffes, and Grevy's zebras. Others care for orphaned or wounded wild animals, specialize in bird-watching or fishing, or have fenced off their estates to make wildlife parks.

These private reserves give visitors a sense of solitude and intimacy with nature and wildlife in a setting of colonial elegance and personal service. Most accommodate no more than two dozen guests. They offer game-viewing drives in open jeeps (à la South Africa) as well as walking tours, night rides, game viewing via horseback and camel, picnics beside water holes, and sundowners on the savanna, all accompanied by the owner of the estate. They permit, even encourage, off-road driving, and when leopards or cheetahs are sighted, there are never more than a handful of other vehicles around.

But this sense of being on safari in the wild is carefully orchestrated. Whereas the national parks are unfenced, large, and lightly patrolled by comparison, these private sanctuaries are comparatively small, fenced, meticulously managed, well groomed, and heavily guarded. Game-viewing vehicles are connected by radio, and scouts are sent ahead to spot the animals. The owners have named many of the animals, some of which are so accustomed to humans that they come right up to the vehicles or living quarters. Little is left to chance. Visitors who pay the price are virtually guaranteed close encounters with the "big five"[100]—or whatever else these luxury zoos have to offer.

Studies done of private reserves have found that those in Africa are, on average, much larger than those in Latin America. Seventy-three percent exceed 2,500 hectares (6,177 acres). Of those private reserves surveyed in 1989, 60 percent in Africa (Kenya, South Africa, Zimbabwe, and Madagascar) were owned by citizens, although a racial breakdown is not given, and 33 percent were foreign owned and 6.7 percent were partnerships between nationals and foreigners. According to the study, a majority (53.3 percent) of these reserves combined tourism and farming, a quarter (26.7 percent) were only for tourism, and 20 percent did research, conservation, and education, with or without tourism. In contrast with private reserves in Latin America, many of those in Africa were set up originally as hunting preserves, and 40 percent (all outside Kenya) continue to make money from hunting safaris.[101] In Kenya, private reserve owners have been among those lobbying most vigorously for a reintroduction of commercial hunting, something the KWS had by 1996 agreed in principle to support.

One of the oldest private reserves in Kenya is Lewa Downs, a 24,686-hectare (61,000-acre) tourism resort and rhino sanctuary managed by William and Emma Craig. This dry, arid scrub country in the shadow of glacier-capped Mount Kenya is the home of two traditional pastoralist groups, the Turkana and the Samburu. The Craig family came to Kenya in 1924 when Will's grandmother, who was a nurse in World War I, won a British government lottery for former soldiers. The prize was a tract of land in Thika, an area of prime farming country outside Nairobi in what was known as the White Highlands. Will Craig, a tall, lanky former bush pilot with a clipped British accent, says that over the years his family moved from agriculture into cattle ranching, but they always cherished a love of wildlife.

More than twenty years ago, Will's parents began using part of their property for wildlife tourism, offering walking safaris—something unheard of at that time in East Africa. They started with four tents and gradually expanded to fifteen double tents and a permanent camp. Some time later, they built three beautiful double cottages, using cut lava stone, wooden pillars, and thatch roofs, in a style similar to that of their main ranch house. A room there costs $400 per night, including meals and game rides. They set up the Lewa Wildlife Conservancy to protect their property by means of a conservation trust. As the price of cattle has fallen, the Craigs have looked to tourism and conservation as their main source of revenue. "Now we're trying to reduce our cattle operations on this land and return it to its original state as much as possible," Will explains.

In the early 1980s, Anna Merz, a wealthy and eccentric British retiree who stayed at the Craig tented camp, proposed the idea of setting up a rhino sanctuary. Lewa Downs had lost its last rhino to poachers, so David Craig, Will's father, agreed to donate the land if Merz contributed the capital. They put up a high, electrified security fence and put out a call for rhinos. Rhino donations came in, including some white rhinos from South Africa, a species no longer found in East Africa. So, too, did funds from various conservation organizations.

Merz, who has written two books and been the subject of several nature documentaries, lives alone with five dogs in a small stone house on the Craigs' estate and spends her days tracking the sanctuary's nineteen rhinos, all of whom she refers to by name. She has short-cropped white hair, and wrinkled, leathery skin oddly reminiscent of her beloved rhinos. Like many of the self-taught European conservationists in Kenya, Merz has thrown enormous time and resources into saving a particular wildlife species, while seeming to remain quite indifferent to the plight of Africa's human species. Merz says that the $300,000 per year needed by her Ngare Sergoi Rhino Sanctuary comes partly from tourism revenues, with the remainder coming from donations.

"Lewa Downs is probably the furthest along in the country as a private conservancy. Basically they've converted over almost completely to tourism," says Steve Turner, director of East African Ornithological Safaris. Turner has leased and refurbished several stone buildings at Lewa Downs to accommodate two dozen bird-watchers. Along the main highway, the Craigs have also built a visitors' center and a luncheon restaurant where tourists can feed white rhinos, take bird-watching walks, and, for $20, go on game-viewing drives. "There's no other place to stop along this road, which gets thousands and thousands of tourists passing each year," says Will Craig. "This center works on the tourism flow. Its peak time is eleven to three, which is down time for our hotel guests. So we use the cars and drivers for game drives from the visitors' center."

The Craigs have also started Lewa Crafts, which Will describes as "periphery businesses to provide jobs in the local area." These include work-shops for wool spinning and rug weaving that employ ten to thirty area women on a piecework basis and for furniture-making workshops that employ fifteen men on salary and commission. They use acacia and other hardwood trees uprooted by elephants, formerly discarded as waste, to make an eclectic inventory of Chippendale corner chairs, luggage racks, folding camp chairs, and four-poster Arab beds. Will Craig plans to start a tannery in the local village (the stench of such an operation is terrible and would not be welcome on his ranch) and a luggage and shoe workshop on his prop-erty. Eventually, he will market all these crafts by mail-order catalog and at the lodge.

Lewa Downs, together with KWS and USAID fund from the COBRA

program, also supports a newer ecotourism project, an eleven-bed *banda* project built on the Ilingwesi Group Ranch, adjacent to the Craigs' ranch. Fences have been removed so that wildlife can migrate between the two ranches, thereby reversing the trend of habitat fragmentation. At $225 per group per night, this community-run facility caters to the local travel market.[102] Also connected to Lewa Downs is a camel trekking concession owned by Reggie Destro Safaris, a small private tour operator. Destro Safaris employs mostly local pastoralists to handle the camels and pays them a per-head fee for use of land for campsites.[103]

One NGO official says that as tourism has stagnated in Kenya, Lewa Downs has "been going down market, expanding its tourism in a hunt to get the right mixture for profitability." These community-based microenterprises are clearly spinoffs from Lewa Downs; at the ranch itself, old colonial master-servant relations are still intact, the biggest profits go to white investors, and visitors learn little—and often seem to care little—about either the country's history and culture or current realities of Kenya's human population.

Will Craig describes what Lewa Downs is doing as ecotourism. "From what I see ecotourism is simply responsible tourism. It's having major respect for where you are, for the countryside, which includes the local community," he says as we talk on the stone porch of his family house, overlooking flower gardens. "And it's minimum number of people and maximum care. On that basis, I keep this hotel to just twelve guests at a time."

Although Lewa Downs is marketed as ecotourism, guests I interviewed there had never heard of the concept. Clad in khaki safari outfits, most were wealthy, conservative Americans who had come via Bush Homes of East Africa, an Atlanta-based company that specializes in upscale tours to private estates in Kenya. Bush Homes is the concept of Phil Osborne, a robust, silver-haired tour operator who says he was first introduced to Africa while working for the CIA in the early 1950s. "What I discovered was a real civility, a dignity I'd never seen before among the hordes and masses." What caught Osborne's fancy was not the civility of Africans but the lifestyle on white settler farms. Even though today there remain only some 100 settler-owned properties in Kenya, Osborne unabashedly credits this minuscule minority with saving Africa's wildlife. "The infrastructure of Africa's wildlife conservation is kept together by this grid of white ranches," he contends as we chat at Lewa Downs.

Later, Osborne sent me some brochures and an article promoting Bush Homes, which reads, in part, "On some of the remaining European-owned farms and ranches in Kenya, it's still possible to experience the intimacy with Africa known by settlers of [Isak] Dinesen's generation."[104] This *Out of Africa* lifestyle is seductive and offers guests great game viewing, but it is out of place in present-day Kenya. The reality is that the fate of Kenya's wildlife depends on the future of the national reserves and their surrounding dispersal areas, not on this handful of white-owned farms.

Although these ranches may provide sanctuary for endangered species, intimate and educative game-viewing experiences for tourists, and menial employment for local people, on other ecotourism fronts they are sadly wanting: they preserve sizable tracts of privately owned land and resources in a few privileged hands; there is no real ownership by or significant income sharing with the surrounding community; they provide little financial benefit to the central government; most do little or no serious scientific research; and they transmit to visitors a distorted, frequently racist, view of modern-day Kenya. Fundamentally, these private reserves are an attempt to maintain family wealth and a lifestyle from a bygone colonial era "under the guise of conservation and ecotourism," says Maasai activist Ole Dapash.

The magnitude of these imbalances was pointed out to me during sundowners at Delamere's Camp at Lake Elmenteita. This tranquil tented camp is a bird and wildlife sanctuary, with a wide green lawn shaded by yellow-barked acacia trees and sprinkled with dozens of bird feeders. When I visited the air was filled with a symphony of chirping, and the pink hue of flamingos colored a distant edge of the lake. At dusk, the staff took the guests via jeep up to a cliff overlooking the lake for drinks and marinated Thomson's gazelle shish kebobs grilled over a charcoal stove. Standing on the windy edge of the cliff, the chief guide, a young Kamba man with a knack for bird calls, talked about the Delameres, the most famous of Kenya's colonial families. With an outstretched arm, he drew almost a complete circle around the lake, pointing out the extent of their property in this part of Kenya. Sixty-four thousand acres, the whole horizon save one narrow slice, belongs to the Delameres. Much of this estate, where beef cattle were raised before the prices plummeted, has now been sheltered in a nature conservancy.

"Yes, we see this as part of ecotourism," explained the camp's Kenyan manager as we sat beside the large fireplace in the open-sided lounge. "We keep everything as natural as possible. There are no nonindigenous plants or wildlife, except for giraffes that we've brought in." The wildlife sanctuary, which has no elephants or predators (except leopards), is a 6,475-hectare (16,000-acre) fenced "peaceable kingdom" of gazelles, impalas, zebras, elands, and buffalo. But it's the 400-odd species of birds that draw most of the guests. Bird-watching tours come mainly from the United States and England. There are four naturalist guides and a staff of between twenty-four and thirty-eight, depending on the season. The twelve luxury tents, complete with electricity and bathrooms, together with a tree house on the other side of the lake, can accommodate a total of twenty-eight guests. With occupancy running at 60 percent, the manager indicated that the three-year-old camp had not yet proved profitable.

The rules are strict, designed to ensure serenity. Even though the camp is located just off a main highway, no day visitors or drop-ins are allowed. All bookings must be made ahead of time in Nairobi. No loud music, noise, or smoking is allowed in the sanctuary. "We don't want the wrong kind of guests," said the manager. "We're near Nakuru and Naivasha [two popular lakes frequented by both Kenyans and foreigners], and it could easily turn into a carnival. We don't allow school tours for locals. It's not a public stomping ground."

Although the sanctuary and all the land belong to the Delameres, the lodge itself was built by Steve Turner, who brings in most of the guests through his Ornithological Safaris. The Delameres are in the process of buying one-third of the lodge's equity from Turner. "It was a business proposition. The Delameres realized that with the presence of game, they could make money from tourism. There are no endangered species, so they cannot pretend to be conserving species," the manager frankly admitted. He added that because the sanctuary is private, none of the revenue goes to the government, although the government, which technically owns the wildlife, must approve all culling—including that of the gazelles served at sundowners.

Turner, who is involved in both Lewa Downs and Delamere's Camp and is himself from a settler family, talked openly with me about the motivation behind establishing private reserves. "These private landowners are under incredible pressure to share their land," he explained. "Africa is no place for whites to be owning huge tracts of land and seeming to do nothing with it. The Delameres and, to a lesser degree, the Craigs are under pressure from locals to utilize the land." He said that in the 1960s and 1970s, vast amounts of land were taken from whites and sold off cheaply. The remaining whites continue to fear they will lose their land if it seems to be underutilized. So, as the director of one Western NGO cynically put it, "They slap on a rhino and say it's a reserve." These white ranch owners, though small in number, command political clout. At one point, the Kenyan government attempted to impose a tax on private lands used for wildlife that was several times greater than the tax for livestock. This caused "extreme consternation, and so it was reversed," explained one top NGO official.

In evaluating the role of private reserves, one hotel manager told me, "Ecotourism really only benefits the private landowners, the white farmers," not those who live near or work on these reserves. Maasai activist Ole Dapash calls the growing number of white-owned reserves, "a worrisome trend." He contends that the struggling African-owned private reserves, such as the Olchoro O'rowu Association in Maasai Mara, Kimana in Amboseli, and other tourism ventures on the group ranches, cannot compete with these European estates, which have "powerful political, economic, and media connections." These white estates are, for instance, the darlings of documentary filmmakers, wildlife photographers, and travel magazine writers who provide them with enormously valuable and nearly free advertising.

Although the private reserves have helped protect and breed endangered species such as rhinos, few other benefits pass from the private reserves to the public parks or national coffers. These upscale reserves are helping to develop a two-tiered wildlife tourism system in Kenya, with the high rollers going to the private parks and those taking package tours to the national parks. "The major problem with settler-owned or corporate-owned game farms," says environmental consultant Robert Hall, is what they "return to the government/national economy. They are not properly taxed." He continues, "These owners cry about their huge expenses to maintain their fences and protect their pet rhinos, but the truth is more complex. These guys have their own air strips, and no one, and I mean no one, knows how many people come and go during a year. Their charges are generally at least $250 to $600 per person per night. And what does the Treasury receive? *Nada*."

This powerful group of white tourism operators has also moved to gain control of the Ecotourism Society of Kenya (ESOK) and recraft its mission to their advantage. Founded in 1993 and officially registered in 1996 shortly after David Western became director of KWS, ESOK is a nonprofit organization headed by Western protégé Chris Gakahu. Under the banner of "Bringing together commerce, conservation and communities," ESOK is composed of tour operators, hoteliers, travel agents, educational institutions, tourism professionals, tourism and conservation organizations, and community and district associations. In a 1995 interview in Nairobi, Gakahu, a biologist with years of field, university, private consulting, and NGO experience, described to me ESOK's ambitious and somewhat conflicting mission as setting standards and helping to certify the training of guides and tour drivers, lobbying the government to give economic incentives to hotels to adopt environmentally friendly practices and systems, "flagging environmentally friendly destinations for potential investors," promoting Kenya's diverse ecotourism options overseas, and providing expertise to local communities wanting to develop tented camps or other ecotourism projects. However, in practice ESOK has not lived up to its pledge to be "a professional society" unrelated to "any particular special interest group." It has established The Ecotourism Partnership, which functions, according to its literature, as "the commercial implementing agency for projects which meet the aims of the Ecotourism Society of Kenya and to provide an impetus to the promotion of community-based wildlife tourism projects" by bringing "together a team of tourism industry professionals who will provide investment and management and marketing skills to such projects."[105]

These contradictory goals have raised eyebrows among some community organizers and ecotourism experts. Says Maasai leader Ole Dapash,

"How can ESOK be objective? It's supposed to be a nonprofit and a watch-dog, but it's gone into business," investing in and promoting a specific list of ecotourism projects. David Western agrees, saying that ESOK was "in-vaded, taken over by white tour operators who set up Ecotourism Partner-ship to try to promote ecotourism for their own benefit. In a move that is very disconcerting, these operators are seeking to stake out huge tracts of land now, anticipating a big growth in the ecotourism industry in the future. And this will create enormous resentment among the indigenous Africans, particularly those who have owned the land from time in memoriam."

Western adds that he believes, "Chris Gakahu has, to his credit, got rid of that group to make sure that ESOK does not have a commercial purpose to its mandate. Whether this will make a big difference to ESOK is unclear. What is needed," Western contends, "is to stake out a very clear role so that it can have a strong influence on the direction of ecotourism in the future. And ESOK certainly hasn't established that yet."[106] To date, ESOK has not been a vigorous industry monitor; it remains to be seen if it will ever evolve into an organization with the capacity and independence to evaluate criti-cally Kenya's tourism industry, to help professionalize the practitioners, and to set standards for sound community-linked ecotourism.

Western, as a central architect of Kenya's present-day community-based ecotourism experiments, goes on to argue that "the antidote" to domina-tion by white-owned ranches and private reserves is "much stronger capac-ity at the community level, a real effort to provide the highest-quality ser-vices, which they don't at the moment, and to really understand the impor-tance of marketing." He adds, "I think that a great many tourists in this day and age would be conscious enough of the value of indigenous operations." Although this is true, the principles and practices of community-based eco-tourism can be implemented on a national scale only if there is broad gov-ernment commitment to this process. And, as President Moi's firing of Western first in May 1998 and again in September demonstrates, the polit-ical will is not there.

Kenya's Ecotourism Scorecard

Kenya has been a trailblazer in ecotourism. It gave birth to Africa's earliest experiments in community-based conservation based on park and tourism revenues and began the first efforts to systematically adopt ecotourism prin-ciples and practices in its national park system. The director of its park ser-vice was the first head of The Ecotourism Society in the United States, and Africa's first nongovernmental ecotourism society was established in Kenya. But Kenya's unstable political climate and widespread economic corruption have increasingly undermined its ecotourism endeavors as well as its tourism industry in general. In the late 1990s, Kenya's troubles multiplied as crime, bad weather, political unrest, and the horrific terrorist bombing at the U.S. Embassy combined to scare off international holiday seekers.

In October 1997, the Kenya Wildlife Society hosted, together with The Ecotourism Society and The Ecotourism Society of Kenya (ESOK), an international workshop titled "Ecotourism at the Crossroads." The Nairobi symposium brought together experts from around the world, but much of the focus was on Kenya. In his opening address, David Western was candid in his assessment of Kenya's progress and problems: "Kenya personifies the best and worst of nature tourism," he told the gathering. "Few countries offer such a golden opportunity to take stock of where nature tourism stands today, warts and all. . . . [T]he workshop will be an acid test of how far ecotourism has come and whether it can indeed offer guidelines for sustainable nature tourism. The test for Kenya is a test for ecotourism throughout the world."[107] In a similar vein, Cornell University professor Charis Cussins predicts that if Kenya's ecotourism experiment fails, its repercussions would be "colossal and immediate, like the recoil of a highly loaded spring." Cussins, an expert in community-based conservation, argues, "This is one of the greatest experiments we've ever had. To lose this case study in local custodianship would be a tragedy, and a tremendous loss to the world." While this experiment is among the world's longest running, its record, when stacked up against the definition of real ecotourism, is very mixed.

1. *Travel to natural destinations.* Since the 1960s, Kenya has been Africa's most popular wildlife tourism destination. Despite the growth of beach tourism, more than 90 percent of tourists visiting Kenya go "on safari" to a game park, even if only for a day, and nearly 80 percent of those interviewed cited nature and wildlife as their major reasons for coming to Kenya.[108]

2. *Minimizes impact.* On this criterion, Kenya's record is fairly poor, particularly in the most popular game-viewing areas. Since the 1970s, the quality of Kenya's national parks and reserves has declined as a result of poorly controlled and, in the half dozen most populated locations, excessive tourism. Protected areas have suffered from the presence of too many lodges, which consume water, wood, and electricity and produce large amounts of waste; off-road driving, which ruins the land and disturbs the wildlife; poaching, which has ebbed and flowed over the years and from park to park; and competition from a rapidly expanding human population and both large- and small-scale farming. With some two-thirds of Kenya's wildlife living outside protected areas, the conflict between humans and wildlife is accelerating rapidly.

   In an article summing up the state of ecotourism in Kenya, Western asks, "Why does Kenya, a pioneer in ecotourism, today lag far behind Latin America and Southern Africa?" He goes on to lament that these days, "Kenya is better known for its tourism gone wrong, conjuring up visions of minibus congestion around lions, harassment of cheetahs, mindless destruction of habitat due to unregulated off-road driving, lodge congestion in parks, and coral reef destruction by rapacious tourists. As a result, Kenya today has the unenviable reputation of being the Costa del Sol of the wildlife world—overcrowded, overrated, and badly abused—with visitors decamping for greener pastures."[109]

3. *Builds environmental awareness.* Here, the record is mixed. While Kenya has excellent tour companies and naturalist guides, one of the most common complaints from tourists is that their guides have poor interpretive skills, lessening the overall quality of the nature tourism experience. In terms of environmental awareness among Kenyans, the country has long hosted a variety of local and international conservation and wildlife organizations, but these have been dominated by white settlers and expatriates and have catered to a black, largely urban, elite. Kenya has wildlife clubs for schoolchildren and some of its leading environmental activists are products of these clubs, but most Kenyans are never able to visit parks and reserves. The Ecotourism Society of Kenya, begun with high hope that it would be a watchdog over the industry, suffered from low visibility, government suspicion, and manipulation by powerful white ranchers and tour operators. Historically, there has been a clash between the environmental practices of the Maasai and other pastoralists, who for centuries have coexisted peacefully with wildlife, and those of the colonialists, who slaughtered wild game for pleasure and set up national parks by evicting the traditional human inhabitants.[110] One of the most promising early developments in the COBRA program has been evidence that at least in the four rural project areas, "community attitudes towards KWS and community-based conservation have changed radically."[111] But across the board, understanding of modern environmentalism runs shallow, and many Kenyans view protection of wildlife as an economic activity controlled by the small white settler class, wealthy foreigners, and politically powerful black Kenyans.

4. *Provides direct financial benefits for conservation.* Until recently, Kenya faced little competition from elsewhere in Africa, and tourism became the country's top dollar earner with little overseas promotion, investment in infrastructure, or national planning and regulation. Similarly, millions of dollars' worth of foreign aid has, since the 1970s, been given to support programs in Kenya's parks and reserves. But through corruption, mismanagement, and ill-conceived projects, little of this money has gone for environmental protection and improvement in the national or county council–controlled parks and reserves. Despite the bans on hunting and trade in ivory, wildlife numbers continue to decline in many of Kenya's parks and reserves. The only exceptions are Amboseli National Park, Maasai Mara Game Reserve, and a few

smaller reserves where the local people are seeing at least some direct benefits from tourism and wildlife protection.

Private reserve owners portray themselves, often condescendingly, as stepping into the breach to do the type of sound wildlife conservation that the government has failed to do. Even though they may offer a short-term solution to, for instance, "the mess in the Mara" and rhino poaching, these privately owned ranches are too small, too lightly taxed, and too removed from Kenya's rural poor to offer long-term benefits for conservation, the national economy, or local communities. In Kenya, as elsewhere, more attention needs to be given to ways in which these private reserves on old colonial estates can contribute financially to the country. Some possibilities include paying a percentage of the gate fee or bed levy, forming genuine partnerships with surrounding communities, establishing more village-run game reserves, assisting local artisans to set up cooperatives, and opening their gates for local schoolchildren to visit and learn about birds and wildlife.

5. *Provides financial benefits and empowerment for local people.* Despite the growth of both private reserves and beach tourism, the heart of Kenya's nature tourism and ecotourism industry remains its national parks and reserves and their surrounding buffer zones. It is in these areas that Kenya has conducted its most innovative and long-term ecotourism experiments. Over the course of three decades, the community conservation schemes in Amboseli and Maasai Mara followed somewhat different paths but produced some common lessons. These experiments are significant because they were large, government-backed initiatives involving the country's foremost tourist attractions, sizable populations, and, at times, international conservation and lending agencies. They represent the most concerted, long-term efforts in Africa to apply ecotourism principles on a national scale.

Both international and national economic and political conditions have undermined and marginalized these efforts to develop ecotourism. During the 1990s, the KWS's nearly 300 community-based conservation projects have aimed to apply ecotourism principles and practices more broadly throughout the park system. Most are revenue-sharing projects; however, the emphasis has increasingly been on capacity building, community investments, and income-generating activities tied to wildlife conservation and tourism. There is a need to better tie revenue sharing with positive community programs to improve wildlife conservation and management.[112]

In terms of employment within the tourism industry, the county councils' deep involvement in Maasai Mara and Amboseli has meant that unlike the situation in Tanzania, significant numbers of Maasai have long been hired as guides, drivers, hotel staff, artisans, and cultural performers. Production of traditional handicrafts "has been an

integral feature of Kenya's tourism development" and capital requirements have been low, permitting small entrepreneurs, including
women, to enter this field.[113]

In terms of ownership, although at the national level much of
Kenya's tourism industry is in the hands of local whites or international corporations, the country does have a well-established and powerful black elite who are involved in tourism enterprises. However, the
imposition of structural adjustment policies and trade and investment
liberalizations beginning in the mid-1980s not only undercut the government's investment in social services and infrastructure but also
allowed foreign competition to undermine the development of local
ownership.

6. *Respects local culture.* On this point, the record is poor. From the outset, Kenya's conservation and tourism policies have been tied to big
   game hunting, colonial control, and Western social and environmental
   values that are at odds with the values and needs of Kenya's rural farmers and pastoralists. In his study of Kenya's environmental values and
   nature-based tourism, John Akama contends that "the socioeconomic
   conditions which led to increasing public support of wildlife conservation and the appreciation of the aesthetic and ethical values of wildlife
   are, most often, non-existent in rural Kenya."[114] While there are some
   promising experiments with cultural centers and artisan cooperatives,
   Kenya's nature tourism continues to suffer all the negative cultural
   abuses of conventional mass tourism. The government and tourist
   industry, fixated on capturing dollars, have not addressed this problem
   with determination and imagination.

7. *Supports human rights and democratic movements.* Political conflicts in
   Kenya have intensified during the 1990s, and rural struggles have
   frequently centered on the use of land, including the question of
   who should control the parks and reserves and the profits from
   nature-based tourism. Although some of the community-based ecotourism projects have explicitly challenged the political status quo,
   most have been rather narrowly focused on income generation and
   social welfare. On the national level, despite the growth of independent NGOs and a proliferation of political parties, opposition to the
   Moi government remains deeply fractionalized. The government has
   moved successfully, although often heavy-handedly, to control and
   confine opposition groups. During the 1990s, tourism in Kenya
   dropped, and in 1997, as political violence and El Niño rains intensified, it plummeted, falling further in the wake of the August 1998 U.S.
   Embassy bombings. Although protests and acts of sabotage have occasionally targeted tourists and tourism facilities, Kenya's prodemocracy
   forces have yet to call for an international boycott by investors and
   tourists. Tourists are therefore staying away from Kenya out of fear

of personal danger and discomfort rather than out of opposition to the country's corrupt and autocratic government. David Western has acknowledged that Kenya has a "tarnished image" and valiantly pledged to develop "new and innovative approaches that will put it back at center stage on the ecotourism map in the coming decade."[115] But as Western's own political downfall illustrates, ecotourism principles and practices cannot be fully and nationally implemented until Kenya has a government committed to public accountability, political democracy, social justice, respect for human rights, and equitable and sustainable economic development.

Notes

1. L. Talbot and P. Olindo, "Kenya: The Maasai Mara and Amboseli Reserves," in Agnes Kiss, ed., *Living with Wildlife: Wildlife Resource Management with Local Participation in Africa*, World Bank Technical Paper No. 130, Africa Technical Department Series (Washington, D.C.: World Bank, 1990), p. 67.

2. Joseph Carvahlo, *COBRA Project: Financial and Economic Analysis* (Nairobi: U.S. Agency for International Development, Bureau for Africa, Regional Economic Development Services Office, East and Southern Africa, September 1991), p. 1.

3. Perez Olindo, "The Old Man of Nature Tourism: Kenya," in Tensie Whelan, ed., *Nature Tourism: Managing for the Environment* (Washington, D.C.: Island Press, 1991), p. 23.

4. David Western, "Ecotourism: The Kenya Challenge," in C. G. Gakahu and B. E. Goode, eds., *Ecotourism and Sustainable Development in Kenya*, proceedings of the Kenya Ecotourism Workshop, Lake Nakuru National Park September 13–17, 1992 (Nairobi: Wildlife Conservation International, 1992), p. 17.

5. John S. Akama, "Western Environmental Values and Nature-Based Tourism in Kenya," *Tourism Management* 17, no. 8 (1996): 568.

6. Ibid., p. 568.

7. Grace Lusiola, "The Role of the COBRA Project in Economic Development of Local Communities," in Gakahu and Goode, *Ecotourism and Sustainable Development*, p. 125; David Western, "Ecosystem Conservation and Rural Development: The Case of Amboseli," in David Western and R. Michael Wright, eds., *Natural Connections: Perspectives in Community-Based Conservation* (Washington, D.C.: Island Press, 1994), p. 15.

8. "Executive Summary," untitled 1991 USAID document on COBRA project, p. 3.

9. Paul Eagles, Jennifer Ballantine, and David Fennell, *Marketing to the Ecotourist: Case Studies from Kenya and Costa Rica* (Waterloo, Ontario: University of Waterloo, Department of Recreation and Leisure Studies, n.d.), p. 3.

10. Western, "Ecotourism: The Kenya Challenge," p. 17.

11. Ibid., p. 18.

12. Olindo, "Old Man," p. 29.

13. Ibid., p. 25.

14. Ibid., p. 29.

15. Carvahlo, *COBRA Project*, pp. 2–3.

16. Raymond Bonner, *At the Hand of Man: Peril and Hope for Africa's Wildlife* (New York: Vintage Books, 1994), pp. 130–131.

17. Nigel Carpenter, Kenya Wildlife Service, "Revenue Generation for the Management and Conservation of Protected Areas" (paper presented at The Ecotourism Society workshop, Costa Rica, October 1995), p. 6.

18. "Executive Summary," untitled USAID document, p. 2. North Americans make up only a modest 14 percent of tourists. Carvahlo, *COBRA Project*, p. 2.

19. World Tourism Organization (WTO), *Yearbook of Tourism Statistics*, vols. 1 and 2 (Madrid: WTO, 1995).

20. Somerset Waters, *Travel Industry World Yearbook: The Big Picture—1996–97*, vol. 40 (New York: Child & Waters, 1997), p. 142.

21. David Western, "Handling the Wildlife Time-Bomb That Is KWS," *The East African*, November 17–23, 1997; Nation reporter and AFP (Agence France Presse), "Travel Warnings Issued," *Nairobi Sunday Nation*, August 9, 1998.

22. Various other articles regarding the embassy bombings and their impact on tourism.

23. Kenya Wildlife Service, "Wildlife Policy 1996," draft, January 15, 1996, pp. 1–2.

24. Western, "Ecosystem Conservation and Rural Development," p. 37.

25. "Executive Summary," untitled USAID document, p. 4.

26. Lusiola, "Role of the COBRA Project," p. 125.

27. "Executive Summary," untitled USAID document, pp. 4–6. Several USAID reports also panned the Kenyan government's performance and the World Bank project. Although wildlife-based tourism was bringing in around $200 million a year, "most of those who border Kenya's parks and reserves received few, if any, tangible benefits from tourism-based utilization," concluded one report. Carvahlo, *COBRA Project*, p. 2.

28. Ibid.

29. Bonner, *At the Hand of Man*, pp. 130–159.

30. Interview with Richard Leakey, Washington, D.C., April 1996; Communications with David Western, June 1998. Western said that by June 1989, well before the CITES meeting, the Ivory Trade Review Group had convinced the United States, Europe, Japan, Hong Kong, and other countries to impose domestic bans on ivory, and this made CITES's international ban inevitable.

31. Interview with Leakey.

32. Kevin Fedarko, "When Elephants Collide: Two Legends of Conservation Vie for the Soul of Kenya's Hallowed National Parks," *Outside*, June 1998, p. 25.

33. "Executive Summary," untitled USAID document, p. 1.

34. Ibid., p. 6.

35. Bonner, *At the Hand of Man*, p. 132; Interview with Leakey.

36. "Executive Summary," untitled USAID document, p. 1.

37. Ibid., p. 13; Lusiola, "Role of the COBRA Project," p. 127; *Mid-Term Evaluation of the COBRA Project Synthesis of Findings and Recommendations* (Washington, D.C.: U.S. Agency for International Development, May 1996), pp. 8–9.

38. Carvahlo, *COBRA Project,* p. 6, 13.

39. Lusiola, "Role of the COBRA Project," p. 126.

40. "After the Investigation, a Damning Report," *Nairobi Daily Nation,* April 2, 1994.

41. Costas Christ, "Kenya Makes Revenue Sharing Top Priority," *The Ecotourism Society Newsletter,* 4, no. 1 (winter 1994): 1–2; Interview with Mark Stanley Price, Africa director, African Wildlife Foundation, April 1996.

42. Interview with Leakey.

43. Fedarko, "When Elephants Collide," p. 26.

44. Western, "Handling the Wildlife Time-Bomb"; Communications with Western, June 1998. Western says that salaries and benefits have always consumed half of the KWS's income.

45. Donatella Lorch, "Noted Kenya Conservationist Resigning in a Political Storm," *New York Times,* January 15, 1994, p. 3; "Richard Leakey: His Early Life, Careers, and Presidential Aspirations," *60 Minutes* (CBS), February 4, 1996.

46. David Western, "Ecotourism at the Crossroads in Kenya," *The Ecotourism Society,* 3rd quarter 1997, p. 1.

47. USAID, *Mid-Term Evaluation,* pp. 8–9.

48. Ibid., p. ii.

49. Kenya Wildlife Service and African Wildlife Foundation, "Summaries and Conclusions from Five Components of the Wildlife Utilisation Study," draft, September 1995; USAID, *Mid-Term Evaluation,* pp. 16–17.

50. Interviews with Meitamei Ole Dapash, 1996–1997; Meitamei Ole Dapash, "The Future of the Maasai People and Wildlife," *Satya,* December 1997; "CITES 1997: What Will Happen to the Elephants?" and "Poaching Holocaust Hits Kenya's Elephants," *Care for the Wild News,* winter 1997; Correspondence with David Western.

51. Fedarko, "When Elephants Collide," pp. 24–25.

52. By contrast, the director of Tanzania's national park service was earning a mere one-fifth of the salary of Western's personal assistant. Economist Intelligence Unit, *Kenya: EIU Country Report,* 1st quarter 1998, p. 19.

53. Reported in Michael McRae, "Survival Test for Kenya's Wildlife," *Science* 280 (April 24, 1998): 510–512.

54. Knowledgeable experts say that despite the problems with the COBRA project, USAID was, in reality, reluctant to shut it down because it fit into one of the agency's priority areas and it justified the size of its mission in Nairobi.

55. Michael McRae, "Crisis Management," *Science* 280 (April 24, 1998): 512; Interviews with World Bank officials, who asked not to be identified, June 1998.

56. Correspondence with Robert Hall, June 1998.

57. Kipkoech Tanui and Esther Im, "David Western Replaced at KWS," *Nairobi Daily Nation,* May 22, 1998; Kipkoech Tanui and Esther Im, "Why I've Lost My KWS Job—Western," *Nairobi Daily Nation,* May 23, 1998; Njeri Rugene and Kenya News Agency (KNA), "Moi Criticises Western," *Nairobi Sunday Nation,* May 24, 1998; Agence France Press (AFP), untitled story, May 23, 1998; David Western, "Press Statement on Termination of My Contract," press release, May 22, 1998.

58. David Western, letter, and Kurt Benirschke et al., letter, "Wildlife Conservation in Kenya," *Science* 280 (June 5, 1998): 1507–1510.

59. Interviews with officials at international conservation organizations based in Washington, D.C., May–June 1998.

60. Luke Odhiambo, "Kenya's Wildlife Service Chief Resigns in Mine Controversy," Agence France Presse, Nairobi, September 18, 1998; Chegu Mbitiru, "Leakey to Head Wildlife Service," *The Nation,* Nairobi, September 25, 1998; other articles and correspondence obtained from the Africa Wildlife Foundation office in Washington, D.C.

61. Talbot and Olindo, "Kenya," p. 69.

62. Western, "Ecosystem Conservation and Rural Development," p. 15.

63. Ibid., pp. 15–17.

64. Ibid., p. 18.

65. Talbot and Olindo, "Kenya," p. 69.

66. J. Waithaka, "Tourism-Associated Impacts in Tanzania," p. 79, and M. K. Koikai, "Why Maasai Mara Is the Most Visited Reserve in East Africa," pp. 8–9, in C. G. Gakahu, ed., *Tourist Attitudes and Use Impacts in Maasai Mara National Reserve,* proceedings of workshop organized by Wildlife Conservation International, Maasai Mara Game Reserve, March 1991 (Nairobi: English Press, 1992).

67. It was originally called the Narok District Council, but to minimize confusion I have referred to it as the Narok County Council, the postcolonial name, throughout this book.

68. Talbot and Olindo, "Kenya," p. 70.

69. C. G. Gakahu, "Visitor Dispersal Strategies in Ecotourism Management" (paper presented at Fourth World Congress of National Parks and Protected Areas, Caracas, Venezuela, February 1992), p. 11.

70. W. Henry, J. Waithaka, and C. G. Gakahu, "Visitor Attitudes, Perceptions, Norms, and Use Patterns Influencing Visitor Carrying Capacity," p. 57, and J. Sindiyo, "Management Proposal for the Mara Dispersal Areas," p. 77, in Gakahu, ed., *Tourist Attitudes.*

71. Koikai, "Most Visited Reserve," p. 9.

72. Christ, "Kenya Makes Revenue Sharing Top Priority," p. 1.

73. Quote contained in correspondence from Robert Hall, a consultant who evaluates international development projects in Africa, with a specialization in environmental, community-based, and institutional issues, June 1998.

74. C. G. Gakahu, "Framework for Establishing Potential Visitor Capacity," in Gakahu, ed., *Tourist Attitudes,* pp. 62–63.

75. Henry, Waithaka, and Gakahu, "Visitor Attitudes," pp. 39–61.

76. Correspondence with Western, June 1998.

77. Interviews; Sindiyo, "Management Proposal," p. 77.

78. Henry, Waithaka, and Gakahu, "Visitor Attitudes," p. 57.

79. Interviews in Kenya, July 1995; Carvahlo, *COBRA Project,* p. 11; John Ole Kisimir, "Who Is Exploiting the Other?" *Nairobi Daily Nation,* July 1, 1998. (Internet: http://www.nationaudio.com/news/dailynation/010798/features/fn3.html).

80. Walter Chin, "Kenya: The Maasai," *Sports Illustrated* (February 20, 1998), p. 66.

81. Kisimir, "Who Is Exploiting."

82. David Western and consultant Robert Hall concurred with my view that Olchoro O'rowu is a successful ecotourism experiment. Correspondence with Western and Hall, June 1998.

83. Interviews and correspondence with Steve Kuluo, Gakahu, Western, and Hall; David Western, however, questions whether Olchoro O'rowu can serve as a model for other community-based ecotourism projects. It is, Western states, "quite different from the type of community-based program that is being set up over much of Kenya." Similarly, consultant Robert Hall adds, "It is one thing to divide Shs. 250,000 among 8 families. It is something else entirely to divide it among 200 families."

84. Gakahu, "Visitor Dispersed Strategies," p. 10.

85. David Drummond, "Impacts of Tourism on the Ecology of Maasai Mara," *Wajibu,* 10, no. 1 (1995): 9–11.

86. Talbot and Olindo, "Kenya," p. 70.

87. Western, "Ecosystem Conservation and Rural Development," p. 30.

88. Ibid., p. 34; Communications with Western, June 1998.

89. Western, "Ecosystem Conservation and Rural Development," p. 35.

90. Ibid., p. 36.

91. Ibid., p. 35.

92. Bonner, *At the Hand of Man,* p. 229.

93. Ibid., p. 230.

94. Western, "Ecosystem Conservation and Rural Development," p. 42.

95. Talbot and Olindo, "Kenya," p. 73.

96. Western, "Ecosystem Conservation and Rural Development," pp. 42–43; "Executive Summary," untitled USAID document, p. 18; Bonner, *At the Hand of Man,* p. 230.

97. Western, "Ecotourism at the Crossroads," p. 2.

98. James McKinley, "Kimana Tikondo Group Journal: Warily, the Masai Embrace the Animal Kingdom," *New York Times,* March 13, 1996.

99. Western, "Ecosystem Conservation and Rural Development," p. 44.

100. Traditionally the "big five" were the preferred hunting trophies—lions, buffalos, elephants, leopards, rhinos—although nowadays camera safaris often substitute cheetahs for buffalos.

101. Claudia Alderman, "The Economics and the Role of Privately Owned Lands Used for Nature Tourism, Education, and Conservation" (paper presented at Fourth World Congress of National Parks and Protected Areas, Caracas, Venezuela, February 1992).

102. Literature from the Ecotourism Society of Kenya; Western, "Ecotourism at the Crossroads," p. 2.

103. International Resources Group, *Ecotourism: A Viable Alternative for Sustainable Management of Natural Resources in Africa* (Washington, D.C.: U.S. Agency for International Development, Bureau of Africa, June 1992), p. 33.

104. Mike Steere, "Manor Stays Give Tourists More Intimate View of Kenyan Wildlife, Land," *Cincinnati Enquirer,* n.d., obtained from Phil Osborne.

105. Interviews with Gakahu, Costas Christ, and Ole Dapash; documents from the Ecotourism Society of Kenya, including "Mission and Values," and "The Ecotourism Partnership."

106. Correspondence with Western, June 1998.

107. Program for "Ecotourism at the Crossroads," conference, October 31–November 3, 1997, Nairobi; Western, "Ecotourism at the Crossroads," p. 4; Fedarko, "When Elephants Collide," p. 26.

108. Carpenter, "Revenue Generation," p. 6.

109. Western, "Ecotourism at the Crossroads," p. 2.

110. Akama, "Western Environmental Values," pp. 567–574.

111. USAID, *Mid-Term Evaluation,* p. ii.

112. Ibid., pp. 2, 7–9, 11, 13.

113. Carvahlo, *COBRA Project,* pp. 10–11.

114. Akama, "Western Environmental Values," p. 567.

115. Correspondence with Western, June 1998; Western, "Ecotourism at the Crossroads," p. 2.

Chapter 10

South Africa: People and Parks under Majority Rule

It is August 1995, and Chris Marais sits in his spacious, tidy office in Kruger National Park, South Africa. All staff members within view, with the exception of the woman who serves us tea, are white. Outside there are flowered lawns, a golf course, a swimming pool, other administrative buildings, several museums, a library, a shop, a police station, a bank with an automated teller machine, a self-service laundry, restaurants, and a dog cemetery (Afrikaners love their dogs). Nearby is the park's largest rest camp—dispersed modules of cottages, houses, tents, and huts with electricity, refrigerators, private baths, and tasteful furnishings, many with air-conditioning. Kruger National Park, located in the country's Northern and Mpumalanga Provinces, along its borders with Mozambique and Zimbabwe, is the flagship of South Africa's world-renowned national park system. Covering a staggering 19,425 square kilometers (7,500 square miles), Kruger is about the size of New Jersey. In addition to the facilities here at its Skukuza headquarters, Kruger has twenty-three other rest camps, including meticulously remodeled whitewashed wattle-and-daub guest houses dating from the 1930s; secluded cottages built of rough stone, wood, and thatching grass; and a tasteful, modern conference facility with theaters, lecture hall, and boardroom. It accounts for almost 80 percent of the National Parks Board's bed-night capacity and earns more than 80 percent of the total revenue. As one of South Africa's most heavily visited parks, Kruger not only pays for itself but also has helped finance other, less well known parks.[1]

The drawing card, of course, is the game, including, according to Kruger's official list, 29,142 zebras, 2,314 hippos, 250–300 cheetahs, 4,600 giraffes, 3,150 kudu, 1,425 waterbuck, 350-plus wild dogs, more than 500 species of birds, and all of the "big five": elephants (7,834), rhinos (220 black and 1,871 white), leopards (600–900), Cape buffalo (15,253), and lions (1,500-plus). The park offers multiple ways to view the game: self-guided tours, with tourists driving their own cars; bush drives with (almost certainly) a white ranger and a black tracker; night drives; guided walking tours; and one- to five-day hikes conducted by armed rangers. In contrast with the rough, vast, and untended wildness of East Africa's game parks, Kruger's paved roads and meticulous planning and grooming make it feel more like a tasteful, tranquil, upscale theme park.

Indeed, over the past century, South Africa has built some of the world's most scientifically managed, best-policed, most luxurious, least expensive, and most exclusive national parks. Subsidized with millions of rand per year in government funding, South Africa's park system served a certain vision of conservation and the pleasures of the white elite. Like South Africa's other game parks, Kruger has been, as one environmentalist explained, run by an "old white boys network": a small community of managers, conservationists, and scientists that was 99 percent white and very ingrown, with a pecking order and an "us-versus-them" mentality. The "them" are the sprawling, impoverished rural communities ringing Kruger and other parks where unemployment ranges as high as 40 percent and political expectations are soaring. In visiting Kruger and other South African parks a few years after President Nelson Mandela took office, I found them, on the surface, surprisingly unchanged by South Africa's transition to majority rule: their senior and mid-level staff and clientele were still overwhelmingly white.

But behind its facade of apartheid-as-usual, Kruger National Park, like nearly every institution in what everyone terms "the new South Africa," has been under tremendous pressure to change. By 1998, when Kruger celebrated its centennial, there was a black African director and the board had instituted a transformation program to remedy past imbalances in hiring and bring in more black visitors.

"We [in Kruger] have had an island existence," says Marais, reflecting on the mentality that guided park management during the era of white rule. Marais, a slight, mild-mannered official with a quick mind and a gentle disposition, explains, "Our view had been that conservationists tended only to wildlife and ecology and left social welfare to others." That view began to rapidly erode as the apartheid wall crumbled following Mandela's release from prison in 1990. In 1992, some South African reporters, social activists, and politicians started writing and talking about the litany of complaints coming from the communities just outside the park's boundaries. A 1992 BBC documentary on conservation in South Africa opened with a scene of angry youths in a township on the edge of Kruger singing, "Weep, Kruger, you shall weep." Kruger, the youths proclaimed, is a place where animals roam free while Africans who enter to collect firewood or hunt an antelope to feed their family are arrested.[2]

The Creation of Apartheid's Parks

When apartheid ended in 1994, 5.52 percent (about 67,340 square kilometers, or 26,000 square miles) of South Africa's total land area was under state-run wildlife protection.[3] This included 16 national parks (with 6 more in the process of formation) and more than 100 provincial or homeland nature conservation areas. A somewhat larger amount (some 80,290 square kilometers, or 31,000 square miles) was protected in 9,000 privately owned game farms and nature reserves that offered upscale hunting safaris and lodges. In addition, there were small protected areas controlled by urban municipalities or regional governments as well as forests and mountain catchments protected by the country's conservation laws.[4] But the expanse and tranquility of these public and private parks and reserves mask the reality that they were all created by evicting tens of thousands of Africans from their homes and lands. Built through forced relocations, protected with military techniques, financed through heavy government subsidies, and run with political and social blinders, South Africa's parks became some of the most luxurious and racially exclusive playgrounds in the world. They are today among the bitterest legacies of apartheid.

The creation of Kruger, South Africa's first park and the second oldest in Africa, began in the 1890s, when Boer farmers trekked into what they called the Transvaal (today the Northern and Mpumalanga Provinces), forcibly evicting an estimated 3,000 Tsonga people from land between the Sabie and Crocodile Rivers. In an act signed by the president of the Transvaal, Paul Kruger, this vast area was proclaimed a game reserve. Like other settlers in the Transvaal, Kruger made a fortune through ivory hunting. Then, however, he became concerned that if the slaughter continued, the elephants and other game would be wiped out within a generation, as had already happened in South Africa's Cape Colony.

South Africa's parks and reserves were created as an emergency response to the decimation and rapid decline of wildlife that began as European settlers cleared and fenced land for ranches, agriculture, mines, and towns. Until the late nineteenth century, whites hunted wild game indiscriminately, sometimes for food, sometimes for trade, and increasingly for pleasure and trophies. Following the Anglo-Boer War at the turn of the century, the British seized control of the Transvaal, created more reserves, and, in 1926, passed the National Parks Act and merged the reserves into Kruger National Park.

From the outset, park authorities had two mandates: to conserve wildlife and to promote tourism. Finding the park largely denuded of game, the first ranger, Major James Stevenson-Hamilton, set about restocking the park and establishing a system of armed patrols and fences, which is still in use. Between 1926 and 1969, Kruger's borders remained substantially the same and Africans within its boundaries continued to be forcibly removed.[5]

In the precolonial era, traditional hunting practices and, often, a conservation ethic that reserved rare species for royalty and ceremonial functions ensured that Africans and wildlife coexisted in equilibrium. It was only with the advent of colonial game reserves that indigenous Africans began to view wildlife with hostility. Not only were Africans forcibly moved to over-crowded and marginal agricultural lands on the periphery of these new reserves; colonial laws also denied them hunting and fishing licenses and the right to use firearms or hunting dogs. They were also forbidden to kill wildlife that wandered outside the reserves and destroyed their crops and domestic animals, and they were banned from collecting any wood or grasses within the reserves. Invariably, the colonial state chose to protect wildlife instead of the local Africans. In times of drought or when water was scarce, Africans were forced to move out. "From 1948 [the year apartheid officially began]," recounted villager James Maluleke, "the park started bringing in lots of elephants. They [the authorities] said people are coming to see the animals so it is better that you move."[6]

Couched in terms of conservation protection and tourism, these harsh policies also helped turn some rural farmers and herders into an impover-ished black proletariat. Through forced labor and prison labor, Africans on the periphery of the parks and reserves were compelled to build roads and clear bush while others provided labor for South Africa's mines and indus-tries. Today, 66 percent of those living in the Northern Province, adjacent to Kruger are subsistence farmers. In 1991, more than two-thirds of the Africans in this province, the poorest province in South Africa, received no income; fewer than a third of adults were literate, and almost a third of chil-dren under the age of five were chronically malnourished.[7]

Historically, South Africa's parks have been closely linked to military and paramilitary personnel and operations. Parks have been used as staging areas, rear bases, and smuggling routes for the region's anticolonial and civil wars. Today, South Africa's military is the country's largest single land-holder,[8] and its properties include parks and reserves. As elsewhere in Africa, the park service includes many former military officers and its tactics mirror military operations. In the 1980s and early 1990s, for instance, Kruger was patrolled by a military unit trained by South African Defence Force instruc-tors, and the border Kruger shared with Mozambique was one of the most strategically sensitive in southern Africa. Close to Kruger's headquarters at Skukuza, a secret rest camp called Jakkalsbessie was built for clandestine ministerial and military meetings with apartheid's allies, and just on the park's edge, at Phalaborwa, there was a clandestine support base for the right-wing Mozambique rebel army the Mozambican National Resistance, known as Renamo.

Although South Africa's national park system was a product of and instrument for white rule, it managed to maintain a benevolent image under apartheid. In the eyes of most white South Africans and much of the Western world, wildlife protection was viewed as "a righteous cause," imple-mented with scientific and technical professionalism and unsullied by the country's policies.[9] While apartheid South Africa was officially shunned by the rest of the world, its park system and conservation efforts continued to receive international accolades.

That South Africa's parks and conservation policies were shielded from negative publicity is due in part to the quiet but influential role of prominent apartheid politicians and businessmen within a leading international conservation organization, the World Wide Fund for Nature (WWF, known in the United States and Canada as the World Wildlife Fund). In recent years, WWF, particularly its U.S. branch, has positioned itself at the center of the ecotourism discourse and movement. Yet in South Africa, as well as elsewhere in Africa, it was, since its founding in 1961, closely aligned with both white rule and the park system's old guard. In 1968, WWF International's president, Bernhard, prince of the Netherlands, suggested to his friend Dr. Anton Rupert, one of South Africa's wealthiest and most powerful Afrikaner businessmen, that he form a national branch of WWF. Rupert agreed, founding the Southern Africa Nature Foundation (now WWF–South Africa), with himself as president and a board composed of other prominent businessmen. Rupert, whose financial empire includes global tobacco interests, also joined WWF International's Executive Committee and for twenty-two years served on its Board of Trustees, where he wielded enormous influence in the organization's inner circles.

Rupert contributed financially to WWF, but his greatest contribution was creation of the 1001 Club, a multimillion-dollar endowment scheme that has given WWF International wide financial and administrative independence from WWF's thirty-odd national sections. Under the scheme, a thousand wealthy individuals—Bernhard was the "1"—were asked to make onetime contributions of $10,000 each to WWF's international headquarters in Gland, Switzerland. Donors were given lifetime membership in WWF and a guarantee of anonymity, but in the late 1980s, some names were leaked to the press.[10] They included several international businessmen involved in circumventing the oil and arms embargo against South Africa as well as sixty—a disproportionately high number—South African contributors, among them prominent members of an even more secretive organization, the Afrikaner Broederbond, an Afrikaner nationalist society dedicated to the preservation of white rule.

WWF International never permitted scrutiny of its decisions, programs, or expenditures, so it is "difficult to know," according to Ray Bonner, who has closely examined WWF, "the extent of the influence that so much South African money has had on the organization's conservation work."[11] Some of its work involved secret military-type antipoaching operations in countries bordering South Africa. In 1989, the British press revealed details of one of the more sordid of these projects funded by WWF International. Code-named Operation Lock, the covert operation employed British mercenaries to train antipoaching units in South Africa and set up sting operations in Namibia and Mozambique. The recruits in these units included Renamo rebels and members of the notoriously brutal *koevoet*, the mainly Zulu counterinsurgency unit in Namibia. (When the *koevoet* was withdrawn from Namibia in 1990, some of its members joined the KwaZulu police, who were widely accused of involvement in the political violence fomented by the Zulu-led separatist Inkatha Freedom Party in that region.) WWF International initially denied these actions had authorized or funded Operation Lock, blaming it on John Hanks, head of WWF International's Africa program, who was subsequently forced to step down. Several years later, Ray Bonner obtained WWF memos proving that Operation Lock had been directly sanctioned by WWF International's director, Charles de Haes (an executive with Rupert's South African tobacco company), and financed by Prince Bernhard.[12]

Stephen Ellis, editor of *Africa Confidential* and one of those who exposed Operation Lock, went a step further, concluding that the South Africa lobby within WWF may also "account for the organizations failure to publicize or publicly condemn the role of South Africa in the international ivory trade."[13] Ellis laid out evidence indicating that between the late 1970s and late 1980s, South Africa had become a main conduit for illegal ivory and rhino horns from the rest of Africa. He cited, for instance, records showing that the apartheid government was exporting to the Far East many more tons of ivory than it had collected from culling. With the end of white rule and the civil wars in Mozambique, Namibia, and (more precariously) Angola, many of the South African–backed covert operations ceased; others—arms and ivory smuggling and support for Inkatha dissidents—were driven further underground. And, overnight it seemed, some of apartheid's collaborators in the national and provincial parks as well as in major conservation organizations such as WWF were proclaiming that local people must become partners in both conservation and tourism through a new strategy known as ecotourism.

Ecotourism in South Africa

Despite such opportunism by the apartheid old guard, the new South Africa widely and innovatively embraced ecotourism. Today, ecotourism is being promoted by the central government; its tourism agency, SATOUR; national and provincial park boards; academic programs at the University of Pretoria and elsewhere; the African National Congress (ANC); and many other groups. And here, more than elsewhere, ecotourism is defined as synonymous with local community involvement, profit sharing, and empowerment through tourism projects and conservation programs.

From the outset, the Mandela government was under enormous pressure to change the status quo in and around the park system. One of the first issues was whether the game parks would continue to exist at all. Throughout the country, marginalized and impoverished communities on the edges of the parks demanded that parkland from which they had been evicted be returned to them; that they be given access to firewood, plants, grazing pasture, water, and other resources inside the parks; and that they get real economic benefits from tourism. Quickly, the new government decided that the parks would not be dismantled, and President Mandela went further, pledging that the ANC would increase the amount of land under protection to 10 percent as recommended by the IUCN.[14] At the same time, the new government committed itself to reorganizing park operations, to carrying out substantial land redistribution, and to developing programs so that people on the periphery would begin to benefit from the parks and from tourism.

As in Cuba, the government embraced international tourism, including ecotourism, as a leading economic activity by which the country could jump-start its economy and move from isolation into full integration in the world economy. In 1993, the Mandela government announced an ambitious campaign to make tourism South Africa's number one industry by the year 2000, and SATOUR projected that the number of foreign tourists would rise from 3.6 million in 1994 to 9 million by the new millennium. One-quarter of these would be overseas visitors, generating some $2.5 billion.[15]

The blueprint for building the new South Africa was, initially, the Reconstruction and Development Program (RDP), the ANC's election campaign platform. The RDP's basic strategy included "participation of communities in management and decision making in wildlife conservation and the related tourism benefits." SATOUR's theme for 1996 was "Explore South Africa, Going Wild in '96," an international campaign that SATOUR officials described as designed to promote the country's ecotourism destinations. As an ecotourism study commissioned by SATOUR states, "The travel industry and, given the nature of South Africa's tourism products, 'ecotourism' in particular are increasingly viewed as a vehicle for redistributing wealth to underdeveloped rural areas in line with the principles of the Reconstruction and Development Programme."[16]

The task was enormous. Even more than Cuba, apartheid South Africa was an international pariah. The ANC-led boycott called on multilateral institutions and foreign countries, companies, and individuals to withdraw businesses and investments from South Africa; to forgo sports, cultural, and educational contacts; and to forgo travel to South Africa. The impact was clearly seen in tourism. Although statistics from the World Tourism Organization purport that even at the height of apartheid, South Africa had more foreign visitors than did any other sub-Saharan African country, these figures are deceptive because they include visitors from other African countries, many of whom came for shopping, business, or work-related activities. For instance, of South Africa's 3 million foreign visitors in 1993, 2.4 million were from other African countries and 618,508 were from other non-African countries, primarily England and Germany. In fact, according to one study, "South Africa was a net exporter of tourism during the apartheid years. Earnings from foreign tourists were some 40 percent less than the amount spent by South Africans abroad."[17] Between 1980 and 1987, tourist arrivals in South Africa fluctuated between a low of 645,000 and peak of 792,000; with the end of apartheid, arrivals jumped 30 percent in 1994 and 42 percent in 1995. By 1996, arrivals totalled over 4.6 million (see table 10.1). South Africa was transformed almost overnight from an international pariah to a fascinating "rainbow nation."[18]

Further, although foreign visitors surveyed showed tremendous support for the country's national parks, visiting game parks was a low priority, largely because of a shortage of accommodations within the parks. On average, foreigners spent only 1.5 days in game lodge accommodations, and only 16 percent visited Mpumalanga Province (formerly the Eastern Transvaal), South Africa's premier wildlife destination. As a SATOUR study concluded, "Although nature is a strong attraction for overseas tourists, the bulk end up staying with friends and relatives and/or hotels rather than game lodges for most of their stay here."[19]

In sharp contrast with the situation in East Africa, tourism in apartheid South Africa's game parks was predominantly domestic. In 1989, for instance, 90 percent of the visitors to Kruger National Park were South Africans, almost exclusively whites,[20] and more than 60 percent of the profits from nature-based tourism came from South Africans. "The local market," a SATOUR study concluded, "was overwhelmingly oriented towards the narrow high-income 'white' segment."[21]

Since the elimination of apartheid, South Africa's tourism attractions, including the nature-based facilities, are being opened and diversified in terms of race, national origin, and, to a degree, class. By 1998, backpacking had become one of South Africa's biggest tourism revenue earners, growing by 400 percent over the previous year. No longer simply cash-strapped students, backpackers these days include growing numbers of overseas professionals and families, many of whom are environmentally, culturally, and politically sensitive. Created for the country's white elite, South Africa's hos-

Table 10.1. South Africa's Tourism Growth

	1976	1981	1984	1988	1990	1992	1994	1995	1996	1997	2000[a]
Arrivals from outside Africa (in millions)	0.340	0.450	0.455	0.400	0.500	0.550	0.700	—	—	—	1.8
Total foreign arrivals (in millions)	—	0.709	0.792	0.805	1.7	2.7	3.7	4.2	4.64	5	9
Earnings (in billions of U.S. dollars)	—	0.658	0.610	0.673	0.992	1.3	1.42	1.43	1.74	2.2	2.5

Source: Correspondent, "Tourist Arrivals Worse in Kenya," *Nairobi Daily Nation*, August 5, 1998 (Internet: http://www.nationaudio.com/news/dailynation/050898/business/business3.html); visitor figures from overseas (outside Africa) from David Grossman and Eddie Koch, *Ecotourism Report—Nature Tourism in South Africa: Links with the Reconstruction and Development Program*, report prepared for SATOUR, August 1995, p. 16; figures for total foreigners and receipts from World Tourism Organization; projections for the year 2000 from SATOUR, in Global Environment Facility (GEF), *Mozambique: Transfrontier Conservation Areas Pilot and Institutional Strengthening Project*, Project Document (Washington, D.C.: GEF, December 1996), appendix 9-1, 9-2; Somerset Waters, *Travel Industry World Yearbook: The Big Picture, 1996–1997*, 40 (New York: Child & Waters, 1997), pp. 139, 146; World Tourism Organization, *Yearbook of Tourism Statistics* (Madrid, Spain: World Tourism Organization, 1995), pp. 12, 13, 26, 27; World Tourism Organization, *Yearbook of Tourism Statistics* (Madrid, Spain: World Tourism Organization, 1986), p. 18; World Tourism Organization, *Yearbook of Tourism Statistics* (Madrid, Spain: World Tourism Organization, 1988), p. 19.

[a]Projected.

Note: Figures are unavailable where there are blanks.

tels and other backpacker facilities are of exceptionally high quality, offering travelers detailed tourist information, transportation, and environmental education.[22]

South Africa's parks were officially opened to all races in the 1980s, but nonwhites were accommodated in separate facilities from whites, to avoid, park officials contended, "incidents." A 1989 study found that even low-income blacks were entering the market, often as day visitors. A subsequent study found that following the April 1994 elections and declaration of affirmative action, "a black executive class, and with it a new leisure traveler, [was] being created overnight."[23] Yet during my monthlong visit throughout much of South Africa in August 1995, I saw only a few black South African tourists in any of the government or private game park resorts, although many school groups were being bused into the parks and the parks were promoting day visitors from surrounding communities.

Kruger National Park: From Fences and Guns to Community Involvement and Ecotourism

The movement toward change in South Africa's national and provincial parks, though not always apparent to outsiders, began in earnest in 1990 with the legalization of the ANC and the freeing of Nelson Mandela. These momentous events sent shivers of anxiety through the National Parks Board's headquarters in Pretoria and its 4,000 park employees, many of whom feared the ANC would dismantle the organization and open the parks to black settlement. This didn't happen, however, for two main reasons. First, South Africa's new leadership recognized the park system as a national asset and a source of hard-currency tourism revenue. Second, the National Parks Board (now called South African National Parks, or SANP), under the leadership of Dr. G. A. ("Robbie") Robinson, who served as chief executive between 1991 and 1997, began to reform the organization from top to bottom.[24]

In Kruger, the process of change was prodded by investigative journalist Eddie Koch of the Johannesburg-based *Weekly Mail & Guardian* and members of a small, dynamic NGO called GEM (Group for Environmental Monitoring),[25] who had been interviewing people in the townships around the park. These investigators asked to meet with Kruger's top management to relay to them what people in the local communities were saying about the park.

In the following months, facilitators were brought in, workshops and meetings were held, and staff members were reshuffled. Park officials who remained began to see that they could no longer focus solely on nature conservation within a delineated microsystem without considering the demands of the "macroenvironment," that is, the people living on the park's periphery. As internal reports put it, management "accepted the fact that higher fences and bigger guns would not ensure a future for the KNP [Kruger National Park]." Under instructions from SANP chief executive Robinson, a new management philosophy, dubbed "an open system approach," was declared. Put succinctly, this new approach held that a successful national park can exist only in a sustainable society and that sustainability can be achieved only if the local communities control access to the financial and human resources.

As part of this "open" approach, Chris Marais, a former Calvinist minister, was, as head of Human Resources, selected to be Kruger National Park's chief liaison to the local communities, a position that had not existed before. In the months preceding South Africa's first all-races elections in April 1994, Marais and a small team of uniformed white Kruger officials began driving out to the bordering townships and holding public meetings. "It was a terrible experience, a total eye opener," recalls Marais. "I had no idea of the hostility. There were two or three incidents when I didn't think we'd get out alive."

With the help of tribal elders, new political leaders, and interpreters, Marais eventually helped to start four community forums: Lubambiswano, representing seventeen villages on the park's southeastern boundary; Hoxane, representing eight communities along the Sabie River; Phalaborwa, representing two townships; and Hlanganani, the largest and most politically turbulent forum, representing twenty-nine communities along the park's western boundary. Although the results have been mixed, the communities' demands are similar, including the three most pressing problems: (1) the communities' lack of resources, including water, wood, and food; (2) the killing of cattle by wild animals; and (3) land claims within the park.

Kruger officials have made some limited headway in dealing with these complex and costly problems: some farmers have been compensated for cattle killed by wild game, and some electric fencing is being installed between the park and the communities. In addition, some simpler issues have been tackled. Actions include giving communities access to ancestral graves inside the parks and beginning a number of "partnership" economic projects, such as buying hotel tablecloths and staff overalls, handicrafts, and vegetables from the local communities; training park guides; and helping traditional healers obtain plants and develop community nurseries. These steps aim, for the first time, to give the local communities a tiny share in tourism profits. But as Marais candidly admitted in an interview with me, "We conservationists like to show small movements and boast we're doing big things." Marais is at once realistic and optimistic. "We've only scratched the surface," he says, adding that the most fundamental change has been that lines of communication are now open. "At first, [the local communities] wanted answers *now*. But the change in attitude since then has been amazing. We walk in and people know us. We've become friends." Marais concludes, "The only thing [we at] Kruger can honestly say we've achieved is a relationship with the people where we can sit down and talk. This is a drop in the ocean."

In 1995, this low-key, methodical dialog erupted in a complex, high-stakes drama in the Punda Maria area, on Kruger's northern edge. The conflict pitted local land claims against mining interests, the military, a coalition of environmental organizations, and the park. The controversy centered on the Madimbo Corridor, an 80.5-kilometer (50-mile) stretch of land along the banks of the Limpopo River just south of the Zimbabwe border. Environmentalists consider this wild and beautiful area of riverine forests, floodplains, and baobab forests South Africa's last pristine wilderness and urge that it be conserved as part of Kruger. Members of the Venda and Tsonga communities, forcibly removed in the 1960s and 1980s so that Kruger could be extended to the Limpopo River, demanded restitution. The South African military, which had occupied this border zone to keep out Zimbabwean guerrillas and refugees, wanted to continue using the corridor for military training and pay compensation to local communities rather than permit them to move back. In mid-1995, while keeping the local communities at bay, the military granted diamond prospecting rights to the Madimbo Mining Corporation, a joint South African–Australian company known to have had ties to the old apartheid armed forces. Members of environmental groups and SANP personnel were outraged. Officials of South Africa's Wildlife Society stated, "If mining goes ahead it will most likely blow any future ecotourism ventures off the map, not to mention the irreversible ecological and archaeological impact."[26]

The displaced Tsonga and Venda people were divided in their response, with some villages opposed and others viewing mining as a potential economic boon in their arid savanna area. One group, the Makuleke, had been forcibly relocated from the Limpopo valley. With the support of an ecotourism consultant, a lawyer, a developer, and some German government funds, the Makuleke proposed to regain ownership of the land but leave it in the park and to build and operate a lodge in a partnership between the local community and the private sector. This plan appeared to be the best solution until diamonds were added to the equation. The prospecting was taking place on land just outside the park but still within the territory from which the Makuleke had been removed. Although environmentalists and park officials immediately warned that mining would irrefutably ruin the land, the mining company promised to follow strict environmental guidelines and to create 2,000 jobs. In contrast, the Makuleke's proposed lodge was slated to create only 33 jobs,[27] but, its supporters argued, the ecotourism project would generate income long after the mining company had closed down.

The Makuleke feared that once again, they would have no voice in how their land was to be used. In an interview published in the *Weekly Mail & Guardian,* tribal leader Gilbert Nwaila denounced the leading conservation organizations and park officials for failing to consult the local communities on the mining issue. "You should tell these people who like wildlife that they should come here and speak to us before they make statements about how our land should be used. And when they come, they should remember we suffered greatly when our villages were destroyed and our homes burnt down so that Kruger could be made bigger. It will be very difficult," the tribal leader concluded, "to convince our people that wildlife is better than mining—and it will be even more so if we are not spoken to properly."[28]

In delicate negotiations lasting for several years, the South African National Parks negotiators were initially somewhat intransigent. By 1997, however, SANP's chief executive, G. A. Robinson, whose commitment to change was often limited by a narrow vision, failure to back senior black staff members, and paranoia about his more conservative enemies inside the parks, had become largely dysfunctional and accepted a generous "golden handshake" retirement package, which was offered to a number of senior white park officials. He was replaced by Masuvo Msimang, who became the first black chief executive of South African National Parks. Then, following the appointment of a new SANP Board Land Claims Committee and with the backing of the board's chairman and environmental affairs minister, SANP negotiators were compelled to adopt a more reasonable stance. In March 1998, the SANP Board and the Makuleke community signed a historic agreement, hailed as a win-win situation, whereby the community agreed not to move back into the park and instead will comanage with SANP any new low-impact tourism developments.[29] While the struggle may not yet be completely resolved, it does signal that in the New South Africa ecotourism is at the negotiating table as a substantial, although as yet largely unproven, alternative. Regardless of the outcome, ecotourism has already helped to shift the terms of the debate to include discussion of the land rights of the local people, the environmental impact of mining and other destructive industries, the long-term economic sustainability of the various alternatives, and the involvement of local people in the economic enterprises.

The Seeds of Change within the Homelands

Permutations of the Kruger National Park experience are being played out all across South Africa, and the country today is a mosaic of ecotourism experimentation. According to many, the earliest experiments occurred, ironically, inside one of apartheid's most odious institutions: the Bantustans. Created in the 1960s and 1970s, South Africa's ten so-called independent "tribal homelands" were formed through the forced relocation of all Africans deemed, according to historian Allister Sparks, "surplus to the white man's needs in the city." In all, some 17 million people—44 percent of South Africa's total population—were stripped of their South African citizenship and relocated in ethnic groupings on just 17 percent of the country's poorest land. The so-called independent government of each ethnic group received "foreign aid" from South Africa and was run by handpicked African collaborators. They were loathed by their African occupants and ridiculed by the world community. The homelands were a political charade and an economic disaster, constituting, as Eddie Koch put it, "overcrowded rural ghettos."[30] One of the Mandela government's first moves was to abolish the homelands and reintegrate these territories into the new South Africa.

It was, however, in two of these homelands—Bophuthatswana (commonly called "Bop"), a fragmented collection of seven impoverished Tswana territories near the border with Botswana, and KaNgwane, on the southern edge of Kruger—that South Africa's ecotourism formed its roots. In 1979, two years after the Bophuthatswana homeland was formed, its repressive figurehead president, Chief Lucas Mangope, announced that his "country" would promote conservation and tourism by forming the 549-square kilometer (212-square mile) Pilanesberg National Park, a compact, biologically diverse stretch of volcanic hills and lush valleys. It was a massive operation for a poor state, and initially it followed South Africa's repressive formula for park creation. Thousands of subsistence cattle farmers, mostly BaKgatla people, members of a Tswana clan who opposed both the homeland and Chief Mangope, were moved out. Their homesteads were razed; alien plants were removed; water was brought in; camps, picnic sites, roads, and an educational center was constructed; and the boundary was fenced. With funding from WWF–South Africa, private companies, and the government, the park was restocked with indigenous wildlife.[31] Only lions were not reintroduced at this time.

Today, the "Bop" park board's headquarters (its official postapartheid name is the Northwest Park Board) in Pilanesberg National Park looks much like Kruger's—an attractive complex of offices located close to public recreational facilities, including restaurants and a bar, swimming pools, game rooms, chalets, a bird sanctuary, and beautifully planted and manicured lawns. In 1995, the official behind the large wooden park director's desk was Hector Magome, the park system's youthful, energetic, and sharp-minded acting director. A Tswana speaker, Magome was one of the park system's highest-level African administrators.[32]

Although Pilanesberg is one of the youngest of South Africa's parks, under Magome and his predecessors, it quickly gained a reputation as the most innovative and community sensitive in the country. "The significance of the Pilanesberg project," wrote ecological consultant David Grossman and journalist Eddie Koch, "lies in the fact that it was the first attempt, at least in greater South Africa, at integrating protected area conservation and community development."[33] The reasons are several. Pilanesberg offered better salary packages and thus attracted better people. By the early 1980s, Pilanesberg's management included a handful of black officials as well as some renegade whites from the national park system who were chafing under its apartheid-driven rigidity. They found Pilanesberg smaller, more intimate, and more flexible, in part because it was set up as an autonomous homeland institution rather than as part of South Africa's civil service structure. From the outset, Pilanesberg instituted revenue-generating projects, including hunting safaris, something that infuriated the national park's old guard. One ethically dubious but lucrative scheme permits big game hunters to shoot endangered white rhinos with tranquilizer dart guns and then have their photographs taken next to their sleeping "trophies." The park also began promoting outdoor rock music concerts at one of its campsites. In a joint venture with a private company, the Pilanesberg board built two luxury lodges and formed its own commercial subsidiary to establish other park facilities.

Although it is a pioneer in income-generating schemes, Pilanesberg, like South Africa's other parks, currently runs at a deficit, which is covered by a government grant.[34] Like all parks in the new South Africa, Pilanesberg is under pressure to become increasingly self-supporting. Under the homeland government, the staff at Pilanesberg set low entrance fees; built a day visitors' complex; set up programs for scholars, students, and teachers; and organized almost 200 youth conservation clubs in the surrounding black communities, all of which made the park more accessible to the mass market and helped build a constituency supporting its survival. "The Parks Board was the only agent of the government from which people could get friendly services," says David Grossman.

Pilanesberg's first director, Roger Collinson, moved over from the Natal Parks Board with, Magome says, "a personal vision long before the rest of the country that parks would do well if local blacks were involved." In the early 1980s, Collinson hired a British social anthropologist, Jeremy Keenan, to survey the surrounding communities to gauge their opinion of the park. Just as Kruger's Chris Marais discovered a dozen years later, Magome explains, Keenan found that "the BaKgatla people were pissed off with the park."

Over the next few years, Collinson and his successor, Levy "Rams" Rammutla (who, like Magome, is a Tswana speaker), instituted a variety of projects and, Magome says, "put us on the map in terms of progressive community projects." These included granting permission for local people to harvest firewood and medicinal plants and to visit ancestral grave sites in the park. Several hundred local people now work in the park or its hotels, and many senior positions are filled by Tswana people. (Most of the white employees hold technical or scientific positions.) The park has also trained local game guards and hunters, and several villages conduct commercial hunting on their own land. In addition, the Bop Park Board began dividing work projects, such as chalet construction, brick making, and road construction, into what Magome terms "chewable chunks" so that small local contractors, rather than big (white) firms, could get contracts. For each project, the park board hires a professional engineer to oversee the contract bidding and construction processes.

Most ambitious was the park's effort to address the BaKgatla's central and long-standing grievance: the fact that they had not received compensation for the loss of their land. In 1992, with the help of Alan Mountain, an environmental consultant hired by the park board, the BaKgatla set up a Community Development Organization (CDO), a legally constituted and democratically elected body to oversee community projects. The park board agreed to contribute to the CDO fund 10 percent of gate revenues, or about R 50,000 (about U.S.$12,500 in 1998) annually and to pay retroactively for all years since the forced removals. Also into the CDO fund goes a percentage of proceeds from concerts and money raised through hunting.

Some CDO funds have been used to bring water to villages and to build classrooms and clinics, but most of the funds have gone into an ambitious scheme to set up a community-owned miniature game park and cultural village, called Lebatlane, on land 32.2 kilometers (20 miles) north of Pilanesberg. Each member of the tribe had originally contributed R 40 (U.S.$10) to purchase this land, which the community planned to use for cattle grazing. But it proved too fragile for grazing, so the community voted unanimously to set up a commercial park for game viewing and controlled hunting safaris. The Bop Park Board donated wildlife to stock the park, and the tribal authority paid R 300,000 ($75,000) to fence the area. Despite initial progress, there have been problems: the road to the park was in terrible condition, marketing proved difficult, and there have been political upheavals within the park board and the CDO. Two years after Lebatlane was formed, no tourists had come, although there had been some limited hunting.

Mountain says that eventually the CDO should become independent of the Northwest Park Board (which superceded the Bop board in 1994), generating its own funds through development projects. He sees the role of the park board as providing "seed funding" and serving as "an island of expertise within a sea of poverty. Its function is to transfer expertise to the community." Among the income-generating schemes being discussed are a women's sewing cooperative, to make park uniforms and overalls for workers in the nearby platinum mines; vegetable gardens to supply the hotels, an upscale hotel to be built on communal land, and a new rest camp and recreational area within the park, to be jointly developed by the park board and the community.[35]

Although there is some grumbling that the community should be more directly involved in running it, Pilanesberg National Park is today solidly supported by those who live around it. Several surveys of the local communities and scientific studies in the early 1990s concluded that conservation, parks, and ecotourism are the most profitable use for this land. According to one survey, using 751 square kilometers (290 square miles) for cattle ranching would provide about 80 jobs at a cost of R 150,000 (U.S.$37,500) per job, whereas wildlife-based tourism would create 1,200 jobs at a cost of R 25,000 (U.S.$6,250) each. Although a Keenan survey in the 1980s revealed some hostility toward the park, in a 1993 survey of Pilanesberg's neighbors, more than 70 percent of those interviewed favored the continued existence of "their park." According to Magome, "Two-thirds of the money generated by wildlife now goes directly to the community." Poaching, a bellwether of local attitudes toward parks, is very low at Pilanesberg.[36]

Sun City

Pilanesberg National Park's success and popularity are due not only to management foresight and community involvement but also to its strategic location relatively close to the Johannesburg–Pretoria axis and, most important, very close to another tourist magnet. Sun City (and its addition, the Lost City) is a vast and garish gambling and entertainment complex rising, Oz-like, out of the arid plain. It was built in the late 1970s by Sol Kerzner, owner of the South African resort chain Sun International, in alliance with Chief Mangope and has been marketed as a fantasy world next to a "real" African experience, the game park. Sun City is the first and most financially successful of a string of pleasure palaces put up in the homelands to circumvent the international cultural boycott against South Africa as well as apartheid's own Calvinist restrictions on gambling and racial intermingling. It was christened by Frank Sinatra and over the years a number of U.S. entertainers performed here under the fiction that Bophuthatswana was an independent country. Writer Allister Sparks describes how, during apartheid, South Africans flocked to Bop and the other "casino-state" homelands for "weekends of sensual permissiveness [including] roulette wheel and blackjack, porn movies, nude stage shows, and the opportunity for cross-colour dalliance."[37] Sun City's doors were always open to white and black, rich and poor. As one guidebook describes, with commendable honesty: "A common sight on the gaming machines is a poor black gambler throwing hard-earned money into the great Moloch with the fixed intensity of one who cannot afford to lose."[38]

As did Pilanesberg, Sun City began with the forced eviction of BaKgatla farmers, and from the outset relations between the community and this tinsel-and-glitz monstrosity were tense. Surrounded by water-starved, impoverished shanties, Sun City pipes in water for its golf courses, swimming pools, lawns, giant wave pool, and artificial rain forest. "It's a huge user of water, and in this area water is a huge issue. Bop's repressive government stilled protests," explains David Fig.

Other than offering menial jobs, it wasn't until the twilight of apartheid that Sun City began to make some overtures to the community. The issue was lions. Sun City's owners urged Pilanesberg's management to introduce lions—which had once lived in the area—into the park so Pilanesberg could be marketed as a "big five" park, in turn, enhancing its draw and that of Sun City. Before making a decision, the park board insisted on canvassing the surrounding communities since lions presented a threat to their livestock. After lengthy discussions, the board agreed to bring in lions if the area was securely fenced. Sun City's owners agreed to pay R 10 million (U.S.$2.5 million) to obtain the lions, put up fencing, and finance their upkeep. The lion project has gone smoothly, and Sun City has subsequently promised to supply the CDO with sewing machines and to buy tablecloths and other linens from the women's cooperative.

Molefe Pilane, former head of the CDO, believes Sun City should do much more. "It's our land and they should be paying rent," he told me in a 1995 interview at his office near Pilanesberg National Park. "We've got oral history which shows our claim." Consultant Alan Mountain agrees, arguing in a 1995 telephone interview that the lion project represented "a beginning" and that Sun City's owners "have to be forced into doing a lot more." Though many see Sun City as anathema to ecotourism, Mountain argues that there can be a "symbiosis" between the gambling casinos, the parks, and rural communities: the casinos are the magnet to attract masses of tourists, some of whom visit the park and help make ecotourism financially viable. "Although I personally find it repugnant," he says, "Sun City is the key to ecotourism. My analysis is that Sun City was by accident conceptually right, but its design was wrong because it does not interface with the community." He contends that if casinos are designed so that they are near game parks and are, for example, co-owned by the tribal authority or local community, they can provide revenues for both conservation and community development. And, Mountain proposes, casinos combined with conservation and ecotourism might offer a viable economic alternative to mining or other financially attractive but environmentally destructive industries: "You have to have ecotourism projects which match other forms of development. For conservation to survive, you have to fight fire with fire."

The Battle for St. Lucia: "Conservation Fight of the Century"

Nowhere has the contest between ecotourism and other forms of development been more evident than at St. Lucia Game Reserve, an extensive wetlands system that includes an 11.3-kilometer (7-mile) stretch of sand dunes along South Africa's northeastern coast, which have been the scene of the country's longest and biggest environmental protest. The dunes, 241.4 kilometers (150 miles) north of the port city of Durban in politically turbulent KwaZulu-Natal Province, form a vital barrier between the Indian Ocean and a beautiful and biologically unique estuary. This is the largest estuarine lake system in Africa and one of the world's great breeding grounds for birds and fish, as well as home of the largest concentration of hippos in southern Africa. Daily, this long body of water is criss-crossed by double-decker tour boats filled with camera-carrying vacationers out to spot hippos, crocodiles, and dozens of species of waterfowl. The tour guide standing beside me points to rolling green dunes in the distance, covered with some of the world's last remaining sand forests. He explains that these dunes are crucial to the life of the estuary, which depends on the shifting balance between seawater and freshwater, and, the guide says, they are endangered: a mining conglomerate, Richards Bay Minerals (RBM), wants to strip-mine these dunes for titanium and other heavy metals, estimated to be worth about $1.5–$3 billion.[39]

The dunes and estuary are part of a nature reserve, one of many parks and protected areas in Maputaland, as this coastal section of KwaZulu-Natal Province is known in the tourism trade. Under apartheid, the KwaZulu portions were a separate homeland, led by Chief Mangosuthu Buthelezi, head of the Inkatha Freedom Party and a leading rival of Nelson Mandela and the African National Congress (ANC). After Mandela's election, Buthelezi, a conservative tribalist, became the main holdout in reintegrating his Zulu homeland into the new South Africa. Under apartheid, this region was a conservation patchwork, with two park authorities—the Natal Parks Board (NPB), created in 1895, and the KwaZulu Bureau of Natural Resources (later named the KwaZulu Department of Nature Conservation, or KDNC), established in 1982—dividing control of the protected areas and natural resources. The divisions followed apartheid's racial dictates, with the game parks in the white-ruled areas staying under the NPB's control and the Zulu, Thonga, and other African areas given to the KDNC. As a result, the two authorities were separate and unequal: the KDNC, the young stepchild of the NPB, was given the smaller, more remote, and less well funded parks.[40] The Mandela government ordered that the two boards be merged into one park authority, a move welcomed in principle but disputed in its details.

The NPB's spectacular parks contain a wide range of facilities—bush lodges, rest camps, safari camps, resorts—with more rooms than any other park system in South Africa. Its annual budget for 1995 was R 128 million (U.S.$32 million), of which only R 50 million (U.S.$12.5 million) was earned through sales and culling of wildlife, entrance fees, accommodations, and its designer line of souvenirs. Government subsidies cover the bulk of expenses, some R 80 million (U.S.$20 million), and despite pressure from the Mandela government to earn more, the NPB's chief executive, George Hughes, balks: "There's a bizarre belief that parks and tourism should pay for themselves and solve the problems of poverty. Tourism cannot be sold as a panacea for all ills. And we [the Natal Parks Board] should never become self-sufficient."[41]

Although Hughes claims that "75 percent to 80 percent of Natal Parks staff is black" and further contends that "one-third of the money going into black communities adjacent to the parks is from ecotourism," he admits that no blacks hold top management positions: "We have no black executives and are unlikely to get any for many years. They need a lot of training and education."

Falling under his jurisdiction is St. Lucia, which, along with Kruger National Park, Cape Town, Sun City, and Durban are South Africa's most popular holiday destinations. According to SATOUR, 75 percent of local and international tourists visit KwaZulu-Natal Province, and the town of St. Lucia depends entirely on tourism. St. Lucia Game Reserve, on KwaZulu-Natal Province's northern coast, was set up in 1895 and further expanded in 1939 to protect both the land and the water. However, in the 1950s, large swaths of coastal land on the edge of the park, including stretches of dune, were planted with nonindigenous pine, Australian eucalyptus, and casuarina trees as part of an ill-conceived afforestation project by the state-owned pulp company. It was believed that this would stabilize the dunes, but instead the exotic species displaced other vegetation, wildlife, and birds. More of St. Lucia's conservation area was lost when the South African Defence Force took over a sizable chunk of land for a rocket-firing and testing range.

Then, beginning in the 1970s, South Africa's government granted prospecting leases for heavy metal mining in the dunes and processing at the port town of Richards Bay, 24.1 kilometers (15 miles) south of St. Lucia. Even though in 1986 the St. Lucia system, including the eastern shore, was declared an internationally important wetland under the Ramsar Convention, the powerful conglomerate Richards Bay Minerals (a subsidiary of Rio Tinto Zinc and South Africa's Gencor) was, three years later, given rights to prospect (but not yet to mine) in these dunes. A year later, the Natal Parks Board formed the Greater St. Lucia Wetland Park, encompassing 2,800 square kilometers (1,081 square miles), including the dunes. It also announced plans to propose that this area be declared a United Nations World Heritage Site, something that could happen only if St. Lucia became a national rather than a provincial park. A mining operation would destroy any chance of having St. Lucia designated a World Heritage Site. Clearly, different government departments were working at cross purposes, headed on a collision course in what was soon to be dubbed "the conservation fight of the century."[42]

Prior to this tug-of-war between mining and conservation interests, the local people had been forcibly removed from St. Lucia. Between 1950 and 1970, two large communities were evicted from the dunes. In the late 1970s, another 3,400 people were moved out so that the South African army could build a missile-testing site. (This area has since been turned into a game reserve.) Those displaced were forced to live as squatters in already overcrowded KwaZulu townships. In response, some invaded Dukuduku State Forest, on the outskirts of the town of St. Lucia, where since the end of apartheid they have negotiated with the Natal Parks Board for the right to stay. These communities subsequently filed claims demanding title to the land and its resources[43]—an option the mining company and the parks board both opposed.

But as apartheid neared its end, both Richards Bay Minerals (RBM) and the conservationists, feeling the winds of change, began wooing the local community. RBM spokesman Barry Clements claimed that if it was permitted to expand into St. Lucia, the company would create "at least 2,500 high-paying jobs" and would replant and rehabilitate the sand dunes, thereby benefiting both the local communities and conservation. RBM began donating to rural development projects and providing start-up money to some 1,500 small entrepreneurs. According to Clements, "This 'battle for St. Lucia' is the greatest hoax in the annals of conservation."[44]

Flanked against RBM is the Campaign to Save St. Lucia, a coalition of some 200 largely white, middle-class environmental and conservation organizations that, together with the Natal Parks Board, argue that nature-based tourism is the more sustainable form of development for this delicate and beautiful area.[45] The coalition estimated that RBM mining in St. Lucia would create a mere 159 new jobs, and it pointed to the abysmal track record of RBM's multinational parent company, Rio Tinto Zinc, in other countries where the company has been accused of engaging in price-fixing and union busting, buying politicians, and plundering the environment. It had not lived up to its promise to rehabilitate dunes at Richards Bay, where it was currently mining. Further, in St. Lucia, mining would disrupt water flows, and this could kill Lake St. Lucia and its surroundings. Opponents claimed that RBM could mine titanium elsewhere than the environmentally sensitive and unique St. Lucia dunes. In 1993, the Campaign to Save St. Lucia collected some 300,000 signatures, including Nelson Mandela's, on petitions to stop the mining.

Then, in December 1993, on the eve of the demise of apartheid, the conservation coalition won a stunning victory: a review panel, headed by a distinguished judge, concluded that mining would permanently damage the dunes. The panel ruled that the dislocated communities should be compensated for their lost land and that the Natal Parks Board should implement ecotourism schemes to both protect the ecology of St. Lucia and directly improve the livelihood of those who had lost their land. The review panel's ruling was based on the findings of a four-year environmental impact assessment by an independent parastatal research council. Although it was financed by RBM and other prodevelopment interests, the assessment was the most extensive ever undertaken in South Africa, and it concluded that "mining would cause unacceptable damage. The Greater St. Lucia area is a very special asset for the nation." The assessment also urged that the area be designated a World Heritage Site. Subsequently, experts contracted by the Ministry of Land Affairs to do a series of six studies also weighed in, even more convincingly, against mining and for ecotourism. As one argued, "The foregone tourist potential of St. Lucia . . . would have effects on the economy because fewer overseas tourists would come to South Africa.[46]

These rulings placed the ball in the Natal Parks Board's court to prove that ecotourism could be an economically viable alternative to mining and could benefit the local communities. Two and a half years later, Gordon Forrest, the NPB's top official overseeing the park's eastern shores, outlined the park's ecotourism proposal: "We're convinced tourism and its multiplier effect can be more profitable. Our argument is that we're here forever, while the mining company is here for twenty years, and then they move out and there's no employment."[47] Pointing to a large wall map at his headquarters in the middle of the St. Lucia park, Forrest said, "We've done a conceptual plan but we have to fine-tune it and decide which areas we will develop. It has twenty-nine development nodes, including a variety of bush camps, hotels, houseboats, and, outside the park, a hotel of more than 1,000 beds." This last, Forrest suggested, might be built on communal land as a joint venture between the community and a private investor. His boss, Natal Parks Board head George Hughes, said that this scheme would "create 432 sustainable jobs in five years."

But these plans are still only on paper, and consultant Alan Mountain calls them pipe dreams: "I'm not promining, but I have to be convinced that the conservation-ecotourism lobby can offer a viable alternative. The pro-conservationists offer wilderness, but they have no program for wealth. Hughes is arguing out of emotion. He has no money to maintain the existing park, much less undertake tourism to counter mining."[48]

The upshot is that the indigenous people who were evicted from St. Lucia are divided, undecided, and suspicious of both mining and conservationists. As a shop steward with the National Union of Mineworkers put it, "Why all of a sudden is there all this activity and protest to save animals when there was no reaction at the time when people faced removal? Is it because this time, there is a threat to the survival of a favourite holiday resort for whites?"[49]

Dukuduku One and Two

In March 1996, residents of the two communities in the forest outside St. Lucia, known as Dukuduku One and Two, were threatening to blockade the town over the Easter holiday to protest the government's failure to consult them before deciding against mining.[50] Both communities claim to be the legitimate owners of the eastern shores, from which they were evicted in the 1950s when the area was declared a state forest. The traditional chief of one displaced group filed a land claim favoring mining, whereas a rival group demanded that its land be returned first before a decision was made about how it should be used.[51] Dukuduku One, an Inkatha Freedom Party stronghold, is made up of the poorest of the poor, who subsist in the forest by growing bananas and sweet potatoes through slash-and-burn farming and "illegal" fishing in the St. Lucia estuary. Community members are skeptical of arguments that they should leave the forest so that it can be utilized for ecotourism. "The nature people are *izigebengu* [criminals]. They arrest us and they destroy our homes. They have destroyed the forest . . . to build their big homes. Now they say we are the ones who are destroying it. Yet we stay here because we like trees. We live in limbo. That is why we build with planks. We have no money and we may have to move at any time. But at least here we are independent," Dukuduku One elders told the *Weekly Mail & Guardian*.[52]

In contrast, residents of the other community, Dukuduku Two, have begun in small but concrete ways to see some tangible benefits from conservation and ecotourism and to receive some modest assistance from the government. The sprawling settlement is located along the paved road leading out of the honky-tonk resort town of St. Lucia. Across a field, at the intersection of two muddy tracks, stands a tiny wooden shack that serves as headquarters of the Dukuduku Development and Tourism Association. The association's only staff member is Leslie Walters, a journalist turned community organizer who has lived in the area for sixteen years and speaks Zulu. Walters says she first encountered the Dukuduku settlement eighteen months earlier when a massive fire drove the residents off parkland where they had been squatting. "I became part of the group looking for an alternative site, and when they were given a new site across the road, I moved across with them. I realized their need for a community-based organization."[53] She says that 95 percent of the estimated 7,000 Dukuduku residents are unemployed and 80 percent are illiterate, but they are fortunate in not being embroiled in the ANC-Inkatha conflicts and in being united under one capable *nduna* (headman), Caiphus Mkhwanazi. Walters, whose husband was a ranger with the Natal Parks Board until his death in 1994, was working largely on a volunteer basis, assisting Mkhwanazi and the community in setting up income-generating, health, and educational projects and in negotiating with the NPB, the government, and the private sector. "From the beginning, they have talked about getting involved in ecotourism because this is such a popular tourist area," Walters says, adding that with majority rule this is becoming a reality. The Mandela government has promised the Dukuduku residents they will not be moved again and has begun providing proper housing sites and services such as electricity, roads, and water.

Walters works closely with two other women who are public outreach officers at the St. Lucia office of the Natal Parks Board. One of their first concessions was to permit the Dukuduku residents and members of other local communities into the park to gather *ncema* grass, used for making traditional Zulu baskets and sleeping mats. According to Gordon Forrest, products made from this grass are now earning the local people R 1.2 million (U.S.$0.3 million) per year. In late 1995, sales to tourists expanded greatly with the opening of a modern handicrafts center at the wharf on the estuary where tour boats dock. The park raised close to R 90,000 (U.S.$22,500) to build the center, which is owned and run by Dukuduku women. Walters says that not only is the center providing employment and income, but it is also helping to revive dying crafts such as carving, beadwork, and basketry.

A number of Dukuduku men found employment in another project, one that Public Outreach Officer Annette Gerber calls "a very positive, win-win" project for the park, the community, and a private businessman. She says that a local businessman, "Mr. Sithole," contacted the NPB asking if he could collect wood from the park to make charcoal. The Dukuduku community had also requested permission to collect firewood inside the park. The park, in turn, wanted to get rid of the nonindigenous pines planted on the dunes. A scheme was worked out for Sithole to hire about thirty local men, who would cut down the unwanted pine trees and turn them into charcoal. Now every day, just inside the park boundary, the sound of a buzz saw leads to a dozen rubber-booted men felling pine trees. Gerber estimates that there are enough alien pines in this area to last for one to two years, and she hopes to extend the project to other areas: "we're trying to find other exotic plantations in the park where they can continue to cut and make charcoal."[54]

The logs are hauled from the park to a large field, where a dozen or so old metal container boxes, left by ships in the port of Durban and donated to this project, sit in a row. When I visited the project site in 1995, gray smoke curled from basketball-size holes cut in the sides and tops of the containers. The end of one container was open and a group of men was carefully loading it with tree trunks. Off to the side, several women were sorting, bagging, and weighing the finished charcoal, which is of exceptionally high grade and suitable for export. Sithole trained the workers, oversees the cutting and cooking operation, and, because he owns a truck, handles the marketing. The workers receive a salary, the community gets free charcoal, and Sithole pays an additional R 1000 (U.S.$250) per month into a community development fund.

In Dukuduku Two itself, Walters has helped start other projects, using funds she raised from the Natal Parks Board and private businesses. These include a créche (day-care center) for preschool children, a nutrition and growth monitoring program, sewing classes, community skills and tour guide training courses, and a scheme to provide every household with a toilet. Next to the clinic, a small nursery grows medicinal plants. The Natal Parks Board has sent the local *nyanga* (medicine man) to Durban for training so that the clinic can offer patients both traditional and Western herbal treatments. Eventually, school groups and tourists will be able to take guided tours in the park and the village to learn about medicinal plants. Walters was preparing three booklets for these tours, on Zulu culture, the fauna and flora of St. Lucia, and ecotourism, which, she explains, "will put across the principal that ecotourism can uplift the quality of life of the local people and the economy of the area."

On the drawing board as well is a truly grand scheme, also mentioned by park official Gordon Forrest: a 1,000-bed hotel, conference center, and tourist campsite, to be co-owned and run by the community and a private investor. Dukuduku Two leaders have presented a proposal to the Natal Parks Board and are looking for international financing. Walters is optimistic: "We have a well-structured community that has worked with the parks in other projects. We have the cooperation of those with experience in running hotels. And we'll have no trouble attracting tourists to St. Lucia. So there is confidence all around." Reflecting on the changes she has seen,

Walters says, "The Dukuduku are now involved in the sensible management of the forest and other resources. So they see that they can generate income and conserve the environment at the same time. In the past, Dukuduku was a conservation disaster, but now it can be a catalyst for conservation into the future."

However, the battle for St. Lucia is not over. In late 1997, after most conservationists had retired from the fight, believing it had been won, the South African government announced it had withdrawn its application to make St. Lucia a World Heritage Site. The decision was prompted by officials of the UNESCO World Heritage Centre, who believed that two other South African sites, Table Mountain and Robben Island, had better chances of approval. An ANC leader in KwaZulu-Natal Province declared that if tourism did not soon become a major force in job creation in the area, the option of mining might be reexamined, and rumors spread that RBM was dusting off its files in preparation for a new mining application.[55]

The South African government must decide whether it will uphold the court ruling endorsing ecotourism or whether, and under what circumstances, it will permit RBM to mine titanium in the St. Lucia dunes. The government must also decide whether or not to honor the land claims of local communities, either by paying them compensation or by allowing them to move back to their traditional areas. These decisions may well be affected both by ongoing conflicts in KwaZulu-Natal Province between Inkatha and the ANC and by discussions as to whether St. Lucia should remain part of the Natal park system or become a national park. While the South African government has repeatedly stated that local communities must be part of this decision-making process, old suspicions die hard and residents of both Dukuduku One and Two remain skeptical that they will receive land, jobs, or other economic and social benefits from either the government or the tourist industry. As the *Weekly Mail & Guardian* warned, "Unless the strident calls for tourism job creation in the area are heeded, perhaps the only option, sadly, will be short-term, vote-getting quick-fix of revenue and jobs from mining.[56]

KwaZulu-Natal Province: Pioneering Joint Ventures with the Private Sector and Local Communities

Although the local communities of St. Lucia have yet to see substantial benefits from ecotourism, elsewhere in KwaZulu-Natal Province there are a variety of ecotourism experiments involving rural villages and private investors. The KwaZulu Department of Nature Conservation (KDNC) was first set up in 1982, as the KwaZulu Homeland's Bureau of Natural

Resources. In its first dozen years, it increased the amount of land under its control from a mere 0.5 percent to 2.5 percent of KwaZulu-Natal Province, including twelve parks, reserves, and protected areas, some newly created and others transferred from the Natal Parks Board. Many of these parks are in the remote, inaccessible, heavily forested border region, and until recently they had little or no tourist facilities.

As elsewhere in South Africa, these conservation areas were formed through forced removals, so the KDNC has been deeply resented by the communities on the parks' peripheries. According to one study, one in three people was moved at least once to create the Kosi Bay Nature Reserve, the KDNC conservation area located on the northern coast near the border with Mozambique. Just before the all-races elections, a KDNC announced it would no longer move people without obtaining their consent and providing compensation.[57]

In addition to the forced removals, the KDNC has been viewed with suspicion for another reason: many former Rhodesian military and intelligence officers joined its ranks, and the KDNC's longtime head, Nick Steele, was himself a former Rhodesian soldier (Steele died in 1996). In 1991, the *Weekly Mail & Guardian* reported that KwaZulu conservation authorities had operated a "secret services" division that spied on local political activists as well as ivory and rhino horn smugglers.[58]

On the other hand, the KDNC, unlike the Natal Parks Board, had from its outset a "policy of sharing" that included community profit-sharing programs and several ecotourism ventures. As Chief Mangosuthu Buthelezi stated in 1989, the Zulu homeland, like Bophuthatswana and other homelands, "has clearly understood that people must be the cornerstone of any conservation effort and that unless conservation is made relevant to ordinary people, it has no hope of gaining their support."[59] Since its inception, the KDNC has admitted local people into protected areas to collect, using traditional methods, wood, bark, reeds, and grasses; to visit ancestral graves; to fish in the Kosi Bay estuary; and to purchase low-priced meat from culling operations. The KDNC has also helped set up several community conservation areas on marginal land no longer suitable for cattle or agriculture. With technical assistance from the department, local communities have started game farms where they raise wildlife for sale to zoos or other parks and run hunting safaris.

As early as 1986, the KDNC included elected representatives of local communities or community liaison officers on their management committees. The department also initiated a scheme to give the three KwaZulu regional tribal authorities 25 percent of all the profits from culling, sale of wildlife, park entrance fees, and tourism-related facilities and services to use for "social upliftment" projects. In 1994, for instance, the Tembe

Tribal Authority received R 200,000 (U.S.$50,000), the Mathenjwa Tribal Authority R 80,000 (U.S.$20,000), and the Mbila Tribal Authority R 68,000 (U.S.$17,000). The program has not been without its problems and critics. Local communities suspect they are being shortchanged, that the park authority is not accurately tallying all its profits. In addition, the money is supposed to be invested in the communities adjacent to the parks and reserves, but it is distributed by the tribal leaders, who at times have simply used all or part of the money for themselves, without public accounting or consultation.[60]

As the end of apartheid neared, it became clear that government funds for parks would be cut and the KDNC would have to raise more of its own budget through tourism-related projects. Unlike the Natal Parks Board, the younger and poorer KDNC had built only campsites and other self-catering facilities in its parks. Now it came up with an innovative scheme to bolster its tourism infrastructure by building hotels and lodges in partnership with private developers and the local community. Under the heading "Eco-tourism . . . What We Aim to Do," a KDNC brochure called this "a three-way agreement with a fair share for each player." The vehicle is a nonprofit tourism development trust company called Isivuno (Harvest), through which the department channels some of the revenue received from park entrance fees, culling, sale of wildlife, and tourism-related activities. Normally, these funds would be turned over to the general provincial coffers, but under this new plan, Isivuno, as the KDNC's commercial arm, was to invest a portion in new revenue-generating projects. The department identified thirty-five sites inside game parks and reserves on which tourist facilities—ranging in size from a 120-bed lodge to 8-bed luxury camps—would be developed.[61] This marks the first time in South Africa that local communities have been involved as partners with both the private sector and the parks in the ownership and management of hotels.

Wilderness Safaris

Isivuno's first two projects have been in partnership with Wilderness Safaris, a South African company with a solid track record in nature tourism throughout southern Africa. One is the Rocktail Bay Lodge, consisting of ten wood-and-thatch A-frame chalets built on stilts under a forest canopy in the Maputaland Coastal Forest Reserve. A wooden walkway runs from the rustic, solar-powered lodge and over the tree-covered dunes to a magnificent, secluded stretch of the Indian Ocean. Because the area is protected as part of the Natal Parks Board's marine reserve, tourists need permits to enter, making this one of the most private beaches in South Africa. The fly-fishing, snorkeling, and swimming are excellent, and during the summer months, loggerhead and leatherback turtles lay their eggs there.

The second project is the Ndumo Wilderness Camp, built in a small reserve in northern KwaZulu Province, right on the border with Mozambique. First established in 1924 and acquired by the Natal Parks Board in 1954, the Ndumo Game Reserve was viewed with hostility by the surrounding Thonga people, who were moved out when the reserve was fenced. During Mozambique's long civil war, Ndumo and the tiny neighboring Tembe Game Reserve had been abused by poachers, refugees, Renamo rebels, and smugglers.[62] In 1989, Ndumo and many other areas were taken over by the KDNC. Conservation authorities long wanted to consolidate the two reserves so that elephants from Tembe could have access to the abundant water in Ndumo's twin rivers. But the 150 families living in the corridor resisted, resenting the fact that they had been forcibly removed from Ndumo and denied access to water within the reserve. In the mid-1990s, the villagers, with the assistance of rural development workers, struck a deal whereby they agreed to move farther south in return for access to a corner of Ndumo, where the Pongolo River flows.[63]

With the 1990 Mozambique peace accord, tourism in this border region again became possible. Ndumo is considered by many to be South Africa's finest bird-watching location, containing more than 400 species, or 60 percent of South Africa's birds, and the reserve's two shallow rivers or pans and its floodplains attract waterfowl, hippos, and crocodiles. Browsing among the acacia, wild fig, and fever tree forest are black and white rhinos, blue wildebeest, red duikers, giraffes, suni antelopes, and other wildlife.

In March 1995, Wilderness Safaris opened the Ndumo Wilderness Camp, which, like Rocktail, is managed as a joint venture between the private company, the KDNC, and the local community. Located in a part of the reserve not open to the general public, the camp's eight luxurious, solar-powered tents are built on raised wooden decks interlinked with walkways made from old railroad ties. Only one tree and seven branches were cut down in building the lodge. Elevated above the tall reeds but under the tree canopy, the lodge is unobtrusively but ideally positioned overlooking a bend in the broad Banzi Pan. Nights are punctuated with the splashing of hippos and crocodiles, and at dawn, the large red-orange ball of the sun appears to rise out of the pan, just in front of the tents.

Ndumo is co-owned by Isivuno and Wilderness, whereas Rocktail is wholly owned by Isivuno. In both projects, Wilderness pays Isivuno a modest annual fee for rent and lease of the land; Wilderness and Isivuno are equal comanagers of both projects. The local tribal authority gets 25 percent of whatever Isivuno receives in rent and management profits, thus making it a partner in both owning and managing the lodges. Profits from management, for instance, are divided as follows: Wilderness Safaris gets 50 percent, Isivuno gets 37.5 percent, and the tribal authority and community nearest the lodge share 12.5 percent (or 25 percent of Isivuno's 50 percent).

As elsewhere, finding a formula for division of profits between the tribal authorities and local communities has been a contentious issue. "We brokered the deals," explained Patrick Boddam-Whetham, an official with Wilderness Safaris, in a 1995 interview in Johannesburg. "We dealt with the local tribal authorities and their communities. But we got into a problem because the two tribal authorities and the chiefs are based far away from the parks. We feared that all the funds from these projects could possibly go only to the local chiefs and not to the tribe which lives near the lodges. So we've set up trusts into which all revenues will be paid, and each trust is administered by trustees elected by the people surrounding the camps." These trusts, in turn, will pay some percentage to their tribal authorities.

Although the blueprint for these joint ventures between the local communities, the private sector, and park authorities is unique, in reality the involvement of and benefits to the local community have so far been fairly minimal. With assistance from Wilderness Safaris, local trustees are receiving training in leadership and accounting, and, typically, local people work at both the Rocktail and Ndumo lodges. The communities have received some funds from the lease payments, but three years after Rocktail Bay Lodge opened, no management profit payments had been disbursed to the community trust fund.

There have been, however, some other tangible benefits. At Ndumo, the community has opened a caravan park on the edge of the reserve and has rented the lodge space for a laundry and parking lot. The Rocktail lodge pays the community for the right to take guests to a hippo pond. "In the past, the village saw hippos as a nuisance, a danger," lodge manager Andy Coetzee tell me. "Now they see them as a resource, and they want to protect them." Both lodges are also buying crafts from the villagers and negotiating to take touring groups to visit a local herbalist, witch doctor, and traditional *kraal*, or homestead. "Our relations with the community are good," says Coetzee, who has lived in this area for more than ten years, speaks Zulu, and has been involved in the negotiations to set up the trust fund. Ndumo's manager, Ian Derrick, concurs. "The people around the periphery are excited we're here. There's 95 percent unemployment, and we're now employing seventeen people. And they like the new projects we're proposing." But, he candidly admits, "The community as a whole and the tribal authorities up in the mountains have not been well informed about what's happening here. It's hard for us to go out and tell them. They've been lied to before by whites, so why would they believe us?"

The managers at Wilderness Safaris say they are talking with the local people about using the income they will be receiving from the lodges to gradually buy out Isivuno's share. If this happens, the local tribe and Wilderness Safaris will become equal comanagers in these lodges. "It's taken years of negotiations with the communities and tribal authorities, but we've come up with a good model here," says Boddam-Whetham, adding that Wilderness Safaris plans to carry out yet another similar project with Isivuno.

Southern Sun's Zululand Tree Lodge

Elsewhere in KwaZulu-Natal Province, several other lodges—all on private land—are billed as promoting ecotourism through conservation and community projects. Just down the road from the huge swath of central Zululand that makes up the Natal Parks Board's Umfolozi and Hluhluwe Game Reserves is the Zululand Tree Lodge, consisting of twenty thatched, wooden tree-house bungalows nestled in a fever tree forest on the Mzinene River within a small private reserve. The lodge's environmentally sensitive construction, which was supervised by experts from the Natal Parks Board, made use of mostly local materials, including handwoven grass mats covering the walls of the bungalows. The unlikely owner is Sun Game Lodges, a division of Southern Sun Hotels, South Africa's largest hotel group. Until the early 1980s, Southern Sun Hotels was linked to Sun International, owners of Sun City and other homeland casino resorts. Southern Sun is owned by a consortium of companies, the majority South African and the remainder British, U.S., and French. It has specialized in traditional four- and five-star high-rise beach resorts and urban business hotels within South Africa, including, even during the international economic boycott under apartheid, all the country's Holiday Inns. Southern Sun owns all its hotels and comanages them with Inter-Continental Hotels and Resorts. With the political changes of the early 1990s, Southern Sun decided to expand into game lodges when the company's largely international clientele requested package tours that included wildlife safaris. "We probably wouldn't have expanded if there had not been a change in government and opening to the world market. Our game lodges are especially aimed at the overseas market and our direct competition is Kenya and Tanzania," explained a Southern Sun executive.[64] Although while Sun Game Lodges is clearly aimed at catching the upward ecotourism curve in the new South Africa, a firsthand inspection revealed that Zululand Tree Lodge has taken a variety of small steps which, when added together, do set it apart as a worthy ecotourism experiment. It has consciously set out to hire workers from the surrounding rural communities, where unemployment and illiteracy both top 50 percent. When it opened its doors in 1995, Zululand Tree Lodge's staff included forty-seven local people, including a ten-member antipoaching team. Only five employees were from outside the area, including the general manager, Andrew Greeff, a career hotel executive.

In an interview, Greeff explained, "As a national company, we see that the government cannot do it on its own but the private sector has to play ball and become a partner. We concluded that we had to begin activities from the bottom up. We take people within our organization and do skills training through a mentorship program. We have a program based on monthly goals and tracking. We're expanding so fast we'll absorb these people." Zululand Tree Lodge's receptionist in 1995 was a black South African, a rare sight then in an upscale South African game lodge. One of the lodge's nature guides was an elderly Zulu man who specializes in walking safaris that came within some six yards—downwind—of rhinos. Before the lodge was opened, this guide had worked for more than twenty years as a tracker in this same reserve, mutely spotting the animals while a white ranger interacted with the tourists.

Zululand Tree Lodge had to work to overcome a legacy of poor relations with the local communities. The reserve had been owned by two white gentleman farmers and used for both hunting and game viewing; Southern Sun had owned an old hotel on the reserve's edge. Local black Africans were barred from the reserve and, in turn, poaching for trophies and illegal hunting for food was rampant. When, in 1993, the lodge was struck by lightning and burned to the ground, Southern Sun decided to purchase the reserve and rebuild the lodge as part of its new ecotourism division. Its first goal, said Greeff, was "to focus on our immediate neighbors." Through a series of meetings with the local chief and headmen, area farmers and businessmen, and officials from the Natal Parks Board and other government agencies, Greeff explained, "We decided this lodge would be built by the local community." Some 240 workers—one per family—were hired on six-month contracts and trained in carpentry, bricklaying, thatching, electrical installation, plumbing, and structural engineering skills. Besides the builder, only five outsiders were brought in as project leaders.

Beyond hiring and training construction workers, manager Andrew Greeff explained that Zululand Tree Lodge, like other Sun Game Lodges, has adopted "a two-pronged plan" of promoting affirmative action through hiring and training nonwhites and facilitating the creation of small, black-owned businesses linked to the hotel chain. One of the lodge's senior staff members works full-time on community and conservation projects. He has established a program to teach local farmers to grow vegetables hydroponically for sale to the lodge and other area hotels. The hotel also purchased a brick-making machine and gave it to the workers so they could make bricks for other projects in the area, including a time-share hotel and conference center. Together with the Natal Parks Board and local officials, the lodge has helped to train and organize conservation teams to remove alien plants on farms and apply environmentally friendly pesticides. Other projects include hiring people to remove unwanted thorn (acacia) trees, install an electric fence around the reserve, take visitors on cultural tours of a traditional *kraal*, and establish an educational program bringing black youths to the lodge and reserve. Some of Sun Game Lodges' environmentally and socially sensitive practices have been adopted and serve to at least superficially "green" hotels throughout the Southern Sun network. Zululand Tree Lodge and other Southern Sun hotels try to buy supplies, including guest toiletries made from natural ingredients, recycled toilet paper, and elephant dung paper, from various community and self-help organizations.

When I asked Greeff to evaluate his personal transition from conventional tourism to ecotourism, he answered, "I feel this concept is the only way we should go. The challenges are exciting and new, and it gives me a great sense of satisfaction. My only problem is that I'm sometimes more focused on community and conservation and forget about running the hotel."

Sun Game Lodges' best-known facility is Bongani Mountain Lodge, located in Mthethomusha Game Reserve, on the southern border of Kruger National Park. A favorite rest spot of President Nelson Mandela, it has been described as "South Africa's prime example of 'rainbow tourism'" because it is a multiple partnership involving the local community, the park service, and private investors. Once part of a homeland, the reserve is now integrated into Kruger. However, the land in the reserve continues to be owned by the Mpakeni people, who receive rent and participate in the reserve's management.[65]

Conservation Corporation

It is Conservation Corporation (also known as Conscorp) that has earned the mantle as the model in South Africa for privately run luxury ecotourism that is committed to providing benefits to its employees and the wider community. A visit to Londolozi and Phinda, two of Conservation Corporation's five lodges in South Africa, shows why. Londolozi is one of three private resorts located in Sabi Sand, which is 646 square kilometers (250 square miles) of *bushveld* (arid scrub brush) private reserves and is situated between two rivers on the western border of Kruger. Londolozi is aesthetically beautiful and bucolic, with whitewashed rondavels, brick-lined walkways, lush green shrubs, arching trees, and splashes of colorful hibiscus and bougainvillea. The dining area is on a wide wooden deck overlooking trees and bushes alive with baboons, elephants, buffalo, and other wildlife.

A short distance behind this restful setting, tucked out of view of the guests, is a small town of 230 people, 150 of whom work for Londolozi. This is Londolozi's most important contribution to ecotourism. Here, the whitewashed rondavels where staff members and some of their families live are painted with bright pictures signifying the occupants' work—a car for a driver, wine bottles and glasses for a bartender, animals for a tracker. There

is an open-sided community center with a large television set and games, a
restaurant selling hamburgers and other fast-food items as well as traditional
African dishes, a store, a laundry, a library, a health clinic, a nursery school,
and an interracial primary school. There are also workshops where people
weave grass mats; sew napkins, tablecloths, and uniforms; and make paper,
bricks, clay pots, and drums. Londolozi employs a full-time community
liaison person, who is the village nurse; she also runs a clinic in Gazankulu,
a sprawling city of 250,000 on the edge of this private reserve, where other
family members live. Two teachers, one white and one black, run the school
and nursery for staff children as well as an adult literacy program; there are
also skills training classes. Paper, cans, and glass are recycled, food scraps are
composted and used on vegetable gardens, and water is recycled.

"Our motto," says Londolozi's managing director, Ronnie McKilvey,
"is care of the land, care of the wildlife, care of the people. We encourage
training and small business development and we provide seed capital and
low-interest loans. Our philosophy is 'don't give a man a fish; teach him to
fish.' We don't believe in aid: it's a black hole, and patronizing," he contends. People pay (modestly) for services, including health care and literacy
and training courses; they also receive dividends from the communally
owned village store. Employees can take out small personal loans but must
pay them back by the end of the month, with 10 percent interest. The profits on these loans go to the community and have been used, for instance, to
build the nursery school.

The village is run by a dozen-member, racially mixed committee elected
by the staff, on which management does not have a vote. McKilvey explains
that most of the white staff members still live outside the village, although
some have opted to live here; five black staff members live in the "white"
area. "We're slowly breaking down segregation, based on performance," he
says. The Londolozi "experiment," begun in 1987, was the company's first,
and McKilvey candidly admits, "We've developed with a lot of trial and
error. There's not a blueprint, and we've made mistakes." One of the ongoing issues is housing. "We try not to split up families. It's up to them if they
bring their family out here," McKilvey says, but the shortage of housing is
also a determinant. Conservation Corporation literature estimates that each
of the company's 150 local employees is supporting at least five dependents,
most of whom live in Gazankulu. Employees can take out home loans to
build houses outside the reserve. By 1995, some twenty-five houses had
been built.

When Londolozi began, the term *ecotourism* had not yet entered the
popular lexicon, at least in apartheid South Africa. In the late 1970s, two
brothers, David and John Varty, decided to turn their family hunting and
vacation lodge into a wildlife tourism lodge. David Varty, who is director
of Conservation Corporation, explains that, "From the outset, we have

described ourselves as conservation developers. We use international tourism, primarily low-density, high-priced tourism, to attract the discerning international traveler to remote parts of Africa. In so doing, we create an economic "exciter" in the region and bring in investment for self-funding conservation efforts and small businesses." He adds, "We created Londolozi as a model not because we're good guys. We know if we want to stay in tourism, we have to have friendly neighbors."

In 1989, Varty teamed up with Alan Bernstein, a wealthy white South African who was managing director of a company focused on attracting international investment to sub-Saharan Africa. They set up Conservation Corporation and began seeking "international investors and more land." Bernstein displayed a tremendous talent for attracting financing, even into white-sand South Africa. By 1990–1991, Conservation Corporation had secured the first substantial new international investment in wildlife tourism and rural South Africa in some eight years, despite the intense civil war and international economic boycott against apartheid. Between 1990 and 1995, the corporation's staff grew from 22 to 1,000.[66] With the end of apartheid, Conservation Corporation rapidly expanded into East Africa and Zimbabwe. By 1998, the corporation had grown from five properties in South Africa to twenty-three properties throughout Africa. Ecotourism expert Costas Christ, who has worked for Conservation Corporation, describes the company's mercurial rise as "a Ben & Jerry kind of story. The Vartys were not rolling in dough. But they and their partners were enlightened whites, all guys in the progressive political and business circles under apartheid. They were young idealists who wanted to do good for the world, and they thought they could do it through business." When Nelson Mandela was released from prison, he went to Londolozi to recoup, praising the village as an example of the type of rural development the new South Africa must pursue.

Varty quips that one of the keys to the company's success was that "we have no scientists in Conservation Corporation, but plenty of MBAs." One of the tasks of these MBAs has been to aggressively raise funds internationally by promoting both Conservation Corporation's sound business practices and its commitment to community development. Unlike other ecotourism ventures, the corporation does not earmark a portion of its tourism profits for its community projects, other than to pay the salaries of its community liaison workers. Instead, it set out to raise community development funds separately, mainly from international donations and to some extent through contributions from its guests. In their ecotourism study, David Grossman and Eddie Koch explain, "The corporation's main vehicle for promoting development is the Rural Investment Fund. This was established to channel capital, obtained from outside funding and donor agencies, into community development programmes that surround the core tourism projects. This institution is designed to spread the benefits of the tourism enterprise, primarily through the mobilization of external funds rather than the redistribution of company profits."[67] A flowchart of Conservation Corporation's "model of conservation development" designed by David Varty graphically illustrates the financial flow. It shows no funds flowing from the corporation's tourism profits into community projects. Rather, the Rural Investment Fund is the source, with its funds flowing first into "sustained resource utilization," "employment and training," "education and health," and "small business opportunities," then upward into "maintenance of biodiversity," "development of local economies," and so forth, all of which ultimately flow into and support "game reserve and tourism facilities." In essence, Conservation Corporation envisions rural development projects bolstering its core tourism enterprises, not vice versa.[68]

Whereas at Londolozi the emphasis has been on improving the lot of the African staff members and their families, at Phinda, another of Conservation Corporation's five South African lodges, social programs are primarily geared toward the surrounding communities. Located in KwaZulu-Natal Province on more than 168 square kilometers (65 square miles) of agriculturally denuded land bought from ten white farmers, Phinda, which opened in 1994, consists of two stunning lodges: the forty-four-bed Nyala Lodge, consisting of large stone rondavels, and the Forest Lodge, comprising sixteen luxury suites raised on stilts and encased in glass.

Conservation Corporation "really cut its teeth on Phinda. It's the company's most cherished baby," says Costas Christ. "With time and care, it has become a model of ecotourism." Environmentally, Phinda represents the largest land restoration project in South Africa. The reserve has been restocked with all the "big five" animals except buffalo, and the bush has been thinned to restore open woodland and enhance game viewing. This has also provided opportunities, as in St. Lucia, for small local entrepreneurs to manufacture and sell charcoal from the cleared wood. Phinda's two rustic lodges make extensive (although not exclusive) use of solar power, recycle bottles and cans, and compost organic waste.

But it is the three extremely poor communities surrounding Phinda—Mnqobokazi, Mduku, and Nibela, with a combined population of about 40,000—on which the corporation's effects have been the most extensive. In 1992, the Rural Investment Fund received a sizable anonymous donation to set up the Phinda Community Development Trust Fund, and by 1995, some $625,000 had been raised. Conservation Corporation committed two staff members to engage in community development and also provided vehicles, a telephone, fax machines, and other office equipment. "Part of the challenge is [finding] how to link First World funding agencies with Third World communities. In that process, we operate like an NGO," explains Les Carlisle, regional development manager for Phinda. "We're playing local government," he adds, "putting in roads, electricity, and so on. If we want things to happen around our parks, we have to make them happen. Local politicians cannot do it."[69]

The Phinda management established, Carlisle says, "a development committee in each of the villages that through the chiefs and *ndunas* identifies projects; then we go seek the funding." Carlisle and his associate, Isaac Tembe, who has a background in community development and accounting, have said no to some projects, but they estimate that they seek funding for about 80 percent of those proposed by the village councils. They explain that they are training villagers so that in time they will have the capacity to raise funds on their own. "Eventually, we'll have hands off and act only as consultants," says Carlisle. The trust funds have been used to build classrooms at a half dozen schools; set up preschools, a health center, and an environmental education center; and provide skills training and adult literacy classes. They have also paid for boreholes, water pumps, and fences and helped to finance small industries such as brick making. The villagers in turn provide the labor for projects, and each household contributes R 20 (U.S.$5) toward the cost of building. Parents pay about U.S.$1 per month to send a child to nursery school.

Most ambitious has been the creation of a multiple-use community game reserve that offers photographic as well as hunting safaris. The safari area, which borders on the Phinda reserve, has been restocked with local animals, with the addition of buffalo, which are not present in Phinda. The Natal Parks Board donated the land, and conservation groups including the Green Trust and WWF have contributed boreholes and solar-powered electric fencing. The reserve, the creation of which was initiated by one of the area's tribal chiefs, is run by the community. Trackers and guides come from the local area, but professional hunters, mostly white, bid to bring in clients. As befits David Varty's diagram, this community reserve actually enhances the attractiveness of Phinda.

Conservation Corporation's investment in the two Phinda lodges and the reserve has been "incredibly high," says Carlisle, and because unlike Londolozi, it is not located in a central nature tourism hub, its occupancy has been relatively low. What got "cut," Carlisle says, were staff housing and programs that are not nearly as high quality or innovative as those at Londolozi.

In assessing the effects of these projects, Grossman and Koch state, "Because of the relative isolation and lack of formal employment opportunities, Phinda probably has a greater relative impact on wealth creation in the surrounding rural villages—via formal employment and the injection of wages into the rural economy—than do the more financially successful private lodges located on the periphery of the Kruger National Park."[70] However, the authors perceptively note that although more research is needed, "indications are that relatively educated individuals qualify for formal employment and that benefits from wages are limited to their immediate family." Whereas a high proportion of women are employed at the lodges, other marginalized groups, especially the aged, receive few benefits. Further, the authors state, all Conservation Corporation projects are based on privately owned land, and there is "no form of direct community ownership or involvement in the management of the core activities of the enterprises." This represents a relatively "passive" form of community participation, although the regional development forum set up by Phinda management does represent, Grossman and Koch conclude, "a real attempt to empower local communities so that they can plan and manage local development programs themselves."[71] Phinda's management, together with the Natal Parks Board, played a role in setting up the Southern Maputaland Development Forum, which includes local tribal authorities, development and conservation groups, community leaders and organizations, and tourism authorities. Its purpose is to debate, at a grassroots level, the development alternatives for the area. This, together with the capacity-building training programs offered by Conservation Corporation community workers, is slowly helping to strengthen the political skills of the local communities, where traditionally the chiefs and *ndumas* have held control.[72]

Although Les Carlisle contends that Conservation Corporation has "developed a model that's exportable," the corporation has in fact had difficulty reproducing its model in eastern Africa and Zimbabwe and has essentially opted for luxury nature tourism without community outreach or a consistent commitment to environmentally sensitive practices (see chapters 7, 8, and 9). The corporation has been constrained by a number of factors. In some cases, it has bought existing properties; it leases rather than owns the land; it has hired people who are not imbued with Conservation Corporation's commitment to community development; and it is operating on foreign turf, where it has little political clout or know-how. According to Costas Christ, Conservation Corporation has been like "a rocket ship taking off with tremendous force and power and speed, and as it went through the atmosphere it began to shake. It became clear that it was having trouble. The time and effort and personal attention given to Phinda was not given to places outside South Africa. Environmental issues and communities have taken a beating."

From Real Ecotourism to Ecotourism Lite and Outright Scams

In the new South Africa, a number of factors and actors have combined to support creative experiments in ecotourism. These include cohesive and vocal rural communities with clear sets of demands, strong leadership, and political skills learned through the struggle against apartheid. The local press has helped to expose the conditions of rural poverty on the perimeters of game parks and reserves and has brought these struggles to national attention. Many environmental groups and activists, as well as policy groups and private consultants, have lent their expertise to assist rural communities and promote ecotourism projects as alternatives to both protectionist conservation practices and more destructive economic activities. The University of Pretoria and other institutions have set up ecotourism projects partly out of a commitment to social and economic justice, but also to help the parks and tourism industry capture the international market and protect against land invasions, sabotage, and other types of rural protest. The Mandela government has strongly endorsed ecotourism as fitting with its development strategies and has devoted government resources and personnel, most importantly through the national tourism agency SATOUR and the South African National Parks, to facilitate ecotourism experiments and promote South Africa internationally.

Luxury and Ecotourism Lite at Sabi Sabi

Yet in South Africa, as elsewhere, some entrepreneurs, conservation organizations, and consultants are using the "ecotourism" label to promote ventures that are not environmentally sustainable, culturally sensitive, or economically beneficial to local communities. A close look at Sabi Sabi, for instance, located in Sabi Sand reserve on the western border of Kruger National Park, reveals that, on a number of fronts, it falls short of the principles and practices of sound ecotourism.

Since the early 1990s, Sabi Sabi representatives have taken part in ecotourism conferences worldwide and have been prominent in similar gatherings in South Africa. Under the slogan of "Come Spoil Yourself," Sabi Sabi has marketed itself as South Africa's premier up-market ecotourism destination, even more luxurious than neighboring Londolozi. Its clientele is 70 percent foreign, mainly German and British, but its U.S. market is increasing. Even with a price tag of about $400 per night, Sabi Sabi is often fully booked several years in advance.

Established in 1980, Sabi Sabi is owned by investment broker Hilton Loon and a group of other wealthy white South Africans. To the casual

observer, Sabi Sabi seems a fine example of competent and carefully run ecotourism. The setting is lovely, the attention to guests beyond compare, and
the game viewing, including walking safaris, night rides, and off-the-road
drives to track the "big five," wild dogs and cheetahs, is superb.

But, according to ecologist and ecotourism expert David Grossman,
Sabi Sabi "is not ecotourism, it's wildlife voyeurism. This is a commercial
business run purely along short-term, commercial lines." In 1994,
Grossman was hired as a consultant by Sabi Sabi to give advice on environmental impact issues. He found that while Sabi Sabi is, for the most part,
environmentally "well managed," vehicles that follow closely behind wildlife
may well interfere with the animal's ability to hunt.

Grossman was most critical of Sabi Sabi's poor relations with its African
staff and the local community located just outside the reserve. So, too, is
Michel Girardin, general manager of Southern Sun's Game Lodges, who
worked for ten years as operations director at Sabi Sabi. Girardin says that
while he and a few other managers tried to implement sound ecotourism
practices, they were overruled and the resort's experiment with ecotourism
"went wrong." My three day stay to this luxurious camp and further interviews seemed to confirm these assessments.

About 80 percent of Sabi Sabi's 180 employees, including trackers,
waiters, bell hops, maids, gardeners, and a variety of workers within the
reserve, are Shagaani, from families who were moved out when the reserve
was originally created. Most of the older staff are illiterate. In a 1995 interview, Sabi Sabi managers Paul Sarty and Mike Simpson said the lodge had at
one time run literacy and skills training programs for its African staff, but
that these had been stopped. Similarly, they explained, a vegetable growing
project with several local farmers had collapsed. Sabi Sabi had no staff person assigned to work on self-help and self-improvement programs with
either the staff or the community living on the edge of the reserve. But, even
so, the two managers contended that "we've done hundreds of things for
community development and conservation. We just don't shout about it."
However, the two managers, as well as Sabi Sabi's brochures, do boast that
this lodge was the first in the area and possibly all of South Africa to promote a black tracker to the position of ranger; not mentioned is that this
ranger left Sabi Sabi with Girardin to join Sun Game Lodges.

Interviews with several of the black staff revealed other problems. A staff
committee, which was handpicked by Hilton Loon rather than elected by
the workers, had not functioned for some time, so workers had no avenue
to express concerns. They said there is no staff health clinic and African staff,
with the exception of the few black rangers, live in a compound described as
over-crowded, run-down, and filthy. Salaries and promotions are not stan-
dardized. One of the black rangers said he had worked three times more
years yet received less salary than a senior white ranger.

Most of the African staff are married but their families are not permitted at Sabi Sabi because, one of those interviewed explained, "there is not enough accommodation and no school for the children." He said that staff works seven days a week for six weeks and then gets six days off to visit their families, most of whom live in Gazankulu, just outside the reserve's boundary. In contrast, almost all of the white staff are single and stay with Sabi Sabi on average a much shorter length of time. Yet, in the current realities in rural South Africa, a black ranger told me he is holding a prized job: "I've only worked at Sabi Sabi. It's a very good job, a very special job. I like the work very much." But stacked up against neighboring Londolozi or other sound ecotourism establishments, Sabi Sabi amounts to little more than ecotourism "lite."

Cross-Border Peace Parks

Meanwhile, on Kruger's eastern boundary plans are underway to create a "peace park" by consolidating this national park with three areas on the Mozambique side of the border and, eventually, incorporating a broad swath of land stretching northeast of Kruger to Gona-re-zhou National Park in southern Zimbabwe and south to the Mozambique coastline above KwaZulu-Natal Province. This cross-border conservation area would become the world's largest wildlife reserve.

Following an end to the Renamo insurgency in the early 1990s and the country's first multiparty elections in late 1994, Mozambique—like South Africa and Zimbabwe—has begun to rebuild its war-torn economy. Building the cross-border park will involve taking down a 80.5-kilometer (50-mile) electrified fence put up in the 1980s to stop Mozambicans from fleeing to South Africa. (This infamous "fence of fire" electrocuted and killed at least 100 Mozambican refugees.) More fundamentally, the project envisions fence mending and cooperation between once hostile neighboring countries and between rural communities and park authorities. In 1996, the World Bank's Global Environment Facility (GEF) granted the Mozambican government a loan of more than $8 million to establish several transfrontier parks.

The advent of peace in southern Africa, together with economic collaboration among the region's countries via the Southern African Development Community (SADC), has stimulated moves to encourage cross-border tourism, including a proposal to introduce a single tourist visa for overseas visitors. In South Africa, the press, major environmental organizations, development agencies, and private consultants and investors have enthusiastically welcomed cross-border parks as among the most promising experiments for protecting biodiversity, improving the quality of life for rural people by providing employment, and expanding nature-based tourism. Powerful players such as WWF's Anton Rupert and John Hanks (who was forced to resign as WWF's international director over the Operation Locks scandal) have endorsed the scheme.[73] Hanks now heads the South Africa–based Peace Parks Foundation. However, to some discerning eyes, the cross-border parks scheme is as problematic as some of its backers.

Stephen Ellis, who has studied the links between the parks, the military, contraband operations, and far-right paramilitary organizations, cautions that some of the old apartheid elite backing the peace park concept may harbor plans to use the territory to destabilize the South African government. According to Ellis, "[M]any white military thinkers are much preoccupied with the necessity to control at least some territory as a means of guaranteeing the physical security of white South Africans. Here the whole Mozambican border has the potential to play a crucial role since it is highly porous. There already exists an important weapons trade across the border."[74]

Blanchard's "Beast-and-Beach" Tourism Project

Such suspicions were heightened by revelations in 1996 that one of the private developers cashing in on the cross-border park plans is James Ulysses Blanchard III, a Louisiana businessman with a passion for gold, guns, and ultraconservative causes. In the 1980s, Blanchard helped finance CIA- and South African–backed right-wing guerrillas in Nicaragua, Angola, and Afghanistan as well as Mozambique. Even though the Renamo rebels in Mozambique fought and eventually lost a dirty, seventeen-year war using child warriors, land mines, and scorched-earth tactics, Blanchard continues to defend them as Christian, anticommunist, free-market capitalists. In 1996, cash-strapped and investment-hungry Mozambican government officials, who are trying to rebuild one of the world's poorest countries, deeded Blanchard 10,360 square kilometers (4,000 square miles), on which he is developing, according to the *New York Times*, "an $800 million ecotourism paradise."[75] The triangle of land along the border links the Maputo Elephant Reserve in Mozambique with South Africa's Tembe Game Reserve and also includes several islands. When news of the secret deal leaked out, Mozambican parliamentarians objected to granting such a large swath of prime coastal and game park property to a foreign developer.

Although some local biologists have endorsed the project as "the only way to save the ecosystem, which the 1992 Rio Summit conference on biodiversity named as one of the 200 most remarkable on the planet," the scheme goes well beyond environmental conservation or even restoration. Plans call for a floating casino, thatched game lodges perched high over watering holes, a marina, a golf course with hippos in the water hazards, an African theme village, an international conference facility, and an antique steam train that would pull rolling hotels made of Orient Express–style sleeping cars through herds of wildlife. Blanchard also plans to sell private homes within his park and to attract hotel chains such as Club Med and Sheraton. Billed as a "beast-and-beach" package, Blanchard's dream scheme faces the reality that civil war and poaching have seriously reduced the "big five" animal species and other attractions. According to the *New York Times*, Blanchard's five-year wildlife reintroduction plan "reads like a cargo manifest for Noah's Ark": 500 zebras, 30 white rhinos, and 25 lions, as well as giraffes, wildebeest, hyenas, wild dogs, and crocodiles.[76]

The project proposes to redo the human population as well, by importing San (Bushmen) from Botswana's Kalahari Desert as another tourist attraction while moving out some 10,000 local subsistence fishermen and farmers. In return for the loss of their land and livelihood, the project pledges to give these displaced poor "'preferential share listing' in the Blanchard portfolio of investment" and first crack at jobs as construction laborers and chambermaids.[77] Blanchard also pledges to provide "social infrastructure for these affected communities, including schools, clinics, community centres, etc."[78]

Under the dictum, apparently, that any private investment is better than no investment, South Africa's influential Endangered Wildlife Trust (EWT) is quietly supporting the project. David Holt-Biddle, managing editor of the EWT's coffee-table-quality publications, *Endangered Wildlife* and *Vision*, calls the Mozambique government's approval of the Blanchard project "one of the biggest environmental stories of the year in southern Africa." Elsewhere, he writes, "Moçambique needs investment, and it needs it sooner rather than later." Only a very close reading reveals that the EWT's Mozambique branch is one of the "interested parties" participating in Blanchard's joint management committee.[79] South African companies also are deeply involved in the project. The development plan was drawn up by the South Africans who created the Sun City casino complex and Pilanesberg National Park. Consultant Alan Mountain, who worked on these projects, argues that ecotourism may have to resort to such conventional tourism attractions in order to be economically viable and stave off even worse forms of environmentally destructive activities, such as mining.[80]

South African companies, capital, and consultants are today enormously influential in building and reshaping nature tourism both domestically and throughout East and southern Africa. National (white) capital has undertaken some of the most innovative and comprehensive ecotourism projects, which are providing tangible benefits to local communities in the new South Africa. However, Sabi Sabi, Blanchard's Mozambique border project, and

Conservation Corporation's shortcomings in Zimbabwe and East Africa illustrate that without clear standards and guidelines for the industry and careful oversight, inspection, and enforcement procedures, ecotourism projects can easily amount to merely ecotourism lite, if not outright scams.

South Africa's Ecotourism Scorecard

Ecotourism is playing a dual role in the new South Africa: helping to reintegrate South Africa into the world economy and helping to redress grievances and redistribute wealth to the country's rural poor. Under apartheid, South Africa was an international pariah, boycotted by both foreign tourists and investors. Most tourism within South Africa was domestic, predominantly run by the white minority; South Africa was a net exporter of tourists; and most investment in tourism was with national capital. The commitment to genuine ecotourism is one of the outgrowths of the antiapartheid struggle. Whereas elsewhere, ecotourism evolved out of environmental movements, in South Africa it has deep roots in the struggle against white minority rule and for a broad-based democracy committed to economic and racial equality and social justice. Ecotourism is seen as a tool for social change, and its principles fit the objectives of the Reconstruction and Development Program (RDP), Nelson Mandela's first blueprint for development. Today, a broad swath of South African society, including government and park officials, the national tourism agency, dozens of NGOs, academics, consultants, environmentalists, journalists, community organizers, rural activists, and private tour operators, developers, and investors, are involved in ecotourism experiments and initiatives. All this adds up to giving South Africa a high rating on the ecotourism scorecard.

1. *Involves travel to natural destinations.* South Africa is a large and enormously diverse country, offering a wide range of tourism attractions. Its wildlife and game parks and reserves, both public and private, are among the finest in the world. Ecotourism and cultural or "heritage" tourism are the most rapidly growing sectors of the tourism industry in the new South Africa.

2. *Minimizes impact.* South Africa's system of national, provincial, and homeland parks has long been considered among the world's best protected and most carefully tended. Visitor numbers are well regulated, poaching is minimal, accommodations well dispersed, and architecture fits the landscape and often utilizes local materials. But this facade of environmental responsibility conceals a great deal of social engineering, and since the fall of apartheid, conservationists have begun to reexamine these practices, with a more critical eye. South Africa's parks were created by evicting tens of thousands of rural Africans, who were forced to live in overcrowded communities on the parks' perimeters

and were denied access to land, water, wood, and other resources inside the parks. But in contrast with the situation in East Africa, South Africa's protectionist school of conservation and park management did not stop there. For decades, apartheid-era scientists and park officials aggressively rearranged the landscape and wildlife—importing the "big five" animal species into parks, culling elephants and other species, putting up electric fences, planting alien trees and shrubs, clearing brush, and cutting (and sometimes paving) roads, all to make the parks more pleasurable for the country's white minority. In some sections of the game parks, there has been even greater impact: golf courses, conference centers, flowered lawns, and so forth. Now there is a realization that some of these practices were not grounded in good science, and as part of a fundamental restructuring and overhaul of the national parks, they are being reassessed. In addition, new ecotourism projects typically strive for low-impact construction and practices, including use of solar power, raised walkways, recycling of water and waste, use of local materials, and incorporation of indigenous designs.

3. *Builds environmental awareness.* Even under apartheid, South Africa's national park system managed to maintain a carefully groomed international image of apolitical excellence and outstanding conservation practices. Today, the principles and practices of ecotourism are being used to help challenge the old order, which narrowly promoted environmental protection at a cost of human exploitation. Environmentalists and social activists who cut their teeth on the struggle against apartheid are today committed to a more holistic and integrated view, one that links conservation to community development. Under apartheid, domestic tourism was overwhelmingly confined to a narrow segment of high-income whites. Now that tourism is expanding beyond a tiny racial and economic elite, it can provide leisure and build support for conservation among a broad cross-section of the population. However, despite the monumental changes since the end of apartheid, supporters of the old order remain powerful in leading environmental organizations, such as the Endangered Wildlife Trust, and within the national park system. These differing visions of conservation and development are being played out in struggles such as those in St. Lucia, Punda Maria, and the cross-border peace parks.

4. *Provides direct financial benefits for conservation.* In the new South Africa, ecotourism profits are flowing more strongly toward community development than toward environmental protection. Under apartheid, South Africa's parks were heavily financed by the government. When apartheid ended, there was a strong movement among the rural poor to dismantle the parks and turn over the land and resources to the original occupants. The Mandela government quickly made it clear that the park system would continue and in fact would

be expanded. But at the same time, the new government declared that the existing level of government subsidies could not be maintained. Park budgets have been cut, and the parks have embarked on a variety of income-generating projects. Ecotourism's contribution to conservation in South Africa is not in direct financial flows but in provision of a new model for operating that is helping the national parks make the transition from white rule to non–racially oriented democratic rule.

5. *Provides financial benefits and empowerment for local people.* More than in the other countries examined in this book, ecotourism in South Africa is grounded in the principle that it must involve and benefit local communities. Ironically, the earliest experiments in the country's community-based conservation and ecotourism were in parks within the Bantustans or black homelands, one of the most hated institutions of apartheid. Today, ecotourism is being used or proposed as a development tool and an alternative to more destructive forms of income generation in many areas of the country. Ecotourism has proved most successful in overgrazed or parched regions, where wildlife can survive better than cattle. It remains to be seen whether ecotourism can be developed as a viable alternative to more lucrative (at least in the short run) alternatives such as mining for diamonds or metals.

In South Africa today, local communities are involved in ecotourism in a wide variety of ways. These range from entitlement to empowerment models and from passive to more active engagement. They include rent or bed night payments made by the ecolodge or private reserve to the local communities; employment; training and education programs; comanagement or co-ownership arrangements between communities and private companies; provision of social services (schools, clinics, wells) and infrastructure (roads, electricity, pumped water); and the purchase of local produce, charcoal and handicrafts. Some of what is marketed as ecotourism is dubious—for example, Blanchard's border park in Mozambique or Sun City as an economic complement to Pilanesberg National Park—but overall there is a level of experimentation and cross-fertilization of ideas that is deepening the definition of real ecotourism.

6. *Respects local culture.* Under apartheid, South Africa's tourism industry either ignored or crudely exploited the country's non-European cultures. Tourism brochures, for instance, showed only white tourists while picturing Africans dancing or selling crafts. Ecotourism, as interpreted in the new South Africa, includes respecting and learning about local cultures and customs and paying a fair price for handicrafts. In KwaZulu-Natal Province, for instance, Kwabhe Kithunga, located on Stewarts Farm, is a cultural village run as a cooperative where artisans demonstrate how they make their round traditional houses, bead jew-

elry, and women's clothing. And ecotourism, together with cultural and "heritage" tourism, are the fastest-growing markets. Typically, ecotours or cultural tours include visits to Robben Island, Soweto, rural communities, and game parks. Although exploitation, particularly of the San (Bushmen), continues in some parks and tourism establishments, the government's commitment to ecotourism as a tool for both conservation and community development provides a platform from which to expose and oppose these practices.

7. *Supports human rights and democratic movements.* The international trade, travel, and investment boycott of apartheid South Africa helped end white rule. This represents the best example to date of how tourists can play a constructive role in assisting popular democratic struggles. Today, the antiapartheid boycott is cited by those struggling for democratic change in Nigeria, Tibet, Burma, and elsewhere. And today, the new South African government is promoting ecotourism and cultural tourism as its passport to international acceptance and respectability.

Notes

1. Douglas Chadwick, "A Place for Parks," *National Geographic,* July 1996, p. 20.
2. Eddie Koch, *Reality or Rhetoric? Ecotourism and Rural Reconstruction in South Africa* (Geneva: United Nations Research Institute for Social Development, August 1994), p. 21.
3. M. Wahl and K. Naude, *National Register of Protected Areas* (Pretoria: Department of Environmental Affairs and Tourism, 1994), p. 21.
4. Koch, *Reality or Rhetoric?* p. 10.
5. Rupert Isaacson, *South Africa: Swaziland and Lesotho* (London: Cadogan Books, 1995), pp. 550–551; Eddie Koch, "Dead Cows, a Long Bicycle Ride, the Fence of Fire, and a Man on the Run," report prepared by the United Nations Research Institute for Social Development and Group for Environmental Monitoring, second draft, January 1995, pp. 6–17.
6. Koch, "Dead Cows," p. 147.
7. 1993 study by the Development Bank of Southern Africa, cited in Koch, "Dead Cows," pp. 141–142, 146.
8. Technically, all land in South Africa is owned by the state and its use is leased.
9. Koch, *Reality or Rhetoric?* p. 17.
10. Among the contributors were such unsavory characters as Zaire's ruthless, corrupt President Mobutu Sese Seko (who was overthrown in 1997); Agha Hasan Abedi, founder of the scandal-ridden Bank of Credit and Commerce International (which was closed in 1991); and fugitive American financier Robert Vesco (who was arrested in Cuba in 1995).
11. Raymond Bonner, *At the Hand of Man: Peril and Hope for Africa's Wildlife* (New York: Vintage Books), p. 69.
12. Ibid., pp. 79–81; Stephen Ellis, "Of Elephants and Men: Politics and Nature

Conservation in South Africa," *Journal of Southern African Studies* 20, no. 1 (March 1994): 59–62.

13. Ellis, "Of Elephants and Men," pp. 59–64; Bonner, *At the Hand of Man,* pp. 67–69.

14. Koch, *Reality or Rhetoric?* p. 12.

15. Ibid., p. 12; Global Environment Facility (GEF), *Mozambique: Transfrontier Conservation Areas Pilot and Institutional Strengthening Project,* Project Document (Washington, D.C.: GEF, December 1996), appendix 9, pp. 1, 2.

16. David Grossman and Eddie Koch, *Ecotourism Report—Nature Tourism in South Africa: Links with the Reconstruction and Development Programme,* report prepared for SATOUR, August 1995, pp. 4–5; David Holt-Biddle, "The New South Africa: Ecotourism Flavor of the Year?" *The Ecotourism Society Newsletter* 6, no. 1 (First Quarter 1996): 2.

17. Study by the Board of Trade and Industries, cited in Grossman and Koch, *Ecotourism Report,* p. 4.

18. Somerset Waters, *Travel Industry World Yearbook: The Big Picture, 1996–1997,* 40 (New York: Child & Waters, 1997), pp. 139, 146; World Tourism Organization, *Yearbook of Tourism Statistics* (Madrid, Spain: World Tourism Organization, 1995), pp. 12, 13, 26, 27; World Tourism Organization, *Yearbook of Tourism Statistics* (Madrid, Spain: World Tourism Organization, 1986), p. 18; World Tourism Organization, *Yearbook of Tourism Statistics* (Madrid, Spain: World Tourism Organization, 1988), p. 19.

19. Grossman and Koch, *Ecotourism Report,* pp. 14–15.

20. Ministry for Administration and Tourism, *White Paper on Tourism: Republic of South Africa* (Pretoria: South Africa Tourism Board, 1992), p. 8.

21. David Grossman and Eddie Koch, *Ecotourism Report:* pp. 14–15.

22. Paul Olivier, "Backpacking Isn't Just for Impoverished Students," *Capetown Saturday Star,* January 3, 1998.

23. Ibid., p. 15.

24. Wilf Nussey, "One for All," *Africa—Environment & Wildlife* 3, no. 4 (July–August 1995): 30; Eddie Koch, "Senior National Parks Board Members Have Pushed Their Own Self-Destruct Button," *Weekly Mail & Guardian,* December 2, 1994.

25. I am indebted to David Fig, a former official of the Group for Environmental Monitoring (GEM) and now a sociology professor at the University of the Witwatersrand, Johannesburg, who helped me plan my research trip, supplied me with key documents and names of people to interview, explained the background of many of the issues regarding parks and ecotourism, and subsequently carefully and thoughtfully read through this chapter's final draft.

26. Eddie Koch, "Corridor That Is Leading to Controversy," *Weekly Mail & Guardian,* August 18, 1995. (Internet: http://www.wn.apc.org/wmail/issues/950818/wm950818-10.html)

27. Interviews with Eddie Koch, David Fig, and Chris Marais, among others; Koch, "Dead Cows," pp. 141–154; Stephanie Dippenaar, "Pik and Dawie on Collision Course," *Weekly Mail & Guardian,* September 22, 1995. (Internet: http://www.apc.org/wmail/issues/950922/wm950922-42.html)

28. Eddie Koch, "Corridor."

29. Correspondence with David Fig, who is chairman of the SANP Board's Land Claims Committee, 1998.

30. Allister Sparks, *The Mind of South Africa* (London: Mandarin, 1991), p. 138; Koch, "Dead Cows," pp. 142, 151.

31. Grossman and Koch, *Ecotourism Report*, pp. 37–38.

32. Interview with Hector Magome at Pilanesberg National Park, August 1995. In the middle of our conversation, Magome suddenly propped his leg up on the desk and rolled up his trousers, revealing dark scars up and down his shins. "I come from one of the poorest families in South Africa," Magome explained. "My body is covered with scars from sores caused by malnutrition. My mother died when I was seven, but shortly beforehand, she took me aside and said she was giving me a new name, 'Hector.' She said it's the name of a bully, of someone who would perservere. She told me I had to learn to be strong. Magome took his mother's words to heart: "In terms of my make-up, I fight. I don't run away." He received a scholarship to study in the U.S. from the Endangered Wildlife Trust, one of South Africa's largest and most mainstream environmental organizations, and came back with two master's degrees. In 1986, he joined the Bop Parks as an assistant ecologist and began moving up through the ranks. In 1997, Magome became the general manager for planning at the South African National Parks in Pretoria.

33. Grossman and Koch, *Ecotourism Report*, p. 42.

34. Ibid., pp. 38–41.

35. Interviews; Grossman and Koch, *Ecotourism Report*, p. 40.

36. Ibid., pp. 42–43.

37. Sparks, *Mind of South Africa*, p. 36.

38. Isaacson, *South Africa*, p. 605.

39. Interviews at St. Lucia, August 1995; Koch, *Reality or Rhetoric?* p. 2; Chadwick, "Parks," p. 41.

40. The Natal Parks Board (NPB) has been South Africa's most wealthy, powerful, and independent provincial parks board and, internationally, it has garnered more acclaim than any other parks board in the country. In 1994, the NPB received the prestigious ASTA (American Society of Travel Agents)/Smithsonian Magazine Environmental Award for its work in both conservation and tourism. In 1995, NPB's Hilltop Camp, a spectacular mountain lodge in the Hluhluwe-Umfolozi Park received a British Airways "Tourism for Tomorrow" award for its environmental sensitivity, quality, and community outreach. When the NPB was founded at the end of the 19th century, there were only fourteen white rhinos left in the world—all in the Umfolozi area of Natal. Today, the NPB is the world's sole supplier of white rhinos and chief supplier of black rhinos to parks, reserves, sanctuaries, and zoos in other parts of Africa, the U.S., Europe, Asia, and even Cuba.

41. Interview with George Hughes, August 1995.

42. Nicky Barker, "The Battle for St. Lucia Is Far from Over," *Weekly Mail & Guardian*, November 14, 1997. (Internet: http://www.apc.org/wmail/issues/971114/NEW531.html).

43. Koch, *Reality or Rhetoric?* pp. 22–23.

44. Telephone interview with Barry Clements, August 1995; Victor Munnik, "St.

Lucia: The Impact on Conservationists, Miners, Scientists, and Mr. Mkhize,"
New Ground, winter 1993, pp. 6–9; Chadwick, "Parks," p. 41.

45. Koch, *Reality or Rhetoric,* p. 2. Endangered Wildlife Trust, *Vision of Wildlife, Ecotourism and the Environment in Southern Africa,* 1996 Annual Report (Johannesburg: Endangered Wildlfe Trust, 1995), pp. 80–90. Only the conservative Endangered Wildlife Trust, which has close ties to business, came out in favor of mining, arguing that RBM has developed "a highly specialized technique . . . for mining coastal dunes." RBM advertises in the Endangered Wildlife Trust's publications, and the trust in turn lists RBM as an "environmentally responsible business in Southern Africa. Munnik, "St. Lucia," pp. 6–9; Koch, *Reality or Rhetoric?* pp. 1–2; J. D. F. Jones, "The Price of a Great African Wilderness," *Financial Times,* January 20–21, 1996; Chadwick, "Parks," p. 41.

46. Jones, "Price of a Great African Wilderness"; Barker, "Battle for St. Lucia."

47. Interview with Gordon Forrest, August 1995.

48. Telephone interview with Alan Mountain, August 1995.

49. *Weekly Mail & Guardian,* November 17–23, 1991, quoted in Koch, *Reality or Rhetoric?* p. 3.

50. Eddie Koch, "'Nature People, Leave Us Alone!'" and "St. Lucia's Villagers Snubbed," *Weekly Mail & Guardian,* March 22, 1996. (Internet: http:// www.wn.apc.org/wmail/issues/960322/NEWS16.html)

51. Interviews with community representatives, August 1995; Koch, *Reality or Rhetoric?* p. 3.

52. Koch, "St. Lucia's Villagers Snubbed."

53. Interview with Leslie Walters, August 1995.

54. Interview with Annette Gerber, August 1995.

55. Barker, "Battle for St. Lucia."

56. Ibid.

57. Koch, *Reality or Rhetoric?* p. 22.

58. Interview in South Africa and U.S., 1995–1998; Ellis, "Of Elephants and Men," p. 66. This division had placed under surveillance anthropologist David Webster who worked near Kosi Bay and was murdered in Johannesburg in 1989. Investigators found that Webster was probably murdered by a death squad set up by South Africa's Special Forces, perhaps because he stumbled on evidence of ivory smuggling. There is suspicion as well that KwaZulu park officials may have been involved in the death of Claire Stewart, another researcher and activist mysteriously murdered in 1993 in the same area.

59. Quoted in Koch, *Reality or Rhetoric?* p. 33.

60. Alexandra Craib, "Maputaland: The People, the Animals, the Beauty—May They All Win . . . ," *Africa Environment & Wildlife* 3, no. 4 (July–August 1995): 46–47; Koch, *Reality or Rhetoric?* p. 33; Department of Nature Conservation, "Policies, Philosophies, and Successes," n.p., n.d.

61. Department of Nature Conservation, KwaZulu-Natal Province, "Policies," n.d., n.p.

62. Pippa Green, "Pockets Full of Land, but No One to Give It To," *Weekly Mail & Guardian,* November 8, 1996; Ellis, "Of Elephants and Men," p. 68; interviews with Zef Nyati, community organizer in KwaZulu-Natal Province, and others.

63. Green, "Pockets Full of Land."

64. When the Sun Game Lodges ecotourism division was being set up, Southern Sun hired Michel Girardin, a well-respected proponent of ecotourism with years of nature tourism experience, to be general manager. In an interview, Girardin contended, "Lodges have to be sustainable wealth-generators for the communities who live around them. They have to see that ecotourism provides tangible benefits—or there will be pressure to use the land for agriculture or industry."

Southern Sun, which is also a subsidiary of South African Breweries, has positioned itself by means other than ecotourism to fit into the new South Africa. In 1994, it joined with a black business consortium in an effort to boost its bid for more casino licenses. Its main rival was Sol Kerzner's Sun International, which had expanded into casinos in Europe, the Bahamas, and the United States. Interviews; Stefaans Brummer, "Cards Are on the Table, but What Is the Game?" *Weekly Mail & Guardian,* September 23, 1994; Farrell Kramer, "Merv Griffin Selling Resorts Casino to Sun International Hotels," AP Business Wire, August 20, 1996.

65. Grossman and Koch, *Ecotourism Report,* pp. 20, 43–55.

66. Interview with Les Carlisle, regional development manager, Phinda, Conservation Corporation.

67. Grossman and Koch, *Ecotourism Report,* p. 29.

68. "The Conservation Corporation Model of Conservation Development," illustrated chart designed by David Varty, obtained from Conservation Corporation.

69. Interviews with Isaac Tembe, community development liaison, and Les Carlisle, regional development manager, August 1995.

70. Grossman and Koch, *Ecotourism Report,* p. 31.

71. Ibid.

72. Ibid., p. 30.

73. Ellis, "Of Elephants and Men," p. 69; GEF, *Mozambique.*

74. Ellis, "Of Elephants and Men," p. 68.

75. Donald McNeil, "Maputo Elephant Reserve Journal: Thinking Big ($800 Million) to Rescue Big Game," *New York Times,* March 7, 1996, p. A4.

76. Joseph Hanlon, ed., *Mozambique Peace Process Bulletin,* no. 19 (September 1997), published by AWEPA, the European Parliamentarians for Southern Africa, Amsterdam (email: awepa@antenna.nl; Internet http://awepa.org); McNeil, "Thinking Big," p. A4.

77. McNeil, "Thinking Big," p. A4.

78. David Holt-Biddle, "The Endangered Wildlife Trust and Blanchard Moçambique Enterprises," *Endangered Wildlife* 22 (March 1996): 9.

79. Ibid.; Holt-Biddle, "Southern Africa—a Situation Report," in *Endangered Wildlife: Ecotourism and the Environment,* fifth annual *A Vision* report (Johannesburg: Endangered Wildlife Trust, September 1997), p. 25.

80. Telephone interview with Alan Mountain.

Conclusion:
The Road Less Traveled

As the millennium draws to a close, ecotourism has opened a bold new direction in how we explore the world. Ecotourism has become the most rapidly growing and most dynamic sector of the tourism market. Yet, it remains, to paraphrase Robert Frost's poem, the less traveled road. Hundreds of millions of tourists still go on conventional cruises, sun-and-sea beach holidays, or mass tourism vacations during which distortions of nature are viewed at palm-fringed poolsides, theme parks, and overcrowded campgrounds. Much of what is marketed as ecotourism amounts to only ecotourism lite, which offers tidbits of nature or minor environmental reforms such as not changing sheets every day or, worse, "greenwashing" scams that use environmentally friendly images but follow none of the principles and practices of sound ecotourism. There are growing numbers of travelers, however, who have walked the path of socially responsible and environmentally respectful tourism.

Even more significant than the increased numbers of ecotourists is the shift over the last two decades of the twentieth century in the paradigm, in the discourse on both conservation and nature tourism. Effective conservation now includes involving and benefiting the people living nearest the protected areas—finding harmony between people and parks—and nature tourism has come to mean not just wilderness experiences but also activities that minimize visitor impact while benefiting both the protected areas and the surrounding human populations. This shift in consciousness and understanding has led to a great deal of experimentation and creativity, most often at the local level—of a project or park—occasionally at the national level, and, more rarely, at the international level.

At the local level, ecotourism principles have become part of many rural struggles over control of land, resources, and tourism profits. Where people the world over find themselves in conflict over parks and tourism, from the gold miners in Costa Rica's Corcovado National Park and the settlers on the Galápagos Islands to the Maasai in East Africa and the displaced communities around Kruger National Park, St. Lucia Nature Reserve, and elsewhere in South Africa, ecotourism is part of the demand and/or the solution. In the most fragile of ecosystems, such as that of the Galápagos, well-run ecotourism is the only option, the only foreign exchange–earning activity that does not lead to irreparable damage. In other instances, ecotourism is clearly more profitable than the alternative economic activities: for example, a study of game farming in Kenya found that wildlife tourism was fifty times more lucrative than cattle grazing; a lion is calculated to be worth $575,000; and a single free-flying macaw in Peru is estimated to generate as much as $4,700 per year in tourism dollars. In the old Bophuthatswana homeland in South Africa, cattle farming could generate only 80 jobs, whereas six luxury lodges planned for a game reserve were projected to create 1,200 jobs, and ecotourism was estimated to be sixty times more profitable than cattle ranching. Even when pitted against the seemingly lucrative industry of mining in St. Lucia, South Africa, ecotourism is calculated to have the potential to provide more jobs for a longer period of time without destroying the sand dunes and the estuary.[1]

But the complexities of involving rural communities in ecotourism and conservation projects are great, and such projects frequently take more time and effort than fast-paced private tourism developers are willing to give. The owners of Oliver's Camp in Tanzania, for instance, spent a year negotiating land-use agreements with three Maasai communities and helping the residents of these villages to create democratic institutions to manage their ecotourism profits.

Often, controversy centers on the definition of the community that should be involved in and benefiting from conservation and ecotourism. Most often, the community is defined as the displaced people living around the immediate perimeter of the park, who, particularly in Kenya's dispersal areas, bear the brunt of wildlife protection. Traditional tribal leaders frequently contend that profits and benefits from tourism should be distributed throughout the entire area under their authority. In places such as Monteverde, Coast Rica, the primary community is a relatively prosperous rural town, whereas in Cuba and, in the past, in socialist Tanzania and Zanzibar, the national government argued that tourism profits should be used to help build social services throughout the entire country.

At the community or village level, there is a wide range of models for involvement. A study by the International Institute for Environment and Development describes a "typology of participation," moving from "passive" to "self-mobilization/active" participation, that is, from local people simply being told what is going to happen or has already happened to communities taking initiatives independently of and sometimes in conflict with external institutions (either government or private).[2] Similarly, there is a range of models for the distribution of profits, from rent for use of land to co-ownership to full community ownership of the park or tourism facilities. Most common is the distribution of revenue in the form of cash pay-

ments or tangible benefits (a road, a clinic, a grinding mill, a classroom, electricity, a truck, etc.) to the local community based on rent for use of land, a
set fee per visitor night, or a percentage of park entrance fees. Although such
compensation can significantly improve daily life in poor rural communities,
it may do little to equip local communities with the educational and technical skills and political know-how they will need to assume an active role in
ecotourism projects and park management and in negotiations with private
sector participants and government authorities.

The ideal is active community participation in the management and distribution of revenues that gives local residents, in the words of David
Grossman and Eddie Koch, "the will, power and skills to improve their standard of living" through the wise use of wildlife and natural resources.[3] But
in reality, many community-based tourism and conservation programs are
"relational" rather than participatory: they seek to improve relationships
between the community and either the state or the private enterprise
through trade-offs rather than to devolve ownership and management of the
protected area or tourism project to the local community. "Without propri-
etorship," write Grossman and Koch, "most forms of participation become
co-optive, cooperative or collaborative arrangements."[4] Frequently, local
communities strengthen their skills and political influence through alliances
with national and international environment, development, and human
rights organizations, scientists, journalists, and academics, who help them
build a counterweight to the power of outside private corporations or negotiate terms with the national government. These external alliances can also
help community-owned ecotourism projects develop internationally acceptable standards of accommodation and effective overseas marketing.
According to David Western, low-quality service and facilities and lack of
international marketing efforts are two of the main reasons why such projects often fail to compete with private sector projects.[5]

Although alliances with NGOs and experts can provide skills, funds, and
political clout, it is difficult for community-based ecotourism to take hold
and expand without strong government support. As John Akama observes
in discussing Kenya, "For local community participation to succeed, local
people need sanctioned authority to enable them to implement programme
responsibilities." As seen in Kenya, Tanzania, and Zanzibar, national governments frequently stifle rural initiatives, hand out lucrative contracts to
politically or economically powerful elites, and cede to the private sector or
local park officials development responsibilities—construction of roads,
wells, schools, and the like—traditionally carried by the state. Although
nearly every developing country is, these days, promoting ecotourism, in
reality much of the implementation has been left to the private sector, with
little overall planning or control exerted by national governments. Over the
past several decades, economic globalization, free trade, and structural

adjustment policies have undercut the capacity of governments in developing countries to provide basic social services or even implement sound government guidelines. A number of governments have devised revenue-sharing schemes with people living around national parks, or undertaken international advertising campaigns promoting ecotourism (South Africa and
Costa Rica), or even set up model ecotourism projects and developed and
marketed a "line" of ecotourism options (Cuba), but none has fully
embraced the principles and practices of community-based ecotourism as a
national development strategy. As Akama puts it, "Probably, the main reason why community-based wildlife tourism programmes fail is the lack of
coherent policies and legislation which delegate responsibility and authority
for tourism development and wildlife conservation from powerful stakeholders (the state, conservation organizations, tourism groups and local
elites) to rural peasants."[6]

The concept of ecotourism has brought new principles and altered
practices to a stratum of the private sector. Over the past several decades,
a number of entrepreneurs, many with backgrounds in environmental
or political movements, have embarked on ecotourism projects with the
conviction that they can do so in a socially and environmentally responsible
manner. These enterprises include, as the case studies in this book show,
outbound tour operators (Wildland Adventures, Tamu Safaris), inbound
operators (Horizontes, Costa Rica Expeditions), rustic and rugged projects
(Rara Avis), tented camps (Oliver's Camp), family-run cabins (Santa Clara
Lodge), modest bungalows (Matemwe Bungalows), community-run lodges
(Moka Ecolodge), scientific centers (La Selva Biological Station, Wilson
Botanical Gardens, Monteverde Cloud Forest Reserve), "soft" ecotourism
(Rain Forest Aerial Tram, Villablanca Hotel, many of the Galápagos Islands'
floating hotels), moderate luxury (Las Tortugas, Ndumo, Rocktail Bay, and
Zululand Tree lodges), and high-end luxury (Londolozi, Phinda). These are
among the finest examples of innovative ecoprojects that benefit, to various
degrees, both conservation and local communities.

In all developing countries, even in Cuba, there is movement away from
government-owned and government-run tourism projects. With the end of
the cold war and the collapse of the Soviet Union, foreign investment and
free trade have become the mantras for economic development, and the private sector vigorously argues for self-regulation, low or no taxation, and a
bevy of government incentives to stimulate investment. However, the
ample examples of ecotourism shams (from Papagayo and Playa Grande's
"green luxury" projects in Costa Rica to the $4 million Nungwi Peninsula
project in Zanzibar and the "beast-and-beach" project along the South
African–Mozambique border); the growth of private parks, which are
undermining national park systems; and the continuing leakage of profits
away from ecotourism projects all highlight a continuing need for govern-

ments to develop clear standards, guidelines, and monitoring procedures, more equitable taxing policies, and investment and promotional strategies that support sound national, particularly community-based, ecotourism enterprises.

Ecotourism is far from fulfilling its promise to transform the way in which modern, conventional tourism is conducted. With few exceptions, it has not succeeded in moving beyond a narrow niche market to a set of principles and practices that infuses the entire tourism industry. Although the large corporate players have endorsed ecotourism, in practice they have mainly undertaken modest, cost-saving reforms that they aggressively market as major ecotourism innovations. At its core, ecotourism is about power relationships and on-the-ground struggles. It will take much stronger grass-roots movements, combined with alliances among activists, experts, and NGOs and carefully planned and implemented national ecotourism strategies, to curb the power of the conventional tourism industry. Although this appears unlikely to happen soon, it is still worth the struggle. Along the way, some excellent models are being built; some local communities are being empowered and their members' lives improved; national parks and other fragile ecosystems are receiving more support; and there is a growing awareness that we cannot continue to play in other people's lands as we have in the past. Despite the constraints, today's traveler does, as Robert Frost suggests, have a choice about which road to take.

Notes

1. Eddie Koch, *Reality or Rhetoric? Ecotourism and Rural Reconstruction in South Africa* (Geneva: United Nations Research Institute for Social Development, August 1994), pp. 6, 10, 2.

2. International Institute for Environment and Development (IIED), *Whose Eden? An Overview of Community Approaches to Wildlife Management* (London: Overseas Development Administration, July 1994), p. 19.

3. David Grossman and Eddie Koch, *Ecotourism Report—Nature Tourism in South Africa: Links with the Reconstruction and Development Program,* report prepared for SATOUR, August 1995, p. 22.

4. Ibid., p. 22; Marshall Murphree, "The Role of Institutions in Community-based Conservation," in David Western and R. Michael Wright, eds., *Natural Connections: Perspectives in Community-Based Conservation* (Washington, D.C.: Island Press, 1994), pp. 403–427.

5. Communication with David Western, June 1998.

6. John S. Akama, "Western Environmental Values and Nature-Based Tourism in Kenya," *Tourism Management* 17, no. 8 (1996): 573.

Index